Evelyn Jacot
201-996-2680
please return

M-2
(Annual % increase)

M-1
(annual % increase)

Unemployment Rate
(all workers)

CPI
(annual % increase)

Rate on 10 year
treasury securities

3 month treasury
bill rate

69 1971 1973 1975 1977 1979 1981

Money, Banking, and the Economy

Second Edition

ALSO AVAILABLE:

Study Guide to Accompany Money, Banking, and the Economy

by Steven Beckman and Janet L. Wolcutt
Wichita State University

Thomas Mayer, *University of California, Davis*

James S. Duesenberry, *Harvard University*

Robert Z. Aliber, *University of Chicago*

Money, Banking, and the Economy

Second Edition

W. W. NORTON & COMPANY
New York · London

Published simultaneously in Canada by George J. McLeod Limited, Toronto.
Printed in the United States of America

SECOND EDITION

Library of Congress Cataloging in Publication Data
Mayer, Thomas.
Money, banking, and the economy.
(Includes Index)
1. Money—United States. 2. Banks and banking—United States. 3. Monetary policy—United States. I. Duesenberry, James Stemble, 1918– (joint author). II. Aliber, Robert Z. (joint author) III. Title.
HG540.M39 1984 332.1′0973 83-13498

W. W. Norton & Company, Inc., 500 Fifth Avenue, New York, N.Y. 10110
W. W. Norton & Company Ltd., 37 Great Russell Street, London WC1B 3NU

ISBN 0 393 95313 0

2 3 4 5 6 7 8 9 0

Contents

PART ONE The Financial Structure

PART THREE Monetary Theory

PART FOUR **Monetary Policy**

PART FIVE **International Money and Finance**

Preface

The extremely favorable response to the first edition elated us. But we have tried hard not to let it go to our heads. There was, we discovered, ample room for improvement. For nothing reveals flaws in a textbook more clearly than extensive class use. Instructors familiar with the original edition will find much that has changed, for the better, we believe.

In preparing this revision, three goals took precedence over all. One, to control the length of the book. Two, to clarify as best we could points that proved ticklish for students. And three, to keep track of the rapid changes brought about both by innovations within, and regulations imposed from outside, the financial system. The first led to a book that is briefer by roughly 20 percent. The second caused us to recast substantially a number of chapters, especially those concerned with theory. And the third meant that we could not stop revising until the book literally was on press. While it is a hard task to bridge the gap that often exists between the wants and needs of the business schools and those of the economics departments, we have tried to do so even more diligently than before, since the first edition saw use in both arenas. Many of the modifications reflect the generous response to a detailed questionnaire that was sent to users and near-users of the first edition.

Rapid change in the financial system is, of course, a major problem for anyone writing a text or teaching in this field. We have covered developments, such as the Garn-St. Germain Act, up to the middle of 1983. But we can hardly expect that upon publication of our text financial innovation will cease. Hence, we include a chapter dealing with the politics as well as the economics of regulatory change, so that readers will be able to interpret the ongoing course of financial evolution.

There are many ways a money and banking text can be written, for the content of the course is limited principally by the hours available to teach it.

We can perhaps best describe this book by explaining how we chose among the various alternatives for coverage and emphasis both in the first edition and now in this new edition.

Our first decision was to offer the instructor the widest latitude possible in fitting the text to his or her preference. This brought us smack up against a critical question: how much space to allocate to institutional description as opposed to monetary theory and policy. Behind that question was our awareness of the "class struggle" that sometimes arises between instructors who prefer to stress theory and policy and a class that prefers to learn about bank management, capital markets, and the operations of the Federal Reserve. This conflict is less severe than it once was. With stresses and strains in the financial system often front-page news, policy debates involve both the functioning of institutions and the theories that influence the actions of monetary authorities. So, without skimping on strictly institutional material, our book does more than describe the activities of banks, financial intermediaries, the central bank, and regulatory agencies; it pays greater attention than most other texts to the impact policy measures have on the financial sector.

The book has the following shape. Parts One and Two, roughly the first two-fifths, deal with financial institutions, the creation of money and bank reserves, and the measurement of money. Part Three takes up monetary theory and inflation. The development of aggregate supply, aggregate demand, and the wage-price spiral provides a bridge to Part Four, on monetary policy. The text ends with a full part on international money and finance.

Less an organizational problem and more a matter of controversy was how much monetarism to include in Part Three on monetary theory. Our solution has been to start with a Keynesian-neoclassical synthesis that makes allowance for many of the points monetarists have raised. This is followed by two chapters on the monetarist approach itself. The first sets forth the quantity theory as developed by Milton Friedman and the Chicago school. The second goes deeper into monetarism by taking up other theoretical models, including those of Don Patinkin and Brunner and Meltzer, and some empirical models, including the forecasting model of the St. Louis Federal Reserve Bank. This second chapter can be omitted without loss of continuity by instructors who want to devote less time to theory.

Having separate chapters on monetarism is, of course, not as desirable as presenting a generally accepted synthesis, but such a synthesis does not exist. We cannot pretend to students that economists agree on macroeconomics and monetary theory. But to reduce the anguish of this admission, we start the theory section with a discussion of why economists disagree and end it by summing up the points at issue between monetarists and Keynesians.

A final comment on the distinctive features of our text. At one time international finance could be treated very briefly, since it had little direct impact on domestic monetary institutions and policy. But this is no longer the case. The United States has become a much more open economy in recent years, and monetary policy is now influenced to a much larger extent by international considerations. Accordingly, after covering the evolution of the international payments system and operations of the foreign exchange market, we conclude with whole chapters on the structure of international banking and the most recent developments in the international monetary system.

The book is organized to permit flexible use in the classroom. In general, we have tried to write chapters so that they will be comprehensible to those who have omitted some of the earlier chapters. This was done at the cost of occasional recapitulation. But it is possible to shift chapters around. For example, some instructors may want to take up the tools of monetary policy along with Part One, while others may want to shift the discussion of central banking from Part One into the discussion of monetary policy in Part Four. Others may want to take up monetary theory before the discussion of institutions in Part One.

A *Study Guide* by Steven Beckman and Janet L. Wolcutt contains highlights, exercises, and problems for each chapter. *An Instructor's Manual,* prepared by the authors, is also available.

Each instructor will, of course, have his or her own ideas about how much time to devote to the increasingly important topic of international finance. Beyond this, a short course stressing institutions rather than theory might well omit chapters 11 (to p. 197), 14–17, 19, 24, and 25, while a course that focuses on monetary policy might want to omit chapters 3, 6, 8, 11 (to p. 197), and 16.

The allocation of various chapters among us was as follows: James S. Duesenberry took primary responsibility for chapters 5, 6, 12–14, 17, and 18; Robert Z. Aliber for Part Five; and Thomas Mayer for the other chapters. We are deeply indebted to a number of economists who read part or all of the manuscript and offered many helpful comments that sent us back to our desks to rewrite and to clarify. The detailed questionnaire sent to several hundred of our colleagues drew an extraordinary response, for which we are grateful. Few chapters escaped the close scrutiny of the respondents. In addition, thorough readings were given every page and paragraph of the first edition by Philip L. Brock of Duke University, Beverly Hadaway of the University of Texas at Austin, Walter Johnson of the University of Missouri at Columbia, and Uri M. Possen of Cornell University. Once again, Wilfred Ethier, of the University of Pennsylvania, reviewed the Part on International Money and Finance. Other reviewers of the first edition should not be forgotten this time around, for they did much to contribute to its success. They are George Bentson, University of Rochester; William Brainard, Yale University; Karl Brunner, University of Rochester; Jonathan Eaton, Princeton University; Milton Friedman, Stanford University; Thomas Havrilesky, Duke University; Arnold Heggestad, University of Florida, Gainesville; Robert S. Holbrook, University of Michigan; David Laidler, University of Western Ontario; Edmund S. Phelps, Columbia University; James L. Pierce, University of California, Berkeley; William Poole, Brown University; and John Rutledge, Claremont Men's College.

Donald S. Lamm at W. W. Norton did much more for this book than any author has a right to ask of an editor. And Drake McFeely and Jacqueline Rifkin, editor and copyeditor, respectively, of the second edition, did a sterling job. Finally, we owe a debt to Marguerite Crown and to Ann Frischia for excellent secretarial services.

Davis, California — T. M.
Cambridge, Massachusetts — J.S.D.
Chicago, Illinois — R.Z.A.

Money, Banking, and the Economy

Second Edition

The Financial Structure

PART ONE

In Part One we shall do two things: lay the groundwork for the subsequent discussion and then look at financial institutions. Chapter 1 takes up the nature of money and how it functions. Chapter 2 looks at the role played in the U.S. economy by financial institutions, banks, savings and loan associations, etc., and explains how claims on them fit into people's portfolios, and why they are so extensively regulated.

The next four chapters look at private financial institutions in some detail. Commercial banks get two chapters, not only because they are so important, but also because most readers come into close contact with them. Other financial institutions are then discussed in Chapter 5, while Chapter 6 treats the money market and the capital market and begins the discussion of what determines interest rates. Chapter 7 then takes up the most important government financial institution, the Federal Reserve System. As will become apparent, the financial system is not working as well as it should, and over the years serious weaknesses have shown up. Hence, the last chapter in Part One looks at proposals for financial reform and at recently enacted reforms.

Introduction 1

It would certainly be an exaggeration to say that *all* our important economic problems are the result of malfunctions in the monetary system, but some of the most important ones are. Inflation is a monetary problem in the obvious sense that it means that our monetary unit, the dollar, is losing value. It is also a monetary problem in a much less obvious way: significant and sustained inflations have occurred only when the quantity of money has risen at a fast rate. Hence, in one sense of the much abused term *cause,* one can say that major inflations are "caused" by a rapid rise in the supply of money. Unemployment, while it has many nonmonetary aspects, is also closely connected with changes in the money supply. If the supply of money rises at a faster than expected rate, this lowers unemployment temporarily, while a sharp decrease in the quantity of money usually increases unemployment temporarily. While one may well argue about which one is cause and which is effect, every recession since 1908 has been associated with a decline in the growth rate of the money supply. And, as we shall show, the relative growth rates of the money supply in various countries are a major factor in determining the exchange rates of their currencies.

Obviously, **monetary theory,** the theory that *deals with the relation between changes in the quantity of money, interest rates, and changes in money income,* is an important topic, and so is **monetary policy,** which is concerned with *how the quantity of money and interest rates should be managed.*

But to understand how money and monetary policy affect the economy one must know something about banks and other financial institutions. This is so because banks create the major part of our money stock, and other financial institutions issue claims on themselves, some of which are also money, and some of which are similar to money. And, of course, financial institutions are the main providers of credit. Beyond this, there is the fact that all of us have day-to-day dealings, whether as depositors or as borrowers, with financial institutions, and we should therefore know something about how they operate. For these reasons, Part One of this book deals with financial institutions, particularly with banks. These chapters are descriptive rather than analytic because there exists no sufficiently specific theory that can explain our financial system in adequate detail. Part Two of this book then deals primarily with how money is created. Part Three takes up monetary theory and inflation, and Part Four discusses monetary policy. Part Five then considers international finance—that is, how the monetary systems of various countries interact. But before getting to these things, we shall take up in this chapter what money is and what it does.

DIFFERENT USES OF THE WORD "MONEY"

We have used the words *money* and *monetary* as though it were obvious what they mean, but this is far from the truth. Actually, a major reason why students often have difficulty in money and banking courses is that they forget that *money* has a very specific meaning in economics. By contrast, in normal conversation the term *money* is used to mean many different things. One of these is just currency, as in the phrase, "do you have any money with you?" But in modern economics money is never defined solely as currency, because currency and checking deposits do the same thing: they pay for goods and services. In fact, only a small proportion of the dollar value of purchases, probably around one percent or so, is paid for with currency. Hence, if we were to define money as just currency we would have great difficulty in relating money to the bulk of all purchases that are made. And it is the very fact that money is related to total purchases that makes money interesting. Since currency and deposits on which checks can be written do the same thing, and since we are interested in what money does, we must include checkable deposits along with currency in the definition of money. One obvious objection to treating deposits as money just like currency is that one cannot make some small payments, such as a bus fare, by check, and that even for larger payments checks are sometimes not accepted. This is perfectly true. But it is also true that if someone buying, say, $10 million of securities tried to pay by currency the deal would, in all probability, fall through. Besides, if we were to exclude checking deposits from the definition of money because checks are not accepted for small payments, should we also exclude some currency notes, such as $1,000 bills? In fact, it helps to think of money as essentially deposits, and of currency as the small change of the system. Although peasants like us use currency for a large proportion of our payments, this is not so for large transactors. They use mainly wire transfers, that is, telex messages or telegrams to transfer money. While no recent data are available one study estimated that in 1978 currency payments accounted for less than one percent of the value of total payments, checks about one quarter and wire transfers roughly three quarters.

But while the popular definition of money as currency is too narrow to be useful in economics, there is also another popular definition of money that is too broad. This definition treats money as a synonym for wealth.

Saying "he has a lot of money" means that he is wealthy. If this particular usage were followed in economics, thus merging money with all other types of wealth, we would be ignoring the distinctive features of money.

A third popular definition of money is to define it as income, by asking, for example, "how much money does he earn?" But defining money as income can be most confusing if we want to discuss, as we later will, whether changes in the money supply bring about equivalent changes in income. Moreover, money is a *stock*, which means that it is a certain amount at any one moment in time, while income is a *flow* over time. If you are told that someone's income is, say, \$5,000, you do not know whether he has a high or low income until you are told whether these \$5,000 are income per year or per week. But someone who carries \$3,000 of currency in his pocket certainly has a large stock of currency.

Instead of defining money either so narrowly as just currency, or so broadly as to include all wealth, economists define money by its functions. Anything that functions as a medium of exchange or a standard of value or, according to many economists, as an extremely liquid store of wealth is considered money. But these functions of money need explaining.

THE FUNCTIONS OF MONEY

Money acts as (1) a medium of exchange, (2) a standard of value, and (3) a store of wealth. Anything that fulfills the first two of these functions is defined as money. (The third function is fulfilled by any valuable asset.)

Medium of Exchange

The medium of exchange function is an obvious one; we use money as an intermediary in exchange. Instead of paying each other with goods and services, we exchange goods and services for money, and then exchange this money for those goods and services we want to acquire. Such a roundabout system of exchange avoids the great disadvantage of barter, the need for a so-called double coincidence of wants. What this rather stuffy phrase means is that to effect barter we have to find someone who wants to obtain the goods and services we have to offer *and,* at the same time, can provide the goods and services we want to obtain in exchange.

In a primitive society with little division of labor, such a person may not be so hard to find, since only a few types of goods are being exchanged and much of the trading is ceremonial and governed by tradition. But in an advanced society with a myriad of commodities it is a different matter. A seller of steel who wishes to exchange it for, say, vanilla ice cream would have to look around a long time before finding someone who has extra vanilla ice cream and, at the same time, wants steel. By contrast, in an economy with money this exchange process is broken into two parts. He first locates someone who wants steel and then someone who has ice cream to sell. It is much easier to locate two such people than to locate a person who just happens to combine both of these characteristics. Another problem with barter is the indivisibility of many goods. For example, a manufacturer of cars could hardly give a farmer, say, one three-thousandths of a car in exchange for a pound of butter.

The inefficiency of direct barter then leads to the possibility of replacing it by *indirect barter*, that is, by a system in which some people exchange their goods not directly for the goods they desire, but for the goods they believe are wanted by those who have the goods they want. The more a product is employed for indirect barter, the more useful it becomes, and hence the greater is the willingness of people to accept it. Ultimately it may be used primarily to effectuate exchange and thus becomes essentially "money."

Despite the great advantage of "money" over simple barter we do find simple barter used occasionally in a modern economy. Barter may reappear to some extent when the monetary system breaks down into a gigantic inflation, with prices doubling, say, every day. In this case money is such a poor store of value that even the very short period of time that must elapse between receiving and spending money is too long to hold it, so that some, though not all, transactions are best conducted by barter.

A more common reason for barter is that prices are not allowed to adjust to equilibrium. There may be price control, and demand may substantially exceed supply at the controlled prices. In this case sellers may be reluctant to sell their goods at controlled prices, that is, for less money than they are worth, but they may be willing to exchange them for other goods. A good example of this type of barter was seen during the Allied occupation of Germany after World War II:

> "Everybody knows that to get cement you must offer coal," said the city fathers of Stuttgart, and they bought liquor brewed in the surrounding countryside, shipped it to the French zone [of occupation] in exchange for cigarettes, shipped the cigarettes to a Ruhr mine and swapped them for coal, brought the coal back to a cement plant in Württemberg, and thus got the cement for reconstruction work.[1]

Another situation where barter is sometimes used is when there are laws setting a minimum price, or if sellers with market power can keep their prices from falling when supply exceeds demand. For example, a country may set a minimum price for a commodity it exports, but then cannot sell all its output at that price. One solution is to barter this commodity with another country that is in the same fix. Then neither country has to admit that its commodity is not worth all that it claims on the market.

Barter also occurs to a limited extent in more normal circumstances, for example, in trading in a car. Apparently barter arrangements have also become significant in countries with very high tax rates, such as Britain and Sweden, as a way of evading taxes.[2]

[1] Horst Mendershausen, "Prices, Money and Distribution of Goods in Postwar Germany," *American Economic Review* 39 (June 1949): 656.

[2] There are "barter clubs" in the United States that allow members to swap goods and services. However, most of this activity involves the use of script as a medium of exchange, and dollars are, of course, used as a standard of value. Hence these transactions are not really barter transactions but are merely transactions in an informal currency. Presumably, a major advantage of this arrangement is that it facilitates income-tax evasion. But barter persists even if there is no tax advantage to it. As late as the early years of this century

Standard of Value

The second function of money is to act as a standard of value, which simply means that we use money as a way of measuring values. We think of, and express, the values of goods and services in terms of money, so that money is the measuring rod of value the same way as a mile or kilometer is a measure of distance. Obviously, a modern economy requires continual comparisons of value; both producers and consumers have to compare the offers of numerous sellers, and this would be hard to do if different sellers denominated their prices in different goods; for example, if one store demands two pounds of butter for a pound of beef, and another store demands ten pencils for a pound of beef, which store is cheaper? A similar problem would arise in deciding whether to buy, say, beef or fish, if the price of beef is expressed in terms of butter and the price of fish in terms of typewriter ribbons. To make rational decisions we would have to know the ratios at which any one good exchanges for all the others.

Suppose that we have a very simple economy with only five commodities, A, B, C, D, and E. If there is no standard of value, and we want to know the exchange ratios of these five commodities in terms of each other, we have to learn ten different exchange ratios (A—B, A—C, A—D, A—E, B—C, B—D, B—E, C—D, C—E, D—E). But if we use one of these five commodities, say A, as our standard of value, we can express the prices of the other four goods in terms of it, and thus we have to learn only four exchange rates (A—B, A—C, A—D, A—E). In general, with N commodities, if there is no standard of value, we have to learn $(N-1)\,N/2$ exchange rates between them. (The first part of the expression is $N-1$ because the exchange rate of a commodity with itself is obviously unity, so that we have to discover the exchange rates of only $N-1$ commodities. For each of these commodities we have to know its exchange rate with every other one, so we have $(N-1)\,N$ exchange rates. But if we know the exchange rate of A with B we already know the exchange rate of B with A and for this reason we divide by 2.)

But if we use one of these commodities as the standard of value, there are only $N-1$ exchange ratios. Hence, a standard of value allows us to achieve an immense economy of effort. Assume, for example, that someone is concerned with 201 items, hardly an outlandish number. Given a standard of value he or she has to ascertain only 200 prices in terms of this standard of value. But in the absence of a standard of value, there are 20,100 exchange ratios.

Another great advantage of a standard of value is that it simplifies bookkeeping. Imagine trying to manage an accounting system in which the entries in the books consist of thousands of commodities. Try to see whether you made a profit or loss.

One particular function of a standard of value, a function that is often

---

barter was used extensively in the more isolated areas of Wales, where there were close-knit communities, so that information costs were relatively low. See Marjorie Sykes, "How to Live without Money," *The Countryman* 83 (Autumn 1978): 40–43.

listed as a separate function of money, is to act as a standard of deferred payment, that is, a standard in which debts are expressed. This use of a standard of value creates serious problems because, as unfortunately we have all found out, the value of money varies over time; the dollar you lent last year will not buy as much when you receive it back this year. In this respect, money is a poor standard of value.

Store of Wealth

The final function of money is to serve as a store of value, that is, as a way of holding wealth. Although this function of money is no more important than the other ones, we will discuss it in more detail because it does bring out a number of important, and not quite so obvious, characteristics of money.

Money has several peculiarities as a store of wealth. One is that it has no, or only trivial, transaction costs. People who decide to hold any other asset as a store of wealth must take the money they receive as income and buy this asset. Later on, when they want to obtain goods or other assets in place of this asset they have to exchange it for money. Both of these transactions, from money into this asset and, later on, from this asset back into money, involve a cost. For example, suppose that someone saves $5,000 to buy a car next year and decides to put these $5,000 into common stock in the meantime. She now has to take the time and trouble to decide which stock to buy, and to call a broker and pay a brokerage fee as well. Then, next year she has again to go to the trouble of calling the broker and paying another brokerage fee. In contrast, by holding these $5,000 as a demand deposit instead, she could have avoided (at the cost of foregoing any potential yield on the stock) both the brokerage costs and the implicit costs represented by the time and trouble required to buy the stock. This is a unique characteristic of money, and in this respect it is superior to all other assets.

A second characteristic of money as a store of wealth is that, quite obviously, its value in terms of money is fixed. This is important because debts are normally stated in money terms. Hence money has a fixed value in terms of debts and certain commitments, such as rental payments. Someone who wants an asset that will allow him or her to pay off a debt has a definite incentive to hold money. To be sure, money is not the only asset that has this convenient characteristic; a bond that matures when the debt is due has it too, but buying and selling a bond involves transactions costs.

The absence of significant transactions costs and the fixity of its value in terms of debts are the two basic characteristics of money as a store of wealth. Two other, but less basic, characteristics are that the value of money fluctuates relative to goods and services, and that some types of money (e.g., currency) have no explicit yield.[3] Hence, if someone wants an asset that will have stable purchasing power over goods and services rather than over debts, money is certainly not the ideal one. Since most of us use money primarily

[3] An explicit yield is a yield that is paid in money, and typically expressed as an interest rate. By contrast, an implicit yield can consist of free services and convenience.

to buy goods it may seem that money is not as good a store of wealth as are assets whose money prices vary. While there is certainly some truth to this contention, it is subject to a major qualification. The prices of various assets and of goods and services do not fluctuate in unison. Hence, people who hold, say, common stocks or inventories of commodities may find that, despite inflation, they are even worse off than they would have been had they held money instead. Certainly, despite the inflation since 1970, someone who bought seemingly sound Penn Central stock that year, just before the company went bankrupt, would have lost more purchasing power than someone who held money instead. Unfortunately, a good inflation hedge does not exist.

Interaction of the Functions of Money

In the United States a single monetary unit, the dollar, fulfills all three functions of money. A dollar bill, for example, is a medium of exchange and a store of wealth, while prices are stated in (abstract units) of dollars. But it is not always the case that all three functions of money are fulfilled by the same monetary unit. For example, in colonial America many merchants used the British pound as their standard of value in which they kept their books, but Spanish coins were a more common medium of exchange since there were more of them around. Similarly, in Britain, until recently, prices of certain high-status goods, for example, expensive clothes, were stated in terms of guineas, a guinea equaling one pound plus one shilling. But guineas were no longer in circulation and the customer paid for these goods with the medium of exchange, pounds and shillings.[4] And in Israel prices of expensive goods are often stated in dollars.

Usually the same unit performs all three functions of money. This is so because it would be inconvenient to use different units as the medium of exchange and the standard of value. For example, suppose that the medium of exchange consists of silver coins, but that the standard of value in which prices are stated is a gold coin. Then at every purchase one would have to do a bit of mental arithmetic to calculate how many silver coins to give the merchant to meet the price set in terms of gold coins. And, as we just pointed out, as a store of wealth the advantage of money is precisely that it is the same unit as the medium of exchange (thus avoiding transactions costs) and as the standard of value (thus having a fixed value in terms of debts). And this requires that all three functions be fulfilled by the same monetary unit.

[4]The guinea was originally a gold coin while the pound was a silver coin. Dealing in gold rather than silver coinage indicates superior social status, hence the use of guineas for prices of prestige goods. There is an extensive history to the use of different types of money by various social classes. The lower classes were sometimes paid in copper while the aristocracy dealt in gold. In ancient Greece, for example, the use of gold by the common people was prohibited at one time because gold could be used to bribe the gods, and this was not something the lower classes were supposed to do. Currently we still have one remnant of this tradition of "high" and "low" money—one should not leave pennies as part of the tip.

M-1

When it comes to defining money, not in a theoretical sense by pointing to its functions, but by specifying the particular *measurable* items that are included in it, some difficulties arise. Some economists emphasize the medium of exchange function, and hence include in money only those items that can be used as a medium of exchange, that is, currency and checkable deposits. This is called *M-1* or "narrow money." Some economists believe that whether checks can, or cannot, be written against a deposit is not so important as long as depositors can quickly and costlessly take funds out of their deposits. They therefore define money in a broader way than *M-1* by including such items as savings deposits. We will discuss both definitions of money in some detail in Chapter 11. For the time being, just think of money as *M-1*, that is, as consisting of the public's holdings of currency and checkable deposits.

TYPES OF MONEY

There are various types of money. **Full-bodied commodity money** is *money that has a value as a commodity fully equal to its value as a medium of exchange.* An obvious example is a gold coin with its value as gold, if sold on the gold market, equal to its face value. A frequently more convenient form of money is representative full-bodied money. This is a monetary unit, such as paper money, that has little intrinsic worth, but can be redeemed in full-bodied money.

If *money does not itself have value as a commodity fully equal to its monetary value, and cannot be redeemed in such commodity money,* it is called **credit money.** All our current U.S. money is credit money.

Currency is **legal tender.** This means that *it has to be accepted in payment of a debt* unless the debt instrument itself specifically provides for another form of payment, such as, for example, the delivery of commodities. But a deposit is not legal tender. A creditor does not have to accept a check and can demand to be paid in currency instead. However, whether or not something is legal tender is *not* the criterion of whether it is money. As long as it is generally accepted in exchange, or used as a standard of value, we call it money.

Nature of Credit Money

Credit money economizes on scarce resources. Instead of using gold or silver, items with a high cost of production, we use items with trivial production costs, entries on a bank's books, paper, or, in the case of coins, some base metals. Money is a token entitling the bearer to draw on the economy's goods and services, and what makes *us* willing to accept it is that *other people* are willing to accept it in exchange for their goods and services. It does not need to have any value as a commodity in its own right any more than the admission ticket to a concert has to be capable of producing music.

This is not to foreclose the issue of whether or not full-bodied money, such as gold coins, or representative full-bodied money is preferable to credit money. While the quantity of a commodity money is governed by the availability of the commodity, the government controls the quantity of credit money. Opinions can reasonably differ on whether it is better to have the quantity of money controlled by accidents such as the discovery of new gold fields, or by governments.[5] Many economists believe that governments, unrestrained by a gold standard or some other rule, tend to increase the quantity of money too fast, which results in inflation. They do this because in the short run raising the quantity of money rapidly has very pleasant results: unemployment falls and so does the interest rate.

Credit money requires considerable sophistication. People have to grasp the idea that something is valuable if other people will treat it as valuable, despite the fact that it has no value in direct use as a commodity. Not surprisingly, credit money is therefore a relatively recent innovation. While there had been episodes of credit money before, in 1930 most of the developed countries were on a gold standard, though credit money in the form of checks did circulate. In general, as one would expect, the evolution of money has been from concrete objects to abstract symbols, that is, from precious metals traded by weight, through coins made of precious metals, to paper money redeemable in precious coins, and to irredeemable paper money and bank deposits. But, as usual, evolution has not followed a straight line. For example, goldsmiths' deposits, which were essentially checks, were used as a means of payment in seventeenth-century England at a time when paper money was not yet acceptable.

THE CASHLESS SOCIETY?

Has the evolution of money run its course, or will it go on? There is a widespread belief that not only will it continue, but that a substantial further step is close at hand. There is much concern now about the rapid growth in the volume of checks to be cleared each year, and the cost that this involves. Moreover, check clearing is a relatively slow process. But computer-based innovations have helped. These innovations take many forms. One is automated clearinghouses that clear checks between banks cheaply. Another, more visible one, is automatic teller machines in many banks that allow customers to make withdrawals and deposits twenty-four hours a day without the intervention of a human teller. These machines need not be installed in the bank itself but can be installed, when the law permits, even in places like shopping centers, thus obviating the need for a branch bank. Moreover, similar machines can be installed at check-out counters in supermarkets and other stores, so that customers can pay by having their accounts debited automatically.

[5]Thus Huston McCulloch has responded to the argument that a commodity standard wastes resources with the following analogy: "A similar argument could be made for bicycle locks and chains. If metal locks could be replaced with symbolic paper locks, resources would be released that could be used productively elsewhere. As long as thieves honor paper locks as they would metal locks, your bike will be perfectly secure. Surely hardened steel and phosphor bronze shackles are evidence of irrationality on the part of those who insist on them" (*Money and Inflation* [New York: Academic Press, 1975], p. 78).

One can allow one's imagination to roam beyond such relatively mundane devices and imagine a completely automated payments system. Income and other receipts would be credited automatically to a person's account by computer. When making purchases the buyer would offer an account number, which the seller would punch into a computer terminal. The payment would thus be automatically transferred to the seller's account. Recurrent payments, such as mortgage payments and utility bills, would be automatically subtracted from the payer's account, as, in fact, is already done in some cases.

However, there are still many obstacles to such a system. In some experiments that have been undertaken the public has been less than enthusiastic about electronic payments, in part because such a system does not provide the choice of delaying payment of bills when an account is low. It is probable that eventually we will move to a widespread electronic payments system, but we are not likely to do so soon. However, most large payments, that is, payments of many thousands of dollars, are already made by wire, and not by check, to avoid delays in the mail. Throughout this book when we refer to transfer by checks we will also mean such wire transfers.

To see one problem with an electronic transfer system consider the following story. Some colonists in a new land were familiar with a monetary system, but had not brought any money with them. Being without a medium of exchange they could still benefit from their familiarity with money by using money as a unit of account. They bartered goods, but they expressed the values of the goods they brought to the market in terms of the standard of value. But, even with a unit of account, barter is cumbersome, so they decided to use a medium of exchange. Since they did not want to tie up valuable goods by using them as a medium of exchange they hit upon the idea of using a credit system. Each colonist was given a line of credit, and one of them served as a clerk who recorded all the transactions, crediting the account of the seller and debiting the account of the buyer. But although this was a great improvement over barter even this system was cumbersome; the clerk was kept busy recording all the transactions and thought that recording very small transactions was a great nuisance. So he suggested that each colonist be given pieces of paper denoting small amounts to be credited to his or her account. They could then pass these pieces of paper to each other to make purchases. This would save a lot of bookkeeping. Only those who accumulate more pieces of paper than needed would turn them in to the clerk who would then credit their accounts. The colonists accepted this scheme and lived happily ever after. They had reinvented currency.

MONEY AND NEAR-MONEY

The fact that the monetary system is evolving rather than static suggests that the distinction between money and "other things" is not clear-cut. At any particular time there may be some items that are just halfway in the process of becoming money. The line of distinction between money and nonmoney is therefore blurry. Where we want to draw this line depends, in part, on what our purpose is, what particular function of money is the most relevant for the problem at hand. For example, if we focus on the medium of exchange function, we want to define money as just those items that generally function as a medium of exchange.

But suppose that we stress the store of wealth function instead. If so, we want to include in the definition of money those assets that are extremely liquid, since it is its liquidity that differentiates money from other stores of wealth. The liquidity of an asset depends on (1) how easily it can be bought or sold, (2) the transactions cost of buying or selling it, and (3) how stable and predictable its price is. Narrow money, at one end of the scale, has perfect liquidity. Since it already is money there is no cost and trouble in selling it, that is, in turning it into money. And the price of a dollar is constant at one dollar. Towards the other end of the scale there are items like real estate, which may take quite some time to sell, involve a substantial brokerage cost, and may have to be sold at less than the anticipated price. We can rank all items by their liquidity, that is by their degree of *moneyness*.

The question now arises where along this spectrum of liquidity and moneyness one should draw the line between money and nonmoney. There is no point at which one can draw an obvious and clear-cut line. Regardless of how broadly or narrowly one defines money there are always some assets that, while excluded from the definition of money, are very close to the borderline. Moneyness is a continuum. We therefore call *items that are excluded from the definition of money but are quite similar to some items that are included,* **near-moneys.**

These near-moneys are items that are very liquid, but not *quite* as liquid as money. Admittedly, this is rather vague, and it is not clear exactly what items should be included. At one end of the spectrum this depends on the definition of money that is used. The other end of the spectrum, where one draws the line between near-moneys and those assets that are too illiquid to be considered near-moneys, is also arbitrary. While stock in corporations is definitely not a near-money, it is not clear whether, say, a government security that matures within one or two years should be considered a near-money.

SUMMARY

1. Money should not be identified with currency alone because the bulk of the value of all payments is made by wire transfers. Nor should money be confused with income or wealth.
2. The functions of money are to serve as a medium of exchange, a standard of value and a store of wealth. As a medium of exchange money avoids the double coincidence of wants required under simple barter. However, under special circumstances barter is still used. As a standard of value money simplifies the comparison of values and facilitates bookkeeping. But when used as a standard of deferred payments money does not function well. As a store of wealth, money is characterized by the virtual absence of transactions costs and by fixity of its value in terms of most debts. Usually the same unit serves all the functions of money.
3. In terms of measurable quantities the term "money" is used here to mean *M-1,* that is checkable deposits plus currency held by the public.
4. Full-bodied money is money that has a commodity value equal to its face value.

Representative full-bodied money is money that can be redeemed for its full face value in full-bodied money. All other money is credit money. The value of credit money is based on the fact that it is generally accepted.

5. There is a trend towards a cashless society in which most transfers are by electronic book entries. But there are many advantages to using checks and currency.
6. Near-monies are items that are not quite as liquid as money, but are highly liquid. Moneyness is a matter of degree.

Questions and Exercises

1. Define: (a) currency, (b) money, (c) income, and (d) wealth. Distinguish between them.
2. Are your average money holdings greater than, roughly equal to, or less than your income, or is this a meaningless question?
3. Explain why demand deposits are included in the definition of money.
4. Explain how a medium of exchange economizes on effort. Do so also for a standard of value.
5. What characteristics distinguish money from other stores of wealth?
6. Explain the meaning of the following terms: (a) full-bodied commodity money, (b) representative commodity money, and (c) credit money. How do they differ?
7. Explain why credit money has value.
8. Discuss the meaning of the term near-moneys. What items are included?
9. Discuss what is meant by liquidity. How would you describe the liquidity of (a) corporate stock, (b) an expected inheritance, (c) a house, and (d) a deposit in a savings and loan association?
10. Rather cynically one may describe the exchange of gifts at Christmas as barter. Why do we use barter at that time instead of giving each other money when money is a so much better medium of exchange?

Further Reading

ALCHIAN, ARMEN. "Why Money?" *Journal of Money, Credit and Banking* 9 (February 1977), pt. 2, pp. 133–41. An excellent discussion of the medium of exchange role.

BRUNNER, KARL, and MELTZER, ALLAN. "The Uses of Money: Money in the Theory of an Exchange Economy." *American Economic Review* 61 (December 1971): 784–806. An excellent discussion of the medium of exchange function of money, but one that assumes some knowledge of economic theory.

FRANKEL, S. HERBERT. *Two Philosophies of Money*. London, St. Martin's Press, 1977. A short book that asks some basic questions about the government's right to manipulate money.

MELITZ, JACQUES. *Primitive Money*. Reading, Mass.: Addison-Wesley, 1974. An interesting discussion of the anthropology of money.

———. "The Polanyi School of Anthropology on Money: An Economist's View." *American Anthropologist* 72 (October 1970): 1020–40. An interesting survey.

RADFORD, R. A. "The Economic Organization of a P.O.W. Camp." *Economica* 12 (November 1945): 189–201. A fascinating description of how "money" arose in a special situation.

The Financial System: An Overview

2

The next four chapters discuss financial institutions in some detail. But first, it is useful to look at the big picture by considering a few salient characteristics of financial institutions and of the financial system in general. Hence, this chapter takes up three basic issues: (1) the reasons why financial institutions exist, (2) how households decide what assets to hold and what claims on themselves to issue, and (3) why governments regulate financial institutions.

THE ROLE OF FINANCIAL INSTITUTIONS

Financial institutions do not produce goods as manufacturing firms do, nor do they transport and distribute goods. So why have them at all? One thing they do—and it is a very necessary activity—is to clear payments for other participants in the economy and thus facilitate the division of labor. For example, a bank clears checks and provides its customers with important bookkeeping services when it sends out monthly statements. Other financial institutions, such as realty firms and stockbrokers, bring potential buyers and sellers together.

An important segment of the financial industry are the **financial intermediaries** who, while they may clear payments, do something else too. They *intermediate by obtaining the funds of savers in exchange for their own liabilities* (such as entries in a passbook), *and then, in turn, make loans to others.* They do not merely bring savers and ultimate borrowers together, but instead sell claims on *themselves* to their depositors and then buy claims on borrowers. Important examples of such financial intermediaries are savings and loan associations, mutual savings banks, and, to some extent, commercial banks.

Essentially, financial intermediaries buy and sell the right to future payments. For example, someone opening an account at a savings and loan association gives it a sum of money in exchange for the right to receive a larger sum back in the future. And the savings and loan then turns around and uses the deposit to make a loan, that is, to make a current payment to someone else, in return for that person's promise to make payments to it in the future.

This activity of trading in current payments and promises for future payments is extraordinarily important. To see this, consider first the extreme case of an economy with no borrowing and lending at all. In such an economy people would still want to save and invest. Many people would want to defer income from the present to the future, either because they expect their income to dwindle as they get older, or their needs to rise, or else because they hope to earn some yield on their savings. But many people would not be able to earn anything on their savings at all because they lack the opportunity to buy a physical asset that produces income, and they would not be able to lend to anyone who has this opportunity. At the same time, those who have the opportunity to acquire highly productive physical assets could do so only to the extent that they could cut back on their own consumption—and this hardly is the way to finance a steel mill! Obviously, such an economy would be very inefficient.

Now let us go to the opposite extreme and not only introduce borrowing and lending, but assume that these activities involve no information costs and no transaction costs. In this case there is a great deal of borrowing and lending. Every household would save until its marginal loss from deferring consumption for one year is equal to the interest rate it can earn from lending these savings, and every investor buys capital assets until the marginal yield on these assets equals the interest rate. Moreover, at the margin, the productivity of a dollar newly invested in every kind of capital has to be equal throughout the economy, for otherwise investors could gain by shifting funds (costlessly) between different sectors. Such an economy allocates its capital very efficiently.

But, in the real world there are information costs and transactions costs. Potential lenders do not have costless knowledge of everyone who wants to borrow, nor do they know the interest each of these borrowers is willing to pay, or the soundness of the potential loans. It is costly for borrowers and lenders to learn of each other's existence, and then lenders have to undertake an often expensive credit investigation of the risk that the borrower will not be able or willing to repay. Moreover, there are transaction costs: loan contracts have to be drawn up, provisions for collateral may have to be made, and so on.

To visualize these problems, imagine that you decide to make a mortgage loan. You first have to locate a potential borrower, and then investigate her credit rating, as well as the current and probable future market value of the house. Then, if you decide to make the loan, you have to draw up a mortgage contract. Obviously all of this is a time-consuming and expensive business, particularly if you try to do it right. And then, once you have made the mortgage loan, you are holding a very illiquid asset, and hence may be in difficulty if you, yourself, suddenly need funds.

But fortunately these costs can be minimized the same way we minimize the costs of most other things. We do not raise and slaughter our own cattle, nor do we make our own furniture. We rely on the division of labor. We do the same in finance by using financial intermediaries.

Advantages of Using Financial Intermediation

Under this system the lender and the ultimate borrower do not go to the trouble of seeking each other out, and since the lender does not take the ultimate borrower's IOU, he or she does not have to investigate the borrower's credit standing. Instead, she gives her funds to, say, a savings and loan association, which, in turn, makes a mortgage loan. Now obviously every financial intermediary levies a charge for services by paying the lender a lower interest rate on the deposit than the rate paid by the borrower. What makes it worthwhile for borrowers and lenders to pay this charge? Let us look at the benefits provided by financial intermediaries.

Minimize cost. We have already mentioned one benefit of using a financial intermediary: it economizes on the information and transaction costs of borrowers and lenders. As a concrete example, consider a corporation that wants to borrow $10 million. Since there are few households able to make a $10 million loan, the corporation would have to scurry around and borrow, say, an average of $10,000 from a thousand households. Since these households would not know that this corporation wants to borrow from them, it would have to seek them out by extensive advertising. And then it would have to convince them that it is a sound borrower. A financial intermediary, say, a savings and loan, on the other hand, is set up to collect the funds of many small depositors. It does not have to let households know that it wants their funds every time a borrower approaches it for a loan. The public already knows that it would like its funds. Moreover, since its deposits are insured, the public does not have to investigate credit standing. To be sure, the financial intermediary itself has to investigate the credit standing of the borrower, but a single investigation by an expert is much less costly than a thousand separate investigations by amateurs.

Long-term loans. A second advantage of financial intermediaries is that they make it possible for borrowers to obtain long-term loans even though the ultimate lenders are making only short-term loans. Much borrowing is done to acquire long-lived assets, such as houses or factories. And someone who borrows to buy such assets does not want to finance them with a short-term loan. Few families would want to finance the purchase of their homes by borrowing on a thirty-day promissory note, and face each month the problem of refinancing the loan. But now consider the same family in its role as lender. Would it want to make a twenty-year loan? Probably not, because it wants to have these funds available in case an emergency arises.

Here is where the financial intermediary comes in. Despite the fact that it has used depositors' funds to make long-term loans, a bank or a savings and loan association can promise its depositors that they can withdraw their deposits at any time. If it has many individually small depositors whose decisions whether or not to withdraw their deposits are independent of each other, then it can predict quite well the probability distribution of deposit withdrawals on any given day and hold small but sufficient reserves to meet such withdrawals. Under normal conditions, the decision whether or not to withdraw a deposit depends largely on the particular circumstances of each depositor, for example, his decision to make a large purchase. Hence, one can, under normal conditions, assume that the decisions of various depositors are independent of each other, so that the law of large numbers applies. However, this fortunate state of affairs does not *always* hold. Suppose, for example, that the public becomes afraid that banks or other financial institutions will fail. It will then try to withdraw deposits on a massive scale. And the financial intermediaries will then not have sufficient liquid funds available to repay these deposits. Until 1934, when the federal government started to insure deposits, the United States suffered numerous financial panics in which many banks failed. Similarly, if interest rates paid to depositors remain constant while other interest rates rise, then many depositors will have an incentive to withdraw their deposits, so that withdrawals will be linked rather than independent. In the 1970s this created a severe problem for savings and loans and for mutual savings banks.

Liquidity. Since many claims on financial intermediaries are liquid they should be distinguished sharply from claims on other borrowers. Suppose you lend $1,000 to General Motors for ten years. In return you get a certificate called a bond that promises to pay you $90 per year, and to return your $1,000 after ten years. Suppose, three years after you have bought this bond, you suddenly need your $1,000 back. General Motors will not pay off the bond for another seven years, and the only way you can get your $1,000 back before then is to sell the bond on the open market to some other investor. The price you will get depends on supply and demand, and may be significantly less—or more—than your original $1,000. By contrast, if you have a deposit in a savings and loan association, you can get your $1,000 back at any time, though, on some kinds of deposits, you lose some of the interest you have previously earned on it.

Risk pooling. Financial intermediaries also pool risks. Suppose there are a hundred loans made, and that it is reasonable to expect that ninety-nine of them will be repaid. Every lender is then afraid that he or she will be the unlucky one. But if the lenders pool their funds, then each lender will lose one percent of his or her loan and no more, thus avoiding the risk of a large loss in exchange for accepting a more certain small loss. Thus by pooling the funds of depositors, financial intermediaries reduce the riskiness of lending.

In summary then, indirect finance has three great advantages: it reduces the risk of lending; it makes loans more liquid than they otherwise would be; and it greatly reduces the information and transaction costs of lenders and borrowers.

Do these advantages mean that all finance takes place through financial intermediaries? Of course not. Since they charge a fee for their services, it is sometimes worthwhile for borrowers and lenders to deal directly. Beyond this, people who want to invest sometimes do not borrow at all, but reduce their own consumption to avoid either the charges of a financial intermediary, or the costs of finding a willing lender. This is likely to occur if the investment project is very risky, so that the potential borrower would have to pay a very high rate of interest to compensate the lender for the risk the lender sees in the project. The investor, say, the proverbial inventor of the better mousetrap, may well think that the risk is much less than lenders think it is, and hence does not want to pay the substantially higher interest rate the lenders require as compensation for assuming the risk.

PORTFOLIO BALANCE

In the previous section we pointed out that financial intermediaries bridge the gap between the types of loans that borrowers want to obtain and that lenders want to make. We will now take this idea up in more detail by looking at the different characteristics of loans that borrowers and lenders prefer.

Most borrowers are not specialists in finance and do not want to pay the costs of acquiring a great deal of information. At the same time they are usually averse to taking risks. Both of these factors suggest that borrowers should try to play it safe.

Avoiding Risk

How can they do this? Financial risks arise not only from holding assets that may decline in value, but also from having outstanding debts that may become due at a time when there are no readily available funds to pay them off. One way to avoid financial risk is therefore to **hedge,** that is, *to have one's assets and liabilities come due at the same time*. Suppose, for example, that you plan to buy an asset costing $1000 that will yield at least $105 each year for ten years and then fall apart. If you finance it by borrowing $1,000 for ten years at a 5 percent interest rate, then the only risk you face is that the asset may not actually pay off as much as $105 a year for ten years. But suppose you finance it by borrowing $1,000 for one year, and plan to obtain additional one-year loans in each of the following nine years. If so, you run an additional risk, because you may not be able to get a new loan at the end of each year or else you may have to pay a much higher than anticipated interest rate on the new loans. Both of these contingencies can be avoided by matching the maturity of the loan and the asset you buy with it.

Although such maturity matching reduces risk, borrowers will not always do it because it may be too expensive. For example, if the interest rate is, say, 6 percent on a five-year loan, and 7 percent on a ten-year loan, some borrowers will be tempted to take out a five-year loan, and accept the risk that they will have to pay a much higher interest rate after five years.

A similar thing is true for lenders. The value to them of a security they purchase is, of course, a positive function of its yield but a negative function of its riskiness. Unfortunately for them there is usually a trade-off here; the higher the yield of a security the greater is its risk. Why should a very sound borrower be willing to pay a high interest rate?

So far we have used the term "risk" rather loosely. One type of risk is **default risk,** that is, the risk that the *borrower will simply not repay the loan,* either due to dishonesty or plain inability to do so. Another type of risk, called **purchasing-power risk,** is the risk that, due to an unexpectedly high inflation rate, the *future interest payments, and the principal of the loan when finally repaid, will have less purchasing power* than the lender anticipated at the time the loan was made. A similar risk is faced by borrowers. A borrower may cheerfully agree to pay, say, 15 percent interest, expecting that a 12 percent inflation rate will reduce the real value of the loan. But inflation may be only 4 percent.

A third type of risk is **interest-rate risk,** that is the *risk that the market value of a security will fall because interest rates will rise.* We will discuss this further later; here we just present the intuitive idea. Suppose that five years ago you bought a ten-year $1,000 bond carrying a 6 percent interest rate, and that the interest rate now obtainable on similar bonds that also have five years to go until they mature is 8 percent. Would anyone pay $1,000 for your bond? Surely not, because they could earn $80 per year by buying a new bond, and only $60 per year by buying your bond. Hence, to sell your bond you would have to reduce its price. But suppose the bond, instead of having five years to maturity, would mature in, say, ninety days; what would its price be then? It would still be less than $1,000 since the buyer would get 6 percent instead of 8 percent interest for ninety days; but since getting a lower interest rate for only ninety days does not involve much of a loss, the bond would sell for something close to $1,000. Hence, while holding any security with a fixed interest rate involves *some* interest-rate risk, the closer to maturity a security is, the lower is this risk. On the other hand, if interest rates fall you gain because your bond is worth more; and the longer the time is until the bond matures, the greater is your gain. But the fact that you may gain as well as lose does not mean that you are taking no risk.

Diversification

All three types of risk are relevant for deciding what assets to include in a portfolio, and what debts to have outstanding. But anyone holding more than one type of asset has to consider, not the risk of each asset taken by itself, but instead the totality of the risk on various assets and debts jointly. Suppose, for example, that someone has a $1,000 debt coming due five years from now; by holding a $1,000 government bond also due in five years, the risk can be eliminated completely on both the debt and the bond. Similarly, suppose someone holds stock in a company that is likely to gain from inflation, and stock in another company that is likely to lose from inflation. The riskiness of a portfolio that combines both of these stocks may be less than the riskiness of each stock taken separately. *A portfolio consisting of assets that are affected in opposite directions by given future events is less risky than are the assets that compose it when taken individually.* Hence a low-risk portfolio need not contain only assets that individually have little risk; sometimes one reduces the riskiness of a portfolio by adding some high-risk assets that offset the risks of other assets in it.

Buying assets with offsetting risks is one example of portfolio diversification. But one can to some extent diversify one's portfolio even if one cannot buy assets with offsetting risks. Suppose, for example, that you have the choice between an asset lasting one year with an expected 40 percent yield, but with a 20 percent chance that it will become completely worthless, or another asset that yields 5 percent, but is virtually riskless. Which asset should you buy? Obviously, this will depend upon your willingness to take risks. Most people are not willing to risk all their livelihood even for an exceptionally high expected rate of return, but many are willing to take a risk with a small proportion of their assets. Hence, they hold some proportion—often only a small proportion—of their portfolio in risky assets. Most large portfolios are diversified, both by containing assets with offsetting risks, and also by containing some assets with small and some with large risks. And one of the major functions of a financial adviser is to tell people how they can diversify their portfolio efficiently.

Table 2.1 Characteristics of Selected Assets (ranked with lowest yield, liquidity, or risk denoted by zero)

Asset	Typical monetary yield	Imputed yield from conveni-ence	Imputed yield from liquidity	Default risk	Interest-rate risk	Purchasing-power risk
M-1	0–1[b]	1	4	0[d]	0	1
Insured savings and time deposits	1 or 3[c]	0	0–3[c]	0	1–2[c]	1
Short-term government securities	2	0	3	0	1	1
Long-term government securities	3	0	2	0	2	1
Corporate bonds[a]	4	0	1	1	2	1
Corporate stock	5	0	1	2	2	2[f]
Physical capital used by households	0	1	0	—[e]	0	0

a. large denomination bonds traded frequently on major exchanges.
b. zero for currency, 1 for some checkable deposits.
c. depends on type of deposit.
d. default risk exists only for deposits of over $100,000.
e. no default risk per se, but risk that capital asset will be less useful than planned.
f. assumes, on basis of recent experience, that inflation depresses real stock prices.

To decide what assets to hold in a portfolio, one has to know the characteristics of selected assets. Table 2.1 shows the typical yields, liquidity, and risks on the following assets: money, saving or time deposits at fixed interest rates in banks or savings and loan associations, government securities, corporate bonds and stocks, and capital held directly, such as an owned home or consumer durables. The first column shows a typical ranking of the monetary yield of these assets. However, this ranking changes from time to time; sometimes deposits have a higher yield than short-term securities, and sometimes short-term securities have a higher yield than long-term securities. Similarly, the yield on stock (that is, the dividend plus capital gains and losses) fluctuates a great deal, and to the chagrin of stockholders it is sometimes negative. The next column shows the imputed yield (apart from liquidity) that an asset may have by providing free services, such as check clearing in the case of deposits, and shelter in the case of housing. The third column shows the asset's liquidity in the sense of the speed and ease with which it can be sold, and the lowness of the transaction costs of buying or selling it. The remaining three columns deal with the three types of risks. Interest-rate risk includes here not only the danger of actually selling an asset at a loss, but also the forgone opportunity cost if interest rates rise. For example, owners of bonds paying 6 percent may hold on to them when interest rates have risen to 9 percent, and thus avoid taking an explicit loss, but they still suffer a loss in the sense that had they not previously bought the 6 percent securities, they could now buy the 9 percent ones.

From Table 2.1 one can see the role that various assets play in portfolios of households. Money is held mainly for its yield in terms of convenience and for its liquidity. Although money is also safe—except for purchasing-power risk—it would be naïve to hold it primarily for this reason because in this respect it is dominated by time deposits. Savings and time deposits, as well as short-term government securities, are held primarily because of their high liquidity and safety, though their yield provides an additional motive. Long-term government securities often have a higher yield, but involve more interest-rate risk than the previously discussed assets. Still they are often included in portfolios to provide safety in the sense of avoiding default risk. Corporate bonds are riskier since they have a default risk. Corporate stock typically has a higher default risk than corporate bonds, but its yield has, over the long run, been higher than the yield on corporate bonds.[1] Capital owned directly has usually a high *imputed* yield such as providing the family with shelter, transportation, and so on, but it is very illiquid.

Another way to look at the seven types of assets listed in Table 2.1 is to consider the types of institutions that issue them. The government issues part of the money stock, currency, and, of course, government securities. Financial intermediaries issue the remainder of the money stock. Financial intermediaries issue saving and time deposits, and corporations issue corporate bonds and stock. With respect to default risk the safest assets are the obligations of the government and of financial intermediaries. It is simple to explain why the government's obligations are safe; since the government has the power to tax, and the power to create money, it can always pay off its debts. But what ensures the safety of the obligations of financial intermediaries? The answer is that the government insures and supervises them. We will take up the insurance systems in later chapters.

GOVERNMENT SUPERVISION OF FINANCIAL INSTITUTIONS

Financial intermediaries are very heavily regulated by both the federal and state governments. For example, one cannot just start a bank the way one

[1] Strictly speaking there is no default risk on corporate stock since it is not redeemable but, all the same, there can be losses.

can start another business. Instead, a prospective bank organizer must obtain special permission, called a charter, from either the federal or state authorities, and this permission is given only sparingly. It will not be given if opening a new bank in the community would seriously weaken an existing bank. Thus, already established banks are protected from competition that could drive them out of business. Moreover, various government agencies supervise banks and financial intermediaries by inspecting the assets they hold and requiring them to get rid of risky ones. Furthermore, to limit the extent to which they can compete with each other the government sets maximum interest rates that financial intermediaries can pay on some types of deposits.

While in other industries the government prosecutes attempts to limit competition, in banking, as in some other regulated industries, it imposes regulations that reduce competition. Why is this? Essentially the answer is that an unregulated banking system would take too many risks. But this does not *necessarily* mean that government regulation is desirable, since it has its own disadvantages. As a general principle, the fact that the private market (or government regulation) suffers from some inefficiencies does not provide a sufficient case to replace it; the alternative might be worse.

What is the argument for government supervision of banks? The first reason is *consumer ignorance*. For competition to work effectively the buyer must be able to evaluate the quality of the product with some degree of efficiency. Otherwise, various producers could succeed by offering a defective product at a low price. Consumers can evaluate most products in either, or both, of two ways. One is through experience. They buy, say, a quart of milk advertised by a new dairy. If they don't like it not much is lost. The other way is by evaluating the product before purchase; for example, they may not buy a car that looks flimsy.

Unfortunately, neither method works well for deciding whether to buy the deposit services of a financial intermediary. The foremost characteristic a household looks for in a financial intermediary is that it be safe and not fail. But experience provides little help here. Once a bank has failed, depositors know that they should not have entrusted their funds to it, but by then it is too late.[2]

The other method of evaluating a product, inspecting whether it is flimsy or not, does not work for financial intermediaries either. Extensive effort and technical knowledge are required to evaluate the soundness of a bank or other financial intermediary. Just looking at the balance sheet won't do. Depositors cannot tell whether the item listed as "loans" consists of loans made to sound or to risky borrowers.

And the financial intermediary has an incentive to buy assets that are

[2]Deposits are not the only example of large and infrequent expenditures on items whose technical soundness it is difficult to evaluate. This is so for houses, too. And here too we have government regulation (building codes) and inspection for safety and health defects that would not be obvious to the buyer. In the absence of such government regulations buyers would probably rely on private housing inspectors and on certificates by the builder. But the certificate of a failed bank would give a depositor little protection, and buildings are easier for a specialist to evaluate than are banks.

too risky from the point of view of the depositor and the economy as a whole. This is so, not because it wants to fail, but because if it makes a risky loan all the additional interest the borrower pays because the loan is risky accrues to it. (The depositor, not knowing that the financial institution is taking these risks, does not ask for higher interest.) But the institution does not bear all the corresponding potential loss, since in the absence of deposit insurance, the depositor stands to lose too. Thus, since the depositor bears part of the risk, the marginal cost of risk taking to both the financial institution and the depositor taken together exceeds the marginal cost of risk taking just to the institution. But in deciding how much risk to take, the financial institution sets the marginal revenue from taking risk equal to the marginal cost that risk imposed on it alone, so that it takes more risk than is justified when one considers the cost of taking the risk to both it and the depositors together.

Some mechanism is obviously needed to prevent financial intermediaries from taking too much risk. One possibility would be extensive consumer information. Thus, in principle, depositors could subscribe to reports, written by accountants and financial analysts, that evaluate banks and other financial intermediaries. However, such reports may not be reliable enough and may be expensive, both in terms of purchase price and in terms of the time it takes to read and evaluate their competing recommendations. But large business firms that have deposits greatly exceeding the insurance limit try to evaluate the soundness of their banks.

Another way to protect the depositor is to insure deposits. One possibility would be to have banks or other financial intermediaries insured by private insurance companies, but there would be the danger that if many large institutions fail, so would the insurance company. Bank failures cannot be predicted from actuarial tables the way deaths, or car accidents, can. However, the government is an institution that can always pay off its debts, and hence we have it insure deposits.[3] But if the government insures deposits (up to $100,000), what protects the government against the danger of banks taking excessive risks? The answer is that the government prohibits financial institutions from buying certain risky assets.

A second, even more important reason, for government supervision of depository institutions (banks, savings banks, savings and loans and credit unions) is that they *create the major part of our money supply.* Thus a wave of bank failures could wipe out a significant proportion of the money stock. And this, in fact, happened in the Great Depression when *M-1* fell by about one-quarter. In Part Three we will discuss how, and why, a reduction in the money stock causes real income and prices to fall. For now, we will merely assert that bank failures that would suddenly reduce the money stock, say, by 20 percent or more, would be a catastrophe. Thus the government has a strong incentive to prevent depository institutions from failing, and one way of doing this is to prevent them from taking too much risk.

[3] Actually bank deposits are insured, not directly by the federal government per se, but by one of its agencies, the FDIC, which has accumulated only a limited insurance fund. But it is hard to conceive of a situation in which the U.S. Treasury would not come to the rescue of the FDIC if this were needed.

Finally, the federal government has in the past tried to use regulation over depository institutions as *a way of subsidizing residential construction and the building industry*. One way it did this was to prohibit savings and loans from making most kinds of business and consumer loans so that they would make more mortgage loans instead. However, this regulation was not very effective, and in 1981 savings and loan associations were given the right to make a limited amount of consumer and business loans. Another way the government tried to subsidize residential construction was to set a ceiling on the interest rates that could be paid to depositors, in the (questionable) belief that depository institutions would then charge lower rates on the mortgages they make. This regulation turned out to be ineffective, and is currently being phased out.

Do these three reasons for governmental regulations mean that the current heavy regulation of banks and other financial intermediaries is justified and not excessive? Not necessarily. While the authors believe that the first two reasons (the difficulty of evaluating the safety of financial institutions, and the need to prevent sharp declines in the stock of money and of near-moneys) justify some government regulations, we are much more skeptical about the last reason (subsidizing residential construction) though, of course, many respected economists disagree with us on these judgments.

Even if one agrees that some controls over banks and other financial intermediaries are needed, it is quite possible that our present level of controls is excessive, and should be reduced. For example, one way of reducing the role of government controls would be to allow private insurance companies to insure bank deposits up to a certain amount, with government insurance taking over beyond that point. It is much easier to make a case for *some* government regulation of financial institutions than to decide just how much regulation is needed, and what form it should take.

SUMMARY

1. Financial institutions play an important role. Among them are financial intermediaries that interpose their own liabilities between ultimate savers and ultimate borrowers. This greatly facilitates saving and investment. Financial intermediaries economize on information and transaction costs, provide liquidity and shorter term assets to savers, and pool risks.
2. Portfolio risk can be reduced by diversifying the portfolio and by holding assets with maturities similar to one's liabilities. Assets are subject to default risk, purchasing-power risk and interest-rate risk. These risks differ for various assets.
3. Financial intermediaries are heavily regulated, often in ways that inhibit competition. The reasons for heavy regulations are prevention of massive failures that, by reducing the stocks of money and liquid assets, could generate a depression; the difficulty people have in deciding whether a financial intermediary is safe; the wish to subsidize certain industries (such as residential construction); and a fear of great aggregations of economic power. While some regulation is justified, it is not obvious that the present level of regulation is.

Questions and Exercises

1. Explain why we have financial intermediaries.
2. Financial intermediaries hold relatively illiquid and somewhat risky assets and yet can issue very liquid and safe claims on themselves. Explain how they can do this magic. Can they do this without limit?
3. Which argument for government regulation of financial institutions do you find most convincing? Which least convincing? Give your reasons.
4. Suppose you had $100,000. How would you distribute your portfolio over various assets? Why? How about if you had $10,000?
5. Many households hold claims on financial intermediaries, and, at the same time, borrow from financial intermediaries. Why don't they "borrow" from themselves?
6. Suppose that you decide to set yourself up as a financial institution and issue $1,000 deposits to each of four customers. Suppose further that the probability of any one depositor demanding repayment of his or her deposit within the relevant period is 20 percent (and that the probabilities of various depositors demanding repayment are independent of each other). How much would you want to keep in reserves to meet potential depositor demand? (Hint: the answer involves more than just a simple number.)

Further Reading

BENSTON, GEORGE. "A Transactions Cost Approach to the Theory of Financial Intermediation," *Journal of Finance* 31 (May 1976): 215–32. A very thoughtful, elegant discussion, though a bit difficult at points.

GOLDSMITH, RAYMOND. *Financial Institutions*. New York: Random House, 1968. This is an excellent survey of the financial system.

GURLEY, JOHN, and SHAW, EDWARD. *Money in a Theory of Finance*. Washington, D.C.: Brookings Institution, 1960. An advanced, seminal treatise.

MOORE, BASIL. *An Introduction to the Theory of Finance*. New York: Free Press, 1968. Chapter two provides a very useful and thorough, yet brief, discussion of portfolio management.

SHAW, EDWARD. *Financial Deepening in Economic Development*. New York: Oxford University Press, 1973. An important discussion of the role of finance in less-developed countries.

The Banking Industry

3

The previous chapter presented a bird's-eye view of financial institutions and their functions. This and the following chapter deal with our most prominent financial institutions, commercial banks or just *banks,* as we will call them. Banks are our most important financial institutions as they create much of our money stock and have such a wide range of activities. We take up banking in considerable detail, both because the behavior of banks is relevant for monetary policy, and because, on a more personal level, readers are likely to deal with banks as depositors, and perhaps as borrowers. In dealing with a bank it is obviously useful to be able to see things from the bank's point of view, and this requires some knowledge of how they operate.

The current chapter deals with the banking industry as a whole, and takes up the way banks are regulated, and how they interact with each other. The following chapter then looks at the individual bank as a profit-maximizing institution and at its assets and liabilities. We postpone discussion of foreign banks in the United States and the foreign activities of U.S. banks until Chapter 28.

A SKETCH OF BANKING HISTORY

Banking is an ancient business. Banks existed already in ancient Babylon and in the classical civilizations, particularly in Rome. But modern banking started in Renaissance Italy where bankers, apart from buying and selling foreign currencies, also took demand and time deposits. These demand deposits were usually transferred orally by the owner visiting the banker who sat behind his bench or table, though checks were not unknown. (Our term *bankruptcy* comes from the Italian custom of breaking the bench of a banker who could not pay off his creditors.) The most famous of these Italian bankers were the Medici family, who for a time ruled Florence and made loans to princes and merchants both in Italy and in the rest of Europe.

In England banking grew out of the custom of goldsmiths, who took in their customers' gold and silver for safekeeping. They then discovered that they could lend such coins out, keeping just a certain proportion as a reserve, since not all customers would come in for repayment at the same time. Moreover they gave their depositors receipts, which these depositors could pass on to other people. Eventually, to make such transfers more convenient, they issued these receipts in round-number sums. They thus became private banknotes; that is, notes repayable on demand by the banker in gold or silver.

In colonial America the first bank, in the modern sense of the term, was the Bank of North America, founded in 1782. Subsequently, banking spread rapidly as the states chartered more and more banks, some of them owned by the state itself. Between 1781 and 1861 over twenty-five hundred banks were organized, but many of them were unsound; almost two-fifths of them had to close within ten years after they had opened.[1]

In 1791, at the urging of Alexander Hamilton, Congress temporarily chartered a national bank, the First Bank of the United States, in part owned by the federal government. This bank, which was much larger than the state-chartered banks, held deposits of the federal government and transferred funds for it to various parts of the country. It also tried to discipline the state-chartered banks that had issued too many banknotes, either by refusing to accept their notes in payment, or by collecting a lot of them and presenting them all at once to the unfortunate bank for redemption in gold.

Not surprisingly, in 1811 when the charter of the First Bank of the United States came up in Congress for renewal, the state-chartered banks tried to kill it. Among the arguments against it were that it was, in part, owned by foreigners, that the bank had dabbled in politics, doubts that the Constitution permitted Congress to charter a bank, and a belief that the bank had too much monopoly power. These arguments were effective. Congress did not renew the First Bank's charter. State banks, now freed from the pressure to redeem their notes, became much more numerous, and as they issued more banknotes and demand deposits, they contributed to an inflation.

But in 1816 the Second Bank of the United States was chartered with the federal government owning one-fifth of the stock and appointing one-fifth of the directors. Although it did a lot of good in curbing excessive expansion by state banks, its charter was allowed to expire in 1836. This occurred in good part because it was opposed by President Andrew Jackson, who was concerned about the concentration of economic power in the Northeast and was an opponent of the bank's president, Nicholas Biddle.

The 1830s also saw another important change in banking. Until then states could charter banks only by a special act of the legislature. This led to much corruption and favoritism. In 1837 Michigan led the way to a new system, called **free banking.** Under this system, anyone who met rather easy

[1] Benjamin Klebaner, *Commercial Banking in the United States: A History* (Hansdale, Ill.: Dryden Press, 1974), p. 48.

conditions could organize a bank and issue banknotes as well as take deposits, checks by this time having come into widespread usage. Although free banking avoided the scandals of the previous system, it developed its own problems. Many new banks were organized and issued their banknotes, and with so many different banknotes around, it was hard to differentiate between genuine and counterfeit notes, or notes issued on nonexistent banks. Moreover, notes of certain banks, considered unsafe or located far away, circulated at less than full face value. Merchants had to look up in registers of banknotes the value of notes presented to them as payment. Moreover a few—though not very many—banks, the so-called wildcat banks, made it hard to present their banknotes to them for redemption in coin by locating in out-of-the-way places. As a result, some banknotes circulated well below their face value, and, in addition, bank failures were common. These problems, as well as the need to develop an additional market for government bonds to finance the Civil War, led Congress to establish the National Banking System starting with the National Currency Act of 1863 (later amended and renamed the National Banking Act). The banknotes, issued by each of the *national banks* chartered by the federal government, were made uniform, and they were safe because each national bank had to deposit $10 of federal government bonds with the Comptroller of the Currency for each $9 of banknotes it issued. (Thus it would put up $1 of capital, borrow $9 from depositors and hold $10 of interest-earning government bonds.) If a bank failed, the holders of its national banknotes were repaid by the Comptroller of the Currency out of the bonds the bank had deposited with him. State-chartered banks were effectively prevented from issuing banknotes by the imposition of an annual 10 percent tax on their notes. There was now a uniform and sound currency that, unlike the previous banknotes, was accepted at par (that is, at full value) throughout the country. Funds could now be transferred all over the country at a cost that could not exceed the small cost of shipping banknotes, and was frequently less. But state banks, though they could no longer issue banknotes, did not disappear, as had been thought they would, because, with the rapidly growing use of checks, they could still provide a medium of exchange, demand deposits.

While the national banking system solved the problem of there being too many types of banknotes and reduced the frequency of bank failures, it was far from perfect. Thus it did not provide an efficient system of check collection. A check passed from one bank to another in a long chain until it was finally presented to the bank on which it was drawn. Hence, if it bounced it would take much too long until this was discovered.

To reduce bank failures the federal government required banks to keep reserves against their deposits. Some of these reserves had to be kept as currency in the banks' vaults, but (except for banks in the three largest financial centers) banks could keep part of their reserves as deposits with banks in larger cities. When these banks then withdrew these reserves the banks in the financial centers would find themselves short of reserves, and had to call in some of the short-term loans they had made to dealers in the money market and the stock market. As a result interest rates would rise sharply. Sometimes a financial panic—in which banks could not get at their reserves—

would result.[2] Banks did, however, develop a device to ameliorate the impact of financial panics. They would jointly stop paying out currency to their depositors, and would pay instead in *clearing house certificates,* which were notes that could be used to make deposits, and hence would be accepted as payments in many cases, albeit often at a discount.

There was no central bank that could adjust the money supply to meet the need for money, and the money supply could therefore not expand along with the demand for money. Hence, there were frequent complaints about a "shortage" of money in the fall when the harvesting season raised the demand for money, and interest rates would rise. (Whether these complaints were justified, in the sense that the supply of money *should* expand along with the demand for it, is another matter, which we will take up in Chapter 23.) A related complaint was that in a financial panic no additional currency was available to meet the increased demand as the public, afraid of bank failures, tried to shift out of deposits, into currency. Bank failures were frequent, particularly among state banks, which, being less heavily regulated than national banks, had grown at a faster rate.

In 1907 the country suffered a severe depression, which along with previous dissatisfaction with the banking system resulted in the appointment of the National Monetary Commission. After exhaustive studies it recommended the establishment of a central banking system, our Federal Reserve System. But there was a great deal of opposition to the creation of a central bank out of fear that it would be run by bankers and lead to a banking cartel. It was not until 1913 that this opposition was overcome and the Federal Reserve Act was signed by President Woodrow Wilson.

We will discuss the Federal Reserve System in considerable detail in Chapter 7, but we will note here the ways in which this new system was intended to solve the problems that beset the National Banking System. Checks could now be cleared through the Federal Reserve instead of routing them through a whole chain of banks. Required reserves had to be kept initially with the Federal Reserve rather than with other banks. (Subsequently banks were allowed to keep them also as currency in their vaults.) The money supply was made more responsive to the demand for money by enabling banks to borrow from the Federal Reserve. But the attempt to make banks safer failed miserably. There were many more bank failures in the period 1931–33 than at any other time.

CHARTERING AND EXAMINATION

Government control over banks comes in several layers. Initially, there is chartering. A prospective bank has to obtain a *charter, either from the federal government* as a **national bank,** or *from its state government* as a **state bank.**

The second layer of government control is the Federal Reserve. Although its main function is the conduct of monetary policy, it also regulates banks. All national banks must, and state banks may, but need not, join the Federal

[2] Besides, some banks would close their doors and fail rather than touch their reserves, so that these reserves did little good.

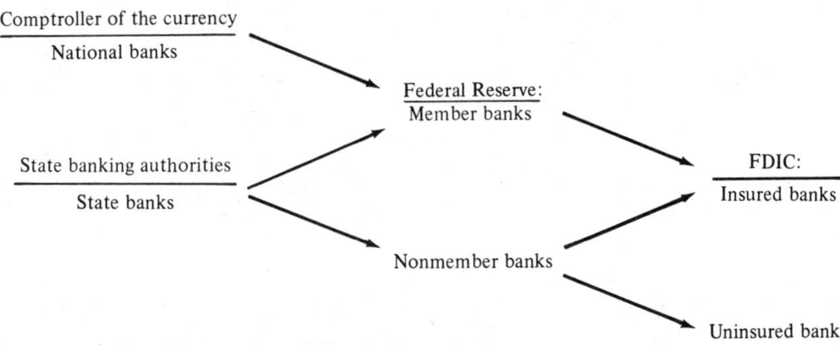

Figure 3.1 The Structure of Bank Regulation

Reserve System, becoming a **member bank**—this term *always refers to membership in the Federal Reserve System.* Third, there is the Federal Deposit Insurance Corporation (FDIC). All member banks *must* join the FDIC while nonmember banks *may* join if they meet the FDIC's admission criteria. The resultant structure of government contacts is shown in Figure 3.1. Table 3.1 shows the relative importance of the various types of banks. It shows that only 30 percent of all banks are national banks, but that, since on the average they are larger than state banks, they hold more than half of all deposits. Only 37 percent of all banks are member banks, but they hold almost three-quarters of all deposits. Practically all banks (97 percent), holding 99.8 percent of all deposits, are insured by the FDIC.

To obtain a charter one must apply either to the Comptroller of the Currency, an office of the U.S. Treasury Department, or to a state official called the superintendent of banks or by a similar name. State requirements, which are generally looser than federal ones, vary and apply only to state banks, and not to national banks located in the state.

A very important requirement for a national bank charter is that the government believes that there is a genuine public need for this new bank, and that its establishment would not take too much business away from existing banks. This is a remarkable requirement since it is so contrary to our general

Table 3.1 Distribution of Banks by Type December 1981

	Percent of all banks	Percent of all bank assets
Uninsured Banks	3.2	0.2
Insured Banks	96.8	99.8
Member Banks	36.8	74.3
National Banks	29.9	57.1
State Banks	6.9	17.2
Nonmember Banks	63.2	25.7
All State Banks	70.1	42.9

Source: U.S. Census Bureau, *Statistical Abstract,* 1982, p. 505.

competitive philosophy of allowing efficient firms to force less efficient ones out of business. In banking we severely curb competition, on the grounds that if a bank fails and cannot repay its deposits, too much of the loss is borne by the FDIC and perhaps large depositors, rather than by the stockholders. However, many, though certainly not all, economists question this departure from the competitive norm, and believe that new banks should be allowed to enter the industry even if this weakens existing banks. Any strong believer in a competitive economy is likely to be critical of our bank chartering system.

After a national bank is in operation it has many contacts with the government. One form of this contact is the **examination.** At least three times every two years, employees of the Comptroller of the Currency, called bank examiners, make an unannounced visit to each national bank. Although preventing fraud is one of the purposes of bank examination, it is not the major one. The main emphasis is on seeing whether the bank is complying with various rules and regulations concerning its asset holdings, if it is carrying assets on its books at a conservative value, and whether any securities held, and loans made, involve excessive risks. If a security is deemed too speculative the examiner can order the bank to sell it, and if repayment of a loan is doubtful the examiner can order the bank to write it off as a loss. Since a bank is required to keep an acceptable minimum ratio of capital to deposits, the write-down of capital that results from writing off loan losses, or from selling low quality securities at a loss, may force it to raise more capital or curb the growth of its deposits. And the fact that it has to write off loans can hurt a bank by reducing the price of its stock. Obviously since the quality of loans and securities is a matter of opinion, disputes between banks and examiners do arise. However, in some cases bank officers welcome the advice of examiners who, as outsiders, can take a more objective view than do the bank's officers.[3]

The examiners may classify a bank as a "problem bank" if it has insufficient capital, or has made unwarranted loans to its officers, directors, or stockholders, has inefficient or possibly dishonest management, or has made an unusual amount of substandard loans. It will then be examined more frequently. If the news that it has been classified as a problem bank leaks out, as has happened occasionally, neither the bank's customers nor its stockholders are likely to react favorably.

However, it is easy to exaggerate the power of bank examiners, particularly in their dealings with a large bank. Such banks are complex institutions, and it is difficult for examiners to acquire enough knowledge to be able to dispute successfully with the bank's officers and lawyers. A senior official of the office of the Comptroller of the Currency was once quoted as saying, "How can I tell David Rockefeller how to run his bank? I've never made more than $40,000 in my life."[4] Small banks, however, offer an easier target. All in all, a recent study discussing bank capital concluded:

[3] Since a bank examiner becomes familiar with the operating methods of many banks and obtains in this way a thorough knowledge of banking, some banks like to hire former bank examiners.

[4] *New York Times*, December 22, 1977, p. 49.

> The lack of objective standards creates difficulties. Except when a bank is asking for a privilege, regulators can only urge or attempt to convince a bank that more capital is required. Arguments as to what is or is not adequate are difficult if not impossible to resolve. . . . The list of enforcement proceedings shows long delays when a bank decides not to cooperate. Examiners do find illegal and illogical actions, but they also miss many. In large banks they can be overwhelmed by details. . . .[5]

Moreover, money brokers have become more active in recent years; they are brokers who take the funds of large depositors, split them into $100,000 units (to get full insurance coverage), and deposit them in those banks and thrift institutions that pay the highest interest rate. Hence a bank that is in danger of failing can take a desperate gamble by obtaining a large influx of brokered funds and investing them in risky but high-yielding assets. By the time the examiners come around and notice by how much the average riskiness of the bank's assets has increased it is too late.

Apart from the chartering authorities the Federal Reserve has the right to examine member banks, and the FDIC to examine insured banks. However, to avoid duplication or even triplication, the "Fed" usually leaves examination of national banks to the Comptroller of the Currency, and examines only state member banks. Similarly, the FDIC usually examines only nonmember insured banks.

FEDERAL RESERVE MEMBERSHIP

As table 3.1 showed, 37 percent of all banks are member banks, and these are mostly national banks. Few state banks, particularly the small ones, have joined the Fed. The most serious deterrent to Federal Reserve membership was that the Fed imposed a much more burdensome reserve requirement on its member banks than the states impose on nonmember banks. However, in response to many member banks leaving the Federal Reserve System, and new banks being reluctant to join it, the differential reserve requirement is being phased out. By 1988 member banks and nonmember banks will have the same reserve requirement, so that the main deterrent to membership will have been removed. Other, but lesser, disadvantages of membership are that it subjects banks to examination by the Fed and that the Fed's regulations are probably more burdensome than state regulations.

What are the offsetting benefits? Until 1980 one benefit particularly important to small banks was that, under normal circumstances, only member banks could borrow from the Federal Reserve. But since then nonmember banks too, as well as other depository institutions that keep reserves with the Fed, can borrow from it. For larger banks the main benefit of membership is that it allows them to attract the deposits of smaller banks in a correspondent relationship. Moreover, Fed membership confers prestige on a bank: it announces to the world that this bank is meeting more exacting

[5] Sherman Maisel et al., *Measuring Risk and the Adequacy of Capital in Commercial Banks* (National Bureau of Economic Research; Chicago: University of Chicago Press, 1981), p. 150.

minimum requirements. For depositors whose deposits exceed the $100,000 insurance ceiling, this *may* be a consideration in choosing a bank.

BANK CAPITAL

Banks have to meet a minimum capital requirement. **Bank equity capital** is the *stockholders' equity in the bank*. It is represented on the balance sheet mainly by outstanding stock, surplus, and retained earnings. In addition to equity capital, banks can count as part of their capital long-term funds they have obtained by selling bonds and notes.

The purpose of a capital requirement is to provide a cushion of safety both for the FDIC and for uninsured depositors. The reason why a large capital stock helps to make a bank safe is because capital represents those funds that the bank can lose without endangering its ability to repay deposits. Suppose that a bank's capital is equal to 5 percent of its assets. Then even if, as a result of making unsound loans, it loses 5 percent of its assets, the depositors' funds are still covered; only the stockholders lose. And protection of stockholders is not a legitimate reason for bank regulation—they are responsible for how they invest.

From the bank's point of view a certain cushion of equity capital is clearly desirable. Not only does it help to protect the bank's stockholders against the danger of the bank failing, but in addition business borrowers, as well as large depositors, are reassured by a high capital ratio. Developing a borrowing relationship with a bank is time consuming, and a firm prefers to borrow from a bank that is likely to be around next year. However, the marginal yield from adding capital declines after some point. Suppose, for example, that a bank already has a high stock of capital relative to its liabilities. The chance of its failing is already so low that adding even more capital does not influence its potential customers much.

At the same time the more equity capital a bank has per dollar of assets, the greater is the number of dollars of capital over which the bank's earnings have to be spread. Assume, for example, that the bank earns a one percent profit on its total assets. If capital equals 10 percent of total assets, then this one percent yield on assets represents a 10 percent yield to the bank's stockholders; on the other hand, if the bank has the same earnings, but only a 5 percent ratio of equity capital to total assets, then the stockholders earn 20 percent on their capital. For each bank there exists therefore an optimal ratio of capital to assets at which the marginal advantage of additional capital is just offset by its disadvantage.

But what constitutes an optimal capital stock—and hence the optimal amount of risk—from the bank's point of view is insufficient capital, and hence excessive risk, from the social viewpoint. If a bank would be the only one to lose if it fails, the social and private costs of risk taking would be the same. But this is not so. If a bank fails, the FDIC has to step in and rescue the insured deposits, and, in addition, depositors with accounts above the insurance ceiling may lose. More importantly, if a large bank fails, or many smaller banks fail almost simultaneously, the public may lose confidence in other banks, and try to withdraw deposits from them, thus causing them to fail. Quite apart from the losses and disruptions this could cause, it could also reduce the stock of money substantially and cause a severe recession.

When a bank decides how much risk it should accept it does not take these external costs of its potential failure into account. It selects a level of risk at which the marginal loss from risk-taking is just equal to the marginal yield from taking this risk. Hence, it takes more risk than is socially optimal. This is why the government is justified in stepping in and limiting the amount of risk a bank takes. It does this both by limiting the riskiness of the bank's loans and securities, and by requiring the bank to hold more capital than it would in the absence of regulations.

The amount of capital a bank should have depends on the bank's size; clearly a bank with $1 million of assets does not need as much capital as a bank with $1 billion. But a $10-billion bank does not have to have a thousand times as much capital as a $10-million bank. A large bank holds more diversified assets, and therefore its losses can be predicted better. Second, fraud is a frequent cause of bank failure. But a, say, $100-million fraud is extremely unlikely. Hence, a $10-billion bank with $300 million of capital is much less likely to be bankrupted by fraud than a $10-million bank with half a million dollars of capital. The amount of capital needed also depends on the diversification of assets. If loans are heavily concentrated in a few industries there is a greater danger that many will turn sour at the same time. Hence such a bank needs more capital.

Another factor that determines the capital required by a bank is the riskiness of its assets. For example, if a bank were to hold mainly government securities it would require a much smaller ratio of capital to assets than if it were to hold mainly loans to risky firms. Hence, the Fed has developed a system that classifies bank assets into several risk classes and then requires different capital/assets ratios for these risk classes.

The federal regulatory authorities, the FDIC, the Federal Reserve, and the Comptroller of the Currency, are concerned about the low capital ratios of banks and have tried to get banks to raise them. As of spring 1983, the Fed had set, for member banks, minimum capital ratios of 6 percent for the smaller banks that serve primarily their local communities and 5 percent for other banks.

BANK FAILURES AND DEPOSIT INSURANCE

In May 1974, the Franklin National Bank, previously the nation's twentieth largest bank with deposits close to $3 billion, faced a crisis. On May 1 the Fed in denying Franklin's request to take over in a merger another financial institution announced that the bank had overexpanded and should retrench its operations. A few days afterwards Franklin announced that it could not pay its usual quarterly dividend (a most unusual event for a large bank), and, also, that it had sizable foreign exchange losses. These foreign exchange losses turned out to be but the tip of the iceberg. In an attempt to expand too rapidly the bank had made a large volume of unsound loans. As the bank's troubles became known large depositors withdrew deposits, while many other banks refused to lend to it. But Franklin was able to offset these deposit outflows by borrowing an unprecedented $1.75 billion from the Fed.

At one time even this would not have sufficed because small depositors would also have withdrawn their deposits. But small depositors did not do so because they knew that small deposits were protected by the FDIC. Had it not been for the FDIC, Franklin National would have failed right away, and its failure *might* have triggered runs on other banks, and hence a financial panic. But this did not happen, and Franklin National was kept afloat until October 1974 when the FDIC was able to merge it into another bank, the European-American Bank. A *possible* financial crisis was therefore avoided, albeit at the cost of the Fed and hence ultimately taxpayers, subsidizing an inefficient commercial bank by giving it very large loans at below market interest rates.

The FDIC commenced operations in 1934 in response to the massive bank failures that had occurred between 1930 and 1933. All but 3 percent of all banks, which hold 0.2 percent of all deposits, are members of the FDIC.[6] This almost universal membership is not surprising since membership in the FDIC gives a bank a great advantage over an uninsured bank in competing for deposits. Since competitive pressures make FDIC membership necessary for nearly every bank, the FDIC, in effect, has veto power over the formation of just about any new bank. In addition to insuring commercial banks the FDIC also insures mutual savings banks (institutions discussed in Chapter 5).

FDIC

In return for an insurance premium paid by the banks, the FDIC insures deposits up to $100,000. If a depositor has several accounts in his or her own name in one bank, the total that is insured is still $100,000. But if an individual has several accounts under different names (for example, a personal account, a joint account with a business partner or a spouse), or if these accounts have different beneficiaries (as in the case of trust funds, for example), then each of these accounts is insured separately for $100,000. Similarly, if a person has accounts in his or her own name in several banks all of these accounts are insured. At present, nearly all accounts are fully insured, but the very few that are not include some very large accounts, so that only about 70 percent of the dollar value of deposits is insured.

But the existence of a $100,000 ceiling does not mean that in most bank failures depositors with larger accounts suffer losses. Such losses are extremely rare because of the way the FDIC handles bank failures. One way, called *deposit assumption,* is that the FDIC merges the failing bank into a sound bank. (As an inducement to the sound bank the FDIC frequently provides a subsidy.) Since the sound bank then takes over all the liabilities of the failing bank, including deposits over $100,000, large depositors do not lose anything.[7] This way of dealing with a failing bank is by far the most common, particularly if it is a large bank, whose failure could result in the bankruptcy of many business depositors, and conceivably even start a run on other banks.

A second way of handling a failing bank, a way the FDIC does use from time to time, is simply to let the bank fail and to pay off deposits up to

[6]The fact that insured banks are *members* of the FDIC is legalistic (but generally used) terminology. Insured banks do not control the FDIC. Its directors are presidential appointees and the funds accumulated by the FDIC do not belong to its members.

[7]However, if you have an outstanding bank loan the FDIC will subtract the value of the loan from the size of your deposit, and pay out only the difference. This offset provision can reduce substantially the amount the FDIC has to pay out.

$100,000. In rare cases the FDIC has temporarily set up its own bank to take over the failing bank's deposits, or has reorganized the failing bank, or made a loan to it.

Since in the past the FDIC has used the merger route for large banks where there are many accounts above the insurance ceiling, it is widely believed that the FDIC will, in effect, protect all deposits in, say any of the twenty largest banks even though the law requires the FDIC to use whichever route is cheapest. This sounds plausible since it may often be uncertain which way is cheaper. However, when a medium-sized bank, Penn Square, failed in 1982 the FDIC just paid off depositors up to $100,000 and let the large depositors take their lumps. At least temporarily this made large depositors in other banks more careful.

In any case, in an indirect way the FDIC protects all depositors. If it were not for the existence of the FDIC, then during a financial crisis small depositors would run all banks that look shaky to them, and this could cause many banks to fail. Since banks hold only a small fraction of their deposits as currency in the bank, and since many of their assets cannot be liquidated immediately, any bank, regardless of how soundly managed it is, can be destroyed if too many of its depositors suddenly try to withdraw their deposits.

An obvious question that arises is why have a $100,000 ceiling. The cost to the FDIC of covering all deposits would be trivial. The main argument against covering all deposits is that this would reduce some of the pressures towards safe management that are currently faced by banks. As long as there is a ceiling there are some depositors, presumably mainly business firms, who have an incentive to monitor a bank's operations and make sure that it is sound. To some extent, banks therefore compete for large deposits by following safe policies. But if all deposits were covered, then this pressure towards safe management would no longer exist. But since it is difficult even for moderate-sized firms to monitor banks, some economists believe that the ceiling should be raised. The FDIC has also considered changing to a system of insuring large accounts at less than 100 percent.

Fully insuring all deposits would also eliminate runs on banks. The establishment of the FDIC eliminated runs by small depositors, and we no longer see long lines of depositors outside banks that are rumored to be in trouble. But such rumors do cause large depositors to withdraw their funds, and to stop other banks from making loans to that bank. Hence, despite the FDIC, a bank reported to be in trouble may still face a massive outflow of funds.

How is the FDIC able to meet claims on it? It has earnings from insurance premiums (one fourteenth of one percent of deposits in 1981) and from securities it previously bought with these premiums. In addition, it can borrow up to $3 billion from the U.S. Treasury, and it is obvious that in case of need Congress would authorize much larger loans. Given the catastrophic experience with bank failures in the 1930s it is almost impossible to imagine the federal government not stepping in to save depositors. The FDIC's loss experience since 1934 has been very favorable. Most years its actual losses have amounted to less than 5 percent of its premium income.

The FDIC's history can be divided into two parts. In the first, from 1934 until the mid-1960s few failures occured and they were small. This may have been due in part to older bankers still remembering the massive bank failures of the Great Depression. In addition banks came out of World War II holding a great stock of government securities which they got rid of only slowly. But as Figure 3.2 shows since the mid-1960s bank failures have grown substantially. And not only were there more failures, but failures were no longer confined to small banks. From 1946 to 1970 the average bank that failed had deposits of about $14 million, while the largest bank to fail had only $40 million in deposits. But in 1972 a large Detroit bank, Bank of the Commonwealth, experienced heavy losses, and the FDIC had to provide it with funds to keep it alive. Then in 1973 there was the first insolvency of a billion dollar bank, the U.S. National Bank of San Diego, the rare case of a very large bank seriously damaged by self-dealing of its president. The following year there occurred the largest bank failure ever, the Franklin National Bank failure, already discussed. And, in 1975 and 1976, two other large banks turned belly up. In 1980 the First Pennsylvania, then the country's twenty-third largest bank, was in difficulty. The FDIC, along with some banks, made a loan to it to keep it alive. In November 1981, it cost the FDIC close to half a billion dollars to merge the failing Greenwich Savings Bank into another savings bank, in its most expensive transaction ever.

But these worries about bank failures should not be allowed to obscure the fact that *perhaps* we have too few bank failures. Failures of banks, as of other firms, fulfill a useful function: they weed out inefficient firms. It requires some failures to keep an industry efficient. However, bank failures are different from failures in most other industries since banks operate with such a high ratio of borrowed funds to their own capital.

The fact that there have been so few bank failures suggests that bank supervision by the FDIC and other agencies has not been an unmixed blessing. It has exacted a cost by limiting the venturesomeness of banks, thus discouraging innovation and experimentation. Since the supervising agencies may be criticized when banks fail, it is in their interest to err on the side of safety.[8] But too much safety has its costs.

A possible solution to this problem would be to "sell" banks the right to take more risk by setting a higher insurance premium for banks that have too low a capital ratio or hold too risky assets. Not only would insuring risky banks (just like poor drivers) at a higher insurance premium allow those banks that want to, to take more risk, but it would also give the FDIC a useful weapon in its arguments with banks. Threatening to revoke a bank's insurance is often not a creditable threat, but threatening to raise its insurance premium would be. On the other hand, there is difficulty in deciding what insurance premium to set. Moreover, it has been argued that the FDIC's losses depend not so much on the riskiness of a bank's assets, as on how soon in the process of failure the regulating agencies become aware of it and close the bank. At present (March 1983) the FDIC is also considering two other proposals. One would force large depositors to share some of the FDIC's

[8] However, insurance has helped to stimulate competition in one important way. New banks, particularly small ones, would find it more difficult to get depositors if these depositors had to worry that they might lose if the bank failed.

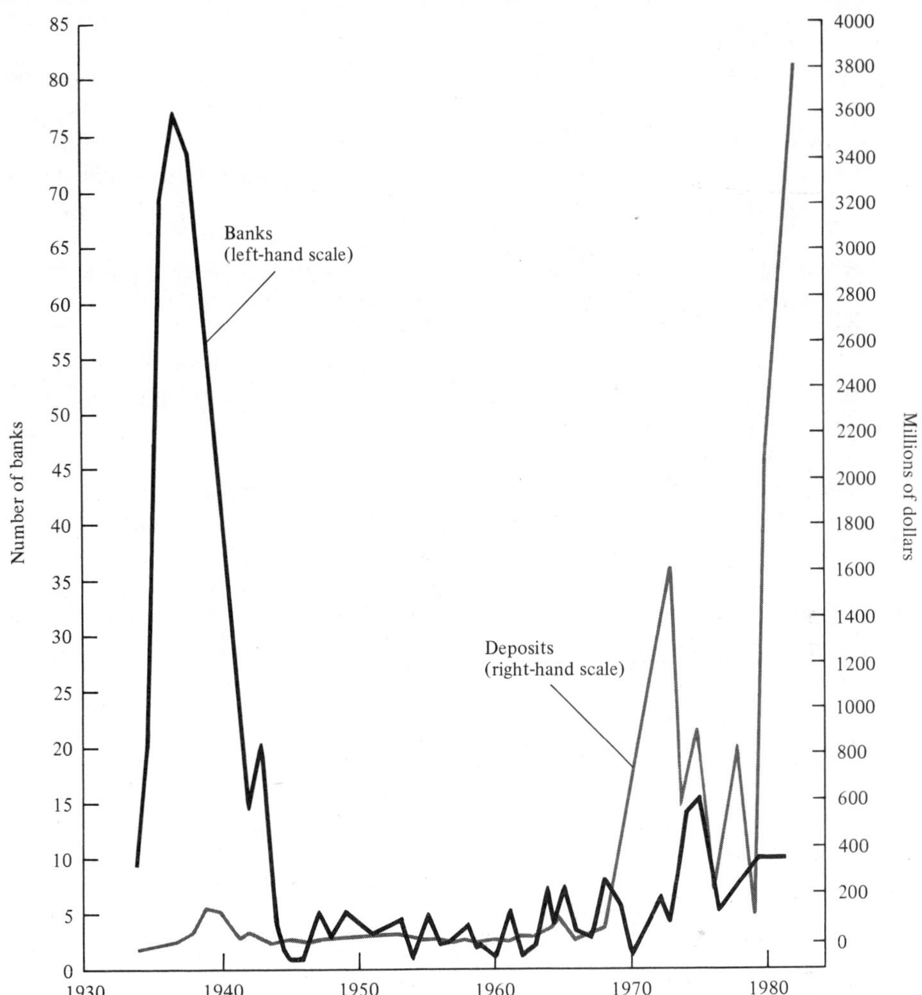

Figure 3.2 Frequency of Bank Failures

Source: FDIC *Annual Report,* 1982, p. 30.

costs in the case of deposit assumptions. This would give them an incentive to pressure banks into being more cautious. The other proposal would require banks to obtain private insurance as well, in the hope that private insurance companies could be stricter than the FDIC.

Savings and loan associations are insured, not by the FDIC, but by the Federal Savings and Loan Insurance Corporation (FSLIC), which operates very much like the FDIC, with the same $100,000 insurance ceiling. Credit unions are insured by the National Credit Union Administration (NCUA).

CHECK CLEARING

We now turn from a serious, but episodic problem, to a minor, but continual one. Suppose that a check drawn on a San Francisco bank is deposited in a

Boston bank. How is this check cleared, that is, presented for payment? Since a vast number of checks, about 65 million per day—have to be cleared, elaborate mechanisms for doing so have been developed. One mechanism is a **clearinghouse.** This is usually an organization of local banks that meets every working day for a few hours. Each bank appears at the clearinghouse, and presents the checks it has received that are drawn on the other banks belonging to the clearinghouse. The banks then offset their claims and liabilities against each other, and any bank with a favorable net balance receives payment.

Checks drawn on banks in other cities usually move through the Federal Reserve's clearing system, either by the receiving bank depositing the check directly with the Fed, or by another (correspondent) bank doing so for it. If the check is deposited in a bank in the same Federal Reserve District (there are twelve of them) on which it is drawn, the Federal Reserve Bank directly debits the account which the bank on which it is drawn has with it. If it is drawn on a bank in another Federal Reserve District, the Federal Reserve Bank passes it on to the Federal Reserve Bank of that district, and this Federal Reserve Bank then debits the account of the bank. The depositing bank gets credit from the Fed after one or two days, depending on the distance the check has to be sent. However, many banks will not permit the depositor to withdraw the funds for several days, sometimes for two weeks or more. This is to protect the bank in case the check bounces.

This system of check clearing may change substantially. In 1980 Congress ordered the Fed to charge banks for check clearing. Previously it had been free. This means that private firms can now compete with the Fed, and if they can clear checks cheaper and better they may succeed in taking away much of the Fed's business. They have already taken over a significant part of the market.

To save time most large payments are made by wire transfers rather than by check. The amounts transferred by wire are immense. In 1981 the Federal Reserve transferred about $240 billion *per day* and, in addition, there are privately operated wire services that compete with the Fed. One of them, run by the New York City Clearing House, that is much used for international transactions, transferred $190 billion per day. Here too, since the Fed is now required to charge full cost for its wire transfers, private operations may take over a larger share of the market.

CORRESPONDENT BANKING

A private network among banks called the correspondent system connects banks and eliminates many of the disadvantages that would otherwise follow from having so many small, isolated banks. Under this system country correspondent banks keep deposits, primarily demand deposits, with larger city correspondent banks, frequently with several of them. These deposits are by no means small, currently amounting to about 3 percent of all deposits.

The city banks pay for these deposits, by providing their country correspondent banks with many services. One important service is the clearing of checks in a more convenient way than the Fed does. In addition city banks provide direct loans to country banks, and also participate with a country bank in making loans that are too large for the country bank to make on its own. Or, conversely, a country bank experiencing too little loan demand can participate in a profitable loan made by the city bank. The numerous other services that city correspondent banks provide to country correspondent banks include the sale or purchase of securities, access to the national money market, investment advice and general business advice, and buying or selling foreign exchange for its customers. Thus city correspondent banks provide many of the services that the head office of a large branch bank provides for its branches.

HOLDING COMPANIES

A holding company is a corporation whose assets consist of a controlling stock ownership in one or more other corporations. This financial device is used in many industries. In banking it is sometimes used to get around restrictive branching laws. In many states in which a bank is not allowed to have branches it can nevertheless form a holding company that holds a controlling stock interest in several banks. But a more important use of holding companies in banking is to avoid the restrictions that prevent banks from entering other industries. Bank holding companies can get permission to have subsidiaries only in those industries that are "closely related" to banking, such as finance companies, companies offering computer services, credit card companies, discount stock brokers, etc.[9] Banks have also used their holding companies to enter certain financial markets in other states, though this use of holding companies is still rare.

The ability to enter these other lines of business is only one of the advantages of forming a holding company. Another important advantage for large banks is that holding companies can generate funds for the bank in ways the bank itself is not allowed to. For example, although a bank itself is not permitted to issue commercial paper (a type of short-term promissory note) and thus borrow short-term funds in this way, a bank holding company can do so in its own name, and then give these funds to its bank.

It is therefore not surprising that nearly all of the country's largest banks are owned by holding companies, and that more than three-quarters of all commercial bank assets are in banks affiliated with a holding company. While the holding company legally owns the bank, de facto the holding company is an organization set up and dominated by the bank. The nonbank assets of the holding company are normally very small compared to the bank.

From the bank's point of view, nonbank subsidiaries have not been successful. Their earnings record has been unimpressive. Moreover, they have increased risk; if one of the nonbank subsidiaries of a bank holding company

[9]To be "closely related" to banking an activity must meet at least one of the following criteria: (1) a significant number of banks have undertaken it for a number of years; (2) it involves taking deposits or lending; (3) it is complementary to banking services, for example, selling life insurance that extinguishes the borrower's debt to the bank in case of death; and (4) it is something in which banks have considerable expertise, for example, data processing.

is in danger of failing this reflects on the bank's reputation. Hence, banks have faced the temptation to prop up these subsidiaries by making additional loans to them, even if these loans are risky. Although the law was drawn up in a way that tries to prevent it, there is still the danger that the failure of a nonbank subsidiary might cause a bank to fail. Fortunately, this danger is greatly reduced because in most cases the nonbank subsidiaries are very small relative to the bank. Some people have also been concerned that a bank might give loans on easier terms to firms that deal with the nonbank subsidiaries of its holding company, and hence these subsidiaries might have an unfair advantage. But whether this is consistent with profit-maximizing behavior for the holding company is disputed.

CONCENTRATION IN BANKING

There are close to fifteen thousand commercial banks in the United States. The ten largest banking organizations held only 17 percent of total domestic deposits in 1977, while the hundred largest held 45 percent. Very few industries have that many firms and so little concentration, and one might therefore think that there is no "monopoly problem" in banking. Indeed, one might wonder whether the problem is not rather that there are too many banks, too many, that is, to reap economies of scale, and to be able to provide a sufficient range of services to bank customers. However, the empirical evidence suggests that once a bank gets above a fairly moderate size economies of scale probably are modest.

In any case, even if we do have too many small banks from the point of view of minimizing bank costs, this does not mean that we do not have a problem of insufficient banking competition as well. While large firms can borrow from banks anywhere in the country, small firms being known only in their locality, can borrow only from a local bank. It is simply not worthwhile for banks elsewhere to acquire the information needed to lend to them. And within a firm's area there may be only one bank. In 13 percent of all rural counties there was only a single bank in 1973.

On a national level there is, of course, much less concentration. Table 3.2 shows the ten largest banks, and Table 3.3 the size distribution of banks.

As far as household depositors are concerned, they generally deal with banks in their own locality, and hence those living in some areas may have insufficient competitive alternatives. However, savings and loan associations and mutual savings banks do provide depositors with an important competitive alternative.

But an insufficient number of banks in a locality is not the only source of insufficient banking competition. Federal regulations set maximum interest rates that banks can pay on certain types of deposits, and in this way reduce banking competition to the detriment of depositors. And banks cannot pay interest on demand deposits. In addition, as in any other industry, there is the danger of collusion.

Many states have tried to prevent the growth of large banking firms by prohibiting or limiting branch banking. However, as the example of some very large Chicago banks illustrates, the virtual prohibition of branching is

Table 3.2 The Ten Largest U.S. Banks, 31 December 1982

Banks	Assets (billions of dollars)	Time deposits as percent of total deposits	Foreign deposits as percent of total deposits	Capital as percent of total assets
1. Citicorp (New York)	$130.0	91%	67%	3.7%
2. BankAmerica (San Francisco)	122.2	83	40	3.5
3. Chase Manhattan (New York)	80.9	83	61	3.4
4. Manufacturers Hanover (New York)	64.0	80	54	3.4
5. Morgan (J.P.) (New York)	58.6	82	58	4.5
6. Chemical (New York)	48.3	73	35	3.4
7. Continental Illinois (Chicago)	42.9	84	55	3.8
8. First Interstate Bancorp. (Los Angeles)	40.9	73	9	4.4
9. Bankers Trust (New York)	40.4	81	55	3.5
10. Security Pacific (Los Angeles)	37.0	79	19	4.0

Source: *Business Week,* 11 April 1983, p. 77.

Table 3.3 Size Distribution of Insured Commercial Banks in the United States, December 31, 1981

Banks with total assets of (in millions of $)	Percent of all commercial banks	Percent of assets
Less than 5.0	5.0	0.1
5.0–9.9	11.5	0.6
10.0–24.9	31.0	3.8
25.0–49.9	24.9	6.5
50.0–99.9	14.9	7.4
100.0–299.9	8.7	10.0
300.0–499.9	1.3	3.6
500.0–999.9	1.3	6.3
1,000–4,900.0	1.1	17.4
5,000 and over	0.3	44.4
TOTAL	100.0	100.0

Source: Based on FDIC, *Statistics on Banking,* 1981, p. 20.

not an insuperable obstacle to a bank becoming one of the largest in the nation. In some states banks may have branches, but only within the same county as their head office or in adjacent counties. In still other states they may have branches, but not in those counties where another bank has its head office. As Figure 3.3 shows, in 1979, twenty-two states allowed their banks to have branches all over the state, eighteen permitted limited branching, and ten opposed branch banking.

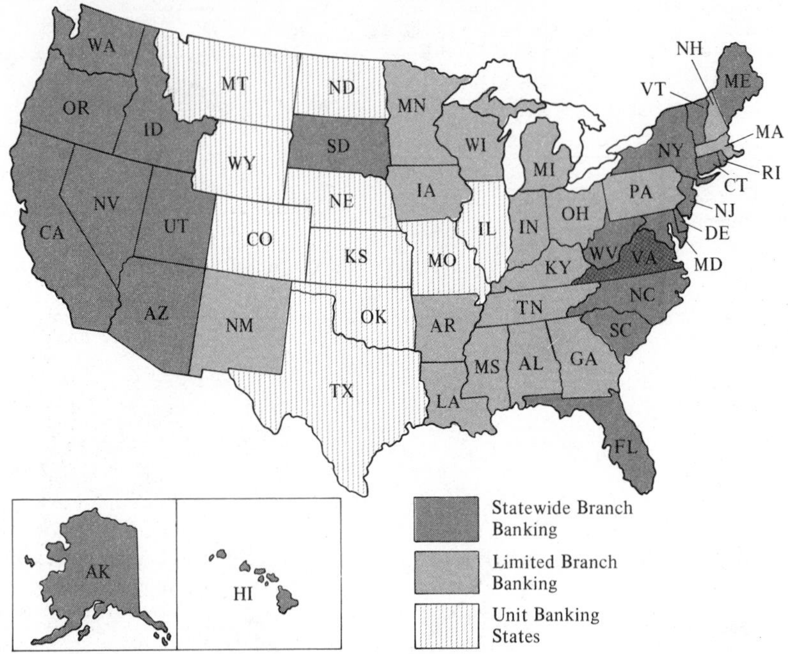

Figure 3.3 Types of Banking Systems

Source: *A Profile of State-Chartered Banking,* Conference of State Bank Supervisors.

Are banks allowed to have branches in different states? There are so many qualifications to the "correct" answer that they may not do so, that it is more correct to say that interstate branching is permitted with one important exception. This is that banks may not open—what to the man in the street is a branch—offices to gather retail deposits in other states. However, banks are allowed to have so-called loan production offices that arrange large and medium-sized business loans in other states. And since there is frequently an understanding that a business borrower will keep a deposit in the lending bank, banks are de facto able to gather business deposits anywhere in the country. Similarly, banks can have in other states so-called Edge Act offices that facilitate foreign trade. (It is therefore not surprising that Citicorp, the holding company of New York's largest bank, has built a big office building a few blocks from the Bank of America headquarters in San Francisco, while the Bank of America has a large office building in mid-town Manhattan.) Moreover, some states have allowed bank holding companies from other states to open banks. Thus there is a reciprocal agreement among several New England states to allow bank holding companies in one of them to acquire banks in the other states. And currently (September 1983) a similar move is afoot in southeastern states. In addition, a few banks that had branches in other states before the prohibition of interstate banking in 1927 have been allowed to keep them.

What little remains of the prohibition of interstate banking is currently under attack. The larger banks are trying to get Congress to eliminate the prohibition of full-scale branches, a move opposed by small banks. There is a widespread expectation that the law will be changed, and large banks are trying to position themselves to take advantage of such a change the moment it occurs. Thus, some have made loans to small banks in other states with a proviso that these loans can be transformed into stock ownership when the law changes. Other bank holding companies have bought finance companies in other states, in the hope of converting them into branches once the law is changed. In 1982 Citicorp, the holding company of Citibank, took over a failing California savings and loan by offering the FSLIC more favorable terms than anyone else, so that it now has a presence in the California retail market. A bank holding company that owns banks in several Western states has given them all almost the same name ("First Interstate Bank of . . .") and has an on-line computer system that allows depositors of one of these banks to withdraw deposits from any of the other banks in the system. Other banks are linked by joint teller machine networks so that a depositor, say, of a New York bank can obtain cash from a machine in California. Moreover, banks are soliciting deposits by mail in other states. With the decontrol of deposit rates they can offer higher rates to offset the convenience of the local bank's neighborhood branches. And with shared automatic teller machine networks depositors can readily withdraw currency from their out-of-state-accounts.

Are the limitations on branching—both intrastate and interstate—justified? It is true that they limit the growth of large banks and hence the aggregation of economic power. But, given the size of the country, it is unlikely that even with completely unlimited branch banking a handful of banks would succeed in dominating the industry as is true in Canada and Britain, for example. The economies of scale in banking are not that great. In California where there is unlimited branch banking, small banks are able to coexist alongside very large branch systems.

The limitations on branching, while serving to limit large aggregations of economic power, have also worked to preserve the monopoly or oligopoly positions of banks in small cities. In a number of localities the market is not large enough to support more than one independent bank, but in addition to this bank it could support a branch of another bank; in these situations branching would reduce monopoly power. Moreover, in other industries, when a firm has a local monopoly it has to worry that if it sets its prices too high it will induce other firms to come into its market area. But, insofar as branching regulations prevent banks from entering another bank's market, a local banking monopoly is more secure in exploiting its monopoly position. Hence, in the view of many economists, the limitation on branching has in many cases worked to preserve small business at the cost of *reducing* competition.[10] However, this view has been challenged on the argument that the empirical evidence shows that the easing of bank-branching laws has not actually increased competition, since banks frequently enter new markets,

[10] What is involved here is the distinction between the popular and the technical concerns about monopoly. On a popular level very large firms are often thought of as monopolists, while economists define monopoly in terms of the elasticity of the demand curve. More liberal branching regulations would result in larger banks, but would increase the elasticity of the demand curve for many banks.

not by starting new branches, but by merging with existing banks in these markets.[11]

Banks have merged for many reasons. Sometimes it is a way to get around the prohibition against establishing branches. At other times it is a way in which capital can flow easily from low growth areas to more rapidly growing areas where the yield on capital is higher. Moreover, many mergers have increased the efficiency of banking by allowing efficient banks to take over lethargic and badly managed ones. Such a device for eliminating mediocre management is badly needed because bank regulations have prevented efficient banks from entering and driving inefficient banks out of business. In addition, mergers have allowed management to satisfy its preference for growth while allowing managers to diversify their assets. And for many small banks mergers have been a way in which the banker can sell out upon retirement and provide new management for the bank.

There has been much concern about the effect of mergers on competition. Clearly, if there are five banks in a city and they all merge, competition is eliminated. But it is much less clear that competition is reduced if banks in different cities merge. It would only reduce competition if, for at least some of the customers, the merging banks are potential competitors, that is, if the market areas of these banks overlap.

The law prohibits mergers that would "substantially" reduce competition, but this is a vague standard that has led to much litigation. Banks operate in many different markets—deposit markets, business loan markets, consumer loan markets, and so on—with some business customers being able to borrow anywhere in the nation and others not. It is therefore hard to define the "market" a bank serves, and hence to determine if a merger would actually reduce competition. Moreover, the Department of Justice, which administers the antitrust laws, and the Federal Reserve have sometimes invoked the doctrine of potential competition by arguing that if a merger is prevented the frustrated acquirer will probably establish its own new branch, thus adding to competition. Obviously such an argument is hard to evaluate, and, on the whole, the courts have not looked kindly upon it.

SOCIAL REGULATION OF BANK LOANS

Traditionally, the purpose of bank regulation has been to ensure the safety of the bank and to deal with the problem of economic concentration. But in recent years, another set of regulations, applicable to other lenders as well as banks, has grown rapidly. These regulations try to protect consumers and prevent discrimination.

Among the oldest of these regulations are state usury laws, that is, laws that set a ceiling on the interest rate that may be charged. The idea behind them is, of course, that a too high rate of interest is unfair to borrowers, and that borrowers have to be protected from exploitation due to insufficient competition among lenders, or due to their ignorance of the financial market.

A major problem with usury laws is, of course, that the lender has a

[11] For a survey of the empirical evidence see Stephen Rhoades, "Competitive Effects of Interstate Banking," *Federal Reserve Bulletin* 66 (January 1980): 1–8.

choice: instead of making the loan at the ceiling rate, he can refrain from making it at all, and lend his funds where they are exempt from the usury laws, for example, out of state. And further, if the interest rate is held below equilibrium, lenders have to ration the available supply of loans among applicants, and will do so by excluding the riskier ones which usually means the poorer applicants. Thus, while usury laws might *perhaps* help borrowers in general, they hurt the really poor who then have to deal with loan sharks or do without loans.

In any case, the scope of state usury laws has been greatly reduced in recent years, in part because of federal legislation, and in part because states have raised their interest rate ceilings.

A federal law, the Truth-in-Lending Law, tries to ensure that borrowers are given sufficient credit information, particularly about the interest rate they are paying. Prior to this law interest rates were often stated in ways that made it hard to understand and compare them. However, the law has the disadvantage of creating costs for the lender, which are, of course, passed on to the borrower. And it is not clear that many borrowers pay much attention to the additional information they are now getting.

Another law deals with creditor rights. Suppose someone buys a defective item on credit and the merchant sells the buyer's IOU to a bank. In the past the buyer was legally obligated to make payment to the bank on this IOU regardless of the defect in the merchandise. This is no longer the case. Furthermore, in response to frequent complaints that minorities, women, and relief recipients faced discrimination in obtaining credit, federal legislation now makes such discrimination illegal, and lenders have to keep records on why they turned down loan applicants.

Several laws prohibit discrimination on the basis of age, race, sex, etc., and also outlaw redlining. In the strict sense of the term redlining means that the lender or insurer figuratively draws a line around a certain neighborhood on a city map and refuses to make sufficient loans or to insure property in this area. However, the term is also used more broadly to encompass discrimination in general. The neighborhoods said to be redlined are usually decaying inner city areas with a high proportion of minority residents, and, critics of redlining argue, a major reason why the areas are decaying is precisely because it is so difficult to obtain mortgage loans there.

Accordingly, the Community Reinvestment Act states that banks and other insured mortgage lenders have an obligation to meet the reasonable credit needs of local low-income communities. When they apply for permission to open branches or to merge with other institutions, the regulatory agency is supposed to treat their performance in serving low-income neighborhoods as a factor in deciding on their applications.

This legislation is based on several arguments. One is that redlining is to a considerable extent just one more manifestation of racial discrimination, that it largely results from white upper-middle-class bankers considering minorities to be unworthy of credit. A second argument is that redlining is a manifestation of laziness; instead of evaluating the loan application on its own merits the lender, without spending any thought on it, simply turns it down because it comes from the wrong neighborhood. A third argument is that banks with branches in decaying neighborhoods drain funds out of these areas by gathering deposits there, and making loans elsewhere. Still another argument is that one of our most serious social problems is the decay of the inner cities, and while the government provides various subsidies for the inner cities, financial institutions should also be required to do their part. Since financial institutions obtain extensive government benefits such as insurance, they can reasonably be asked in turn to help the government in salvaging the inner cities.

Opponents of the Community Reinvestment Act and similar legislation raise a number of issues. Thus, they question whether redlining actually exists to any large extent, because if a bank were to pass up any sound loan it would be reducing its own profits. Banks use certain rules of thumb to cut down the cost of credit investigation, but the use of such rules is in the public interest because otherwise too many resources would be used in investigating credit applications. But, by being willing to pay a higher interest rate, potential borrowers in decaying areas can often induce lenders to do this extra work. Hence, they argue that the reason why so few mortgage loans are made in decaying areas is that there are few sound applicants for mortgage credit there. Of course, in declining neighborhoods there are many people who want to borrow, but the loans they want are usually risky, and banks are supposed to avoid risky loans. Hence, the argument runs, requiring banks to make a certain proportion of their loans in decaying areas means imposing a tax on banks because these loans are risky and banks will shift this tax onto their customers. Moreover, even if under ideal conditions it might be desirable to curb redlining by legislation, in actual practice such legislation is likely to be inefficient, to result in much red tape, and to be evaded. For example, a bank with a branch in a low-income neighborhood might simply close that branch, so that this neighborhood would no longer be part of the area in which it is supposed to make loans.

One reason that this whole debate about redlining has arisen is that there are so few minority banks, despite some limited attempts by the federal government to foster them. They are hindered by the general poverty of the inner city, which results in their having an inordinate number of small—and hence costly—deposits, and by relatively high losses on business loans. These high loan losses are in large part due to the fact that minority banks try to make loans not only on the basis of economic soundness but also on the basis of social usefulness. There is therefore considerable debate about whether these minority banks can help to raise inner-city income significantly. But it has been suggested that they can do so indirectly by providing minorities with the economic leadership role that seems naturally to attach itself to bankers. Turning from minority banking to what is really majority banking, banks run by women and making a special effort to cater to women as customers have been established in some major cities because of a belief that many other banks discriminate against women. Of course, these banks also accept the business of male customers.

SUMMARY

1. Banking has a long history. In the United States, there were two national banks chartered by the federal government and their demise was followed by a period

of free banking. This in turn was followed by the National Banking System that provided safer banks.

2. Banking is heavily regulated by the federal or state chartering authorities, by the FDIC, and, for member banks, by the Federal Reserve. Entry into banking is restricted and banks are examined.
3. Banks are required to maintain a capital ratio to protect the FDIC and depositors. Since this ratio exceeds what banks would hold on their own, this is an area of continual conflict between banks and the regulators.
4. Nearly all deposits are now insured up to $100,000, and the most common way in which the FDIC handles bank failures also protects larger deposits. The main purpose of the deposit ceiling is to give large depositors an incentive to watch the bank's safety. In recent years, bank failures have increased substantially, but it is by no means clear that they are excessive.
5. Checks are cleared through local clearinghouses, the Federal Reserve or by private firms. The latter form of clearing may grow.
6. Banks have extensive correspondence relationships that provide small banks with services from large banks.
7. A common form of bank organization is the holding company. This allows banks to enter certain other industries and to raise capital in ways they otherwise could not.
8. Although banking is an industry with many firms and with a low concentration ratio on the national level, there is still a problem of banks having excessive market power on a local level. There are restrictions on bank branching, but they are declining. Interstate branch banking while formally prohibited is in many ways an actuality.
9. In recent years various types of discrimination in granting credit, such as redlining, have been outlawed. Lenders are also required to provide extensive information to borrowers.

Questions and Exercises

1. "Banking is so different from other industries, that limiting entry to protect existing banks from excessive competition is not only justified, but is needed." Discuss.
2. Look up the branching regulations of your state. Then write an essay either defending or criticizing these regulations.
3. Banking is much more heavily regulated than other industries. How can this be justified?
4. Discuss the following proposals to loosen up deposit insurance:
   - *a.* Allowing banks to obtain insurance from private insurance companies instead of the FDIC.
   - *b.* Insuring depositors instead of banks, and permitting depositors, who would pay for the insurance premium, to decide whether they want to buy this insurance;
   - *c.* Insuring only the accounts of households, and not of businesses.
5. Describe the process by which checks are cleared.
6. Critically discuss:
   - *a.* "Banks should be allowed to decide on their own how much capital they want; after all, they are the ones who lose if it turns out that they have insufficient capital."

b. "Banks should be required to keep a capital to deposit ratio of at least 25 percent."

7. What do you think is the most serious *current* problem facing bank regulation? (Articles on current banking problems can be found frequently in *Business Week.*)
8. Write an essay either defending or criticizing:
   a. usury laws;
   b. regulations prohibiting redlining.

Further Reading

BENSTON, GEORGE. *Bank Examination. The Bulletin* (New York University Graduate School of Business Administration) nos. 89–90 (173). A very thorough and scholarly discussion.

———. "Optimal Banking Structure." *Journal of Banking Research* 3 (Winter 1973): 220–37. An excellent survey of a voluminous literature.

———. "The Persistent Myth of Redlining." *Fortune,* 13 March 1978, pp. 66–69. An interesting challenge to the view that banks redline.

———. "Mortgage Redlining Research: A Review and Critical Analysis," in Federal Reserve Bank of Boston, *The Regulation of Financial Institutions,* Boston, Federal Reserve Bank of Boston, 1979, 144–95. A very useful survey, but see also the comments by Robert Schafer (pp. 200–202).

BUSER, STEPHEN, CHEN, ANDREW, and KANE, EDWARD. "Federal Deposit Insurance, Regulatory Policy and Optimal Bank Capital, *Journal of Finance* 36 (March 1981) 51–60. A probing discussion of FDIC behavior.

CHASE, SAMUEL, and MINGO, JOHN. "The Regulation of Bank Holding Companies." *Journal of Finance* 30 (May 1975): 281–92. A thoughtful survey of the problem.

HAVRILESKY, THOMAS, and BORRMAN, JOHN. *Current Perspectives in Banking.* Arlington Heights, Ill.: AHM Publishing Corp., 1976. An interesting collection of readings.

KLEBANER, BANJAMIN. *Commercial Banking in the United States: A History.* Hinsdale, Ill.: Dryden Press, 1974. A compact and useful source of information.

LAWRENCE, ROBERT, and TALLEY, SAMUEL. "An Assessment of Bank Holding Companies." *Federal Reserve Bulletin* 62 (January 1976):15–21. A short, but authoritative assessment.

MAISEL, SHERMAN (ed.). Risk and Capital Adequacy in Commercial Banks. Chicago: University of Chicago Press, 1981. A highly sophisticated analysis of bank capital adequacy, the FDIC premium, and related issues.

ROSENBLUM, HARVEY. "Bank Holding Companies: An Overview." *Business Conditions* (Federal Reserve Bank of Chicago), August 1973, pp. 3–13. A useful survey.

SCHAFER, ROBERT, and LADD, HELEN. *Discrimination in Mortgage Lending.* Cambridge, Mass.: MIT Press, 1981. This study presents an empirical argument that discrimination in lending does exist.

SCOTT, KENNETH, and MAYER, THOMAS. "Risk and Regulation in Banking: Some Proposals for Federal Deposit Insurance Reform." *Stanford Law Review* 23 (May 1971): 857–902. A discussion of issues in deposit insurance.

The Banking Firm

4

In the previous chapter we discussed the structure of the banking industry, and the regulatory environment in which it operates. This chapter, by contrast, focuses on the bank as a firm, and sees how this bank firm operates to maximize its profits. Before turning to the details of banking two general characteristics should be mentioned. First, banks face a peculiar balance sheet situation. A large proportion of their liabilities are short-term, while most of their assets are longer term. Although, under normal conditions, banks can predict deposit withdrawals fairly well, they still have to worry about occasional, unexpectedly large withdrawals. A bank that is illiquid and cannot meet its depositors' checks fails even if its assets exceed its liabilities. Hence, banks have to make sure that they hold sufficient liquid assets. This is costly because liquid assets generally pay a lower rate of return than do other assets.

Second, banks are heterogeneous. There are very small banks as well as very large internationally oriented banks. Some of these large banks, the Bank of America is the prime example, have an extensive branch network, and hence finance small business as well as major corporations. But other large banks, such as the Harris Trust Company of Chicago, for example, so-called wholesale banks, deal mainly with large corporations.

BANK ASSETS AND LIABILITIES

A bank is a dealer in debts. It issues its own debts (mainly deposits) and it holds the debts of borrowers. Both types of debts are recorded on the bank's balance sheet, which is simply a double-entry statement of assets and liabilities. We can therefore study the banking business by looking at each item on the balance sheet of this dealer in debts. Table 4.1 shows a balance sheet for all U.S. banks in 1981, and we will discuss all items listed in it, starting with the liabilities side.

Table 4.1 Assets and Liabilities of All Banks, June 1982
(percent distribution)

Assets		Liabilities	
Cash and due from depository institutions—total	11.1%	Total deposits	74.9%
Currency and coin	1.2	Demand	19.8
Balances with Federal Reserve Banks	1.2	Savings	13.1
Demand balances with commercial banks in the U.S.	1.8	Time	42.1
All other balances with depository institutions	3.2	Federal funds purchased and securities sold under repurchase agreements	9.4
Cash items in the process of collection	3.8	Other liabilities	8.2
Securities—total	19.9	Total liabilities	92.5
Obligations of the federal government and government corporations	10.1	Capital account—total	7.4
Obligations of states and political subdivisions in the U.S.	8.6	Subordinate notes and debentures	0.4
All other securities	1.1	Equity capital	7.1
Federal funds sold and securities purchased under repurchase agreements	4.9	Total liabilities and capital	100.0
Loans, gross—total	56.7		
Commercial and industrial loans	20.9		
Real estate loans	16.8		
Loans to individuals	10.7		
Loans for purchasing and carrying securities	0.6		
Other loans	5.8		
Adjustment for possible loan losses and unearned income on loans	−1.8		
Net loans	54.8		
Other assets	9.3		
TOTAL	100.0		

Source: *FDIC 1982 Statistics on Banking,* Table 106.

Checkable Deposits

One type of deposit is a deposit against which checks can be written. Federal government regulations limit the types of such accounts that banks can offer, but these regulations are in the process of being relaxed. At this writing, banks can offer the following types of checkable accounts. First, there are demand deposits. Banks may not pay interest on demand deposits. However, as so often happens the law is an imperfect barrier against economic pressures. In effect banks do pay *implicit* interest on demand deposits by providing free (or below cost) services. Thus on accounts above a certain minimum banks do not charge for check clearing and provide services, such as payroll preparation for firms. Firms with large deposits can also borrow at a lower rate. Moreover, in states that permit it, banks have established numerous branches, thus substituting convenience to depositors for direct interest payments.

Second, on the so-called "money market accounts," authorized in 1982, banks can pay an (unregulated) interest rate. However, there are certain restrictions on this type of account. The minimum balance must be at least $2500 and each month only six "preauthorized transfers" such as checks or telephone orders to the bank to make a payment are permitted and only three of these may be checks. However, these restrictions are likely to be eased in the future, and in the meantime banks can set up an arrangement whereby they transfer some funds from this account to a checking account that has no limit on the number of checks.

Third, there are NOW accounts on which banks may pay 5½ percent interest. (They can, and do, of course, provide additional implicit yield via free services such as check clearing.) Fourth, on Super-NOW accounts banks can pay an unregulated interest rate, but must require a $2500 minimum balance. And since they are required to keep reserves against Super-NOW accounts, the interest rate that banks offer on these accounts is below that on money market accounts. Corporations are not permitted to have NOW or Super-NOW accounts. (Although these terms, "Now accounts," "Super-NOWs," and "money market accounts," are frequently used many banks have their own proprietary names for them.)

Before leaving checkable deposits there are two special types of checks that may need explanation. One is a *certified check*. This is a check on which the bank has guaranteed to make payment. This avoids the risk that the drawer of the check may not have sufficient funds in the bank to cover it by the time it clears. (The bank covers itself by subtracting the amount of the check from the depositor's account right away.) Such a certified check is therefore sure to be good unless it is forged or obtained by fraud. It is accepted in some situations when a personal check is not. An *officer's check,* often called a cashiers' check, is similar. It is a check drawn on the bank itself, which a depositor buys for a fee from the bank. Checkable deposits are not shown separately in Table 4.1 because, apart from Super-NOWs, they are de jure (but not de facto) savings deposits.

Savings and Time Deposits

One type of savings deposit is the passbook account, but savings accounts can also be evidenced by a written agreement between the depositor and the bank rather than by a passbook. Another type, certificates of deposits, usually abbreviated as CDs, is for a fixed sum. Although households can cash their CDs before the stated maturity date, Federal Reserve and FDIC regulations impose an interest penalty for this. This penalty also exists for fixed-maturity passbook accounts but not for other passbook accounts.

Large depositors can purchase negotiable CDs, whch are issued only by relatively well known banks. They are negotiable, which means that the purchaser can reclaim the funds prior to the maturity date by selling the CD on the money market. Then, at maturity, the bank pays off the CD to whoever is holding it. Such negotiable CDs are purchased almost only by business and governments since the minimum denomination is $100,000 and the normal denomination is $1 million or more. They are highly liquid assets since there is an active market in them. The maturity of negotiable CDs is usually a year or less and is often set to suit the convenience of the particular purchaser. There is no interest ceiling on CDs above $100,000; interest rates on them are determined by the market. As will be discussed in Chapter 8 the ceiling on smaller time deposits, called the Regulation Q ceiling, is currently being phased out.

Miscellaneous Liabilities

In addition to their deposits, banks have a set of miscellaneous liabilities. One of these is purchased federal funds. *Federal funds* are *not* funds belonging to the federal government as the name might suggest. Instead, they are deposits usually held at the Federal Reserve and traded among themselves by banks and some other institutions, such as savings and loans, mutual savings banks, government security dealers, and government agencies. They have the characteristic that they are transferred immediately with the Fed giving the receiving bank credit the same day. The lending bank wires the Fed and tells it to transfer some of its reserves to the borrowing bank's account. However, federal funds can also take other forms; for example, a city bank can borrow the correspondent balances a country bank keeps with it.

It is a very large market, and the big money-market banks use the federal funds market at times, not just to obtain the funds to meet their reserve requirements, but also to obtain funds for additional lending. The total amount borrowed in recent years has been substantially more than the required reserves of these banks. Most loans are made on a one-day basis, and it is a way in which banks can quickly obtain more reserves, or lend excess funds. Many small banks enter this market—typically as lenders—through their city correspondent banks. The great majority of banks are active in this market. Although it is actually a market for loans, in the language of the money market, transactions in it are described as "sales" and as "purchases." The *interest rate that the selling bank charges* is called the **federal funds rate,** and it is an important indicator of the balance of supply and demand in the money market.

Another liability is "securities sold under repurchase agreements." Repurchase agreements, also called "repos" or RP's, work as follows: a bank "sells" a security to someone with an agreement to repurchase it at a certain date at an agreed-upon price. In essence it is just like a loan the bank has received since it has to repurchase the security, and is therefore a liability of the bank. Such repurchase agreements can be used to pay interest on what is, in effect, a demand deposit. Banks have agreements with some corporations that towards the end of the day when all incoming checks have already been cleared they "sell" the corporation a security for all the funds in its demand deposit above a certain minimum, with an agreement to repurchase the security the next morning, so that the corporation has the funds available to meet incoming checks. In this way the corporation receives one day's interest on the overnight loan of its funds. However, most repurchase agreements are for longer than just overnight. Some banks also make repurchase agreements with household depositors. Since banks have to repurchase the securities they have "sold" they are entered on the balance sheet as liabilities.

The next item on the balance sheet is "other liabilities." This catch-all item includes various borrowings by a bank. Another liability item is outstanding acceptances. Acceptances arise in a rather complicated way. A firm selling to another firm on credit may not know enough about the buyer to feel safe in accepting its promise to pay. This is particularly likely with a foreign customer, in part because it is more difficult to sue in a foreign court than in a court in one's own country. But while the seller does not want to take the customer's IOU, he is willing to take the IOU of the customer's bank. Hence, a financial instrument, called a banker's acceptance, was developed. To explain it, let us back up and look first at a transaction *not* involving a bank. The seller draws up an order to pay by a certain date on the buyer and releases ownership of the merchandise when the *buyer "accepts" the order to pay by writing "accepted" across it.* It is now a **trade acceptance** and is legally binding. Alternatively, the buyer can make an arrangement with his or her bank allowing the seller to draw the order to pay, not on the buyer, but on the buyer's bank. *When the bank writes "accepted" on this order to pay,* it becomes a **banker's acceptance.** Since the bank is liable to make the payment on it, it is listed on the bank's balance sheet as a liability. However, the buyer is supposed to make payment to the bank by the date the bank has to make its payment on the acceptance. The bank lends its reputation, not its funds, to the buyer who usually has to pay a small fee for this service. The seller receiving the banker's acceptance, need not hold it to maturity but can sell it (at a discount from face value) in the money market.

The final item subsumed under other liabilities includes items like bills the bank has not yet paid, accrued salary, and so on.

THE BANK'S ASSETS

Primary Reserves

The first three assets listed on the left side of the balance sheet in Table 4.1 compose the bank's primary reserves. They are currency and coin in the bank (also called vault cash), reserves with the Fed, and demand deposits with domestic banks, that is, correspondent bank balances. These three items form the bank's first line of defense against a deposit or currency outflow.

In connection with these three items let us look at required reserves. As already mentioned the law was changed in 1980 to phase in the Fed's reserve

Table 4.2 New Reserve Requirements

	Initial rate[c] (in percent)	Range within which Fed can vary requirement[d] (in percent)
Normal Reserves:		
Transaction Accounts:		
On deposits of:		
Less than $25 million[a]	3	—[e]
$25 million and over[a]	12	8–14
Nonpersonal Time Deposits	3	0–9
Supplementary Reserves[b]	0	0–4

Note: The first 2.1 million reservable liabilities are exempt from the reserve requirement. This $2.1 million figure will be raised each year by 80 percent of the increase in total reservable liabilities.

a. The $25 million breaking-point will be increased each year after 1981 to reflect 80 percent of the increase in total transaction accounts in that year.

b. Imposition requires affirmative vote of five governors.

c. Although this is called the initial rate it will be phased in and reached only in 1984.

d. In extraordinary circumstances the Fed may for 180 days set reserve requirements outside this range.

e. Fed cannot vary this requirement except as indicated in note c.

requirements for all depository institutions (commercial banks, mutual savings banks, savings and loans, and credit unions) that have *transactions accounts,* that is, deposits transferable by check. They have to keep a certain percentage of these transactions accounts plus a (lower) percentage of their time deposits (other than those of individuals) as reserves. However, subsequent legislation exempted from the reserve requirement institutions with less than two million dollars of reservable deposits, and, as indicated in the footnote to Table 4.2, this cut-off point will be raised each year.[1]

The new reserve requirement system is being phased in and will be in full operation in September 1987; until then the reserve requirements are a changing mixture of the old and new systems.[2] Table 4.2 shows what reserve requirements will be in 1987 when the new system is in full operation.[3]

The new system imposes no reserve requirements on time deposits with a maturity of four years or more, or on time deposits owned by individuals and sole proprietors rather than by corporations or partnerships. The Federal Reserve if it wishes can eliminate the reserve requirement on other time deposits by setting the reserve ratio at zero. The purpose of the reserve requirement is to control the supply of money, and Congress did not want to decide whether time deposits are money. The Fed has considerable power to vary the reserve requirements; thus in extraordinary circumstances it can

[1] There are also reserve requirements against so-called Eurodollar liabilities. Eurodollars will be discussed in chapters 11 and 31.

[2] For member banks the switch to the new system will take about 3 years; for others it will take until September 1987.

[3] During the phase-in period the applicable reserve requirements can be found on page A-18 of the current month's *Federal Reserve Bulletin*.

set it for 180 days at any level it wants to, though it then has to pay interest on the additional reserves thus required.

Member banks have to keep their reserves as vault cash or as reserves with the Fed. Most are kept in the latter form. Other institutions can keep them also as deposits with member banks (or certain government agencies) that then, in turn, pass them on to the Fed. Reserve requirements do not have to be met on a continuous basis, but only as an average over a two week period.[4] Thus a bank can keep low reserves for, say, ten days, and then make it up by keeping very high reserves for the next four days. There is also a two day lag in the sense that the two weeks over which deposits are measured end on a Monday, but the two weeks over which the corresponding reserves are figured end on the following Wednesday. This two day lag allows banks to determine their average deposits for the two week period on Tuesday, and to adjust their reserves by Wednesday to meet the requirement.

The Fed does not pay any interest on normal reserves. Hence, one can think of the reserve requirement as a requirement to make an interest-free loan to the government. In this respect it functions as a tax. For example, suppose the interest rate is 10 percent and a bank has to keep 12 percent reserves. If so, for each dollar of deposits it is foregoing 1.2 cents (12 cents $\times$ 10 percent) of interest income per year. But the main reason we have reserve requirements is not that this is a good tax. Nor is it to ensure the safety of the depositor's funds. This is the function of deposit insurance and of the examination process that tries to ensure the safety of all the bank's assets, not just of a small reserve ratio. Instead, as will be discussed subsequently, the function of the reserve requirement is to allow the Fed to control the quantity of money.

Another item on the balance sheet—cash items in the process of collection—is also extremely liquid, representing as it does checks and similar instruments that have just been deposited in the bank and that the bank has sent on for clearing. However, a bank does not count these cash items in the process of collection as part of its primary reserves because it knows that they are approximately offset by checks drawn by its own depositors on it that are currently in transit and will have to be paid.

Securities and Loans

Beyond its primary reserves a bank holds mainly *loans and securities*. These two items are known as **earning assets.** One part of these earning assets compose its **secondary reserves.** These are *assets that are not quite as liquid and safe as primary reserves, but still are very liquid*. They therefore provide the bank with a second line of defense if its primary reserves are insufficient. Unlike primary reserves they earn a modest income though their yield is less than that on less liquid and less safe assets.

[4] Banks can make up a reserve deficiency of no more than 2 percent during the following period, and can meet up to 2 percent of their reserve requirement by excess reserves they held the previous period.

It is not possible to identify secondary reserves on a bank's balance sheet, since the items constituting the secondary reserves are classified together with other items. One item included in secondary reserves is short-term government securities. Others are bankers acceptances, commercial paper (short-term promissory notes issued by large and very sound corporations), and call loans—loans mainly to brokers and security dealers on which the bank can demand repayment in a day.

Banks do not put all their available funds other than primary and secondary reserves into loans; they also hold fixed income securities, mainly those issued by federal or state and local governments. Federal securities provide banks with an asset that has no default risk and has a very wide market. State and local government securities provide income that is exempt from federal taxes, and buying the securities issued by local governments in its area helps a bank to obtain the deposit business of those governments. Although such securities are usually safe with respect to default risk, if interest rates have risen, a bank selling a bond with, say, 15 years to maturity can make a substantial loss. And if it holds the bond to maturity it is still making a loss in terms of opportunity costs.

Banks believe that they should place some of their funds into securities rather than into loans, that too high a ratio of loans to deposits is dangerous. Conventional ideas about the acceptable ratio of loans to deposits have varied over time, and they have increased along with the actually experienced loan-to-deposit ratio—an example of rules conforming to behavior. In 1982 the ratio was 75 percent; in 1948 when it was 29 percent, a 75 percent ratio would have been considered an outrage.

Loans involve personal relationships between the banker and the borrower. Hence, they differ sharply from security purchases in which the bank buys securities usually from a dealer on the open market and does not know the borrower personally. Moreover, while a bank can sell a security again in the open market, there are fewer facilities for selling a loan, and the bank normally holds it until maturity.

Business loans. Banks have a strong comparative advantage in making commercial and industrial loans. Retail banks, though not the large wholesale banks, make most of their loans to fairly small, local borrowers. Such loan applications require the evaluation of someone on the spot, as the local banker is. This gives banks a powerful advantage over large, distant lenders, such as insurance companies. Contrast, for example, the position of a bank and an insurance company in making a loan to a local grocery store and in buying a corporate bond. The bank knows much more about the local grocery store than the distant insurance company does and, hence, is in a much better position to decide whether to make it a loan. By contrast, the insurance company with its large staff of security analysts can reach a much more sophisticated decision about buying a corporate bond than can the typical bank.

An important characteristic of bank lending to business is credit rationing. A bank, unlike other firms, does not stand ready to provide as much of its product, loans, as the customer is willing to pay for. A fruit store will normally be happy to provide the buyer with, say, ten times as much as he normally buys, but a bank will usually not be ready to make a borrower ten times the normal loan. Similarly, a bank will not make loans to just anyone who applies for one, even if she is willing to pay an interest rate high enough to offset the fact that this loan is risky. Banks ration loans among applicants, both by turning away some loan customers and by limiting the size of loans to others. A major reason why banks, unlike other sellers, limit the amount of their product they provide to each customer is surely that the bank takes a risk. It hands over its funds, and cannot be certain that it will be paid.

Credit rationing has both its defenders and its critics. The defenders point out that a banker's evaluation of loan requests acts as a check on the overoptimism of the firm's management. By scrutinizing loan requests, granting some, and denying others, the banker provides the economy with the services of a more or less objective outsider. The critics of credit rationing, on the other hand, point out that it allows banks to favor large depositors over other borrowers. Moreover, the critics argue, it gives bankers, particularly in small towns, a lot of arbitrary power, and it can be used as a weapon in forcing tie-in sales.

One factor that plays an important role in credit rationing is the existence of a customer relationship between the banker and the business borrower. Most of the business loans that banks make are to previous borrowers; it is a repeat business. Firms establish a customer relationship with a particular bank (or in the case of a large firm, with several banks) and, as long as the arrangement is mutually satisfactory, continue both to borrow from this bank and to keep deposits with it. This customer relationship comprises more than just a borrower-lender relation. The firm also uses other services of the bank, such as the provision of foreign exchange, the preparation of payrolls, etc. These services are often profitable and important for the bank. Large firms establish their customer relationships primarily with large and medium-sized banks, not only because such banks can provide these ancillary services, but also because national banks (and in many states, state banks) are allowed (with some exceptions) to lend to any one borrower an amount equal to no more than 15 percent of their capital, except on fully secured loans where the maximum is 25 percent.

This customer relationship implies that the bank has an obligation to take care of the reasonable credit needs of its existing customers. A bank is therefore not a completely free agent in making loans; it has to accommodate the reasonable demands of its customers. To do this it may have to turn away other potential customers, even though these new customers would be willing to pay a higher interest rate than do existing customers. Similarly, it may have to ration loans among its existing customers rather than turning some of them down altogether. Or else, it may have to sell some of its securities, or obtain the funds needed for extra loans by raising the interest rate it pays on large CDs. In the short run such actions may be costly for the bank, but are necessary to maximize long-run profits.

The existence of stable banking relations provides a major benefit: information. Over the years a bank learns much about its customers. If these customers were to change banks frequently, this information would become worthless to the firm's old bank, and its new bank would have to spend resources to acquire this information. But there is also a disadvantage. In a period of tight money, preexisting customer relationships lead to discrimination against new firms. At a time when banks have difficulty in meeting the loan demands of their existing customers, they are reluctant to take on new ones. Hence, new firms with highly productive uses for capital may find it hard to obtain loans.

The maturity of bank loans varies widely. Banks make many **term loans,** loans *usually having a maturity of from one to five years,* and some are even for longer. A borrower can use these term loans to finance fixed investment. They are often amortized, that is, repaid in installments just like a consumer loan. On term loans the bank can protect itself by imposing certain restrictions on the borrower, such as limiting the amount of other debt that can be incurred.

Another way in which banks sometimes take care of the customer's need for long-term capital is to purchase capital equipment and lease it to the customer. Thus, banks own ships, airplanes, even cows. Such equipment leasing gives the bank the tax benefit of accelerated depreciation, while, if certain conditions are met, the leaser gains from the fact that its balance sheet does not show a debt, as it would had it borrowed from the bank to buy the item directly.

Instead of a term loan, a borrower may prefer to get frequent short-term loans. One way to do this is under a **line of credit.** This is an *arrangement whereby the bank agrees to make loans to a firm almost upon demand up to a certain amount.* Lines of credit are usually established for a year. Under a firm line of credit the bank is more or less committed to make loans, and frequently charges a fee on the amount of the line that is *not* used, in addition to the interest on the amount that *is* used. As an alternative, a firm may obtain a revolving credit arrangement whereby it can borrow up to a certain amount, and then repay the loan at will without penalty. Later it can then borrow again up to the designated amount. A firm can also obtain a formal commitment from a bank to make it a loan in the future. For this it frequently has to pay a small fee. As Table 4.3 shows, in early November 1982 about 70 percent of the dollar value of all business loans was made under some form of loan commitment such as a line of credit or revolving credit.

A bank frequently requires business borrowers who have a line of credit, and many who don't, to keep a *compensating or supporting balance* in the bank. This means that the firm has to keep as a demand deposit, say 10 percent of its line of credit, or under other arrangements, say 15 percent of its outstanding loans. Compensating balances may be set as an average balance during the life of the line of credit, or more burdensomely, as a minimum balance. A compensating balance requirement is not legally binding, but if the borrower does not adhere to it the bank may refuse further loans, or may charge a higher interest rate on any subsequent loan. There is much variation in the compensating balance requirements of various banks. Some have rigid policies, while others merely consider the potential borrower's deposits as one factor in deciding on a loan request.

The compensating balance requirement raises the effective interest rate.

Table 4.3 Commercial and Industrial Loans Made, November 1–6, 1982[a]

Size of loans (thousands of dollars)	Percent of all loans	Percent of value of all loans	Average maturity (number of months)[b]	Percent of dollar amount of all loans made: under commitment	with floating rate	Average interest rate (percent)[b]
			Short-Term Loans			
1–24	72.1	2.7	3.6	40.8	32.5	15.6
25–49	11.9	1.7	3.6	35.8	39.5	15.3
50–99	5.3	1.5	4.1	64.5	70.8	13.8
100–499	7.3	5.6	4.8	54.4	65.4	13.8
500–999	.8	2.4	3.2	68.9	65.0	12.9
1000 and over	2.7	86.1	.8	72.8	21.6	10.8
All loans	100.0	100.0	1.2	70.1	26.4	11.3
			Long-Term Loans			
1–99	87.6	9.5	43.9	44.1	49.0	15.2
100–499	9.0	11.5	26.4	32.4	67.9	14.0
500–999	1.2	5.1	45.3	69.6	81.6	13.0
1000 and over	2.2	73.9	49.6	87.5	82.7	11.5
All loans	100.0	100.0	46.2	76.1	77.8	12.2

a. Excludes construction loans and land-development loans.

b. Average for loans weighted by their dollar amounts.

Source: *Federal Reserve Bulletin* 69 (February 1983), A 27.

doesn't he earn interest on the comp. bal.?

Suppose the bank makes a $100,000 loan at an 8 percent interest rate with a 10 percent minimum compensating balance requirement. The borrower can then use only $90,000 of that, but still pays 8 percent on $100,000, or $8,000, which is equivalent to 8.9 percent on the $90,000 actually used. However, in many cases the borrower has a partially offsetting benefit; the compensating balance can be drawn down if things get really bad.

Another requirement frequently imposed on a borrower is to provide the bank with collateral for the loan so that, in case it is not repaid, the bank can sell the collateral to pay it off. The collateral, which may consist of securities, inventory, and so on, often, though not always, exceeds the value of the loan. This protects the bank in case the collateral's market value declines. Sometimes the bank may not require collateral as a condition for the loan but may offer the borrower a lower interest rate if collateral is provided.

The interest rate charged on bank loans varies, of course, along with open-market interest rates, though with a lag. Table 4.3 shows the interest rates charged on loans in November 1982. It shows that the larger the loan the lower the interest rate. This is not surprising since the interest rate paid has to compensate the bank for the cost of making the loan, and the cost of making a $10 million loan is not a thousand times the cost of making a $10,000 loan. This does not mean that the average borrower who obtains a small loan could lower the interest rate by taking out a large loan; instead, if the loan is made at all, the interest rate would be higher, because a large loan to a small firm is risky.

Many loans are made at the *prime rate*. This is a rate established by each bank for large loans to its best—or at least better—customers. The prime rates of various banks *tend* to move together. Some banks set the prime rate by a formula based on the cost of funds to them, while others set prime rates equal to those of large banks.

Since only strong firms can borrow at the prime rate, getting the prime rate is prized as an important symbol. However, particularly in periods when banks are scrambling for loan business, many top firms can borrow at (unannounced) rates below the prime rate. Thus a survey by the *American Banker* (March 11, 1982) found that "almost 90% of the 500 largest industrials with sales greater than $400 million were offered short term bank borrowings in 1981 at below the prime . . . rate." Some large firms are offered the alternative of borrowing at a small fixed margin over the London Interbank Offered Rate (LIBOR) that is, the rate at which large international banks lend to each other in London.

Loans to firms that do not receive the prime rate are often scaled up from the prime rate. For example, the loan agreement may state that the interest rate will be half a percent above the prime rate.

As Table 4.3 shows, the interest rate charged is frequently a variable rate, rather than a fixed rate; as the prime rate on newly contracted loans changes, the rate on many previously made business loans changes along with it. Sometimes, however, the loan agreement contains a "cap" on how high the interest rate can rise.

Real Estate Loans. These loans account for almost a third of all bank loans. Residential mortgages may be insured or guaranteed by the Federal Housing Administration (FHA) or the Veterans Administration (VA). FHA and VA mortgages involve little risk for banks, but have the disadvantage that the maximum interest rate that the bank may charge is limited, though this ceiling can often be avoided by discounting the mortgage note using the points system in addition to charging interest. (Under the points system a customer signs a promissory note, say, for $50,000. The bank then gives the customer only, say, $48,000 for this $50,000 note, thus obtaining an additional $2,000 of interest.) Mortgage loans are long-term loans that can seriously reduce the bank's liquidity. But the actual maturity of mortgage loans is much less than their apparent maturity, since they are amortized (that is, repaid in installments) and, in addition, are frequently repaid when the house is sold. Moreover, a secondary market for mortgage loans, particularly FHA and VA loans, has developed on which banks can sell their mortgage loans. In addition many mortgages are made at variable interest rates, so that banks do not lose so much on these loans when interest rates rise.

Consumer Loans. Another major outlet for bank funds is consumer lending which accounts for about 20 percent of total bank loans. One substantial advantage of consumer loans for banks is that they are liquid. Since they are usually short term and amortized, their turnover is fairly rapid.

Most consumer loans are made for the purchase of durables, which then serve as collateral for the loan. Banks make consumer loans both directly and indirectly through dealers by financing loans originated by the dealer. However, banks also make general purpose loans to consumers. Among these are credit-card loans on which the bank receives not only interest from the borrower, but also a commission from the vendor. Some banks have set up an arrangement by which credit-card holders can have their checking accounts credited and the card debited automatically if the balance in the checking account is insufficient to meet incoming checks. Other banks have set up similar arrangements for automatic loans to customers who do not have the bank's credit card. On the whole, U.S. banks are moving towards the British overdraft system, under which the depositor can overdraw the account, with the bank treating the overdraft as a loan.

The interest rate charged on consumer loans is higher than on business loans. The reason is that the cost of making such loans is also high because these are relatively small and short-term loans. For example, if it costs a bank \$50 to set up and take care of monthly payments on a \$2,000 two-year loan, it must charge approximately 1.2 percent just to cover this cost. Nonetheless, banks usually charge a lower interest rate on their consumer loans than do other consumer lenders because they avoid the riskier loans that other lenders are more ready to make. Losses on consumer loans usually run between 0.75 and 1.25 percent of outstanding loan volume.

Banks also make loans for the purchase of securities. Such loans are made, not only to households, but also to security dealers and brokers who use them to finance their customer's purchases, as well as their own security holdings. *Loans to security dealers and brokers are often made on a* (*renewable*) *one-day basis* (referred to as **call loans**) and are therefore extremely liquid for banks.

Still another type of bank loan is the student loan. This loan is offered at a relatively low interest rate since it is subsidized by the federal government, which also guarantees repayment. This guarantee has had to be invoked much more frequently than was expected when the legislation authorizing it was passed.[5]

Foreign Loans. Many large banks, as well as some medium sized banks, have banded together into so-called syndicates to make large loans to foreign firms and foreign governments. Loans to foreign governments are safer than loans to foreign or domestic firms in one respect: a country—unlike a firm—is not likely to go out of business. However, they are riskier in another way since, if a foreign government refuses to repay, the bank cannot go to court, have the country declared bankrupt, and all its assets distributed among creditors. Instead, the sanctions against a country just walking away from its debts are twofold. First, its assets that are located elsewhere, for example, bank deposits in another country, or ships in foreign ports, can be seized. This makes it hard for a country to carry on normal foreign trade. Second, and more seriously, a country that has defaulted on its debts cannot borrow in the international capital market.

While these sanctions are sufficient to prevent countries from defaulting

[5]The last two entries under loans in Table 4.1 are accounting adjustments. Banks have to set aside a reserve against potential loan losses. To obtain the net value of loans these reserves have to be substracted, and the same is true for any unearned income that is included in the face value of some loans.

in normal times, they can turn out to be insufficient to prevent default when a country is hit by a severe problem, such as a catastrophic drop in export earnings. Thus, in 1981 when the Polish economy was in crisis, Poland declared itself unable to repay outstanding loans. U.S. and European banks that had made large loans to Poland and other East European countries on the assumption that as a last resort the Russians would bail out any of these countries, now found that there was no Russian umbrella. There was talk about declaring Poland in default, both on these bank loans and on loans made by the governments of various countries. In part for political reasons default was avoided; Poland agreed to continue to pay interest on the loans and the banks agreed to reschedule, that is, extend them. Moreover, they made additional loans to Poland, thus in effect lending Poland part of the money it used to pay interest on the original loans.

In 1982 and 1983 there were more actual and threatened defaults. Argentina, Brazil (both of which have massive foreign debts), and Rumania refused to make scheduled loan repayments. Mexico also asked its lenders to reschedule outstanding loans by stretching their maturities. In addition, these countries wanted to obtain additional credit. These defaults or near-defaults were due to several factors. One obvious one is that these countries had borrowed more than they should have. A second is the severity of the 1981–82 recession, the most severe since the 1930s, which sharply reduced the prices of raw materials exported by many debtor countries. A third factor is that in early 1983 nominal interest rates declined much less than the inflation rate. Hence the real rate of interest that these countries had to pay rose sharply. And in the case of Mexico a major factor was the decline in oil prices.

In asking banks to reschedule their loans and to make new loans these debtor countries were not powerless. They could threaten that unless they got what they asked for they would default. If so, then the banks would have to write off these loans on their books as losses, something they were most reluctant to do, since it would reduce their profits and their capital. By contrast on a rescheduled loan the banks can, at the very least, postpone recognizing the loss for accounting purposes, and if things turn out well they will be repayed. Hence debtor countries have a big bargaining chip. Thus, the *Wall Street Journal* (July 29, 1982) reported a U.S. banker as saying "I find it absolutely hilarious when I hear bankers talking about getting tough with the Poles. . . . In some ways it is the Poles who are in the driver's seat."

These near bankruptcies created a serious problem. In mid-1982 the loans that the ten largest banks had made to third world countries equalled 169 percent of their equity capital! There was fear that if several large debtor countries default some banks might fail, or at least have their capital (and hence lending capacity) severely impaired. On the other hand, the alternative of having the federal government, directly (or through the IMF) make loans to these countries to bail out the banks is also not an appetizing choice.

Rescheduling the loans of weak borrowers occurs also on domestic loans. It is a fairly common procedure when a large borrower is unable to repay.

In such cases banks have an incentive to avoid forcing the borrower into bankruptcy because they would then have to write off the loan as a loss. By rescheduling the loan they, at the very least, postpone recognizing the loss for accounting purposes, and at best, allow the borrower to recover and repay the loan in full. This gives the borrower some power.

Other Assets

Apart from the major assets discussed so far, the banks' balance sheet contains a number of minor assets listed in Table 4.1 as "Other Assets." Included in this category are items such as "customer's liabilities on account of acceptances," which is the counterpart of the acceptance item listed as a liability. When a bank accepts a draft for a customer the customer incurs a liability to the bank and this is an asset for the bank. Additional examples of "Other Assets" are federal funds sold and bank premises.

ASSET AND LIABILITY MANAGEMENT

Having looked at the various assets and liabilities of banks, let us now look at how banks manage these assets and liabilities. Banks try to avoid risky assets even if they could earn a high rate of return on them. Generally, the losses banks make on business loans run well below one percent of their outstanding loans. Since rising interest rates can substantially reduce the price of the bonds they hold, banks risk making larger losses on them, but are able to avoid recognizing these losses for accounting purposes by holding on to their low-yielding bonds rather than selling them. The extent to which banks avoid risk varies, of course, from bank to bank, and also from time to time. After some spectacular bankruptcies or right after a financial crisis has been narrowly averted, banks tend to be more cautious.

Banks try to develop their loan business. For example, their officers call on corporations served by other banks and bid for their business. Sound companies, particularly large ones, do not have to approach their bankers "hat in hand."

On the liabilities side, a traditional banker, say of 1910 vintage, would be appalled by what banks do now. Before the Great Depression typically only middle- and upper-class families held demand deposits. A textbook published in 1916 described the process of opening a bank account as follows:

> There are so many ways in which a bank may be defrauded . . . that the officers must be very careful to whom they extend the privilege of opening an account. . . . One of the pleasantest ways to open an account with a bank is to be introduced by a depositor in good standing. . . . It is not always possible to arrange for a personal introduction. In such a case, a properly written letter addressed to an officer and signed by a depositor in good standing, or even by a mutual friend, will be of material assistance. . . . If it is impossible for a person to obtain either a personal or written introduction to the bank he had chosen, he may make application for the opening of an account without an introduction and have the assurance that such a procedure will not militate against him, if he presents his case properly. It is true that some banks will not, under any circum-

stances, open an account with a person unknown to them. In fact, it is good banking practice not to accept accounts from strangers. . . .[6]

This is a far cry from the way banks act now, chasing after depositors with singing commercials.

Prior to 1966, banks took their liabilities as more or less given from the outside. The traditional banker was more concerned with the assets side of his balance sheet than with obtaining deposits.

This story is still a fair description of the way many small banks behave, but it is no longer true for large and medium-sized banks. During the early 1960s, several things happened that made these banks active seekers after short-term funds. One was that firms wanted to borrow more and, as we saw, banks are obligated to meet the reasonable credit needs of their good customers; they were therefore under pressure to obtain more funds. Second, by the early 1960s banks had run down their government securities substantially, and many of the government securities they did hold were pledged as collateral for public deposits or were held as needed secondary reserves.[7] Third, large banks serving large corporations found it difficult to obtain additional funds the conventional way from their depositors because these corporations had learned various ways of economizing on their deposit holdings. Thus, these banks had to find new ways of acquiring funds. At the same time, by the 1960s the attitude of bankers had changed; many of those whose outlook toward risk had been shaped by the Great Depression had retired, and a new breed of more confident profit-oriented officers had taken charge. Moreover, in 1961 a new financial instrument, the large negotiable CD, was developed.

The large negotiable CD meant that banks can now issue a security that is similar to a Treasury bill in the sense that the owner does not have to hold it to maturity but can sell it at any time on the money market. This greatly broadened the market for large CDs. *Large and medium-sized banks can now—at a price—obtain additional deposits whenever they wanted them by offering large CDs carrying a slightly higher rate of interest.* In general, the rate a bank has to pay on its CDs depends on its size, both because large banks are better known and because the market believes that the FDIC is less likely to let a large bank fail with losses to depositors than a medium-sized bank.

And large CDs are not the only instrument of liability management. Another one is a repurchase agreement (RP); that is, an arrangement under which a bank "sells" some of its securities with a commitment to buy them back again, say, the next day, at a fixed price. In effect the "buyer" is making a loan to the bank. Another method of liability management is to have the bank's holding company issue commercial paper, or securities, and to make the funds thus obtained available to the bank. Still another way in which large banks obtain funds is to buy Eurodollars. An American bank

[6] Joseph F. Johnson, Howard M. Jefferson, and Franklin Escher, *Banking* (New York: Alexander Hamilton Institute, 1916), pp. 266–68.

[7] Many governments require banks holding their deposits to pledge specific government securities as collateral in case the bank fails.

can borrow (that is, "buy") dollars from its own European branch or from other U.S. or foreign banks. In addition, banks can buy federal funds and they can borrow from the Fed. Large banks can, and do, purchase a great volume of funds by these means; at one time borrowed funds amounted to more than a quarter of the liabilities of large banks.

Small banks cannot play this game. Since they are not well enough known, and since they could only deal in small amounts, they would face prohibitive transactions costs in the large negotiable CD market and the Eurodollar market. However, through their correspondent banks, they enter the federal funds market, and they can borrow from the Fed. Moreover, by offering a higher interest rate, they can obtain funds from money brokers.

THE MATURITY MATCH BETWEEN ASSETS AND LIABILITIES

A bank cannot just look at either its assets or its liabilities in isolation, but has to watch the match-up between the maturity of its assets and liabilities. Banks face the temptation of having much longer maturities for their assets than for their liabilities. One reason is that their loan customers often want term loans and want them at fixed interest rates rather than at floating rates, so that they can predict future interest costs. In other words, they want banks to provide the service of assuming the risk that interest rates will rise in the future. Second, usually, though by no means always, short-term interest rates are lower than are intermediate-term and long-term interest rates. This gives banks an incentive to finance their intermediate- and long-term loans and security holdings by borrowing short-term, say in the CD market. Third, the large banks think they have enough expertise to try to forecast interest rates. Hence, at times when they expect interest rates to fall, they are tempted to buy long-term securities to lock in the high yield, and to finance this purchase with short-term funds whose cost they expect to decline.

But a substantial mismatch of the maturities of assets and liabilities creates a substantial risk. Suppose a bank expects interest rates to fall, and therefore buys long-term bonds and finances their purchase by issuing, say, 90-day CDs. It then turns out that the bank is wrong, that interest rates rise instead of falling. After 90 days the bank is then earning, say, 10 percent on its bonds while paying 13 percent on the CDs it issued to finance their purchase. If the bank has bet very heavily on its guess it may be in serious trouble; its income is eroded by the 3 percent interest differential, and the market value of its bonds portfolio has fallen. In the late 1970s, a large bank, First Pennsylvania, got into serious difficulties in this way.

Banks cannot easily avoid *some* mismatch between the maturities of their assets and liabilities, but they can limit it in several ways. One way is to keep their securities portfolio fairly short-term, and to make a large proportion of their term loans at floating interest rates (even though their customers may object). Moreover, they can resist the temptation to speculate on changes in interest rates. Beyond this they can offset the greater maturity of their assets than of their liabilities by using the forward market. This is a market in which one can buy or sell certain government securities and CDs for future delivery. A bank can sell government securities or CDs which it does not own for future delivery. Then, if interest rates do rise, so that the prices of government securities and CDs fall, it can make delivery by buying them cheaply on the market, thus gaining a profit that offsets the losses on its long-term fixed assets. Conversely, if interest rates fall, its losses on its forward market deals are offset by the capital gains on the long-term assets it holds. Like a wheat farmer it can reduce risk by hedging.

In these ways banks have succeeded, by and large, in avoiding substantial interest rate risk. If interest rates rise the earnings on their assets rise by about as much as their costs do.

OTHER BANKING ACTIVITIES

Taking deposits, making loans and holding securities are not the only activities of banks. In 1980 close to 20 percent of the income of large wholesale banks came from sources other than interest income. Many banks earn a substantial income by providing services such as advice and payroll preparation, as well as by acting as dealers in the money and foreign exchange markets. Banks can also speculate in the foreign exchange market by holding foreign currencies at one time, or selling them short at another. Moreover, they can speculate in the domestic money markets by, for example, selling federal funds early in the week, expecting to buy them back at a lower price later on. Then there are bank trust departments which control very large amounts of capital. Only about one-quarter of all banks have them, and a relatively small number of bank trust departments account for the bulk of trust department assets. They only administer funds for wealthy households, estates, pension funds, and so on. For some trust funds the bank provides only investment advice, but for much the greater part it has sole investment responsibility. Banks can, and do, invest these funds, unlike their own assets, in common stocks as well as in fixed-income securities.

There has been some concern about these trust activities of banks, and proposals have been made to take trust departments away from banks and to turn them into separate institutions. The main arguments for this are, first, that trust departments allow banks to accumulate great economic power, and second, that banks might not separate their trust and commercial banking activities as they are supposed to do. For example, if a bank in its capacity as a lender hears of unfavorable developments ahead of the firm's other stockholders it might have its trust department sell this stock to the detriment of other stockholders. But banks are not supposed to do this, and whether this actually occurs on a significant scale is a matter for debate.

Apart from personal trusts, the larger banks also handle trust matters for corporations. They administer corporate pension funds, send out interest and dividend payments on corporate bonds and stocks and register bond transfers. These activities can be a profitable part of the customer relationship for the bank.

SUMMARY

1. Banks issue checkable deposits and savings and time deposits. Other bank liabilities include federal funds bought, bankers' acceptances, and capital.
2. Their primary reserves consist of vault cash, interbank deposits, and deposits with the Federal Reserve.
3. All sizable depository institutions with transactions accounts or nonpersonal time deposits must hold reserves set—within limits—by the Federal Reserve.
4. Bank loans are the biggest bank asset. Banks ration credit. Business firms have a customer relationship with banks, and are able to get term loans as well as short-term loans. They often have a line of credit, but have to keep compensating balances, and frequently, have to offer collateral. The best customers can often borrow below the prime rate, but many other customers have to pay more than the prime rate. On many term loans the interest rate is variable.
5. Mortgage loans are an important part of a bank's assets, though they are relatively illiquid. In addition, banks make consumer loans and security loans.
6. Large and medium-sized banks now manage their liabilities by actively buying funds in the CD market and the federal funds market. Large banks rely heavily on such purchased funds.
7. Banks have to watch the maturity match between their assets and liabilities. They are tempted to hold assets that are much longer term than their liabilities, but this is risky.
8. Banks earn fee incomes from various activities, and the biggest banks have very large trust departments.

Questions and Exercises

1. Describe the way large banks manage their liabilities.
2. Describe the current system of reserve requirements for member and nonmember banks. Do you think it is proper and equitable?
3. Describe CDs, both negotiable and nonnegotiable ones.
4. Describe:
   a. bankers' acceptances,
   b. cashier's check,
   c. federal funds,
   d. primary reserves.
5. Describe credit rationing. Why do banks do this?
6. Describe the customer relationship of banks. Is this desirable?
7. Describe the following characteristics of business loans:
   a. lines of credit,
   b. compensatory balances,
   c. collateral,
   d. the prime rate.
8. Suppose a banker tells you that in his twenty-five years as a loan officer he has never made a loan that went into default. Should you congratulate him for sound business judgment?
9. Describe the functions of bank trust departments.
10. "Capital requirements on banks should be lowered. If they have a smaller proportion of their funds tied up in capital they can make more loans." Discuss.

Further Reading

BREWER, ELIJAH. "Bank Funds Management Comes of Age." Federal Reserve Bank of Chicago, *Economic Perspectives,* March / April 1980, pp. 3–10. A very useful survey.

FRIEDMAN, BENJAMIN. "Credit Rationing: A Review." *Board of Governors, Federal Reserve System, Staff Economy Study #72,* 1972. An excellent discussion of the large literature on credit rationing.

HAVRILESKY, THOMAS, and BOORMAN, JOHN. *Current Perspectives in Banking.* Arlington Heights, Ill.: AHM Publishing Co., 1976. An interesting collection of readings.

HAYES, DOUGLAS. *Bank Funds Management.* Ann Arbor, Mich.: University of Michigan, Graduate School of Business Administration, 1980. A compact discussion of how banks manage funds.

HODGMAN, DONALD. *Commercial Bank Loan and Investment Policy.* Urbana, Ill.: University of Illinois Press, 1963. An interesting argument that the deposit business of banks takes precedence over their lending business.

LINDOW, WESLEY. *Inside the Money Market.* New York: Random House, 1972. A fascinating discussion of liability management as seen by a banker.

SILBER, WILLIAM L. *Commercial Bank Liability Management.* Chicago: Association of Reserve City Bankers, 1978. An interesting and detailed survey.

WEINTRAUB, ROBERT. *International Debt: Crisis and Challenge.* Fairfax, Va.: Department of Economics, George Mason University, 1983. A stimulating discussion.

Financial Intermediaries 5

Most of us have a hard time saving, but when we do manage to save something we find it difficult to invest in an increasingly complex economy. A number of other institutions beside commercial banks serve to intermediate between savers and investors, and provide an alternative to direct finance. These institutions include mutual savings banks, savings and loan associations, credit unions, life insurance companies, and pension funds.

Most Americans depend on these financial intermediaries to do their investing for them. Some sacrifice of investment income is required to pay the cost of operating financial intermediaries, but most people, especially those of modest means, are willing to pay that price for the safety and convenience offered by intermediaries. Wealthy individuals buy common stocks and may hold municipal bonds for tax-free income, but few American families hold common stocks, and even fewer hold tax-exempt bonds. Most families invest their savings in commercial banks and other intermediaries. Table 5.1 shows the distribution of household financial assets among the different kinds of directly held securities and financial intermediaries. Table 5.2 shows how the flow of household saving has been distributed among different kinds of securities and financial intermediaries.

In Chapter 2 we discussed the rationale for the use of financial intermediaries. In this chapter we will review the development of several of the more important kinds of intermediaries. In addition to the ones mentioned above we will consider the role of consumer finance companies and of several important federal financial agencies.

THRIFT INSTITUTIONS: A PROFILE

The thrift institutions, mutual savings banks, savings and loan associations, and money market funds provide the best and most important example of

Table 5.1 Household Balance Sheet, 31 December 1982
(billions of dollars)

Assets		Liabilities	
Deposits and credit-market instruments (1)	$2,802.3	Credit-market instruments	$1,676.4
Deposits	1,980.9	Home mortgages	1,103.7
Checkable deposits and currency	312.5	Other mortgages	34.8
Small time and savings deposits	1,297.9	Installment consumer credit	343.4
Money market fund shares	206.6	Other consumer credit	84.6
Large time deposits	163.8	Bank loans n.e.c.	35.3
		Other loans	74.6
Credit market instruments	821.4	Security credit	25.4
U.S. government securities	360.6	Trade credit	22.4
Treasury issues	276.3	Deferred and unpaid life insurance premiums	16.5
Savings bonds	68.3		
Other Treasury	280.0		
Agency issues	84.3		
State and local obligations	155.3		
Corporate and foreign bonds	73.5		
Mortgages	186.6		
Open-market paper	45.4		
Corporate equities	1,306.2		
Mutual fund shares	89.9		
Other corporate equities	1,216.3		
Life insurance reserves	244.6		
Pension fund reserves	931.7		
Security credit	27.7		
Miscellaneous assets	82.2		
TOTAL: Financial Assets	$5,394.5	TOTAL: Liabilities	$1,740.7

(1) Excludes corporate equities.

Source: Board of Governors of the Federal Reserve System, Flow of Funds Accounts, May 23, 1983.

Table 5.2 Annual Change in Financial Assets of Households (dollar amounts in billions)

Year	Savings associations	Mutual savings banks	Commercial banks	Credit unions	Life insurance reserves	Pension fund reserves	Credit and equity instruments	Money market fund shares	Total[b]
1960	$ 7.6	$ 1.4	$ 2.7	$0.5	$ 3.2	$ 8.3	$ 6.2		$ 31.6
1965	8.5	3.6	14.9	1.0	4.8	12.1	2.8		55.1
1970	11.0	4.4	27.0	1.2	5.5	18.4	− 1.2		75.1
1971	28.0	9.9	28.1	1.7	6.3	21.1	− 8.9		98.3
1972	32.7	10.2	29.0	2.5	6.9	22.6	6.0		122.2
1973	20.2	4.7	35.3	3.6	7.6	25.4	32.0		142.7
1974	16.1	3.1	34.1	2.6	6.7	29.6	36.6	$ 2.4	138.5
1975	42.8	11.2	24.6	5.4	8.7	34.9	27.0	1.3	162.8
1976	50.6	13.0	37.9	6.0	8.4	44.0	23.9	0.0	199.5
1977	51.0	11.1	37.7	7.8	11.5	54.6	27.7	0.2	223.0
1978	44.9	8.6	40.1	6.4	12.0	61.8	51.9	6.9	254.9
1979	39.3	3.4	33.3	3.2	12.5	54.3	67.7	34.4	271.4
1980	42.1	7.4	74.8	6.9	11.5	77.5	25.7	29.2	286.0
1981[a]	13.7	3.1	39.9	1.3	12.3	87.3	19.5	107.5	304.9

a. Preliminary. b. Includes checkable deposits and currency not classified elsewhere.

Sources: Federal Home Loan Bank Board; Federal Reserve Board. Savings and Loan Source Book—1981.

the functions of financial intermediaries outlined in Chapter 2. As we indicated there, they reap economies of scale and the benefits of diversification, and create liquidity by pooling the assets of many individual savers.

Our present financial arrangements reflect the origins and historical evolution of our financial institutions and markets: At one time there was a clear division of function between commercial banks and thrift institutions. Commercial banks specialized in demand liabilities (bank notes and checkable deposits) and provided short-term loans to business. Savings banks and savings and loan associations provided savings deposit services for households and held long-term assets, especially home mortgages.

Commercial banks have long been active in the savings account and mortgage markets. More recently thrift institutions have begun to provide checkable deposits (NOW and Super-NOW accounts) and have broader powers to provide consumer credit and to make loans to business. Clearly, the deposit institutions are becoming more alike. However, it will be some time before the differences among them disappear. A review of their history may help to explain some transitional problems.

Savings Banks

Mutual savings banks were organized early in the nineteenth century to encourage saving among the growing artisan class in cities like Boston, Philadelphia, and New York. Mutual savings banks are controlled by self-perpetuating boards of trustees. Earnings, in excess of operating costs, are either paid out as interest to depositors or added to surplus as a cushion against losses.

Most of the mutual savings banks operate in New England and New York, with a very small number in other states. Most mutual savings banks are state chartered and regulated by state banking commissioners. Under recent legislation, savings banks may now, if they wish, obtain federal charters and some have done so. They have been conservatively managed and have had few failures. Between 1930 and 1933 only ten mutual savings banks failed, while over nine thousand commercial banks and over five hundred savings and loan associations failed. The Massachusetts savings banks set up their own insurance fund so that many of them do not belong to the FDIC.

Savings and Loan Associations

Savings and loan associations originated as self-help associations. A group of people who wanted to finance their own houses agreed to pool their savings in order to build homes. Savings and loan associations now operate in much the same way as savings banks. They differ from savings banks, however, in several important respects.

First, many savings and loan associations are now organized as corporations rather than as mutual associations. There are only a few "stock" savings banks. Because of their origin, their investment powers are more limited. Savings and loans were restricted to mortgage loans and government securities until the law was changed in 1980.

The two thousand federally chartered savings and loans hold about 60 percent of all deposits. The remainder is held by over 2500 state-chartered associations. Eighty-five percent of deposits are insured by FSLIC, which is similar to FDIC. Most of the remaining deposits are insured by state-operated funds.

State-chartered associations are examined and supervised by state banking commissions. Federally chartered associations are supervised by the twelve regional Home Loan banks. The Home Loan Bank System was founded in the 1930s after the failure of a large number of savings and loan associations. Each regional bank is nominally owned by the federally chartered associations in its area, but their activities are controlled by the Federal Home Loan Bank Board, appointed by the president. The Federal Home Loan Bank Board sells securities on behalf of the twelve regional Federal Home Loan banks to finance loans to member associations. Thus the Home Loan Bank System provides its member associations with a "lender of last resort." However, the lending capacity of the system is more limited than in the case of the Federal Reserve. Ordinarily the Home Loan banks must charge borrowing associations a rate that covers its own borrowing costs. In emergencies the Home Loan Bank Board may borrow directly from the U.S. Treasury.

Money Market Funds

Money market funds first became important in 1974 when short-term interest rates rose to record levels, and had an explosive growth in 1979–82 when rates again rose sharply. The funds, organized by brokerage firms and firms managing mutual funds for stocks and bonds, invest in treasury bills, commercial paper, and bank CDs. They arrange with banks to honor checks drawn by fund shareholders on the funds account. When the bank presents the check the fund liquidates assets and, of course, reduces the number of shares credited to the person drawing the check.

Credit Unions

Credit unions have grown rapidly in recent years. They are cooperative organizations like savings banks but are often sponsored by employers. Employers often provide free office space and arrange for payroll deduction savings plans. Credit unions usually provide consumer credit and mortgage credit to their members.

INVESTMENT PORTFOLIOS OF THRIFT INSTITUTIONS

The thrift institutions have always invested heavily in home mortgages. Their concentration on mortgages reflects their comparative advantage over other investors in mortgage investment as well as legal restrictions. The thrift institutions have an advantage over other intermediaries in the mortgage field. The managers of local offices can readily keep up with changes in real-estate values, zoning laws, and tax changes in the immediate area. Thrift institutions also hope to attract deposit business from mortgage borrowers.

Table 5.3 Savings and Loan Associations' Balance Sheet, 31 December 1982 (billions of dollars)

Assets		Liabilities	
Mortgages	$482.4	Deposits	$580.8
Consumer credit	20.2	Federal funds and security RPs	15.1
Other assets	203.4	Credit market instruments	70.4
Demand deposits and currency	5.5	Corporate bonds	3.2
Time deposits	14.0	Mortgage loans in process	—
Federal funds and security RPs	15.4	Bank loans n.e.c.	1.2
U.S. government securities	88.0	Federal Home Loan Bank loans	66.0
Treasury issues	13.6	Profit taxes payable	.6
Agency issues	74.4	Miscellaneous liabilities	14.2
State and local obligations	.8		
Open-market paper	8.8		
Miscellaneous assets	70.9		
TOTAL: Financial Assets	$706.0	TOTAL: Liabilities	$679.9

Source: Board of Governors of the Federal Reserve System, Flow of Funds Accounts, 2nd quarter 1983.

Because of legal restrictions, savings and loan investment portfolios consist mainly of real-estate loans, U.S. government securities, and cash, though under the 1980 law this has changed to some extent. Table 5.3 shows the aggregate balance sheet for U.S. savings and loan associations. Over 80 percent of savings and loan assets are invested in real-estate loans.

Savings and loans have specialized in mortgages on single-family homes, but they also lend to apartment developers and provide commercial mortgages for developers of shopping centers and other office and store buildings. Savings and loan associations make construction loans to builders. They advance funds as construction proceeds and are repaid when the building is sold. They also make mortgage "commitments" to builders, agreeing to make mortgage loans to the purchasers of homes in a tract development when the homes are completed and sold.

While the demand for mortgage credit is fairly steady, savings and loan associations have to adjust their policies to fluctuations in deposit inflows. When there is a temporary decline in deposit inflow they may borrow from the Federal Home Loan Bank (FHLB). However, in very tight money periods, they have had to ration their lending more severely. They may limit new commitments to deposit customers and builders with whom they have a continuing relationship. When their deposit inflow is large they repay the Federal Home Loan Bank and temporarily build up their holdings of government securities. In the longer run, of course, savings and loans adjust mortgage rates upward when they cannot meet demand for new commitments, and downward when they have surplus funds.

The investment activities of mutual savings banks are somewhat more complex because they have broader lending powers than the savings and loans. Mutual savings banks can buy corporate bonds and even some stocks and they have limited consumer-lending powers. Table 5.4 shows their balance sheet. Nonetheless, because they have a comparative advantage over insurance companies and pension funds in mortgage lending, mutual savings

Table 5.4 Mutual Savings Banks' Balance Sheet, 31 December 1982
(billions of dollars)

Assets		Liabilities	
Demand deposits and currency	5.2	Deposits	$157.1
Time deposits	1.8	Miscellaneous liabilities	7.9
Federal funds and security RPs	5.3		
Corporate equities	3.2		
Credit market instruments	151.3		
U.S. government securities	23.9		
Treasury issues	6.0		
Agency issues	17.9		
State and local obligations	2.5		
Corporate and foreign bonds	18.9		
Mortgages	94.5		
Consumer	4.3		
Commercial paper	7.3		
Miscellaneous assets	7.5		
TOTAL: Financial Assets	$174.2	TOTAL: Liabilities	$165.0

Source: Board of Governors of the Federal Reserve System, Flow of Funds Accounts, 2nd quarter 1983.

banks have placed about two-thirds of their funds in mortgages. Commercial mortgages make up about one-third of their mortgage portfolio. Since the savings banks are concentrated in states with relatively slow population growth, mutual savings banks often lend on mortgages in areas outside their home state.

Because they have the option of buying corporate bonds, mutual savings banks have an investment choice and are willing to shift funds into the bond market whenever bond yields rise relative to mortgage yields. As we shall see in the next chapter, their exercise of this choice is one of the links between bond and mortgage rates.

Together the thrift institutions hold about $500 billion in mortgages, nearly half of the total from all sources. Since they play such an important role in the mortgage market, any reduction in their lending activity affects the rate of residential construction. Because the home-building industry is large and politically powerful, the competitive problems of the thrift institutions have produced a good deal of political controversy and much legislation to assist the thrift institutions and to provide alternative sources of mortgage financing.

THE COMPETITION FOR THE CONSUMERS' DOLLARS

The thrift institutions face two kinds of competition. They must compete with commercial banks which offer savings deposits and certificates like those offered by thrift institutions. They must also compete with marketable securities—bonds, stocks, treasury bills—and with money market funds.

Households now hold over 15 times as much in time and savings deposits as at the end of World War II. Thrift institutions increased their share of the "savings market" from about 45 percent in 1945 to 60 percent in 1960.

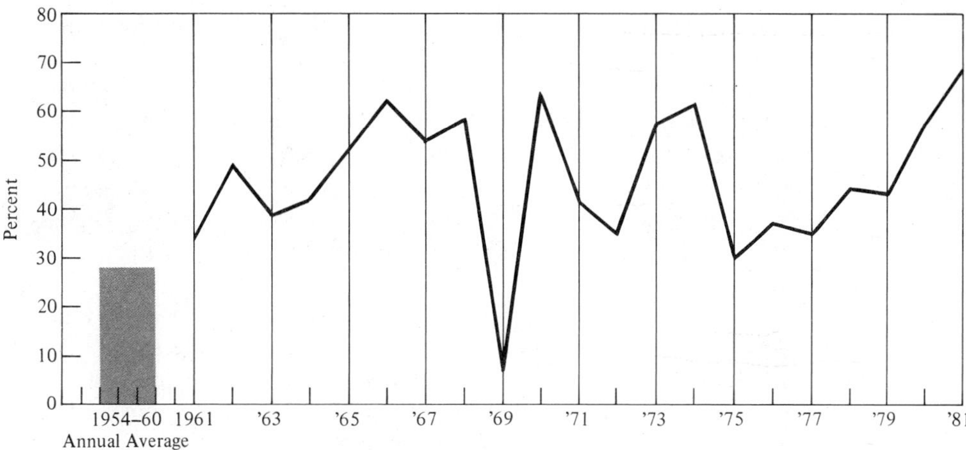

Figure 5.1 Commercial Bank Share of Gains in Savings Deposits.

Source: *Savings and Loan Fact Book,* 1981.

Thereafter, the share of commercial banks has moved erratically with a small net gain (see Figure 5.1).

On average, household investment in marketable securities has absorbed only a few percent of household savings. On a number of occasions, however, rapid increases in money market rates have induced households to shift funds from thrift institutions directly into marketable securities or money market funds.

To understand the changes in the competition for savings, it is first necessary to examine the factors determining the rates offered on deposits in an unregulated market. We then have to take into account the influence of government regulation of deposit rates.

Setting Deposit Rates

In the past two decades, financial institutions have been competing vigorously for savings deposits. Altogether more than fourteen thousand banks, six thousand savings and loans, and six hundred mutual savings banks with a total of nearly fifty thousand offices have sought to attract the savers' dollars.

In most urban areas there is vigorous competition among a number of institutions offering savings deposits. Consumers can choose among several banking offices located near home, place of work, or shopping center. When the rates offered are the same, consumers often choose one institution over another on the basis of locational convenience, hours of business, or because they like the clerks. Some households keep their savings account with the bank that gave them a mortgage loan. Commercial banks are generally supposed to have an advantage in attracting savings accounts because they offer "one-stop banking," enabling customers to keep a checking account and savings account in the same office. Many studies show that convenience is a dominant consideration. However, as we will discuss below, thrift institutions are now able to issue what are in effect demand deposits.

Customers are clearly responsive to interest-rate differentials as well as to locational and convenience factors. Changes in the rates paid by different institutions have a significant influence on their share of the local market for savings deposits. The interest rates paid by both banks and thrift institutions, and hence the difference between them, has been limited by Regulation Q. But, since Regulation Q is being phased out, in the following we will consider a free market.

The competition among different institutions in the same market tends to narrow the spread between the rate earned on assets and the rate paid to depositors. The spread between the earnings on assets and rates paid to depositors at times may be more than enough to cover operating costs and a good return to capital. The high return to capital will then tend to create new competition. New institutions may be founded or existing institutions may open new branches. The result will be higher rates and greater convenience as the new entrants to local markets compete for deposits. At the same time costs per dollar of deposits increase, with more offices per dollar of deposits. In the long run then, there is always a tendency for deposit rates to move with long-term security yields in a way that limits the spread between rates earned and rates paid.

When long-term interest rates fluctuate in a narrow range the result of competitive pressures is clearly determined and poses no problems. Some difficulties of adjustment arise when market rates show a rapid trend. These difficulties have been apparent in recent years when long-term rates have risen rapidly. To see how these problems arise we have to take a closer look at the rate-setting process.

Competition among banks is a little like competition among gas stations. The products offered are basically very similar but differentiated from one another by the convenience factors mentioned above. Because of those factors the elasticity of the supply of deposits to an individual bank or banking office is limited, especially in the short run. If one bank pays a little less than a rival, it will lose some customers but not all of them. In fact in a period of a year or two it will lose only a fraction of its business. On the other side if it raises its rate it will gain only a limited amount of deposits.

When long-term interest rates rise, each bank management will find it profitable to raise deposit rates to attract new deposits. Of course, they will wait for a while to see if the rate increase will persist. It is not good public relations to move rates up and down frequently. But, if the market rate increase is deemed permanent, deposit rates will tend to rise.

The general rule is that the rate should be raised to the point at which the marginal interest cost of obtaining a dollar of new deposits, plus increases in total operating cost per dollar of new deposits, just equals the net rate of return per dollar of new investments.

But how much does it cost to get additional deposits? If the deposit rate is increased, additional interest must be paid on *all* savings deposits, old as well as new. The marginal cost in interest paid per dollar of new deposits may be much higher than the deposit rate itself. How much higher will depend on the elasticity of supply of deposits.

The elasticity of the supply of deposits to any institution will depend on a number of factors. The response of individual depositors to rate changes will depend on the size of their deposits and on the loss of convenience that may be involved in switching from one bank to another. In addition, elasticity of the supply of deposits to any one institution depends on how its competitors respond when it makes a rate change.

Effects of a Deposit-Rate Rise

Figure 5.2 shows the choice facing a typical thrift institution when a rise in the rate of return on new assets occurs. The horizontal axis shows the amount of the bank's deposits; interest rates are shown on the vertical axis. At the start our bank has deposits A, and pays interest rate r_1 on deposits. r_1 is also the rate paid by competing institutions. The supply of deposits line shows the increase in deposits the bank thinks it can get by raising its deposit rates, if all competing institutions keep their rates at r_1. The marginal cost of funds line shows the corresponding marginal cost of funds—the increment in interest costs per dollar of deposits gained. Additional operating costs of servicing new deposits are assumed to be zero. Marginal cost must be above the interest rate since the increased rate must be paid to old depositors as well as new ones. For example, suppose the bank initially paid 5 percent and had 100 million dollars of deposits. Its interest cost is 5 million dollars. Suppose it believed that it could attract 40 million dollars of new deposits by raising its rate ½ percent. At 5½ percent its interest costs would rise to 7.7 million dollars (5½ percent times 140 million dollars). Total interest costs would

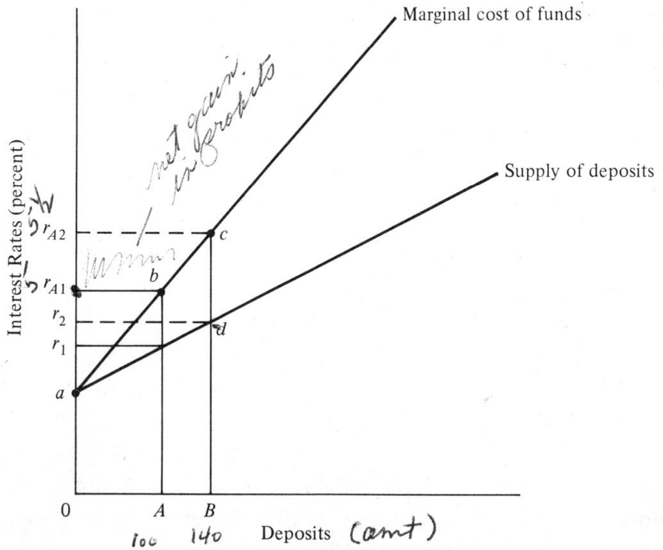

Figure 5.2 Deposit-Rate Choice

have to rise 2.7 million dollars to attract 40 million dollars of deposits. The increment in interest costs per dollar of new deposits is 6¾ percent (2.7 ÷ 40 = .0675). It won't pay for the bank to raise its rate by ½ percent unless new assets will bring in at least 6¾ percent.

In Figure 5.2 the initial earnings rate on assets is r_{A1}, just equal to marginal cost at the initial volume of deposits, so that marginal cost of funds just equals marginal revenue from deposits. If the interest rate on new assets rises to r_{A2}, it will pay the bank to raise its deposit rate until r_{A2} equals marginal cost at deposit volume B with the deposit rate read off the supply curve at r_2. That is not the end of the story, however. Other institutions will be in the same position and will raise their deposit rates too. The supply curve for our bank will shift upward.

The upward shift in the supply curve, and in the corresponding marginal cost of funds schedule, will lead to a further rise in rates. The second rise will be smaller than the first. After several "rounds" of competitive rate increases, rates will stop rising. The amount of deposit-rate increase induced by, say, a one percentage point rise in bond and mortgage rates will depend on a number of factors. It will obviously depend on the elasticity of deposit supply as perceived by savings and loan association or mutual savings bank managers. In markets with many small institutions the elasticity may appear high. The outcome will approach the purely competitive one, with deposit rates rising as fast as mortage rates. In markets with only a few competitors each management will fear that any rate increase will be matched by its rivals. If individual institutions think they cannot increase their market share, they will expect to gain deposits only from commercial banks or by competing against marketable securities. They will be assuming a much lower supply elasticity than in the more competitive case.

The net change in profits of thrift institutions resulting from a rise in mortgage rates and the resulting rise in deposit rates will depend on the percentage gain in deposits. The amount of deposits gained by the thrift institutions from a deposit-rate increase will depend on what is happening elsewhere in the market.

For any single bank the net effect of a rise in mortgage rates depends on whether other market rates also rise, the rate responses of other thrift institutions, and the rate responses of commercial bank competitors. If only the mortgage rate increases and rival institutions keep their rates fixed, any single institution is bound to gain. It will raise interest costs just enough so that the added interest cost required to attract the last (marginal) additional dollar of deposits just balances the earnings on an additional dollar invested in new mortgages. It will increase profits on all the deposits gained up to the last one. The area $r_{A1}r_{A2}bc$ in Figure 5.2 shows the net gain in profits.

In other cases the increase in deposits will be less and, in fact, it may turn out that thrift institutions can lose by a rise in mortgage rates. To take the extreme case, suppose that all market rates, not just the mortgage rate, increase and that commercial banks as well as thrift institutions are in active competition for deposits. All institutions will raise their rates, but cannot jointly induce households to switch from marketable securities to savings deposits unless they raise rates by *more* than the increase in mortgage and other market rates. And households are not likely to increase their total saving by very much either. The effect of rate increases by banks and thrift institutions will largely cancel out and they will be left with more or less the same deposits as at the start. They will, however, be paying more in interest to depositors.

The rise in interest cost would not matter so much if the total earnings of thrift institutions went up with earnings on new assets. Then they would get more earnings and pay more to depositors. Mortgage contracts run for a long time. The interest receipts of a savings and loan association come from mortgages written at various dates in the past. When mortgage rates go up, average recorded earnings of savings and loan associations rise only as old mortgages are paid off and new ones are written at higher rates. This is a slow process. In Chapter 8 we will describe a new form of mortgage that does not generate this problem. Some data on the relationship between deposit interest rates and mortgage earnings are shown in Figure 5.3. In a period of rising rates, thrift institution mortgage earnings average much less than current mortgage rates. Because of the earnings lag, it is not only possible, but highly probable that a general unexpected rise in interest rates can reduce

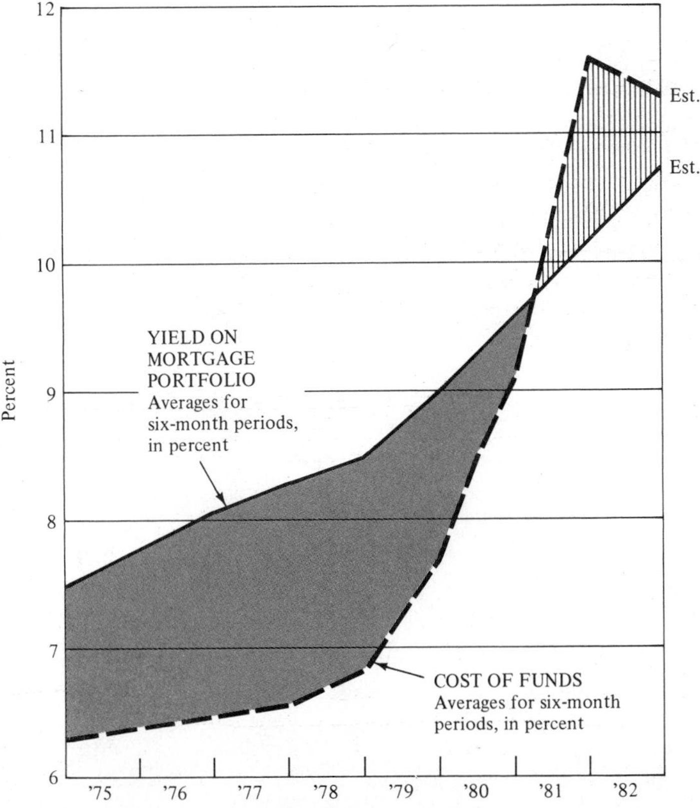

Figure 5.3 Savings and Loan Finances 1975–82

Source: *The New York Times*, Dec. 30, 1982, page D4.

thrift institutions' net earnings and even turn them into net losses. Moreover, that proposition is true even when each individual institution adjusts rates to maximize net earnings under the circumstances facing it. Maximizing net earnings may in fact mean minimizing net losses.

BANK COMPETITION AND REGULATION Q

In the last section we noticed the effect of commercial bank competition on the response of thrift deposits to increases in rates. Since 1933 the deposit rates paid by commercial banks have, in fact, been limited by the Federal Reserve System. Acting under legislation passed in 1933, the Federal Reserve Board issued **Regulation Q,** which *set the maximum, or ceiling, interest rates that commercial banks may pay on time and savings deposits.* Changes in the Q ceiling have had an important influence on the competitive position of commercial banks and thrift institutions.

History of Rate Competition

For the first decade after World War II the thrift institutions competed vigorously among themselves but were not much affected by competition from other commercial banks or marketable securities. In New England the mutual savings banks had always dominated the saving market. In other areas, especially in rapidly growing ones like California and Florida, demand for mortgages was strong. Savings and loans could readily lend on mortgages at interest rates that enabled them to pay rates on savings deposits well above those offered by commercial banks.

Commercial bank rates were held down by the Federal Reserve Regulation Q, but until 1957 most banks did not want to pay rates above those permitted by the Regulation Q. In the absence of commercial bank competition, the thrift institutions grew rapidly, increasing their share of total savings deposits from 45 percent in 1946 to 60 percent in 1957.

After the tight money period of 1955–57, the commercial banks began to seek new sources of funds. At their request, the deposit-rate ceiling was moved up several times between 1957 and 1965. As banks raised their rates, and went in for advertising and promotion of savings accounts, the thrift institutions also raised their rates. In terms of the price-setting analysis displayed in Figure 5.2, the increase in commercial bank savings deposit rates caused an upward shift in the deposit supply curve faced by thrift institutions. However, the gap between thrift and commercial bank rates narrowed and the commercial banks' share of the market stopped falling. The rise in rates not only slowed the deposit growth of the thrift institutions but also ate into the net earnings available for additions to capital. By 1965 the average net earnings of the savings and loans were reduced to less than ½ percent, and a few inefficiently managed associations were in the red.

Thus the thrift institutions, and especially the savings and loans, were in a poor position to deal with the impact of the Vietnam war boom. Faced with a slow growth in demand deposits, strong loan demand, and rising interest rates, commercial banks raised rates quickly after a rise in the deposit-rate ceiling in late 1965. Thrift institutions also raised rates but not so much.

At the same time a sharp rise in Treasury bill rates drew funds from all types of savings accounts into open-market securities. The commercial banks lost deposits to open-market securities but gained at the expense of thrift institutions while the latter lost both ways. Saving deposit inflows to commercial banks in 1966 were only slightly below the 1965 level while the flow to thrift institutions fell by almost 50 percent.

In the fall of 1966 the Federal Reserve Board *reduced* the Q ceiling on consumer savings deposits at commercial banks. At the same time, under new legislation, the Federal Deposit Insurance Corporation and the Federal Home Loan Bank Board were empowered to set deposit rates for federally regulated savings and loan associations and mutual savings banks. Once the Q ceiling stopped rising, and was applied to the thrift institutions, competition for savings deposits was limited to advertising, convenience branches, longer hours, and promotion gimmicks—"a free toaster with every new account." With rate competition eliminated, the thrift institutions were able to maintain their share of the savings deposit market. Their share of consumer time and savings deposits has declined only slightly since 1966.

The use of the Q ceilings to suppress competition for deposits was originally regarded as a temporary expedient in the expectation that the "high", i.e., 6 percent rates of 1966 would not persist. In fact, of course, interest rates showed a strong upward trend for many years. The widening gap between ceiling rates and market rates increased the importance of the competition between marketable securities and deposits.

Open Market Competition. Before 1965, the rates paid by thrift institutions were generally above or close to the rates paid on bonds. Thereafter, market rates on bonds rose much faster than thrift rates and households bought significant amounts of long-term corporate bonds.

Long-Term Certificates. Since the difficulties of the thrift institutions were in large measure due to the practice of "lending long and borrowing short" the regulatory authorities encouraged thrift institutions to lengthen the maturity of their liabilities. The Q ceilings on deposit certificates were increased so that higher rates could be paid on funds committed for long periods. This change strengthened thrift institutions in competition with bonds and reduced deposit volatility.

Short-Term Rates. A more serious problem arose from the wide fluctuation in the yields on short-term securities. A substantial proportion of time and savings deposits is normally held by households with large total assets. These families do not need immediate access to all their funds though they presumably want to keep them in a safe, liquid form. Moreover, they are knowledgeable about financial markets. In tight money periods the rates on Treasury bills rise well above those offered by banks and thrift institutions. During each tight money period since 1966 the *rise in short-term interest rates had drawn funds away from thrift institutions,* causing a sharp fall in the net inflow of thrift deposits. This process is called **disintermediation.** In ensuing easy money periods short-term rates fall and the interest-sensitive funds return to thrift institutions. This cycle of feast and famine caused concern about the stability of thrift institutions. They have not suffered significant net deposit losses and have not had to sell off their mortgage portfolios. But in each tight money period it appears that they *might* have to sell off mortgages or take losses, or even become insolvent.

The episodes of actual or threatened disintermediation in 1966, 1969, and 1974 lasted only a few months. A more prolonged period of difficulty for thrift institutions began in mid-1978. Interest rates began to rise in mid-1978. Short-term rates moved upward erratically for nearly three years, and then fluctuated around a much higher level than the one ruling in early 1978.

Household purchases of treasury securities rose at the expense of thrift deposits as they had in earlier episodes of rising rates. But the effect of the rise in rates was strongly influenced by institutional changes which were in turn largely due to earlier credit crunches. The most important of these changes were the development of Money Market Funds and Certificates.

Money Market Funds

As noted earlier money market funds first became significant in 1974. Since they are far easier to acquire than large denomination bank CDs, commercial paper or even treasury bills, they provided an easy way for households to take advantage of high market rates. Thus they intensified the effect of variations in short-term market interest rates. When interest rates rose in 1978–9 the public responded with enthusiasm, placing about $30 billion per year in money market funds in 1979 and 1980. By 1981 the word of high yield safe liquid assets that were available had spread to relatively unsophisticated investors who placed over $100 million in money market funds in 1981. They absorbed one-third of the total increase in liquid assets; deposits at thrift institutions actually fell.

As we note below, the shift of funds had a severe impact on home construction and was a major factor in the recession. It also left a permanent mark on the financial markets. The growth of the money market funds hastened the trend toward payment of market interest rates on all kinds of deposits. Recent legislation is discussed below.

Money Market Certificates. In 1978 banks and thrift institutions were authorized to offer money market certificates (MMCs). The six month certificates carry interest rates linked to the treasury bill rate. In one way they were remarkably successful. They attracted a huge volume of funds—$200 billion by the end of 1982. Most of those funds were shifted from existing deposits but the offer of money market certificates may have reduced the loss of funds to thrift institutions. In 1982 banks and thrift institutions were authorized to offer a three month certificate at a rate linked to the bill rate.

While the MMCs may have helped to limit the outflow of funds from thrift institutions, they proved to be very costly. Most of the funds attracted to MMCs were switched from other accounts at lower interest rates. Thus the offer of MMCs led to a sharp rise in interest expense for the thrifts. The overall rise in interest costs led to operating losses (expenses in excess of current revenues). A number of institutions were forced to merge with stronger ones as operating losses depleted their capital.

EVALUATING CEILINGS

The imposition of ceilings has generated a great deal of controversy. Proponents of the ceilings have maintained that they were necessary to prevent widespread failure of financial institutions and to maintain the flow of mortgage funds for residential construction. Opponents of the ceiling argue that they have discriminated against the less wealthy households, led to inefficient resource allocation, and protected inefficient firms. Moreover, they have argued that protection of the mortgage market and residential construction is not an important social objective, that a relatively small rise in mortgage rates would provide a sufficient volume of mortgage funds, and that failure of a few financial institutions with insured deposits is not very costly to society.

Effect of Ceilings on Net Earnings

As we noted earlier, the profit-maximizing deposit rate for any one institution depends on the rate that can be obtained on new assets. When mortgage rates rise, therefore, we expect that the profit-maximizing deposit rate for each institution will rise. That is the force that makes deposit rates follow security-market rates.

But what is true for each individual firm is not necessarily true for the group. The gain for any firm from raising deposits in response to a rise in mortgage and bond yields is obtained by raising its rate relative to its rivals. It thereby attracts deposits from them and earns the higher market rate on new assets. But if they all move together in response to the rise in market rates, their rate increases cancel out. They do not gain deposits from one another. Their gain in deposits results from attracting funds from the bond or other markets. The depository institutions therefore get only a small gain in deposits and only a small rise in earnings. But they have to pay higher rates on all deposits. The rise in mortgage and deposit rates therefore produces smaller rather than larger profits while depositors gain.

The imposition of ceiling rates checked competition for savings and enabled the thrift institutions to keep deposit rates below their average earnings on assets. In effect the imposition of ceilings protected thrift institution profits from competition just as a government-sponsored cartel would have done.

Ceilings and the Risk of Failures

Imposition of the ceilings undoubtedly raised thrift institution and commercial bank earnings over what they would have been under free-market conditions. In the case of the thrift institution the ceilings also prevented an absolute decline in net earnings. The general rise in market rates after 1965 produced only a gradual increase in thrift institution earnings. When the rise in market rates started, their earnings came from a portfolio of mortgages that had been negotiated at the rates in effect in the late 1950s and early 1960s. Earnings from those old mortgages did not rise when market rates rose. The thrift institutions benefited from the rise in market rates only as total deposits rose and old mortgages were repaid, which permitted new investment at higher rates. Average earnings lagged behind the market rates and the net earnings of savings and loans in 1966 were only about ½ percent of deposits. A ½ percent increase in deposit rates in 1966 would have put the average association in the red.

In fact, of course, the earnings of associations varied widely. Some large, efficient associations had wide earnings margins while smaller or less efficient associations were already having problems before 1966.

Many associations could not have increased rates without incurring operating losses. In the absence of the ceilings those associations would have faced a dilemma. If they raised rates and showed operating losses their reputations would have suffered, and they would have run the risk of heavy withdrawals. Moreover, their relatively small capital cushion would not last long in face of operating losses. On the other hand, if they did not raise rates, they would lose deposits to other institutions. To meet substantial deposit withdrawals, they would have to sell mortgages carrying rates below the current market rate. These mortgages would have to be sold at less than book value. The associations' capital would show a decline and eventually liquidation would be necessary.

Ceilings permitted the weaker associations to survive in the face of the upward trend in interest rates but the sharp rise in interest rates in 1980 led to the forced merger of a number of weak institutions. Indeed, it may be argued that the "success" of the ceiling regulation in preserving weak institutions during the 1970s only made the industry more vulnerable.

After several years of congressional debate over a variety of proposals for eliminating the ceilings and improving the competitive position of the thrift institutions, legislation enacted in 1980 provides for gradual elimination of the ceiling over a six-year period. It provides broader lending powers for thrift institutions and permits banks and thrift institutions to offer interest-bearing checking accounts (NOW accounts). These measures and other financial reform issues are discussed in Chapter 8.

Thrift institutions had operating losses of over 6 billion dollars in 1981 and 10 billion dollars in 1982. By late 1982 several hundred institutions holding nearly half the total assets of thrift institutions had net worth of less than 3 percent of deposits.

In response to these difficulties Congress passed the Garn St. Germain Act intended to limit the number of failures and forced mergers and to improve the competitive position of the thrift institutions. The act authorizes commercial banks and thrift institutions to offer instruments competitive with money market funds. Most of them are offering (under a variety of names such as "Capital Accounts") accounts paying as much or more than money market funds and offering similar limited checking privileges. These accounts are insured, and have proven attractive to depositors—so much so, that some observers have predicted the demise of money market funds. Others expect that the funds will lose part of the market but continue to attract investors by making it easy to shift assets to or from a money market fund into or out of securities.

New regulations also permit depository institutions to pay at any rate they wish on accounts of over $2,500. These "Super-NOW" accounts move the banking system closer to a regime of free competition for deposit accounts. In time we may expect to see a market based on interest rates for all accounts at all deposit institutions. At the same time, however, service charges are likely to become more important.

The act also authorizes thrift institutions to make commercial and agricultural loans. This change together with the changes in interest rate regulations brings us closer to a unified banking system.

The FDIC and FHLB are authorized to issue promissory notes backed by deposit insurance funds. The notes may be issued to institutions whose net worth has fallen below 3 percent of deposits. The insuring agencies receive a claim against the institution's assets (but in the event of liquidation the insuring agency's claim could not be exercised until after depositors had been paid). The legislation is intended to shore up the confidence of depositors and to permit savings banks and savings and loan associations to continue operating in the face of operating losses and depleted capital. Given time they may be saved from failure by a decline in interest rates which will bring their costs into line with income. These and other issues in banking structure are discussed in Chapter 8.

THE MORTGAGE MARKET

In the past two decades variations in residential construction expenditures have played an important role in business fluctuations. Because the thrift institutions have invested so heavily in mortgages their problems have affected the rate of construction.

Many, though not all, economists believe that the decline in thrift deposits in 1966 led to severe rationing of mortgage credit and consequent reduction in residential construction. Housing starts in 1966 were 20 percent below 1965. Within the year they fell even more.

In 1969, short-term interest rates again rose sharply and savings deposits fell even more sharply than in 1966. The inflow to thrift institutions declined by one-third from 1968. Though this could have cut their mortgage lending by one-third, the resulting impact on the housing industry was cushioned by a very large expansion of mortgage lending by federal credit agencies described later in this chapter. Nonetheless, housing starts declined by 25 percent between the beginning of 1969 and the beginning of 1970. It should be noted that the activities of federal credit agencies may increase interest rates and draw more funds from thrift institutions. Figure 5.4 shows how savings and loan deposits were affected by the rise in Treasury bill rates in the even more severe credit crunch of 1973–74. Housing starts fell by more than 50 percent from their peak in 1973 to the trough in 1974, though other factors, for example, a large number of unsold condominium units as well as disintermediation, were responsible for the decline.

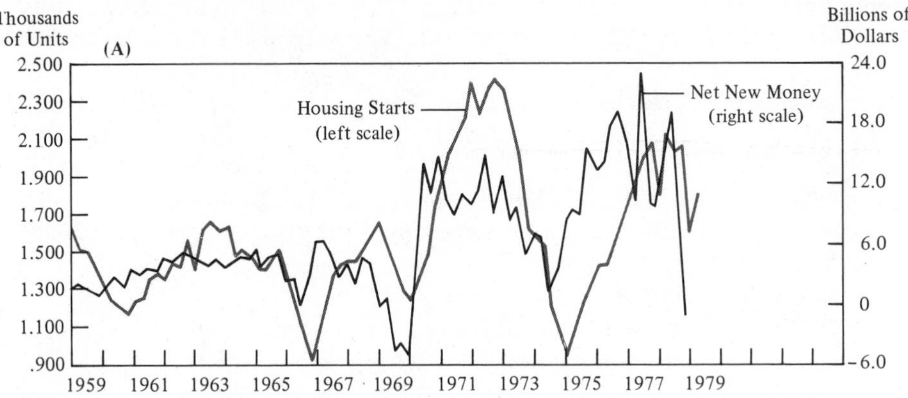

Figure 5.4A Housing Starts and Net New Money

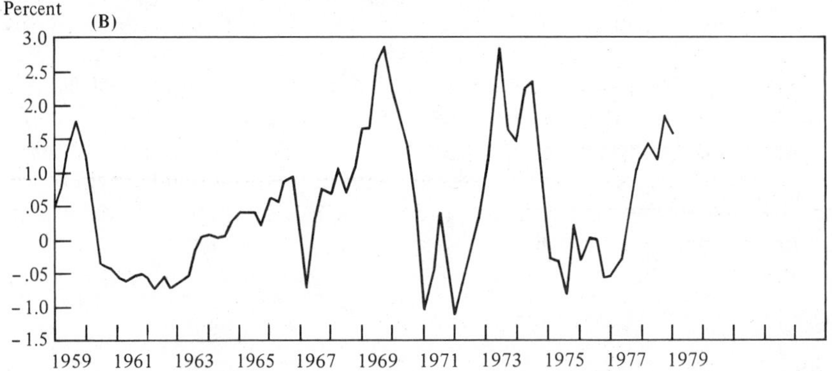

Figure 5.4B Interest Rate Differential (six-month treasury bill minus time deposit rate)

Source: Neil Berkman, "Mortgage Finance and the Housing Cycle," *New England Economic Review*, September/October 1979.

The sharp rise in interest rates which began in mid-1978 led to the most severe depression of the postwar era. Other factors, e.g., a reaction to earlier speculation on housing prices may have been at work, but high interest rates clearly played a major role.

There is a clear association between tight money, rising interest rates, and reductions in housing construction. However, there is as usual some controversy as to the causal factors involved. Since houses last a long time, their value is more sensitive to change in interest rates than the values of other capital goods. One would therefore expect residential construction to be adversely affected by rising interest rates regardless of the channels through which mortgage credit flows. It is widely believed, however, that variations in the flow of funds to the thrift institutions cause a greater variation in residential construction than would be expected from the rise in mortgage interest rates as such. As already noted there is a good deal of evidence that mortgage lenders ration credit during periods of tight money and that the gap is not filled by other lenders. However, some economists do not find this evidence convincing and believe that the rise in mortgage rates is sufficient to explain the decline in residential construction during tight money periods.

INSURANCE AND RETIREMENT SAVINGS

Household claims against life-insurance companies and pension funds are comparable in size to their holdings of time and savings deposits at commercial banks and thrift institutions. These institutions play a dominant role in the market for corporate bonds and have become increasingly important holders of common stock. Both kinds of institutions have grown in the post-war years, but pension-fund growth has been especially rapid.

Life Insurance

Life-insurance companies have been in operation for over two hundred years, but their growth and importance accelerated with urbanization and industrialization as people found themselves less able to rely on their children for support in their old age. Farmers and owners of small businesses have less need for life insurance because they can rely on their family farm or business to provide for dependents in case of the death of the principal earner. Moreover, they usually find it necessary to invest all their savings in the farm or business. Industrialization created a salaried middle class that could save and needed to provide for dependents. Life insurance is a way to provide for dependents but it usually also combines insurance with investment.

It is possible to buy life insurance without building up an asset. The holder of a term-insurance policy pays a premium just equal to the probability of death for his or her age group (plus sales and administrative costs). The insurance company with a large number of similar policies collects just enough in premiums to cover the death benefits to those who die in the current year plus its costs. The policyholders do not build up any claim, and the insurance company's assets are only a fraction of a year's premiums. However, term-insurance rates rise with age, and become painfully high just as the insured person begins to think seriously of the possibility of death.

Many people find a so-called ordinary-life, or level-premium, policy more attractive than term insurance. The holder of an ordinary-life policy pays a more expensive premium in early life than he or she would for a term premium. The insurance company invests the excess premiums and accumulates the earnings in a reserve account. The ordinary-life premium remains constant. It is calculated so that the total premiums paid plus earnings on reserves less expenses will always cover death benefits. In effect, holders of ordinary-life policies pay in advance for their insurance so that they will not have to face increasing term-insurance premiums. In the process they build up an investment in the life-insurance reserve. If a policyholder cancels his or her policy he or she is entitled to get back most of the reserve against the policy. The amount that can be returned to the individual is called the cash surrender value. Policyholders may also borrow against the reserve at a rate specified in the policy.

With rising population and income the amount of insurance in force has grown rapidly; life-insurance reserves grow annually at a rate of about 6 billion dollars.

Since life-insurance contracts run for many years and promise a fixed minimum rate of interest on reserves, life-insurance companies invest most of their insurance reserves in long-term assets. Since their investment income is not taxed at the regular corporate rate they invest only limited amounts in tax-exempt state and local securities. Their liabilities are fixed in dollar amounts, so life-insurance reserves are not ordinarily invested in common stock. This is an example of the portfolio hedging we discussed in Chapter 2. That leaves mortgages and corporate bonds as the principal investment outlet for life-insurance funds. At times life-insurance companies have invested substantial amounts in single-family home mortgages. In recent years, however, they have concentrated on commercial mortgages for relatively large offices, shopping centers, and apartment buildings, leaving the retail mortgage business to local thrift institutions and banks.

Pension Funds

The same forces of industrialization and urbanization that have generated the need for life insurance have also created the need for retirement saving. Increasing length of life and the widespread practice of mandatory retirement have intensified the need for retirement funds. The Social Security System, developed in the 1930s, provides a basic retirement income for nearly everyone, but many people wish additional retirement support. Anyone who wishes to can, of course, do his or her own saving and investment during working life and then retire on the income from his or her savings, gradually liquidate capital, or buy an annuity. However, there are tax advantages to saving through a pension fund. Many unions have negotiated for employer-funded pension plans and have been willing to take part of their wage increases in the form of pension contributions. Table 5.5 shows how rapidly pension funds have grown. Employer contributions to retirement funds approved by the Internal Revenue Service are treated as wage costs for tax purposes. Since employees pay no tax until benefits are received, they defer taxes by saving through a pension fund.

Employer-sponsored pension funds are administered by either a bank trust department or an insurance company. The contributions are invested by the fund manager mainly in corporate stock or bonds. Because the number of employees covered by pension funds has grown rapidly, and because wage rates have been rising, the contributions on behalf of current employees exceed the benefits paid to retired employees, and the assets of pension funds have been rising rapidly.

Other Forms of Insurance

Other insurance companies, principally marine, fire, and casualty companies, have much smaller financial assets than life-insurance companies; still

Table 5.5 Private Pension Plans: Coverage, Contributions, Benefits, and Assets, Selected Years, 1940–80

Year	Workers covered (thousands)	Contributions (millions of dollars)			Benefits		Assets, end of year (billions of dollars)
		Total	Employer	Employee	Number of beneficiaries (thousands)	Amount of payments (millions of dollars)	
1940	4,100	310	180	130	160	140	2.4
1945	6,400	990	830	160	310	220	5.4
1950	9,800	2,080	1,750	330	450	370	12.1
1955	14,200	3,840	3,280	560	980	850	27.5
1960	18,700	5,490	4,710	780	1,780	1,720	52.0
1965	21,800	8,360	7,370	990	2,750	3,520	86.5
1970	26,300	14,000	12,580	1,420	4,750	7,360	137.1
1975	30,300	29,850	27,560	2,290	7,050	14,810	212.6
1980	35,800	68,970	64,840	4,130	9,100	35,177	407.9

Source: Alicia Munnell, *The Economics of Private Pensions.* Brookings Institution, Washington, D.C., 1982.

the 60 billion dollars they hold is not negligible. Their sources of funds and investment patterns are quite different from those of the life-insurance companies. Marine, fire, and casualty companies offer fire, theft, and accident liability insurance to home owners, automobile owners, and to businesses. There is much more variation in their payments for losses than in the death-benefit payments of life-insurance companies. They have to have a substantial amount of capital obtained from sale of stock or plowed-back earnings. Their capital is invested in financial assets. In addition they collect premiums in advance and have the use of the policyholders' funds until losses are paid. (If premiums are collected at the start of the policy year and losses are evenly distributed they have the use of half a year's premiums.)

Marine, fire, and casualty companies have to keep part of their assets in liquid form, for example, in Treasury bills, commercial paper, or bank CDs, but the bulk of their funds are invested in long-term assets. Since they are fully taxed corporations these companies, like banks, prefer municipal bonds to corporate bonds. They also hold substantial amounts of corporate stock. Like the pension funds, they are prepared to switch from bonds to stock or vice versa in response to changes in yields. Marine, fire, and casualty companies are the only group of institutions whose portfolio choices provide a direct link between the yields on municipal bonds and anticipated yields on common stock.

MUTUAL FUNDS

A good many people enjoy following the stock market, studying brokers' research reports, and making their own investment choices. They boast about the winners and keep quiet about the losers. Others, who want to invest in common stocks, because they hope for a better yield than they can get on fixed-income securities, find the task of investment management an onerous one. Wealthy people can afford to pay investment counsel and can buy a diversified portfolio of stocks without paying too much in brokerage charges. People with $10 or $20 thousand to invest in stocks cannot afford to pay too much for investment advice and find it difficult to get a diversified portfolio. Mutual funds solve their problem.

Common-stock mutual funds issue shares at, say, an initial price of $100 per share. They invest the proceeds, less a commission, in common stock. The value of the funds' shares fluctuates with the fortunes of the stocks held by the fund. The net asset value of a share is computed daily. After the initial offering the fund stands ready to sell new shares each day at the net asset value of existing shares or to redeem existing shares at the same price. When new sales exceed redemptions the fund buys additional stocks; when redemptions exceed new sales the fund must sell some of its holdings. The commission mentioned above is called a loading and usually runs about 4 percent. Most of the loading charge is used to pay commissions to brokers and other selling expenses. Many funds do not charge any loading. These no-load funds pay no sales commissions and spend little on advertising. Mutual funds are managed by professional money managers.

The investment managers get an annual fee, usually one-quarter percent to one-half percent of asset value. The remainder of dividends earned is paid to the holders of the fund's shares. If it pays out all dividends, the fund need not pay income taxes, but its shareholders must pay income tax on the dividends they receive. If the fund sells stock at a profit, it pays out a capital gains dividend, taxable to the fund's shareholders at capital gains rate.

Mutual funds provide a good example of the functions of intermediaries. Since they operate on a relatively large scale, they can provide professional investment management at relatively low cost per dollar invested. They can also manage and monitor a diversified portfolio to reduce risk at relatively low cost in management and brokerage charges.

A number of stock-market studies question the value of professional investment advice. There is no proof that any fund management can beat the market averages. However, few investors can buy all the stocks in Standard & Poors five-hundred-stock index, much less the fifteen hundred in the New York Stock Exchange Index. Whatever the merits of fund managements, they attract a continuing flow of funds from investors who want stocks but do not want to either throw darts or spend a lot of time and effort choosing investments.

There are a variety of types of funds. Some announce that they will invest for growth and capital gains. They do not say so but their shares involve a relatively high risk of loss as well as a chance of big gains. At the other end of the spectrum, balanced funds buy a variety of securities including bonds as well as stable dividend stocks and some growth stocks.

Though they have grown rapidly since World War II and have assets of over 60 billion dollars, stock mutual funds still own only about 5 percent of all common stock. Nonetheless, they provide an opportunity for equity investment to a large number of people, who would otherwise find it difficult to participate in the equity market.

FEDERAL CREDIT AGENCIES

The federal government sponsors a number of agencies that act as financial intermediaries. Altogether there are over seventy different agencies that borrow either in financial markets or from the Treasury and make loans for some special purpose. Their total outstanding loans amounted to $129 billion in 1978. These agencies lent $27 billion in 1978.

There are two types of rationale for the federal agencies. First, some agencies provide an outright subsidy to an activity considered desirable by the Congress. The Rural Electrification Administration provided 2 percent loans to rural cooperative electric utilities for many years. Second, many credit agencies were created because Congress was convinced that the private financial system was not working properly. The Farm Credit agencies (the twelve Banks for Cooperatives, the twelve Federal Intermediate Credit Banks, and twelve Federal Land Banks) were created in the 1930s when the farmers complained that they could not obtain sufficient credit from the small banks who served them. The Farm Credit agencies sell securities guaranteed by the Treasury and lend the proceeds to farmers through a complex network of local institutions. The farm borrowers pay interest rates that cover the interest on the guaranteed securities plus administrative costs. No outright subsidy is involved, but the farmers get the benefit of the superior credit standing of securities guaranteed by the U.S. Treasury. The Farm Credit agencies have over $40 billion of securities outstanding.

The most important federal credit agencies are those providing home mortgage credit. The Federal Home Loan Bank Board sells its own securities in the open market and lends the proceeds to twelve regional Federal Home Loan banks, which lend in turn to savings and loan associations, which finally make mortgage loans.

The Federal National Mortgage Association (FNMA) also sells securities in the open market and buys federally insured mortgages from banks and other lenders. FNMA makes commitments to buy mortgages from three to twelve months in the future, so that developers building a large number of houses can be assured that mortgage financing will be available when the houses are completed.

The FNMA and FHLBB serve as intermediaries in drawing funds from the general credit market into the mortgage market. They help to create a unified national mortgage market. They also provide a source of funds for mortgages that is independent of the growth of deposits at the thrift institutions. Their activities have greatly expanded since 1965 when the growth of deposits at thrift institutions began to fluctuate. The large increase in agency securities has provoked some controversy. Some security analysts argue that the increase in the volume of securities of federally sponsored agencies has an adverse effect on other security issuers. Others maintain that intermediation by government agencies serves to perfect the market and to provide low-cost pooling of risks.

The Federal Financing Bank began operations in 1974. The FFB borrows from the Treasury and in turn buys loans previously made by a variety of federal credit agencies or makes direct loans to borrowers whose obligations have been guaranteed by a government agency. The FFB reduces the cost of federal credit programs since the Treasury can borrow at lower cost than federal credit agencies.

SUMMARY

1. While (with one exception) mutual savings banks are state chartered, federally chartered savings and loan associations hold more than half the total assets of that industry.
2. They are supervised by the Federal Home Loan Banks, which also make loans to them.
3. The portfolios of savings and loan associations consist primarily of mortgage loans and construction loans.
4. While mutual savings banks have more diversified assets, mortgage loans do account for about two-thirds of their total assets.
5. Between them, mutual savings banks and savings and loan associations account for nearly half of all outstanding mortgage loans.
6. Thrift institutions face competition for savings not only from each other, but also from commercial banks and from open-market securities, such as government bonds.
7. As a result of this competition their savings flow has been very erratic. When open-market rates rose, thrift institutions could raise their deposit rates to hold onto their savings flows. But since the interest they earned on their previously made mortgages was fixed, they faced large potential losses.
8. In 1966, to protect the thrift institutions, the federal government lowered the maximum interest rate banks could pay on savings and time deposits under Regulation Q, and imposed such interest-rate ceilings on thrift institutions too, albeit at a one-half of one percent higher rate.
9. But this was only a partial solution because it did not prevent competition from higher yielding open-market securities, and hence thrift institutions lost deposits. As a result mortgage loans were much less available. There were periodic credit crunches, even though thrift institutions tried to protect themselves from disintermediation by issuing term certificates.
10. Regulation Q led to much controversy. Some contend that without it there would have been massive failures of thrift institutions, and there is much controversy over whether Regulation Q actually helped the mortgage market. Among the disadvantages are discrimination against small savers, the protection of inefficient institutions, and periodic disintermediation.
11. Pension funds have experienced rapid growth and like life-insurance companies can switch their investments readily between various types of assets.
12. Mutual funds are a quite different type of intermediary; they allow small investors to hold indirectly a highly diversified portfolio.
13. There are also a number of government financial intermediaries that borrow either on the open market or from the U.S. Treasury. These government financial intermediaries are particularly important in the residential mortgage market.

Questions and Exercises

1. As net worth increases, the proportion of financial assets invested through financial intermediaries tends to decline. Why?
2. Financial intermediaries can invest in long-term assets, even though their deposits may be withdrawn without notice. Why is this possible? Are any risks involved?
3. Intermediation reduces the costs and risks of investment. Explain.
4. During the 1950s the share of time and savings deposits held in mutual savings banks and savings and loan associations increased; later on the share of time and savings deposits held in thrift institutions declined. Explain.
5. A decline in mortgage rates may sometimes increase the reported profits of savings and loan associations. Explain.
6. Regulation Q has tended to reduce the efficiency of financial institutions. Why?
7. Many economists believe that Regulation Q has encouraged policies that discriminate against the poorer depositors at banks and thrift institutions. Why?
8. A rapid increase in short-term interest rates can cause a sharp reduction in housing starts. Trace the connection between short-term interest rates and housing starts.
9. The growing use of term and group insurance reduces the amount of life-insurance reserves relative to the amount of insurance in force. Explain.
10. Life-insurance companies invest most of their resources in long-term assets. Why?
11. What is a mutual fund? Why do many small investors find them attractive?

Further Reading

ARCELSUS, FRANCISCO, and MELTZER, A. H. "The Markets for Housing and Housing Services." *Journal of Money, Credit and Banking* 5 (February 1973). A review of the evidence of the effects of rationing and other factors on the volume of residential construction.

BENSTON, GEORGE J. "Savings, Banking and the Public Interest." *Journal of Money, Credit and Banking* 4, no. 1, part 2 (February 1972). This long essay analyzes many of the issues relating to the regulation of savings banking.

BLOOM, MARSHALL, CROCKETT, JEAN, and FRIEND, IRWIN. *Mutual Funds and Other Institutional Investors*. New York: McGraw-Hill, 1970. A major study of the operation of mutual funds and the impact of institutional investors on the operation of the stock market.

FEDERAL RESERVE BANK OF BOSTON. *Housing and Monetary Policy*. Conference Series no. 4, Boston: 1970. This volume contains essays by economists, government officials, and officers of financial institutions on the effects of monetary policy and regulation of financial institutions on problems of residential construction.

———. *Policies for a More Competitive Financial System*. Conference Series no. 8, Boston: 1972. The essays in this volume evaluate a number of proposals for changes in the structure of the financial system and the regulation of financial intermediaries.

GURLEY, JOHN G., and SHAW, EDWARD S. *Money in a Theory of Finance*. Washington, D.C.: The Brookings Institution, 1960. A path-breaking, theoretical analysis of the role of financial intermediaries in the economic system.

MELTZER, ALLAN. "Credit Availability and Economic Decisions." *Journal of Finance* 29 (June 1974). This essay presents evidence indicating that rationing plays only a limited role in accounting for the instability of housing construction.

PROJECTOR, DOROTHY, and WEISS, GERTRUDE. *Survey of Financial Characteristics of Consumers*. Washington, D.C.: Board of Governors of the Federal Reserve System, 1966. Reports the results of one of the largest and most detailed surveys of the ownership of various financial assets.

TURE, NORMAN B. *The Future of Private Pension Plans*. Washington, D.C.: American Enterprise Institute for Public Policy Research, 1976. A review of the development of private pension plans and of issues in their regulation.

U.S. LEAGUE OF SAVINGS AND LOAN ASSOCIATIONS. *Savings and Loan Fact Book*. Chicago: 1977. This annually published volume contains a wealth of data on the operations of savings and loan associations, mortgage markets, and residential construction.

WELFLING, WELDON. *Mutual Savings Banks*. Cleveland:The Press of Case Western Reserve University, 1968. A history of savings banks together with an analysis of their operations and regulations.

Capital Markets

6

A growing, changing economy needs vast amounts of capital to take advantage of changing technology, and to provide plants and equipment for a growing labor force. Much of the saving that is the ultimate source of the needed capital is done by households who do not own businesses and farms. They want to put their savings to work. Businesses and governments want to invest in physical capital but do not have the needed savings. In a large, complex economy a very elaborate set of arrangements is needed to bring savers and investors together. We noted in Chapter 2 how financial intermediaries assist in that process, but they are only part of the system of capital markets. The function of the capital markets is to provide arrangements so that households, businesses, and governments that want to invest more than they save can bid for the funds of other spending units who have surplus funds.

There cannot, however, be a single pool of funds up for competitive bids. There have to be separate markets for long-term funds and short-term funds; some borrowers are well known, others have to establish their credit worthiness. Some loans involve collateral, some involve monthly payments or lots of bookkeeping. The markets for small loans are different from those involving large sums. The capital markets thus consist of a network of submarkets each dealing with a different type of loan or security. Nonetheless, these submarkets are closely linked so that interest-rate movements will draw funds from one market into another. Moreover, the pattern of financing demands is constantly changing. As the relative supplies of different kinds of securities change over the business cycle, interest rates must change in order to induce lenders to shift their pattern of security purchases and induce borrowers to change their methods of financing.

In this chapter we will examine the adaptation process in the markets for short-term assets, then in the markets for long-term securities, and finally look at the interaction between the two sets of markets. We will be mainly concerned with the way in which changes in interest differentials bring about an adjustment to changing supplies and demands for securities. In Chapter 12 our concern will be the level of interest rates.

SURPLUSES AND DEFICITS

Disputes over deficits in the federal government are familiar to almost everyone, especially in the last few years when deficits of over $100 billion have been recorded. While we do not hear as much about deficits in other sectors of the economy, these deficits are often as large as those of the federal government. For purposes of financial analysis, a household or business has a **surplus** *when saving exceeds investment,* and a **deficit** *when investment exceeds saving*. While most households usually have a surplus, many will show deficits in years when they buy automobiles or houses. State and local governments seldom record deficits in their ordinary operations; however, they often borrow for construction of schools and other public buildings. Businesses usually run deficits during booms. Of course, they are making profits then; but they are spending even more for investment than they are saving, so they have to borrow. Federal deficits usually rise during recessions, when tax revenues decline, while expenditures continue to rise, or during wars, when expenditures outrun taxes.

Since 1965 the federal government has reported a surplus in only one year. Businesses have shown deficits every single year, while households in the aggregate have had surpluses every single year. It is important to note, however, that there is a lot of variation within these groups. Some businesses have surpluses even when there is a deficit for business as a whole, while many households have deficits even when there is a substantial surplus for the whole household sector.

When we add up all the surpluses and deficits for households, businesses, and governments, they will always just balance. You can see why if you remember that for the economy as a whole saving always has to equal investment. A surplus for each sector is defined as the excess of saving over investment for that sector (when the figure is negative we call it a deficit). When we add up the differences between saving and investment for all the sectors, that's exactly the same as taking the difference between total investment and total saving, and we know that that has to be zero.

But to bring total surpluses and deficits into balance, the financial markets have to match the supplies and demands for each separate kind of financial asset (from the point of view of a financial investor with a surplus) or liability (from the point of view of a borrower with a deficit). To understand the nature of that problem we must first make a quick examination of the methods used to finance particular kinds of expenditures. Figure 6.1 shows the distribution of amounts borrowed by major sectors of the economy.

Financing Deficits

Spending units with deficits may be able to finance a deficit for a particular month or year by using cash or selling financial assets accumulated in earlier

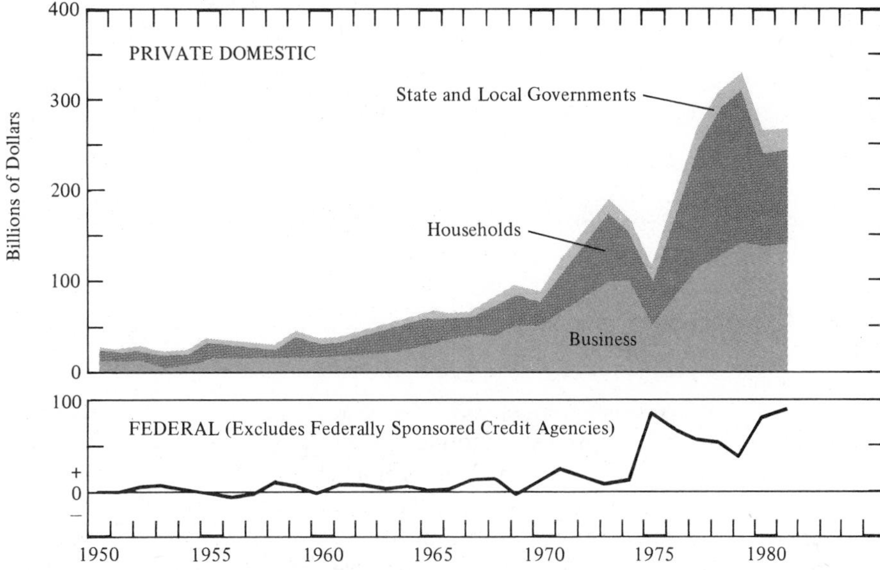

Figure 6.1 Major Nonfinancial Sectors: Net Funds Raised
Annually

Source: *Federal Reserve Chart Book,* 1982, p. 45.

periods when they had a surplus. In fact, large amounts of short-term deficits are financed in that way. Firms may then borrow to replenish liquid assets. Thus, particular types of borrowing are not necessarily associated with particular expenditures, but special forms of financing are commonly used for purchases of durable goods and housing. A substantial proportion of automobiles and other durable goods purchases are financed with installment credit, provided either by banks or consumer finance companies. Gross extensions of consumer credit vary closely with durable goods sales. However, households are always making payments on outstanding debts. Almost all home purchases are at least partially financed with mortgages. The gross volume of mortgage loans is much larger than the amount of residential construction since new mortgages are often taken and old mortgages repaid when existing homes are sold. In addition home owners make regular monthly payments, thus reducing the total mortgage credit outstanding on their mortgages. For both reasons the net flow of mortgage credit is much smaller than the gross amount. The net increase in mortgage credit goes up and down with the amount of residential construction but the two do not exactly match.

Except for limited amounts of seasonal borrowing in anticipation of tax receipts, state and local governments do not—or at least are not supposed to—run deficits on their current operations. Most of their borrowing is directly connected to particular construction projects. They issue bonds to build schools, college dormitories, or water and sewer systems. Because of increasing population and strong popular demand for all kinds of public facilities, state and local debt has been growing rapidly ever since World War II.

As might be expected and as Figure 6.2 shows, business financing is

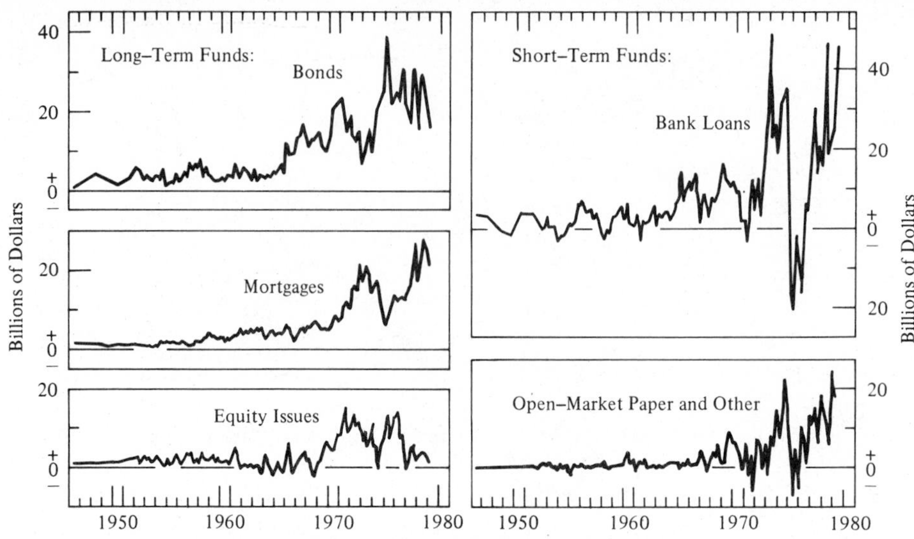

Figure 6.2 Net Funds Raised by Nonfinancial Corporations
Annually, 1946–51; seasonally adjusted annual rates, quarterly, 1952–

Source: *Federal Reserve Chart Book,* 1982, p. 62.

more complex than government or household financing. Except in the case of office and store buildings, where mortgage financing is often used, business financing is not usually tied to particular expenditure projects. Businesses use a wide variety of sources of funds. Much of their investment is financed from their own retained earnings. But they may also sell new shares of stock, issue bonds, borrow from banks, or sell commercial paper. Moreover, corporations operate on both sides of the market, lending as well as borrowing. To provide for short-term fluctuations in receipts and expenditures they build up substantial holdings of demand deposits, bank CDs, and Treasury bills. One corporation may hold commercial paper issued by another. Moreover, corporations supply trade credit to smaller firms, that is, they ship their goods and allow the firm that is buying them, say, ninety days to make payment on them.

In choosing among alternative sources of finance, corporate treasurers have to balance a number of conflicting considerations. Other things equal, they would like to borrow as cheaply as possible, but they also want to arrange their financing so as to limit the risk of bankruptcy. Short-term borrowing is often cheaper than long-term debt. However, the firm that relies too heavily on short-term debt might have trouble if market interest rates rise rapidly, if lenders short of funds decide to ration credit more stringently, or if the firm's credit rating declines. Therefore, most firms want to finance only a small fraction of total assets with short-term debt. They also want to limit their total debt so as to limit the risk of bankruptcy in a depression. Moreover, even when bankruptcy is not an important concern, it is necessary to consider the effect of debt finance on the value of the stock. An increase in fixed interest charges will increase the variability of the corporation's net earnings and that may reduce the price of the stock.

Instead of borrowing, the corporation can obtain equity capital by retaining part of its earnings or issuing new shares. The tax law favors retention of earnings. The stockholders must pay income taxes on dividend receipts. If, on the other hand, the corporation retains part of its earnings and reinvests them profitably, the corporation's earnings will increase. The increase in earnings will be reflected in the price of the stock. The stockholders will then obtain capital gains, which are taxed at lower rates, instead of dividends. Moreover, they can, if they wish, hold the shares for a long time, thus postponing tax payments. Because of the tax law, corporations seeking additional equity capital tend to rely much more heavily on retained earnings than on the issue of new shares.

Treasurers like to have a substantial amount of liquid assets on hand. By holding liquid assets they obtain flexibility to choose an advantageous time to borrow and avoid the risk of needing funds at a time when banks are cautious about expanding their loans. But to hold liquid assets they have to borrow in advance. It will usually cost more to borrow than the interest they receive on their liquid assets.

Most firms try to maintain a balance among sources of funds—equity from retained earnings and sale of shares, long-term debt, short-term debt. The mix they choose reflects the risks of the business and the relative costs of different kinds of financing. Firms with stable markets use more debt financing than cyclically sensitive businesses. Changes in the relative costs of different kinds of finance will cause shifts in the sources used and in the amount of liquid assets held.

In the short-run, however, most firms adjust to the changing balance of receipts and expenditures by varying their holding of liquid assets and their short-term debt. When they feel their short-term debt is too high and their liquid assets too low, they will issue bonds or sell stock. Thus their long-term financing will reflect their average deficit while liquid asset holdings and short-term debt respond to short-term changes in their position.

CAPITAL MARKETS: A PROFILE

The process of transfering funds from households, businesses, and governments with surpluses to those with deficits involves far more than the collection and disbursement of funds. For each loan or security issue, lenders must evaluate the credit standing of borrowers; interest rates and terms of payment must be arranged. Moreover, since individual lenders frequently shift from a surplus position to a deficit position, or change their view about the prospective value of securities, there must be facilities for trading in existing securities. These processes are carried out through a variety of arrangements that bring borrowers and lenders together.

You can take a tour of a stock exchange, but most other financial markets do not have physical identity. They exist in the form of organizations that buy and sell securities and well-established arrangements for bringing buyers and sellers together. The market organization for each type of transaction reflects the characteristics of the loans or securities involved and the numbers of buyers and sellers involved in the market. Security markets are usually classified as **primary markets,** *for new securities,* and **secondary markets,** *for trading in old securities.* They are also divided between **open markets,** *where buyers and sellers compete in a kind of auction market,* and **negotiated markets,** *where borrowers negotiate terms with lenders directly.* Markets are also divided into short-term markets for bank loans, Treasury bills, and other short-term securities and long-term markets for bonds, stocks, and mortgages. In the next section we will consider the organization and functions of short-term markets giving particular attention to the close linkages among the markets for different types of short-term security. Then we will consider the long-term markets.

SHORT-TERM SECURITY MARKETS

In considering the organization of the short-term markets we have to discuss the markets for short-term Treasury securities, commercial paper, bank certificates of deposit, federal funds, and bank loans. Figure 6.3 shows the amounts of funds raised by the different kinds of short-term loans and security issues.

The secondary market for U.S. Treasury securities involves a volume of transactions far larger than the activity of the stock exchanges. The volume of transactions in Treasury bills and other short-term Treasury securities can reach twenty billion dollars in a single day. Purchases and sales of existing government securities are usually made through government security dealers, some in banks, some affiliated with large brokerage houses. The

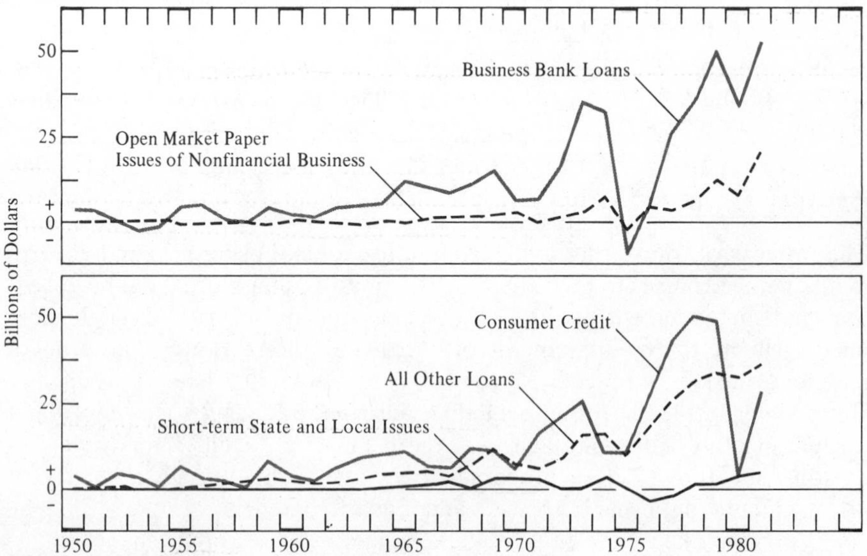

Figure 6.3 Short-Term Borrowing
Annually

Source: *Federal Reserve Chart Book,* 1982, p. 47.

dealers borrow from banks and buy an inventory of Treasury securities. At any time each dealer stands ready to offer to buy or sell government securities. Dealers make their profit from small spreads between their buying and selling prices. The dealer spread for transaction in Treasury bills is less than five hundred dollars for a million-dollar transaction. Usually they hold securities for only a brief time but because of the very large volume of activity their average inventory runs to above five billion dollars.

Commercial Paper

Commercial paper is one of the oldest forms of business financing in the United States, dating back to the 1830s. The securities called commercial paper are *promissory notes of well-known corporations* that, unlike the promissory notes given for bank loans, may be bought and sold. Although it is an old form of financing, it has played a relatively small role in the credit markets until recent years. Much of the commercial paper is issued by finance companies.

Commercial paper is issued in two ways. Large issuers, particularly the "captive" finance companies of the automobile producers, such as the General Motors Acceptance Corporation, have salesmen to sell commercial paper directly to banks and corporations. Smaller issuers sell their commercial paper to dealers, who in turn sell it to banks and corporations. A number of the government bond dealers also act as dealers in commercial paper. There is also a resale or secondary market for commercial paper and the dealers who participate in the issuance of new commercial paper buy "secondhand" commercial paper from banks and corporations and resell it to others.

Bank Certificates of Deposit

A third important component of the short-term securities markets is the market for **negotiable certificates of deposit** (CDs), the *transferable promissory notes issued by commercial banks.* These certificates are very similar to commercial paper except for the fact that they are issued by banks. Commercial banks generally sell their certificates of deposit directly without the assistance of dealers or brokers. A large proportion of the sales of certificates of deposits is made to their own customers, though large banks may also sell to others. Each bank sets the rate on its own issues of certificates of deposits each day. Since the market is highly competitive, it must match the rates offered by competing banks. Corporations, state and local governments, or banks that wish to resell certificates of deposit before the maturity date do so using the network of dealers who also serve the Treasury bill and commercial-paper markets.

The market for federal funds described in Chapter 4 is also an important component of the short-term securities markets. Bank loans were discussed in Chapter 4. We need only note here that the market for bank loans is linked to the open short-term securities markets in three ways: banks obtain funds for loans from the open market by selling CDs and buying federal funds; they supply funds to the market by buying short-term assets; and they finance dealers in securities.

FUNCTIONS OF THE SHORT-TERM MARKET

The short-term markets perform three important functions. First, these markets make it possible for businesses and governments to finance their short-term deficits and invest their short-term surpluses quickly and cheaply. Second, the short-term markets serve to integrate the banking system so that the deposits of individual banks can in effect be pooled in a national credit market. Third, much of the adjustment to cyclical and seasonal changes in surpluses and deficits of businesses, governments, and households is made through the short-term market.

Each day thousands of businesses find that their receipts exceed their payments, while others find themselves in the reverse position. They can of course build up their bank deposits when they are running a temporary surplus and draw them down when the balance of receipts and payments swings the other way. But since demand deposits yield no explicit interest, corporate treasurers prefer to invest temporary surpluses in interest-bearing securities that can be sold when they need cash. To do that, they need securities that are safe and readily salable at low cost. Treasury bills, commercial paper, and negotiable certificates of deposit meet these requirements very satisfactorily. By trading in the secondary markets for these securities, corporations in effect pool their surpluses and deficits so that they cancel out, without recourse to the banking system or to the sale of securities to the general public. State and local governments also participate in this pooling of surpluses and deficits. Because of the timing of tax receipts many governmental units have surplus funds for a period after collection of taxes. They invest their surplus funds in Treasury bills and other short-term securities and sell them later on when their budget shows a seasonal deficit. Corporations and state and local governments also finance one another by buying securities issued by other corporations or state and local governments.

Corporations and state and local governments also finance one another indirectly using the commercial banking system as an intermediary. Businesses frequently borrow from banks to finance temporary deficits. The banks in turn obtain the funds by selling certificates of deposit to other corporations. The effect is the same as though one corporation had made a loan to another but the two corporations need never have any direct contact. The "lending corporation" obtains a lower rate of interest on the certificate of deposit that it buys than the bank obtains on the loan. The lending corporation, in effect, is paying the bank for its specialized services in evaluating the credit of the borrowing corporation and administering the loan.

The processes just outlined serve to cancel out many of the short-term surpluses and deficits of individual corporations and state and local governments. However, corporations usually run a net deficit and must borrow funds from the household sector. While a few wealthy households may buy commercial paper directly or buy short-term securities of local governments, most of the net short-term financing of both businesses and governments is obtained from the banking system, even though households may in some sense be the ultimate suppliers of the funds. Corporations usually borrow from banks with which they have a well-established relationship and state and local governments usually borrow their short-term funds from local banks. However, loan demand at individual banks may not match the growth of deposits at those banks.

Short-term credit markets serve to pool the funds of all banks so that banks whose deposit growth is large relative to their loan demands may supply funds to other banks in the reverse position. This adjustment takes place in several different ways. Banks faced with particularly strong loan demand may sell Treasury bills or commercial paper that was purchased at an earlier time when they had surplus funds. These securities may be bought by another bank that has greater deposit growth than loan demand. And if they are bought instead by a household or corporation, the buyer pays for them by writing a check on his or her bank, so that the funds are transferred between banks in an indirect way. Large banks, with strong loan demand, issue certificates of deposit and these may be bought by smaller banks with temporary surplus funds. To serve their large customers, banks may arrange for other banks to "participate" or share in large loans. Finally, banks with surplus funds may sell federal funds to banks who need funds. This interchange of short-term assets creates a national pool of funds so that customers of one bank can gain access to funds supplied by depositors in other banks that may be in different parts of the country. In the business-cycle upswing when businesses are borrowing heavily, large city banks will have the heaviest loan demand and will draw funds from suburban banks whose deposits are growing faster than loan demand.

Households obviously play an important role in the short-term markets as suppliers of funds to commercial banks. They do not participate directly as borrowers in the open markets for short-term securities but they do obtain funds from the short-term market indirectly by borrowing funds from banks or finance companies. Households obtain large amounts of installment credit from banks and finance companies. Their demands for bank credit obviously compete with other demands for bank credit. In addition, finance companies obtain most of their funds either by borrowing from banks or by issuing their own commercial paper. Through banks and consumer finance companies, households are often important competitors for short-term funds. They supply funds through money market funds as well as through banks.

The federal government is also an important participant in the short-term securities markets. The Treasury finances a large part of its deficits by sale of additional Treasury bills and other relatively short-term securities. In addition, the federal financing agencies such as the Federal Home Loan banks and Federal National Mortgage Association (FNMA) finance most of their operations by issue of short-term securities.

Balancing Cyclical Swings

As already noted, businesses finance cyclical variations in their deficits by increasing borrowing from banks and by reducing liquid asset accumulation when deficits increase. They reduce their borrowing and acquire liquid assets when deficits decline. The federal government also adjusts to changes in the size of its deficit by varying the increase in its short-term debt. At times these changes are offsetting; the government deficit may increase while business deficits decrease. Businesses then buy Treasury bills and borrow little from banks while the Treasury sells its securities to businesses and banks. At other times businesses have heavy deficits while the Treasury deficit is small. There are times, however, when both businesses and governments have large deficits while households have unusually large surpluses. Much of the household surplus will be reflected in commercial bank deposits, which will be channeled into business loans or acquisition of Treasury securities.

The swings in the deficits and surpluses of different sectors of the economy can be balanced off within the short-term security markets a good part of the time. At times, however, there may be excess demand for short-term credit, which will have a significant effect on long-term mortgage and bond markets. We will discuss the interactions between long-term and short-term markets in the section on term structure. First, however, we need to discuss the operations of the short-term markets in more detail to see how the different submarkets are linked together.

Short-Term Interest-Rate Linkages

The markets for the different types of short-term credit are closely integrated. The interest rates in these markets move together because each class of market participants can choose to raise funds or supply funds in more than one way and can shift its asset portfolio or liability structure in response to changes in interest rates. A corporate treasurer needing funds to cover a short-term excess of payments over receipts can choose among selling the liquid assets (commercial paper, CDs, and Treasury bills) he holds, issuing new commercial paper, or borrowing from a bank.

Differences in interest rates and other costs involved in raising funds from alternative sources will be considered in making the choice. Corporate treasurers faced with a short-term excess of receipts over payments may acquire commercial paper, bank CDs, or Treasury bills, or fail to renew bank loans or commercial paper already outstanding.

If the interest rate on any one type of short-term credit tends to rise relative to other short-term rates, some treasurers will change their mode of adjustment to short-term cash-flow problems. A rise in Treasury bill rates relative to commercial-paper rates will cause some treasurers to sell commercial paper rather than Treasury bills, while those with surplus funds will buy Treasury bills rather than commercial paper. Thus the amount of Treasury bills demanded will rise and the amount supplied decrease while the reverse will be true for commercial paper. These adjustments will tend to hold the rates for different kinds of short-term credit together. Banks, of course, play a central role in these market adjustments since they deal in all forms of short-term credit and act as both borrowers and lenders. Small banks switch their liquid asset holdings between Treasury bills, commercial paper, CDs of large banks, and overnight federal fund loans to large banks in response to rate changes. The large banks price their loans to business in relation to the cost of raising short-term funds and, of course, try to obtain funds in the cheapest market.

Since the different types of short-term credit are such close substitutes for both banks and corporations it is hardly surprising that the interest rates involved move together. Figures 6.4 and 6.5 demonstrate this.

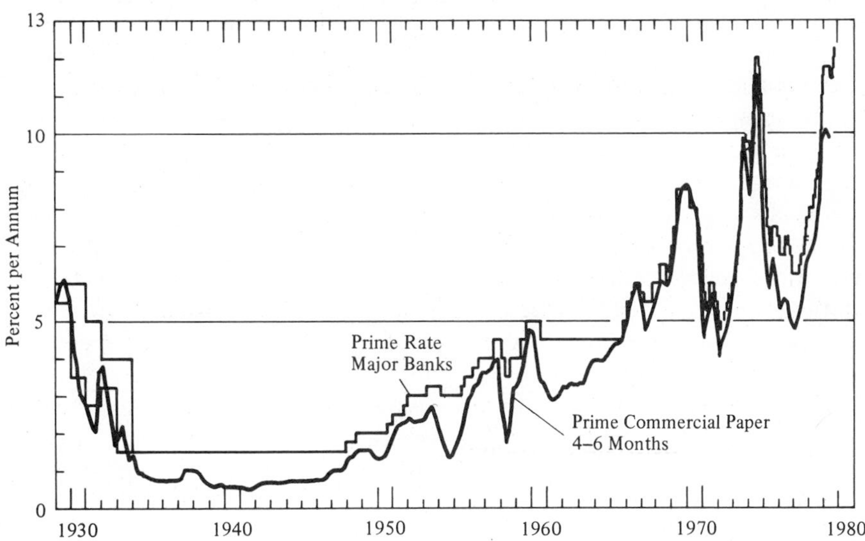

Figure 6.4 Short-Term Interest Rates: Business Borrowing
Prime rate, effective date of change; prime paper, quarterly averages

Source: *Federal Reserve Chart Book,* 1982, p. 99.

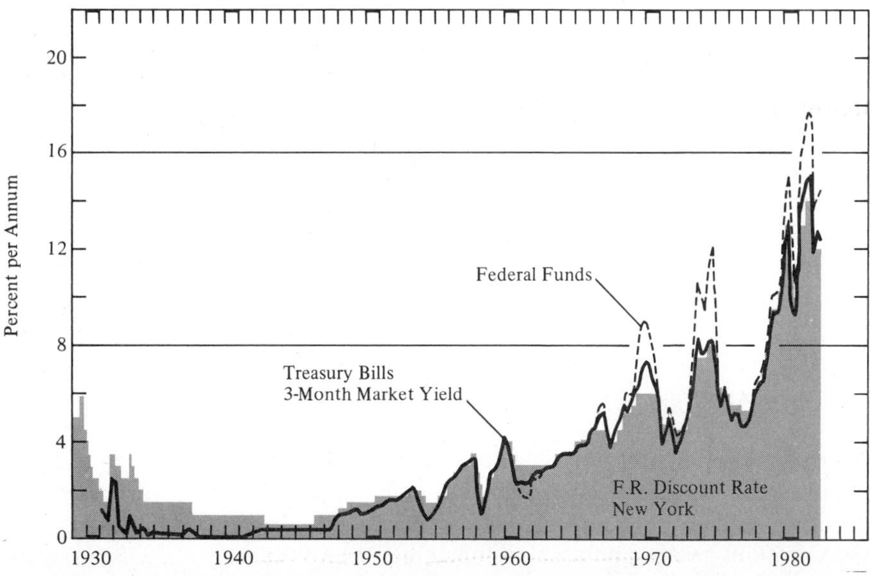

Figure 6.5 Short-Term Interest Rates: Money Market
Discount rate, effective date of change; all others, quarterly averages

Source: *Federal Reserve Chart Book,* 1982, p. 98.

Indeed it may seem surprising that the structure of short-term interest rates varies as much as it does. Treasury bills, commercial paper, and bank CDs appear to be very similar instruments. They all run for short periods, can be sold before maturity, and are issued by borrowers with high credit ratings. From the standpoint of the buyers they differ in two respects: their risk, or more accurately the trouble of avoiding risk, and their marketability, the cost and speed with which they can be resold.

Treasury bills usually carry a slightly lower interest rate than other short-term securities because of their ready marketability. Because the outstanding volume is so large and because they are so widely held there is an active and continuous market for Treasury bills. Dealers are prepared to buy or sell Treasury bills in amounts as large as $50 million on a moment's notice at a very low charge. Other short-term securities can be sold in the secondary market, but it may take longer and cost more.

Treasury bills, of course, are regarded as completely riskless while there is always at least a bit of risk of repayment problems for commercial paper, even that issued by the largest and best-known corporations, or for the CDs of even the largest banks. Some banks and corporations buy commercial paper or CDs to earn a very slight differential in interest rate over the Treasury bill rate. Others are more risk averse and will prefer Treasury bills unless the rate spread is much larger.

The differential between the yields on Treasury and other securities may vary for two reasons. First, concern over risk varies; for example, after Penn Central went bankrupt, many commercial-paper buyers became concerned over risk, and commercial-paper rates rose relative to Treasury bill rates. Second, the distribution of liquid asset holdings varies so that sometimes the more risk-averse asset buyers become relatively more important and the spread between bills and short-term securities widens. For example, at times foreign countries buy up a large amount of U.S. dollars to keep the dollar from falling relative to their own currencies. They tend to use these dollars to buy Treasury bills rather than CDs or commercial paper, and this has sometimes lowered—as in 1978 and 1979—the Treasury bill rate relative to other short-term rates. Thus, as a first approximation, all types of short-term credit can be regarded as nearly homogeneous substitutes with rates moving together in the major swings in credit conditions. But from day to day and week to week the special factors affecting different short-term credit markets can cause significant differences in the spreads among rates.

LONG-TERM MARKETS

The long-term capital markets provide financing for home buyers and for commercial building through the mortgage market. They finance schools, hospitals, and other public facilities through the municipal bond market. Corporations seeking permanent financing turn to the markets for corporate stock and bonds. Foreign corporations and governments also sell substantial amounts of securities in the U.S. long-term capital markets. Finally, the U.S. Treasury and various federal credit agencies sell long-term bonds and their securities are widely held and actively traded. Figure 6.6 shows the amounts of long-term funds raised in the capital markets.

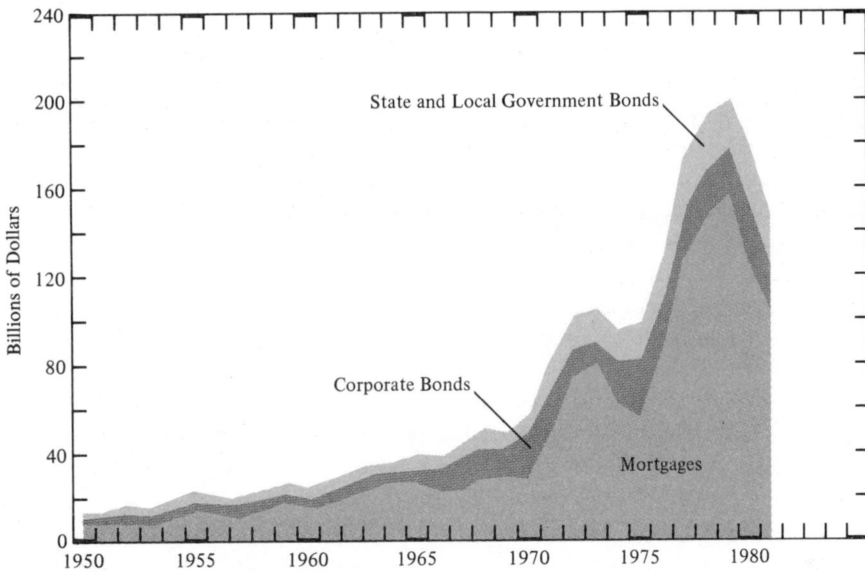

Figure 6.6 Long-Term Borrowing
Annually

Source: *Federal Reserve Chart Book,* 1982, p. 46.

The securities issued and traded in the long-term markets are far less homogeneous than short-term securities, and the markets in which they are issued and traded reflect the differences among long-term securities.

Bond Markets

Investment banking firms specialize in the issue of long-term corporate, municipal, and foreign bonds as well as common stock. A corporation proposing to sell securities arranges with an investment banking firm to underwrite the securities. The investment banking firm undertakes to buy the entire issue at an agreed-upon price. It then sells the issue piecemeal to life-insurance companies and pension funds in the case of foreign and corporate bonds; or to banks, marine, fire, and casualty companies, and wealthy individuals in the case of municipal bonds. If the issue is a large one, the investment banking firm may form an ad hoc group called a syndicate, joining with other investment banking firms and brokerage houses to share the risk. The syndicate tries to sell the bonds at a price a little above the buying price. If they have guessed the market correctly, they sell out the issue quickly and make money. When they misjudge the market they may have to sell part of the issue at a loss. To protect investors, the Securities and Exchange Commission (SEC) requires that a corporation provide much information when it sells a large bond issue. Providing this information and meeting all the required government regulations is expensive. Some corporations sell a whole bond issue directly to insurance companies or pension funds at a negotiated price. These sales are called private placements. By using this method the seller avoids paying the underwriter's profit and the cost of SEC registration for a public issue.

Competitive bidding is usually required by law for the bond issues of state and local governments and public utilities. Competition among investment banking firms and brokerage houses for these issues is very sharp. Sometimes the interest rates offered differ only in the fourth decimal place. Competitive bidding is, of course, inconsistent with private placements.

The secondary markets for corporate and municipal bonds are limited. Most issues are held to maturity. There is some trading in old bonds on the New York Stock Exchange, and financial institutions sometimes trade bonds privately. Municipal bonds may be resold through brokers but the market is poorly organized because there are so many relatively small issues outstanding.

Because Congress has placed limits on the maximum interest rate payable on long-term bonds, the Treasury has been able to make only a few long-term issues in recent years. Nonetheless, there are large amounts of long-term U.S. Treasury securities outstanding. They are widely held and actively traded. The dealers who are so active in the short-term market also trade in long-term Treasury securities and the secondary market is better organized than the other bond markets.

The Stock Market

In the bond markets the volume of new issues is large relative to the amount of secondary trading. The reverse is true of the markets for common stocks. Daily trading on the stock exchanges can exceed 5 billion dollars, while new common-stock issues run to only a few billion dollars per year. Indeed, in some years, the value of stock retirements (when companies buy back their own stock) has exceeded the value of new issues. The importance of the stock market cannot be judged by the volume of funds raised through stock issues. Though most corporations obtain equity capital by the retention of earnings, the opportunity to raise equity capital may be vitally important to a limited number of rapidly growing firms. Without the opportunity to sell equities they would have to sell out to some larger firm. The survival of independent, growing firms strengthens the competitive process.

Moreover, the stock market values the performance of managements and exerts pressure for efficiency and innovation. When a firm's management does not appear to be exploiting the opportunities available to it, the company's stock will be priced at a level that encourages a takeover bid by another firm.

Finally, the stock market provides capital indirectly. Stockholders are willing to forgo dividends so that firms can retain earnings and reinvest. The stockholders hope that successful investment of retained earnings will produce higher earnings with increased dividends later on, and ultimately a higher price for the stock. They are prepared to forgo dividends in the hope of a capital gain. An active stock market makes it possible for investors to realize their capital gains at any time by selling some of their stock. If it were not for the fact that the stock markets permit investors to sell their stocks, many of them would not be so willing to hold as much stock as they now do.

New common-stock issues are usually sold through underwriters as in the case of bonds. Secondary trading in existing stocks is carried on through the New York Stock Exchange, the American Stock Exchange, and several regional exchanges. The shares of smaller unlisted corporations are traded through brokers in the so-called over-the-counter (OTC) market.

Residential Mortgage Markets

In many ways the residential mortgage market is the most complex of all the credit markets. It is by far the largest of the long-term credit markets. The annual net increase in mortgage debt exceeds $100 billion in most years and the gross flow of mortgage credit is still larger, sometimes reaching $200 billion. The market for mortgages on single-family homes is almost necessarily a retail market in which millions of families arrange for mortgages with several thousand commercial banks, mutual savings banks, savings and loan associations, and other lenders. Although mortgage contracts are fairly well standardized, lenders must evaluate each property separately to be sure that its value exceeds the amount of the mortgage. Since foreclosures are expensive, lenders also want to know about the financial position of the borrower to assure themselves that the required payments will be made.

Most of the mortgage financing for purchase of existing homes is provided by local financial institutions—commercial banks, mutual savings banks, and savings and loans. Those institutions also provide the financing for single homes built for the owner or by small building firms. Mortgage financing for large tract developments and for apartment buildings can be obtained from a wider range of sources. Insurance companies provide mortgage credit for some large apartment projects. In the West and South, mortgage "banks" act as intermediaries between distant financial institutions and local builders of tract developments and apartments. These firms—not really banks at all—arrange mortgages on properties meeting the specifications of the lender, collect payments, and do all the legal work for a fee. Their operation has helped to make a national mortgage market.

Savings and loans, mutual savings banks, commercial banks, and, to a lesser extent, insurance companies provide most of the funds for home financing. However, the Federal Home Loan Bank Board (FHLBB) and the Federal National Mortgage Association (FNMA) also play an important role in the mortgage market. FHLBB sells bonds in a national security market and lends to savings and loan associations, which in turn, lend to local mortgage borrowers. FNMA, originally a federal agency and now a private corporation, also sells its securities in the national market and then buys mortgages from financial institutions.

Another federal agency, the Government National Mortgage Association (GNMA), guarantees securities backed by federally insured mortgages. These securities are issued by thrift institutions, which originate the underlying mortgages, and are sold to pension funds, insurance companies, and individual investors.

These institutions provide a source of mortgage funds not dependent on the flow of deposits to banks and thrift institutions. Thus, in spite of the local character of mortgage markets, funds may be drawn from any part of the country to any other area. After many years of evolution a unified national mortgage market has been developed.

The changes just noted have affected the response of mortgage markets to fluctuations in short-term market rates. As we showed in Chapter 5 the flow of funds to thrift institutions is strongly influenced by variations in short-term market rates. In the credit crunches of 1966, 1974, and 1979 the inflow of funds to thrift institutions was sharply reduced. Mortgage interest rates rose, but not enough to clear the market. Lenders chose to ration their loans rather than to raise the price enough to choke off loan demand. Lenders were concerned about their long-term relations with builders and realtors. Each wanted to move cautiously to avoid setting too far ahead of the pack.

By 1980 the situation had changed in a number of respects. The growth of the market for GNMA mortgage backed securities provided a national standard for mortgage rates independent of local competitive considerations. In addition the lenders had to pay market based rates for large amounts of funds raised through money market certificates. They could not afford to offer the going rate for MMC funds unless they could get at least as high a yield from investments. Mortgage rates rose much faster in 1980–82 than at any time in history.

VALUATION IN LONG-TERM MARKETS

Long-term capital markets differ from the markets for shorter-term assets because of an important difference in the investment risks involved in the two markets. An investor who buys a short-term security has only to worry about the credit worthiness of the borrower. If the borrower remains solvent the lender will receive a fixed payment in a few months. Long-term lenders too have to worry about credit risk. In fact, they have to worry more because there is more time for a change in the borrower's fortunes before repayment is due. But long-term lenders have an additional risk. For one reason or another a long-term investor may want to sell the bonds before they mature. Even if the borrower's credit standing remains good, the price of bonds can fall before they mature if the interest rates have risen since they were issued.

Valuing Bonds

For example, a $1,000 Treasury bond due in 1998 with a 3½ percent annual interest payment sold for $851 in 1983. The fall in price was not due to a deterioration in the Treasury's credit standing but to the general rise in interest rates. In 1983 new long-term bonds with $1,000 maturity value could be sold at $1,000 with an annual interest payment of 10½ percent. No one will pay one thousand dollars for a bond promising thirty-five dollar interest payment plus repayment of principal in twenty years when he or she can get an annual interest payment of one hundred dollars and repayment of principal at the same date. Obviously, the old bonds with the low interest payment must sell for less than one thousand dollars. To find out how much less, we use the present-value approach to valuing contracts for future payments.

Start from the proposition that the promise—even if guaranteed—of one dollar in the future is always worth less than one dollar in hand now. The reason is that money in hand now can be invested at interest. If I invest one dollar now at 7 percent, I will have 1.07 dollars in a year. Conversely, if I want one dollar a year from now, I can invest \$1/1.07 or \$.934 and get one dollar in a year. If you promise one dollar in one year I will give you only 93¢ now for your promise, even if I have absolute faith in your honesty and ability to pay. \$1/1.07 = .934 is called the present value of one dollar discounted at 7 percent for one year. What about the value of one dollar to be paid in two years? One dollar invested for the first year produces \$1.07; the whole \$1.07 can be invested for the second year at 7 percent, and principal and interest at the end of the second year will be worth (\$1.07) (\$1.07) or \$1.145. To get one dollar in two years invest \$1/1.145 or \$.873. This is the present value of one dollar discounted at 7 percent for two years.

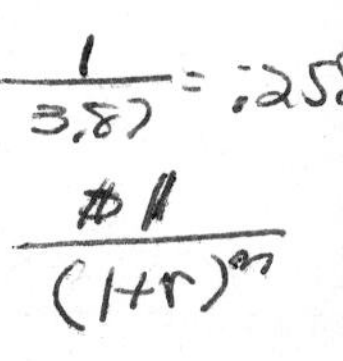

Following the same procedure the present value of one dollar discounted at 7 percent for twenty years is one dollar divided by 1.07^{20} or \$.258. In general, the present value of one dollar discounted at any interest for any number of years is $\$1/((1 + r)^n)$. Notice how small the present value has become when discounted for a period as long as twenty years. That is because the denominator in the calculations reflects the compounding of interest and grows rapidly as the time period increases. The curve marked 7 percent in Figure 6.7 shows how present value declines with the increase in numbers of years

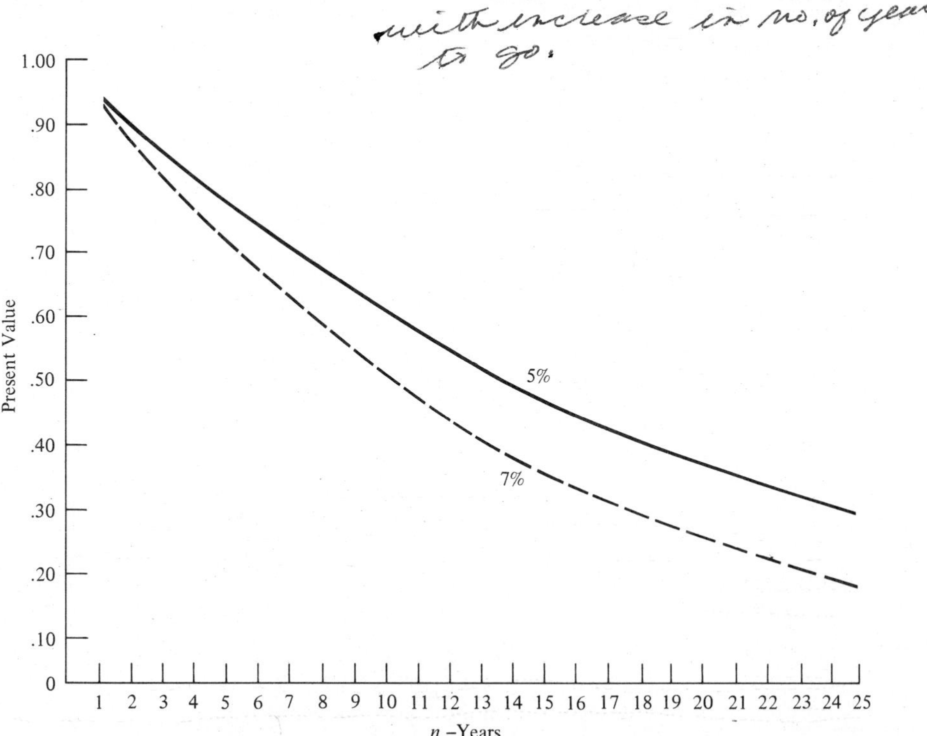

Figure 6.7 Present Value of One Dollar

of discounting. Of course, the rate of decline of present value also depends on the interest rate used. At 5 percent the numbers in the denominators of present-value calculations are always smaller (present value larger) than at 7 percent. The curve marked 5 percent in Figure 6.7 illustrates the difference.

To value a bond we have to calculate separately the present value of each of the interest payments and the present value of the final repayment of interest, and then add them up. Because the present value of payments due in the distant future is more sensitive to interest-rate changes than payments due in the relatively near future, the prices of long-term bonds will fluctuate much more in response to interest-rate changes than will the prices of shorter-term bonds.

Valuing Common Stocks

Bond valuations are based on more or less secure promises of future payment of interest and principal. Equity investors, on the other hand, often appear to show little concern for dividends. They seem to be a lot more interested in the prospective change in the price of the stock than in the current dividend. The day-to-day gyrations of the market are hard to understand. Commentators can always explain what happened yesterday but are not very good at predicting tomorrow. The only really safe prediction of stock-market behavior is the one made many years ago by J. P. Morgan. When asked what the market would do he said, "It will fluctuate." Nonetheless, the underlying basis of stock prices is the same as that of bond prices. The value of a stock depends upon the present value or the payments that the actual or prospective stockholders expect to receive.

Lots of people buy stocks that have never paid a dividend. Small, growing companies may reinvest all their earnings. Investors expect that earnings will continue to grow and that eventually the company will start to pay dividends. Other companies have losses but are expected to "turn around" under new management or because they have a new product line. Some firms limp along barely surviving for years. The value placed on their stock may have the same explanation of Samuel Johnson's description of second marriages: "the triumph of hope over experience." But in most cases stocks are valuable because there are good reasons for believing that they will pay dividends in the future. When everyone becomes convinced that there will never be any dividend payments, a stock becomes worthless.

The so-called investment value of a stock is the present value of the expected future dividends. One may imagine a company that is expected to pay a fixed dividend for an indefinite period. In that case the stock will be valued in the same way as a perpetual bond. A perpetual bond promises interest payments "forever" with no principal payment. The value of a perpetuity of one dollar discounted at 5 percent is twenty dollars. It takes a capital sum of twenty dollars to generate interest of one dollar per year. In the case of a stock we would expect discount rates to be relatively high because future dividend payments can never be certain.

A steady dividend is unusual in a growing economy. A typical company usually hopes to grow and increase its earnings over time by reinvesting part of its profits. Consider, for example, a company currently earning two dollars per share after taxes and paying a one-dollar dividend. The company reinvests one dollar, and expects to earn 10 percent after taxes on its reinvested profits. Earnings will grow at 5 percent per year and, if the company always pays out half its earnings, dividends will also grow at 5 percent. We now have to value a growing stream of earnings. To do so, we apply the present-value method as in the case of bonds. The prospective stream of dividends is \$1.05, $\$1.05^2$, and so on, in successive years. Discounting this stream of dividends at r percent per year we have

$$\text{Present value} = \frac{1.05}{1+r} + \left(\frac{1.05}{1+r}\right)^2 + \cdots$$

This is equivalent to present value $= 1/(r - .05)$. If, for example, r is 10 percent, present value is $1/(.10 - .05)$ or 20 times dividends or ten times earnings. The price-earnings ratio increases with the prospective growth rate and decreases with the discount rate applied to future earnings.

More complicated cases arise for companies expected to grow unusually rapidly for a time, and then settle down to a more ordinary rate of growth. There are tables that give present values for two-stage growth paths. They show that an expectation of unusually high earnings growth for a period of ten years or so will justify very high ratios of price to current earnings. That is the explanation of the high price-earnings ratio of "growth stocks."

The theory of investment value has a perfectly sensible logic, but its application rests on a number of assumptions about the future. To calculate investment value one must assume a future earning stream and apply a discount rate. Any student of the stock market knows that earnings for next year are hard to predict, let alone the growth paths for earnings years ahead. The price of a stock can suddenly rise or fall in response to information leading to a revaluation of earnings prospects. Moreover, discount factors can change. They will be influenced by competing long-term bond yields, but they can be influenced even more by changes in confidence or lack of it about the future of the economy or of the particular company.

On the whole the stock market reacts quickly to new information relevant to the values of stocks. Many investors are ill-informed or inactive, but studies of stock-price movements show that the active, well informed investors cause prices to reflect any available information about the values of stocks. One might think that if a stock has been rising for some time, it is likely to continue to rise and is therefore a good buy. But this is not so. Investors have bid up its price to a level so high that the stock is just as likely to fall as to rise from then on. It is impossible to "beat the market" unless one has information that others lack or luck.

Inflation and Common-Stock Prices

It used to be thought that common stocks were a good hedge against inflation. An all-around rise in prices, wages, and other costs should raise dollar earnings in proportion to prices and leave the real value of earnings and stock prices unchanged. In fact, when inflation comes as a surprise, companies with outstanding long-term debt should gain. Earnings before interest should rise in proportion to prices and contract interest remains the same, so earnings after interest should increase relative to prices.

The response of stock prices to a fully anticipated, but not yet realized, inflation depends on the accompanying change in interest rates. Anticipated inflation will raise the projected growth of nominal earnings, but it will also raise interest rates. If the increase in interest rates exactly balances the anticipated increase in prices, the increase in the numerator in the present-value calculation is canceled out by the increase in the denominator. In general, we do expect interest rates to rise with anticipated inflation, but the change in interest rates need not be exactly the same as the change in the expected rate of price increase. In fact, as almost everyone knows by now, common stocks have been a poor hedge against inflation in the last decade. In the period of 1966–82, stock prices rose at an average annual rate of about 3.0 percent, while the consumers price index rose at a 6.2 percent rate. After taxes, corporate earnings have not kept up with prices. The tax system has worked against them. In calculating profits, many firms value the cost of materials drawn from inventory at the price they originally paid for them, rather than at the replacement costs. These corporations earn paper profits in the rise in the value of materials. The profits are not real since the materials drawn from inventory must be replaced at higher prices. Nonetheless, they have to pay taxes on those paper profits. In the same way depreciation on fixed capital is based on historical rather than replacement costs. Hence, the tax code does not allow firms to subtract from their taxable income a sufficient and realistic amount for depreciation. Their taxable income is therefore overstated, they have to pay more taxes, and this reduces the after-tax profits that are available for stockholders. In addition the stock market's evaluation of earnings has been adversely affected by investor fears that efforts to fight inflation will lead to a recession or price control.

SPECIALIZATION AND COMPETITION IN LONG-TERM CAPITAL MARKETS

The markets for long-term debt are linked together but the different kinds of long-term debt are not such close substitutes as the short-term securities. Each type of long-term security has special features that make it more attractive to some groups of investors than others. The interest on municipal bonds is exempt from federal income taxes. Wealthy individuals and fully taxed corporations including banks will buy them at substantially lower yields than taxable corporate bonds. The tax advantage is much less significant to insurance companies, mutual savings banks, and savings and loan associations, which do not pay the regular corporate income-tax rate.

Mortgages are less attractive to most investors than corporate bonds because there are significant costs associated with acquiring and servicing them. The costs of collecting payments and making sure that taxes and insurance payments are kept up is considerably higher per dollar invested than the cost of managing a corporate bond portfolio. In addition, the lenders cannot invest safely without acquiring considerable expertise in the local real-estate market involved. Those negative considerations are more important to some investors than others. Savings and loan associations have to invest in mortgages because of restrictions on their investments. Savings and loan associations, mutual savings banks, and commercial banks with suburban branches can acquire and maintain information on residential markets more cheaply than other investors. Moreover, depository institutions expect to gain deposits by making mortgage loans to local customers. Thus, we find the savings and loan associations specializing in home mortgages, while mutual savings banks split their portfolios between home mortgages and corporate bonds. Commercial banks buy substantial amounts of home mortgages but put a larger share of their long-term investments into municipal bonds because of the tax advantages these yield to them.. Life-insurance companies prefer corporate bonds and commercial mortgages on office buildings and shopping centers.

Institutional participation in the stock market is limited. Pension funds and marine, fire, and casualty companies together own about 15 percent of the common stocks. But most stocks are owned by individuals either directly or through mutual funds or bank trust departments. As noted earlier, corporate bonds are mainly held by life-insurance companies and mutual savings banks.

Since each type of lender specializes in a limited range of securities, the long-term market appears to be partially segmented into a number of separate compartments. The supply of funds to the different kinds of lenders follows a pattern unrelated to shifts in the offerings of different kinds of securities. If the long-term markets were completely separate from one another, supply and demand for each type of security would have to be balanced separately in each segment of the market. It would then be possible for interest rates in the different markets to move independently of one another.

In fact, however, the compartments in the security markets are far from watertight. Most lenders participate in more than one market. Their choices among the different securities help to link markets together directly. Insurance companies, for example, operate in both the commercial mortgage market and the corporate bond market. A rise in the supply of corporate bonds will first push up corporate bond yields and then induce insurance companies to buy more corporate bonds and less commercial mortgages. Commercial mortgage rates will then be pulled up, so that they move with the corporate bond yield. There are several of these competing portfolio pairs: corporate bonds versus home mortgages for savings banks, mortgages versus municipal bonds for commercial banks, common stocks versus corporate bonds for pension and endowment funds, and common stocks versus municipals for wealthy individuals.

In addition, all the markets are linked to the market for long-term U.S. securities. Almost all institutional investors hold substantial amounts of longer-term U.S. securities. A rise in the yield of any one type of asset will cause lenders specializing in that asset to sell U.S. securities so as to buy the asset in question. The resulting rise in yields on U.S. securities will cause lenders

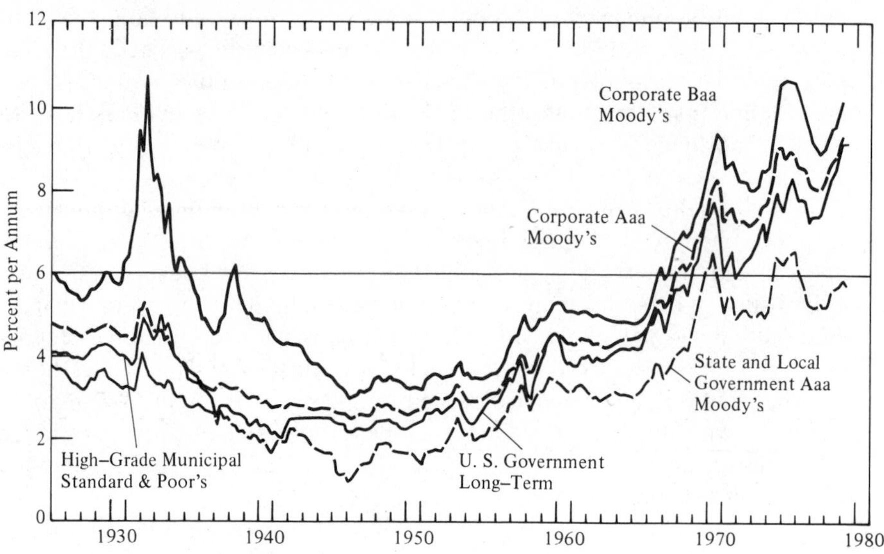

Figure 6.8 Long-Term Bond Yields
Quarterly averages

Source: *Federal Reserve Chart Book,* 1982, p. 97.

specializing in other assets to try to sell them in order to buy U.S. securities. This shift will pull up the yields of those assets so that all the yields will move up together.

In spite of the specialization of financial institutions and the apparent segmentation of long-term security markets, the bond markets appear to function reasonably well. Yields on different types of securities do move together (see Figure 6.8). The differences in yields appear on the whole to reflect differences in taxes, risk, and costs of placement and servicing of different kinds of securities in a fairly rational way. This reflects the fact that various markets can be tied together so long as a sufficient number of participants on the margin move readily from one market to another in response to interest-rate changes. As usual in economics, the action is at the margin.

However, the linkages among the long-term markets are not nearly so tight as in the short-term markets. The spread between municipal and corporate bond yields varies considerably because of the wide variation in commercial bank demand for municipals. When demand for bank loans is growing more rapidly than deposits, commercial banks often sharply reduce their purchases of municipal bonds. More bonds must be sold to individuals. That requires that one of two things happens: wealthy individuals in tax brackets above the 46 percent rate applicable to banks increase the proportion of municipal bonds in their portfolios, or individuals in lower tax brackets are induced to buy municipals. In either case, the yield of municipal bonds will have to rise sharply relative to the yields of other assets. When commercial banks have rapid deposit growth they return to the municipal market and yields of state and local bonds fall relative to others. The differential tax treatment of competing investors is ultimately responsible for the shifts in the relative yields of municipals.

As noted earlier, the mortgage market is the most glaring example of market failure in our capital markets. The variation in thrift institutions' demand for mortgages leads to imbalances in the supply and demand for mortgages. As noted in the last section these shifts in demand for mortgages are only partly reflected in interest-rate changes. These shifts often produce rationing rather than volatile fluctuations in interest rates.

You will notice that the two problem areas—the municipal and mortgage markets—are ones in which the long-term market is affected by activity in the short-term market. Variations in demand for short-term bank loans are responsible for variations in bank demand for municipal bonds. Variations in short-term interest rates are primarily responsible for variations in the flow of funds to thrift institutions and thereby for shifts in demand for mortgages. These are obvious cases, but there are other more pervasive links between the movements of short-term interest rates and those of long-term rates. This rather tricky and controversial subject is considered in the next section.

TERM STRUCTURE

We have seen that the yields on different types of short-term securities all move together, though with some variations in the spreads among the rates on different short-term assets. We have also seen that rates on all the different kinds of long-term securities show similar patterns but with wider variations in the spreads among different rates. In both cases the rates are held together because security buyers are willing to substitute one kind of security for another in response to changes in the relative yields. Sellers will also change their methods of financing if one source of funds appears to be cheaper than another. The same thing applies to the relation between yields on short-term securities and yields on long-term securities. Figure 6.9 shows the rates on short-term commercial paper and the rates on long-term corporate bonds. If you examine it closely you will note that both rates usually move up and down at the same time; they show common trends, and the short rates move up and down much more than the long rates. The short rates in the period were usually below the long rates but occasionally short rates rose above the long rates.

Figure 6.9 shows rates for two kinds of securities: commercial paper maturing in six months and corporate bonds maturing in twenty years. At any one time there are securities available maturing at a variety of dates from one day to thirty years or more ahead. Figure 6.10 shows actual yields on Treasury securities. The yield is shown on the vertical axis. The horizontal axis shows the number of years to maturity. The rising yield curve is typical of recession periods, when investors think that short-term yields are abnormally low. As we'll see later, the yield curve will slope downwards at times when investors think that yields are abnormally high. Changes in yield curves reflect the investment decisions of investors in the financial markets as well as the decisions of security issuers.

Though some investors, like insurance companies, tend to specialize in longer-term securities, they are not locked into any rigid investment pattern. An insurance company can put investment funds received from premiums

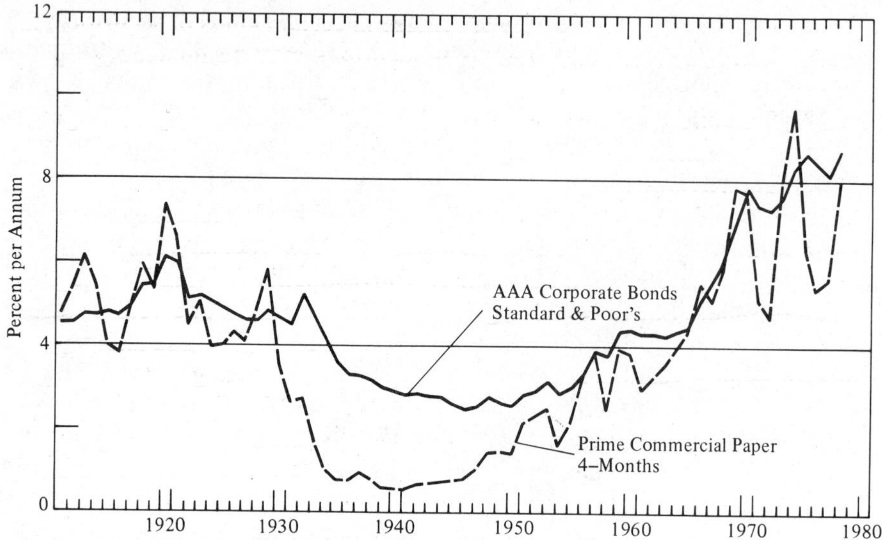

Figure 6.9 Long- and Short-Term Interest Rates
Annually

Source: *Federal Reserve Chart Book,* 1982, p. 96.

and from repayments of maturing bonds into short-term securities, if their yields appear sufficiently attractive. A bank will shift toward longer-term securities if their yields look better than those on short-term assets. In this respect long- and short-term securities are linked together in the same way as different kinds of securities of the same maturity.

The linkage is a good deal more complex than in the case of competing securities of the same maturity. It involves two kinds of elements. First, as

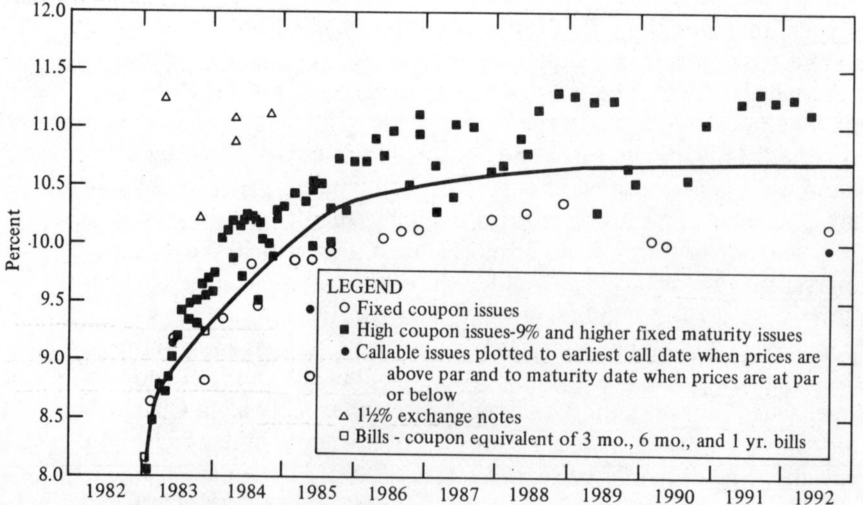

Figure 6.10 Yields of Treasury Securities, October 29, 1982

in other cases in which investors specialize in certain kinds of securities, the relative yield of long- and short-term securities may be influenced by the relative amounts of those securities outstanding, and by the distribution of financial resources as between those institutions specializing in long-term securities and those specializing in short-term ones. As we shall see, there is some controversy over the importance of this consideration.

Second, yield curves are clearly influenced by expectations about the future of interest rates. A buyer choosing between Treasury bills and commercial paper is choosing between two investments running for the same length of time. A buyer choosing between a bond and a one-year Treasury bill is choosing between an investment running for a year and another running for twenty years. To compare them he or she has to guess what future interest rates will be when the Treasury bill matures. The comparison depends very heavily on the investor's expectations about the future. It follows that yield curves will be influenced by the way investors form their expectations about future movements of interest rates.

Many economists take the view that only expectational factors are important in determining yield curves. In the next section we will show how yield curves are determined when only "permanent investors," who want to hold bonds to maturity, are in the market. In the following section we will show how the same approach applies to investors who may wish to sell bonds before maturity. In both cases we assume that expectations about the future are given. We must then consider briefly how investors form expectations about future rate movements. Finally, we have to examine how the maturity distribution of outstanding bonds and the resources of different kinds of financial institutions influence yield curves.

Permanent Investors

The importance of expectations in determining the shape of the yield curve can be shown by a simple example. An investor with funds available for two years can either purchase a one-year bond now and use the proceeds (including interest) to buy another one-year bond a year from now or he or she can purchase a two-year bond now.

To make a wise choice three things should be known: the yield on two-year bonds now; the yield on one-year bonds now; and the yield on the one-year bonds that will be available a year from now. The first two figures are found in the newspaper, but the third involves a guess, and this guess may be the crucial element in the decision. Suppose, for example, that one-year bonds now yield 4 percent, but our investor thinks that short-term interest rates are going to rise to 6 percent in the coming year. In that case one dollar invested in two successive one-year investments will produce \$(1.04) (1.06) at the end of two years. (One dollar invested now produces \$1.04 at 4 percent in one year, 1.04 dollars invested for the second year at 6 percent produces 1.04 times 1.06 dollars.) What yield is required to make a single two-year investment equally attractive? If the yield on two-year bonds is R percent per year the investor will have $\$(1+R)^2$ at the end of two years so $(1+R)^2$ must equal (1.04)(1.06). It turns out that $R=5$ percent will be close to right. Exactly the same argument holds if we consider a three-year bond versus three successive one-year investments, or for that matter a twenty-year bond versus twenty successive one-year investments.

The following example will show how yield curves are related to the pattern of expected future interest rates. The economy is in a recession. The current rate on one-year securities is 4 percent, but investors foresee a vigorous recovery with rising rates. They expect the rate on one-year securities to rise to 5 percent in a year with a continued rise to 6 percent a year later and to 7 percent in another year at the peak of the boom. Thereafter, their foresight runs out, but investors expect that the boom will peter out and that thereafter rates on one-year securities will fluctuate between 5 percent and 7 percent with an average of 6 percent. Accordingly, the yield on a one-year security will be 4 percent, on a two-year security it will be about 4.5 percent. Yields will gradually rise toward 6 percent as the maturity increases.

Holding-Period Yields

The expectations theory outlined above assumes that investors intend to commit themselves for some considerable length of time. If they buy long-term securities they plan to hold them to maturity. If they buy short-term securities they plan to keep reinvesting in short-term securities. Some investors, like insurance companies, *do* plan to hold the securities they buy, but others may consider buying long-term securities even though they only want to hold them for a year. Or they may consider buying long-term securities to hold for a year and then reconsider whether to sell them or to continue holding them. Those investors are not directly interested in average yields over a long period. They are concerned with comparing the yield on one-year securities with the yield on long-term securities over a holding period of, say, a year.

If security prices stayed the same, the holding-period yield on a one-year investment would simply be the annual interest payment divided by the price. A bond paying six dollars per year and selling for one hundred dollars is said to have a "coupon" yield of 6 percent because a set of dated coupons each redeemable for six dollars is attached to the bond.

The one-year holding-period yield will exceed or fall short of the coupon yield by the percentage change in price during the year; for example, if the bond with the 6 percent coupon were purchased for ninety-five dollars at the start of the year and sold for ninety-seven dollars at the end, the holding-period yield would be 6.32 percent plus 2/95 or 8.42 percent. If it sold for ninety-three dollars, the holding-period yield would be 6.32 percent minus 2/95 or 4.22 percent.

Any investor who buys a bond maturing in more than one year wants to obtain a first-year holding-period yield at least equal to the yield on a one-year bond. That requirement is closely related to the requirement that the yield on a long-term bond should depend on the expected short yield in future years. Go back now to our first example of a choice between a two-year bond and two successive one-year investments. We assumed there that the initial one-year rate was 4 percent, and the expected one-year rate a year hence 6 percent. The equivalent average yield for a two-year bond is approximately 5 percent. Suppose a two-year bond is issued at one hundred dollars with a five-dollar annual coupon interest payment. What will its price be a year hence? In the second year it must yield 6 percent, but it pays only a five-dollar coupon. Its price at the end of the first year, and start of the second year, must be ninety-nine dollars to produce a 6 percent holding-period yield—5 percent coupon yield, 1 percent gain in price from ninety-nine to maturity price of one hundred. For the first year the holding-period yield will be 4 percent—a 5 percent coupon yield less a 1 percent capital loss. In each period the holding-period yield equals the one-year yield. This kind of calculation can be extended to any number of years in the future.

Thus for any given set of expectations about future short-term yields, investors will accept the same bond yield whether they plan to hold the bond for one year or until maturity.

Expectations and Timing

The holding-period yield on a security is clearly the yield that is relevant to the decisions of a speculator considering whether to hold bonds for a short period, but it is also important to other investors. Speculators play a relatively small role in bond markets. The bond markets are dominated by issuers who will sooner or later need long-term financing, and by institutional buyers who normally invest most of their assets in long-term securities. However, the holding-period yield is relevant to the timing of bond issues and bond purchases. An insurance company may plan to keep most of its assets in long-term investments, but it can hold short-term securities when its investment managers expect the holding-period yield on bonds to be lower than the current short-term yields. They can invest in short-term securities until the holding-period comparison becomes more favorable to bonds. In the same way, corporate treasurers may borrow short-term funds while planning to refinance by a bond issue. For example, a corporation buying a new factory has the option to finance it initially by issuing short-term security, and later on when those securities become due, to redeem them by issuing long-term bonds. The question is whether to bring out the issue now or wait until next year. If the holding-period yield on bonds is below the current short-term yield, now is the time to make the issue; otherwise it is better to wait.

The effect of these considerations is to move the holding-period yield for bonds toward equality with the current short-term yield. If everyone thinks the holding-period yield on bonds is below the current short-term yield, borrowers will tend to issue more bonds, investors will hold back on purchases, and bond prices will have to fall enough to raise the holding-period yield to equality with the short-term yield.

So far we have been concerned with the arithmetical relationship between yields and prices of long-term securities and expectations about future yields on short-term securities. In our examples we have supposed that we know what investors expect to happen. That provides only half a theory of yield curves. The other half of the explanation depends on the theory of how investors form their guesses about the future. Two kinds of considerations enter into the formation of expectations. First, investors may try to judge the future of interest rates from their past history. Second, investors try to understand the economy and use their information to deduce in a logical or "rational" way how interest rates will move in the future.

Many investors lack confidence in their ability to make a very accurate analysis of the future path of interest rates. Nonetheless, they have to make decisions and they may therefore be forced to assume that the future will be like the past. The simplest forecast of short-term interest rates is to assume that they will stay where they are. However, short-term interest rates jump around from day to day and week to week. Most investors will think that they can improve their forecast by using an average of rates for a few months back to iron out the random fluctuations. Moreover, they know that there are business fluctuations so that rates move up and down cyclically. They do not want to assume short-term rates will stay at the peak level or at the trough level. A more reasonable assumption is to suppose that future rates will tend to equal the average of past rates over three or four years. If current rates are above the average of the past few years, investors then expect them to fall back to normal; if current rates are below the average of the past few years, investors expect them to rise toward normal. If investors form their expectations in that way, long-term yields will show common cyclical fluctuations. But long rates will show cycles with a much smaller amplitude than short rates. Long and short rates will show similar trends since the "normal" rate is gradually adjusted upward in response to a rising trend in short rates.

Rational Expectations

Those Kiwi-fish expectations—the Kiwi fish swims backwards because it doesn't care where it's going, it only wants to know where it's been—would make sense for an investor who has no source of information except the past history of rates. In fact, of course, most investors try very hard to use all available sources of information. They make or buy forecasts of the economic outlook and try to anticipate changes in fiscal and monetary policy. Instead of basing their forecasts on mechanical or arithmetical projections based on the past history of rates they try to form rational expectations that take into account all the information available that might help them to forecast. The theory of rational expectations is still a matter of controversy and its implications have been fully worked out only for cases where investors are assumed to believe in a fairly simple model of the economic world.

However, it does have important implications that can help us to understand how security markets work. First, the rational-expectations theory implies that at any one time investors have already made full use of all the information available at the time. It is sometimes thought that information percolates through the market gradually. If something happens to increase the value of a security the "smart money" finds out first and acts to drive up prices, other investors catch on a little later and push prices up some more until the new information is fully reflected in security prices. That does not seem to happen. There is enough "smart money" so that all the price rise implied by any event occurs very quickly. In particular, if short rates rise, perhaps because the Federal Reserve has changed its monetary policy, or because business investment is picking up, and there is a reason for thinking that the new level of rates will persist, long-term yields will respond at once, not gradually as implied by the backward-looking approach outlined earlier. Second, the rational-expectations theory has important implications about the way security markets respond to policy actions. If the central bank follows any regular pattern in guiding short-term interest rates the market will take that pattern into account. Suppose, for example, that the Fed always pushes down short rates in a recession and gets them back up in recovery. When a recession occurs the market will act to bid up yields even before the Fed has done anything. But the extent of the rise in long-term yields will be limited by the expectations that short-term yields will be depressed for only a short time. The expected action of the Fed is built into the security prices. Some further implications of the rational-expectations approach are discussed later in Chapter 26.

Inflation and Term Structure

The theory of rational expectations can be applied directly to the relationship between expectations of inflation and the structure of interest rates. We have yet to discuss the determination of the absolute level of short-term interest rates, but we are giving away no secrets by asserting that experience shows that a high rate of inflation is generally accompanied by high interest rates. It follows that when investors anticipate an acceleration in the rate of inflation, they expect that all interest rates will rise sooner or later. Investors may believe that inflation will accelerate for any of a variety of reasons, for example, an expansion of government expenditures or a rapid growth in the money supply. Whatever the reason they will respond by holding back on bond purchases until rates have risen to a level consistent with their expectations about inflation. If they are right, short-term rates will eventually rise, but at the moment of the change in expectations, long-term rates will rise relative to short-term rates.

Supply and Demand Factors

Expectations about future interest rates must play an important role in determining the term structure of interest rates. However, the expectations approach does not provide a complete theory of term structure except under some rather special conditions. The expectations approach provides a complete explanation if all buyers and sellers of securities have exactly the same expectations about future interest rates and the market participants hold their expectations with certainty or are indifferent to risk. In the latter case they seek to maximize the *expected* short-term holding-period yield on their portfolio and act in the same way as they would if they were certain of the outcome.

Given those two conditions the prices of bonds of any maturity must move in such a way as to equate their holding-period yields with current short-term yields. Moreover, the structure of yields will be the same regardless of the quantities of securities in the market. An increase in the volume of bonds outstanding and a corresponding decrease in the volume of short-term securities outstanding will have no effect on the pattern of yields.

What happens if the participants in the market disagree about the future of interest rates? At times there will be investors who expect short-term yields to rise rapidly in the near future while others expect them to rise slowly or not at all. The latter group will be willing to buy bonds at yields only a little above the current short-term yield. The first group will want a big spread before they will buy bonds. Now the relative quantities of long- and short-term bonds will matter. If the volume of bonds is small they can all be sold to the investors who think short-term rates will not rise much, and the bond yield will be only a little higher than the short yield. If there are more bonds and less shorts, some of the bonds will have to be sold to the group expecting more rapid short-term rate increases, and, to induce them to buy, bond yields must be higher relative to the short yield.

In practice there may be a continuous spectrum of opinion. Moderate changes in the distribution of outstanding securities will have some effect on yields but not a very large one.

A very similar argument applies to the willingness of investors to take risks and to the degree of certainty of their expectations.

Differences of opinion about expected future interest rates, differences in uncertainty about the future, and different degrees of concern about risk all tend to make the spread between long- and short-term rates depend on the relative volumes of securities of different maturities outstanding.

Attitudes toward the risk involved in long-term investment are not just a matter of personal taste; they also reflect the nature of the investor's liabilities. Insurance companies, for example, have long-term liabilities promising a fixed interest rate on insurance reserves. They need not worry much about capital losses on bonds because they will not have to sell them. On the other hand if they hold short-term securities, rates might fall and they might not earn the contract interest. They will usually prefer to hold long-term securities when expected long-term yields equal short-term yields. Commercial banks on the other hand may have to liquidate securities if deposits decline or loan demand surges. They prefer shorts to longs at equal expected yields. Because of institutional differences in risk position the spreads between long- and short-term yields may depend on the distribution of assets among the different financial intermediaries as well as on the relative quantities of securities outstanding.

VALUING WEALTH

The bulk of the wealth of any market economy consists of claims direct or indirect against income-producing property: land, houses, offices, factories, and other equipment. The claims are stocks, corporate bonds, mortgages, and deeds to houses. Their aggregate value depends on the present value of the income they will produce as estimated by the securities markets. Thus the value of corporate securities depends in part on the judgments of security buyers about the future movements of corporate earnings. But the valuation of securities also depends on the interest rate used to discount future income. Thus a fall in interest rates, other things equal, should increase the present value of any given future stream of income. That conclusion applies not only to corporate securities but to farmlands, houses, and unincorporated businesses. Thus, if interest rates fall while prospective property income remains the same, total wealth should increase.

Wealth and Government Debt

Most of the national wealth consists of claims against private property, but the holders of state, local, and federal securities certainly think of them as part of their wealth whether they hold them directly or indirectly through intermediaries. However, it is difficult to estimate the net increase in wealth resulting from increases in government debt.

When federal or state governments issue bonds, the bondholders have more assets. The public has an offsetting liability to pay more taxes of some sort but their tax liability is mixed up with all the other taxes and constitutes a relatively small part of the total tax burden. If the taxpayers are fully aware of their future tax liability and discount their future taxes at the same rate as the yield on the bonds, the implicit liability has the same value as the government bonds and there is no net increase in wealth from the bond issue per se. Prospective future income may be increased by the expenditures financed by government debt but in many cases, for example, in defense expenditure, government purchases financed by debt will not increase prospective future income.

However, it is not likely that taxpayers discount the future at the same yield as that paid on bonds. They are likely to discount uncertain future tax liabilities at a rate much higher than the yield on government bonds so that the issuance of debt causes a net increase of total nominal wealth.

Correspondingly, an increase or decrease in interest rates will cause a decrease or increase in the net wealth associated with government debt in the same way as in the case of private wealth.

Finally, in connection with government debt we have to take account of the power of the federal government to issue some interest-free debt in connection with its money-supply operations. When the government issues currency it is issuing interest-free debt. The currency is always someone's asset, but since no interest payment is required there is no offsetting tax liability. In fact the U.S. government does not issue much currency but the Federal Reserve does. Since the Federal Reserve holds one dollar in U.S. bonds for every dollar of currency issued and returns the interest received to the Treasury (after paying its own expenses), the effect of currency issues on the debt burden is the same as though the Treasury issued currency directly, and sold fewer interest-bearing bonds to the public. The Federal Reserve also acquires Treasury debt through open-market operations when it wants to increase bank reserves. Thus any increase in bank reserves through open-market operations gives the Treasury a free ride in the same way as an increase in demand for currency.

We noted earlier that an increase in interest-bearing government debt increases perceived wealth to the extent that the public "undervalues" the resulting increase in expected tax liability. We may suppose, for example, that because the taxpayers do not fully anticipate future debt service liabilities, or discount them at a higher rate than the interest rate on government bonds, each dollar of additional debt adds, say 75¢, to perceived wealth.

Now consider the effect of an open-market operation to increase bank reserves or to offset the reserve drain from increased currency demand. The open-market operation is in effect an exchange of non-interest-bearing for interest-bearing debt. After the open-market operation the public holds less interest-bearing debt and more non-interest-bearing debt. They hold the same amount of assets but their prospective tax liability is reduced and therefore their net wealth is greater. A dollar of non-interest-bearing debt adds one dollar to wealth. We assumed that one dollar of interest-bearing debt adds 75¢ to wealth. The open-market operation therefore increases net wealth by one dollar (increase in non-interest-bearing debt) less 75¢ (from the decrease in interest-bearing debt) for a net gain of 25¢.

Real Versus Nominal Wealth

So far we have discussed wealth in nominal terms, but it is the real value of wealth that counts. The real value of private wealth should be independent of the price level. If all wages and prices double the nominal value of property incomes from profits or rent should double and, given the interest rate, the nominal capital value of claims to profit and rent should also double. But since all other prices have doubled the purchasing power of those claims should remain unchanged. Individual debtors gain from a price level rise while creditors lose but those gains and losses cancel out.

The wealth associated with government debt and the money base, however, is stated in nominal terms and its real value is affected by changes in the price level. When the price level rises, the real value of the money supply declines and the moneyholders as a group are poorer. To be sure, for that part of the money supply that consists of bank deposits there is an offset since the banks who are the debtors for these deposits are better off as a result. (As creditors banks lose too, but those who borrowed from them gain.) However, for that part of the money supply that consists of currency everyone is poorer. Moreover, as prices rise the real value of government bond holdings is reduced, and so people feel poorer unless, as discussed before, they believe that their tax burden will now fall too. This change in real wealth resulting from this decline in the real value of currency and government debt is called the "real balance effect."

We have now noted a number of different ways in which wealth can change. Wealth based on private property can change in real value if either the expected future value of property income increases or the capital value of a given stream of prospective property income receipts changes. In the short run prospective future property income will change with business-cycle fluctuations. In the long run the accumulation of physical capital tends to increase expected real property incomes. The valuation of property incomes can change if the uncertainty of the outcome changes or if the interest rate falls.

Total real wealth can also be increased by the accumulation of government debt and by the exchange of interest-bearing for non-interest-bearing government debt through open-market operations, while the price level remains unchanged. Finally, a given stock of interest-bearing and non-interest-bearing government debt will decline in value if the price level rises.

It is important to recognize that the price-level factor and the other routes for changing wealth are not independent. The magic of wealth creation by increasing government debt or money supply is limited by the fact that too much of it may raise prices thereby causing a decline in the real value of wealth to offset the increase generated by deficits and open-market operations.

SUMMARY

1. The capital markets perform the task of transferring very large amounts of funds from surplus spending units to deficit ones.
2. On an annual basis over $200 billion of funds pass through the credit market.
3. If we counted the short-term shifts in surplus and deficit positions of individual households, businesses, and governments the amount transferred would be far larger. These transfers involve credit evaluation, collection of monthly payments for mortgage and installment credit, and a good deal of legal work, so they are far from a routine matter.
4. In order to perform the transfer function the markets have to operate in such a way as to match the kind of liabilities borrowers wish to issue with the kind of assets lenders wish to hold. They do this in two ways: 1) by intermediation: liabilities issued by borrowers are held by intermediaries who in turn issue a type of liability more attractive to the lenders; 2) by adjusting the relative yields of different kinds of assets in such a way as to induce borrowers to issue the kind of liabilities lenders want, or to induce lenders to accept the kind of liabilities borrowers want to issue or both.
5. For this to happen interest rates must be flexible and markets for different kinds of securities must be linked together so that all types of securities are competing with one another directly or indirectly.
6. The test of performance is that intrinsically similar kinds of securities should pay similar, risk-adjusted interest rates regardless of their origin.
7. On the whole, U.S. capital markets seem to meet that test. Credit markets are geographically unified so that interest rates are similar throughout the country. Institutional specialization does not create segmented or compartmentalized markets. However, the market for municipal bonds is significantly affected by the differential tax treatment of financial institutions.
8. On the whole, the short-term markets are very well integrated, and so, with certain exceptions, are the long-term markets.
9. The two sets of markets are also closely linked but the relationship between long- and short-term rates is heavily influenced by expectational considerations. There

is also some evidence that the investment specialization of financial institutions does influence the relation between long- and short-term interest rates.

Questions and Exercises

1. All short-term open-market interest rates tend to move up and down together. Why?
2. Treasury bill rates are almost always lower than commercial-paper rates. Explain.
3. Cite some reasons why spreads between Treasury bill and commercial-paper yields may vary from time to time.
4. Markets for short-term securities serve to link together all sectors of the capital market. Explain.
5. Since the volume of new equity issues is relatively small, the stock market's role in the capital markets is really not very important in spite of the attention given to the stock market in the press. Comment.
6. Markets for bonds and mortgages are dominated by financial institutions. Each type of financial institution specializes in certain types of security, therefore, the long-term security markets operate in separate compartments that have little effect on one another. True or False? Explain your answer.
7. What is meant by a *yield curve?*
8. A falling yield curve usually indicates that investors expect bond yields to (a) rise or (b) fall. Choose one and explain.
9. The annual increase in the wealth held by Americans is equal to the annual net saving of businesses, households, and government during the year. True or False? Explain.
10. Does an increase in government debt increase wealth (a) always, (b) sometimes, or (c) never?
11. An open-market operation does not generate wealth. People just exchange bank deposits for government debt. Is this (a) always, (b) sometimes, or (c) never, true?

Further Reading

BAUMOL, WILLIAM J. *The Stock Market and Economic Efficiency*. Fordham University Press, 1965. This study reviews the theory and evidence of the efficiency of the stock market as a means of allocating capital among competing uses.

BOARD OF GOVERNORS OF THE FEDERAL RESERVE SYSTEM. *Joint Treasury–Federal Reserve Study of the U.S. Government Securities Market*. 1969. This is a summary of an exhaustive study of the operations of the market for U.S. government security.

DOUGALL, HERBERT E., and GAUMNITZ, JACK E. *Capital Markets and Institutions*. 3d ed. Englewood Cliffs, N.J.: Prentice-Hall, 1975. This short text describes each of the major capital markets and provides a wealth of detail on the volume of transactions and the decision-making process of the major participants.

FEDERAL RESERVE BANK OF BOSTON. *Financing State and Local Governments*. Conference Series No. 3, 1970. The papers in this volume discuss policy issues relating to the organization of the market for state and local securities and the role of tax-exemption in those markets.

FEDERAL RESERVE BANK OF BOSTON. *Issues in Federal Debt Management.* Conference Series No. 10, 1973. The papers in this volume discuss the number of policy issues relating to the organization of the market for U.S. Treasury securities and the possible effects of alternative and management policies by the Treasury.

FORTUNE, PETER. "Tax-Exemption of State and Local Interest Payments: An Economic Analysis of the Issues and an Alternative." *New England Economic Review,* Federal Reserve Bank of Boston, May/June 1973, pp. 3–20. This paper proposes an alternative to tax-exemption of state and local security and analyzes its implications.

HURTLEY, EVELYN H. "The Commercial Paper Market." *Federal Reserve Bulletin* 63 (June 1977): 523–36. This article explains the organization of the commercial-paper market, reviews the history and outlines the factors accounting for differences in yields on commercial paper and other short-term instruments.

KUZNETS, S. SIMON. *Capital in the American Economy.* National Bureau of Economic Research, New York, 1961. Though out of date in some ways, this volume offers a broad perspective into the history of saving capital formation in the United States.

LIGHT, J. O., and WHITE, WILLIAM L. *The Financial System.* Homewood, Illinois: Richard D. Irwin, Inc., 1979. This volume discusses the organization of the capital markets in terms of the decision-making processes.

MELTON, WILLIAM C. "The Market for Large Negotiable CD's." *Quarterly Review,* Federal Reserve Bank of New York, Winter 1977–78, pp. 22–34. This paper gives a detailed description of the market for commercial bank certificates of deposit. It outlines the organization of the market for each of the major short-term securities.

Central Banking 7

In this chapter we will discuss our own central bank, the Federal Reserve System, in some detail; but before doing so, we have to look more generally at what central banks in developed noncommunist countries do.

THE CENTRAL BANK: A PROFILE

Despite their name, central banks are not "banks" in the same sense as commercial banks. They are governmental, or quasi-governmental, institutions that are not concerned with maximizing their profits, but with achieving certain goals for the entire economy such as the prevention of commercial bank failures, high unemployment, and so on. Central banks, even if in a formal sense owned by private stockholders, carry out governmental functions, and are therefore part of the government.

Origin of Central Banks

Central banks have developed in two ways. One is through a slow process of evolution, the prime example being the Bank of England, which started out as a commercial bank, but acquired over the years the added powers and responsibilities that slowly turned it into a central bank. In this process of evolution it is hard to say when it ceased to be a commercial bank and became a central bank. In contrast to the Bank of England, many central banks did not just grow into central banks but, like the Fed, were central banks right from the start. Such a central bank is from the outset owned de facto by the government, although it may, like the Fed, have private stockholders. When a bank acts as a central bank, that is, determines its actions on the basis of the public interest rather than its stockholders' interest, it operates as a public institution even if the stockholders formally elect all of its chief officers.

PURPOSES AND FUNCTIONS OF CENTRAL BANKS

The two most important functions of central banks are to control the quantity of money and interest rates and to prevent massive bank failures, but they also have certain "chore functions."

Controlling the Money Supply

The reason why we need a central bank was put succinctly by the nineteenth-century British economist and financial journalist Walter Bagehot, when he wrote, "money will not manage itself." Each commercial bank, as it obtains reserves, expands its deposits. With no central bank, the growth rate of deposits and hence of the money stock would depend upon what could be completely arbitrary factors that change bank reserves, and it may differ sharply from the appropriate rate.

Lender of Last Resort

A related reason for having a central bank is the need to guard against bank failures, particularly if there are many relatively small banks. This is not to say that central banks always did prevent widespread bank failures; the Fed certainly did not do so in the 1930s. But a central bank *should* act as a *lender of last resort*, that is, as an institution able and willing to make loans to banks in a crisis when other banks cannot, or will not, do so. The reason the central bank is able to make loans at such a time is that, as we will see in Chapter 10, it has the power to create reserves. (This implies that it is not a profit-making institution; otherwise it would create such reserves also at times when they are not needed and this would be inflationary.) In the United States, one defense against bank failures is, of course, the FDIC, but the Fed stands ready to backstop the FDIC by acting as a lender of last resort. If it were not for this, the threatened failure of a large bank with many deposits above the $100,000 insurance ceiling *might* occasionally set off a run on other banks by big depositors.

Being ready to act as a lender of last resort is an extremely important function of a central bank. It is easy to forget this because potential financial panics arise only rarely. Hence when one looks at the day-to-day activities of a central bank its lender of last resort function seems irrelevant and unimportant. But one can say a similar thing about a fire extinguisher! Don't forget, therefore, that, although a central bank does not *normally* act as a lender of last resort, it must always stand ready to do so, even if it means that it must temporarily abandon other goals such as fighting inflation.

Chore Functions

One set of chore functions consists of services the central bank provides for commercial banks. Thus it acts as a banker's bank, holding most of the reserves of commercial banks. These reserves have no physical existence; they are just entries on the liabilities side of a central bank's balance sheet.

Since the central bank holds reserves for commercial banks it frequently also clears checks for banks.

In addition to its services for commercial banks, a central bank provides many services to the government. Thus it acts as the government's bank. The government keeps an account at the central bank, writes its checks on this account, and, in some countries, sells its securities through the central bank.

Another group of services to the government arises directly out of the central bank's close relation with commercial banks. Thus the central bank typically administers certain controls over commercial banks. For example, the Fed controls bank mergers and examines member banks. In a number of countries the government has imposed controls (so-called exchange controls) over the purchase of foreign assets by its residents, and these controls are often administered by the central bank.

In some countries, in particular the less-developed countries, the central bank also makes loans to the government. And, in fact, a number of central banks—the Bank of England again is the prime example—originally started out as commercial banks that made loans to the government and got certain privileges in exchange. But having the central bank make loans to the government can turn out to be a bad practice because the central bank often cannot deny funds to the rest of the government. And when the government spends these borrowed funds they become additional reserves to commercial banks. Thus the central bank may find itself creating bank reserves, and indirectly, money, not because it believes that the increase in the money stock is desirable, but because it has no choice. To prevent this, in the United States the Fed is not allowed to lend to the Treasury directly. However, what cannot be done openly can be, and is, done indirectly by using the public as an intermediary; the Treasury sells securities to the public, while the Fed buys the same amount of government securities from the public.

Another function of a central bank is to issue currency. In many countries all the currency notes in circulation are issued, that is, placed into circulation, by the central bank, though sometimes the Treasury issues some currency notes as well. Since worn currency notes have to be withdrawn from circulation and new ones issued, this task is far from costless.

The central bank acts as an adviser to the government. Particularly in the area of international finance, governments rely strongly on the advice of their central banks.

Other Aspects of Central Banking

Before leaving the topic of central banks in general there are two items to be discussed: the relation of central banks to the rest of the government, and their ability to create reserves.

Central bank-government relations are complex. Although they are part of the government, central banks maintain a certain detachment from the rest of it. Thus they usually have much more independence from the administration than do such government agencies as the Treasury Department.

Central banks have the power to create reserves. Unless there is a law stating that the central bank must keep, say, 20 cents in gold for each dollar of its outstanding currency notes and deposits, it can create as many reserves for the commercial banks as it wants to. After all, these reserves consist, apart from currency, merely of entries on the central bank's books.

THE FORMAL STRUCTURE OF THE FEDERAL RESERVE SYSTEM

The United States started a central bank only in 1913 when President Wilson signed the Federal Reserve Act. In 1907 an unusually severe financial panic with many bank failures had finally convinced enough people that a central bank was needed. Even then there was much opposition to it because of a fear that Wall Street would be able to use it as a tool to dominate Main Street. The opposition was eventually overcome as it became increasingly clear that a lender of last resort was needed. But, given the great concern that a central bank could lead to a powerful cartel of banks on the one hand, or to political control over banking on the other hand, a careful and elaborate system of checks and balances was written into the Federal Reserve Act.

At its start, the Federal Reserve System was looked upon more as a cooperative enterprise of bankers, whose main function was to pool the previously dispersed reserves of banks, than as a government agency concerned with the goals of high employment and price-level stability. But although its structure has changed less than its functions, the Federal Reserve System we have today is not the system that was originally set up in 1913. It has been changed both by major pieces of legislation, particularly the banking acts of 1933 and 1935, and by the slow evolution in modes of functioning that is a matter of internal organization and practice rather than of statutory change. The Federal Reserve Act of 1913 envisioned a highly decentralized system. Some people even saw the Fed not as a single central bank but as twelve confederated regional central banks. But over the years the Federal Reserve has become more centralized. The twelve regional Federal Reserve Banks, most of all the initially extremely powerful New York Bank, have lost power to the Board of Governors in Washington.

The major features of the Federal Reserve System, however, have not changed. It still consists of twelve Federal Reserve Banks and the Board of Governors.

The Federal Reserve Banks

The locations of the twelve Federal Reserve Banks, and their branches, are shown in Figure 7.1. The assets of various Federal Reserve Banks are far from equal. More than half the assets are held by just three: New York, Chicago, and San Francisco. The New York Bank alone accounts for about 30 percent of all Federal Reserve assets. Apart from its size, the New York Bank is the "first among equals" because its location gives it direct contact with the country's main money market. Hence, it is this Bank that carries out all the purchases and sales of securities on behalf of the whole Federal

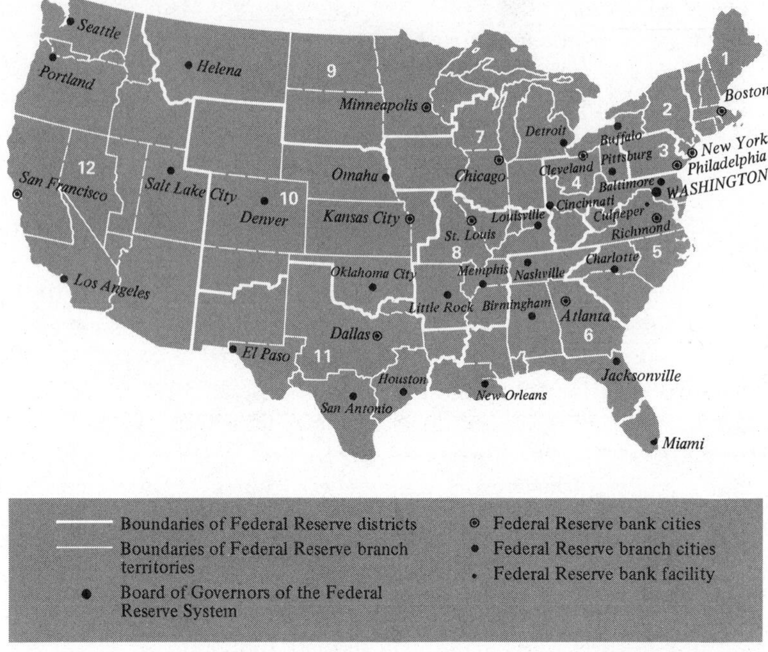

Figure 7.1 Federal Reserve Banks and Their Branches By Location

Source: Federal Reserve Bulletin.

Note: Alaska and Hawaii are in the 12th district.

Reserve System. In addition, it is the Federal Reserve System's contact point in many, though not all, its dealings with foreign central banks and international institutions.

Each of these Federal Reserve Banks is controlled by a board of nine part-time directors. Three of these directors, called class A directors, are elected by the member banks, and are bankers themselves. Member banks also elect three class B directors. These must be people experienced in industry, commerce, or agriculture, and may not be officers, employees, or stockholders of banks. In other words, the three class A directors are balanced by members of business groups that borrow from banks. To prevent domination by any particular size group of banks, member banks are divided into large, medium, and small banks, and each of these groups votes for one class A and one class B director. But actually, neither class A nor class B directors are "elected" in the proper sense of the term since there is usually only a single candidate for each election. Frequently the single candidate for the election as a class B director, and often also the single candidate for the class A directorship, is someone suggested to the banks by the president of that Federal Reserve Bank.

Finally, there are three class C directors. These are not elected by the member banks. They are appointed by the Board of Governors to embody the broader public interest beyond that of banks and their borrowers. One of these class C directors becomes the chairman of the board, and another the vice-chairman.

It is sometimes said that the member banks elect the majority of the Federal Reserve Banks' directors, but this is misleading. When one takes account of the fact that in addition to the appointed class C directors, the president of the Bank often de facto nominates the class B directors, and apparently in many cases even the class A directors, it is more accurate to say that in actuality the Federal Reserve System selects the majority of the directors.

In describing the various classes of directors we were careful to avoid saying that any of the three classes "represents" a particular group, because all directors are supposed to represent the public interest rather than the narrow interests of bankers or borrowers. The public interest, however, is like the proverbial elephant described by the blind men. One's social background, associations, and experience affect one's perception of the public interest.

There have been many complaints that the directors are selected only from "establishment types" and that until recently women and minority groups, as well as labor and consumers, were virtually unrepresented even among the class C directors. Part of this is due to the fact that the main function of the directors is not to make monetary policy, but rather to guide the Bank's president in his administrative work of running the bank, a task in which those with business experience of their own have an obvious advantage. However, by participating in the selection of the Bank's president, and also by informing him of their views on policy, which, however, he is free to ignore, the directors do have some influence on policy, so that the criticism that the directors are unrepresentative cannot be dismissed entirely.

The chief executive officer of each Federal Reserve Bank is its president. He or she is chosen by the directors with the approval of the Board of Governors. In recent years he or she has frequently been someone initially suggested to the directors by the Board of Governors. Most of the recently appointed presidents, unlike most of the directors, have been professional economists.

The Federal Reserve Banks examine member banks, pass on some bank-merger applications, clear checks, withdraw worn currency from circulation, and issue new currency. But, in addition to these chore functions, the Federal Reserve Banks have some policy functions too. Each "sets" a **discount rate,** that is, *the rate the Fed charges on its loans to banks and other depository institutions in its District*. But this rate has to be approved by the Board of Governors, and furthermore, the Board of Governors, by its power to approve or disapprove the existing discount rate, can force a Federal Reserve Bank to change its current rate. Hence, the only real power the Federal Reserve Banks have over the discount rate is the power to advise, and to delay a change in the discount rate for as long as two weeks. However, each Federal Reserve Bank administers its own discount window, that is, under general rules applicable to all Federal Reserve Banks, it makes the particular decision when a bank or other depository institution in its District applies for a loan. A more important policy role of the Federal Reserve Banks is, as will be described later, to participate in the Federal Open Market Committee.

Still another function of the Federal Reserve Banks is to provide the Federal Reserve System with local contacts. Despite the vast amount of information that flows into Washington, statistical data become available only with some delay. However, by talking to local business the Fed is able to obtain some indication of economic developments right away. Another important function of the Federal Reserve Banks is to explain, and justify, Fed actions to the local business community, and thus to generate political support for the Fed. This is an important, though informal, part of the directors' job. Finally, each Federal Reserve Bank has a competent staff of economists who carry out research, not only on local conditions, but also on monetary policy and related problems.

The Board of Governors

At the apex of the Federal Reserve System is the Board of Governors (sometimes called "Federal Reserve Board") located in Washington, D.C. The seven governors are appointed by the President of the United States with the advice and consent of the Senate. They can be removed only for "cause," something that, so far, has never happened. They serve a fourteen-year term and cannot be reappointed after serving a full term, which is supposed to remove them from needing to seek the President's favor, or fearing his threats. In the ideal case all governors serve out their full fourteen-year terms which are staggered. If so, there would be only two vacancies on the Board every four years, so that within a single term a President could not dominate the Board. But the chairman's term, as chairman, though not as a board member, is only four years so that each President can appoint his own chairman. These provisions are examples of the checks and balances built into the Federal Reserve System.

However, not all of them have worked well. Most Board members retire before their full fourteen-year terms are up, sometimes because of age and sometimes for financial reasons. In the period 1960–82, of the twenty-two governors who were appointed, only six—little more than one-quarter—served for as long as seven years. Hence, usually more than two vacancies occur on the Board during any one presidential term. For example, there were four vacancies on the Board during President Carter's first three years in office. Moreover, when a governor resigns the President can, if he wants to, appoint someone to the remaining years of the former governor's term. This not only means that some governors have a less than fourteen-year term, but also that they are then eligible for reappointment to a full term of their own and might therefore be tempted to favor the president's view. The majority of the board members are professional economists, some of whom had previously been staff economists in the Federal Reserve System.

The Board of Governors makes monetary policy; it controls the discount rate and, within limits, can change reserve requirements. Together with other members of the Federal Open Market Committee (FOMC) it controls the most important tool of monetary policy, open-market operations. In addition, its chairman is one of the main economic advisers to the President, as well as to Congress. And governors sometimes also act as U.S. representatives in negotiations with foreign central banks and governments. Beyond this, chairmen frequently press their views on fiscal policy and other economic issues in statements to Congress and to the general public. The Board has a large and competent staff of economists to aid it in this work.

Despite the fact that determining monetary policy is by far the Board's most important task, much of its time is spent on bank regulatory problems. For example, it passes on many bank-merger applications and decides the permissible lines of nonbank activity for bank holding companies. And it administers the laws that prohibit discrimination and untruthful statements in lending. In these activities the Board of Governors' control extends beyond banking to credit in general. Closer to home it exercises some rather loose supervision over the Federal Reserve banks, which have to submit their budgets to the Board for approval.

The Federal Open Market Committee

The focal point for policymaking within the Federal Reserve System is the FOMC, which meets about eight times a year and sometimes holds telephone conferences between meetings. This committee consists of the seven members of the Board of Governors whose chairman is also chairman of the FOMC and five presidents of the Federal Reserve Banks.[1] The Federal Reserve Banks rotate in these five slots on the FOMC except for the New York Bank, which has a permanent slot. However, those Federal Reserve Bank presidents who are not currently members of the FOMC are usually present at its meetings and participate in its discussions, though, of course, they do not vote. But since the FOMC tries to reach a consensus rather than just rely on a majority, their presence, even in a nonvoting capacity, gives all Bank presidents some influence over FOMC decisions.

The FOMC's function is to decide on **open-market operations,** that is, *Federal Reserve purchases and sales of securities*. The FOMC does not carry out security purchases or sales itself. Instead, it issues a directive telling the New York Federal Reserve Bank the open-market policy it should follow for the accounts of all the Federal Reserve Banks. But although the FOMC's power is limited to open-market operations, it provides a forum for discussing the use of all the Fed's tools. Figure 7.2 summarizes the allocation of the Federal Reserve's tools among its various components.

There are some other Federal Reserve components, but they are *much* less important than the FOMC. One is the Federal Advisory Council, which consists of one commercial banker (usually a president of a large commercial bank) from each district. As the name implies, this committee advises the Board of Governors, but that is all. Figure 7.3 summarizes the structure of the Federal Reserve System.

[1] Although the law permits the first vice-president of a Federal Reserve bank to serve on the FOMC in place of its president, this is normally not done, except when a president is unable to attend a meeting.

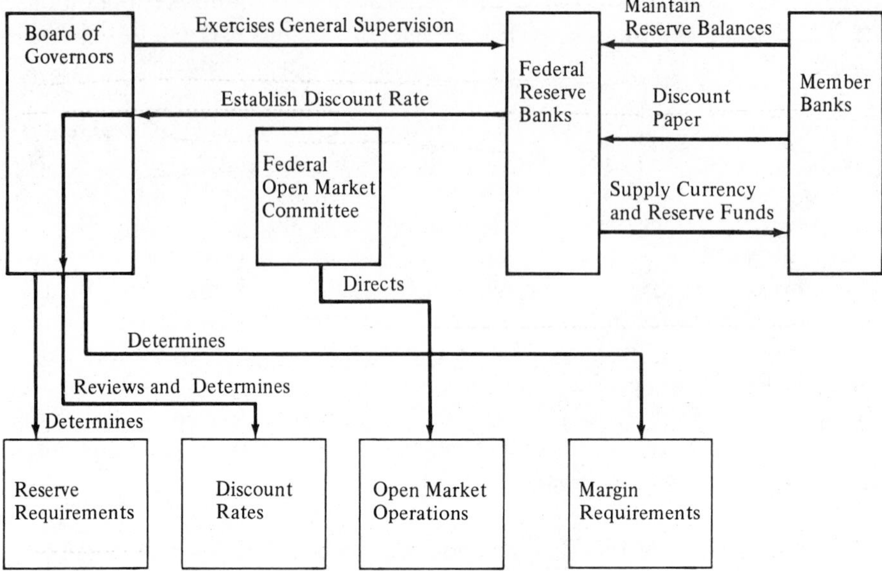

Figure 7.2 Allocation of the Federal Reserve's Tools

Source: Adapted from Board of Governors Federal Reserve System, *The Federal Reserve System, Purposes and Functions* (Washington, D.C., 1974), p. 50.

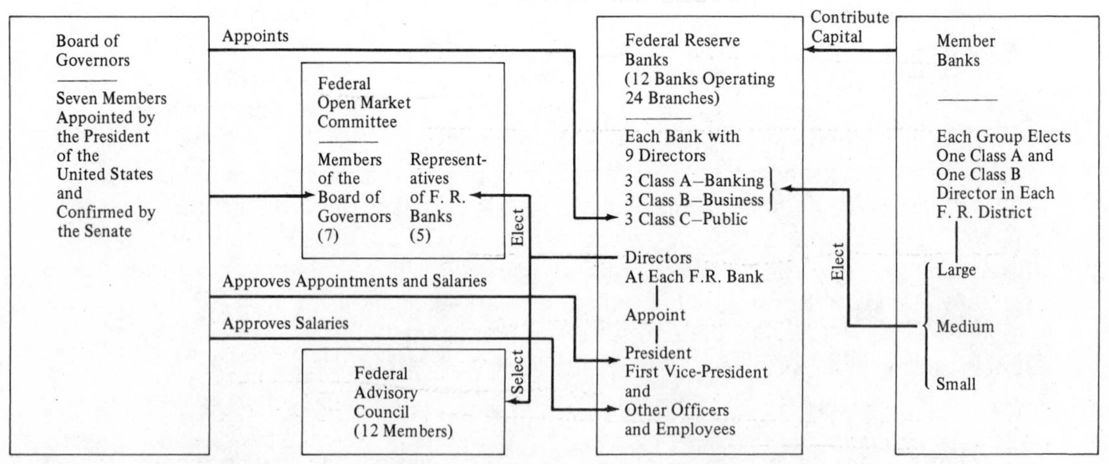

Figure 7.3 The Structure of the Federal Reserve System

Source: Board of Governors, Federal Reserve System, *The Federal Reserve System, Purposes and Functions* (Washington, D.C., 1974), p. 18.

THE INFORMAL STRUCTURE OF THE FEDERAL RESERVE SYSTEM

Merely to know the formal, legal aspects of an organization is rarely sufficient. The Fed, like any organization, has developed certain traditions and other attributes that powerfully affect its operations. These informal aspects are neither definite nor clear-cut. They involved the distribution of power within the Fed, the constituency of the Federal Reserve, and its behavior as a bureaucracy.

Distribution of Power within the Federal Reserve

The distribution of power over monetary policy within the Federal Reserve System and among "outsiders" is, of course, a matter of judgment. However, based on his experience as a Fed governor, Sherman Maisel has given an estimate of the distribution of power, shown in Table 7.1. However, there

Table 7.1 An Estimate of the Distribution of Power Over Federal Reserve Policy

Insiders	Percent	Outsiders	Percent
The chairman	45	The administration	35
Staff of the Board and FOMC	25	Congress	25
Other governors	20	The public directly[a]	20
Federal Reserve Banks	10	Financial interests	10
		Foreign interests	5
		Other regulatory agencies	5
TOTAL	100		100

a. Includes the press, economists, lobbyists, and general public.
Source: Sherman Maisel, *Managing the Dollar* (New York: W. W. Norton, 1973), p. 110.

are two qualifications to Table 7.1. First, the distribution of power cannot be quantified precisely; as Maisel states, "Other knowledgeable persons would certainly draw charts with different weights."[2] For example, one former senior Fed official believes that the chairman has more power than Table 7.1 suggests. Second, the distribution of power depends, in part, on the strength of the personalities involved. For example, a President who takes great interest in monetary policy exercises more influence than one whose main concern is foreign policy. It also depends on the particular issue. The FDIC has more influence on matters like bank capital ratios than it does on monetary policy.

The chairman's power is based on five sources. First, as the head of the Board, his opinions and statements carry great weight with the public. Second, a number of decisions do not even come before the Board, but are taken by the chairman himself as the Board's representative. For example, it is the chairman, and not the whole Board, who meets with the President.

[2] Sherman Maisel, *Managing the Dollar* (New York, W.W. Norton, 1973), pp. 109–11.

Third, the chairman arranges the agenda and exercises the leadership role at the Board's meetings. Fourth, the chairman maintains supervisory powers over the Board's staff members, who therefore have a greater incentive to please him than other Board members. Finally, the foregoing powers of the chairman give him an aura of authority, which tends to induce other board members to vote the way he does.

The Federal Reserve's Constituency

To refer to the Fed's constituency is to use the term in a broader sense than when it is applied to a congressperson's geographic constituency. A government agency tends to view itself as a spokesman for a particular group, and tries to represent this group's interests within the government. In return, the agency receives direct and indirect political support from its constituency. As former Secretary of the Treasury and current Secretary of State George Shultz put it: "Advocacy government is part of our unwritten constitution."[3] An example of this is the Department of Agriculture acting as spokesman for farmers and receiving support from congresspersons elected from rural districts. The Department of Labor has a similar relation to labor unions. This does not mean that these agencies necessarily disregard the public interest; rather the public interest is supposed to emerge as a consensus of the views of various groups as expressed by "their" government agencies. Admittedly, the view of the public interest that does emerge can too often be summarized as "more for me," and the power of various groups is not always appropriate.

It seems plausible that the Fed views itself as having two major, and perhaps two minor, partly overlapping constituencies. One major constituency consists of banks and the financial community. There is a great deal of populist criticism of the Fed for representing financial interests. But it is far from clear that this criticism if valid.

The other major constituency of the Fed is composed of the fixed-income groups who stand to lose by inflation. Several government agencies (such as the Departments of Agriculture and Labor) represent producer groups. Someone should represent those who lose when producers raise their prices, or the government adopts excessively expansionary policies. The Fed has assumed some of this task, at least in the sense of worrying more about inflation than most other government agencies do. Whether or not it has worried sufficiently about inflation, or has become an engine for inflation, is another issue.

Two other, *but* minor, constituencies that the Fed *may* have are the financial press and academic economists. With the Fed being in the news so much it obviously wants to get a favorable reception, by the press and also by academic economists, who, at times, have been sharply critical of it, both in their writings and in their testimony before Congress. But it is hard to say

[3] "Reflections on Political Economy," *Journal of Finance* 29 (May 1974): 325.

to what extent, if any, the Fed's policy has been influenced by its concern about the opinions of these two groups.

The Federal Reserve as a Bureaucracy

Interest groups outside the Fed are not the only beneficiaries of its concern; to a considerable extent it probably also takes good care of its own institutional interests. The modern theory of bureaucracy argues that a government agency is not a Platonic philosopher-king, interested only in the public welfare. It is also concerned with its own survival and prestige, which it can easily rationalize as being indirectly a concern for the public welfare.

Assuming that the Fed is actually concerned with its own strength as an institution, how would one expect it to behave? First, it would, whenever possible, avoid conflicts with powerful people who could harm it. In practical terms this means that, for example, it would be tempted to follow expansionary policies that in the short run would meet Congress's and the administration's wish to keep interest rates down. Second, one would expect it to try to maintain its power and autonomy: to be unwilling, for example, to give up any of its policy tools, even those tools that are not very useful. Third, an organization that is trying to maintain its power and prestige is unlikely to admit that it made mistakes in the past, since to do so may suggest that it could conceivably be making mistakes currently too.

Fourth, a way for an organization to protect itself from criticism is to act myopically, that is, to pay a great deal of attention to the direct and immediate impact of its policies, and to pay too little attention to the longer run or less direct damage these policies may do. This is so because the organization is more likely to be blamed for those bad effects of its policies that are immediately visible and clearly its fault, than for those bad effects that could be the result of many other causes. Finally, the Fed has an incentive to announce vague targets, so that if it misses its target this will not be obvious.[4] In any case, many central bankers tend to think of their task as an art that is practiced better by relying on the intuition of knowledgeable people than on rigorous analysis. For example, the preeminent central banker of the pre-World War II period, Sir Montague Norman, was once asked to state the reason for a decision he had made. He replied: "Reasons, Mr. Chairman? I don't have reasons. I have instincts."[5]

Do central banks in general, and the Fed specifically, really behave in this way? Some economists have argued that this is so, but the subject is still very much open to debate.

Some economists have criticized the Federal Reserve for trying to protect itself against criticism by not making enough information about its actions available to the public. While there may be much truth to this criticism,

[4] A central bank is not the only one who faces this temptation. A student who announces to her parents that her goal this semester is to get all As is taking a bigger risk of disappointing them than another student who announces that his goal is the much more difficult task of transforming himself into a thoughtful and perceptive person.

[5] Quoted in Andrew Boyle, *Montague Norman* (London: Cassel, 1967), p. 327.

compared to foreign central banks, however, the Fed is a veritable chatterbox. In addition to occasional studies, the Board publishes each month the *Federal Reserve Bulletin,* which contains articles on current developments, a record of previous FOMC actions, detailed financial statistics, and so on. And the Federal Reserve Banks issue without charge their own publications containing articles on banking, local economic conditions, and monetary policy.

FINANCES OF THE FEDERAL RESERVE SYSTEM

The outstanding stock of the Federal Reserve Banks is owned by its member banks, who receive a fixed 6 percent dividend on this stock. The fact that the member banks own all the stock of the Federal Reserve Banks is sometimes taken to mean that they own these Federal Reserve Banks. But this is completely misleading. Ownership means two things: the right to appropriate all the net earnings, and the right to control the property. Member banks have no claim on the residual earnings of the Federal Reserve Banks. They get their 6 percent dividend, regardless of the Fed's earnings. Similarly, they have little control over the Federal Reserve Banks, and none over the Board of Governors. Hence, they do *not* control the Fed.

The net earnings of the Federal Reserve Banks come from the securities they hold, and to a much smaller extent from interest on the loans they make. They also earn income by charging financial institutions for the services they perform for them, such as clearing checks. But where do the funds that the Fed invests in securities come from? The main source is the issuance of Federal Reserve notes. Suppose the Fed prints $1 million of Federal Reserve notes and ships them to a bank that asks for them. It then debits that bank's reserve account. If it wants to keep total bank reserves constant it then offsets this by buying $1 million of securities in the open market. Hence, on its books its liabilities for outstanding Federal Reserve notes are up by $1 million, but so are its government security holdings. Apart from this, the Fed can buy securities in a way which is akin to deposit creation by banks. It simply pays for the securities by giving banks credit on their reserve accounts. Similarly, when it makes loans to member banks it just writes up their reserve account.[6]

Out of the earnings on this capital the Fed pays its dividends on member bank stock (which amounted to 0.5 percent of net earnings in 1982). After taking care of these items it places a relatively small amount into its surplus account; the great bulk of net earnings ($12 billion in 1982) is normally turned over to the U.S. Treasury. There is no law requiring the Fed to do this; though if it did not, there would be a law requiring it.

[6]It may seem that when a member bank deposits reserves with the Fed the Fed obtains funds, which it can invest and hence earn interest on. But the total amount of currency and reserves is fixed. Assuming that there is no change in currency held by the public, then the only way one bank can obtain more reserves is for another bank's reserves to decline. Hence, there is no change in the total reserves, and hence in the earning assets, held by the Federal Reserve.

FEDERAL RESERVE INDEPENDENCE

The Fed has a great deal of independence, much more than other government agencies. While the President of the United States with the advice and consent of the Senate appoints new governors as vacancies occur, and chooses his own chairman, once he has made these selections *officially* he does not have any more power over the Federal Reserve; in principle the Fed could ignore his wishes completely. To be sure, in a legalistic sense the Fed is a "creature of Congress," but Congress is neither set up to exercise day-to-day control over it, nor, under present legislation, has it the right to do so. Thus, while the Fed reports its targets for the growth rate of the money stock to Congress, *in principle,* it could ignore any congressional reactions to these targets.

Actual Independence

But, as usual, the formal situation as set forth in legislation is only part of the story. Actually, the President and Congress have considerable influence over the Fed. One source of the President's influence is moral suasion; the governors are reluctant to oppose the views of the one person elected by the whole nation; they go along if they feel they can do so without dereliction of duty. Second, the Fed is continually active in Congress, trying to obtain certain legislation or to block other legislation. It wants the support of the President in these legislative struggles, and hence has an incentive to keep on good terms with him. Third, the chairman wants the President's goodwill, so that when the President appoints a new governor, it will be someone the chairman prefers. Thus, in 1977 one study found:

> The Federal Reserve shifted course in the fundamental sense easing or tightening significantly in 1953, 1961, 1969, 1971, 1974 and 1977. Except for 1971, these were years when the presidency also changed hands; and except for the changeover from President Kennedy to President Johnson, these were the only years when the presidency changed hands. Considering further that the thrust of monetary policy, which began to ease in 1961, eased significantly during Johnson's presidency from its first year (1964) it may be reasonably urged that the dominant guiding force behind monetary policy is the President. Congress plays only a "watchdog role." . . . The historical record shows that in each administration monetary policy fitted harmoniously with the President's economic and financial objectives and plans.[7]

Moreover, to ward off undesired legislation and to obtain the legislation it does want, the Federal Reserve probably bends at least to some extent to congressional pressures. At the same time, the Fed's independence protects Congress from having to make hard choices. Some people think that Congress knows that it can take a politically popular but wrong stand and rely on the Fed to play the role of the "heavy" nay-sayer.

[7]Robert Weintraub, "Congressional Supervision of Monetary Policy," *Journal of Monetary Economics* 4 (April 1978): 349–50. The experience since this was written until now (March 1983) is probably consistent with this.

In general, the Fed cannot take the continuation of its independence for granted. It is to some extent "a prisoner of its independence." It may have to give in on some issues to prevent Congress from taking away some of its independence.

But the influence of the President and Congress should not be overestimated; on some issues the Fed can mobilize an extraordinarily powerful lobby of bankers in each congressional district to pressure Congress into preserving its independence. Congress, by and large, doubts its ability to challenge the Federal Reserve, in part because the Fed claims to possess esoteric knowledge about monetary policy, and to safeguard us from explosive inflation. Moreover, there is usually little political benefit in challenging the Fed.

All in all, as Sherman Maisel has written,

> . . . independence is both ill-defined and circumscribed. . . . Although no legal method exists for the President to issue a directive to the System, its independence in fact is not so great that it can use monetary policy as a club or threat to veto Administration action. The System's latitude for action is rather circumscribed. . . . In any showdown, no nonrepresentative group such as the Fed can or should be allowed to pursue its own goals in opposition to those of the elected officials.[8]

INDEPENDENCE: PROS AND CONS

Does the Fed have too much or too little independence? From time to time this question becomes a political issue, and it *may* sooner or later become a major issue in a presidential election. Political debates about the Fed's independence do not result so much from fundamental disagreements about the proper role of the Fed in the government (an issue that evokes little public excitement). Instead they occur because of strong disagreement about the policy that the Fed is following. One way to change this policy is to bring the Fed under the control of those in Congress or the administration who oppose this policy. Another way is to frighten the Fed enough so that it will change its policy. Thus in 1982 several bills to reduce the Fed's independence gained powerful support in Congress. Shortly thereafter the Fed changed its policy, *perhaps* in part because of these threats.

We will discuss the pros and cons of monetary policies in Part Four. Here we just discuss more general arguments about the Fed's independence. Although these arguments sound abstract and philosophical they are relevant to what may soon become a major political issue.

The Case for Independence

There are several arguments on both sides of the independence issue. Supporters of independence argue that monetary policy, and hence the value of the dollar, is too important and too complex an issue to be left to the play of political forces. As a former chairman of the Board, William McChesney Martin, put it:

[8] Sherman Maisel, *Managing the Dollar,* pp. 24, 136.

> An Independent Federal Reserve System is the primary bulwark of the free enterprise system and when it succumbs to the pressures of political expediency or the dictates of private interest, the ground work of sound money is undermined.[9]

In this view the political process is myopic: being overly concerned with the next election, it overplays the importance of short-term benefits, and hence is unwilling to make those hard and unpopular decisions—such as tolerating more unemployment in the short run—that are needed to obtain the long-run benefits of a stable price level. Moreover, politicians, if they can, are likely to use the central bank to finance increased government expenditures without raising taxes. In addition, pressure groups impart an inflationary bias to government policy. Hence an independent central bank largely removed from political pressures is needed to ensure justice to those who lose from inflation. Anyone familiar with the case for a gold standard will probably see a similarity with the argument that the gold standard guards against unwise inflationary actions.

Another variant of this argument puts it in terms of a "*political business cycle*." Before an election the government is tempted to adopt too expansionary a monetary policy, which results in lower interest rates and lower unemployment just before the election. The resulting inflation and rising nominal interest rates then occur only after the election. At that point the government adopts restrictive policies, which it hopes the public will have forgotten by the time of the next election.

The Case against Independence

Critics of central bank independence reject these arguments. They believe that it is fundamentally undemocratic to say that elected officials should not be trusted to judge monetary policy. To be sure, monetary policy involves difficult decisions that need a long-run point of view, but the same thing is true of foreign policy or defense policy. Moreover, for better or worse, the public holds the President responsible for the economic conditions that result from *all* the policies followed during his administration. Hence, he should have control over monetary policy, one of the most important of these policies.

In addition, some economists maintain that the Fed has not used its independence well and therefore should be deprived of it. At times it has tolerated inflation, as in the late 1960s and 1970s, and in other years, the 1930s, for example, it has had a deflationary bias and allowed too much unemployment to develop. In addition, its independence has not really removed it from politics. Instead, it has had to become a political animal in order to defend both its actions and its independence. Moreover, its independence allows the Fed too much leeway to indulge in that characteristic weakness of a bureaucracy, continuous overemphasis of narrow, parochial interests.

[9] Quoted in A. Jerome Clifford, *The Independence of the Federal Reserve System* (Philadelphia: University of Pennsylvania Press, 1965), p. 18.

Finally, monetary and fiscal policies should be integrated, and adequate integration cannot be achieved, the opponents of Fed independence claim, merely by a process of informal consultation. Rather it requires that the Fed be part of the administration. Giving the President control over the Fed need not necessarily weaken its influence, but might even strengthen it. If it were part of the administration, the Fed's counsel would then be better heeded by the administration.

Possible Compromises

These pro and con arguments may give the misleading impression that the choice is between two irreconcilable extremes. But this is not so. Even if the Fed were to lose its formal independence, and become a part of the administration, there would still be at least an attempt to keep it out of partisan politics. Moreover, as just pointed out, the independence that the Fed currently has is far from complete.

On a more practical level, the relevant debate does not deal with such "fundamental" issues as the Fed's complete independence, but focuses on proposals for relatively minor reductions in its independence. For example, one proposal would make the chairman's term of office coincide better with the president's so that each president could appoint his own chairman a year after he took office. Other proposals would shorten the terms of the governors or eliminate the FOMC and shift its work to the Board of Governors. A more radical proposal would put the Secretary of the Treasury on the FOMC, and an even more radical one would make the Fed turn all its gross earnings over to the Treasury and to finance its activities through congressional appropriations. This would give Congress much more control over it.

SUMMARY

1. Central banks are not "banks" in the conventional sense; they are institutions concerned with managing the money stock, preventing financial panic by acting as lenders of last resort, and with other governmental tasks. Many of them originated as commercial banks, but over time have assumed governmental functions.
2. Central banks perform services, such as holding reserves and check clearing for banks, and also act as the government's bank, doing such chores as issuing currency. Central banks can create reserves for the banking system.
3. The Federal Reserve System has become more centralized since its establishment in 1913. Its current organization is shown in Fig. 7.3.
4. Each Federal Reserve Bank has nine directors chosen in a way that provides checks and balances. While formally the Federal Reserve Banks are "owned" by member banks, this does not give member banks ownership in any meaningful sense. These Federal Reserve Banks carry out most of the operating chores of the System, and have a limited influence on monetary policy.
5. The Board of Governors consists of seven members appointed by the President. Together with five Reserve Bank presidents, they serve on the Federal Open Market Committee. This Committee controls the Fed's most important tool, open-market operations.

6. Within the Federal Reserve, the chairman has a great deal of power; among outsiders, the Administration and Congress have the most power over the Fed. The major constituencies of the Fed are the financial community and fixed income groups. The Fed also has its own interests in preserving its power and independence.
7. The Fed finances its activities from charges for its services and from interest earnings.
8. The Fed's independence is circumscribed. Historically it has gone along with the President's overall views on monetary policy. There are numerous arguments for and against Fed independence.

Questions and Exercises

1. The term *central bank* is a misnomer; it is nothing like a bank. Discuss the extent to which this statement is true for the Federal Reserve System.
2. Why do countries have central banks?
3. What does the term *lender of last resort* mean?
4. Discuss the chore functions of the Federal Reserve.
5. What monetary policy functions are carried out by
   a. the Federal Reserve Banks,
   b. the Board of Governors,
   c. the FOMC?
6. Critically discuss: "The Federal Reserve Banks have nothing at all to do with monetary policy; they only undertake the chore functions of the Federal Reserve System."
7. The Federal Reserve System is an example of a system of "checks and balances." Describe these checks and balances.
8. What does it mean to say that the Federal Reserve has constituencies? What are they?

Further Reading

ACHESON, KEITH, and CHANT, JOHN. "Bureaucratic Theory and the Choice of Central Bank Goals: The Case of the Bank of Canada." *Journal of Money, Credit and Banking* 5 (May 1973): 637–56. A pioneering application of bureaucratic theory to central bank behavior.

GALBRAITH, JOHN A. *The Economics of Banking Operations*. Montreal: McGill University Press, 1963. Chapter Seven gives a useful and compact discussion of central banking.

KANE, EDWARD. External Pressures and the operations of the Fed," in Raymond Lombra and Williard Witte (eds.). *The Political Economy of Domestic and International Monetary Relations*. Iowa City, Iowa: University of Iowa Press, 1982. A superb discussion of the Fed as a political animal.

———. "The Re-Politization of the Fed." *Journal of Financial and Quantitative Analysis* 9 (November 1974): 743–52. An important contribution to the debate about the Fed's independence.

MAISEL, SHERMAN. *Managing the Dollar*. New York: W. W. Norton, 1973. Provides important insights into Fed behavior by a former member of the Board of Governors.

MAYER, THOMAS. "The Structure and Operation of the Federal Reserve System: Some Needed Reforms." In U.S., Congress, House Committee on Banking, Currency, and Housing, *Compendium of Papers Prepared for the Fine Study*. 94th Cong., 2d sess., 1976, 2: 669–726. A survey of the Fed's organization with proposals for changes.

WEINTRAUB, ROBERT. "Congressional Supervision of Monetary Policy." *Journal of Monetary Economics* 4 (April 1978): 341–63. An important discussion of the extent to which the Fed is actually independent.

Financial Evolution 8

So far we have dealt with the financial system as it now is. But many of the interesting problems relate to *changes* in the system. It would therefore be appropriate at this point to present a theory of financial evolution. Unfortunately, we do not have such a theory. Hence, what we do instead in this chapter is to describe and attempt to explain some recent financial changes. The purpose of this is to provide a feel for how the financial system adapts, or fails to adapt, to certain shocks. In addition, this chapter also discusses certain proposed reforms that may be enacted in the future.

THE INCENTIVES FOR CHANGE

As a starting point consider a financial system that is in full equilibrium. It makes efficient use of existing technology which remains unchanged. Consumer tastes and incomes are constant. The quantities of financial assets are in accord with their relative prices, such as the interest rate, which is the relative price of a dollar now compared to next year. In the political arena the power of those who would gain from changes in laws and regulations is balanced by the power of those who would lose from such changes. Under such conditions the financial system remains unchanged. But a mere listing of these conditions shows that change is likely.

But while change is normal, since the mid-1960s the financial structure has changed at an unusually rapid pace. One reason for this is technological innovation. The computer revolution has greatly reduced the cost of transferring funds between various types of assets. For example, if all entries had to be recorded manually into ledgers, then money market funds would have to levy higher charges, and hence be less popular.

Another cause of the rapid change has been the great rise in interest rates. Three-month Treasury bill rates, which averaged 2.7 percent in 1960–

62, averaged 12.1 percent in 1980–82. If interest rates on all assets would have risen equally this would not have provided an incentive to shift from certain assets to others, or to develop new types of assets. But not all interest rates did rise equally. No explicit interest is paid on demand deposits, and Regulation Q held down the interest rate on savings and time deposits. This provided a strong incentive to switch out of such deposits into other assets, and to invent new types of assets that would provide the services of deposits but would escape interest rate regulations. At the same time there was a shift in political power as a political association of the elderly, the Grey Panthers, joined those who fought to eliminate the Regulation Q ceiling.

The opportunity for profitable financial innovation therefore existed, and the response was not long in coming. If banks cannot pay interest on demand deposits how about paying interest on something that functions just like a demand deposit, but can pay interest because legally it is not a demand deposit? Hence a savings bank had the clever idea of allowing its depositors to pass on to other people (and thus use just like a check) its orders of withdrawal, similar to those used to withdraw currency. The Negotiable Order of Withdrawal (NOW account) was born.[1] In the meantime other entrepreneurs developed the money market mutual fund, an institution that grew rapidly until 1983 when it declined again.

Depository institutions had to meet this competition from money market funds. To do this some used "sweep accounts." In these accounts deposits above a certain agreed-upon level were automatically swept into a money market fund so that they could earn interest. In addition, many institutions used the repurchase agreement mechanism, whereby they automatically "sold" a security to the depositor who had excess funds in his demand deposit.

By the early 1980s the regulation prohibiting explicit interest payments on demand deposits was in shambles. Small depositors had their NOW accounts and larger depositors their sweeps and repurchase agreements. And both had their money market funds. As money market funds run by stock brokers allowed their customers to write even small checks against their money market accounts, banks and thrift institutions faced even more competition. The law prohibiting interest payments on demand deposits had not been repealed; instead it had been made more or less irrelevant by the market. This is a familiar story; lobbies have enough political strength to block needed changes in the law, but they lack clout in the marketplace.

The same factors that were making the prohibition of interest payments on demand deposits ineffective were also undermining the Regulation Q ceilings on interest rates paid on time deposits. Thrift institutions were therefore in serious trouble.

[1] NOW accounts started in Massachusetts and New Hampshire where savings banks have available a state deposit insurance system, and hence can avoid being subject to FDIC regulations. To protect the competitive position of financial institutions in other New England states the federal regulators had to allow institutions in these states to have NOW accounts too. They then had to permit them in New York, and finally nationwide.

ALTERNATIVE POLICIES

The obvious solution would seem to be to repeal Regulation Q and have thrift institutions pay a competitive rate of return. But, as discussed in Chapter 5, their earnings on mortgages, made when interest rates were lower, did not suffice to pay the higher interest rates required to stay competitive when interest rates rose. There is no simple solution to this problem. The basic mistake was made many years ago when we developed a financial structure based on the assumption that there would be little or no inflation, so that interest rates would stay fairly low. Until the 1960s this assumption seemed reasonable, but this does not help matters now. As it became clear that something had to be done a number of remedies were tried, mostly in the hope that with a bit of patchwork the system could survive long enough either for thrifts to get rid of their old low-yielding mortgages or for market interest rates to come down again.

Price Discrimination

One possible way for the thrifts to compete more effectively for deposits without an excessive increase in their interest costs is to use more price discrimination. Not all deposits are equally sensitive to interest rate competition. A depositor keeping five hundred dollars in a savings deposit for one year might not find it worthwhile to learn about other assets, or to buy money market fund shares. By contrast, someone who is considering how to hold $10,000, for, say, five years, should certainly be concerned about the interest rate differential. If a money market fund pays 5 percent more than a deposit this differential amounts to $2,500 over the five years. The obvious strategy for the thrift industry is therefore to have the regulators set a higher rate on large, and on longer term savings than on other savings.

This strategy was followed extensively; thus, in 1978, mutual savings banks and savings and loans were allowed to offer six month $10,000 *money market certificates* paying one quarter of one percent more than the Treasury bill rate. Subsequently they were allowed to issue longer term deposits with similarly floating rates. But to some extent such a policy of price discrimination is self-defeating. As floating rate deposits are extensively advertised depositors become more aware of the interest rate differential, and hence less willing to hold low-yielding deposits. By March 1980, when, as will be discussed shortly, the law was changed, money market certificates accounted for about 30 percent of all savings and loan deposits. Moreover, such price discrimination not only creates inefficiencies, but is unfair since it discriminates against those who do not have $10,000 available.

Maturity Matching

Another solution is to get rid of what caused the problem in the first place, a mismatch of the maturities of assets and liabilities. Suppose that savings and loans had financed their mortgage portfolio, not by issuing short-term deposits but had, instead, issued liabilities with maturities equal to those of their mortgages. In this case they could afford to pay a competitive rate of interest to *new* depositors and finance this by their earnings on *new* mortgages. Old depositors would simply be stuck with a lower rate the same way as are those who, say, twenty years ago bought bonds. Such a lengthening of the maturity of liabilities actually occurred for some time as savings deposits declined relative to CDs. However, the growth of six-month money market certificates, money market accounts, and Super-NOWs worked to shorten maturities again.

Alternatively, one could shorten the maturity of the thrifts' assets so that if the interest rates they have to pay depositors rise then, with only a relatively short lag, the interest rate they receive on their assets rises too. One way of doing this would be to shorten the maturity of mortgage loans, say to five years. Such short mortgage loans were prevalent in the 1920s in the U.S. and are widely used in Canada. Borrowers would usually "repay" the mortgage loan by taking out another loan at the then prevailing interest rate.

A number of mortgage instruments have recently been developed that represent to some extent a return to the short-maturity mortgage. These are variable interest rate mortgages, which are long term in the sense that the loan is repaid over, say, twenty years, but their interest rate varies from time to time, along with some other interest rate such as the cost of funds to savings and loans.

There is much opposition to variable rate mortgages. Opponents claim that they shift the risk of interest rate fluctuations onto households who cannot predict what their mortgage costs will be in the future. However, this argument confuses nominal and real interest rates. Sharp increases in nominal interest rates are *usually* the result of sharp increases in the inflation rate and—on the whole—household income, and hence the ability to pay mortgage interest rises along with the inflation rate. If a 5 percent increase in the inflation rate raises the nominal interest rate on a variable interest mortgage from 10 percent to 15 percent, then the real rate of interest on the mortgage is constant. (In fact, the after-tax real rate has fallen because homeowners who itemize deductions can deduct interest paid from income subject to tax.) By contrast, on a so-called fixed rate mortgage the real rate falls when the inflation rate rises.

This does not mean that variable rate mortgages, or short-term mortgages, present no problems. While average household income may rise along with the inflation rate, any particular household may find that its money income increases much less, and with a variable rate mortgage, mortgage interest therefore takes a larger share of its income. Moreover, nominal interest rates do not always move in unison with the inflation rate. Thus the inflation rate fell from 12.4 percent in 1980 to 8.9 percent in 1981, a 3.5 percent drop, while the three-month Treasury bill rate *rose* by 2.6 percent. Furthermore, variable rate mortgages are complex, and some borrowers may not fully understand what they are getting into.

Finally, variable rate mortgages do nothing to resolve a very serious problem. This is that borrowers are repaying their mortgage loans at a faster than desired rate. Suppose that the inflation rate is 10 percent, while the mortgage rate is 15 percent, and that a family takes out a 90 percent mortgage on a $100,000 home. At the end of the year the value of the house has risen to $110,000 so that, disregarding the repayment made on the mortgage during the year, the mortgage is now equivalent to only 82 percent of the value of the house ($90,000 ÷ $110,000) compared to the previous 90 percent. The family has thus been forced by inflation to repay (through its 15 percent interest payments) 8 percent of the value of the house during this year.

This problem of fast repayment is avoided by another type of mortgage that keeps monthly interest payments constant as the inflation rate and interest rate rise, by increasing the outstanding amount of the mortgage. Another type of mortgage, the graduated payments mortgage, starts with low monthly payments which rise over time. But such mortgages have the problem that at times the value of the mortgage may exceed the (depreciated) value of the house, so that the borrower may be tempted to walk away from the mortgage and let the lender take over the property. Moreover, these contracts are complex and may confuse the borrower.

Greater use of variable rate or shorter term mortgages are not the only way in which to reduce the maturity of thrift institution assets. Another possibility is to lift the restrictions that limit the consumer and business loans that thrift institutions may make. Since such loans have a much shorter maturity than do mortgage loans, thrift institutions could lower the average maturity of their portfolios by shifting partly out of mortgage loans into business and consumer loans. This has much support among economists who prefer a free market solution to government fiat. And in 1982 thrift institutions were given more (but still limited) power to make consumer and business loans.[2]

There is much opposition to giving them further power to make business loans by those who are afraid that this would substantially reduce the volume of mortgage loans. But there are some offsetting factors. First, if thrift institutions shift from mortgage loans to business loans and mortgage interest rates rise relative to interest rates on business loans, some other lenders will shift into mortgage loans. Moreover, as thrift institutions earn more on business loans they will attract more deposits, so that the amount available for mortgage loans *might* actually increase. Third, even if mortgage funds become less available and mortgage interest rates rise, residential construction may not be reduced very much. If mortgage rates rise potential homebuyers can obtain funds in other ways, for example, by selling some of the securities they own. Finally, would a decline in residential construction really be so bad? To be sure, we want additional housing, but we also want additional business capital.

In any case, neither making variable rate mortgages nor getting permission to make more business and consumer loans helps thrifts with their *immediate* problem, which is large volume of old low-yielding mortgages in

[2]The extent to which savings and loans will take advantage of these powers is unclear, because special provisions of the tax law give them an incentive to keep no more than 15 percent of their assets in a form other than residential mortgages and federal securities.

their portfolios. Policies to shorten asset maturities in the future are a bit like throwing a drowning man a free ticket to swimming lessons.

Eliminating Regulation Q

This is, of course, the most fundamental solution. But it was strongly opposed by the thrift industry, in large part because Regulation Q gave it a great competitive advantage over commercial banks; on most types of deposits thrift institutions could pay a one-quarter percent higher interest rate than commercial banks. All the same, the elimination of Regulation Q is appealing to anyone who believes in free markets. It eliminates disintermediation and the resulting rationing of mortgage credit that distorts resource allocation. It also gets rid of much excessive nonprice competition and of discrimination against small depositors. On the other hand, if the elimination of Regulation Q means that deposit rates substantially exceed the rate that thrift institutions earn on their mortgages, then either there are massive failures or else the government has to subsidize thrift institutions.

FINANCIAL REFORM

Thus every solution has its problems. But something *had* to be done, and in 1980 and 1982 there were important financial reforms. But before considering their specifics it is useful to look at some underlying factors.

Background

In the 1970s the average inflation rate was close to 7½ percent, and as a result interest rates rose substantially. This made obsolete many financial laws and regulations which had been adopted on the assumption of relatively low interest rates. One of these, Regulation Q, has already been discussed. Another one is the prohibition of explicit interest payments on demand deposits. As long as the interest rate was, say, 2 percent, this regulation was not so disruptive. But when interest rates rose into the double digits, the prohibition of interest on checkable deposits led to inefficiencies. It provided a strong incentive to hold fewer demand deposits, even though this meant spending more resources on managing one's cash balance; such as a corporation hiring someone to monitor its cash balance continuously. In addition, banks competed for customers by providing a greater range of free services than is consistent with efficiency. Many customers would have preferred to get interest instead of some of the free services.

Moreover, as interest rates rose it became more expensive for member banks to keep reserves with the Federal Reserve on which they earned no interest. Hence, many banks left the Fed.

Still another problem arose in many states due to their usury laws. At a time of no inflation, when the interest rate on Treasury bills is, say, 3 percent, an interest rate of 12 percent seems very high, but if the inflation rate is 12 percent too, and the Treasury bill rate is 15 percent, a usury law ceiling of 15 percent on personal loans means that few families can find someone willing to lend to them. The obvious solution is to raise the usury law ceiling. But voting for this ceiling can be costly for politicians.

These problems did not arise all of a sudden. The plight of the thrift institutions created a crisis already in 1966 when for the first time the Regulation Q ceiling was made seriously restrictive. Interest rates started to rise in the late 1960s. But financial reform was long delayed. This should not be surprising. As Donald Hester has written:

> Historically, American monetary reforms have almost always been the result of unusually severe failures of the financial system or of war. The two early national banks surely facilitated war debt finance; and the National Banking Act was obviously a consequence of the Civil War. A series of sharp financial crises led to the founding of the Federal Reserve System, and most other major agencies regulating financial institutions emerged during the Depression. . . .
>
> The very pessimistic conclusion is that enlightened preventive maintenance of the financial mechanism is unlikely to occur. To be sure, legislation affecting financial institutions will be enacted, but it is likely to be the outcome of smoky cloakrooms and take the form of inadequately illuminated riders.[3]

There are several reasons for this. One is that, while it may be easy to get agreement that some change is needed it is much harder to agree on exactly what the change should be. But a much bigger obstacle is that any meaningful reforms take something away from some industries that won't sit still for this. And some industries, such as the building industry-savings and loan "complex," have great political power. Hence, unless there is a strong countervailing constituency for financial reform Congress is not likely to accept any reforms such powerful industries oppose.[4] Imagine that a senator votes for a bill strongly opposed by banks and savings and loan associations. There are a very large number of these in his or her state, and their managers may now support the opposition candidate. And what countervailing support does the senator get in exchange? Will the general public be much influenced by a vote on a perhaps obscure piece of legislation dealing with an issue most voters think is too complex for them to understand? Moreover, many voters look upon bankers as being specially knowledgeable in this area, so that bankers' opposition is likely to cost dearly. Besides, change generates uncertainty, and people like things the way they are.

What *does* help the cause of reform is that there are potential gainers as well as losers. For example, banks lose if thrift institutions are allowed to make consumer loans, but thrift institutions obviously gain. One might therefore expect that the political pressures from potential gainers and losers would more or less cancel out, and that the issue can be decided on its

[3] Donald Hester, "Special Interests: The FINE Situation," *Journal of Money, Credit and Banking* 9 (November 1977): 653–55.

[4] Should one blame Congress for heeding the "special interests" and not the objective economists who propose reform? *Perhaps not*. Put yourself in the position of a senator who is told by an academic economist that a certain proposal would raise public welfare, and by a lobbyist that it would seriously hurt his industry. Public welfare should certainly be put in first place, but the economist talking about what would increase it may well be wrong. On the other hand, the lobbyist, though perhaps exaggerating, is not likely to be wrong in saying that his industry would be hurt since it is much easier to judge impacts on an industry than on the whole economy.

merits. But this is usually not the way it works. Various types of financial institutions have enough power to keep others out of their turf, but not enough to invade the others' turf.

The obvious solution for such a situation where each pressure group can hold its own territory is to present a reform package that allows these groups to make trades. Several such packages were tried during the 1970s, but never passed Congress.

THE DEPOSITORY INSTITUTIONS DEREGULATION AND MONETARY CONTROL ACT (DIDMCA)

But in March 1980 financial reform finally arrived. The immediate reason for the passage of DIDMCA was that the courts had invalidated certain powers that depository institutions had been given under an interpretation of the old law. The only way to preserve these powers was to change the law, which meant that the various types of depository institutions were forced to reach agreement on a compromise package. In any case, Regulation Q was becoming less and less effective. With depositors switching to money market certificates, thrift institutions were paying approximately the market rate of interest on a rapidly growing share of their deposits.[5] And had the government tried to "cap" the interest rate on money market certificates, thrift institutions would have suffered a substantial outflow of funds in large part to the money market funds. At the same time organizations representing depositors were putting political pressure on Congress. All in all, it was becoming less and less feasible to exploit depositors. In addition, the inflation rate was accelerating sharply. This gave Congress an incentive to overrule the banking industry, and to give the Federal Reserve the control over the reserve requirements of nonmember banks that it claimed it needed for effective monetary control.

DIDMCA provided for an end to Regulation Q. It established a committee, the Depository Institutions Deregulation Committee, consisting of the secretary of the Treasury and the heads of the federal agencies regulating depository institutions. This committee was instructed to phase out Regulation Q in an orderly fashion by 1986. However, it must proceed with due regard for the safety and soundness of thrift institutions. Since any rise in the ceilings threatens some thrift institutions this is a hard task. Not surprisingly, while the committee has been criticized by the savings and loan industry for moving too fast, others have criticized it for moving too slowly.

Another important provision of DIDMCA (and we can only discuss the important ones) permitted nationwide NOW accounts, thus ending the anomaly that federal law allows such accounts in some states but not in others. It also set aside a court decision that had invalidated automatic transfer accounts and remote terminals of savings and loan associations.

In addition, it eased certain restrictions on the mortgage loans of savings and loans, and gave them permission to invest up to 20 percent of their

[5] In 1977 deposits with a fixed interest ceiling accounted for 87 percent of the total liabilities of thrift institutions; by 1981 they accounted for only 26 percent.

assets in consumer loans, commercial paper, and corporate securities. Mutual savings banks also received permission to make business loans up to 5 percent of their assets subject to certain geographic restrictions.

Another important provision eliminated state usury law ceilings on mortgage loans, and for a three-year period let the usury ceilings for other loans fluctuate along with the Fed discount rate.[6] In addition, as described in Chapter 4, reserve requirements were lowered, but extended to cover all transactions accounts and nonpersonal time deposits, and the Federal Reserve was ordered to charge for its services but to extend its lending to all depository institutions keeping reserves with it. And the deposit insurance ceiling was raised from $40,000 to $100,000.

FROM DIDMCA TO THE DEPOSITORY INSTITUTIONS ACT OF 1982

DIDMCA was a great step forward, but did not solve the whole problem. With the Regulation Q ceiling being phased out rather slowly money market funds were still growing at the expense of thrift institutions. Moreover, thrift institutions were meeting increasing competition for deposits from banks. But while the phase-out of Regulation Q was not proceeding fast enough to protect the deposit base of thrift institutions it was too fast to protect the thrift earnings. In 1981 and 1982 they were paying a higher rate on deposits than they were earnings on their assets. As a result of these losses their net worth fell. In 1975 insured savings and loans had a ratio of net worth to total assets of 5.8 percent. By September 1982 this ratio had fallen to 3.4 percent. In mid-1982 more than one-sixth of all savings and loans had a net worth ratio below 2 percent, which is about the minimum required by the Federal Home Loan Bank Board. Help was needed.

And in October 1982 the (Garn-St. Germain) Depository Institutions Act did provide such help. To permit depository institutions to compete better with money market funds they were allowed to offer the money market accounts (described in Chapter 4) which can offer an interest rate competitive with money market funds.[7] In addition it provided that by the beginning of 1984 the Regulation Q ceiling be the same for thrift institutions as for banks.

To deal with the immediate emergency, the FDIC and the FSLIC were given expanded powers to merge failing institutions into sound ones. They could, if necessary, merge institutions across states lines and, if necessary, even merge thrift institutions into banks. To prevent failures from occuring troubled savings and loans were offered what are in effect loans from the

[6] States were given the right to override these usury law provisions if they acted by April 1, 1983. Thus these usury law changes did not really take power away from the states, but allowed them to ease their usury laws without the state legislators having to vote for it.

[7] In the meantime several states have allowed their state chartered banks to own money market funds. The Garn-St. Germain Act also eliminated reserve requirements for the first $2 million of reservable deposits, and it overrode state laws that had invalidated "due on sale clauses." (These are provisions in mortgage contracts that make the mortgage fall due when the property is sold.)

FSLIC on which they have to pay interest only if they have net earnings. If they fail the FDIC takes a loss. Obviously this amounts to a substantial subsidy.

Apart from the Garn-St. Germain Act savings and loans were also given other help. The Federal Home Loan Bank Board lowered the required net worth ratio, and several accounting changes were authorized that allow savings and loans under certain conditions to increase the net worth shown on their books even though their actual net worth is unchanged.

But what helped thrift institutions even more is that interest rates declined, thus reducing the basic problem they faced. However it is far from clear whether this means that the problem is solved. First, interest rates may rise again, and second, over time as the public shifts out of passbook savings accounts into money market accounts thrift institutions will face higher interest costs.

Money market funds are not the only intruders on the banks' terrain. Nondepository institutions, and even nonfinancial corporations, have also moved in. For example, American Express, which is the leading credit card company and is the biggest seller of travelers checks, owns a large overseas bank, as well as a big brokerage house that has a money market fund. Sears Roebuck has bought a large brokerage firm with a money market fund, and is thus set up to collect what are, in effect, deposits in its numerous retail stores. Given the size of Sears (it has almost 25 million active credit cards outstanding) banks are afraid of this type of competition. Indeed, Citicorp, the largest bank holding company, is said to be toying with the idea of spinning off its domestic banking operations, so that it will be able to compete with other firms unhindered by the regulatory restrictions that are imposed on banks but not on other firms. Some firms like Household Finance have indeed bought banks, and then sold off their loan portfolios so that they are not legally defined as banks, and hence not subject to various regulations such as the prohibition on interstate branching. Not surprisingly, this development caused much concern. Brokerage firms have used this device so that they can offer accounts that have FDIC insurance. Thus in early 1983 the FDIC announced that it was considering new regulations that would reduce the intrusion of other firms into banking. William Isaac, the FDIC chairman stated:

> Sears, Roebuck and National Steel both own federally insured savings and loans which now have commercial lending powers and checking authority. In other words, they are banks. In my judgment a bank shouldn't own a steel company. Why should a steel company be permitted to own a federally insured savings and loan?[8]

THE REGULATORY STRUCTURE

Another problem is the way depository institutions are regulated. Commercial banks and mutual thrift institutions can decide whether to operate under a federal or a state charter. For example, in 1979 when the New York State

[8] *New York Times,* January 28, 1983, p. 31.

banking commissioner did not permit a large bank, Marine Midland, to merge into a foreign bank, the Hong Kong and Shanghai Banking Corp., Marine Midland simply handed in its state charter and took out a national charter instead. Not only can a bank decide its chartering agency, but a state bank can also choose whether or not to be a member bank. Giving banks the right to decide whether they want to abide by the stricter federal regulations, or by the generally more relaxed state regulations, may seem strange.

Not only can banks choose their supervising agencies, they can play one off against the other. Many economists believe that since the regulatory agencies do not want to lose banks from their supervision, they compete among themselves for banks by limiting the severity of their regulations. This "competition in laxity" has drawn much criticism from those who are concerned that banks are permitted to take too many risks.

By no means do all economists agree that such alleged competition in laxity is bad. Many argue that it provides a useful counterweight to the inherent tendency of bank regulators to impose excessive regulation, and to discourage risk-taking too much. Bank regulators have an incentive to be too severe because they get blamed if they allow banks to do something that results in some bank failures. But they do *not* get blamed by the public if they prohibit something, say, a new type of loan, that would actually have been quite safe. If they prohibit it nobody ever finds out about its safety. Insofar as this bias in the regulators' own reward and punishment system outweighs the bias that results from the pressures brought to bear by the banking industry, and from the regulators' tendency to be "nice" to their industry, regulations tend to be too severe, and some competition among regulating agencies is desirable. For example, NOW accounts would probably not have developed if all depository institutions were regulated by a single government agency.

From time to time, bills are introduced in Congress to limit "competition in laxity" by abolishing one or more of the federal regulatory agencies. This would also have the advantage of reducing complexity and duplication of effort. One solution would be to centralize federal bank supervision in a single government agency. But which one? State banks would not like to be regulated by the parent of national banks, the Comptroller of the Currency, nor would nonmember banks like to be regulated by the Federal Reserve. In one way the FDIC would be the logical choice since it has to pay up in case of bank failure; but this very fact may make it too cautious. Hence, some economists have proposed creating a new agency that would do nothing except regulate banks, but others are afraid that such an agency could be captured by the industry it is regulating.

A related issue is the Federal Reserve's role in bank regulation. The Board of Governors now has to spend much of its time on this. Hence, some economists believe that it should be relieved of this task, so that it can spend more time on monetary policy, and also so that it would be less likely to be influenced in its monetary policy by any special concern about banks. But the Fed believes that the information it gains from bank supervision is useful to it in making monetary policy.

SUMMARY

1. As a result of the computer revolution and high interest rates, financial change was particularly rapid in the 1970s and early 1980s.
2. Money market funds, nationwide NOW accounts, and deposit sweeps undermined both the prohibition of interest payments on checkable deposits and Regulation Q.
3. Several remedies were tried to aid ailing thrift institutions. One was price discrimination. Another was to reduce the maturity of thrift institution assets by shifting to variable rate mortgages. Thrift institutions tried to get permission to make more short-term consumer and business loans to reduce the maturity mismatch of their assets and liabilities. Attempts to lengthen the maturity of their liabilities were unsuccessful.
4. Other problems that arose due to high interest rates include a too-low usury law ceiling in many states, a strong incentive for depository institutions to undertake more nonprice competition, and for member banks to become nonmember banks.
5. Financial reform was clearly needed, but is difficult to achieve, given the power of each industry to preserve its terrain and the difficulty of fashioning an acceptable trade-off.
6. In 1980 financial reform did come. DIDMCA set up a committee to phase out Regulation Q. It also permitted nationwide NOW accounts, gave the thrifts additional lending powers, and greatly weakened state usury laws.
7. Unresolved problems include the viability of banks and thrift institutions in face of competition from money market funds and from other corporations, and federal supervision which many economists would like to see greatly simplified, in part to reduce competition in laxity.

Questions and Exercises

1. State in your own words why inflation has created a need for financial reform.
2. In many discussions of financial reform it is said that equity requires that various institutions are allowed to compete on a "level playing field." Do you think this is meaningful, and if so, what does it mean?
3. Write an essay arguing that thrift institutions should be given a federal bail-out. Then write an essay arguing the opposite.
4. What do you think is the biggest need for financial reform right now?
5. Go over the various provisions of DIDMCA and show why they are a trade-off by discussing who lost and who gained from them.

Further Reading

CARRON, ANDREW. *The Plight of the Thrift Institutions*. Washington, DC: Brookings Institution, 1982. A good discussion of the problem and possible solutions.

CARGILL, THOMAS, and GARCIA, GILLIAN. *Financial Deregulation and Monetary Control*. Stanford: Hoover Institution Press, 1982. A highly useful discussion of DIDMCA and its background.

FEDERAL RESERVE BANK OF BOSTON. *Policies for a More Competitive Financial Sys-*

tem. Boston: Federal Reserve Bank of Boston, 1972. A series of useful papers on a wide range of issues.

GARCIA, GILLIAN, ET AL. "The Garn-St Germain Depository Institutions Act of 1982," Federal Reserve Bank of Chicago, *Economic Perspectives* 7 (March / April 1983): 3–32. An excellent survey.

KANE, EDWARD. "Accelerating Inflation, Technological Innovation, and the Decreasing Effectiveness of Banking Regulations." *Journal of Finance* 36 (May 1981): 355–67. An excellent discussion of the war between the regulators and the innovators.

MAYER, THOMAS. "Competitive Equality as a Criterion for Financial Reform." *Journal of Banking and Finance* 4 (1980): 7–15. A discussion of the meaning of equity in financial reform.

MCNEILL, CHARLES, and RECHTER, DENISE. "The Depository Institutions Deregulation and Monetary Control Act of 1979." *Federal Reserve Bulletin* 66 (June 1980): 444–53. A useful summary of complex legislation.

MELTZER, ALLEN. "Major Issues in the Regulation of Financial Institutions." *Journal of Political Economy* 75 (August 1967): *Supplement* 482–501. A stimulating plea for greater reliance on free-market processes.

MORAN, MICHAEL. "Thrift Institutions in Recent Years." *Federal Reserve Bulletin* 68 (December 1982): 725–38. A useful survey of recent developments.

U.S. CONGRESS, SENATE COMMITTEE ON BANKING, HOUSING, AND URBAN AFFAIRS. *Compendium of Major Issues in Bank Regulations*. 94th Cong., 1st sess., 1975. A large number of papers on many detailed aspects of bank regulation by economists, lawyers, and regulators.

The Supply of Money

PART TWO

The growth rate of the supply of money is a factor of great, perhaps overwhelming, importance in determining the course of a country's economy. Over the long run it dominates the behavior of prices. Hence, we will spend much time in this book discussing how the money stock is—or should be—growing, and how this affects the economy. In this part we will take up how money is created and measured. Chapter 9 deals with the definition and measurement of money, and Chapter 10 explains how the banking system can create money on the basis of additional reserves. Where these reserves come from is discussed in Chapter 11.

The Measurement of Money

9

Chapter 1 defined money in quite general terms. The time has now come to be more specific, and also to see how money is measured.

THE A PRIORI AND EMPIRICAL APPROACHES

There are two major approaches to defining money. One, called the *a priori approach,* is a rather philosophical one that focuses on the nature of money. It searches for the one characteristic that most distinguishes money from other things, and then defines money in terms of this characteristic. This is surely the way we usually define something.

To the question, what is *the* distinguishing characteristic of money, there is a simple answer: it is its medium of exchange function. This is the function that is unique to money; nothing else is a general medium of exchange. By contrast, the store of wealth function is not unique to money; money shares this function with many other things. Hence, the a priori approach defines money as anything that is a generally accepted medium of exchange.[1]

The a priori definition of money has the advantage of providing, at least on an abstract level, a fairly clear-cut differentiation between those items that are money and those that are not. Items that can normally be used to make payments, such as demand deposits, and travelers checks are money, while time deposits are *not*. Hence, this approach defines money as *M-1* plus transactions accounts and travelers checks.

[1]The standard of value function is also unique to money. But one cannot use it to define money since it is an abstraction rather than a concrete unit. Thus, it is meaningless to ask, for example, whether the standard of value increased at a 5 percent rate last year.

While the a priori definition of money focuses on what is distinctive about money, that is, on its essence, the rival **empirical definition** *focuses instead on what makes the money supply important*. Money is important for policy for two reasons. One is that changes in the money supply have a major, and numerous economists would say a dominating, impact on nominal income. The second reason is that the Fed can control the supply of money. Since economists are interested in policy, variables that the government can control are, obviously, more strategic to them than other variables, such as expectations, that may also have a powerful effect on nominal income, but cannot be controlled so easily.

The empirical definition of money therefore defines money, not by any inherent characteristics, but as that liquid asset, or collection of liquid assets, that (1) has the most predictable impact on nominal income, and (2) can be controlled by the Fed. In addition, supporters of the empirical definition of money prefer to use a variable for which data for many years exist, so that we have more observations to test our theories by.

Many—probably most—economists believe that the monetary measure that has the closest relation to income is *M-1*, but some, Milton Friedman, for example, believe that the broader measure, *M-2* (shown in Table 9.1) is more closely related to income. With respect to the controllability criterion, now that reserve requirements on personal savings and time deposits (which are included in *M-2*) are being phased out, *M-1* will probably be superior. But it is far from certain whether this difference in controllability will be substantial.[2]

Which is better, the empirical or the a priori definition? Those who adhere to the a priori definition argue that the empirical definition is inadequate because it misses the essence of money and is subject to erratic shifts. Thus, it may define money as *M-1* at one time and as *M-2* at another time depending on which of these shows the closest correlation with income. This seems arbitrary to supporters of the a priori definition. Besides, the advocates of the empirical definition do not agree among themselves about which measure of the money stock is the best "handle" in controlling income. Supporters of the empirical definition such as Milton Friedman, on the other hand, see nothing wrong with the definition of money changing from time to time, and each of them believes that he or she has evidence that allows one to choose between *M-1* and *M-2*.

Fortunately, this disagreement is unimportant. It is essentially a dispute about the ownership of the word *money*, and is not a disagreement about how the economy operates. Thus, one could accept the a priori definition of money as *M-1*, and yet if it turns out that *M-2* has the more predictable effect on income, and is the more readily controllable total, one could think and talk mainly about *M-2*, using some word other than *money*, say, *bread*, if one does not like to say *M-2*. On the other hand, one can go along with the empirical definition, and use the term *money* for, say, *M-2*, while being fully aware of the fact that the item that is the medium of exchange has a unique and interesting characteristic.

[2] The measure for which the longest run of data is available is old M_2, currency plus all deposits in commercial banks.

Table 9.1 Measures of Money and Liquid Assets, January 1983

	Billions of dollars (seasonally adjusted)	Percent
M-1		
Currency	134.2	27.8
Travelers checks	4.1	0.9
Demand deposits	239.4	49.6
Other checkable deposits	104.4	21.7
Total	482.1	100.0
M-2		
M-1	482.2	24.0
Small time deposits	797.4	39.7
Savings deposits	335.1	16.7
Money market deposit accounts	189.1	9.4
Money market mutual fund balances (general purpose and dealer)	166.7	8.3
Overnight repurchase agreements	40.1	2.0
Overnight Eurodollars	7.2	0.4
Consolidation adjustment[a]	−7.8	−0.4
Total	2010.0	100.0
M-3		
M-2	2010.0	
Large time deposits	310.7	83.6
Money market mutual fund balances	46.1	12.9
(institutions only)		1.9
Term repurchase agreements	40.6	
Consolidation adjustment[a]	−4.1	1.7
Total	2403.3	100.0
L		
M-3	2403.3	82.1
Short-term Treasury securities	216.9	7.4
Commercial paper	113.5	3.9
Term Eurodollars	81.0	2.7
Savings bonds	68.1	2.3
Bankers acceptances	45.3	1.6
Total	2928.1	100.0

a. Adjustments to prevent double counting. For example, the estimated demand deposits and vault cash that thrift institutions hold as reserves against savings and time deposits are subtracted.

Note: For precise definitions of various items see footnotes in Board of Governors, Federal Reserve System, *Statistical Release H.6.*

Source: Board of Governors, Federal Reserve System, *Statistical Release H.6.*, June 24, 1983.

THE MEASURES OF MONEY

Table 9.1 shows the various measures of money as defined by the Federal Reserve. Of these *M-1* and *M-2* are by far the most important. *M-3* is used only occasionally, and *L* (which is not really a measure of money in the usual sense) is hardly ever used.

M-1, sometimes called "narrow money," consists of items that can be spent immediately, that is, currency, travelers checks, and those deposits in commercial banks, mutual savings banks, and savings and loan associations against which unlimited checks can be written, as well as share drafts in credit unions.

M-2, also called "broad money," adds to *M-1* some items that while not quite as liquid, are still extremely liquid. These are savings deposits, time deposits of less than $100,000, deposits against which a limited number of checks can be written, and shares in (noninstitutional) money market funds. It also includes overnight repurchase agreements, as well as other repurchase agreements of less than $100,000 and overnight Eurodollar deposits at Caribbean branches of U.S. banks held by U.S. residents other than banks.[3] These Caribbean Eurodollars are more liquid than Eurodollars held in Europe because Caribbean banks are in the same time zone as the U.S. East Coast banks, so that their deposits can be transferred by telex whenever East Coast banks are open. Money market shares are included because checks can be written against them, though in many cases only checks of $500 and over. Some money market funds do not deal with the general public, but only with large institutional investors, such as insurance companies. These are excluded from *M-2*. Savings deposits are extremely liquid since the depositor can usually withdraw them by visiting the bank and presenting the passbook. Hence, they too are included in *M-2*. Small time deposits—that is, time deposits of less than $100,000—are very liquid in the sense that they can normally be redeemed on demand, albeit at an interest penalty. Hence, the Fed includes them too in *M-2*.

Large time deposits are excluded from *M-2* because they function to a large extent like securities, many of them being negotiable, so that they can be sold on the money market. Hence, the Fed includes them in the broader measure, *M-3,* rather than in *M-2*. *M-3* also includes repurchase agreements issued for periods longer than overnight, and shares in those money market funds that deal primarily with institutions. The final measure, *L,* is more a measure of highly liquid assets in general than of money.

These definitions (or close variants of them) were first adopted by the Fed in 1980. Before then it used a different set of definitions. M_1 was defined as currency plus demand deposits in commercial banks. M_2 added savings and small time deposits in commercial banks to M_1, and M_3 added to M_2 savings and small time deposits in thrift institutions. Since the Fed presented the new definitions of money only in 1980 much of the work that economists have done in the past has used the old definitions of money. Hence, when we refer to this work we will have to use these old definitions. To differentiate between the old and the new we will use a hyphen, e.g., *M-1,* for the new definitions and a subscript, e.g., M_1, for the old definitions.

Figure 9.1 shows the behavior of *M-1, M-2,* and *M-3* in recent years, and illustrates the considerable divergence between their growth rates. Hence, *it does* make a difference how money is defined.

ALTERNATIVE DEFINITIONS AND MONEY SUBSTITUTES

The definitions currently used by the Fed are not graven in stone, and as the financial system changes and new financial instruments are developed the

[3]It may seem inappropriate to refer to Caribbean deposits as "Eurodollars," but it is standard usage.

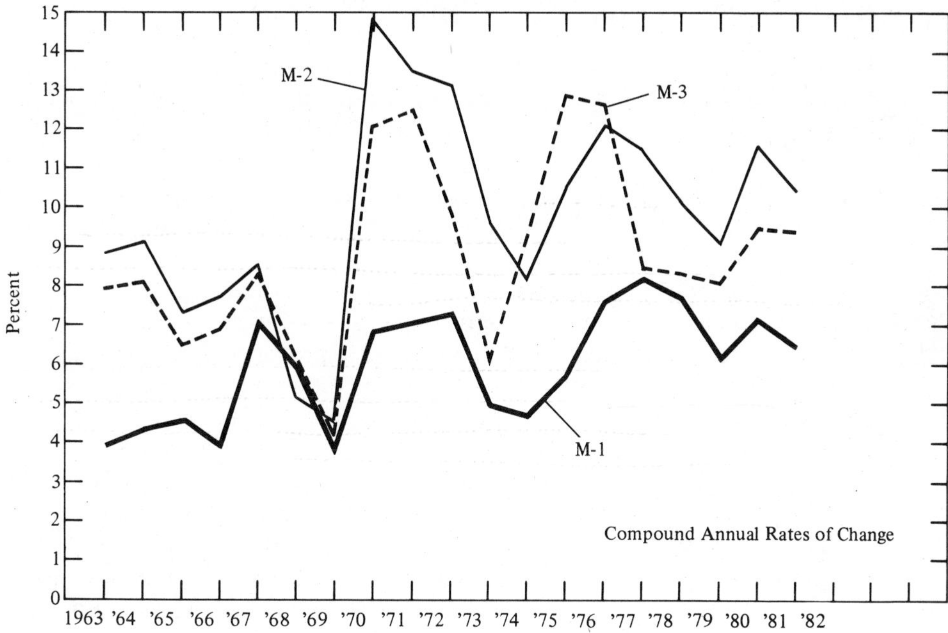

Figure 9.1 Behavior of Various Measures of the Money Stock, 1963–82

Fed is likely to change these definitions. Even now they are not beyond criticism. For example, some economists are uneasy about the Fed's treatment of money market funds.

Whichever way one defines money there will be some near-moneys that are similar to money and make the measurement of something called "money" rather arbitrary. The most obvious example is credit cards. One can think of a credit-card line of credit as a substitute for holding money—or as money itself. Lines of credit, such as those provided by credit cards, are like money in the sense of providing a widely, though not quite generally, accepted medium of exchange. However, they differ from money in one important way: money is part of a person's wealth, but a line of credit is not; for example, wouldn't everyone rather receive a $1,000 check as a gift than have the ceiling on their credit-card credit raised by $1,000?

Similarly, in recent years many American banks have adopted a common practice of British banks, the extension of overdraft privileges. These banks allow certain customers to write checks in excess of their demand deposits, and these overdrafts are treated as automatic loans.

Another troublesome problem is created by Eurodollars. The volume of Eurodollar deposits held by nonbanks was estimated in 1982 as about 313 billion. More generally, does it make sense to talk about the U.S. money stock in isolation? Some economists point out that large firms can hold foreign currencies to meet their needs for transactions balances by selling them on the foreign exchange market just before they make payments in dollars. Others consider Eurodollars to be more akin to highly liquid securities than to money since most of them are large CDs.

MEASURING MONEY AS A WEIGHTED AGGREGATE

Perhaps the solution is to measure money in a more sophisticated way. So far the discussion has been in terms of a simple dichotomy: an item either is—or is not—money, and there is nothing in between. But this is a crude procedure. Why not allow for the obvious fact that for the empirical definition of money the difference between those items included in money and other highly liquid assets is a matter of degree rather than of kind? This suggests that one should measure money as a *weighted average* of various components rather than as their simple sum. For example, currency might be given a weight of one, and savings deposits a weight of, say, 0.3. The problem is then to find some way of assigning appropriate weights to various monetary components. One way is to use the interest rate paid by a monetary asset as an (inverse) measure of its moneyness. Financial assets provide two yields, liquidity, i.e., moneyness, and interest. In equilibrium the total perceived yields on assets must be equal; thus the less explicit interest an asset pays, the greater must be its implicit yield in the form of moneyness. Hence, one can use the interest rates paid on an asset as an (inverse) weight of its moneyness. One can then combine various assets into a monetary total by weighting them in this way. This approach is still new and experimental, but seems promising.

REFINING THE MONEY MEASUREMENTS

So far we have discussed some broad issues in defining and measuring money. Now to get more specific. It is easy to say that demand deposits should be counted as part of the money stock, but do we really want to include all types of demand deposits? No, we do not. We are interested in the size of the money stock, not because this is knowledge that ennobles a person's otherwise drab life, but only because changes in the money supply bring about changes in expenditures, and hence in nominal income. This suggests that we should include only those deposits that affect expenditures.

It follows that the deposits of the federal government should not be counted. Federal government expenditures are not influenced at all by the Treasury's money holdings. They are set by congressional authorization and, in some cases, by the behavior of the economy. The U.S. Treasury is never constrained in its expenditures by having insufficient money—it can always borrow more. For this reason U.S. government deposits—but not state and local government deposits—are excluded from the money supply.

Another item that is excluded is currency held by banks in their vaults. We exclude this because it too does not affect the bank's expenditures. And for the same reason interbank deposits are excluded too. In addition, we also exclude cash items in the process of collection, that is, checks, etc., currently in the process of clearing. This is done on the, perhaps somewhat doubtful, assumption that those who wrote these checks have already deducted them from their outstanding balances. And what affects expenditures are the deposits that people *think* they have. These adjustments are not the only ones that are made to bank deposits to calculate the money stock. For example, deposits at certain corporations set up by banks to facilitate foreign trade have to be added in.

HOW RELIABLE ARE THE DATA?

We now come to a painful topic. The frequently used early estimates of the growth rate of the money stock are very poor. The way we know this is that the initially published data are substantially revised later on. This is illustrated by Table 9.2 which shows the results of a revision made in February 1983. (And such revisions are made throughout a five-year period.) The mean absolute change in the money growth rate that resulted from this revision was 4 percent for *M-1* and 2 percent for *M-2*. This is equivalent to the difference between an expansionary and a restrictive monetary policy! Hence errors in estimating the money growth rate can give a misleading picture. For example, in March 1978 the data showed a sharp retardation of the money growth rate for several months that some economists thought would lead to a recession. But when the data were revised shortly afterwards, this no longer seemed plausible.

The unreliability of the data until several years afterwards when they have been completely revised has two major implications. First, one should not get upset about data showing that money was growing at a highly undesirable rate for a short period of time. Over a period of, say, three or six months, errors tend to average out, but the weekly data on the growth of the money stock that are published in many newspapers are, in all probability, going to be revised substantially. When one adds to this the fact that the actual weekly growth rate of money fluctuates very erratically in any case, it follows that the publication of the weekly money stock figures could constitutionally be banned under the Supreme Court criterion of being material without any redeeming social value. Second, the Federal Reserve has to make its current policy on the basis of preliminary data. And since these data do not give a reliable indication of what the current monetary growth

Table 9.2 Growth Rates of Money: Old and Revised Series

Period	*M-1* Old	*M-1* Revised	Absolute Difference	*M-2* Old	*M-2* Revised	Absolute Difference
	(compounded annual rates of change, seasonally adjusted)					
December 1981–January 1982	23.1%	21.5%	1.6%	13.0%	10.6%	2.4%
January 1982–February 1982	− 3.4	0.5	3.9	4.5	3.8	0.7
February 1982–March 1982	2.7	1.6	1.1	11.8	9.0	2.8
March 1982–April 1982	11.5	1.9	9.6	10.5	4.2	6.3
April 1982–May 1982	− 2.4	8.6	11.0	11.3	10.5	0.8
May 1982–June 1982	− 0.3	2.7	3.0	6.8	9.5	2.7
June 1982–July 1982	− 0.3	2.7	3.0	10.3	11.0	0.7
July 1982–August 1982	10.9	10.8	0.1	15.3	15.5	0.2
August 1982–September 1982	14.9	13.6	1.3	5.2	8.8	3.6
September 1982–October 1982	22.6	15.5	7.1	8.3	8.1	0.2
October 1982–November 1982	18.3	14.4	3.9	12.2	9.9	2.3
November 1982–December 1982	9.2	11.4	2.2	7.9	9.1	1.2
Average			4.0			2.1

Source: Federal Reserve Bank of St. Louis, *Monetary Trends,* March 3, 1983, p. 1.

rate is, the Fed can hardly be expected to achieve the precise growth rate it desires.

One reason for the poor quality of the preliminary data is that smaller depository institutions report their deposits only infrequently, so that the Fed has to estimate their deposits at other times. In addition, there are a number of technical difficulties in estimating the money stock. For example, as pointed out above, cash items in the process of collection are deducted from the deposit total. But, actually, not all of them should be deducted since, for example, some of them relate to items that are not included in the money stock.

But the biggest source of errors is that the money data, like most economic statistics, are adjusted for seasonal variations. For example, the demand for money always increases at Christmas, and to reduce seasonal fluctuations in interest rates the Fed adjusts the supply of money for such seasonal variations in demand. To prevent these seasonal changes in supply from distorting the figures, the money stock for each month is divided by a seasonal adjustment factor that should cancel out these seasonal variations. If the seasonal pattern is constant, then this is a simple procedure that does not lead to significant errors. But the seasonal pattern is unstable; for example, in a year when the public feels prosperous its demand for money at Christmas may rise by more than it does in another year in which it feels pessimistic, and hence less generous. Obviously, such a variable seasonal pattern is hard to adjust for. This difficulty of adjusting the data for varying seasonal effects is by far the most important reason why the preliminary money stock data are so bad. In 1982 the Fed published *M-1* growth rates estimated by its usual method of eliminating seasonals, and by a then new experimental method. Here are the results for the first half of 1982:

Table 9.3 Annualized Monthly Growth Rate (percent)

	Usual method	Experimental method
January	21.0	11.4
February	− 3.5	1.3
March	2.7	6.4
April	11.0	4.5
May	− 2.4	0.5
June	− 1.6	1.3
Averages:		
First three months	10.4	9.5
Second three months	3.1	3.4

The month-to-month growth rates are radically different. For example, the April growth rate shown by the usual method is an extremely high one, that if continued for some time would be highly inflationary. But the alternative method of seasonal adjustment shows only a moderate growth rate. Seasonal adjustments have to cancel out over the year; if one month has a seasonal adjustment coefficient of more than 100 percent, another month must have one of less than 100 percent. Hence, it is not surprising that for the three-month growth rates the two methods yield *fairly* similar growth rates.

If the errors in the money-stock figures were constant, for example, the money stock always being overstated by, say, 5 percent, these errors would not matter because they would not affect money *growth rates,* which is what matters in predicting *changes* in income. But, unfortunately, this is not the case. Thus, if the error in the seasonal adjustment factor is positive for one month, it must be negative for another month since over the whole year the seasonal adjustment factors cancel out.

One reason why the money growth figures are so bad is that small percentage errors in estimating the money *stock* can purely as a matter of arithmetic result in very large percentage errors in the estimate of how fast money has grown over a short period of time. For example, suppose that the actual money stock stood at $1,000 billion at the start of the month, and at $1,004 billion at the end of the month. This is a growth rate in annual terms of approximately 4.8 percent (0.4 percent times 12). But suppose that the money stock at the end of the month is estimated by mistake as $1,006 billion, an error of only 0.2 percent. The growth rate then appears to be about 7.2 percent instead of 4.8 percent. The shorter the period of time covered by the data, the greater is the error in the growth rate that results from a small mistake in estimating the stock at either the beginning or the end of the period.

Someone trying to gauge the growth rate of money has to worry not only about errors in the data, but also about erratic, and hence essentially meaningless, factors that cause the money growth rate to vary from time to time. Many people who watch the money growth rate are uninterested in such erratic changes that are likely to wash out soon, but would like to know what the underlying money growth rate is. Accordingly, one study asked the following question: suppose the estimated money growth rate is *x* percent, and one wants to set out a range so that the probability is two-thirds that the *true* growth rate falls within this range. How much would one have to add or subtract from *x* percent to get this range? This figure is given by a statistic called the "standard error." It is shown in Table 9.4. To illustrate its interpretation assume that the estimated *M-1* month-to-month growth rate is 6 percent. This 6 percent should be interpreted as a best guess with a two-thirds chance that the true underlying growth rate is between 1½ and 10½

Table 9.4 Standard Errors of Money Growth Rates (percent)

Growth rate measured:	*M-1*	*M-2*
monthly	4.5	3.5
quarterly	1.7	1.3
half-yearly	0.8	0.6

Source: David Pierce, "Trend and Noise in Monetary Aggregates," in Board of Governors, Federal Reserve System, *New Monetary Control Procedures,* vol 1, Washington, D.C., 1981, p. ii.

percent. Since a 1½ percent growth rate is a highly restrictive policy, while a 10½ percent growth rate is a highly expansionary policy, this table illustrates that month-to-month growth rates have little meaning. But over a six-month period the range around the estimated 6 percent growth rate is only 5.2 to 6.8 percent.

SUMMARY

1. There are two general approaches to defining money. The a priori approach focuses on the essence of money. This leads to the *M-1* definition. The empirical approach focuses on that collection of monetary assets that has the closest correlation with nominal income and is readily controlled by the Fed. Some economists think that it is *M-1* and others think it is *M-2*.
2. *M-1* is defined as currency, checkable deposits, and travelers checks. *M-2* adds to *M-1* savings deposits, small time deposits, money market fund shares, overnight repurchase agreements, and Eurodollar deposits of U.S. residents held in Caribbean branches of U.S. banks. *M-3* adds to this large time deposits, and term repurchase agreements. *L* is a much broader measure.
3. Eurodollars and credit cards create problems for measuring meaningful monetary totals. One approach to measuring money combines various components by giving them different weights.
4. Federal government deposits, vault cash, interbank deposits, and cash items in the process of collection are excluded from money.
5. The published data are subject to substantial revisions over time, largely due to faulty seasonal adjustment.

Questions and Exercises

1. Write an essay defending:
   a. the a priori approach to the definition of money.
   b. the empirical approach to the definition of money.
2. Describe a change in Federal Reserve or FDIC regulations that would induce you to make a change in the definition of money.
3. Look up recent data on the relative growth rates of *M-1, M-2, M-3*. Is there a significant divergence between them? If so, to what do you ascribe it?
4. Discuss why we exclude from money:
   a. government deposits.
   b. cash items in the process of collection.
5. Should food stamps be included in *M-1* or *M-2?*

Further Reading

ADVISORY COMMITTEE ON MONETARY STATISTICS. *Improving the Monetary Aggregates*. Washington, D.C.: Board of Governors, Federal Reserve System, 1976. A storehouse of technical details on how the money data are constructed and on how they could be improved.

BARNETT, WILLIAM, OFFENBACHER, EDWARD, and SPINDT, PAUL. "New Concepts of Aggregate Money." *Journal of Finance* 36 (May 1981): 497–505. A good discussion of measuring money as a weighted aggregate.

BRYANT, WILLIAM. *Money and Monetary Policy in Interdependent Nations*. Washington, D.C.: Brookings Institution, 1980. An argument that one needs to look beyond a country's borders in defining money.

FRIEDMAN, MILTON, and SCHWARTZ, ANNA. *Monetary Statistics of the United States*. New York: Columbia University Press, 1970. Chapter Three gives a cogent and powerful defense of the empirical approach to the definition of money.

HART, ALBERT. "Regaining Control over an Open-ended Money Supply." U.S. Cong., Joint Economic Committee, *Special Study on Economic Change*, vol. 4, Washington, D.C., 1980, pp. 85–143. An important discussion of the erosion of the concept of money.

LAIDLER, DAVID. "The Definition of Money: Theoretical and Empirical Problems." *Journal of Money, Credit and Banking* 1 (August 1969): 508–25. A very clear discussion that is easier than many of the other items cited here.

LAWLER, THOMAS. "Seasonal Adjustment of the Money Stock: Problems and Policy Implications." *Economic Review* (Federal Reserve Bank of Richmond) 63 (November-December 1977): 19–27.. A thorough discussion of a technical issue.

SIMPSON, THOMAS. "The Redefinition of Monetary Aggregates." *Federal Reserve Bulletin* 66 (February 1980): 97–114. This is the Fed's statement of how it now defines money, and its reasons for adopting its definitions.

U.S., CONGRESS, HOUSE, SUBCOMMITTEE ON DOMESTIC MONETARY POLICY, COMMITTEE ON BANKING, FINANCE, AND URBAN AFFAIRS. *Measuring the Monetary Aggregates*. 96th Cong., 2d sess., February 1980. A useful compendium of economists' views.

YEAGER, LEYLAND B. "The Medium of Exchange." In *Monetary Theory*, edited by Robert Clower, pp. 37–60. Baltimore: Penguin Books, 1969. A rousing and subtle defense of the a priori approach to defining money.

The Creation of Money 10

In this chapter we explain how banks and other depository institutions create money; approximately 70 percent of *M-1* consists of their deposits. What is important here is to *understand* the underlying principles that permit such money creation, and not to allow oneself to become mesmerized by the numerical examples or the algebra. But before taking up deposit creation we deal with a much easier topic: the creation of currency.

CURRENCY

The creation of currency is simple and straightforward. The U.S. Bureau of the Mint and the U.S. Bureau of Printing and Engraving, both agencies of the U.S. Treasury Department, buy various types of metal and paper and turn them into coins and paper money. How they do so interests counterfeiters, not economists.

Once these coins and currency notes are received by the public they are counted as part of the money supply. When someone withdraws currency from a bank it then replenishes its currency supply by "buying" currency from a Federal Reserve Bank, which debits the bank's account for this currency. The amount of currency in circulation therefore depends upon how much currency the public wants, given its total money holdings, that is, deposits plus currency. While it is getting a bit ahead of the story, monetary policy never tries to control the supply of currency directly.[1] It operates by

[1] Well, almost never. In some countries, as well as in the Confederacy during the Civil War, a certain monetary policy affecting currency has been used. This is a so-called monetary reform when a highly inflated currency is called in and replaced by a new issue on a less than one-to-one basis. (Bank deposits are frozen and also converted into new deposits on a less than one-to-one basis.) In this way the quantity of money is reduced in one fell swoop. This was done, for example, after World War II in a number of European countries in which the quantity of money had been increased greatly during the German occupation.

changing interest rates and the supply of money. It is entirely up to the public to determine what proportion of its money holdings it wants to hold as currency. The Fed and the Treasury then supply the banks with whatever currency they need to meet the demands of the public.[2]

CHECKABLE DEPOSITS

When someone deposits a dollar of currency this results in several dollars of deposits. This may seem bizarre since it suggests that something is created out of nothing, and thus to contradict the law of conservation of matter and energy. But this puzzle disappears once one sees what a deposit actually is.

The Nature of Deposits

What actually is a **deposit?** It is not a physical object like currency, but merely *a property right evidenced by an entry in the bank's books*. You cannot see a deposit, or hold it in your hand, any more than you can hold in your hand the right to a jury trial or someone's promise. This is confusing because when we speak of someone drawing a deposit out of the bank and receiving currency in exchange for the deposit, there certainly is a tangible item, currency, being withdrawn. But when you "draw out your deposit" what you are actually doing is *exchanging* your right to receive payment from the bank in the future for currency *right now*. When banks create deposits, they no more create something out of nothing than the Supreme Court does when it creates a new legal right. In neither case does what is created have any physical existence. It is important to keep this in mind; otherwise, the subsequent discussion of deposit creation becomes incomprehensible.

Two Special Cases: 100 Percent Reserves and 100 Percent Currency Drain

As one more preliminary to multiple deposit creation here are two special cases in which it does *not* occur, and this will provide a clue as to why it does occur in more realistic situations.

One hundred percent reserves. The first special case is one in which the law in its awful majesty requires that the bank keep 100 percent reserves against its demand deposits. Consider what happens when someone deposits $10,000 of currency. We can see this best by looking at a **T account,** *a condensed version of the bank's balance sheet,* which leaves out all previous entries, and shows just the ones we are currently considering. Such a T account now shows:

(1)

Assets		Liabilities	
currency	$10,000	deposits (my deposit)	$10,000

[2]The exceptions to this are trivial or rare. One is a coin shortage when the mints cannot keep up with the unexpectedly high demand for certain coins. For example, in 1974 there was a shortage of pennies. Another exception was the closing of banks in 1933, to prevent further runs on them.

This bank is now in equilibrium; it has exactly the reserves that the law says it must hold against its deposit. Has there been multiple deposit creation? Certainly not. A $10,000 deposit has been created against a $10,000 of currency reserves. This is a one-to-one ratio; there is nothing multiple about it.

Loans in currency only. Consider another unrealistic case in which the required reserve ratio is only, say, 20 percent, but in which a borrower when granted a loan takes the proceeds entirely in the form of currency, and continues to hold this currency. In this case, since the required reserve ratio is less than 100 percent, the above T account does not represent an equilibrium for the bank. It can increase its profits by lending out $8,000 of the initial $10,000 deposit or by buying an $8,000 security, keeping the other $2,000 as a reserve against its deposits. Its T account now, after it has made a loan, looks as follows:

(2)

Assets		Liabilities	
currency	$2,000	deposits	$10,000
loan outstanding	$8,000		

This bank is now in equilibrium; it holds just the reserves it must hold against its deposit. But again, there has been no multiple deposit creation: the bank initially received $10,000 of currency, that is reserves, and has $10,000 of deposits outstanding, so that deposits have increased in a one-to-one ratio to reserves.

MULTIPLE DEPOSIT CREATION

Now drop the peculiar assumption that a borrower, or seller of a security, holds the proceeds of a loan in the form of currency. This is most improbable because someone is not likely to borrow and pay interest unless he or she wants to use the money to make a purchase. And whomever he or she buys from is not likely to hold currency either, but will deposit the funds into a bank or other depository institution. One can assume, as a first approximation, that *all* the proceeds of a sale will be deposited. (Later on an allowance will be made for the fact that this assumption is not *quite* correct.) We will now also assume that there is a 20 percent reserve requirement, that the public does not increase its time deposits and that depository institutions use all their available reserves to make loans or to buy securities instead of holding some idle reserves.

How Multiple Deposit Creation Occurs

Consider now again a situation where someone deposits a $10,000 check obtained from selling a security to the Fed into bank A. When the check has cleared this bank's T account now looks as follows:

Bank A

(3)

Assets		Liabilities	
reserves with the Fed	$10,000	deposits	$10,000

And, as before, since the bank has $8,000 more than the required 20 percent reserves, it increases its loans, and writes up the borrower's deposit account by the amount of the loan. Its T account is:

Bank A

(4)

Assets		Liabilities	
reserves with F.R.	$10,000	deposits	$18,000
loans outstanding	$ 8,000		

The borrower does not keep the loan idle, but uses it to make a purchase. And the seller now deposits the $8,000 check received into, say, savings and loan B, which sends it to the Fed for clearing. After it clears, bank A's T account is:

Bank A

(5)

Assets		Liabilities	
loans outstanding	$8,000	deposits	$10,000
reserves with F.R.	$2,000		

Its reserves, $2,000, are now just sufficient to cover the $10,000 deposit it has outstanding, so it is in equilibrium. However, savings and loan B has now received $8,000 of deposits and reserves, which gives it the following T account:

Savings and Loan B

(6)

Assets		Liabilities	
reserves with F.R.	$8,000	deposits	$8,000

But there is no reason why B should want to keep 100 percent reserves against the deposit. It needs to keep only $1,600 ($8,000 times 20 percent) reserves and can use the remainder, $6,400, to make a loan or buy a security. When the borrower, or seller of the security, spends the $6,400 the recipient deposits the check into bank C, which sends it to the Federal Reserve for clearing. As a result, B's T account becomes:

Savings and Loan B

(7)

Assets		Liabilities	
reserves with F.R.	$1,600	deposits	$8,000
loans outstanding	$6,400		

B is now in equilibrium, having just the $1,600 reserves it needs, and no more. But the story continues with C, which has received $6,400 of deposits and reserves. It, too, will keep only 20 percent, that is, $1,280, as a reserve against the $6,400 deposit, and use $5,120 to buy a security or make a loan, which, by the now familiar process, will become a deposit in D, so that D can now lend out 80 percent of it, $4,096, which, in turn, will become a deposit in E, and that depository institution will again lend out, or buy a security with, 80 percent of this.[3]

In this process, deposits are being created by every depository institution in the chain; there are deposits of $10,000 in A, $8,000 in B, $6,400 in C, $5,120 in D and $4,096 in E, and so on. In other words, there is **multiple deposit creation;** *the initial deposit has called forth a series of subsequent deposits*. The two salient reasons why this occurs are, first, that no institution keeps a 100 percent reserve against its deposit and, second, while each one loses an equivalent amount of reserves when it makes a loan or buys a security, it loses these reserves not to thin air, *but to another* depository institution that then expands its loans or security holdings.

The Deposit Multiplier

How much does the multiple deposit creation amount to? We have a series here that goes as follows: $10,000, $8,000, $6,400, $5,120, $4,096, and so on, each figure being 80 percent of the preceding one. (There is, of course, nothing special about the 20 percent reserve ratio. It is just a number picked arbitrarily. Had a 50 percent reserve ratio been used, the sequence of deposits would have been $10,000, $5,000, $2,500, $1,250, . . .) Such a sequence forms a geometric progression

$$R[1+(1-r)+(1-r)^2+(1-r)^3+\ldots]$$

and its sum is

$$D=\frac{1}{r}R$$

where D stands for deposits, r is the reserve ratio, and R is the initial increase in reserves that occurred when bank A obtained a $10,000 deposit. With a 20 percent reserve ratio the total of deposit creation amounts to (1/0.2) $10,000, that is, $50,000. Hence, we have here a deposit multiplier ($1/r$) of 5. The **deposit multiplier** is the *change in deposits* per dollar change in reserves. (Unlike the Keynesian multiplier that relates some autonomous expenditure item, such as investment, to income, this multiplier relates reserves to the deposits.)

Another way of explaining the creation of $50,000 of deposits is as follows. The process of a depository institution making a loan, losing reserves to another depository institution making a loan, and so on, continues until all of the original $10,000 of extra reserves has become required reserves. (Strictly speaking, of course, the process never comes to a stop, but we can allow for this by rounding to the nearest dollar.) If the required reserve ratio

[3] As an exercise, write out the T accounts for C, D, and E.

is 20 percent, then, when all of the $10,000 has become reserves, deposits must be equal to five times required reserves, that is, to $50,000.

The above example of the deposit multiplier is highly unrealistic. For example, B received $8,000 of reserves and deposits and then lent out exactly $6,400. Obviously, it is not likely to make a loan of just that amount. In actuality, banks do not look at particular receipts of reserves and deposits, and then try to lend out 80 percent of these particular receipts. Instead, banks have a continual inflow and outflow from a large number of transactions. Each morning a bank looks at the total inflow and outflow of reserves during the previous day, estimates the major changes likely to occur during the current day, and then decides whether it should expand or contract its loans and investments. There is no reason to tie particular loans closely to particular reserve receipts. As a result, there can be a significant delay between the acquisition of reserves and the full expansion of deposits.

MULTIPLE DEPOSIT CONTRACTION

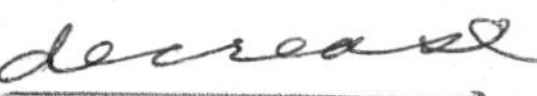

Now take the opposite cases where reserves decrease. This time assume that the reserve ratio is 25 percent, so that we get some variation into our figures. Assume also that there are no excess reserves being held. When a customer of mutual savings bank A buys a $10,000 security from the Fed, the Fed debits A's reserve account as the check is cleared. Its T account now looks as follows:

Mutual Savings Bank A

(8)

Assets		Liabilities	
reserves with F.R.	−$10,000	deposits	−$10,000

But since A kept only $2,500 of reserves against the $10,000 deposit it is short $7,500 of reserves and has to replenish them by selling a security or calling in a loan for $7,500. When it does so, and the check it receives is credited to its account, its T account—considering both the initial and the new transaction—becomes:

Mutual Savings Bank A

(9)

Assets		Liabilities	
reserves with F.R.	−$10,000 +$ 7,500	deposits	−$10,000
loans and securities	−$ 7,500		

Mutual savings bank A is now in equilibrium. It has lost $10,000 of reserves and made this up both by reducing its required reserves and by obtaining new reserves. But it has merely shifted part of its reserve shortage to another depository institution since by selling a security or calling a loan it received a check drawn on bank B.

As this check clears, bank B's T account becomes:

Bank B

(10)

Assets		Liabilities	
reserves with F.R.	−\$7,500	demand deposits	−\$7,500

Bank B kept \$1,875 (=\$7,500 × .25) against the \$7,500 deposit, and it is now short \$5,625 (=\$7,500 − \$1,875) of reserves. Hence, it too sells a security, or else calls in a loan, for \$5,625. Its T account becomes:

Bank B

(11)

Assets		Liabilities	
reserves with F.R.	−\$1,875 (= −\$7,500 + \$5,625)	demand deposits	−\$7,500
loans and securities	−\$5,625		

Bank B has therefore lost reserves equal to exactly 25 percent of its decline in deposits, and hence is no longer short of reserves. But when it obtained \$5,625 by selling a security it received a check drawn on a deposit in bank C. As this check is cleared, bank C is short of reserves, its T account looking like this:

Bank C

(12)

Assets		Liabilities	
reserves with F.R.	−\$5,625	demand deposits	−\$5,625

Bank C does not have to worry about \$1,406 (=\$5,625 × .25) of this loss in its reserves because its deposits have fallen too. But it is still short \$4,219 of reserves. So, suppose that it sells a security for \$4,219 to a customer of bank D. It now has sufficient reserves again, but bank D is short \$3,164 (\$4,219 × .75) of reserves. So *it* sells a security, thus passing the problem on to bank E, and so on.

In this process, deposits are decreasing again in a geometrically declining sequence. They fell by \$10,000 in A, by \$7,500 in B, by \$5,625 in C, and so on. Applying the formula for the sum of a declining geometric series again, we can see that deposits must fall by \$40,000 or

$$\frac{1}{r}R = \frac{1}{.25}\$10{,}000.$$

Thus, multiple deposit contraction is just as possible as multiple deposit creation, and not surprisingly, the two are symmetrical though the numbers differ because we used different reserve ratios.

LEAKAGES FROM THE DEPOSIT CREATION PROCESS

The story told so far is that of a multiplier process in which required reserves are the only leakage that absorbs the reserves with which the story started out. But there are also other leakages, excess reserves, currency holdings by the public, and reserves held against nonpersonal time deposits which we now take up. In doing so it is convenient to think of the term "deposits", which we have used in a vague way so far, as checkable deposits.[4]

Excess Reserves

A bank or other depository institution will frequently hold excess reserves to avoid either borrowing from the Fed or buying deposits in the CD market, or else having to sell short-term securities. However, excess reserves of banks are typically small. In the period 1981–82 they accounted for less than one percent of total reserves and in only one month of this period did they equal as much as 1.1 percent of total reserves.

How can we introduce excess reserves into the demand-deposit creation process? The simplest way is to think of them as functioning just like required reserves. Suppose a bank gets a $10,000 deposit and lends out only, say, 85 percent of it, holding 15 percent as reserves against this deposit. It does not matter for the deposit creation process whether all of these 15 percent represent required reserves, or whether, say, 14 percent are legally required and 1 percent are excess reserves. In either case, as the bank lends out $8,500, the next bank receives an $8,500 deposit. Hence, now that banks hold some legally excess reserves the demand-deposit multiplier is not $d = 1/r$, but $d = 1/(r+e)$, where e is the *percent of a dollar of deposit that banks hold voluntarily* as **legally excess reserves.** If the required reserve ratio is 14 percent and banks hold 1 percent legally excess reserves, the deposit multiplier is 1/.14 + .01 or 6.67.

Deposits into Currency

As the volume of deposits expands and income rises along with it, people exchange some of their additional deposits for currency. Suppose that for each dollar of additional deposits the public wants to hold, say, 30 cents more currency. The 30 cents of currency that depository institutions have to pay out to the public for every dollar of new deposits are lost to the deposit-creation process just as much as are the 14 cents that, in this example, they have to keep as required reserves. A bank receiving a $10,000 deposit keeps $1,400 as a legal reserve, $100 as a legally excess reserve, and pays out to the public $3,000 as currency. Hence it can lend out, only $5,500, which then becomes a deposit in the next bank. So the extended formula for the demand deposit multiplier is

$$d = \frac{1}{r + e + k},$$

where k is the proportion of each dollar of demand deposits that the public withdraws as currency. In this example, we have

$$d = \frac{1}{.14 + .01 + .30} = 2.22.$$

[4]More precisely they are deposits against which unlimited checks can be written.

Checkable Deposits into Nonpersonal Time Deposits

As checkable deposits increase some of them will be transferred into nonpersonal time deposits. It may seem that a term for nonpersonal time deposits could simply be added to the denominator as was done for excess reserves and for currency. But this is not so. When a depository institution holds additional reserves or a person withdraws additional currency, this sum is completely lost to the deposit creation process; the next institution in the chain does not get any of it. But this is not the case for a dollar shifted into a time deposit. Here the dollar stays in the system. All that happens is that reserves have to be held against it, and it is just these reserves (and not the time deposit itself) that is lost to the deposit creation sequence. Hence, the leakage is not t, the nonpersonal time deposit ratio, but $t(r_t)$ where r_t is the required reserve ratio against nonpersonal time deposits. And insofar as no excess reserves are kept against personal time deposits (which do not have a legal reserve requirement) these deposits do not result in a leakage at all. Thus to adjust the checkable deposits multiplier for the shift into time deposits one must add to the denominator the leakage into time deposits per dollar of demand deposits *times the legal reserve ratio against time deposits,* that is

$$d = \frac{1}{r + e + k + t(r_t)},$$

where t is the proportion of checkable deposits that are shifted into nonpersonal time deposits, and r_t is the reserve ratio (legal plus excess) held against these time deposits. Suppose that t is 20 percent and r_t is 5 percent; the multiplier then is

$$d = \frac{1}{.14 + .01 + .30 + .2(.05)} = 2.17.$$

This multiplier, 2.17, is less than a third of the 7.14, which it would be if the required reserve ratio, 14 percent, were the only leakage.

FROM MULTIPLIER TO STOCK OF DEPOSITS: THE MULTIPLICAND

Previously, when there was only one leakage, required reserves, we showed that the stock of deposits, D, is $D = (1/r)R$, where r is the required reserve ratio and R the volume of reserves. What happens when we introduce the other leakages?

Suppose someone finds a \$100 bill and deposits it. Some depository institution now has excess reserves of $(1 - r)$ \$100, and it goes ahead and expands its deposits in the same way as if it had received the \$100 from someone depositing a check received from the Federal Reserve in payment for securities. Hence, an increase in currency that is deposited leads to multiple deposit creation just as much as an increase in reserves with the Fed.

But suppose the \$100 bill is not deposited. Then it would serve to satisfy the public's demand for currency, kD, so that some other \$100 is now deposited instead, since the total demand for currency is, in the first instance, unchanged. (Only as deposits go up will more currency be demanded.) Hence, once one introduces the currency leakage, the multiplicand is no longer R, but is $R+C$ which is called the *base.*

How about the other leakages? They do not change the multiplicand. Those reserves that leak into excess reserve holdings or into required reserves against nonpersonal time deposits are already part of total reserves, R.

The Money Multipliers

The main reason for discussing the deposit multiplier is that it permits one to calculate the money multipliers. To go from checkable deposits to *M-1* one must add currency.[5] Since the public is holding a proportion k of its checkable deposits as currency each dollar of checkable deposits results in k dollars of currency being held. Total currency holdings are $kD=k\,\frac{1}{r+e+k+t(r_t)}\,(R+C)=\frac{k}{r+e+k+t(r_t)}\,(R+C)$. Adding this to checkable deposits which are $D=\frac{1}{r+e+k+t(r_t)}\,(R+C)$, one gets

$$M\text{-}1=\frac{1+k}{r+e+k+t(r_t)}\,(R+C).$$

To get *M-2* one must add to *M-1* various items shown in Table 9.1. Denoting the ratio of these items to checkable deposits by x, we have $x=\frac{x}{r+e+k+t(r_t)}(R+C)$, where x is the stock of items to be added to *M-1*. Adding this to *M-1* we get $M\text{-}2=\frac{1+k+x}{r+e+k+t(r_t)}\,(R+C)$. So far we have assumed that no reserves, either required or excess, are held against

X. To make allowance for such reserves one merely has to add to the denominator a term, $x(r_x)$, where r_x is the reserve ratio held against the items included in *M-2* but not in *M-1*. This gives $M\text{-}2=\frac{1+k+x}{r+e+k+t(r_t)+x(r_x)}\,(R+C)$.

MONEY-SUPPLY THEORY

We could end the story at this point and say that there is a fixed money multiplier determined by r, e, k, t, and r_t. One can take the average values of these coefficients and easily calculate the money multiplier. But why assume that the values of these leakage coefficients are fixed? While the legal reserve requirements are set by the Fed the others depend on how the public wants to hold its assets. Since these decisions of the public are susceptible to economic analysis we need not take these leakage coefficients as "given," but can see how they change with economic conditions.

The excess reserve ratio, e, that banks want to hold depends, on the one hand, on the interest rate that banks could earn by investing these excess reserves, and, on the other hand, on the benefits that banks expect to obtain from holding them. A profit-maximizing bank keeps excess reserves up to a point at which the marginal (opportunity) cost of idle reserves (the yield obtained from investing them minus the cost of investing) is equal to the marginal benefit to banks (the avoidance of the cost of obtaining additional

[5] We ignore the complication that the money stock includes travelers checks, but excludes interbank and federal government deposits.

reserves if the bank runs short of reserves, multiplied by the probability that the bank will actually run short).

The public's desired currency ratio *k* depends on the opportunity cost of holding currency, that is, on implicit and explicit yields on deposits as well as on the interest rate paid on securities. If this latter interest rate rises the public will switch into securities. But people are *much* more likely to pay for their security purchases by running down their deposits than their currency holdings, so that the ratio of currency to deposits is raised. The currency ratio also depends on income or wealth because these variables measure the extent to which people can afford to forgo earning interest on deposits or securities to obtain the convenience of holding currency, and on retail sales, the variable that measures the work to be done by currency. Some economists believe that the currency ratio also varies with tax rates because in transactions on which taxes are evaded it is safer to use currency rather than checks which leave records. Another factor influencing the currency ratio is the rise in the drug trade and other illegal transactions in which payment is made by currency and not by check.

The nonpersonal time-deposit ratio, *t,* depends on the interest rate on time deposits compared to the yields on demand deposits and on securities. Obviously, if banks raise the interest rate they pay on time deposits, while neither the yields on demand deposits nor on securities rise, the public will want to hold more time deposits. And the time-deposit ratio also depends on total wealth, since time deposits are one way of holding wealth.

Thus, income, wealth, and interest rates are factors determining *e, k,* and *t,* and hence the money multiplier. As income rises and interest rates increase, one would expect *e* to decline somewhat. But since it is already small to start with, this does not make very much difference. At the same time, with income and retail sales, as well as interest rates on securities, all rising, *k* rises too.

Hence, the deposit multiplier is partly endogenous, that is, affected by the demand for money, so that even if the Fed keeps bank reserves constant, the stock of money tends to rise as income increases, and fall as income falls—in other words, to behave procyclically. This analysis of money creation, which makes the *money multiplier partially endogenous by allowing* e, k, *and* t *to vary,* is called **money-supply theory** to distinguish it from the mechanistic "textbook" approach that takes the money multiplier to be a constant.

THE "NEW VIEW" OF MONEY CREATION

Although money-supply theory is a substantial advance over the simple mechanistic approach, it has been challenged in recent years by some economists who believe that it does not go far enough. Their approach is unfortunately called the New View, though by now there is nothing new about it.

Adherents of the New View ask why banks and thrift institutions would necessarily want to supply more deposits merely because their reserves have increased. Don't they, like other firms, set their level of output at the point that maximizes profits rather than producing the maximum feasible output? Surely we would not accept an analysis of the volume of steel sold that tells us that it is determined only by the amount of iron ore, etc., that steel companies have available. A profit-maximizing bank will look at demand (marginal revenue) as well as at costs in determining its output. But the deposit creation story just told looks only at the supply side, the maximum quantity of deposits that banks can create. Does the public's demand for deposits not matter at all? Does the public meekly accept whatever volume of deposits the banks can supply? Couldn't one go to the opposite extreme, and assume instead that banks are always able to create all the deposits that the public is willing to hold, so that the volume of outstanding deposits is determined by the demand for deposits? Suppose, for example, that the public wants to hold more total deposits. Banks would then find that they can "sell" deposits to the public at a lower imputed yield, that is, at a lower cost, and would therefore expand their total deposits.

But how would banks obtain the required reserves? To start with, since the public wants to hold more deposits, it will presumably deposit some of its currency holdings into banks and this raises bank reserves. Second, banks can increase their reserves by borrowing from the Fed. Moreover, the increased demand for total deposits can also be met by banks raising the (implicit or explicit) yield on time deposits, thus inducing some depositors to shift from checkable deposits to time deposits. Given the difference in reserve requirements, with personal time deposits having no reserve requirement at all, this reduces the reserves that have to be kept against the average dollar of deposits.

Hence, the New View argues, the supply of reserves is not as critical to the creation of money, particularly of *M-2,* as the traditional approach suggests.

Fortunately, the conflict between the two approaches is not as serious as may appear at first. Suppose that we start out with an equilibrium situation in which banks are producing their optimal volume of deposits, so that their marginal revenue from holding the public's deposits just equals the marginal cost of servicing these deposits. Now suppose that the Fed makes more reserves available. One of the costs of servicing deposits is the forgone interest from holding reserves against these deposits. But with more reserves available, interest rates fall, and as a result the marginal cost of servicing deposits falls too. Marginal costs are now less than marginal revenue, so that banks expand their volume of deposits. Hence, critics of the New View believe that, as the traditional view predicts, when banks obtain additional reserves bank deposits increase.

Moreover, these critics argue that although the traditional approach analyzes bank deposits in a way very different from that used for other goods, this does not necessarily mean that it is wrong. Deposits differ radically from other goods: an increase in their supply, after some time, raises the demand for them. It does so because, as will be shown subsequently, an increase in the money supply raises nominal income. And the higher is nominal income, the greater is the demand for nominal money. Hence, when banks supply more deposits, after some time, the demand for deposits increases too, so that the yield on deposits does not necessarily have to rise to induce the public to hold more deposits.

In any case, money-supply theory is much less vulnerable to the New

View's criticism than is the crude "textbook" multiplier, since it allows the leakage coefficients to be determined by economic conditions. For example, suppose that income rises. This raises interest rates, and hence, changes e, k, and t. Money-supply theory therefore makes some room for the demand factor stressed by the New View, but gives it much less emphasis than the New View does. In a sense, it is a simplified version of the New View that gambles on the assumption that the leakage coefficients are stable enough so that one can avoid the full complexity (and it is a very great complexity) of the New View. *If*, in actuality, most of the observed changes in the money stock are due to changes in the volume of bank reserves, rather than in the money multiplier, then the relatively limited analysis of fluctuations in the money multiplier that money-supply theory gives us may be sufficient.

SUMMARY

1. Currency is created by the Bureau of Engraving and Printing. Banks buy it from the Fed and put it into circulation.
2. Multiple deposit creation is a more complex topic. It is necessary to realize that deposits are not physical objects, but merely book entries. Deposit creation is therefore a set of rules that explains under what conditions banks can make certain book entries. Multiple deposit creation would not be possible if depository institutions had to keep 100 percent reserves, or if those who borrow from them or sell securities to them would keep the funds as currency rather than redepositing them. Ultimately, what makes multiple deposit creation possible is that the funds one bank or other depository institution loses when it makes a loan are received by another one.
3. Simple examples of multiple deposit creation show a decreasing series of deposits created by various depository institutions in a chain. Multiple deposit contraction operates by the same mechanism as deposit expansion.
4. There are various leakages from the deposit creation process. The ones discussed are required reserves, excess reserves, and the flows into currency and time deposits.
5. The deposit (transactions accounts) multiplier can be used to derive the *M-1* multiplier $(1+k)/[r+e+k+t(r_t)]$. The *M-2* multiplier is $(1+k+x)/[r+e+k+t(r_t)+x(r_x)]$. The multiplicand is $R+C$.
6. Money supply theory shows why the various leakages in the money multiplier are not constant, and why the money multiplier rises in expansions.
7. The New View argues that the traditional money multiplier approach is too mechanistic, that one must look at the profit maximizing behavior of banks and bring in the demand for deposits.

Questions and Exercises

1. Carry out the example set out on p. 181 through to bank G. Assume that G just holds the reserves it receives and does not make additional loans. On this assumption what is the deposit multiplier?
2. What happens in the example of deposit creation on p. 181 if the proceeds of the loan made by B are redeposited in B?

3. Set up an example of the deposit creation process using a 50 percent reserve ratio. Work it through for four banks.
4. Work out an example of deposit *contraction* using a 10 percent reserve ratio. Follow it through for six banks.
5. How would you answer a banker who claims that banks cannot create deposits, that they can lend out only the money deposited with them?
6. Carry the example of deposit contraction on pp. 183–184 forward and assume that F has excess reserves, and hence does not have to call a loan. What is the deposit multiplier now?
7. Suppose that we have an economy in which there is only a single bank, which has a reserve ratio of 20 percent. If someone deposits $1000 of currency in this bank, how much can this bank lend out?
8. Why do changes in income and wealth affect e, k, and t?
9. Explain the New View in your own words. How can adherents of the traditional view try to answer it?

Further Reading

BRUNNER, KARL. "The Role of Money and Monetary Policy." *Review* (Federal Reserve Bank of St. Louis) 50 (July 1968): 9–24. A strong criticism of the New View.

BURGER, ALBERT E. *Money Supply Process*. Belmont, Calif.: Wadsworth Publishing Co., 1971. Chapters 1–4 give an extremely thorough and detailed discussion of the deposit and money multipliers.

CACY, J. "Alternative Approaches to the Analysis of Financial Structure." *Monthly Review* (Federal Reserve Bank of Kansas City) 53 (March 1968). A good survey of the New View.

JOHANNES, JAMES, AND RASCHE, ROBERT. "Predicting the Money Multiplier." *Journal of Monetary Economics* 5 (July 1979): 301–25. This article develops a way of predicting the money multiplier with a high degree of accuracy.

FEDERAL RESERVE BANK OF CHICAGO. *Modern Money Mechanism: Workbook*. Chicago: Federal Reserve Bank of Chicago, 1961, pp. 1–14. A very clear and lucid discussion of deposit creation.

PESEK, BORIS. "Monetary Theory in the Post-Robertsonian 'Alice in Wonderland' Era." *Journal of Economic Literature* 14 (September 1976): 867 ff. The latter part of this article is a forceful and stimulating criticism of the traditional view of deposit creation. For the traditionalist's response, see the debate in the *Journal of Economic Literature* 15 (September 1977): 908–27.

TOBIN, JAMES. "Commercial Banks as Creators of 'Money.' " In *Banking and Monetary Studies*, edited by Deane Carson, pp. 408–19. Homewood, Ill.: Richard D. Irwin, 1963. A sharp critique of the traditional explanation of deposit creation.

Bank Reserves and Related Measures

11

In the preceding chapter we discussed how the banking system can create deposits equal to a multiple of the reserves it receives. In this chapter we discuss where the reserves come from. Any individual bank can obtain reserves by competing them away from some other bank, perhaps by selling a large CD to one of that bank's customers. But obviously the depository institutions system as a whole cannot gain reserves this way. It can obtain reserves only from some entity outside itself, that is, from either (1) the Fed, (2) the U.S. Treasury, (3) the domestic public, or (4) foreigners.

BANK RESERVES

The way in which bank reserves change is set out in a standardized accounting framework published by the Federal Reserve and carried every Monday in the *Wall Street Journal*.[1] Table 11.1 shows a condensed example. It is arranged so that factors that increase bank reserves are listed first, followed by those that decrease bank reserves.

Factors that Increase Bank Reserves

The first of these items consists of the open market operations that the Fed carries out precisely for the sake of changing bank reserves. Suppose the Fed buys these securities directly from a member bank. It pays for them by crediting the selling bank's reserve account, so that the bank's reserves go up automatically. The bank's and the Fed's T accounts look as follows:

[1] The data come from entries on the Fed's and Treasury's balance sheets.

Table 11.1 Weekly Published Federal Reserve Data—Member Bank Reserve Changes, March 16, 1983

	Change from week ending March 9, 1983 (millions of dollars)
Purchase of U.S. government securities, securities of U.S. government agencies, and acceptances	+$820
Borrowings from F.R.	+ 266
Float	− 565
Other Federal Reserve assets	+ 171
Gold stock	—
SDR certificates	—
Treasury currency outstanding	+ 692
Currency in circulation	+ 679
Treasury cash holdings	+ 4
Treasury, foreign and other deposits with the F.R. banks	+ 5
Other F.R. liabilities and capital	− 2
TOTAL	+$700

Source: *Wall Street Journal,* March 21, 1983.

Bank

(1)

Assets		Liabilities	
reserves with F.R.	+		
securities held	−		

Federal Reserve

Assets		Liabilities	
securities held	+	deposits	+

Suppose now that the Fed had bought these securities, not from a bank, but from General Motors. General Motors gets a check, which it deposits in its bank, and the bank clears the check by sending it to the Fed for credit. Its T account becomes:

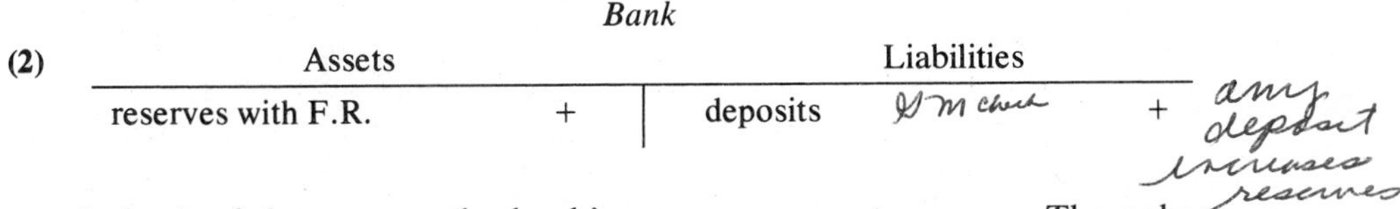

Bank

(2)

Assets		Liabilities	
reserves with F.R.	+	deposits	+

In both of these cases the bank's reserve account goes up. The only difference is that in the second case demand deposits go up automatically, whereas in the first case, where the Fed bought the securities from a bank, deposits go up only when the bank uses the reserves to make a loan or to buy another security. (The Fed's balance sheet is the same in both cases.) Conversely, when the Fed sells a security to a nonbank, bank reserves fall, and the T account of the buyer's bank shows:

Bank

(3)

Assets		Liabilities	
reserves with F.R.	−	deposits	−

The next item, borrowings, refers to the loans that depository institutions can obtain from their Federal Reserve Banks. The Fed makes these loans by crediting the borrowing institution's reserve account, so that we have the following T account entries:

Bank

(4)

Assets		Liabilities	
reserves with F.R.	+	borrowings from F.R.	+

Federal Reserve Bank

Assets		Liabilities	
loans to banks	+	deposits	+

And when the bank repays the loan the Fed will take the amount of the loan out of the bank's reserve account, so that the T account will show negative entries for all of these items, and the reserves will therefore disappear.

Float, the next item, works like a loan from the Fed. If the Fed were to give credit for a check it is sent for clearing at exactly the same time that it debits the account of the bank on which the check is drawn, then there would be no float. But the Fed credits the account of the depositing bank after one or two days, despite the fact that, due to transportation delays and so on, it may take longer than this before the check is debited against the account of the bank or other depository institution on which it is drawn. As a result of one bank's reserve account having been credited for the check, while the other bank has not yet been debited, total reserves increase for a short time. Thus the T accounts of the bank that received the check, and the bank upon which the check was drawn, look as follows:

Receiving Bank

(5)

Assets		Liabilities	
reserves with F.R.	+	demand deposits	+

Drawer Bank

Assets	Liabilities
reserves with F.R. unchanged	demand deposits unchanged

For both banks together therefore reserves have temporarily increased. When the check finally is debited to the drawer bank, its reserve account is debited, and the increased reserves and deposits generated by float disappear.

Another factor raising bank reserves is an increase in Other Federal Reserve Assets. Whether the Fed buys paper clips, or foreign currency from another central bank, it does so by drawing a check on itself. When the check is deposited and cleared the Fed credits the reserve account of the bank that received it. Here are the relevant T accounts when the seller has deposited the Federal Reserve check, and it has cleared:

Commercial Bank

(6)

Assets		Liabilities	
reserves with F.R.	+	deposits	+

Federal Reserve Bank

Assets		Liabilities	
paper clips	+	deposits	+

Then there are various U.S. Treasury operations that change bank reserves. The first of these are changes in the U.S. gold stock. If the Treasury sells gold the check it receives in payment is debited against the reserve account of the bank or other depository institution on which it is drawn.

The next item, special drawing right certificates, we defer until later (see footnote 3) and turn now to Treasury currency in circulation. Since currency held by depository institutions is part of reserves, an increase in outstanding Treasury currency that lands up in banks obviously increases bank reserves. But how about Treasury currency that is held by the general public? We will make allowance for that part of Treasury currency by subsequently subtracting—as a factor of decrease—currency held by the public.[2]

FACTORS THAT DECREASE BANK RESERVES

Bank reserves decrease if certain items increase. One of these is currency in circulation, that is, currency held by the public. Clearly, if someone withdraws $1000 from a depository institution, then vault cash, and hence reserves, decrease by $1000. A similar story applies to the next item—Treasury cash holdings. If the Treasury holds more currency, and the public's currency holdings are constant, then the depository institutions must be holding less currency and hence fewer reserves. (If the increase in the Treasury's currency holding comes from a reduction in the public's currency holdings, then a rise in one factor that decreases reserves—Treasury cash holdings—is fully offset by a fall in another factor that decreases reserves—currency held by the public.)

The Treasury deposits tax payments and receipts from sales of its securities initially into depository institutions. But since it writes its own checks

[2]What about Federal Reserve currency in circulation? This is already taken care of indirectly by taking account of the factors that change the Fed's balance sheet, such as loans. The proceeds of these loans can be taken either as a credit to the bank's reserve account with the Fed, or if the bank wants to, by having the Fed ship Federal Reserve currency to it.

on its account with the Fed from time to time, it has to transfer funds from its accounts with depository institutions to its account with the Fed. When this happens the Fed credits the Treasury's account and debits the accounts of the depository institutions.[3]

The T accounts are:

Depository Institutions

(7)

Assets		Liabilities	
reserves with F.R.	—	demand deposits of U.S. Treasury	—

Federal Reserve Bank

Assets		Liabilities	
		member bank deposits	–
		U.S. Treasury deposits	+

Some foreign governments also keep accounts with the Fed. When they transfer funds from their deposits with banks (or checks they have received drawn on U.S. banks) to the Fed, then bank reserves fall the same way as they do when the U.S. Treasury transfers deposits to the Fed. And the same is true when certain other institutions that hold deposits with the Fed, such as the U.N. or the FDIC, increase their deposits with the Fed.

The final item is other Federal Reserve liabilities and capital. Suppose that a new member bank buys stock in the Fed, thus raising Fed capital. It pays for this stock by having the Fed debit its reserve account, so that total bank reserves fall. Other Federal Reserve liabilities are brought in to keep the books straight. Previously we treated all the increase in other Fed assets as though it meant an increase in bank reserves because the Fed pays for these assets. But insofar as these assets have not yet been paid for—so that Federal Reserve liabilities increase—bank reserves have actually not yet increased. Hence, we must now compensate for this by subtracting the increase in Fed liabilities.

THE FED'S CONTROL

All of these factors changing reserves can be classified into two groups: those that are controlled by the Fed and can therefore be used to change reserves,

[3]Now consider SDR certificates. These are Special Drawing Rights, a form of international reserves created by the International Monetary Fund (IMF). When the IMF distributes additional Special Drawing Rights, as it does from time to time, the Treasury as a matter of government bookkeeping adds their dollar equivalent to its account at the Fed. Hence, occasionally there is an increase in Treasury deposits with the Fed that does not result in a decrease in bank reserves. To make up for the fact that we are treating *all* increases in the Treasury deposits at the Fed as though they were decreases in bank reserves we have to add increases in Special Drawing Rights back in by treating them as a factor that increases bank reserves.

and those that are beyond the Fed's immediate control. One factor the Fed can obviously control is its purchase or sale of securities. To a considerable extent it can also control borrowings from it by changing the discount rate. All the other factors, called "operating factors" or "market factors," are not normally controlled by the Fed. Hence, to control reserves the Fed has to forecast changes in these operating factors, and if need be offset them by open market operations. Its forecasts are necessarily subject to some error and this limits the Fed's control over bank reserves, and hence the money stock, in the short run. Of course, over a longer period of time such errors wash out.

THE RESERVE BASE AND OTHER MEASURES OF RESERVES

The time has come to look at several important concepts that are widely used in discussions of monetary policy.

The Base. A frequently used measure of Fed policy is the behavior of the base, sometimes also called "monetary base." One can think of the base in terms of the accounting framework of "sources" and "uses." From the uses side, it consists of reserves and currency in circulation. From the sources side, it consists of all the factors determining reserves discussed in this chapter except currency in circulation. Since currency in circulation is included in the base, an increase in it, although it decreases reserves, does not decrease the base.

Adjusted Base. In gauging whether monetary policy has been expansionary or restrictive the base can sometimes give misleading results. Even if the base has not expanded at all, monetary policy could still be expansionary if the reserve requirements ratio was reduced, thus raising the money multiplier. And the average reserve requirements ratio may fall even if the Fed does nothing, if deposits shift from depository institutions with a high reserve ratio to those with a lower reserve ratio. Hence, to evaluate monetary policy one should make an adjustment to the base for the change in the average reserve requirements ratio. This is done in the following way. Suppose the average reserve requirements ratio has fallen, thus releasing, say \$100 million of required reserves. This \$100 million is then added to the base to get the adjusted base.

Unborrowed Reserves. Depository institutions are, at least to some extent, reluctant to be in debt to the Fed. If so, when they obtain additional reserves the first thing they do is to repay these loans rather than to use the reserves to make loans or buy securities. If this view is correct—and this is disputed—then deposit creation depends less on total reserves or the base than on *unborrowed reserves,* sometimes called *"owned reserves."* To obtain owned reserves all one has to do is to subtract from total reserves the amount that depository institutions have borrowed from the Fed.[4]

[4]Sometimes the term "unborrowed reserves" is defined somewhat differently; "seasonal borrowings" (which will be discussed subsequently) are not subtracted from total reserves.

Table 11.2 Reserve Concepts

Measure	Definition
Base or monetary base or high-powered money	reserves of depository institutions plus currency held by the public
Adjusted base, extended base or net base	base adjusted for changes in reserve requirements
Reserves	reserves of depository institutions
Unborrowed reserves	reserves minus borrowings from the Fed[a]
Excess reserves	total reserves minus required reserves
Free reserves	excess reserves minus borrowings from the Fed[a]

a. Borrowings that are subtracted do not include seasonal and extended borrowings.

Free Reserves. This measure subtracts from unborrowed reserves the reserves that have to be kept against existing deposits in an attempt to measure the reserves that will be used to expand deposits.

Table 11.2 shows various reserve and base measures.

Which of these is the best measure in the sense of predicting how the money stock will change? This is an unsettled issue. The adjusted base is obviously better than the base since the money multiplier applicable to it has one less variable, changes in the required reserve ratio, and hence one thing less that has to be estimated with some error.

The base has an advantage over bank reserves because it takes account of currency holdings of the public which are ignored by reserves. But, on the other hand, it gives currency holdings too much importance by counting a dollar of currency held by the public as equal to a dollar of reserves held by banks, despite the fact that a dollar of bank reserves, unlike a dollar of currency, can result in several dollars of money.

Unborrowed reserves and the unborrowed base are better measures than total reserves or the total base if—*but only if*—banks are reluctant to expand deposits on the basis of the reserves they have borrowed from the Fed. Excess reserves and free reserves are usually not good measures. Suppose the data show that excess reserves have increased. This need not be a signal that deposits will increase; excess reserves may have increased just because the federal funds rate has fallen, while the discount rate has not, so that banks find it worthwhile to hold more excess reserves.

THE RESERVE BASE, THE MONEY MULTIPLIER, AND THE MONEY STOCK

The Fed can exercise good control over the monetary base through its open market operations by offsetting changes in the market factors, such as float. Does this mean that it also has good control over the supply of money? This depends upon its ability to predict changes in the money multiplier. If the money multiplier is stable, or otherwise highly predictable, the Fed could attain its target for the money supply very easily. If it wants the money supply to increase by, say, $10 billion, and it knows that the money multiplier applicable to the base is 2.5, it would simply raise the base by $4 billion. But is the money multiplier so highly predictable?

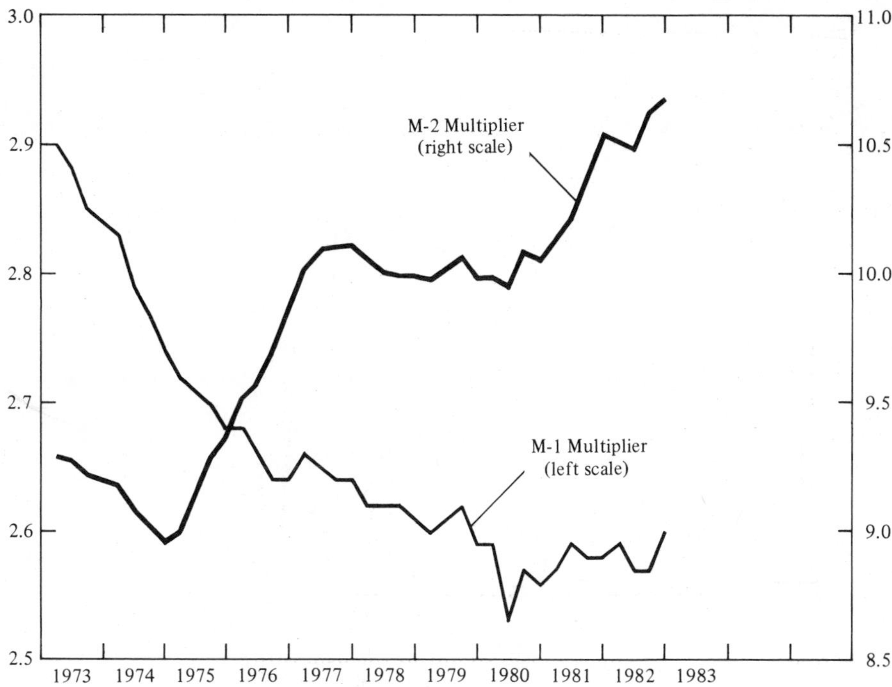

Figure 11.1 The Money Multiplier *1972*

Note: Money multiplier is the M_1 multiplier applicable to the adjusted base, and includes one leakage that has not been discussed. This is the leakage into federal government deposits (which are excluded from the money supply). This leakage is quite minor, usually being less than 0.02. And it must be multiplied by the reserve requirement against demand deposits, so that its effect is trivial.

Source: Unpublished data provided through the courtesy of the Federal Reserve Bank of Saint Louis; Board of Governors, Federal Reserve System, *Banking and Monetary Statistics, 1941–1975,* and *Annual Statistical Digest;* Council of Economic Advisers, *Economic Report of the President, 1979.*

As Figure 11.1 shows it has been declining at a fairly steady rate. The fact that the money multiplier is declining rather than constant does not create a problem since the Fed can make allowance for a steady decline. The real issue is whether there is so much erratic variation, so that the Fed cannot predict accurately how the money supply will vary as it changes the monetary base.

The relation between changes in the adjusted base and changes in *M-1,* as shown in Figure 11.2, is a relatively close one. But is it close enough? What is involved here is a rather subtle trick of arithmetic. Assume that the Fed predicts that the money multiplier for the month will be 2.500, and it actually turns out to be 2.525. Such an error of one percent looks like a very good forecast, but it may be large enough to get the Fed into trouble. It means that for a given size of the base the money supply is one percent greater than the Fed predicted. This is more serious than it seems. Suppose the Fed is aiming at an annual money growth rate of 6 percent, which is approximately 0.5 percent per month. Now due to the error in estimating the money multiplier all of a sudden money is growing at a 1.5 percent rate this month, three times as fast as intended. It is growing at a more than 18

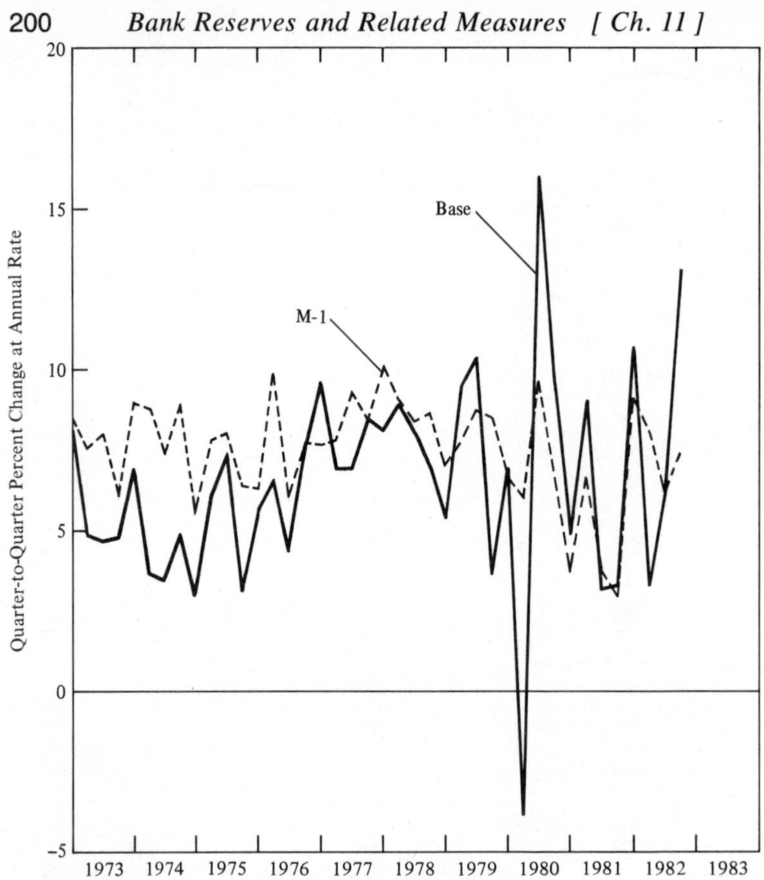

Figure 11.2 Changes in the Adjusted Base and in *M-1*

percent *annual* rate, which, if continued, would be highly inflationary. Hence, despite its "accurate" estimate of the money multiplier the Fed may be subject to much criticism.

SUMMARY

1. Reserves are created or destroyed by Fed security purchases and loans, by increases in float and in Fed assets, by Treasury gold purchases or sales, as well as by changes in Treasury currency outstanding, currency in circulation, Treasury cash holdings, certain deposits with the Federal Reserve, and other Federal Reserve liabilities and capital.
2. Important measures of reserves are the base, adjusted base, unborrowed reserves, excess reserves, and free reserves.
3. The money multiplier has been declining in a fairly stable manner. But even a small error in predicting it can have large effects on the money growth rate when this is expressed as an annual rate of growth.

The Fed decreases member bank reserve balances (restricts credit) when it sells govt. securities in the market + vice versa.

Questions and Exercises

1. Given the following data calculate the change in bank reserves:

	Change
1. Fed security purchases (including repurchase agreements)	10
2. Gold stock	−10
3. Currency in circulation	15
4. Acceptances bought by Federal Reserve	− 3
5. Treasury currency	10
6. Float	− 3
7. Other Federal Reserve liabilities and capital	1
8. Other deposits with F.R. banks	− 1
9. Other Federal Reserve assets	5
10. Foreign deposits with F.R. banks	5
11. Federal Reserve loans	20
12. Treasury deposits with F.R. banks	− 5
13. Treasury cash holdings	− 5

2. Take the data given in the previous example: (a) eliminate the figure shown for Fed security purchases, and (b) add the following:

14. Member bank deposits at the Fed	− 3
15. Currency held by banks	− 2
16. Currency held by nonbank public	5

   Now calculate Fed purchases of securities.

3. Take each of the items in question 1 and explain in your own words the effects of this item on bank reserves. Do not merely state whether its increase raises or lowers reserves, but explain why.
4. Evaluate the following statements:
   a. When the Treasury buys gold, the money stock increases because the country now has more gold.
   b. An increase in float increases the money stock because it means that there are more checks in transit, which, in turn, means that people are receiving more money. This increases the money stock.
   c. An increase in currency in circulation raises bank reserves because some of this currency will be deposited in banks.
   d. When Federal Reserve loans increase, bank reserves decline because by increasing the liabilities of banks to the Fed it reduces their *net* assets with the Fed.
5. Take each of the items in Table 10.1 and set up, wherever relevant, the T accounts for commercial banks, the Fed, the Treasury, or the nonbank public.
6. Look at the factors supplying and absorbing bank reserves in last Monday's *Wall Street Journal.* Write a paragraph explaining in your own words what has happened.
7. Define and discuss the relation between: reserve base, extended base, high-powered money, free reserves, unborrowed reserves.
8. "The money stock depends upon the actions of the Fed, the Treasury, the commercial banks and the public." Explain this statement.

Further Reading

BERGER, ALBERT. *The Money Supply Process*. Belmont, Calif.: Wadsworth Publishing Co., 1971. A very thorough and comprehensive survey of the factors that determine the money stock.

FEDERAL RESERVE BANK OF NEW YORK. *Glossary: Federal Reserve Statements*. New York: Federal Reserve Bank of New York, 1972. A useful explanation of various technical terms.

NICHOLS, DOROTHY (Federal Reserve Bank of Chicago). *Modern Money Mechanics*. Chicago: Federal Reserve Bank of Chicago, 1971. A simple and clear discussion of the factors changing bank reserves and of deposit creation.

Monetary Theory

PART THREE

This Part deals with the factors that determine changes in nominal income with particular emphasis on the money supply. We will first take up the Keynesian theory and then the quantity theory and monetarist approach. Since the material in this Part is controversial, before taking it up one should consider how one goes about choosing between rival theories.

To decide what theory to accept we first have to know what it is we want from a theory. The seemingly obvious answer, "the truth," is so broad as to be almost meaningless. Instead, there are several different tasks that a theory can perform. One of these is to be a framework for organizing what we already know. Instead of memorizing a vast number of individual facts, we simply learn a theory that helps us to recall these facts at will. For example, the theory that highways are more crowded on weekends than on weekdays permits us to plan our trips without memorizing on what days the traffic is bad. In microeconomics marginal analysis is used for this purpose; instead of learning about the particular factors considered by each individual firm in deciding about its price, such as how a particular customer will react, we learn the generalization that a firm sets its price so that marginal revenue equals marginal cost.

Another function of a theory, one that is not so widely known, is to be a fruitful strategy for further research. A theory is not a static entity that exists in unchanged form once it has escaped the great thinker's mind. Instead, if it is an important theory, it is a growing thing that is being continually revised. Hence, someone confronted with two theories might very reasonably prefer the one that at present is *less* accurate and reliable, if it is likely to be the more fruitful one in the sense of being more open to interesting developments. Thus a philosopher of science, R. G. A. Dolby, has written that a new theory "is likely to be received favorably by such young scientists if it appears simple, coherent and plausible. But the way in which the new approach generates promising prospects for further research is probably the most important factor of all."[1]

The third function of a theory is a familiar one: to predict future events, and to explain why past events occurred. Presumably, when people say that a theory should tell them "the truth," it is primarily this function of a theory that they have in mind.

Thus a theory has more than a single function. This raises the distinct possibility that several theories may be useful, though they disagree on some points. Even within the confines of using a theory just to predict, more than one theory may be helpful. For example, one theory may predict better for the short run, and the other theory for the long run; one may do better in predicting nominal income, the other in predicting real income. Thus the fact that at so many points in economics we have more than one theory is not really quite as bad as it looks.

But still it would be nice if economists were to agree more. Why don't they? One reason is that various economists place different degrees of emphasis on different problems, and, as just mentioned, for different problems different theories may be preferable. For example, the Keynesian theory has its *comparative* advantage in analyzing the short run, while the quantity theory of money has its *comparative* advantage in analyzing the long run.

Another reason why economists disagree (though it is probably a much less important reason than most people think) is differences in value judgments. Now, in principle, value judgments should not influence what we predict will happen. But this is not so even in the physical sciences.[2]

Third, deciding which theory is the more convenient organizing principle is largely a matter of "scientific taste," and deciding which theory is likely to be more fruitful in the future involves much guesswork. Not surprisingly economists frequently disagree on such issues.

Fourth, economists, unlike physical scientists, have a long tradition of trying to be helpful to policymakers by answering every important question, even if it means

[1]R. G. A. Dolby, "Sociology of Knowledge in Natural Science," *Science Studies* 1 (January 1971): 20.

[2]Consider, for example, the decision whether a certain chemical is a safe food additive. One cannot settle the question with certainty, but can only say that it is safe at a certain level of probability. Suppose that the additive, if actually bad for people, only gives them a slightly upset stomach. One may say that it is safe if the probability that it actually *is* safe is as high as 99 percent. But suppose that it can kill people; then a 99 percent probability that it is actually safe is not sufficient to call it safe. (See Richard Rudner, "The Scientist *Qua* Scientist Makes Value Judgments," *Philosophy of Science* 20 [January 1953]: 1–6.)

taking a guess. In recent years as pollution and similar problems have become important issues, physical scientists too have been forced to answer questions on which they have little information—and they also disagree frequently.

Fifth, much disagreement among economists is about the political feasibility of certain policies, rather than about economics per se. An economist might advocate a (high employment) balanced budget not because she thinks that this is the best imaginable policy, but because she thinks that this is the best that can be done, given the political pressures. Another economist might be more optimistic about what the political pressures permit.

Finally, but perhaps most importantly, while physical and biological scientists can settle many issues by laboratory experiments, in economics experiments are generally not possible. One would hardly recommend that the Fed adopt a policy that *may* cause a recession merely to find out if it actually does so. To be sure, economists can use statistical techniques (mainly regression analysis) to try to disentangle the effects that particular variables have had on the economy, but that is a very poor substitute for controlled experiments.[3]

What is a reasonable response to this disagreement? One obvious step is to see if it really is a disagreement on matters of substance, or if, as often happens, seeming disagreement is merely the result of different ways of expressing the same point. But suppose that there is genuine disagreement on points of substance. One response that is often reasonable is to take both views seriously. Suppose, for example, that one theory predicts that a certain action, say raising interest rates, will lead to a recession, while another theory claims that it will have little effect. Even if the Fed believes that the latter theory is more likely to be right, it may well decide not to raise interest rates. Or suppose that one group of economists believes that wage-price guidelines are needed to stop inflation, while another group believes that inflation will not end unless the budget is balanced. An administration that is eager to stop inflation quickly may well decide to "accept" both theories, despite their disagree-

[3]One reason for this is that our data often lack a close correspondence to the variables that our theory tells us are important. For example, Keynesian theory places much importance on the marginal efficiency of investment, but there are no data that measure this variable, and hence we have to use some more or less imprecise proxies for it. Another problem is that several theories can produce a close fit to past data, and it is hard to decide which one gives the best fit; this may well vary from period to period. Moreover, when we use these theories to predict into the future, neither one may perform well. This is so because information on the past could be used to formulate the theories, so that it is not surprising that they fit well to the past data. But when used to predict, where they do not have this advantage of having, so to speak, seen the "answers" to the examination ahead of time, they do not do as well. Another important reason is that when two variables show similar fluctuations, it is easier to say that they are related, than to determine which one is cause and which one is effect.

ment, and impose wage and price guidelines as well as balancing the budget. Finally, remember that economists are doing much research trying to resolve their disagreements. By studying several theories you put yourself in the position of being able to understand these resolutions as they occur.

Money, Interest, and Asset Prices

12

In previous chapters a lot of attention has been given to the determination of the supply of money. We must turn our attention to the demand for money.

This chapter has two functions. On the one hand it can be regarded as a completion of our discussion of capital markets. After we have examined the factors determining demand for money, we will show how the processes that equate supply and demand for money serve to exert an important influence on the level of interest rates and asset prices. On the other hand the chapter will also serve as an introduction to the discussion in the following chapters of ways in which money can influence prices and the level of output for the economy as a whole.

THE MEANING OF MONEY

The "meaning of money" sounds a little like a title for a philosophical treatise. Our objectives here are more pedestrian. We just want to note three ways in which careless use of the term *money* can lead to confusion. First, we must distinguish between real and nominal quantities of money. Second, we must avoid confusion between money, wealth, and income. Third, we must note that the definition of money is a source of controversy and confusion.

Real versus nominal money. The fact that money only has meaning in relation to the prices of goods and services is the most fundamental proposition of monetary theory. The *real* quantities of physical assets—cars, houses, land, watches, and what-have-you—are invariant to changes in the level of prices. If all prices double there is no change in the number of cars or houses. Nor is there any change in their barter exchange values. When the price of my Volkswagen was $3,000 and the price of my house was $30,000 I could sell my house and buy ten Volkswagens. If Volkswagens go to $6,000 and the house to $60,000 I can still trade my house for ten VWs.

But if instead of a house I had $30,000 in the bank I would find that after the price level changed I could buy only five VWs instead of ten. At the doubled price level, $60,000 would have the same economic meaning to me as $30,000 at the original price level. Prices translate arbitrary nominal units of money into real values in terms of goods and services.

This brings us to an important point. The real quantity of money can be changed in two ways. First, the nominal quantity of money supplied can change while prices are fixed. Second, prices can change while the nominal quantity of money remains fixed.

We cannot measure the price or value of money absolutely because we are unable to combine all the different goods and services money can buy. But it does make sense to say that the value (price) of money goes down when the price level of goods goes up. However, there is another "price" for money. The interest rate is the rental price of money. When the interest rate is 5 percent you can rent, that is, borrow, $100 for one year for $5.

We will see later on that there are interactions between the two prices. The price level or value of money does affect interest rates. On the other hand there is a feedback from interest rates to price-level movements. In this chapter we will be concerned with the way both kinds of prices affect the demand for money, that is, the amount people are willing to hold.

Money versus wealth and income. We noted in Chapter 1 that while money may be part of wealth, it is not the same thing. Wealth can be held in many other forms.

A related question is whether increasing the aggregate money stock directly increases aggregate wealth. The answer from our discussion in Chapter 6 is that the amount of nominal wealth created by an increase in money supply depends on how the increase in money comes about. The effect of an increase in money supply on real wealth also depends on whether the increment in money supply causes a change in the price level.

Which Definition of the Term *Money*?

We have discussed alternative definitions of money in a separate chapter. We will often use the term *money* in a general way when it is not necessary to be more precise. We will, however, try to point out how the response of demand for "money" to changes in interest, wealth, and income depends on which of the several definitions of money discussed in Chapter 11 is used.

THE ECONOMIC IMPACT OF MONEY

The fact that money measures are only meaningful in terms of a price level has been known for a long time. Inflation is a very old phenomenon. The Greeks and Romans had plenty of experience with it, and certainly realized that a denarius didn't go as far in Nero's time as in the days of the Republic.

In modern times discussion of the economic impact of money goes back to the seventeenth century when people were reacting to the effects of gold and silver imports from America. A little later there was raging controversy over trade policy. Mercantilist policy aimed at increasing exports of goods while restricting imports, with the difference paid in gold or silver. Proponents of mercantilism took it for granted that a country was better off if it had more gold and silver. Others argued that gold and silver do not produce anything and that too much of these metals only drives up prices.

Controversy centered on two alternative propositions, one holding that more money stimulates trade and the other that more money drives up prices. The money-stimulates-trade doctrine usually gained popularity in periods of depression. Its proponents assumed, at least implicitly, that prices were fixed and that there were unemployed resources. In that case, if more money led to more spending, it would also lead to more employment and output.

The more-money-raises-prices school assumed that prices were flexible and that production could not be increased in the short run. In that case, if an increased money supply induced more spending, prices would rise but not output or employment. Since the seventeenth and eighteenth centuries were periods of rising money supply and rising prices, this argument carried conviction. Nonetheless, the money-stimulates-trade doctrine reasserted its strength in the periodic depressions.

These disputes are of far more than historical interest. Modern monetary analysis is much more sophisticated and precise and has a stronger empirical base than the pamphlets of the seventeenth century. Nonetheless, there is still room for dispute. Indeed, criticism of Federal Reserve policy is the economist's favorite indoor sport. The central issue in the critique is the conflict between the desire for more rapid growth of money supply to stimulate trade—that is, to increase employment and output—and the fear that rapid money supply growth will accelerate inflation.

In this and the next six chapters we will work to synthesize the true insights underlying both those slogans. We will find that under some circumstances more money does stimulate trade. In some circumstances it just drives up prices, and sometimes it first stimulates trade and then drives up prices. Meanwhile, we have to proceed step by step and avoid slogans.

When the moral philosophers and pamphleteers of the seventeenth and eighteenth centuries tried to work out the consequences of an increased money supply, they found it necessary, first of all, to develop a theory of what people would do with more money—hoard it, spend it, or lend it.

The Demand for Money

In their search for understanding of the impact of changes in money supply on economic activity and prices, seventeenth-century writers recognized that the key to the puzzle lay in the demand for money. Why do people hold money in the first place? It does not make an obvious contribution to the production process. Nor does it, except in the hands of misers, give the kind of satisfaction that ordinary goods and services provide.

On examination, though, it appears that money does contribute to productive efficiency and it does provide utility to its owner just as any durable good does. In Chapter 1 we discussed the superior efficiency of a money economy over a barter economy, and considered the social efficiency of a money economy. Now we are interested in the returns from holding money as perceived by individual households or firms. Part of the return is associated with the medium of exchange or transactions function of money. Another part of the return arises from the safety and convenience of money as a form of wealth, a store of value.

TRANSACTIONS DEMAND FOR MONEY

The use of money makes it possible to split the exchange process into two parts. People sell goods or services for money at one time and then, at leisure, use the money to buy other goods and services, ultimately having exchanged one set of goods and services for another. In the interval between transactions they are holding money. The ratio of the amount of money they hold to the annual value of transactions depends, in part, on the average length of the interval between the receipt of money from sale of goods and services and the payment of money for purchase of goods and services.

For households, the ratio of average money holdings to annual expenditure for goods and services will depend on how often the members of the household get paid. Consider the following simple case. A family receives a paycheck of $1,000 per month. They do not save anything, and spend the whole $1,000 each month, so they have a zero bank balance at the end of each month just before the next check arrives. They spend at a steady rate—$33.33 per day in a thirty-day month. When they receive each check they are holding $1,000. Their bank balance gradually declines to zero by the end of the month. It jumps to $1,000 on the first and the cycle repeats. The time pattern of the family's bank balance is shown in Figure 12.1. On the average their balance is $500; half of one month's pay, or 1/24th of a year's income.

If the paycheck came weekly, the family's money holdings would follow a similar pattern, but the average amount of money held would be only half a week's pay or 1/104th of a year's pay, only about a quarter as much as in the other case.

Of course, reality is a little more complicated. Nobody spends at a steady rate. People are likely to pay their rent on the first of the month, pay other bills around the tenth, and do their grocery shopping on Fridays. The important points, however, are that they do have to hold money because there is a time interval between receipt and expenditures, and that the average ratio of money held to expenditures depends on factors such as the frequency of wage payments and whether goods and services are paid for at the time of purchase or charged and paid for monthly.

Very similar considerations apply to businesses. The paychecks that families receive usually come from businesses, and the money they pay for goods and services goes back to businesses. The same money can just pass back and forth between them. In a simple but unlikely example we may suppose that businesses accumulate money from sale of goods and services

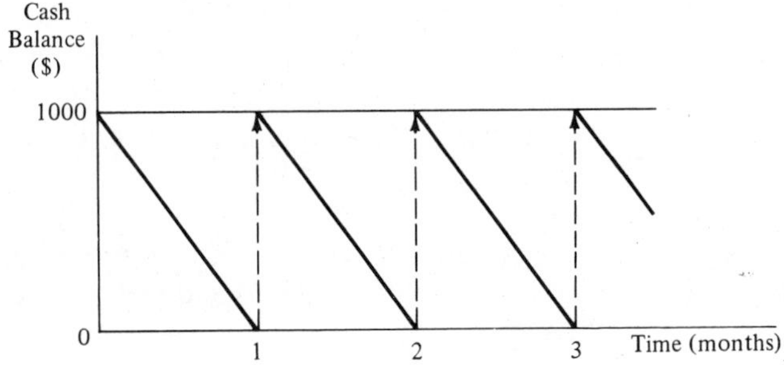

Figure 12.1 Time Pattern of Household Cash Balances

to households during the month and pay out all their receipts in wages and dividends at the end of the month. Their cash balances would follow the mirror image pattern of the household shown in Figure 12.1.

In a closed economy with no purchases from outside, with, say, one hundred families each earning $1,000 a month, the total cash balance of the two combined is always $100,000; it is all in the hands of businesses at the end of the month, then all in the hands of households on the first. Then household money holdings gradually decline, business holdings gradually rise, until businesses again have it all at the end of the month. The GNP of this economy is $100,000 per month—1.2 million dollars per year. Total transactions are twice as much ($1.2 million annual income payments, $1.2 million sales of goods and services). Combined money holdings of households and businesses are 1/12th of a year's GNP, 1/24th of a year's transactions.

Of course we have drastically oversimplified. Businesses have to make payments to one another as well as to labor. The timing of receipts and payments does not work out so neatly as in our example. Still, the amount of money held for transactions purposes does depend on the structure of the payments system. The amount of money required for a given real GNP at a given price level does depend on the organization of the payments system, especially on the frequency of payments.

That idea was recognized early in discussions of the demand for money. William Petty, the first economist who tried to measure the national income of England in the seventeenth century, described the "circle of payments" from household and business and back again. He wrote:

> . . . for the expense being forty millions, if the revolutions were in such short circles, *viz.*, weekly as happens among poorer artisans and laborers who receive and pay every Saturday, then 40/52nd parts of one million of money would answer those ends. But if the circles be quarterly according to our custom of paying rent, and gathering taxes, then ten millions were requisite.[1]

The idea that the amount of nominal money people want to hold is simply a fixed proportion of total annual nominal expenditures or, alternatively, that the amount of money balances people want is proportional to total annual

[1] Charles Henry Hull, ed., *Economic Writings of Sir William Petty* (London: Cambridge Univeristy Press, 1899), pp. 112–13.

expenditures held sway for over three hundred years. The basic equation of exchange $M = kYP$ where M is money demand, Y is real output, P the price level, and k is the ratio of money holdings to total annual expenditure, or, in real terms, $M/P = kY$, was generally accepted. It was also agreed that k was mainly determined by the structure of the payments system. The equation could be reversed to read $PY = M/k$. Disputes raged, not over the value of k, but over the circumstances under which a rise in M would make output rise or make prices rise. Those problems will occupy us in the next eight chapters, but there is a lot more to be said about the demand for money.

Holding Precautionary Balances

The description of receipt and expenditure patterns summarized in Figure 12.1 suggests a dull, repetitive life. Many individuals have a regular monthly pattern of wage and salary receipts and routine expenditures. They may also have dividend receipts quarterly, and royalties annually. On the payments side, income taxes have to be paid quarterly, college tuition two or three times a year, and property taxes annually. Those receipts and payments may be predictable but because they are large, people may give more care to the sums involved than to their monthly salary checks and routine expenditures. Businesses, of course, have all sorts of lumpy expenditures, for example, capital goods purchases and dividend payments. They may have irregular receipts from contract payments or from floating a bond issue.

Receipts and payments are not only irregular, they are often unpredictable. Households are often faced with large unexpected expenditures for home or auto repairs. Their receipts vary because family members may sometimes become unemployed, or at other times get a lot of overtime work.

Because their receipts and payments are lumpy, irregular, and partly unpredictable, most households do not want to end the month with no money, waiting for the postman to bring the check. If their assets are large enough, they usually want to have some readily available liquid assets to absorb the unevenness in the flow of receipts and payments, and they want to avoid borrowing when things do go wrong. Businesses, of course, have similar problems. Their sales vary unexpectedly, and they cannot predict when major outlays for repairs may be necessary. They too usually want to have a cushion of liquid assets so they don't have to rush to negotiate a bank loan every time their cash flow predictions go wrong. Keynes labeled funds held for these purposes precautionary balances. The fact that there are irregular or lumpy receipts and payments, and some unpredictable ones, does not destroy the basic idea of a close link between the level of aggregate income and expenditure and the demand for money. The scale of irregular payments and of unusual receipts and expenditures varies with the level of income. The irregularities of receipts and expenditures are smoothed in the totals for a large population. Their existence does not undermine the proposition that the structure of the payments system strongly influences the ratio of aggregate money holdings to aggregate income expenditure.

VELOCITY OF MONEY

For some purposes it is convenient to ask how much money people want to hold in relation to income and expenditure. But, especially when we are asking how money affects expenditure, it is sometimes useful to ask how fast money moves around the circle of payments from income to payments for goods and services and back again to income. As D. H. Robertson put it, we can think of "money sitting or money on the wing." We are unable to measure how fast any individual dollar moved but we can ask how many dollars worth of transactions per year are made with the average dollar. In 1982 approximately eighty trillion dollars of transactions were made in the United States. The average money supply *M-1* was $460 billion. The average dollar changed hands nearly two hundred times during the year. The *ratio of the annual volume of transactions to the stock of money* is called the **transactions velocity of money.**

A more commonly used concept is the income or circuit velocity of money. The number of times the average dollar goes around the circle from expenditure to income and back to income is the ratio of GNP to money stock. In 1982 GNP was approximately $3,000 billion and the average money stock (*M-1*) was $460 billion, so the circuit velocity of money was over 6.6 times per year.

Transactions velocity is always much higher than income velocity because total transactions include both income and expenditure payments and the expenditure payments include payments for intermediate goods as well as final products. GNP includes auto sales, but total transactions also include payments for coal to make steel, and payments for steel to make the cars. In addition, total transactions include transactions in financial assets and for sales of existing land and buildings. Nonetheless, the two move roughly together.

We can rewrite the equation of exchange as $MV \equiv GNP$. The three-bar equality sign is used to indicate that the equation is an identity. It is always true because V is defined as $V = \text{GNP}/M$, which is just another arrangement of the equation of exchange. (The previously discussed equation, $M = kYp$, is also an identity.)

Since the equation is essentially a definition, it tells us nothing about the real world. But it does serve to remind us of some connections between money and other things that must always be true. In particular, any increase in M must be accompanied by either a decrease in V or an increase in output, prices, or both.

Actually velocity varies a good deal, as can be seen in Figure 12.2. You can see that in 1945 the average dollar traveled the income circuit about two times. In 1929 and 1965 the average dollar went around the income circuit nearly four times a year, and in 1982 the average dollar went around the circuit about six times a year.

Velocity also varies a good deal in the very short run. In fact quarter-to-quarter movements of velocity are closely associated with quarter-to-quarter movements of GNP.

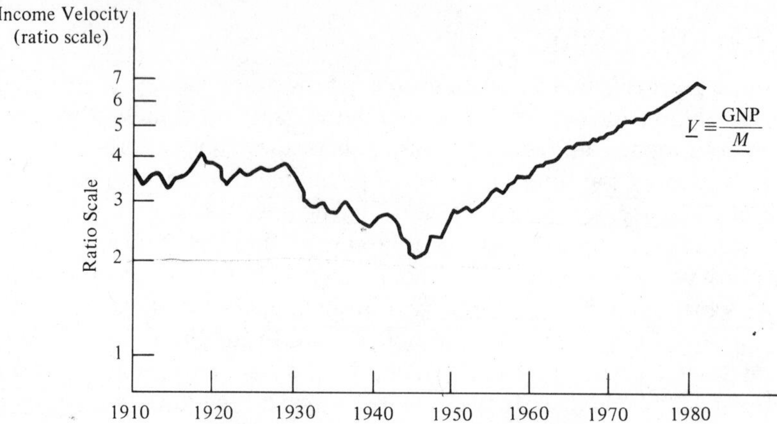

Figure 12.2 Income Velocity of Money in the U.S., *1910–82*

There are many causes for variations in velocity. There have been important changes in institutional arrangements for making payments. There are some reasons for believing that there are economies of scale in the use of money so that although demand for money increases with the level of income and transactions, it does not increase proportionately. The short-run changes in velocity may simply reflect the fact that people do not adjust money holdings to short-run changes in income. Milton Friedman has argued that people adjust money holdings to "permanent income," that is, to the average expected income over the long run. In that case velocity will tend to rise whenever there is an unusually rapid rise in income.

In addition, however, it appears that the demand for money at a given level of income also depends on the level of interest rates.

TRANSACTIONS DEMAND AND THE INTEREST RATE

Our discussion of payment cycles, irregular receipts, and payments and precautionary balances shows that households and firms will often have money that they will not immediately disburse. They may expect to have funds idle for a day, for a week, several months, or in the case of precautionary balances, for an uncertain period. It is usually possible to earn more interest by investing any cash not needed immediately and then disinvesting when it is needed. Whether investing is worthwhile depends on the kind of investments available, how much it costs to buy and sell them again, how much risk is involved, and what return they will pay. The length of time for which funds can be invested and the sum involved are also revelant.

Businesses usually use short-term marketable securities as alternatives to holding demand deposits. In Chapter 6 we discussed the way corporate treasurers use short-term securities to get interest on temporarily idle funds. There we were mainly interested in their choice among alternative securities. Now we want to focus on their decisions as to whether to invest or not.

Treasurers of large corporations keep careful track of cash flows and project future receipts and outlays. That adds a good deal to overhead and would not be worthwhile if interest rates were not high enough to justify short-term investments. Suppose a treasurer finds that his cash-flow projection indicates that one million dollars can be invested for a week. If he invests in Treasury bills yielding 8 percent he will earn about \$1,600 that week, more than enough to cover the dealer's spread, which will amount to \$500. The transaction would obviously be less attractive at a lower interest rate. It would also be less worthwhile if only, say, \$100,000 were involved, or if the funds were available for only three days.

When interest rates are low, only firms with surplus funds that are either large, or available for a long time, will find it worthwhile to reduce demand-deposit holdings by making temporary investments in securities. As interest rates rise, smaller amounts, or amounts available for shorter periods, can be profitably invested. Thus the proportion of liquid assets businesses hold in demand deposits will be relatively large when interest rates are low, and relatively small when they are high.

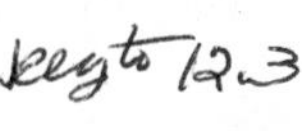

Notice that both payments and receipts of businesses get larger when GNP is larger. Their total liquid asset holdings are likely to grow in rough proportion to GNP. Thus at any given GNP their demand for money will be a downward sloping function of interest rates. But at a higher GNP they will hold more money and more securities at any given interest rate. In Figure 12.3 the line marked Y_0 shows business demand for money at different interest rates with GNP = Y_0. The line Y_1 shows their demand for money in relation to interest rates at the higher GNP, Y_1.

The situation for households is very similar in principle. Most households use bank or thrift institution accounts or money market funds instead of short-term securities. To decide in what form temporarily available funds should be kept one must balance interest earnings against the time, trouble, and cost of moving funds from one form to another. And, just as in the case of businesses, the amount of interest earned depends on the level of interest rates, the sum involved, and the time for which it can be invested.

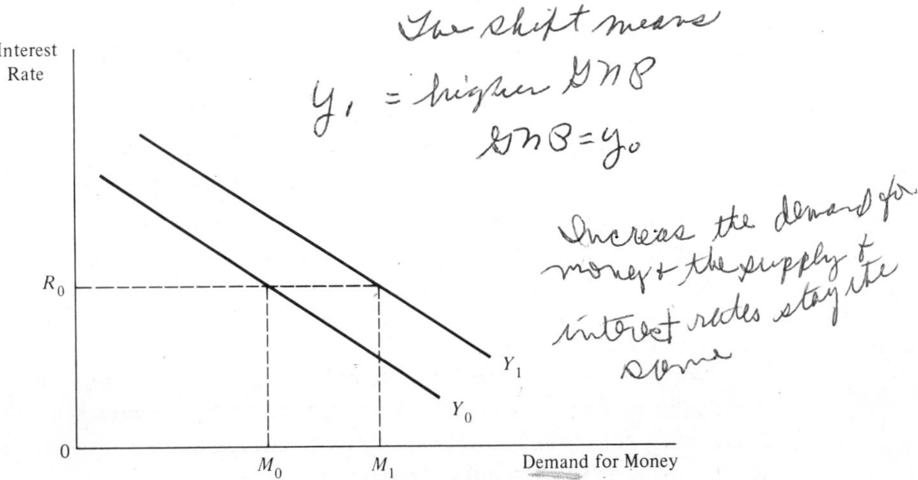

Figure 12.3 Business Transactions Demand for Money

Although the exact holding time is unpredictable, precautionary balances for a "rainy day" are likely to be investable for relatively long periods, so they can be attracted into the highest yielding liquid assets. Funds being accumulated for a one-time payment—real-estate taxes, or an annual insurance premium—may be on hand for several months, but whether it is worthwhile putting them into a money market fund or bank capital account depends on the amount and the interest rate differentials.

MONEY AS AN INVESTMENT

In our discussion of transactions and precautionary demand, we regarded money as an asset held only because receipts and payments of individual households and firms are not perfectly synchronized, regular, or predictable. Those considerations are directly connected with the use of money as a medium of exchange. There are, however, other reasons for holding money that are more closely associated with the role of money as a store of value. In fact, until a couple of hundred years ago, money was far and away the most important financial asset. There were no common stocks or marketable bonds and no array of savings banks, insurance companies, and other financial institutions. Most people held their wealth in the form of land, houses, or unincorporated businesses. There were, of course, some mortgages, some trade debt. Lawyers and others often acted as intermediaries in arranging personal loans, often at high rates. There is always considerable uncertainty in the value of land, houses, and independent businesses. Any wealthy person who wanted to reduce the uncertainty in the value of his total portfolio found that the easiest way to do so was to hold part of his wealth in the form of money. Anyone who wanted to avoid the cares of owning physical assets or the risks and problems of making personal loans, directly or indirectly, found that money was a relatively attractive way of holding wealth.

The role of money as a financial asset held for investment, as opposed to transactions reasons, was recognized early in the game but it was not given a major role until the work of two famous economists, Alfred Marshall and A. C. Pigou, who successively held the chair of political economy at Cambridge University. The work of Marshall and Pigou not only recognized the importance of money as an asset in investment portfolios, but also treated decisions about money holding in that context as a matter of rational choice in the balancing of risk and return on an investment portfolio.

However, they did not carry that notion very far. When dealing with the theory of the relation between prices and money in the long run, they were content to use a summary formulation in which they assumed that aggregate wealth is proportional to aggregate income and that demand for money can be approximated as a fixed proportion of wealth, k_1, plus a fixed proportion, k_2, of income. On those assumptions, demand for money is given by $M = k_1W + k_2Yp$, where W is wealth and Y is real income and p prices. If the ratio of wealth to income is w, then W can be replaced by wY and the money demand equation can be rewritten as $M = k_1wYp + k_2Yp$, or $M = (k_1w + k_2)Yp$. In short $M = kYp$ where $k = (k_1w + k_2)$.

This equation is called the **Cambridge Equation.** Since the velocity of money is defined as the ratio of Y to M, you can see that since $k = \frac{M}{Yp}$, V is just the inverse of the Cambridge k.

Marshall particularly was interested in short-run business-cycle problems as well as in long-run price theory. In explaining the depressions and financial panics of the nineteenth century, Marshall placed great emphasis on the variability of k. He attributed variations in k to fluctuations in business confidence. The resulting variation in the velocity of money caused corresponding variations in nominal money expenditures and therefore led to fluctuations in prices and output.

During the great depression of the 1930s another Cambridge economist, J. M. Keynes, related changes in k to expectations of changes in interest rates. Keynes argued that people who are "bearish" on bonds, i.e., who fear a rise in bond yields and a fall in bond prices will prefer money to bonds. The "bulls" holding opposite views will wish to hold bonds rather than money. The price of bonds will have to move to a level at which there are just enough "bears" to hold all the money, and just enough "bulls" to hold all the bonds.

James Tobin of Yale generalized Keynes's approach by arguing that even when investors think it just as likely that interest rates will rise as fall, they will still want to hold a safe asset to reduce the risk on their total portfolio. The greater the proportion of wealth held in money, the lower the percentage change in the value of the total portfolio from a given percentage change in bond prices. Investors can then be regarded as trading-off risk for return by varying the proportion of the money and other assets in their portfolios. The average return on the portfolio depends on the excess of bond yields over the yield on money and on the proportion of the portfolio held in bonds. The average return on their total portfolio increases as they shift toward progressively greater proportions of bonds and smaller proportions of money in their portfolio. But the risk they bear increases at the same time. As in any other commodity choice, investors will stop increasing the share of risky assets in the portfolio when the additional reward from more risky assets just balances the value they place on avoiding additional risk.

Different investors will have different views as to the risks involved at any one time, and they will also have different tastes for risk versus return. "Plungers" may borrow as much as they can to maximize return. Most investors, however, will place a progressively higher value on avoiding additional risks as they become more fully invested in risky assets. Most of them will decide to dilute the risk of their portfolio by holding some money. However, the reward they get for taking risks changes with interest rates. The bond-to-wealth ratio at which marginal risk aversion balances the return from additional bond holdings will increase as bond yields rise relative to the yields on riskless assets. Conversely, the optimum money-to-wealth ratio will decline. Tobin's argument thus leads to just the same conclusion that Keynes reached. Speculative demand for money will fall as bond yields rise relative to liquid asset yields.

The Keynes-Tobin model of asset demand for money applies most directly when a single well-defined type of money is the only riskless asset. The asset demand for money will tend to increase as the excess of the yield on risky assets over the yield, if any, on money balances declines. The ratio of that differential to a measure of risk is called the "market price of risk."

The Keynes-Tobin model cannot be applied literally because there are many kinds of "money" paying different interest rates and because there are other liquid assets not included in any definition of money. Nonetheless, the theory helps to explain why many people are prepared to accept relatively low yields on riskless assets. It also helps to provide the underlying logic for empirical studies of demand for money. Before considering empirical results we can use the theory to draw some general theoretical conclusions about the relation between interest-rate movements and demand for money. In doing so we must, of course, take account of transactions as well as asset demand for money.

TOTAL DEMAND FOR MONEY AND LIQUID ASSETS

So far, we have considered the transactions and investment demand for money separately. Now we must consider the total demand. When we do so we find that the definition of money becomes important, because some assets can be used as media of exchange while other money-like assets serve only as stores of wealth.

In analyzing the demand for any particular monetary aggregate, it seems natural to treat transactions and investment demand separately and then add them together. In fact, the separation between transaction and investment needs for liquidity is somewhat artificial. Liquid assets are held to cover regular payment cycles, as a means of holding funds from irregular or unexpected receipts, and to provide for irregular or unpredicted outlays. An investor holding liquid assets avoids certain investment risks while at the same time avoiding the cost and inconvenience of many transactions in illiquid assets or frequent resort to borrowing. Those benefits have to be considered jointly in deciding whether they justify the reduction in investment yield which is usually involved. Suppose, for example, that interest-bearing NOW accounts are the only liquid asset. Then, the investor has to divide his portfolio between money (NOW account) and risky assets. At the margin, the difference between the NOW account yield and the expected yield elsewhere should be equal to the value to the investor of the benefit (in terms of cost, convenience, and risk) of $1 more or less held in the NOW account. That benefit will tend to decline as the amount of liquid assets in relation to income and wealth increases. Accordingly, we expect that the share of wealth held in liquid form will rise as the difference between the yield on other assets and the NOW account yield becomes smaller.

A somewhat more complex situation arises when interest is paid on some liquid assets but not on the demand deposits and currency used as transactions media; in that case we might expect investors to choose the level of total liquid assets just as in the case cited above. They might then choose the level of demand deposits and currency by balancing the convenience value of ready money against the loss of interest. Business firms can do the same thing when Treasury bills and other marketable securities are available to them. A variety of other liquid assets, e.g., money market funds, and deposit certificates of various maturities complicate the picture still further.

All the different kinds of liquid assets are close substitutes for one another. Each has its own advantages and disadvantages for each investor group. Economies of scale in transactions costs are important in some cases. Indeed, some assets are available only in large denominations. Others involve special knowledge or financial sophistication. The operation of Regulation Q has further complicated the picture. Thus, households with modest assets and little knowledge accept a return of only 5½ percent on their savings accounts while better informed households can earn 8 percent from money market funds. Those who can tie up their funds for a few months can earn a much higher return than those who want them available on demand. In these circumstances the demand for each type of liquid asset depends on its own yield, the yield on each of the other liquid assets, as well as the yields on risky assets of all kinds.

The demand for each of the "monetary aggregates" is the sum of the demands for its components. Thus, *M-1* is a mix of noninterest-bearing demand deposits, NOW accounts, and some other interest-bearing checking deposits. *M-2* adds money market funds as well as time and saving deposits. The mix of liquid assets has changed rapidly in the last few years in response to financial innovations induced by rising interest rates and changes in regulation. It is worth noting that the ratio of total liquid assets (*L*) to GNP has remained more stable than its composition throughout the post-war period.

EMPIRICAL STUDIES

Economists have worked hard at empirical testing of theories of demand for money and measurement of the response of money demand to changes in income, wealth, and interest rates. There are literally hundreds of studies of demand for money for the U.S. and other countries. As usual the results agree in some respects, disagree in others. We can report here only a few of the main conclusions and note some unsettled issues.

In a general way it can be said that empirical studies confirm the broad qualitative conclusions of the last section. Demand for any liquid asset increases with income and wealth. It increases with its own yield and falls when the yields on competing assets rise.

The question whether income or wealth is more important is problematic mainly because they move together. We have to recall that two kinds of wealth are involved, human and nonhuman. Human wealth is usually measured as a moving average of actual past income. Most studies making the comparison show that money demand at a given date is more closely associated with a moving average of past income than with current income.

Measurement of the relative importance of nonhuman wealth and income is difficult because they both grow with similar trends. A number of studies using data for long periods have indicated that either income or wealth must be involved in the explanation of demand for money, and that if both are used together variations in wealth leave little for income to explain. On the other hand, one of the most thorough studies of postwar data, done by Stephen Goldfeld of Princeton, concluded that income performs better than wealth in explaining money demand. He added, however, that short-run changes in wealth help to explain the data. Probably then, income and wealth play independent roles in determining demand for money, but it is difficult to disentangle their relative importance.

It also turns out to be difficult to separate the influence of the returns on different types of assets since they all move more or less together. Short-term and long-term interest rates move together in business cycles though short-term rates fluctuate over a wider range. On the whole they give equally good explanations of the demand for money. The reported demand elasticities are, of course, much higher for long-term rates than for short-term ones because the latter move so much more. The hypothesis that equity yields should be relevant is difficult to test because the prospective yield on equity cannot be readily measured. We can measure the dividend component, but the prospect for capital gain is in the eye of the beholder. Finally, recent studies in the U.S. indicate that the rates paid on time and savings deposits are an important factor in determining the demand for money. Goldfeld's 1973 study reported interest elasticity of about 0.2 for *M-1* assuming equal changes in time deposit and commercial paper rates and allowing about two years for the full effect of a rate change to be felt.

Recent Instability in Money Demand

While empirical studies of demand for money agree as to broad qualitative conclusions about the direction and order of magnitude of the response of demand for money to changes in interest rates, income, and wealth, agreement is far from complete. Moreover, none of the empirical estimates have been wholly successful in predicting demand for money. Indeed, since 1975, they have all been notably unsuccessful.

Prior to 1975 short-run forecasts of demand for money showed substantial errors. However, an overprediction for one period of a few months was usually canceled out by an opposite error a few months later. There was clearly room for improvement, but the forecasters seemed to be on the right track. After 1975, however, money-demand forecasters were thrown into confusion. Forecasts of money demand have erred by wide margins. At first it was thought the prediction errors were an aberration, perhaps associated with the oil shock and the recession; however, the forecast errors persisted and have, indeed, grown larger.

In trying to explain what happened, economists have pointed to changes in regulations noted in Chapter 11 that blur the distinction between demand and savings deposits. There is widespread agreement that much of the difficulty is due to financial innovations, such as money market funds, NOW accounts, and "Super-NOW" accounts paying high interest rates. Banks developed new devices to help their corporate customers to reduce their holdings of demand deposits while maintaining the availability of their funds for transactions purposes.

At the beginning of 1980, NOW accounts became available nationally. In recognition of the changes just noted and the prospect of a substantial shift from demand deposits to NOW accounts the Fed changed its money stock measures as noted in Chapter 11. Use of the new definitions for monetary aggregates helped to improve the stability of money demand functions but did not solve all the problems of the money managers.

Predictions of short-run movements of the redefined monetary aggregates have remained unsatisfactory. There was, for example, a significant underprediction of the change in velocity of *M-1* from 1980 to 1981 and a marked decline in 1982–83. In spite of the innovations of the past decade, the relation of total liquidity to GNP has remained quite stable. That consideration has led some economists within the Federal Reserve System to propose that total liquidity rather than any of its components should be used as a policy target.

The relation of monetary aggregates to interest rates and GNP is likely to remain unstable until the financial system has adjusted to the recent spate of regulatory changes. The system may evolve toward one with market interest rates on all kinds of deposits. In that case, the demand for deposits will be unresponsive to changes in the *level* interest rates on deposits and other liquid assets but very sensitive to differences in rates paid on different types of liquid assets.

MONEY SUPPLY, INTEREST, AND INCOME

So far we have been concerned with various partial aspects of the demand for money. The object of analyzing demand, however, is to enable us to understand the interaction among interest rates, money supply, and income. To get an overview of that interaction, we must neglect, but not forget, some of the complexities arising from the existence of a variety of moneylike assets.

For simplicity, first assume that income and wealth move closely together so that income can be used as a proxy for both. Second, suppose that the only money is currency, and non-interest-bearing deposits. Third, assume that there is only one interest-bearing security. Under those circumstances, it is clear that the demand for money tends to rise with income and to fall as the interest rate rises.

Those simplifications give us, as they should, a basis for a relatively simple theory of interest-rate determination. In Figure 12.4 the curve marked Y_0 represents demand for money associated with some given income level Y_0. The vertical line $\overline{M}$ is the fixed money supply. Then the equilibrium interest rate is R_0. The vertical line M' corresponds to a larger money supply. Demand and supply for money are equated at the lower interest rate R'. In general, when nominal income is fixed, a larger money supply reduces the short-term interest rate.

Figure 12.5 shows a set of money-demand curves, each corresponding to a different level of nominal income. Y_0 is the lowest nominal income; Y_1 a higher one, and so on. The vertical line at $\overline{M}$ shows the money supply. M' as before shows a larger money supply. Ignore it for the moment.

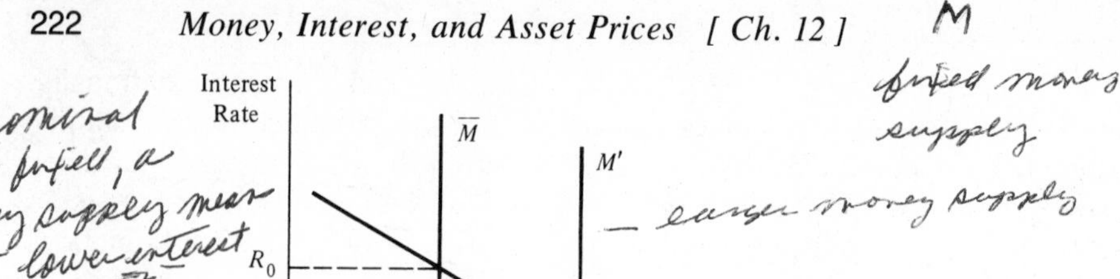

Figure 12.4 Determination of the Interest Rate

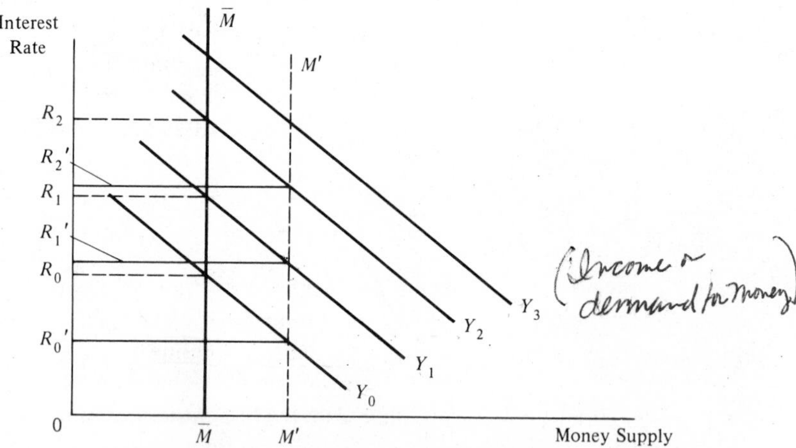

Figure 12.5 Effect of Changing Income on Equilibrium Interest Rate

You can see that $\overline{M}$ intersects Y_0 at R_0; it intersects Y_1 at a higher interest rate R_1, and so on. Clearly, when money supply is fixed the equilibrium interest rate rises as income rises.

In Figure 12.6 the information in Figure 12.5 has been replotted with R on the vertical axis and Y on the horizontal axis. The upward sloping line LM is derived from the points R_0Y_0, R_1Y_1, and so forth, on Figure 12.5. The **LM curve** *shows the equilibrium interest rate for each level of nominal income and a given money supply*. It strongly emphasizes the fact that a rise in money income must be accompanied by a rising interest rate if money supply remains fixed. Notice that a change in money supply shifts the whole LM curve. We will make a great deal of use of the LM curve in the next three chapters. In Figure 12.7 the line LM is the same as in Figure 12.6. The lower line $L'M'$ is derived in the same way as LM from Figure 12.5 using the larger money supply M' and plotting the alternative equilibrium points R'_0Y_0, R'_1Y_1, and so on.

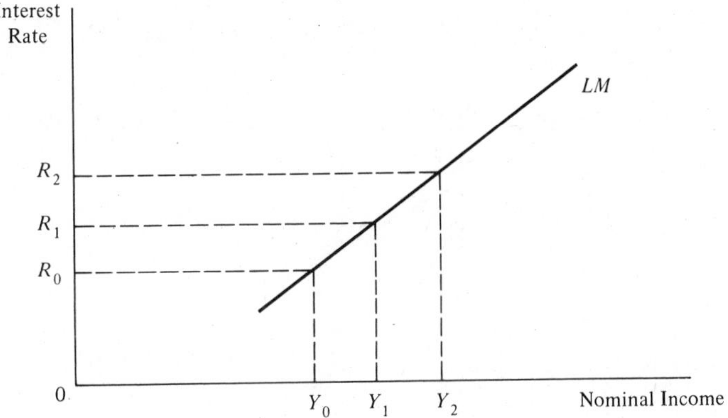

Figure 12.6 The *LM* Curve

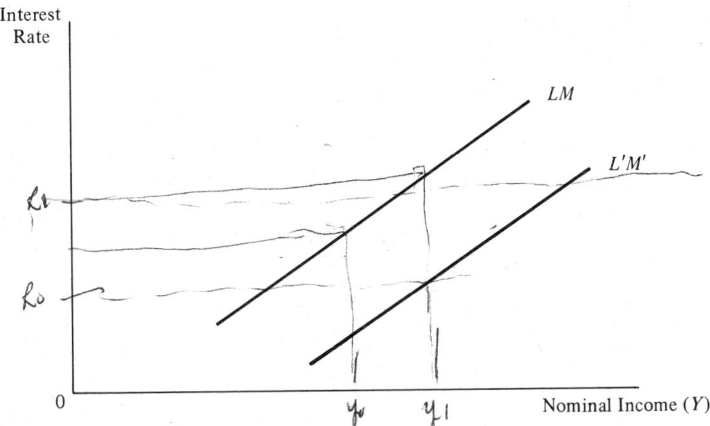

Figure 12.7 Increase in Money Supply Shifts the *LM* Curve

Changing Price Levels

In our discussion so far we have not distinguished between nominal and real magnitudes. As long as prices stay constant this does not matter. But, in a world of inflation, nominal income can change a lot while real income remains the same. It is very important to make the distinction between real and nominal magnitudes. In fact, the analysis of the relation between money supply and inflation is based on just that distinction. We started this chapter by emphasizing that monetary magnitudes are significant in real rather than nominal terms. We now have to follow that up and try to adapt our analysis of the relation of money supply, interest rates, and income to one relating nominal money supply, real income, price level, and interest rates. We could have said real money supply, real income, and interest rate, but we want to be able to deal with the central fact that the Fed determines nominal money supply. The *New York Times* reports the market reaction to each week's

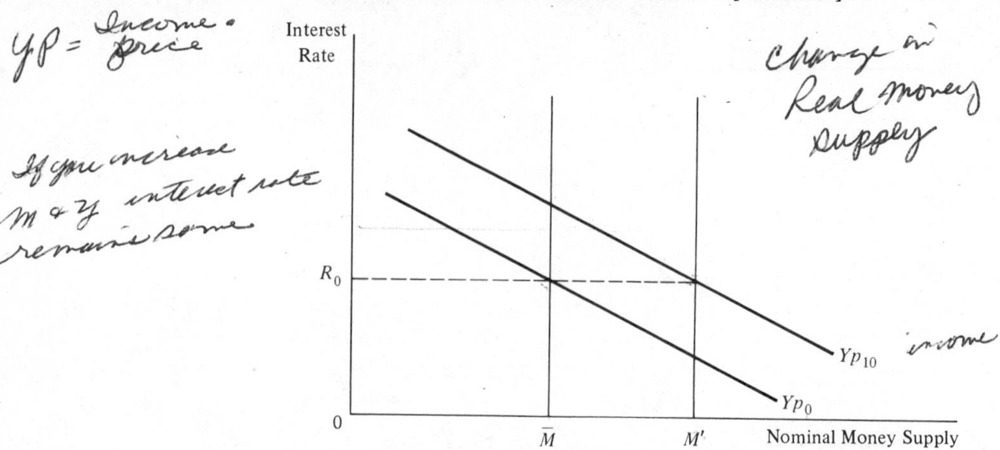

Figure 12.8 Effect of Price-Level Change on Interest Rate

change in nominal money supply. It never reports changes in real money supply. At least in the short run, prices are influenced by a variety of forces other than money, so that the Fed determines nominal money supply, while other things determine prices. The two together determine the change in real money supply. In the long run, money supply may be a major determinant of price levels but that is not true from month to month.

With a little mathematics the whole *LM* analysis can be shown in real terms. The basic equation for the demand for money (*L*) can be written

$$M = L(R)Y \cdot p$$

where *M* is nominal money, *R* is interest rate, *Y* is real GNP, and *p* the price level. If we divide both sides by *p* we have

$$M/p = L(R)Y.$$

We can now derive the *LM* curve in real terms exactly as we did using Figures 12.5, 12.6, and 12.7, replacing *M* with M/p. Notice that we can change the real money supply, either by changing nominal money supply, while prices remain constant, or by changing prices while nominal money supply remains constant. With a given nominal supply, a rise in the price level reduces real money supply and shifts the whole *LM* curve to the left; while a lower price level shifts the whole curve to the right.

A graphical example may help clarify the mathematical equations. In Figure 12.8 the solid line Yp_0 is just the same as in Figure 12.4. The vertical line $\overline{M}$ shows the initial nominal money supply. Now suppose the price level moves up 10 percent, while real income stays the same. Yp_{10} shows the new money-demand curve. At each interest rate, people want to hold just 10 percent more money because with the same real income their nominal transactions are all inflated by 10 percent. M' is just 10 percent bigger than $\overline{M}$ so that M/p is unchanged by the price-level change, and (surprise) it intersects Yp_{10} at the same interest rate R_0 as the intersection of $\overline{M}$ and Yp_0. We get the same combination of interest rate and real income when we keep the real money supply constant. Alternatively, if money supply remained at $\overline{M}$ the real money supply would have fallen and, as Figure 12.8 shows, the interest rate would have risen. You can see that if we plot an *LM* curve with real income on the horizontal axis, the *LM* curve corresponding to any given nominal money supply will be higher when the price level rises.

DEMAND FOR ASSETS VERSUS DEMAND FOR MONEY

Determining the interest rate or the level of asset prices by equating the supply and demand for money seems a little artificial. When there are only two assets "money" and "bonds" it makes no difference whether we say that the interest rate equates supply and demand for money or for bonds. If the money supply increases we may say that the interest rate must fall to induce investors to raise the share of money in their portfolio. That is the same as saying that the price of bonds must rise to induce investors to reduce the share of bonds in their portfolios.

If we substitute liquid assets for "money" and risky assets for "bonds" we can generalize the model and assert that an increase in the supply of liquid assets tends to raise prices of risky assets. However, that approach has a number of limitations. It doesn't differentiate among types of risky assets. Moreover, other factors beside the supply of liquid assets can affect the prices.

Economists have developed a number of more pragmatic approaches for analysis of the links between money and the large number of assets and asset prices appearing in real markets. Three leading approaches to be discussed are the money-market and term-structure approach, the capital-market-model approach, and the three-assets approach developed by Brunner and Meltzer.

Money Market and Term Structure Approach

The simplest approach is a two-step one. We first analyze the movements of short-term interest rates on the assumption that from week to week and month to month most of the activity in balancing supply and demand for money takes place in the market for Treasury bills, bank CDs, and commercial paper. This is called the money-market view of interest rates. Then we link all other interest rates and asset prices to short rates by taking account of the term structure consideration in Chapter 6. We look at those steps one at a time.

The money-market view of short-term interest rates. We already noted that some economists think that demand for money is much more responsive to the yields on short-term securities and time deposits than to any other yields. They argue that investors seeking a hedge against risk will hold Treasury bills, time deposits, or other liquid assets rather than money because they get a better return. Money will be held mainly for transactions purposes, and transactions demand at a given level of income will be determined by yields

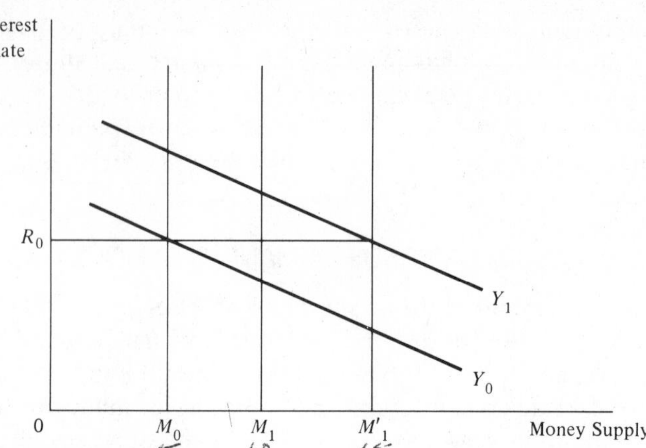

Figure 12.9 Equilibrium Interest Rate at Alternative Levels of Income and Money Supply

on the other liquid assets that can be quickly and cheaply converted into money.

That argument leads to the use of a demand for money equation which makes demand for money depend on GNP and time and savings deposit rates, which can be regarded as a constant in the short run. In that case all the work of equating supply and demand for money in the short run has to be done by changes in the short-term interest rates (including those on money-market certificates).

With a given time-deposit rate the demand for money can be represented by quantity of money on the horizontal axis and the short-term interest rate on the vertical axis. In Figure 12.9 the solid lines show an initial equilibrium for the income Y_0 and money supply M_0. The line Y_1 shows money demand for a high level of income a year later. The vertical lines M_1 and M'_1 show alternative levels of money supply a year later. You can see that the movement of the short-term interest rate can be regarded as the result of a race between growth of income and growth of money supply. When money supply increases more than enough to compensate for the increased money demand due to increased income the short-term interest rate falls. When money supply does not grow so much the interest rate rises.

Generally nominal GNP rises from quarter to quarter with only an occasional small decline in recessions. At the same time nominal money supply almost always increases from quarter to quarter. However, quarter-to-quarter percentage changes in both money supply and GNP vary widely and the differences between them may vary even more so. It is the difference that counts.

In a recession nominal GNP tends to show little change, while money supply increases, so that short-term rates fall. In booms, when GNP is rising relatively rapidly there are two possibilities. Most of the time the Fed more or less "accommodates" the boom, providing more money as GNP increases. However, it does not usually go all the way. It increases money-supply growth but not enough to prevent a gradual rise in interest rates. Sometimes though, out of fear of inflation, the Fed holds down money-supply growth and short-term interest rates rise rapidly. It is important to recognize that the relation between income, demand for *M-1* and short-term interest rates can be shifted by a variety of institutional changes discussed earlier. Such changes may either offset or accentuate the interest-rate response to the relative growth rates of income and GNP.

The Fed has often preferred to set an interest rate target and supply the money required to achieve it. In terms of Figure 12.9 that is equivalent to selecting an interest rate R_0 and letting the demand determine the money supply. With income Y_0 the required money supply would be M_0, but with income Y_1 a larger money supply is required.

Term and risk structure. If short-term interest rates can be analyzed in terms of income movements and Federal Reserve action, it is possible that other rates are determined by the factors considered in the discussion of term structure in Chapter 6. We suppose that long-term rates respond to the actual movements of the short rate, and the expectations of future short-rate movements, and we apply the term-structure theory. Bond buyers and sellers know what has happened to short rates, and they guess what will happen to GNP, what the Fed will do to money supply, and thereby what will happen to future short rates, and then decide whether it is a good time to buy or sell bonds. Their decisions determine the long-term bond prices and yields. The same argument applies to stock but in that case investors also have to judge the implications of their GNP forecasts for future corporate profits and dividends. In this elaborate guessing game, expectations about inflation can play a central role. They may influence bond and stock prices directly or indirectly.

Bond-market participants may guess the rate of inflation and use their guess to deduce Federal Reserve policy. If they think that inflation will accelerate they may conclude that the Fed will hold back on the money supply and thereby raise short-term interest rates. That will lead to lower bond prices and higher bond yields. But expectations of inflation may also influence bond yields directly. Corporate treasurers will be more willing to pay high rates to raise funds for capital goods purchases if they expect prices to rise. Either way we can be pretty sure that expectations of accelerating inflation will raise interest rates. We will return to that subject after the discussion of inflation in later chapters.

The Capital-Market Model Approach

The money-market approach for short-term interest rates coupled with the term-structure analysis of the relation between short rates and others is a useful device. However, many economists think that it leaves out important aspects of the behavior of capital markets and financial intermediaries. They prefer to think of a system of linked capital markets, which is built up by analysis of the portfolio decisions of households, corporations, governments, and all the different kinds of intermediaries. In this analysis the supply and demand for each type of asset (from the buyer's point of view) or liability (from the issuer's point of view) is derived from analysis of the decisions of each type of investor. The yield on each type of asset must be the one that brings the supply and demand for that asset into balance. All the markets are linked, however, because the supply and demand curves depend on the yields of other assets. You may regard the discussion of market interactions in Chapter 6 as a crude form of capital-market analysis with the addition that the short rate is determined by the money-market approach. A number of very elaborate statistical models of capital markets have been developed and some of them are now used in large econometric models designed for forecasting.

The Brunner and Meltzer Approach

Another way of dealing with the multiple-asset problem has been proposed by Brunner and Meltzer. They feel that the model of interest rates based on bonds-money economy is too simple, not to say deceptive. They feel that the term-structure approach gives money too limited a role. On the other hand, since they are interested in some general theoretical conclusions about income determination they feel that the detailed capital-market models place too much emphasis on the details of capital-market structure. In their view those details are important only in the very short run.

Brunner and Meltzer feel the most useful way to analyze capital markets is to split them into three pieces: the money market, the debt market, and the market for real capital. In their view expenditures for goods and services are given by the wealth embodied in the three types of assets, and the relative prices of those assets and of currently produced goods and services. We shall discuss their theory in more detail in Chapter 16.

THE INCOME-EXPENDITURE APPROACH VERSUS THE MONETARIST APPROACH

Now that we have surveyed the development and empirical testing of theories of demand for money we have to return to the question of the use of those theories.

Many people are interested in demand for money because they are trying to predict the course of interest rates over the next few months and sort out the probable influence of Federal Reserve action on stock prices. The influence of money does not stop with its direct effect on securities markets. Everyone recognizes that changes in money supply exert an important influence on movements of aggregate output and prices. Indeed, so-called monetarist economists think of money as the dominant influence on nominal GNP and prices.

In dealing with those matters there are two basically different approaches. One, called the *income-expenditure approach,* begins by analyzing the factors causing households and businesses to vary their expenditures on goods and services. From that point of view changes in money supply are regarded as one factor, albeit an important one, influencing expenditures decisions. Moreover, money exerts its main influence indirectly through its influence on interest rates and asset prices. The game plan for income-expenditure analysis is to examine the determinants of expenditures on goods and services assuming a given level of interest rates and asset prices to find what income goes with each level of interest rates. The result is then coupled with the *LM* curve to find the equilibrium level of income for a given money supply. That equilibrium is one in which the income and interest rate on the *LM* curve are consistent with the interest rate and income from the first step. We will go into more detail on this in the next chapter.

The income-expenditure approach gives money a significant role in determining the rate of expenditure on goods and services, but it allows all sorts of other factors to do so too. Moreover, changes in money supply exert their influence only indirectly. A change in money supply first ripples through financial markets as people use money to bid up prices of financial assets. The resulting changes in interest rates and asset prices then exert their influence on consumption and investment decisions. The other approach is not necessarily inconsistent with the income-expenditure approach but it starts from the idea that money supply exerts a dominant influence on expenditures. Accordingly, monetarist analysis starts with the idea that an increase in money supply influences expenditures in many ways. One, but only one, of those links between money and expenditure is the effect of money on interest rates and asset prices. The monetarist approach is outlined in more detail in Chapters 15 and 16.

In the next two chapters we deal with the Keynesian or income-expenditure approach. In doing so we first use a simple model whose monetary component is derived from the *LM* curve. In Chapters 15 and 16 we review monetarist analysis of expenditures. We then turn to the analysis of inflation. Finally we try to sum up the arguments and the agreements and disagreements of Keynesians and monetarists.

SUMMARY

1. Money is an important asset in our economy.
2. Changes in the supply of money play a major role in determining the prices of all other assets.
3. The demand for money arises from the two main functions of money, as a store of value and as a medium of exchange.
4. The demand for money as a medium of exchange stems from the fact that households and businesses must hold money during the intervals between the times when they receive payments from the sale of goods and services, and the times at which they make payments for goods and services. By taking time and trouble and using other liquid assets as substitutes for money, households and businesses can economize on the amount of money they hold. The extent to which it is worthwhile to economize in the use of money depends on the level of interest rates. Consequently, the transactions demand for money depends on the level of income and transactions, but it also depends on the level of interest rates.

5. The demand for money as an asset or a store of wealth stems from the fact that the nominal value of money is fixed so that money is a riskless asset, at least in nominal terms. The demand for money as an asset increases with total wealth, but the proportion of total wealth held in money form depends in part on the difference between the interest yields on money holdings and prospective yields on other assets. The asset demand for money may also depend on the public's views about the amount of risk involved in holding other assets.
6. Empirical studies support the view that demand for money depends positively on the level of income and on the level of wealth, and negatively on the difference between the interest rate paid on money holdings and the interest rate on other assets.
7. In equilibrium the available money supply must be held by someone. If we are given the rates paid on commercial-bank time deposits included in the money supply, we can show that the equilibrium interest rate is the one that equates the supply and demand for money.
8. We can also show that for a given supply of money the equilibrium interest rate rises with the level of income.

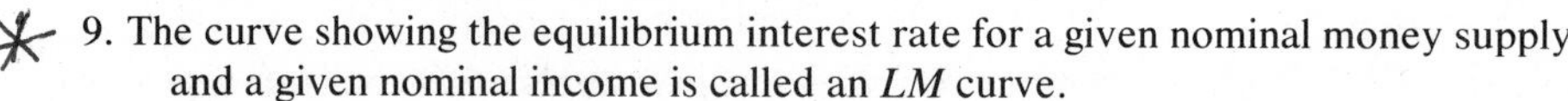

9. The curve showing the equilibrium interest rate for a given nominal money supply and a given nominal income is called an *LM* curve.

Questions and Exercises

1. Using diagrams like those in Figure 12.7, show how the *LM* curve will shift in response to a reduction in money supply.
2. If more people received their paychecks monthly instead of weekly, the transactions demand for money would tend to increase. Explain.
3. An increase in savings-deposit rates tends to increase the velocity of *M-1*, but will have less effect on *M-2*. Explain.
4. Some people hold money to reduce the risk of change in the nominal value of their assets. Name some nonmoney assets that can serve the same purpose.
5. "Short-term interest rates are determined by the supply and demand for securities such as Treasury bills and commercial paper." "The Fed can influence short-term interest rates through its control of bank reserves and money supply." Are the two statements consistent? Explain how they can be reconciled.
6. Draw an *LM* curve with real income on the horizontal axis. How will the curve shift if the price level rises while nominal money supply remains fixed?

Further Reading

BAUMOL, W. "The Transactions Demand for Cash: An Inventory Theoretic Approach." *Quarterly Journal of Economics* 66 (November 1952): 545–56. This paper gives a formal exposition of the theory of transactions demand for money, emphasizing the trade-off between the cost in terms of interest forgone by holding an inventory of money and the benefit of reduction in the cost of making financial transactions.

BRUNNER, KARL, and MELTZER, ALLAN H. "Predicting Velocity: Implications for Theory and Policy." *Journal of Finance* 18 (May 1963): 319–54. An empirical study of the influence of interest rate, wealth, and income on the demand for money over a long period.

FRIEDMAN, MILTON. "The Demand for Money—Some Theoretical and Empirical Results." *Journal of Political Economy* 67 (June 1959): 327–51. An important exposition of Friedman's views on the demand for money, with tests of his views and competing ones.

FRIEDMAN, MILTON and SCHWARTZ, ANNA J. *A Monetary History of the United States, 1867–1960*. Princeton, N.J.: National Bureau of Economic Research, 1963. This very large volume gives a detailed history of the causes of changes in the money supply over nearly a century, together with a detailed analysis of the response of the economy in each period.

GOLDFELD, STEPHEN M. "The Demand for Money Revisited." *Brookings Papers on Economic Activity,* 1973: 3, pp. 577–638. A statistical study of alternative formulations of the demand for money equation.

LAIDLER, DAVID. *The Demand for Money: Theories and Evidence*. 2d ed. New York: Dun-Donnelley, 1977. This book provides the most comprehensive view of the development of the theory of demand for money and the current state of the art. Summarizes a very large number of empirical studies.

PORTER, RICHARD, SIMPSON, THOMAS, and MAUSKOF, EILEEN. "Financial Innovation and Monetary Aggregates." *Brookings Papers on Economic Activity,* 1979: 1, pp. 213–29. This paper offers an explanation of an apparent downward shift in the demand for money in terms of changes in practices of banks' development of new substitutes for money.

TOBIN, JAMES. "The Interest Elasticity of Transaction Demand for Cash." *Review of Economics and Statistics* 38 (August 1956): 241–47. A classic exposition of the theory of the transactions demand for money.

———. "Liquidity Preference as Behavior Towards Risk." *Review of Economic Studies* 25 (February 1958): 65–86. This paper develops the theory of the demand for money as a means of avoiding the risk involved in holding other financial assets.

Income-Expenditure Theory

13

The development of the market-oriented industrial economies over the past three hundred years or so has been marked by a phenomenal but uneven growth in output. The output level of each decade has exceeded the level of the previous one, but there have also been significant fluctuations in output. Until the Second World War, major depressions marked by sharp price declines and widespread unemployment occurred every decade or so with a couple of minor recessions in between.

Those fluctuations in output, prices, and employment culminated in the Great Depression of the 1930s, a worldwide catastrophe that almost brought capitalism to an end and produced permanent changes in the structure and government policy of the market economies.

Even before the 1930s economists devoted a lot of effort to explaining fluctuations in output and prices. Neoclassical economics provided a basic framework for understanding the long-term growth process and the long-run adjustment of market economies to population growth, capital accumulation, and technological change. Short-run fluctuations were treated separately under the heading of "business cycles," but in spite of a good deal of effort, no theory of short-run output fluctuations was ever widely accepted.

In attempting to deal with short-run fluctuations in prices and output business-cycle theorists often resorted to play-by-play accounts. They recognized, for example, that business investment expenditures were more volatile than consumer expenditures and sought explanations for investment booms and slumps. At the same time they recognized that an investment boom would increase employment and income for consumers and lead to a rise in consumer expenditures. They tried to trace through the resulting cumulative process. Then they examined how the boom might be checked.

For example, rapidly rising prices and output could push up interest rates, slow investment expenditures, and throw the whole process into reverse.

Much of their difficulty lay in the absence of adequate data on short-run movements of demand and in the lack of any systematic framework for the analysis of the interactions among the components of demand. In seeking an explanation of the Great Depression of the 1930s, John Maynard Keynes made effective use of the income-expenditure approach. That approach emphasizes the fact that decisions to spend are strongly influenced by income or expected income. At the same time it asserts that "one person's expenditure is another's income." By contrast, the mainstream of classical theory had looked upon expenditures as being determined by the quantity of money. Keynes used national income accounts as a conceptual framework, together with a few bold generalizations about the response of consumers to changes in income, the response of interest-rate changes to changes in income and money supply, and the response of investment to changes in interest rates. With those elements he was able to give a systematic account of the factors controlling the total reaction of output to an initial change in investment or government expenditure. Keynes's work has been much criticized and elaborated in the last forty years, but it did get the analysis of short-run fluctuations in output off to a fresh start.

But Keynes had very little data to work with. The practical significance of his analysis was greatly increased by the publication, shoftly after the appearance of the "General Theory of Employment, Interest, and Money," of the first set of comphrensive annual national accounts. These data, the fruit of many years of work by Simon Kuznets and the National Bureau of Economic Research, provided the basis for empirical measurement and testing of the relationships in Keynes's model and for its application to practical policy problems. Though many of Keynes's conclusions have been challenged or modified, the systematic analysis of interactions between income and expenditure in terms of national-income-account categories still forms the basis of most short-run forecasting and a great deal of policy analysis.

In this chapter we will first outline the structure of the national income accounts and then proceed to outline the main features of the Keynesian income-expenditure approach. In order to see the forest for the trees, we will concentrate on the simplest, most central features of the model. In the following two chapters we will consider a number of complications, especially those relating to the impact of monetary policy on changes in economic activity.

THE STRUCTURE OF THE NATIONAL INCOME ACCOUNTS

The national income accounts are based on a double-entry bookkeeping system for the nation. The central concept is the *measure of the aggregate value of the nation's output of goods and services*—**gross national product** or **GNP**. The idea is to measure and add up the output of all the nation's farms, factories, drugstores, doctors, universities, and so on.

In principle, it is simple to estimate the value of, say, coal, steel, and automobiles among other things produced in 1984. But does the sum of those values mean anything? It really cannot because the value of automobiles produced in any year includes the value of steel used in their manufacture. The value of steel produced includes the value of coal used to make it. Thus, in this example the coal is included three times and the steel twice.

A more useful way to measure output is to include only the "value added" for each production unit. **Value added** for a business firm is the *value of its total output less the value of materials and services purchased from other firms.* Thus, each firm's contribution to production is counted only once and the total is independent of the number of stages of production through which an intermediate product passes. Thus the U.S. GNP for any year, say 1984, is the sum of the value added during 1984 by each producing unit. The producing units include farms and business firms of all types. GNP also includes the value added by independent professionals such as lawyers, by nonprofit organizations like universities and churches, and by governments.

The value-added approach to measuring output not only solves the "double-counting" problem, but it also leads to a direct relation between the value of output and the incomes of factors of production. In fact, it turns out that if we keep the books balanced and follow the usual accounting conventions, the value of production in a year is identical with the total income of households, businesses, and governments.

Table 13.1 Income Statement of Typical Firm

Sales *Plus:*		$20,000
Inventory increase		1,000
Value of production		21,000
Less: Expenses		16,600
Purchased materials	$5,000	
Wages and salaries	10,000	
Interest payments	500	
Depreciation charges	1,100	
Profits		4,400
Less: State and local taxes		400
Profits before income taxes		4,000
Less: Corporate income taxes		1,800
Profits after income taxes		2,200
Less: Dividends		700
RETAINED EARNINGS		$ 1,500

Table 13.1 shows the calculation of profit for a hypothetical firm. Table 13.2 shows the same information arranged to show that value added by the firm is exactly equal to incomes paid to households and government plus the profits of the firm. The latter are divided into dividends, corporate income taxes, and profits retained by the firm. Of course, that conclusion results from the definition of profits as a residual after everybody else has been paid.

Table 13.2 Income Statement of Typical Firm: An Alternative Presentation

Value added by firm		Incomes paid by firm		
Value of production	$21,000	Households		$11,200
Less: Purchased materials from other firms	5,000	Wage and salaries	$10,000	
		Interest payments	500	
		Dividends	700	
		State and local governments		400
		Federal government		1,800
		Retained by firm		2,600
		Depreciation	1,100	
		Retained earnings	1,500	
VALUE ADDED	$16,000	TOTAL INCOME		$16,000

GNP As Final Product

There is another way to solve the double-counting problem. Instead of taking the value-added route, double counting can be eliminated by only counting production sold to final users. Thus, in the steel, coal, and automobile example we could just count the autos and not bother with the steel and coal. More generally, GNP can be regarded as the sum of the value of goods and services sold to consumers, capital goods such as machinery, factory, and office buildings sold to business, and goods and services sold to government. To these we would add residential construction, additions to inventories, and the excess of exports over imports. The latter item reflects the fact that some U.S. production is sold abroad, while some of the goods purchased by consumers and businesses are imported.

The total value of products sold for consumption, investment, or government purchase, plus exports minus imports, has to be exactly equal to the sum of the value added by all producing units. In effect the value of any final product, for example, an automobile, can be built up from the value-added contributions of the auto dealer, the auto manufacturer, the suppliers of raw materials to the auto manufacturer, parts manufacturers, suppliers of raw materials to them, and so on. Those contributions include not only the physically identifiable elements of the final car but energy for heat, light, and power, and services of lawyers, insurance companies, advertising agents, and so on.

Double-Entry System

Gross national product regarded as the sum of the value-added contributions of all producing units can thus be readily broken down into classes of final products or into expenditures by different kinds of purchasers of final products. At the same time, the value-added contribution of each producing unit breaks down into income payments of different kinds—wages, rents, profits, taxes. Total GNP will therefore be equal to the sum of the national totals for the various income elements. Thus the national income accounts are a double-entry system in which the components of the product side—consumer expenditure, investment, government purchases, exports less imports—add up to GNP, while the components of the income side—wages, profits, and so on—add to the same total.

We have seen that the total GNP is always distributed in income to households, businesses, and governments. That conclusion results directly from the definition of GNP and the definition of profits as the residual claim to value added for each production unit. Definitions, however, do not tell us anything about the relative size of the shares of GNP going to various sectors or about how those shares are likely to vary over the business cycle. In fact, the distribution process is fairly complicated for two reasons. First, the distribution takes place in two stages. The primary distribution divides the GNP between business gross profits (before depreciation) and household income, wages, salaries, rents, and interest, with a small share going directly to government in sales taxes. There are secondary distributions involving business payments of corporate income taxes to government out of profits, business payments of dividends to households, household payments of income taxes to government, and government payment of transfers (such as social security) to households. Second, the shares of income going to profits vary systematically over the cycle.

Initial Distribution of National Income

The primary distribution of GNP divides gross national income into three parts. First, government levies sales taxes and property taxes on business and these indirect business taxes are a first charge on output. Second, households receive wages and salaries, interest and rent from business. Third, what is left is the gross profit of business, which is divided into capital consumption allowances (more commonly called depreciation) and profits.

The share of indirect taxes, mainly excise, sales, and property taxes in GNP, depends, of course, on governmental decisions in the setting of tax rates and the choice of commodities subject to tax. If tax rates were set and left alone, the share of GNP going to indirect taxes would, of course, depend on the sales volumes of the taxed commodities. In fact, however, state and local governments are constantly adjusting tax rates. The revenue from these taxes ultimately reflects the willingness of the public to pay taxes for government services and the resolution of political conflicts over the share of the tax burden paid by various groups. In fact, in the postwar period, the ratio of indirect taxes to GNP has varied in a fairly narrow range.

The share of corporate profits in GNP shows a rather complex pattern. From the late 1940s until the late 1960s, there was little trend in the ratio of gross corporate profits to GNP, but there were marked cyclical variations in the ratio. Corporate profits rose more than proportionately during booms and fell more than proportionately in slumps. Those changes in the share of corporate profits reflect the changes in labor productivity associated with short-run variations in capacity utilization. Prices seem to be adjusted to the trend of labor cost per unit of output, so that short-run variations in labor productivity and labor costs are reflected in profits. During the late 1960s and early 1970s, the share of corporate profits in GNP showed a downward trend, even after allowance for cyclical factors. There has been a good deal of dispute over the cause of the shift, but in recent years the share of corporate profits has shown an upward trend.

Secondary Distribution of National Income

After the primary three-way split of gross national income, various redistributions occur. First, corporations allocate part of their gross profits to depreciation allowances in recognition of the fact that the plant and equipment used in the productive process is wearing out. Second, corporate net profits are divided among corporate income taxes, dividends, and retained earnings for investment in the business. Third, there is an interchange between households and governments. Households pay income and social security taxes to governments. On the other hand, governments make transfer payments—social security, welfare, pensions, Medicaid—to households. *The net received by households from wages, salaries, rents, interest, dividends, and transfer payments, less taxes,* is called **disposable income.** We will make much use of that concept when we discuss the determination of consumer expenditures.

Real Versus Nominal GNP

The basic data for the national income accounts are measured in value terms. GNP measured by the final-product approach is obtained by adding up the value-price times quantity—of all the different kinds of output produced in the year. Thus the statement that the GNP in 1982 was 4 percent greater than in 1981 reflects both the changes in physical outputs and the changes in prices between the two years.

We need value data for many purposes, but changes in real output are even more important. Accordingly, we have a set of national income accounts in real or constant dollar terms. We cannot measure real GNP directly as we cannot add the output of apples, oranges, bicycles, and trucks. We combine the outputs of diverse goods and services by weighting them by their relative prices. Thus, we regard one $4,000 car as the equivalent of forty bicycles valued at $100 each. To get changes in the price level out of the picture we use the prices of a single base year for the value-weighting process. 1972 is the base year currently in use. In principle, we get the GNP in 1972 dollars for 1982 by multiplying the 1982 output of each product by its 1972 price and adding them up. We get the 1981 GNP measured in 1972 prices in the same way. When we compare the two constant dollar figures, the increase from 1981 to 1982 has been purged of the effects of inflation. The change reflects only changes in output since the same prices are used in each case.

In these days of persisting inflation there is a lot of difference between the movements of constant dollar GNP and those of GNP in current value or nominal GNP, as shown in Figure 13.1.

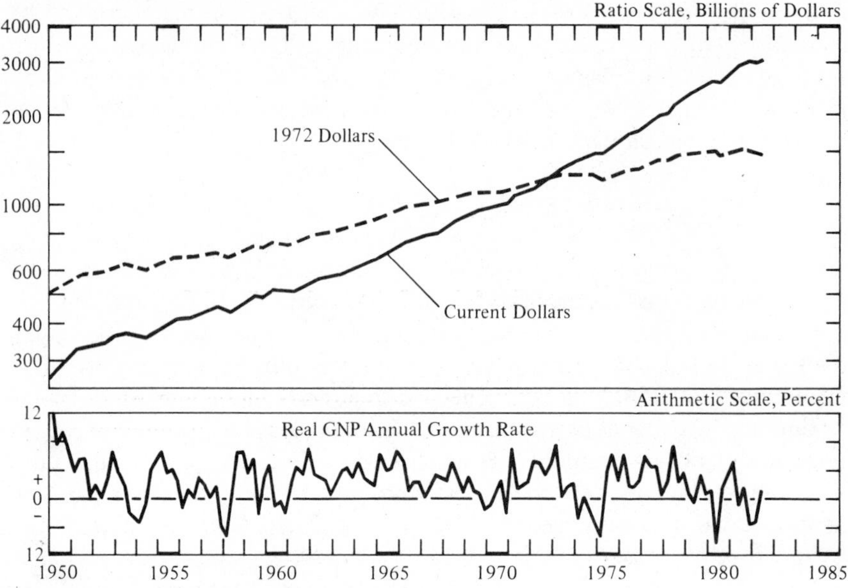

Figure 13.1 Gross National Product
Seasonally adjusted annual rates, quarterly

Source: Board of Governors of the Federal Reserve System, *Historical Chart Book,* 1982, p. 12.

POTENTIAL OUTPUT

You can see from Figure 13.1 that real GNP has been increasing for many years. In some periods its rate of growth is relatively high, in others real GNP grows slowly and occasionally actually declines a little, but the trend is distinctly upward. The upward trend of real GNP reflects the growth of our labor force, and the increased productivity from improved technology, better education, and a continuing increase in the stocks of all kinds of capital goods.

The upward trend of real GNP could not occur without a continuing increase in our capacity to produce, but it does not follow that the increase in real GNP for any one year is the same as the increase in capacity to produce. The rate of growth of real GNP is erratic while the capacity to produce output grows fairly steadily.

In the analysis of unemployment, capacity utilization, and changes in prices and wages, it is useful to compare the actual constant dollar GNP with some measure of the aggregate output that could be produced in practice. The maximum theoretical GNP for a given labor input, say, an average workweek of forty hours for all of the labor force, would be produced if capital and labor resources were being used in the most efficient way. Resources are utilized with maximum efficiency if (1) it is not possible to produce more of one good without producing less of another, and (2) the amount of good A that must be given up to produce more of another good B just corresponds to the amount of A that consumers will give up to get another unit of B. In an unchanging world a competitive price system should produce just that result.

In practice we never achieve the most efficient utilization of our resources for two reasons. First, taxes, subsidies, regulations, and elements of monopoly prevent the price system from working perfectly. Second, prices have to be constantly adjusted to a moving target. In a world of change the accumulation of capital, changing technology, the growth of the labor force, and changes in its age distribution and educational level cause continual changes in the optimal distribution of resources. Moreover, individual workers are always entering and leaving the labor force, while firms frequently either have to lay off workers or expand employment. No price system can keep up with all those changes, so there are always some resources that are at least temporarily underutilized or used in relatively inefficient ways. There will be unemployment in some occupations while there are unfilled vacancies in others. There will be excess capacity in some industries while others are working overtime. In practice a certain amount of unemployment is inevitable. Even in World War II unemployment did not fall below one percent of the labor force and at that time there were widespread labor shortages and inflation in spite of the use of rationing and price and wage controls. A practical definition of an economy's "potential output" has to allow for a level of unemployment at which labor markets are in balance—a level at which upward pressures on prices in markets with excess demand are roughly in balance with downward pressures in markets with excess supply. For a number of years after the Second World War there was general agreement that labor markets would be roughly in balance at an unemployment rate of around 4 percent. More recently, economists have accepted the view that changes in the structure of the labor market require an unemployment target of 5 percent or even 6 percent. (That change will be discussed more fully in Chapter 18.) Potential output changes from year to year, even with a given level of unemployment, because of the growth of the labor force and its productivity.

THE CIRCULAR FLOW OF INCOME AND EXPENDITURES

When we try to analyze the economic processes underlying the national income accounts data, it is useful to think of the national accounts as measuring a circular flow of expenditures for goods and services, and income payments for services used in production. The accounts should be thought of as measuring flows because all the national income data have a time dimension. The amount of water in a system of pipes is measured in gallons. But the rate of flow of water past a given point is measured in gallons *per minute*. In the same way gross national product and its components are measured in billions of dollars *per year*.

The simplest form of circular flow is shown in Figure 13.2. In the diagram we assume that all income goes to households in wage payments, and that households spend all their income on consumption goods. The heavier upper line shows the flow of consumer expenditures—payments from households to producing firms. The lighter upper line shows the flow of consumer

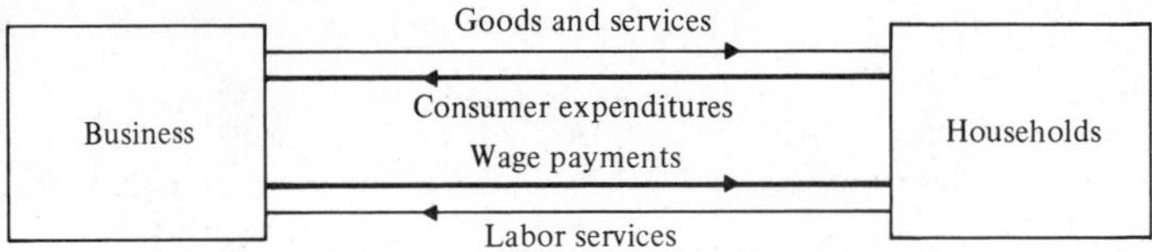

Figure 13.2 Circular Flow I

goods from firms to households. The heavier lower line shows the wage payments from firms to households, while the lighter lower line shows the flow of labor services from households to firms. The rates of flow of consumption expenditures and wage payments have to be equal, and, of course, both equal GNP. One measures the final product side of the accounts, the other the income side. In the continuing process we do not raise the chicken-egg question of whether the expenditures cause the production and income or vice versa.

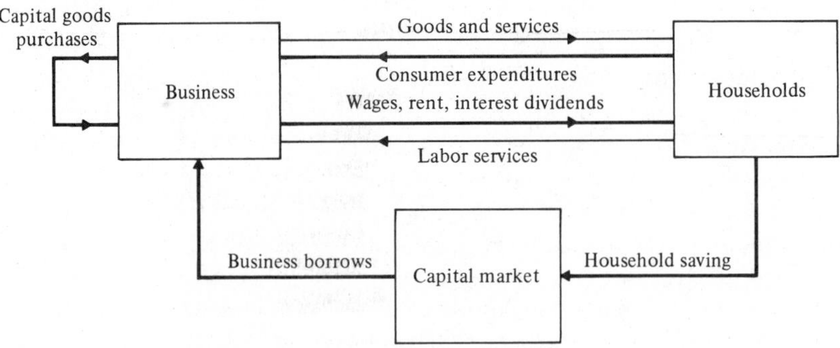

Figure 13.3 Circular Flow II

Figure 13.3 shows a more realistic circular-flow picture. When we take account of investment and saving, the new diagram differs from the earlier one in three ways. First, we have shown a side flow of investment-expenditure payments from firms buying investment goods to those producing them. Second, households do not have to spend all their income on consumption. They may save and lend their savings to investing businesses through the capital market. Third, businesses can also save. The flow of payments from businesses to households is not equal to the whole GNP, but to GNP less depreciation and corporate retained earnings.

Figure 13.4 shows the additional complications arising from the introduction of government. Households and businesses make tax payments to government. Government purchases goods from business, and makes transfer payments to households. Finally, the government may run a deficit and draw funds from the capital market or run a surplus and lend to businesses through the capital market.

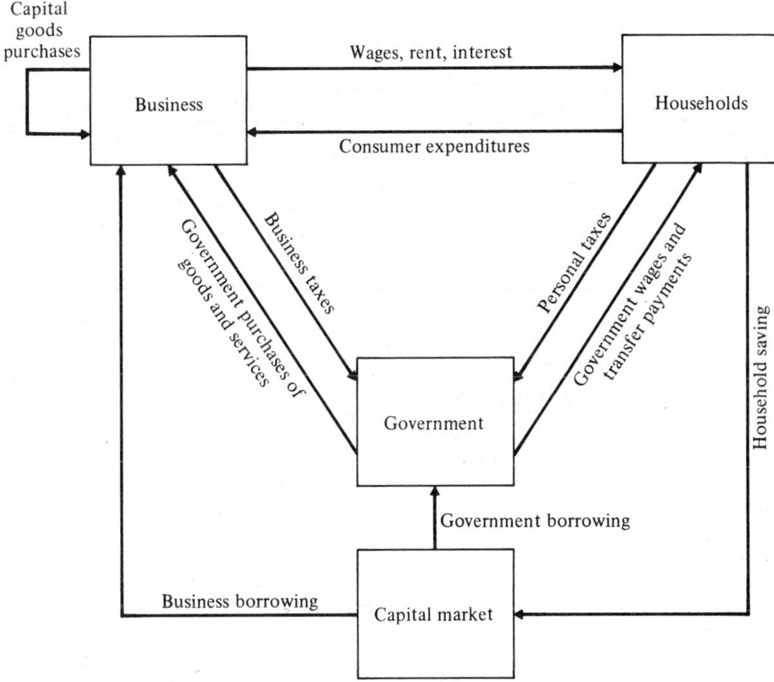

Figure 13.4 Circular Flow III

Equilibrium Circular Flow

In the real world the rate of flow of the various kinds of expenditures on goods and services is always changing, prices are changing, and income payments to various groups are always in flux. Moreover, it is clear that changes in any one part of the system will influence other parts. When the government canceled its support of the supersonic transport (SST), the reduction in government expenditures was felt in every part of Seattle. And since people in Seattle buy things made elsewhere the change was reflected in economic activity throughout the country. It is obvious that an attempt to trace step by step the way in which government expenditures, tax rates, or money supply affect the economy is certain to be a tedious and complicated process. Indeed, we are likely to get lost in the mass of detail, leave out some of the interactions, and get the wrong answer.

We can learn a lot and avoid some mistakes by asking a simpler question. Under what conditions would a circular-flow process be in equilibrium in the sense that it keeps on repeating itself with the various flows in the system maintained at constant rates? To make sense out of that question, we have to assume some fixed characteristics of the economy with which we are dealing. At a minimum, we have to specify the labor force and capital stock of our economy and therefore its potential output measured in, say, 1972 dollars. Since we are going to be concerned with the effect of economic policy variables, we also specify the money supply, the real rate of government expenditures, and the tax rate and transfer payment formulas.

If a circular flow is to repeat itself, there must be a certain consistency between the given factors just mentioned and the rate of flow of GNP and its components. Moreover, there must be a certain consistency between the GNP and its constituent flows. First, the rates of household consumption and saving must be consistent with the rate of flow of GNP, the share going to households, and the tastes of consumers. Second, the rate of investment must be consistent with the prospective returns on investment and the interest rate. Third, producers have to sell their output. Total expenditures for goods and services must equal total production. Fourth, the amount of real money balances businesses and households want to hold must equal the amount available. You will recall from the last chapter that the demand for real money balances depends on real income and the interest rate. Fifth, the price level must be constant. The various elements in the circular flow can be measured either in money terms or in real, constant dollar terms. To have constant flows measured in both real and nominal terms the price level that links the two must be constant. Finally, the real flows must be consistent with the potential output of the economy. Real GNP cannot exceed potential output. It is physically possible for real GNP to fall short of potential output. However, it can be shown that a steady state equilibrium with output substantially below potential output is at least unusual, if not impossible.

PRICE ADJUSTMENTS AND QUANTITY ADJUSTMENTS

We noted above that in an equilibrium steady circular flow, production must equal expenditures. That condition is a little trickier than it sounds. More precisely, the equilibrium condition is that production must equal expenditures including *planned* but not *unplanned* inventory. Planned inventory investment motivated by the need for bigger stocks of raw material and finished product as production and sales growth is just like any other investment expenditure, but the unplanned inventory investment arising from an excess of production over sales of final product is a sign of disequilibrium. Unplanned inventory investment must be zero in equilibrium.

As already noted, firms can try to eliminate any difference between production and sales by a quantity adjustment (changing production and employment) or by a price adjustment. In a world of change, both kinds of adjustment are occurring all the time. But it will make our exposition easier if we first examine quantity adjustments, assuming that prices are fixed, and then turn to price adjustments.

In this section, the relations among real GNP, real investment, real government expenditures, and real consumption are analyzed. In particular, we will show how the responses of real consumption and real GNP to changes in real investment and government expenditures are influenced by the factors determining the share of GNP going to consumers and by the desires of consumers to save. That analysis gives us a limited insight into the impact of fiscal policy on the economy. It is important to remember, however, that the conclusions are only partial. To complete the analysis we must take account of monetary factors and allow for changes in the price level.

Goods-Market Equilibrium

The first requirement for a steady state circular flow is balance between the flow of production (GNP looked at from the production or value-added point of view) and the total that businesses, governments, and households want to spend on goods and services. The total of actual expenditures for consumption, investment, and government purchases is always equal to the value of production if we count inventory accumulation whether desired or not as part of expenditures. But clearly, firms will change their rate of production if they are accumulating unwanted inventories because they are unable to sell their output. Thus, if a steady rate of production is to be maintained, the sum of expenditures, government purchases, and investment in fixed capital plus any *planned* inventory investment must equal the value of production. That condition is not necessarily fulfilled.

In the simplest case, we could suppose that the real expenditures of households, businesses, and governments are just given arbitrarily. Then all the adjustment would be on the production side. In fact, however, real expenditures are likely to be influenced by real income. In particular, consumer expenditures are strongly influenced by the level of disposable income. If that is so, then production is determined by expenditures while at the same time expenditures are at least partly determined by production. To analyze the implications of the mutual determination of expenditure and production, we make use of the concept of the consumption function.

The Consumption Function

Economists have long recognized that consumer expenditures are likely to respond to changes in income. Almost everyone finds it intuitively plausible that (other things equal) real consumption expenditures will be higher when real disposable income is high rather than when it is low. Keynes gave that notion a central role in his analysis of short-run changes in income and production. He labeled *the relation between real income and real consumption* the **consumption function.** According to Keynes, "the fundamental, psychological law, upon which we are entitled to depend with great confidence, both a priori from our knowledge of human nature and from the detailed facts of experience, is that men are disposed, as a rule and on the average, to increase their consumption as their income increases, but not by as much as the increase in their income."

Since Keynes's time, economists have devoted a lot of theoretical and empirical work to the analysis of consumption, and used much more complex formulations of the relation between income and consumption than the one embodied in Keynes's statement. We will discuss the consumption function in the next chapter, but for the purpose of showing how the income-consumption interaction works, a simple adaptation of Keynes's observation will suffice. A simple form of the consumption function is $C = AY + B$. C is real consumption, Y is real GNP. A indicates the increase in real consumption per dollar increase in real GNP. It reflects the increase in real

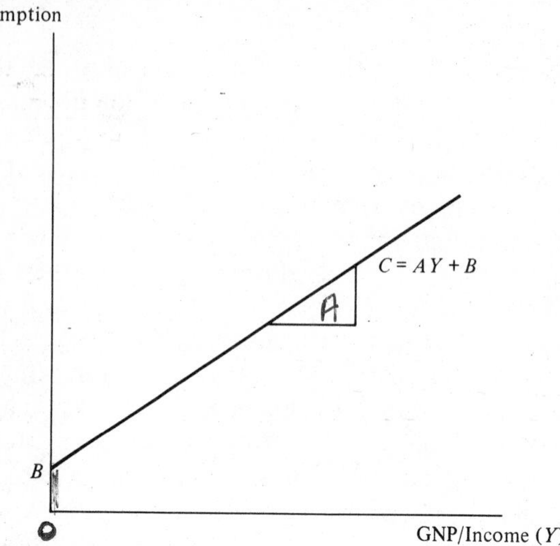

Figure 13.5 The Consumption Function

consumer expenditures per dollar of increase in real disposable income as well as the increase in disposable income per dollar of GNP. The increase in disposable income depends on the increase in tax receipts less transfer payments and the increase in earnings retained by corporations per dollar increase in GNP. For example, if disposable income increases by 60 percent of any increase in GNP, while households spend 90 percent of any increase in disposable income, A would be .54. The constant B reflects all factors affecting consumer expenditures other than GNP. Thus, B includes consumption out of those transfer payments not related to GNP. In the next chapter, we will show that it also reflects such factors as the real wealth of households. For the moment, however, just take B as given.

The equation $C = AY + B$ is shown graphically in Figure 13.5. The height of the line C at $Y = 0$ is B. A is the slope as shown in the little triangle. Figure 13.6 shows total expenditures by adding fixed rates of investment and government expenditures to consumer expenditures at each level of GNP. $C+G$ represents consumption plus government expenditure, $C+I+G$ represents consumption plus government expenditures and investment. Thus, the height of $C+I+G$ shows total desired expenditures at each GNP. GNP, on the other hand, is the rate of production.

Figure 13.6 also includes a 45-degree line. All points on the 45-degree line satisfy the condition that total expenditures (measured vertically) equal total production (measured horizontally).

At point E_0 where the 45-degree line intersects the $C+I+G$ line both equilibrium conditions are satisfied. Consumers are spending the amount they want for the GNP, Y_0, while total expenditure equals production. Y_0 is the only GNP that satisfies both conditions. At any smaller GNP desired expenditure exceeds production. At any larger GNP production exceeds desired expenditure.

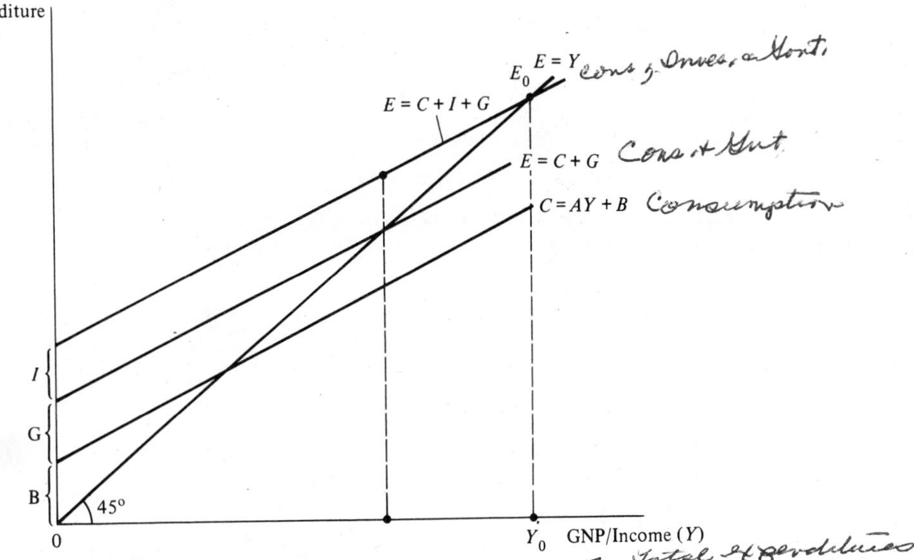

Figure 13.6 Equilibrium of Production and Expenditure

Changes in $I + G$: The Multiplier

Now let us consider what happens when $I+G$ changes. In Figure 13.7, the line C is the same consumption function used before, and the line $C+I+G$ is the same as Figure 13.6. The equilibrium position is at E. The line marked $C+I'+G'$ represents total expenditures for a higher level of $I+G$. The new equilibrium is as E'. Notice that Δy is more than the increase in $I+G$. In fact the increase in equilibrium GNP is about twice the increase in

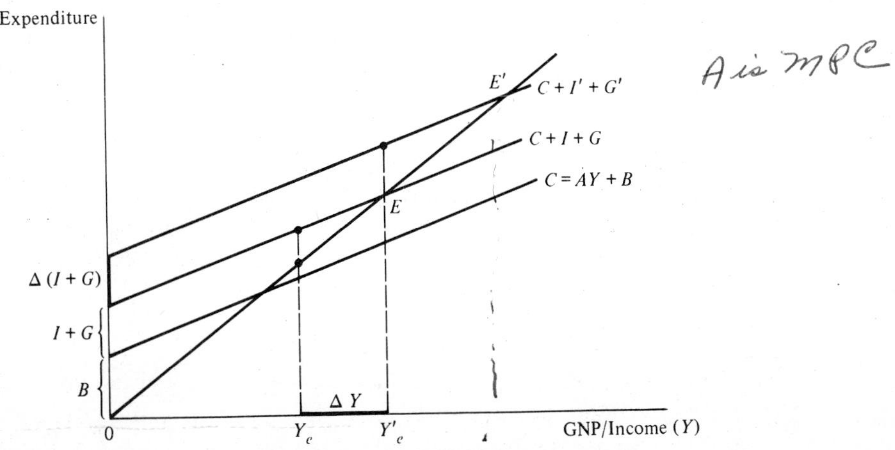

Figure 13.7 Changes in Equilibrium Income

$I+G$. That has to be so because the consumption function slopes upward. Each one-dollar increase in government and investment expenditures directly increases GNP by one dollar. Those expenditures increase disposable income. Households with more disposable income are induced to spend more on consumption. The total increase in GNP is a *multiple* of the initial increase generated by more government purchases or investment expenditures. With a little algebra the ratio of the increase in equilibrium GNP to the increase in government purchases or investment can be calculated.

There is a simple algebraic equivalent to our 45-degree line diagram. The equation of the $C+I+G$ line is given by adding $I+G$ to C so that $C+I+G=AY+B+I+G$. The production-expenditure-equilibrium calculation is $C+I+G=Y$.

We have therefore that

$$Y=AY+B+I+G$$

or

$$Y-AY=B+I+G$$

or solving for Y

$$Y=(B+I+G)\frac{1}{1-A}.$$

Thus the equilibrium GNP is equal to the sum of government expenditures, investment, and the part of consumer expenditures not affected by GNP—all *multiplied* by $1/(1-A)$. Since A is less than one, the multiplier must be greater than one. Any increase in I, G, or B will produce an increase in real GNP, which equals the initial change multiplied by $1/(1-A)$.

If A is close to one, the consumption line has a steep slope and the multiplier will be very large. If A is near zero, the consumption line is nearly flat, and the multiplier will be small. A is the income-consumption feedback coefficient.

Thus the size of the multiplier will depend on the way consumers divide increased disposable income between consumption and saving. The *ratio of increased consumption to increased disposable income* is called the **marginal propensity to consume** (MPC). The higher the MPC, the higher the multiplier.

The size of the multiplier will also depend on the share of additional income going to consumers. That will depend in part on the share of GNP going to profits, but it will also depend on the share going to indirect taxes and personal income taxes.

Fiscal Policy

The multiplier equation $\text{GNP}=(B+I+G)\cdot 1/(1-A)$ can give some insight into the basic elements of fiscal policy. With fiscal policy the government can cause changes in GNP in three ways: by changing purchases of goods and services; by changing transfer payments; or by changing tax rates. First, an increase in the rate of government expenditures for goods and services changes

G, and thereby changes GNP by G times the multiplier. Second, an increase in transfer payments can change either A or B. For example, an increase in social-security benefits can increase B in the multiplier equation because it makes disposable income higher at every level of GNP. On the other hand, an increase in unemployment benefits can reduce the amount of disposable income change for each change in GNP. And third, by changing tax rates, governments can influence the size of the multiplier, since tax rates affect share of income going to consumers.

That is fiscal policy in one easy lesson. Unfortunately, there are all sorts of complications, so don't jump to any conclusions yet!

INTEREST RATES, INVESTMENTS, AND INCOME

Investment and Interest Rates

Any change in the rate of investment will cause a change in equilibrium GNP by an amount equal to the multiplier times the initial change in investment. All sorts of things influence the level of investment, but the link between interest rates and investment deserves special attention in a book on money and banking. We will discuss the determinants of investment in detail in the next chapter, but at this point we will simply assert that other things equal, a rise in interest rates tends to lower the rate of investment. Figure 13.8 shows a hypothetical relationship between the level of interest rates and the rate of investment. At interest rate R_0 we get investment rate I_0. At the higher rate R_1 we get lower investment I_1, and at the lower interest rate R_2 we get investment I_2.

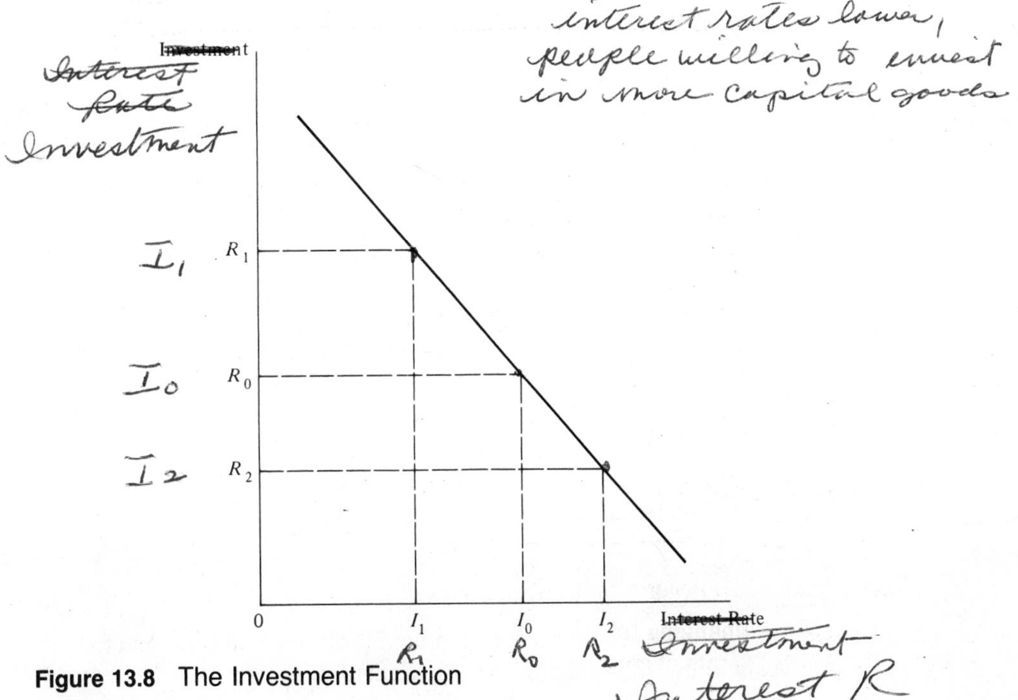

Figure 13.8 The Investment Function

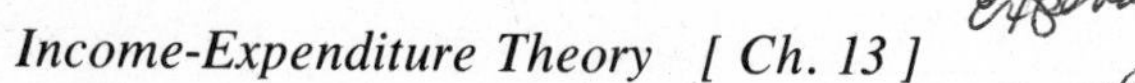

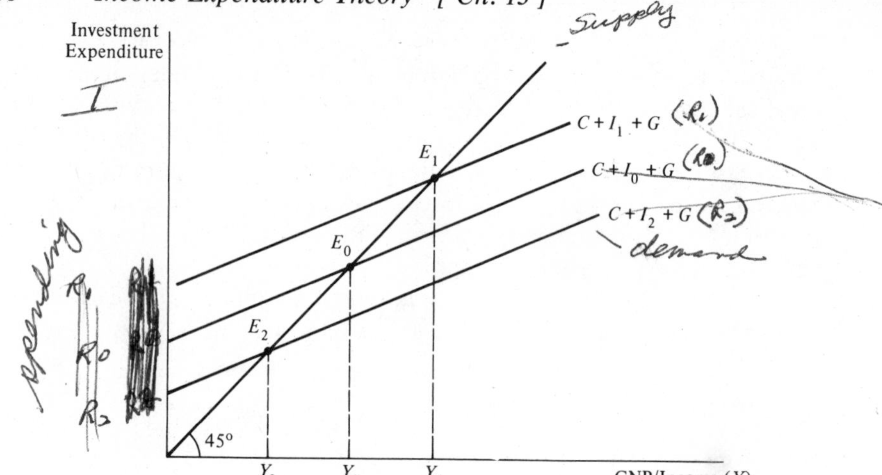

Figure 13.9 Deriving the *IS* Curve I

The *IS* Curve

Now we want to link the level of interest rates to the level of GNP. That can be done very simply by transferring the hypothetical responses of investment to interest-rate levels shown in Figure 13.8 to the 45-degree line diagram. In Figure 13.9 we show three $C+I+G$ lines that correspond to the interest rates (R_2, R_0, and R_1) shown in Figure 13.10. The middle one has investment I_0 corresponding to interest rate R_0; the lower one has investment I_2 corresponding to higher interest rate R_2; the higher one has investment I_1 corresponding to lower interest rate R_1. The level of government expenditures and the consumption function are the same in all three cases. You can see that as the interest rate moves up the equilibrium GNP moves down and vice versa. The effect of a one percent change in interest rates on GNP is the effect of the interest-rate change on the rate of investment times the multiplier.

If the equilibrium GNP corresponding to each level of interest rates is plotted we will get a downward sloping curve as in Figure 13.10. Since the curve is for *equilibrium incomes where planned saving equals investment* it is called the ***IS* curve** (investment-saving equilibrium curve).

The *IS* curve can be represented algebraically by rewriting the multiplier equation with investment treated as a function of the interest rate instead of as a constant.

$$Y=[B+G+I(R)]\frac{1}{1-A}.$$

$I(R)$ is shorthand to indicate a relationship between the level of interest rates and the rate of investment like the one shown in Figure 13.8.

The Position and Slope of the *IS* Curve

Each point on the *IS* curve represents an equilibrium level of income for the rate of investment corresponding to the indicated interest rate.

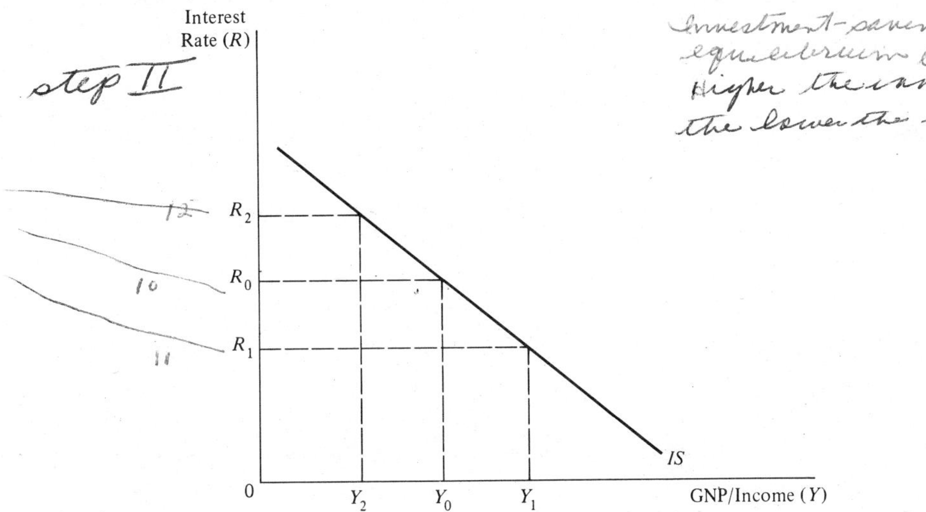

Figure 13.10 Deriving the *IS* Curve II

The position and slope of the curve will be affected by any of the fiscal policy actions discussed earlier. Thus an increase in real government expenditures will shift the curve outward by the amount of the expenditure increase times the multiplier $1/(1-A)$. A reduction in personal income tax rates will increase the multiplier. It will shift the curve outward because a larger multiplier applies to government expenditures and other elements not directly affected by the interest rate. It will also flatten the curve since a larger multiplier applies to investment, which increases as the interest rate falls.

The *IS* curve summarizes the effect of changes in the interest rate on the level of income, taking multiplier effects into account. A fall in the interest rate first increases the rate of investment and then induces increases in consumption expenditure so that the total increase in GNP is a multiple of the increase in investment generated by the fall of interest rates.

Thus the slope of the *IS* curve depends on two factors: the slope of the investment function, which determines increases in investment resulting from the given fall in interest rates, and the size of the multiplier, which determines the ratio of the total GNP increase to the initial increase in investment.

IS and *LM* Curves

The *IS* curve is a device used to show how interest rates are related to GNP. Since the curve slopes down to the right, low interest rates are associated with high incomes. The curve is based on considerations relating to markets for goods and services and has nothing to do with financial markets. We simply take the interest rate as given and look for a consistent level of income and production.

But in the previous chapter we showed that the level of interest rates (for a given money supply) depends on the level of income. We summarized

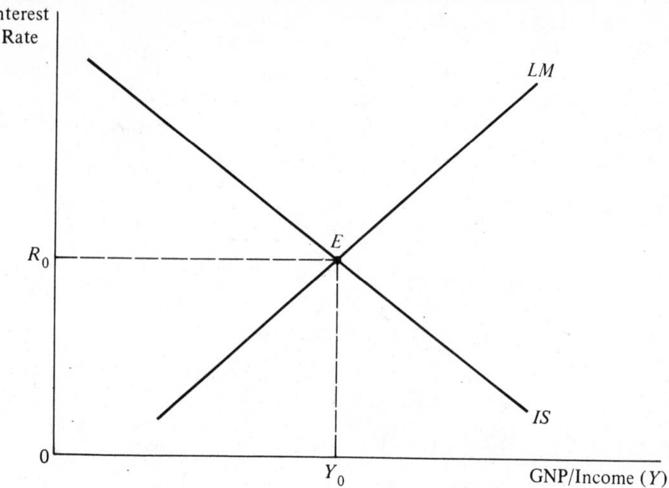

Figure 13.11 Equilibrium Income Determined by *IS–LM* Curves

the income-interest-rate relationship with the *LM* curve, which showed that (given some real money supply) an increase in income is associated with an increase in interest rates.

The *IS* curve relates low interest rates to high income, and the *LM* curve relates high income to high interest rates. Do the two curves contradict one another? No, this is another case of mutual or simultaneous causation. Both the goods market and the money market have to be in equilibrium at the same time. All interest-income combinations on the *IS* curve are equilibrium positions for the goods markets but most of them are not equilibrium positions for the money market. All interest-income combinations on the *LM* curve are equilibrium positions for the money market but most of them are not equilibrium positions for the goods market. However, at a point where the curves cross both markets are in equilibrium. Figure 13.11 shows the *IS* and *LM* curves together with the equilibrium point at R_0Y_0.

From your studies in other economics courses you will probably have anticipated that this is leading up to the point where one curve will slope down while the other slopes up, and the answer is where they cross. However, it is important to remember that the two curves are devices for summarizing a lot of information. The *IS* curve shows the net effect of a change in interest rates on GNP. It takes into account both the direct response of investment to interest rates and the multiplier effect of changes in investment on consumption expenditures. The *LM* curve condenses the long story about financial markets, money substitutes, and demand for money in relation to income.

Together the two show that given the factors underlying the *IS* and *LM* curves, there is only one equilibrium set of rates of flow of real GNP and its components. The underlying variables are all in real terms. The equilibrium real GNP depends on a level of real government expenditures and transfer payments, real capital stock, and real money supply.

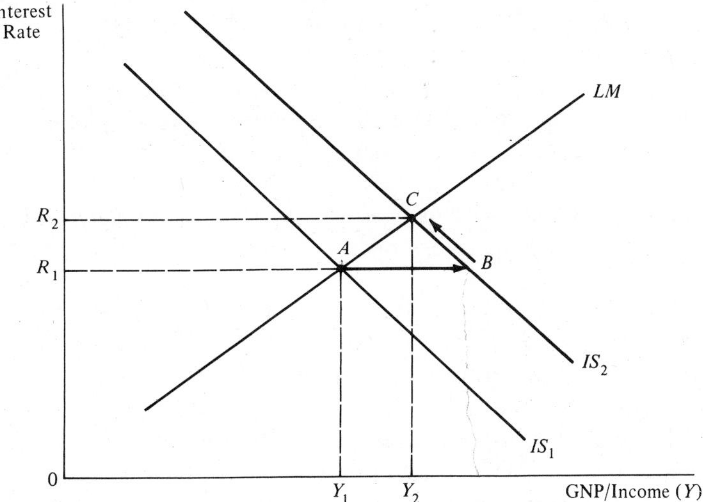

Figure 13.12 Effect of Shift in *IS* Curve

At every point on the *IS* curve, one of the conditions for circular-flow equilibrium is fulfilled: production equals expenditure at the indicated interest rate. At every point on the *LM* curve another condition for circular flow of equilibrium is satisfied: demand for money at the indicated interest rate and income equals supply of money. Both conditions are satisfied at the interest-rate-income combination at which the two curves intersect.

IS–LM curves and fiscal policy. We can get a better insight into the significance of the money-market equilibrium condition by reexamining our discussion of fiscal policy. You will recall that we ended our brief introduction to fiscal policy by noting that there were complications yet to be considered. The necessity of satisfying the money-market equilibrium condition is one of them. We can see how it comes into play by assuming a shift in the *IS* curve and following through the whole response assuming a fixed interest rate—ignoring the *LM* curve—and then see how the reaction of the financial markets produces a reverse feedback offsetting part of the initial change.

In Figure 13.12 the curves IS_1LM show an initial equilibrium at *A*. Now suppose that an increase in government expenditures pushes the *IS* curve out as shown by the line IS_2. The new equilibrium is at point *C* but the economy does not automatically jump to this point. If the interest rate remains constant for a while the rise in government expenditures will raise GNP, and then generate a step-by-step multiplier process that would increase income to point *B*. That development, however, would throw the money market out of equilibrium.

The rise in income would increase demand for money for transactions purposes. Business firms would seek to sell securities and increase their cash holdings. Others would borrow from banks, which would in turn sell securities. Since by assumption the money supply is fixed, interest rates would have to rise to induce the public as a whole to get along with the same amount of money in spite of the rise in income. Some people would increase their money holdings but others would reduce them.

As interest rates rise, investment will be cut back, reducing incomes. Thus there will be a gradual rise in interest rates accompanied by falling investment and income. The movement is shown in Figure 13.12 by the arrow along the curve IS_2. It will continue until the rise in interest rates and the fall in income have brought the money market back into balance. The whole system will be in a new equilibrium at *C* where the new *IS* curve crosses the *LM* curve.

In fact, of course, interest rates will start to move up as soon as government expenditures rise, so that investment will begin to fall before the multiplier response to government expenditure is completed. Simultaneous adjustment process is represented by the arrow from *A* to *C* showing the net effect of the increase in government expenditures offset by the decline in investment associated with rising interest rates.

The size of the total response to fiscal policy depends in part on the size of the ordinary (fixed interest rate) multiplier, but it also depends on the slopes of the *IS* and *LM* curves. In Figure 13.12 the final equilibrium income at *C* is about halfway between the starting point at *A* and the simple fixed interest multiplier equilibrium at *B*. However, that result is an arbitrary byproduct of the way the hypothetical *IS* and *LM* curves were drawn.

The actual outcome depends on the relative slopes of the *IS* and *LM* curves. If the *LM* curve is steep, the increase in government expenditure will have little effect on GNP. The rise in public expenditure will crowd out investment by pushing up interest rates. With a steep *LM* curve a small rise in income will drive interest rates up a lot, and with a flat *IS* curve the rise in interest rates will have a strongly adverse effect on investment.

In the opposite case, with a steep *IS* curve and a flat *LM* curve an increase in government expenditure can drive up income without raising interest rates much. Moreover, the rise in rates will not cut investment much so there will be little crowding out. GNP will rise almost as much as you would expect from a simple multiplier calculation.

IS–LM curves and monetary policy. In the last example a change in fiscal policy was represented by a shift in the *IS* curve. In an analogous way a change in monetary policy can be represented by a shift in the *LM* curve. The *LM* curve shows the equilibrium interest rate associated with each level of income with a given money supply. As we showed in the last chapter, in the short run, which is what we are dealing with here, an increase in the money supply will reduce the interest rate at any given level of income. Alternatively a given interest rate will be consistent with a higher income when money supply increases. So an increase in *M* causes the *LM* curve to shift down to the right. In Figure 13.13 the *IS* and *LM* curves are the same as in Figure 13.12. The curve LM_2 shows the effect of an increased money supply. The new equilibrium point is at γ where *IS* and LM_2 cross, but as before it will take time for complete adjustment.

When the money supply increases no change in income has occurred, so the interest rates should drop quickly to keep the money market in equilibrium. With income the same, interest rates should drop to the level indi-

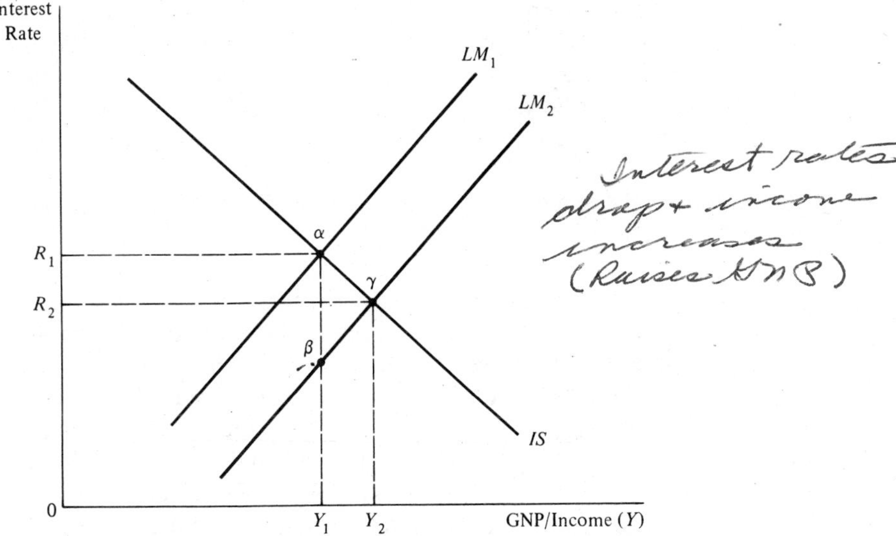

Figure 13.13 Increased Money Supply Raises GNP

cated by point β (old income on new *LM* curve). Then the lower interest rates should stimulate investment and raise income, but with the higher income, interest rates should rise again thus limiting the tendency for investment to rise. The new equilibrium is at γ, where the money market is in balance with a higher income, a lower interest rate, and a higher ratio of money to income than at the start. The interest rate is lower than at the start but higher than the one corresponding to β at the initial level of income.

The magnitude of the GNP change resulting from a given change in money supply depends on the relative *IS–LM* slopes. However, the effects of the slopes on the magnitudes of the income response to monetary changes are exactly opposite those in the fiscal policy case.

With a steep *LM* curve an increase in money supply has a big effect on interest rates and with a flat *IS* curve interest rate changes have strong effects on investment and income.

In general, monetary policy is more effective the flatter the *IS* curve and the steeper the *LM* curve, just the opposite of the fiscal policy case. Note, however, that this whole discussion assumes that prices are constant. As we will show in Chapter 15, once prices are allowed to vary substantially, this result only holds in the short run. Remember that the *IS* curve will be flat if investment responds strongly to a change in interest rates. The *LM* curve will be steep if demand for money (at a given income) does not respond much to interest rates. In that case a little money moves the interest rate a long way.

A capsule summary of debates over monetary policy put forward by James Tobin of Yale declares that there are three possible positions: "money does not matter; money matters; only money matters." In terms of *IS–LM* analysis, money matters most when the *IS* curve is flat and the *LM* curve is steep. Money matters least in the opposite case.

At this point you might expect us to cite some empirical evidence to give you some idea how to choose among those positions. We are going to wait until the next chapter for that for three reasons. First, the empirical evidence cannot be examined without considering the theory of investment in more detail. Second, it turns out that there are reasons for expecting consumption as well as investment to respond to interest rates. Third, there are aspects of the response to changes in money supply that do not fit into the *IS–LM* model very neatly.

Before going on to those complications, however, we have to get price changes into the picture. In our discussion of the possible effects of changes in fiscal and monetary policy, we have so far assumed fixed prices. Consequently, movements of *IS* and *LM* curves, generated by monetary and fiscal policy, must be reflected in output changes. In the next section, we will see that when prices can vary, all or part of the impact of an initial change in fiscal or monetary policy may be translated into price instead of output change.

PRICES AND THE AGGREGATE-DEMAND CURVE

The level of prices must enter the picture because the price level influences the real money supply. We noted in the last chapter that the real money supply can change in two ways. First, the nominal money supply can change while prices remain fixed. Second, prices can change while nominal money supply remains fixed. With a fixed money supply a fall in prices increases the real money supply and a rise in prices decreases the real money supply.

Corresponding to each real money supply there is an *LM* curve. Thus for any given nominal money supply there is a whole family of *LM* curves, one for each price level. Figure 13.14 shows an *IS* curve together with two *LM* curves corresponding to alternative price levels and real money supplies. There is an *LM* curve for each price level and a different intersection

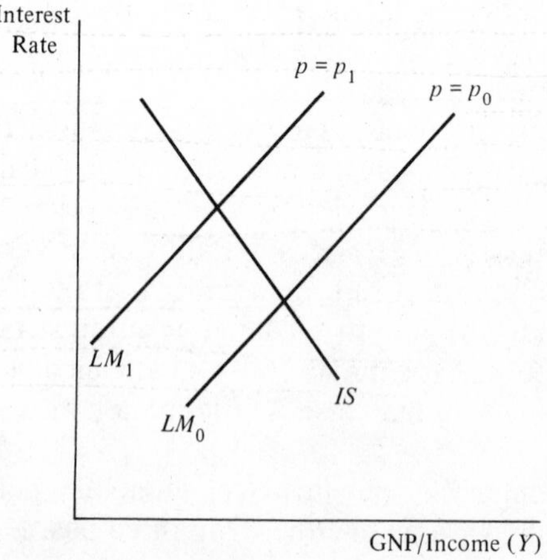

Figure 13.14 Effect of Change in Real Money Supply

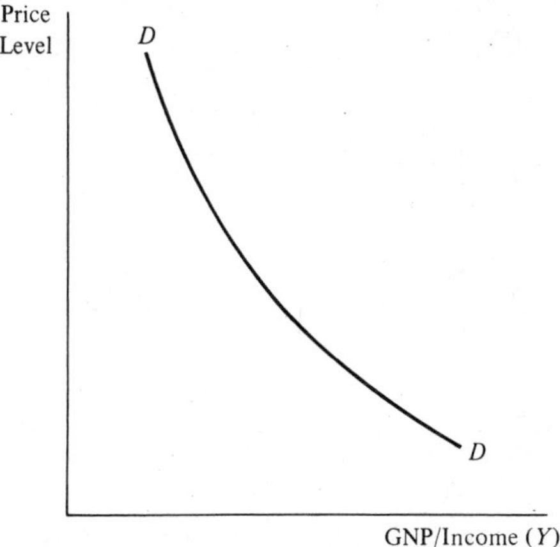

Figure 13.15 The Aggregate-Demand Curve

of *IS* and *LM* for each *LM* curve. As the price level declines the *LM* curve shifts down to the right and the equilibrium value of *Y* at the *IS–LM* intersection moves to the right.

If we plot the equilibrium values of *Y* for alternative price levels, we get a downward sloping curve like *DD* in Figure 13.15. *DD* is an aggregate-demand curve showing the relation between the price level and the quantity of output demanded.

Effects of Price Level Changes

The downward sloping aggregate-demand curve indicates that aggregate real demand will be greater, other things equal, when the price level is low than when it is high. It is important to stop and think why that should be so. Why should a lower price level lead to more aggregate real demand for goods and services? The answer is simple enough if you followed the argument up to this point. The aggregate-demand curve is drawn for a given nominal money supply. The real money supply corresponding to a given nominal money supply is greater when the price level is lower. The *LM* curve shifts to the right when the real money supply increases and the rightward shift in *LM* moves the equilibrium real output to the right.

Thus the effect of the real money change for a given drop in the price level depends on the slopes of the *IS* and *LM* curves in just the same way as the effect of a given nominal change in *M* with a fixed price level. So far we are leaving aside the effect that a drop in the price level has on consumption by changing wealth. When this is added in the next chapter, you will see another reason why the aggregate-demand curve slopes downward.

If the *LM* curve is steep and the *IS* curve is flat, a fall in the price level will cause a relatively large rise in real demand. In the opposite case, the price-level change will not have much impact.

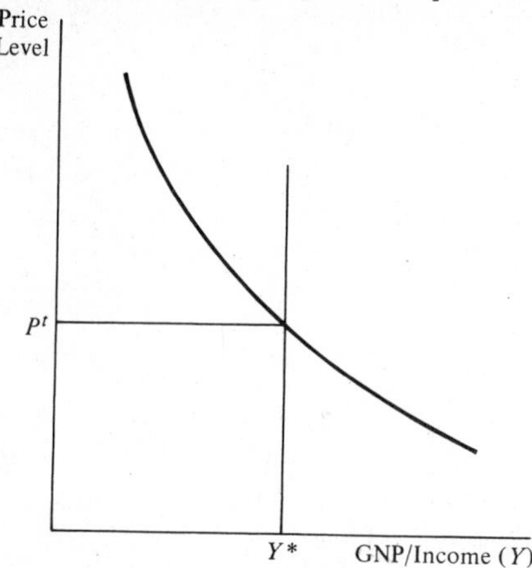

Figure 13.16 The Equilibrium Price Level

Price Level and Potential Output

The only real circular-flow equilibrium in both money and real terms is one with constant prices and constant outputs. In terms of real GNP and output there is only one such equilibrium position. Real GNP has to equal potential output. Otherwise, there will be some tendency for prices to change. Correspondingly, there is only one price level for any set of real *IS* and *LM* curves that will be consistent with the condition that real GNP be equal to potential output. In Figure 13.16 *DD* shows an aggregate-demand curve for given real government expenditures, tax rates, propensity to consume, and real capital stock and a given nominal money supply. Y^* is potential output. If actual real output is to equal Y^* the price level must be p^t, where the demand curve intersects the vertical line at Y^*.

In general, there is reason to believe that there is always some positive price level that would make aggregate real demand equal to potential output. We will discuss that issue more fully in the next chapter after we have taken account of some additional factors that help ensure that an equilibrium exists.

The real question is not whether any equilibrium exists, but whether we can "get there from here." Can prices be expected to adjust enough to keep real aggregate demand at potential output when potential output is growing, and the elements of *the real* IS *and* LM *curves* are changing?

We can provide some insight into the role of the price level in aggregate supply and demand analysis by considering some patterns of movement of aggregate-demand curves and the factors underlying them.

Perfectly Flexible Prices Versus Fixed Price Level

At one extreme it is possible to imagine that the price level is perfectly flexible in the sense that prices move continuously to equate aggregate demand with potential output no matter how the aggregate-demand curve shifts. In that case, changes in government expenditures and taxes and changes in the money supply as well as any events in the private sector affecting the aggregate-demand curve will be immediately translated into price changes while actual real output is always equal to potential output.

At the other extreme we can suppose that prices are rigidly fixed. If the price level remains permanently fixed, output is demand determined. Any shift in the aggregate-demand curve will be reflected in a change in real output up to the point of full capacity output. Thus, an increase or decrease in government expenditure or a change in taxes will shift the *IS* curve and the demand curve. An increase in *M* will shift the *LM* curve to the right, cause a shift in the aggregate-demand curve and an increase in output. As long as the intersection of the aggregate-demand curve with the fixed price line occurs to the left of Y^* it is physically possible, although economically unlikely, that prices can remain fixed. However, when the intersection is to the right of Y^* prices cannot remain fixed unless we have price control or rationing.

If we look at price-level movements over a long period, we do observe a good deal of fluctuation. At the same time there is a lot of variation in unemployment and capacity utilization. Clearly, neither of the extreme cases is realistic. Prices are not fixed, but they are not so flexible as to offset all shifts in aggregate demand.

Much of the observed cyclical fluctuation in output can be explained if we assume that prices and wages adjust gradually and incompletely to short-run movements in the position of the aggregate-demand curve.

THE AGGREGATE-SUPPLY CURVE

The concept of potential output is a straightforward one in a simple economy, making a single product by one technique. In a real economy making many products with a variety of complex and changing technologies, the notion of potential output becomes less clearcut.

As noted earlier, relative prices must constantly change in response to changes in technology, taste, and relative factor supplies. In practice it is impossible for prices to adjust quickly enough to clear all markets for factors and products.

As a result the specialized labor and capital resources required for some products will be in short supply while other resources are underutilized.

In the shortage sectors firms can increase production only by working overtime, using obsolete plant, and employing poorly trained or unqualified workers. Prices will tend to rise in those sectors while they may fall in sectors with excess capacity.

A level of demand high enough to utilize all resources would create many shortages. On the other hand, if aggregate demand is so low that there are no shortages at all there will be much excess capacity and unemployment.

In the high-demand-many-shortage case lots of prices will be rising and none falling. In the opposite case many prices should be falling and none rising. At intermediate levels of aggregate output some prices will be rising and some falling. At some level of output the *average* price level should be stable with some prices rising and others falling. We can define potential

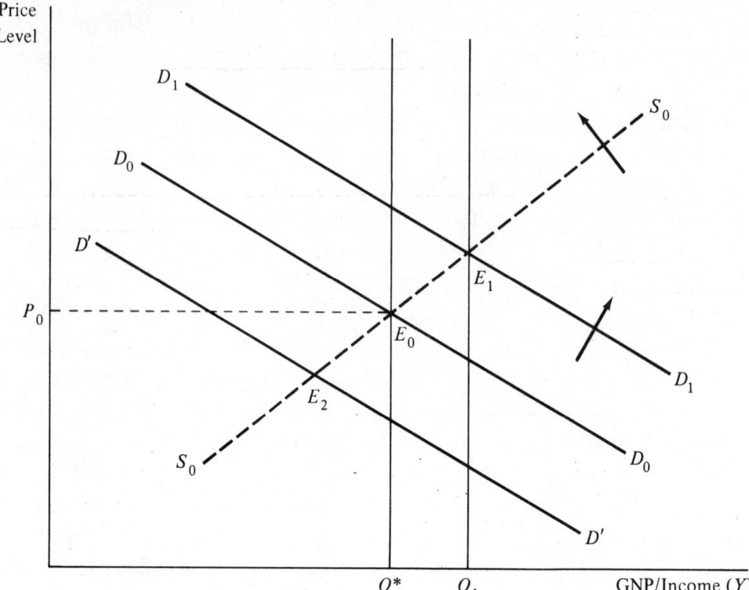

Figure 13.17 Interaction of Shifting Aggregate-Demand and Aggregate-Supply Curves

output as the output at which upward and downward pressures on prices are in balance. Suppose that we start from an initial equilibrium price level at potential output. Now suppose that the aggregate demand curve shifts.

In sectors with excess capacity and available labor, increased demand will be met with increased output and little increase in price. In sectors with more fully utilized resources, prices will rise more and output less. But total output and average price level will both rise. A downward shift of aggregate demand should reduce both prices and output.

If aggregate demand shifts up and down over the business cycle, we can envisage a short-run cyclical supply curve showing the price-output response to cyclical fluctuations in demand. In Figure 13.17 the vertical line at O^* represents potential output and the curve D_0D_0 the average position of demand. It intersects O^* at P_0. P_0 is a price index, an average of prices, and we suppose that (with demand D_0D_0) relative prices are more or less in equilibrium. Some are a little above equilibrium, some below. Correspondingly some firms having vacancies get by with the use of overtime. Some workers are unemployed.

Now suppose that demand is shifting up and down. D_1D_1 shows the "peak of the boom" demand curve, $D'D'$ shows the "trough of the slump" demand curve. S_0S_0 is the short-run supply curve or the cyclical price-output response curve. It passes through the equilibrium point E_0 since the prices and outputs corresponding to P_0, O^* are the baseline from which price and output adjustments take place when demand shifts.

In a boom prices and output move up along S_0S_0 *to* E_1, then as demand shifts down they follow the short-run supply curve back down and at the trough of the slump reach E_2. If demand fluctuates up and down, price level fluctuates but does not show any trend. The fluctuations in demand lead to alternating mild inflation and deflation accompanied by fluctuations in employment and output.

Cyclical fluctuations are superimposed on the long-term upward trend of output. Potential output increases from year to year. Ordinarily, the aggregate-demand curve also shifts to the right as money supply and government expenditures increase. As a historical matter, investment demand at a given interest rate has on the average tended to grow with the scale of the economy. New, capital-intensive technologies have maintained the prospective return on investment in spite of continuing increases in capital per worker. But there is no reason why the rightward shift of the aggregate-demand curve should just keep pace with the growth of potential output from year to year.

We shall discuss short-run price adjustment again in Chapter 18 but the general conclusions we have just reached will hold so long as the race between aggregate demand and potential output is a fairly close one, with the movements of aggregate demand sometimes requiring a modest price increase and sometimes requiring a modest decline. The story will even work fairly well for a large "one-shot" rightward shift in aggregate demand. In a wartime inflation, for example, the aggregate-demand curve shifts sharply rightward under the combined impetus of an increase in real government expenditures (only partly offset by tax increases) and an increase in money supply as the government covers part of its deficit by creating new money. When the war is over, the government's real expenditures are reduced but the increase in money supply does not go away. In the end, the equilibrium price level is higher than at the start.

A gradual price-level-adjustment approach works as long as the adjustment of prices to any one change in the equilibrium price level is not affected by expectations of continuing price change. That will be so when shifts in aggregate demand relative to potential output are relatively small and when the gap between actual and potential output is sometimes positive and sometimes negative. It may be true in wartime cases if everyone expects that the inflationary pressure of the war will soon be over.

Sometimes, however, the aggregate-demand curve shifts outward faster than potential output and continues to shift outward by at least enough to compensate for the resulting rise in prices. That starts a continuing inflation period. When people expect inflation to continue, economic behavior changes in a number of important respects. We shall postpone those reactions to later chapters dealing with inflation. In those chapters, we will also discuss some factors influencing price change other than the gap between aggregate demand at the current price level and potential output. A realistic discussion of inflation can hardly omit the influence of supply shocks from changes in oil, food, and raw material prices.

SUMMARY

1. The objective of income expenditure analysis is to show how the expenditure decisions of households, businesses, and governments interact to simultaneously determine the equilibrium level of real and nominal GNP, the interest rate,

and the price level. Income-expenditure analysis is based on the use of the national income accounts.

2. The national income accounts provide a double-entry bookkeeping system for the nation. The expenditure side of the accounts shows the breakdown of final purchases into expenditures for consumption, different kinds of investment, and government expenditures. The total value of goods and services purchased during the year is called the gross national product (GNP).
3. The income side of the accounts shows the breakdown of the incomes received by households, businesses, and governments. It can be shown that the total value of those incomes must exactly equal the total of GNP expenditures.
4. The consumption function relates the rate of expenditures for consumption to the disposable income of households, and then, taking account of the distribution of GNP, relates the level of consumption expenditures to the level of GNP.
5. The level of production of goods and services is in equilibrium for a given rate of government expenditure and a given rate of investment, when total production (GNP) equals the amount that households want to spend for consumption, plus the amount spent by businesses and governments. The equilibrium reflects the fact that GNP depends in part on the level of consumer expenditures, while consumer expenditures themselves depend on GNP.
6. The level of GNP will change by a multiple of any change in the sum of investment and government expenditures. The ratio of increase in GNP to increase in investment and government expenditure is called "the multiplier."
7. The investment-demand function relates the rate of investment to the level of interest rates.
8. By combining the previous equilibrium analysis of GNP with the investment-demand curve, we can trace out a relationship between the level of interest rates and the equilibrium level of GNP.
9. The curve showing the set of interest rate / GNP combinations, consistent with equilibrium in the goods market, is called the *IS* curve.
10. Given the factors underlying the *IS* curve and given the *LM* curve corresponding to some particular real money supply, there is only one combination of interest rate and GNP consistent with the *IS* equilibrium in the goods market and the *LM* equilibrium in the money market.
11. With a given nominal money supply, the real money supply varies with the price level. Consequently, for any given nominal money supply, there is a different *LM* curve for each price level.
12. At progressively lower price levels, we find that the *LM* curve shifts to the right. Accordingly, the intersection of a given *IS* curve with the *LM* curve occurs at progressively higher levels of real GNP as the price level falls.
13. By plotting the *IS–LM* intersection, corresponding to a number of different price levels (keeping nominal money supply constant), we can derive an aggregate-demand curve. If we plot the price level on the vertical axis and real GNP on the horizontal axis, the curve slopes downward to the right. The intersection of the aggregate-demand curve with an aggregate-supply curve determines the equilibrium price level.
14. The position of the aggregate-demand curve and, therefore, of the equilibrium price level can be shifted by changes in any of the factors underlying the *IS* curve—for example, government expenditures, taxes, or other factors—that might affect investment. It can also be shifted by changes in the nominal money supply.

Questions and Exercises

1. Discuss the effect of each of the following on the *IS* curve:
   a. an increase in the rate of government purchases of goods and services;
   b. a reduction in personal income-tax rates;
   c. an increase in Social Security benefits.
2. An increase in the nominal money supply tends to shift the aggregate-demand curve to the right. Explain in terms of the *IS-LM* curve.
3. The size of the multiplier depends on the ratio of disposable income to GNP as well as on the propensity to save. List some of the factors that may influence the relations between disposable income and GNP.
4. The size of the multiplier affects the slope of the *IS* curve. Explain.
5. The aggregate-demand curve slopes downward to the right. Why? List some factors that influence the slope of the aggregate-demand curve.
6. If potential output rises while the aggregate-demand curve remains fixed, the equilibrium price level must fall. How does the reduction in price level lead to an increase in real output?

Further Reading

COUNCIL OF ECONOMIC ADVISERS. *Annual Report*. Government Printing Office, Washington, D.C. The first chapter of each council report usually contains an analysis of the causes of changes in GNP during the preceding year. The student will also find the tables at the end of the report a useful source of data on GNP and its components as well as on price changes and changes in employment and unemployment.

HICKS, JOHN R. "Mr. Keynes and the Classics: A Suggested Interpretation." *Econometrica* 5 (April 1937): 147–59. In this paper Professor Hicks introduced the *IS-LM* intepretation of Keynes's theory.

KEYNES, JOHN MAYNARD. *The General Theory of Employment Interest and Money*. New York: Harcourt Brace & Company, 1936. This important but difficult to read and often paradoxical work has played a major role in shaping modern macroeconomics.

OKUN, ARTHUR M. "Potential Output: Its Measurement and Significance." Proceedings of the Business and Economic Statistics Section of the American Statistical Assn., 1962, pp. 98–104. This paper gives a detailed discussion of the concept of potential output, a methodology for measuring it, and major factors determining changes in potential output.

SAMUELSON, PAUL A. "The Simple Mathematics of Income Determination." In *Income, Employment and Public Policy,* by Lloyd A. Metzler et al., pp. 133–155. New York: W. W. Norton, 1948. A useful summary for those who are willing to follow some relatively elementary mathematics.

STEWART, KENNETH. "National Income Accounting and Economic Welfare." *Review* (Federal Reserve Bank of St. Louis) 56 (April 1974): 18–24. This paper discusses various criticisms of GNP as a measure of economic welfare and explains some important attempts to provide a better measure by adjusting GNP to take account of such considerations as the cost of pollution.

U.S. DEPARTMENT OF COMMERCE, OFFICE OF BUSINESS ECONOMICS. *Readings in Concepts and Methods of National Income Statistics*. Springfield, Va.: National Technical Information Service, 1976. These papers explain the structural framework of the GNP accounts in great detail and also how the department goes about measuring the GNP and its components from the statistical sources available.

U.S. DEPARTMENT OF COMMERCE, BUREAU OF ECONOMIC ANALYSIS. *The National Income and Product Accounts of the United States, 1929–74.* Washington, D.C.: Government Printing Office, 1976. This volume provides a set of tables for all components of GNP for the whole forty-five-year period.

———. *Survey of Current Business.* Washington, D.C.: Government Printing Office. Issued monthly. Each issue contains the national income data. The July issue provides more detailed tables.

Investment, Consumption, and National Income

14

The income-expenditure approach emphasizes the mutual determination of consumption, investment, GNP, interest rate, and price level. In our first survey of the income-expenditure approach, we used the simplest possible description of the reaction of consumption to disposable income and of investment to interest rates. In our concern to emphasize the big picture of the whole system, we had to neglect important aspects of the determination of investment and consumption expenditure.

In this chapter we will examine in much more detail investment, consumption expenditures, national income, and the sources of change and instability within the system.

DETERMINANTS OF INVESTMENT

A growing economy must devote a substantial proportion of its total output to the production of capital goods—machinery and equipment, trucks, ships, planes, and railroad equipment, factories, office and store buildings. It must do so in order to take advantage of new technology and to provide plant and equipment for a growing labor force. Moreover, a growing population with rising income is prepared to pay for more and better housing requiring substantial expenditures on residential construction. Finally, as the economy grows, it requires increasing inventories of materials, work in process, and finished goods at each stage of the production and distribution process.

In the U.S. investment expenditures of all kinds have averaged around 15 percent of GNP in the years since World War II. In some rapidly growing countries, like Japan, the share of investment in GNP has been almost twice as high. Investment is only one of many factors responsible for Japan's high rate of growth, but it has certainly played an essential role in the growth process.

From a long-run point of view, capital formation is important to the growth of potential output, but variations in the rate of investment also play a major role in accounting for short-run variations in aggregate demand and output. Investment expenditures are much more volatile than consumption expenditures, so that in spite of their modest average share of total output, variations in the rate of investment account for a large proportion of the cyclical variations in the level and growth rate of aggregate output.

Plant and Equipment

In the U.S. business investment in plant and equipment accounts for two-thirds to three-quarters of total capital-formation expenditures. It includes the building of factories and their equipment as well as transportation and construction equipment and office and store buildings. These expenditures are made by thousands of business firms of all sorts, and their investment decisions involve a great variety of technical and market considerations. The paperwork underlying a firm's decision to build a new plant, costing a couple of million dollars, may fill a book as large as this one. The work on a 100-million-dollar glass plant may fill a whole set of filing cases. The work behind an investment decision may involve an elaborate market analysis, as well as all sorts of engineering studies. In these days, of course, environmental-impact statements, health and safety regulations, and zoning conflicts generate more paper.

In spite of their variety when considered in detail, a few basic forces provide the motivation for most plant and equipment investment. Any investment expenditure is worth considering because it promises to bring in more revenue to the investor, or because it is expected to reduce future costs of some sort. Any firm's investment decision involves two parts: an evaluation of the amount and timing of the prospective additional revenues or reduced costs resulting from the investment; and a comparison of those revenues or cost savings with the costs of the capital goods involved. Since the prospective revenues or costs will occur in future years, while the investment expenditure is immediate, a comparison of the present value of future revenues with the initial capital costs is involved.

Sources of Investment Opportunity

Opportunities for firms to increase revenues (reduce costs) in the future by capital expenditures arise from a number of sources.

Maintenance costs. Anyone who owns a car knows that as mechanical equipment grows older, maintenance costs rise. At some point before the equipment becomes completely broken down, it will be worthwhile to examine whether the present value of maintenance and operating costs on the old equipment will exceed those for new similar equipment by enough to justify replacement.

Technological improvement of equipment and processes. Continuous technological progress has been one of the outstanding characteristics of market economies for the last three hundred years. When new technology moves from the laboratory and the pilot plant into practical use, it has to be embodied in new equipment. Firms will often find that the cost reduction available from the purchase of new equipment, embodying new technology, justifies replacing old equipment, even when replacement would not be justified on a maintenance cost basis.

New products. A great deal of investment is required for the production of new products. A substantial proportion of consumer expenditures today pays for products that did not exist thirty years ago. Black and white as well as color televisions, modern stereo equipment, instant cameras, and frozen foods are just a few examples.

Expanding output. In the long run, aggregate demand must grow to keep pace with the growth of the labor force and with increases in productivity. Demand growth for old products, as well as new, can generate new opportunities for profitable investment.

As demand grows, existing firms find their plant fully utilized and may have to meet the demand by overtime, extra shifts, or by using obsolete equipment. At some point it will become profitable for someone to build new capacity to avoid the extra cost involved. Because capital goods are durable, investment decisions must be based on expectations of demand conditions in the future. In fact, the observed growth of demand up to any date is important only to the extent that it helps to predict the level of demand in the future.

Although rising maintenance costs, technological change, new products, and aggregate-demand growth are separate forces generating investment opportunities, the potential return from any particular investment project may arise from the joint operation of more than one of those factors. For example, the cost saving from replacing old equipment may arise from both the high maintenance cost of the old equipment and the lower operating cost of new equipment embodying new technology.

Evaluating Investments

At any time, thousands of firms are faced with opportunities to reduce cost or increase revenue by acquiring new plant or equipment. They have to calculate whether the potential cost savings or added revenues are large enough to justify the capital outlay in question. As already noted, the investment decision involves comparison between capital outlay now and a stream of returns from reduced costs or increased revenues over a number of years in the future.

A firm facing a single investment opportunity can decide whether to accept or reject the investment by making a simple present-value calculation. Present value of the returns from the investment can be calculated in exactly the same way as in the bond- and stock-value calculations used in Chapter 6.

$$\text{Present value} = \frac{R_1}{1+r} + \frac{R_2}{(1+r)^2} + \cdots \frac{R_n}{(1+r)^n}$$

where r is the discount rate and R_1, R_2 . . . R_n are the revenues or cost savings expected each year as a result of making the investment. The project is worth doing if the present value is greater than the cost of the initial investment.

In practice, the problem proves to be more difficult. The initial capital costs are fairly well known, but anyone who has had anything to do with a construction project knows that various unforeseen difficulties may raise costs above the initial estimates. The projected revenues or cost savings are even more uncertain. They are predicated on estimates of future sales, prices, and wages. Moreover, the new equipment may suddenly be made obsolete by new technological developments. New competing products may wipe out the market for the output. Firms making investment decisions may protect themselves against these contingencies by making conservative estimates of prospective revenues or cost savings. Alternatively, they may use their best estimates of the revenues and costs in computing the expected returns in the present-value equation. They can allow for risk by discounting future returns at a rate higher than the going interest rate. The higher discount rate has the effect of deflating distant prospective returns by more than the early ones, thus reflecting the greater uncertainty of estimates of conditions in the more distant future.

In many cases, one design for an investment project is clearly better than any available alternative. In other cases, however, alternative types of equipment or building materials may be available, and it is necessary to choose between them. Each of the alternatives may pass a present-value test, but they are mutually exclusive—if one is accepted, the other will be rejected. In that case it is necessary to compute the present value of the difference between the costs and returns from the alternative designs.

For example, the firm may have to choose between cheap equipment with relatively short-service life or sharply rising maintenance costs and equipment that is more expensive but more durable. To choose between them, the firm needs to compute the difference in the present value of the two options.

An important variation on the mutually exclusive options problem is postponement. It often happens that a firm knows that sooner or later it will have to replace a piece of equipment or a plant, just as we all know that sooner or later we will have to replace the old car. A present-value calculation may show that it is worth building a new plant, but it may also turn out that the option of partial replacement or renovation to delay the construction of a complete new plant is still better.

The Effect of Tax Rates on Investment

Whenever investment falls relative to GNP or when the Congress becomes concerned about the need for more investment to raise the growth of productivity, proposals to change corporate income taxes in order to stimulate investment are heard. This is hardly surprising, because corporate tax rates can have a very important influence on investment returns and on the risks of investment. We can see how taxes affect investment by examining their effect on present-value comparisons.

As before, suppose we have to decide whether to purchase capital goods. The investment is expected to generate a stream of before-tax returns R_1, R_2, . . . R_n. In the absence of taxes, we compute the present value of the project by discounting the prospective returns. Now, however, suppose that there is a 50 percent corporate income tax. If it applied to all returns, the present value of the prospective returns would be simply cut in half.

In fact, however, the tax does not apply to all the returns. The tax applies only to the return net of depreciation. You may have already noticed that the evaluation of investments by the present-value approach did not involve depreciation. If we evaluate investment by that approach, depreciation appears only as an accounting adjustment. But when we allow for corporate income taxes depreciation plays an important role in reducing the portion of total cash returns taken by taxes.

The after-tax return for any year is computed as follows:

gross return $= R$
depreciation $= D$
taxable income $= R - D$
tax $= t(R - D)$
after-tax return $= R - t(R - D)$, or $R - tR + tD$.

Thus the present value of the return from investment depends on three elements: (1) the gross return; (2) the tax on the gross return; and (3) the reduction of taxes obtained by deduction of depreciation allowances.

If we like, we can think of the present value of tax saving from depreciation as a reduction in the cost of the asset. It is the government's contribution to the cost of the asset, while the government also gets a part of the cash returns as they come. Notice that if the investing company has other taxable income, it gets the tax benefit of the depreciation allowance, even if the project is a failure and produces no revenue.

The present value of the tax deduction for depreciation allowances can be influenced by changes in tax regulations affecting the timing of depreciation allowances. Total depreciation can never exceed the original cost of the depreciating asset (unless it is resold), but the distribution of depreciation during the life of the asset can be changed. With simple "straight-line" depreciation, an equal amount of depreciation is allowed for tax purposes each year. The straight-line depreciation allowance for a $100,000 asset, lasting twenty years, is $5,000 per year. Other depreciation formulas allow firms to take more depreciation and reduce taxes more in the early years of the investment's life and correspondingly less in the late years. While the arithmetic sum of tax deductions under these formulas is the same as with straight-line depreciation, its present value is greater because the present value of a dollar saved in the early years is greater than the present value of a dollar saved a long time from now. Changes in the tax regulations, permitting faster depreciation in the early years of an investment's life, should encourage investment. Another device for encouraging investment is the investment tax credit. Under legislation passed in 1962, firms are permitted to deduct a percentage of the cost of new equipment from taxes at the time of purchase. In effect, the government pays part of the cost of new equipment. It is important to note that, under present law, depreciation allowances are based on the cost of plant and equipment at the time of acquisition. In an inflationary era, the tax savings from depreciation allowances do not rise with price level and after-tax revenues fall relative to before-tax revenues.

Inflation Expectations

The stream of prospective returns from an investment (the *R*s in the present-value equation) involves both price and quantity elements. If the project is a labor-saving one, the return consists of a reduction in the number of hours of work employed for a given output, multiplied by the appropriate wage rate. If the project is intended to increase output, the return consists of the increased output multiplied by the difference between the price per unit of product and the unit cost of the labor and materials employed. In our discussion of the evaluation of investment projects, we implicitly assumed constant prices, but nowadays inflation is a fact of life, and expectations about future price changes are likely to play an important role in investment decisions.

The importance of inflation expectations is most obvious if we consider the choice between making an investment now or postponing for a year. Consider a case in which the interest rate is 4 percent, and prices are expected to be stable. A firm's management decides that is just about a toss-up whether to build now or wait a year. Now consider the same choice when the management expects construction costs to rise by 7 percent in the next year. If the interest rate were still 4 percent, it would clearly be better to build now, since the investment required by the postponement alternative will be higher by 7 percent, while the build-now option is unchanged. In fact the build-now option would be preferable to delay at any interest rate up to 11 percent. At that rate the interest saved by postponement would just cancel the higher investment cost from a year's price rise, and the two plans would again be a toss-up. A more general approach involves systematic adjustment of the stream of prospective returns for expected inflation. Suppose that as before we have to compute the present value of an investment project in order to compare it with the cost of the capital goods involved. Suppose that the returns are expected to rise at *i* percent per year. Then, if we assume that the returns are collected at the end of the year, the expected return at the end of the first year is $R_1(1+i)$; the return at the end of the second year is $R_2(1+i)(1+i)=R_2(1+i)^2$, and so on.

The evaluation of the investment proposal now involves comparing the price of the capital good (which remains unchanged) with the present value of the prospective returns, taking expected inflation into account. We now have

$$\text{present value} = R_1(1+i)/(1+r) + R_2(1+i)^2/(1+r)^2 + \ldots R_n(1+i)^n/(1+r)^n.$$

You can readily see that expected inflation offsets the effect of the interest rate on the discounted values of future returns. In fact the present-value formula can be rewritten as

$$\text{present value} = R_1/(1+r-i) + R_2/(1+r-i)^2. \ldots$$

Thus a one percent rise in the expected inflation rate has exactly the same effect on present value as a one percent reduction in the nominal interest rate. The present value of an investment depends on *the difference between nominal interest rate and the expected inflation rate.* This difference is called **the real rate of interest.** Notice two points. First, the real rate can be changed either by a change in the nominal rate with given inflation expectations, or by a change in inflation expectations with given nominal rate. Second, in times of inflation the nominal rate becomes a poor measure of the restrictive or expansive impact of monetary policy. Nominal interest rates usually rise during periods of inflation, but they sometimes lag behind inflation expectations so that the nominal rate may be rising while the real rate is falling.

Finally the above conclusions must be modified to take account of the effect of the tax treatment of depreciation and interest payments.

INTEREST RATES AND INVESTMENT: THE INVESTMENT-DEMAND SCHEDULE

So far we have been considering investment projects taken one at a time. We now want to consider the effects of interest rates on the aggregate rate of investment for the economy as a whole. To see how the level of interest rates affects investment, we can perform a hypothetical experiment. Suppose first that the going real interest rate on corporate bonds is 5 percent. Each of the many firms making investment decisions has its own views on the factors determining the prospective future revenues or cost savings from various investment options. They are faced with a certain set of prices for capital goods. Given all the relevant information, each firm will make a certain set of choices undertaking some projects now, choosing to postpone others, and rejecting others altogether. In the aggregate their decisions will lead to expenditure of, say, 200 billion dollars in a given year.

Now to make our hypothetical experiment, suppose that the corporate bond yield is 7 percent instead of 5 percent, while everything else remains the same. In what way will individual firm decisions and aggregate investment differ in the 7 percent case by comparison with the 5 percent case?

From our previous discussion it should be clear that the higher interest rate will lead to decisions generating a smaller amount of investment than the two hundred billion dollars of investment generated by the lower one. First, in simple one-option investment choices, there will be a certain set of projects in which the present value of prospective returns evaluated at 5 percent exceeds the required capital outlay by only a small margin. When the present-value calculation is made with a 7 percent discount rate, the present value of the returns will be smaller and in some cases will fall short of the required capital outlay.

Second, in the case of mutually exclusive alternatives the higher inter-

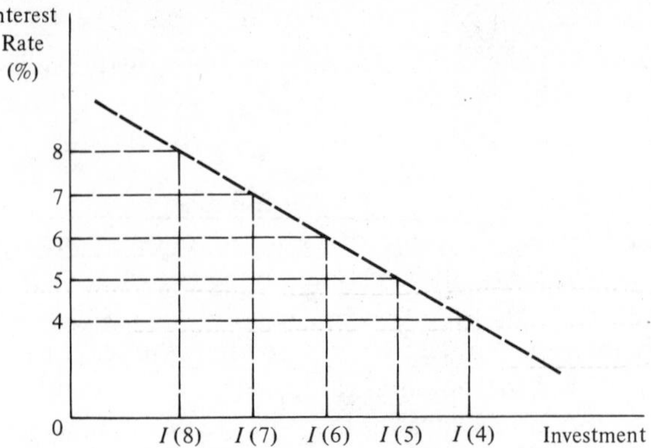

Figure 14.1 Investment-Demand Schedule

est rate will reduce the benefits from expenditure on greater durability. The extra outlay for durability (or low maintenance cost in later years) remains the same, while a reduction in maintenance costs or deferral of replacement is deflated by a larger discount factor with the 7 percent rate than with the 5 percent rate. At the 7 percent rate, less durable alternatives with less initial outlay will be chosen, thus reducing total investment.

Third, the higher rate will favor postponement or renovations. Thus all things considered, the 7 percent rate will produce less investment (other things equal) than the 5 percent rate. Figure 14.1 shows the amount of investment at several rates. The dotted line shows what we might expect if we made a whole set of hypothetical experiments with rates ranging from 4 percent to 8 percent.

Shifts in Investment Demand

Each increase in the stock of capital as a result of investment tends to push the investment-demand schedule down. On the other hand, increases in the expected level of output push the investment-demand schedule up. In a sense the net movement of the investment-demand schedule is the result of a continuing race between the growth of the capital stock and the actual and expected growth of output.

The central role of the "race" between accumulation of capital through investment and the growth of output is confirmed by numerous empirical studies. Empirical studies indicate that variations in the ratio of output to capital stock account for much of the observed variation in the ratio of business fixed investment to GNP. Because the growth of the capital stock varies less than the growth of output, variations in the ratio of capital stock to output are most strongly influenced by the growth of output. Empirical studies show that a large part of the variation of investment can be explained by the average rate of growth of output over three- or four-year periods. *The link between the level of investment and the rate of growth of output* is called the **acceleration principle.** Investment tends to increase when output growth accelerates.

Of course, that is not the whole story. Changes in interest rates and taxes have a significant role in determining investment. Moreover, investment decisions will certainly be influenced by expectations about future movements of output. Business-management expectations about the economic outlook reflect their judgments about prospective changes in fiscal and monetary policy, as well as their views about the growth of potential output in the longer run. Management may believe that, because of (or in spite of) government policy output will follow a path that stays close to potential output. In that case the effect of short-term variations in output growth will be limited. Investment will not be cut back drastically in a recession if an early recovery is expected. In a boom, management will be cautious about stepping up investment plans if it expects output to level off or decline in a short time. Nonetheless, many decisions about the timing of investment projects will be affected by judgments about the movement of demand over the next couple of years. That is why many business firms spend money for forecasts of GNP movements over the next year or two. Prospective changes in government policy always play an important role in those forecasts.

Shifts in investment demand are both a cause and a consequence of movements of aggregate demand. As we have just noted, variations in the growth of real output tend to cause variations in the rate of fixed investment. Thus, a rapid increase in aggregate demand will lead to an upward shift in investment demand, which will, in turn, contribute to the growth of demand. One is tempted at this point to envisage endless sequences of feedbacks from demand growth to investment and from investment to demand growth. In fact, however, rising interest rates are likely to check the interaction process before it goes very far.

INTERACTIONS

Technological change, new products, growth of demand, and the aging of existing equipment are the source of opportunities for investment. Variations in the rate of growth of demand appear to be the most important determinant of *variations* in investment opportunities. However, variations in taxes and interest rate may also play an important role in two ways. Variations in interest rate may speed up or slow down the response of investment to demand growth or technological change. They will also influence choices as to expenditure per unit of capacity on those projects which are undertaken.

We might say that the influence of such factors as the rate of growth of output are reflected in the zero interest rate intercept of the investment function while the interest rate response noted above shows up in the slope of the investment function.

Residential Construction

The construction of new homes and apartment buildings accounts for around one-fourth of the total capital outlays in the United States. Expenditures for additions and alterations have amounted to $15 billion in recent years. In principle, the logic of investment in residential construction is similar to the decision logic for any other investment project. The same kind of choice between present capital outlays and future benefits is involved. But because it accounts for such a large volume of investment, the special characteristics of residential construction deserve more attention. Moreover, the financing arrangements for residential building make this type of investment particularly sensitive to changing financial conditions.

Because buildings last a long time, they are likely to be sold several times before they are demolished. The valuation of existing buildings makes a good starting place for an attempt to understand investment in residential construction.

Investment Decisions

A prospective buyer of rental housing has to calculate the present value of the expected net revenues from his investment. In doing so, he must estimate future gross rents and allow for operating costs and property taxes. His after-tax receipts will be affected by income tax deductions for local taxes, depreciation, and interest payments.

A developer considering a new building project can estimate the costs for constructing a certain type of building, add land-site costs, and his direct expense for architects, engineers, and legal costs. He can then compare those costs with his own present-value calculation of net rental income. Prospective single house buyers must make similar calculations. Their rental estimates will reflect their own tastes but they must consider market rents because they may want to resell the house.

Building Costs and House Prices

Rents move gradually in response to the changing balance between the growth of the housing stock and the increase in demand generated by rising income and population. Rents cannot long remain below the level required to cover the costs of the most efficient builders. In rapidly growing areas rents must be high enough to induce a rate of building which will balance the growth of demand.

Mortgage Markets and Residential Construction

The basic factors driving the demand for home building tend to move rather slowly and steadily. Population grows slowly at only one or two percent per year. The annual addition to the stock of houses is also a very small fraction of the existing stock. The growth of income varies a good deal from year to year, but most people consider their average income rather than their current income in choosing their housing accommodation. Taxes, maintenance costs, and construction costs vary, but not enough to cause violent year-to-year shifts in the rate of building. Finally, nominal mortgage interest rates have risen over the years, but after allowance for inflationary expectations, the rise in real mortgage interest rates has been very small until 1980 and so have the annual variations. One might expect therefore that expenditure on residential construction would show little cyclical fluctuation. Unfortunately for the home-building industry, the opposite is true. Housing starts and residential construction expenditures vary more widely than any component of GNP except inventory investment.

Most economists attribute the instability in housing construction to events in financial markets. Interest-rate changes influence all kinds of investment but they have been particularly important for housing. Interest rates affect housing in three different ways. First, a rise in real interest rates reduces the present value of expected revenues as it does with any investment. Because buildings are long-lived this effect may be more important for construction than for equipment. Second, a rise in nominal interest rates due to inflation makes housing more attractive to people in high tax brackets since interest is deductible now and the capital gains tax comes in the future at a lower rate. On the other hand, the higher monthly payments may discourage some low income buyers.

Third, as explained in Chapter 6 the problems of the thrift institutions have amplified the effects of interest rate changes on home building.

INVENTORY INVESTMENT

Inventory investment accounts on the average for only about one percent of GNP expenditures, but it is one of the most volatile components of GNP. Variations in the rate of inventory investment account for a significant part of the variation in the growth of demand and have played an important role in each recession since the Second World War.

Retailers and wholesalers carry inventories because their sales vary erratically, while it takes time to obtain merchandise from suppliers. If they do not have goods in stock when customers are ready to buy, they may lose a sale to a rival. In deciding how much inventory to carry, they have to balance the cost of storage and interest on their investment in inventories against the gain in sales from having goods on hand. It is not worth raising the average inventory if the probable gain in sales from holding it just balances the carrying cost. Actual inventory will vary around the target average precisely because sales do vary erratically.

Manufacturers carry inventories of finished goods in order to be able to fill orders promptly. In addition they hold inventories of finished goods to smooth production. Since it is costly to hire and dismiss labor for frequent variations in production, manufacturing firms try to maintain steady production rates while sales fluctuate. When sales increase, firms will let inventories decline for a while, then step up production by enough to rebuild inventories as well as to match the increased sales rate. The reverse will be true when sales decline.

Manufacturers also hold inventories of materials and components and work in process. They hold material inventories to ensure that production can continue in the face of delays or interruptions of supplies and because it is cheaper to transport and handle relatively large batches of materials. Work-in-process inventories are directly linked to the production process. They are relatively unimportant for simple, quickly produced items, but producers of complex capital goods like aircraft, ships, or generators have large inventories of partly finished products because each item takes weeks or months to complete.

Planned inventories tend to vary more or less proportionately with final product sales so that the rate of inventory investment tends to vary with the growth of the goods component of GNP. That produces an acceleration effect. The rate of inventory investment tends to rise when the rate of growth of goods output accelerates, thus temporarily giving an additional fillip to the growth of demand.

The ratio of inventory to final sales may vary for a number of reasons. Work-in-process inventory will rise when new orders exceed shipments. As production increases in response to orders, the work in process in the pipeline rises. When finished product shipments catch up with orders, the flow of shipments out of the pipeline balances the flow in from new orders, and work-in-process inventories level off. When orders decline, shipments will be maintained for a while, but work in process will decline. Firms may also change their inventory targets in response to changing judgments about the availability and cost of materials and supplies. In an upswing, purchasing agents will increase orders if they fear that prices will rise or that suppliers will be unable to fill the orders promptly. Their efforts to protect themselves may increase the already high utilization of capacity and add to pressures on prices. Purchasing agents may trim inventory targets in a downswing for the opposite reason.

The factors noted above have caused significant variations in the rate of inventory investments, but the "big swings" in inventory investment seem to be connected with the problems of adjusting production to sales. Inven-

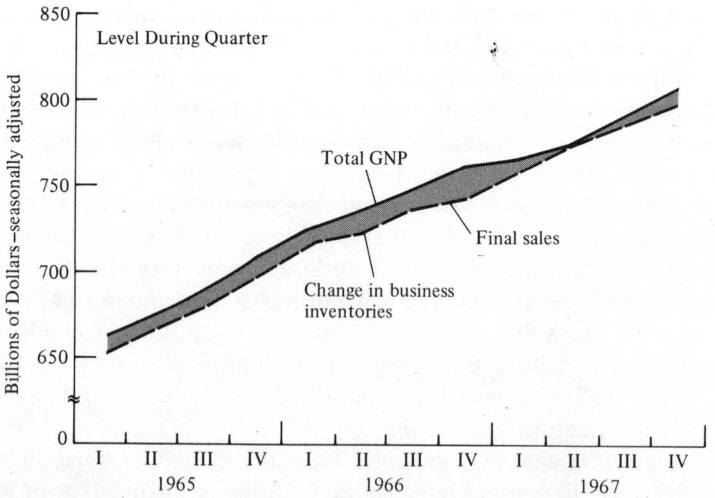

Figure 14.2 Total Gross National Product and Final Sales *1965–67*

Source: *Annual Report of the Council of Economic Advisers,* February 1968, p. 44.

tory accumulation is after all the difference between production and final product sales. A relatively small change in the gap between production and sales can result in significant unplanned inventory accumulation. A substantial adjustment of production may then be required if producers try to bring inventories back to normal in a short period. Figure 14.2 shows the course of the very large inventory swing in the 1965–67 period.

You can see how inventory investment rose in late 1966 when production (GNP) rose in spite of a slowdown in growth of final sales. In 1967, the growth of final sales accelerated while the growth of production slowed. Inventory accumulation declined and became negative.

MONEY, WEALTH, AND CONSUMPTION

In the previous chapter we introduced the notion of the consumption function and used the simplest possible relation between disposable income and consumption in order to see how the pieces of the income-expenditure model fit together. Now that we have worked out the whole model, we can consider a more complicated and realistic treatment of consumption. In particular, we want to show how changes in money supply influence consumption directly.

Consumer expenditures make up about 60 percent of total GNP. Even small variations in the ratio of consumption to disposable income can play an important role in the fluctuations of aggregate demand. On the average, American households save about six-and-one-half percent of disposable income, and spend the balance on consumption; but the savings rate is sometimes as high as eight percent and sometimes as low as three percent. A shift of a couple of percentage points in the ratio of consumption to disposable income, one way or the other, can make the difference between a boom year and a recession. Any realistic theory of income determination has to give some explanation of short-run variations in the savings rate. Moreover, crude empirical generalizations are always dangerous in economics. If we do not know why they hold, we do not know what kind of changes in circumstances will make them break down. In the case of personal saving, a simple empirical rule is dangerous because savings rates differ greatly from country to country. In Japan the personal savings rate is close to 25 percent of disposable income. In this section we are going to consider first some of the basic motivations for saving and their implications for the responses of consumers to changes in wealth. From that discussion we will be able to see why changes in money and wealth influence consumption expenditures.

The Life-Cycle Approach to Consumption and Saving

In our society there are only a few people who save because they have more income than they can use, or because they are misers, or because it is the right thing to do. Most people find that it is hard to save, and they only do so to achieve some definite purpose. They save for the down payment on a house, to start a small business, to prepare for future college expenses for their children, and very often to prepare for retirement. A relatively small number of people plan to leave estates for their children or to give bequests to charitable or educational institutions. You will notice that, except in the last case, the object of saving is to accumulate for a time and then to dissave when it is time for children to go to college or when retirement actually occurs. Because so many of the factors motivating saving have to do with the changes in circumstances that occur as people grow older, the saving theory built on those considerations is called the **life-cycle theory of saving.**

The central proposition of this theory is that *saving and dissaving occur because families do not receive income at the same time they wish to spend it.* To time the expenditure of limited resources efficiently, it is necessary to plan ahead and at some times spend less than current receipts, and at other times more. To do that properly, families have to guess the pattern of future income, anticipate special consumption problems like college expenses, choose a plan for consumption and saving for future years, and finally, carry out the first step of the plan in terms of current consumption and saving. That all sounds very difficult and it is. Most people have only a vague idea of how their income will change. They plan for college expenses, but most of today's parents did not anticipate current tuition rates.

Since people usually do not forecast their incomes correctly, they often have to go back to the drawing board to plan anew how to distribute total resources over the remaining years of life. Those resources include expected future income receipts, and wealth currently on hand. Planning for the future is complicated because it is difficult to judge what the future will bring; yet the implications of an individual's views about his future prospects are fairly simple.

As a first approximation suppose a man wants to spend a constant amount per year in each of the n remaining years of life. He starts with some initial wealth w and expects to receive a certain average income $\bar{Y}$ for the remainder of his life. His total lifetime resources are then $w+n\bar{Y}$. If he spends $\bar{C}$ per year and plans to leave no estate, his total consumption $n\bar{C}$ must equal total resources. That is, $n\bar{C}=w+n\bar{Y}$. Therefore $\bar{C}=w/n+\bar{Y}$. In most years his current income Y will differ from his expected average income. His saving in any year will be $Y-\bar{C}$ or $Y-\bar{Y}-w/n$. In particular his preretirement income will be above average, and his postretirement income will be below average. Thus before retirement $Y-\bar{Y}$ will be positive, and he will usually be a positive saver. After retirement $Y-\bar{Y}$ will be negative and he will be dissaving by liquidating his accumulated wealth in order to finance consumption expenditures.

Those relatively simple considerations have some important implications for aggregate saving. First, notice that the lifetime saving of the individual who saves only for such things as retirement will be zero. He saves in one part of life and dissaves an equal amount at other times. Does that mean that the only net saving for the nation is accounted for by rich people who leave large estates? It would mean that if population and income were constant. In that case the positive saving of people of working age would be just canceled by the dissaving of retired people. In fact, of course, the growth of population implies net saving for the nation, even if no individual leaves anything behind. When population is rising, the number of people in each working-life-age group—for example, those between thirty and forty—is larger than the number in each retired-age group—say, sixty to seventy; so that the positive saving of those of working age outweighs the negative saving of those in retirement. That tendency is reinforced by the upward trend of per capita income. Young people today are anticipating a higher average lifetime income than did their predecessors thirty or forty years older, who are now entering retirement age. Correspondingly, those young people are saving for a higher retirement income than their parents have. The positive saving of the working-age group outweighs the negative saving of the retired group. Thus the life-cycle theory accounts for positive aggregate saving, even if no individual has any net saving over his whole life.

The life-cycle theory has another important implication. If each individual is seeking to accumulate assets for retirement, the amount he saves at any time will depend not only on his current and expected future income but also on the real value of the assets he owns. At any time, the past saving of the population is embodied in capital goods and houses. Thus the value of physical assets valued at cost will rise with accumulated saving. However, the real and nominal value of wealth can deviate from the sum of past savings.

The market value of wealth generally deviates from the cost of accumulated physical assets because prices, interest rates, and expectations of future profits and rents change all the time.

The nominal value of wealth is equal to the present value of the property income from private assets, plus the net present value of interest-bearing government debt, plus the value of non-interest-bearing government debt (currency and bank reserves). The real value of government debt, whether interest bearing or not, will decline when prices rise or increase when prices fall. The real value of private property as a whole will not be directly affected by price change, though private debtors will gain from price increases while the creditors will lose.

Changes in interest rates will affect the value of all assets except non-interest-bearing government debts. A rise in interest rates obviously depresses bond prices. It is also apparent that stock prices are adversely affected by increasing interest rates. It also follows directly from present-value calculations that a rise in interest rates reduces the value of directly held physical assets. Of course, the interest rate relevant to the valuation of common stocks and physical assets is the real rather than the nominal interest rate.

The life-cycle theory indicates that consumer expenditures are likely to vary with wealth as well as with income, responding positively to both. While the wealth associated with a given level of income can change for a variety of reasons, there are two reasons that play a particularly important role in monetary theory. First, a reduction of real interest rates tends to raise the real value of wealth relative to income, and therefore shifts the consumption line upward. That consideration makes consumption as well as investment responsive to the real interest rate. Second, a fall in the price level increases the value of real balances and therefore increases wealth and consumption. Thus the price level enters the picture in two ways: through the real balance effect just mentioned, or through a price change raising or lowering the real money supply and the resulting lower or higher interest rates. Finally, to the extent that money supply is increased by currency issues or increases in bank reserves, an increase in the money supply increases real balances even without a price-level change.

Limitations of the Life-Cycle Theory

The life-cycle approach provides a rationale for the savings behavior of many people. However, it has to be qualified in a number of ways. In particular, it does not deal very well with the estate-building objectives of relatively high-income people. It may not apply well to a large number of relatively low-income families who have difficulty enough in making ends meet from month to month, without planning for the distant future.

The life-cycle hypothesis can, in principle, be extended to cover saving or estate-building purposes as well as for retirement. However, the assumptions required seem a little unrealistic. People planning for retirement usually have a fairly clear idea of the amount they will need to accumulate. People who hope to leave estates do not need to have a very precise objective. Very wealthy people may just spend what they want and leave an estate that is simply a residual. Middle-class people may save enough to provide for retirement with some cushion. If things go well, they will not need to liquidate all their assets before death. However, if they have heavy medical expenses or suffer losses from inflation, they will sell off their houses and other assets, leaving little behind them. Those considerations affect our view of the response of savings and consumption to changes in asset values. According to the life-cycle theory, capital gains and losses will have a direct effect on consumption. Households that suffer capital losses should reduce current consumption, planned consumption in retirement, and planned estate by the same percentage. It seems more probable that people with a rather imprecise estate-building objective will maintain most of their consumption objectives and let the estate take the blow. That consideration somewhat weakens the conclusion of the life-cycle theory.

There is also some doubt about the applicability of the life-cycle model to the lower end of the income and wealth scale. The chronic problem of poverty among the elderly indicates that a large number of people have difficulty carrying out a life-cycle plan. Private pension plans have tax advantages, and Social Security has proved advantageous to relatively low-income families. That may account for their popularity, but many people find pension plans and Social Security attractive as a means of getting the retirement problem off their hands. A high proportion of the population does almost all of its saving through pension funds, life insurance, and mortgage payments. They hold very little in liquid assets or stocks and bonds.

The result is that the behavior of half or more of the population may deviate from the life-cycle model in several respects. First, they may not save as much as would be expected from life-cycle considerations. Second, their consumption may be unaffected by changes in asset values. Third, their consumption will be directly linked to relatively short-term movements in income.

Short-Run Variations in Consumption

The life-cycle theory is intended to explain the trend of the average level of saving without giving much attention to short-run movements. In its unqualified form, the theory implies that households concerned with lifetime planning will not be much affected by short-run variations in disposable income. However, many households are forced to respond to short-run variations in disposable income, because their liquid asset holdings are small. Households who save mainly through pension funds, life insurance, and mortgage payments have to adjust their consumption expenditures when income declines. They can cushion the decline by drawing down whatever liquid assets they have and by borrowing, but many will also have to cut consumption expenditures. They will, of course, tend to increase expenditures when income rises again.

In adjusting to changes in income, most households find it is easier to reduce expenditures on durable goods than to reduce their payments for food, rent, or other nondurables and services. Making an old car last another year reduces their living standard only a little and can save a considerable amount in monthly automobile payments. Moreover, when unemployment rises, even households not directly affected may refrain from taking on new commitments for installment payments for fear that their incomes will fall. When disposable income is advancing rapidly many households will only gradually increase their expenditures on nondurables and services, but will use the slack in their budgets for installment payments on new durable goods. Variations in expenditures on consumer durables induced by changes in the growth of disposable income are accentuated by the resulting variations in the size of the stock of durable goods in the hands of consumers. In the recovery from a recession, purchases of autos and other durables will be increased as consumers make up for the purchases postponed during the recession. After a couple of years of rapid expansion, sales of durable goods may level off or decline because consumers have acquired large numbers of new cars and other durables during the upswing. Empirical studies show that sales of autos and other consumer durables vary much more than other consumer expenditures and contribute substantially to short-run fluctuations in aggregate demand.

THE AGGREGATE-DEMAND CURVE AND PRICE-LEVEL CHANGES

Our discussion of the consumption function showed that an increase in wealth will tend to increase consumption for a given current income. We noted that wealth may increase for several reasons. Expectations of future property income may improve. The real interest rate may fall. The real net value of government debt and of currency and bank reserves may rise either because the nominal stock of those assets increases (while price level remains constant) or because the price level falls. Any increase in wealth, whatever its cause, tends to increase consumption relative to income and therefore shift the *IS* curve to the right.

Shifts in the *IS* curve due to price-level change have an important effect on the aggregate-demand curve. In Chapter 13 we derived an aggregate-demand curve showing increase in real income with lower prices. In that derivation, the link between price and real income depended entirely on the *LM* curve. The real money supply corresponding to a given nominal money supply increases as price level falls. The *LM* curve shifts down to the right, as the real money supply increases and intersects the *IS* curve at a higher level of real income.

We must now take account of the fact that, since a fall in the price level increases real wealth and consumption, the *IS* curve will shift to the right when the price level falls. The two effects reinforce one another, since each tends to flatten the aggregate-demand curve. Moreover, the significance of the interest sensitivity of demand for money and of investment demand in determining the response of aggregate demand to price level is changed in a number of ways. First, through wealth effects a fall in interest rates can increase aggregate demand, even if investment demand is insensitive to interest rates. Second, even if the demand for money is very interest elastic, producing a flat *LM* curve, an increase in real money supply and in the real net value of government debt will shift the *IS* curve to the right when the price level falls.

The last point has a special theoretical importance. It ensures that the aggregate-demand curve will always intersect the potential output line at some positive price level, however low.

THE EQUILIBRIUM PRICE LEVEL

Now we will try to be more precise about the relation between the equilibrium price level and the factors underlying the *IS* and *LM* curves. The key to understanding the determination of the equilibrium price level is recognition of the fact that the price level determines the real value of nominal magnitudes affecting economic decisions. Thus the *LM* curve links real money supply, real income, and interest rate. The price level determines how much real money supply corresponds to a given nominal money supply. It is clear that if the nominal money supply is doubled and at the same time the price level is doubled, the position of the *LM* curve is unchanged. How about the *IS* curve? Some of the elements underlying the *IS* curve do not involve any nominal magnitudes. The investment function relates real investment to real interest rate. Its position is determined by real capital stock and expected real output. The investment function should be just the same at a higher or lower price level, but other relationships do involve nominal magnitudes. The consumption function is basically a relation between real consumer expenditure, real income, and real wealth. Some of the wealth is based on nominal holdings of money and government debt. Moreover, the *IS* curve is partly determined by government purchases, transfer payments, and taxes. Some of these fiscal policy factors are usually stated in nominal terms, for instance, cents-per-gallon gasoline taxes. Income tax laws provide personal exemptions stated in dollar terms, and the tax rate rises with nominal income.

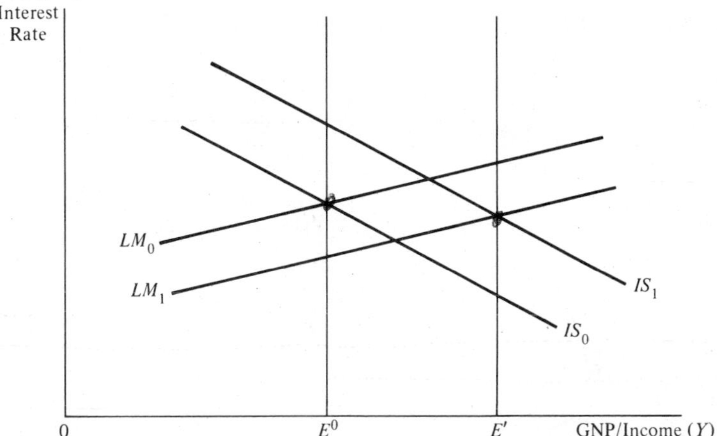

Figure 14.3 Changes in Price Levels Shift *IS* and *LM* Curves

Suppose we draw the *IS* curve with real income on the horizontal axis and with given values for all the nominal factors just mentioned and a given price level. The price level determines the real value of government purchases, wealth, and so on, and therefore determines the position of the *IS* curve.

Now reconsider the equilibrium price level. Figure 14.3 shows curves IS_0 and LM_0 for a given set of nominal magnitudes—money supply, government debt, government purchases, gasoline taxes, and other items—at a given price level p_0. The *IS* and *LM* curves intersect at E^0 to the left of the potential output line. The economy is at a partial equilibrium for less than full employment so that the price level is too high.

At a lower price level all the nominal magnitudes will have higher real values. The *LM* curve will shift rightward as shown by LM_1 and so will the *IS* curve, IS_1. At p_1 the two curves intersect at potential output, E′. So p_1 is an equilibrium price level.

If we now double all these nominal magnitudes and at the same time double prices and wages, the real value of all the nominal magnitudes in the system will be unchanged, and the *IS* and *LM* curves will be unchanged, still intersecting at potential output. But notice that that result holds only when *all* nominal magnitudes are changed together. If, for example, the money supply is doubled but there is no change in government debt, transfer payments, and the other magnitudes, the equilibrium price level will not be twice as high.

Notice also that the position of the *IS* and *LM* curves can be shifted by other factors. The investment function can be shifted by technological factors or by the expected growth of output. The consumption function can be shifted by changes in age distribution or changes in the expected growth of income. To keep actual output at potential output, the equilibrium price level has to change to offset the upward or downward shift in the *IS* curve, resulting from shifts in the real factors as well as the nominal ones.

Changes in Prices Versus Differences in Price Level

In using the concept of an aggregate-demand curve and an equilibrium price level, it is important to remember that the aggregate-demand curve shows the effect on the demand for real output of the difference between one price level and another. The argument used to derive the aggregate-demand curve does not take into account any effects of the process of changing prices on the behavior of consumers or investors. When prices move rapidly, either upward or downward, the process of change will in itself have effects not fully reflected in the derivation of the aggregate-demand curve. Rapid price changes will affect expectations about future prices and thereby influence the behavior of consumers and investors. Further complications arise from the existence of fixed price contracts. Creditors lose in unexpected inflations and gain in deflations. Conversely, debtors gain in inflations, lose—even go bankrupt—in deflations. The net response of consumers and investors to those redistributions is not reflected in the construction of the aggregate-demand curve. Thus, even perfect price flexibility does not guarantee that real GNP will always grow with potential output.

In fact, however, prices do not always adjust very rapidly. When the aggregate-demand curve shifts to the right faster than potential output, prices will rise but there is usually some increase in output. When the aggregate-demand curve does not grow as quickly as potential output, prices may decline but output will not keep pace with its potential.

The historical record shows that over the long run actual output has followed the trend of potential output. Prices, aggregate demand, and potential output have somehow been mutually adapted to one another. The adjustment has not been a one-sided one. Sometimes prices do all the work of bringing the actual price level to the equilibrium determined by potential output and a given aggregate-demand curve. At other times policy is changed to adapt the aggregate-demand curve to potential output and the existing price level.

SHORT-RUN FLUCTUATIONS IN OUTPUT

Over a very long period the trend of actual output has followed the trend of potential output. In the short run, however, actual output often deviates significantly from potential output. Those deviations occur because the growth rate of aggregate demand is uneven, and prices do not move quickly enough to cause the compensating movements along the aggregate-demand curve, which would keep actual output at potential. In this section we give a very brief outline of the major factors responsible for the uneven growth of aggregate demand. Factors involved may be classified first into those associated with changes in the supply and demand for money on the one hand, and nonmonetary factors on the other. Nonmonetary factors, in turn, can be divided into primary factors arising from changes in fiscal policy, technology, and long-term expectations, which affect the investment-demand function and the consumption function, and into further movements of consumption and investment demand induced by prior changes in the rate of growth of

GNP. It is important to note that, while we may treat these factors separately for expositional purposes, the monetary and nonmonetary factors always interact so that the effect of a change in one factor depends on what is happening to the others.

"Real" Sources of Instability

Our analysis of the factors underlying the *IS* curve suggests that the primary sources of nonmonetary instability are likely to stem from changes in fiscal policy or from changes in the factors underlying investment demand.

Prior to the Great Depression, government outlays were rather small relative to GNP in peacetime, so that changes in fiscal policy during peacetime were seldom a substantial cause of economic instability. Many economists believe that rapid changes in government expenditures during and after wars, which have been only partially offset by tax increases, have played a major role in the history of business fluctuations. Since the Great Depression the scale of peacetime government expenditures has increased in most of the developed market economies and fiscal policy has therefore played a greater role. Nonetheless, the most important variations in fiscal policy have been associated with wars. The Second World War, the Korean War, and the Vietnam War were far and away the most important events in the history of economic instability in the last forty years. As our discussion of the record of monetary policy will show, money-supply changes during those episodes worked to intensify rather than to offset the instability generated by fiscal policy. Wars aside, frequent changes in federal expenditures and tax policy appear to play a substantial role in the short-run fluctuations in economic activity. These changes in fiscal policy have often been made with a view to offsetting instability generated elsewhere in the economy. However, the record of success in the timing of changes in fiscal policy for stabilization purposes has been a very mixed one.

The extent of the shift in aggregate demand generated by changes in fiscal policy depends in part on whether changes in money supply intensify or offset the change in fiscal policy. When money supply does not expand to accommodate an increase in government expenditure, the extent of the shift in aggregate demand depends, as noted earlier, on the slopes of the *IS* and *LM* curves and on the magnitude of real balance effects.

Rapid shifts in demand can and often have been generated by the private sector as well as by government. Changes in expectations about the profit prospects of major industries, such as railroads, have often caused sharp variations in investment demand. Investment demand has often also been affected by speculative booms in securities and land. Many economic historians have attributed much of the instability of the nineteenth century to the uneven pace of development of major new industries and to the erratic pace of development of frontier areas. The Florida land boom and the stock-market boom of the 1920s provide more recent examples of spectacular speculative booms. Changes in expectations may affect expenditures by consumers as well as investment outlays. For example, the sharp fall in automobile demand in 1974–75 is often attributed to the uncertainties arising from the acceleration of inflation at that time as well as to fears about the availability and price of gasoline. As in the case of fiscal policy, the change in aggregate demand resulting from shifts in investment demand or in the consumption function depends in part on monetary factors.

Induced Shifts in Demand

Any sustained change in the rate of growth of output, regardless of its origin, produces further repercussions throughout the economy. Changes in the growth of output can induce sharp changes in the rates of investment in plant and equipment, in inventories, and in expenditures for consumer durables.

An increase in the rate of growth of GNP, whether generated by government spending or an investment boom in some sector of the economy, can increase consumption spending through the multiplier, and the resulting improvement in capacity utilization can cause further increases in sectors not originally involved in the investment boom. When the original impetus weakens, the whole process can go into reverse.

Inventory cycles have played an important role in each recession since World War II. A rise in the rate of growth of income will tend to increase the rate of inventory investment, and that, in turn, will contribute to a further increase in the rate of growth of income. Exhaustion of the original impulse that set off the boom will not only slow down the growth of income directly, but will cause inventory investment to decline and might even cause an absolute drop in output. In that case producers will have excessive inventories, and they will for a time attempt to reduce them so that inventory investment becomes negative. That, of course, will make the situation even worse, causing a further decline in income and accentuating inventory problems. Because inventory investment is only a small part of the total, it will usually be possible to work off excess inventories. Nonetheless, the inventory mechanism can cause a fluctuation in output out of proportion to the original impulse that changed investment and the rate of growth of output.

Finally, variations in the rate of growth of GNP appear to cause disproportionate fluctuations in demand for automobiles and other consumer durables. Of course, all three processes interact with one another. Together they can cause much wider fluctuations in GNP growth than one would expect by taking them one at a time and adding their separate effects.

But, as already noted, the operation of multiplier and accelerator is modified in important ways by events in the monetary sector. Monetary and financial factors have always played an important role in business fluctuations. In the Gold Standard era before the World War I, financial panics and sharp contractions in money supply were a feature of every major depression, while rapid money growth helped to fuel investment booms on the upswing. Indeed, it was widely believed that business fluctuations could be greatly reduced if monetary stability could be achieved. The Fed owes its existence to that belief.

As things have worked out, monetary policy has sometimes served to limit or offset the destabilizing factors discussed above. At other times, the Fed has played a passively permissive role by providing enough money supply growth to accommodate the demand generated by other factors without a rise in interest rates.

Finally, sharp changes in policy have sometimes played a destabilizing role. For example, an accommodating monetary policy together with an expansive fiscal policy may start a boom. If the Fed suddenly checks money supply growth, it may cause a recession. It may not be possible to choke off the boom without causing a recession.

The complex interactions among the rates of growth of GNP and its major components make it almost impossible to check excessive demand without at times braking too hard. That may occur even when the restraining effect of monetary policy results from a failure to increase money growth rather than from an actual slowdown of money growth. Inflation introduces still more complex interactions between real and nominal magnitudes. Those considerations underlie much of the dispute between monetarists and Keynesians. The Keynesians suppose that a great variety of factors can influence the behavior of the economic system. While recognizing that "money matters," they suppose that fiscal policy and all sorts of development in the private sector also matter. Moreover, they think that both monetary and fiscal policy must be verified with circumstances. No policy formula will work all the time. Most monetarists agree that lots of things besides money affect economic events, especially in the short run. But they think that a lot can be gained by taking advantage of some properties of money which permit us to assert (with some qualifications) some simple and useful propositions about nominal movements in relation to money supply. We turn to those propositions in the next two chapters and then contrast them with the Keynesian view.

SUMMARY

1. Investment in plant and equipment, residential construction, and inventories makes up about 15 percent of total GNP, but accounts for a much larger fraction of fluctuations in the growth rate of GNP.
2. Inventory investment, though accounting for only about one percent of total output on the average, accounts for a much larger proportion of fluctuations in output.
2. In the long run inventory investment may be regarded as driven by the growth of output. In the short run, however, inventory investment reflects changes in the flow of orders for durable goods. It is often seriously disturbed by lags in the adjustment of production to final sales of goods.
4. The demand for housing services tends to rise with increasing population and rising real per capita income. Continued outward shift in the demand for housing services is matched by a continued growth in the supply of housing from new construction.
5. At any one moment, the equilibrium price of housing services will depend on the demand for housing services and the existing stock of houses. The price of houses will equal the discounted value of their rental services and will therefore be influenced by the interest rate.
6. A fall in interest rates will raise the present value of houses and stimulate new construction, while a rise in interest rates will depress housing prices and reduce

the rate of construction. However, much of the actual fluctuation in the rate of residential construction has resulted from the variation in the availability of mortgage credit as well as from variations in the interest rate.

7. Prospective profitability of investment in plant and equipment depends on the size and character of the existing stock of capital equipment, on technical change, and on expectations about the growth of demand in the future. It is also influenced by taxes and expectations about the prospects for future inflation. Finally, an investment is worth making if the present value of the prospective future returns exceeds the price of the capital goods involved in making the investment.
8. The present value of the prospective stream of returns from an investment will vary with the interest rate. As in the case of housing, a rise in interest rates will reduce the present value of prospective returns and discourage investment, while a fall will increase the present value of prospective returns and stimulate investment.
9. Thus for both residential construction and plant and equipment, we may assert that, other things equal, there will be more investment at low interest rates than at high ones. Accordingly, there is a downward sloping demand curve for investment.
10. However, it is important to bear in mind that the other-things-equal clause covers a large number of factors. Variations in the stock of capital goods and housing, changes in expectations about the growth of future income, changes in technology, and changes in tax rates may cause shifts in the investment demand function that are much more important than the movements along the investment demand curve caused by variations in interest rates after adjustment for inflation expectations.
11. In the life-cycle theory of consumption, saving is explained in terms of the fact that the time profile of income receipts for households does not match the pattern of their expenditure needs. In particular, most households have to save in order to prepare for retirement.
12. The theory implies first that households will be relatively insensitive to short-term variations in their disposable income. Second, it implies that their saving behavior can be influenced through changes in the market value of the assets that they hold. What counts is the real value of assets, so the saving of holders of money and other claims fixed in nominal value will be influenced by changes in the price level. Changes in interest rates will affect the valuation of all assets.
13. Thus the aggregate rate of saving will be affected by changes in price levels and interest rates, as well as by changes in income.
14. The life-cycle theory is subject to two kinds of important qualifications. First, it may not apply well to very wealthy households. While they are small in number, they own a disproportionate part of total wealth. That consideration at least dilutes wealth effects emphasized in the life-cycle theory. Second, the theory may not hold very well for a large group of relatively low-income families who find it difficult to save. Their consumption behavior is likely to be much more responsive to short-run changes in disposable income than one would expect from a literal application of the life-cycle theory.
15. Changes in interest rates and price levels can influence wealth and thereby influence consumption.
16. In principle there always is a price level that will be consistent with the full use of the economy's potential output. However, the process of changing prices can

itself be a destabilizing force. The result is that actual output may often differ from potential output.

17. Once the growth of output is changed by any initial disturbance, from monetary policy, fiscal policy, or some source in the private sector, further shifts in investment and consumption demand are likely to occur.

Questions and Exercises

1. List some of the effects of tax policy on the prospective returns from investment in plant and equipment. Use present-value equations to illustrate your answers.
2. An increase in the rate of growth of output tends to raise the level of plant and equipment investment. Explain.
3. If business firms expect prices to rise each year, they will tend to invest more. Why?
4. A rise in interest rates can offset the effect of inflation expectations on investment. Illustrate using the present-value equation.
5. It is assumed that Social Security benefits will be permanently increased by 10 percent. How will personal savings be affected? Does it make any difference how the increased benefits are financed?
6. If lower birth rates cause the growth rate of U.S. population to decline, the personal savings rate is likely to fall. Why?
7. Would you expect the reduction in savings rates to occur at the same time as the decline in population growth?
8. Other things equal, a reduction in stock prices tends to increase the amount people want to save at a given level of income. Why?
9. List as many different causes of the shifts in the *IS* curve as you can.
10. Which ones reflect changes in monetary policy? Which ones reflect fiscal policy? Which ones reflect changes in the private sector?
11. Review the channels through which monetary policy affects the aggregate-demand curve. Give an example of each.
12. If prices were perfectly flexible all short-run shifts in aggregate demand would be reflected in prices, not in output. Explain.
13. Any initial shift in aggregate demand tends to induce further shifts in the same direction. Give some examples.

Further Reading

ANDO, ALBERT and MODIGLIANI, FRANCO. "The 'Life Cycle' Hypothesis of Saving: Aggregate Implications and Tests." *American Economic Review* 53 (March 1963): 52–84. The basic exposition of the life-cycle hypothesis and its economic significance.

BOSWORTH, BARRY. "Analyzing Inventory Investment." *Brookings Papers on Economic Activity*, 1970:2, pp. 207–28. This paper offers a comprehensive explanation of the factors involved in short-run variations in inventory investment.

———. "The Stock Market and the Economy." *Brookings Papers on Economic Activity*, 1975:2, pp. 257–91. This paper reviews the evidence on the effect of fluctuations in stock prices on variations in consumer expenditures.

CLARK, PETER K. "Investment in the 1970s: Theory, Performance and Prediction." *Brookings Papers on Economic Activity,* 1979:1, pp. 73–114. A painstaking review of the performance of alternative theories of investment in the explanation and prediction of business-investment expenditures.

DUESENBERRY, JAMES. *Business Cycles and Economic Growth.* New York: McGraw-Hill, 1958. Chapters four and five provide a detailed analysis of the behavior of business firms in making investment decisions.

———. *Income, Saving and the Theory of Consumer Behavior.* Cambridge: Harvard University Press, 1952. Presents a theory of saving and consumption that stresses emulation.

EISNER, ROBERT. *Factors in Business Investment.* Cambridge, Mass.: Ballinger Publishing Co. (for the National Bureau of Economic Research), 1978. This volume provides tests of alternative theories of investment based on the records of a large sample of business corporations.

FRIEDMAN, MILTON. *A Theory of the Consumption Function.* Princeton, N.J.: Princeton University Press, 1957. This classic work presents Friedman's version of the consumption function together with a number of empirical tests of his and alternative hypotheses.

JORGENSON, D. W. "The Theory of Investment Behavior." In *Determinants of Investment Behavior,* edited by R. Ferber, pp. 129–56. New York: Columbia University Press, 1967. This article outlines the pure theory of investment decision and provides tests of a realistic empirical version of the theory.

KOPCKE, RICHARD W. "The Behavior of Investment Spending during the Recession and Recovery, 1973–76." *New England Economic Review* (Federal Reserve Bank of Boston), November/December 1977, pp. 5–41. This article tests the performance of alternative investment theories in light of the experience of the major business cycle of 1973–76.

MAYER, THOMAS. *Permanent Income, Wealth, and Consumption.* Berkeley: University of California Press, 1972. A review of alternative theories of consumption with an examination of evidence for and against each alternative.

MODIGLIANI, FRANCO. "Monetary Policy and Consumption." In *Consumer Spending and Monetary Policy: The Linkages,* pp. 9–97. Boston: Federal Reserve Bank of Boston, 1971. This essay presents the results of a large econometric model and shows how changes in monetary policy can influence consumption through their effects on income, interest rates, and wealth.

———. "The Life Cycle Hypothesis of Saving, the Demand for Wealth and the Supply of Capital," *Social Research* 33 (Summer 1966): 160–217. An excellent exposition of the life-cycle hypothesis.

The Monetarist Approach 15

The theory that was just discussed is neo-Keynesian. In this and the following chapter we look at a rival approach, called the quantity theory or monetarism. Proponents of this approach have made numerous criticisms of Keynesian theory, many of which have to a considerable extent been incorporated into Keynesian theory. But by no means have all been incorporated. This is why we will now take up this quantity theory or monetarist "counterrevolution." Its conflict with Keynesian theory should not be exaggerated; *some* economists, rightly or wrongly, believe that it is actually just another brand of Keynesianism. Moreover, in the case of moderate Keynesians and moderate monetarists it is sometimes difficult to tell the players apart without a scorecard.

There are several versions of monetarism. This chapter takes up the basic idea that underlies all these versions, and then deals with Milton Friedman's version. The following chapter deals with other versions. But first a few words about the terms *quantity theory* and *monetarism*. Unfortunately, the terminology is not standardized; some economists call themselves quantity theorists, and others with similar views call themselves monetarists. We will not use these terms as synonymous. Instead we will use **quantity theory** to refer to *the twin propositions that changes in the money stock are the most important causes of the historically observed changes in money income, and that changes in the money stock tend to bring about proportional changes in nominal income*. **Monetarism** will be used to denote the quantity theory *plus* some other propositions described later in this chapter.

THE QUANTITY THEORY—BASIC PRINCIPLES

The basic idea—and research strategy—of the quantity theory is to look directly at equilibrium in only one market, the market for money. For example, suppose that the money market is not in equilibrium, that the demand for money exceeds the supply. People then try to build up their money holdings by cutting back on their net expenditures—either investment or consumption—so that aggregate demand falls. Conversely, if people have more money than they want to hold, they run down their money holdings by spending more on consumption or investment. *Hence changes in aggregate demand can be explained as a result of people holding more or less money than they want to.*

As previously discussed, desired money holdings depend on the price level, real income, real wealth, and the expected real opportunity cost of holding money. In this functional relationship one of these variables, the price level, has an important and special characteristic. Suppose prices double while all the other variables in the demand-for-money function remain constant. What will happen to the *real* quantity of money demanded? If people are aware that prices have doubled and behave rationally then the answer is: nothing. The real value of the determinants of the demand for real money is unchanged. But if the public wants to hold the same *real* quantity of money when prices double, it will have to hold twice as much *nominal* money; and similarly if prices fall by, say, 10 percent, it will want to hold 10 percent less nominal money. The demand for money therefore is strictly proportional to the price level. No such relationship necessarily holds for any of the other determinants of the demand for money.

To begin the examination of the quantity theory we temporarily introduce the simplification that only two assets exist, money and goods—and no securities. Suppose now that as a result of, say, Fed open-market operations the public initially holds more (real and nominal) money than it wants to. It is easy to predict what will happen. People will try to exchange the excess money for goods, and hence aggregate demand will increase. Conversely, if, perhaps due to Fed open-market sales, actual money balances are below desired levels, the public will try to accumulate more money by cutting back on its expenditures, and aggregate demand will fall.

Although each person can reduce his or her money stock very easily by buying goods, this is not true for the whole economy. As one person gets rid of money by making a purchase, the seller's money holdings go up. How then can the public as a whole bring its money balances into equilibrium? The answer is that as people spend their excessive money balances, sellers face increased demand for their products, and hence raise their production and prices so that nominal incomes increase. And as nominal incomes increase, so does the nominal amount of money people want to hold. Hence, as this process continues, a point is reached at which nominal money balances are no longer excessive. The economy is now back in equilibrium.

If we take the special case where real income is fixed, and only prices respond to the increased aggregate demand, we get a nice and simple result: prices have to rise in strict proportion to the excessive money balances. For example, if 10 percent more money is created than the public wants to hold at the existing price level, prices will rise by 10 percent. This is then a new equilibrium because the public is holding the same *real* quantity of money (M/P) as before. Hence, in this simple case where real income is fixed, and there are no securities, we readily get the traditional quantity theory result that prices vary in strict proportion to the quantity of money.

In the more complex case where real income is not fixed, the story is different because there are now two factors that induce people to hold the previously excess money balances: the rise in prices and the rise in real income. Hence, in this case prices rise less than in proportion to the excessive money balances.

So far we have dealt only with an economy in which there are no securities, so that people could spend their excessive money balances only on goods. When one makes the analysis more realistic by introducing securities, people spend some of their excess money balances on securities rather than on goods. Excess money balances therefore raise security prices, and hence lower interest rates. This stimulates investment and consumption, so that aggregate demand increases. But *initially* (and we postpone discussing what happens subsequently) aggregate demand increases by less than it does in the case where there are no securities because, with the interest rate having fallen, the public wants to hold more money than before. For example, if the nominal money stock increases by 10 percent and real income is constant, prices may increase (in the first instance) by, say, 7 percent (which increases the demand for nominal money by 7 percent) with the additional 3 percent of money being held because interest rates are lower.

This process can readily be expressed in terms of the previously discussed Cambridge equation, $M = kYp$, where M is the money stock and k is the proportion of nominal income, Yp, that people want to hold as money. Suppose that initially M is 100 and k is $1/5$, so that Yp is 500. If M now rises to 200 and k is unchanged, then Yp rises to 1000. But if the fall in interest rates raises k from $1/5$ to $1/4$, then Yp rises only to 800.

Does this mean that the quantity-theory proposition that an increase in the money stock raises nominal income proportionately applies only in a world without securities? Of course not. As we will show later the 7 percent rise in nominal income in our example is not an equilibrium; eventually the interest rate will rise back to its previous level, and income will rise by the full 10 percent by which the money stock has increased.

The process just described shows how income is determined by the interaction between actual and desired money balances. No mention was made of the marginal propensity to consume and the marginal efficiency of investment. This is so, because once one knows by how much people want to change their money holdings, one can derive *as a residual* how much they will spend, since any part of income not spent on commodities or securities must have been added to money holdings.

RECENT DEVELOPMENTS OF THE QUANTITY THEORY

Although the quantity theory has a long history, it fell into disrepute in the 1930s, in part because it seemed at the time that this theory could not explain the Great Depression, and partly because of the publication in 1936 of Keynes's theory. Although some economists continued to advocate the quantity theory, most economists became Keynesians and treated the quantity theory as little more than ancient superstitition.

Only in the mid- and late-1950s did the quantity theory again become a serious rival to the Keynesian theory. There were several reasons for its revival. One was that, contrary to the prediction of many Keynesians, upon the conclusion of World War II the American economy did not revert to the depressed conditions of the 1930s, but instead underwent inflation. Second, one seemingly great benefit of the Keynesian revolution had been its demonstration that by manipulating expenditures and taxes, the government can keep the economy close to full employment. But it turned out that there were serious political as well as economic difficulties in actually changing government expenditures and tax rates in these recommended ways, so that Keynesian theory appeared to be less useful than it had originally seemed. Third, the time was ripe for a change. Economists had expended much effort along Keynesian lines and were now ready for something new.[1]

But the resurgence of the quantity theory should not be attributed merely to impersonal historical events; surely it is also due to the fact that several extremely able economists advocated this theory. Don Patinkin of Hebrew University restated the quantity theory in a rigorous way that avoids many of the crudities that infested earlier expositions. Milton Friedman, of the University of Chicago, and many of his former students provided a framework that allows one to test empirically the proposition that changes in the quantity of money dominate changes in income. The tests they, as well as Clark Warburton, formerly of the FDIC, have performed provided supporting evidence. Moreover, Friedman and Anna Schwartz of the National Bureau of Economic Research argued in a lengthy study that the experience of the Great Depression should be interpreted as confirming the prediction of the quantity theory rather than that of the Keynesian theory. Subsequently they showed that in both the United States and in Britain, longer run movements in nominal income were highly correlated with movements in the money stock. And two economists, Leonall Andersen and Jerry Jordan, then at the Federal Reserve Bank of St. Louis, presented data that they argued show that changes in the money supply have much more impact on nominal income than do changes in fiscal policy. Since the 1960s, Karl Brunner of the University of Rochester and Allan Meltzer at Carnegie-Mellon University have jointly presented empirical evidence that the demand for money is stable in a way that supports the quantity theory and have built a new theoretical model that is in important ways more elaborate than the Keynesian model. As a result of all of this work quantity theorists and monetarists are no longer a disreputed sect among economists. While they are a minority, they are a powerful minority. The monetarist "counterrevolution," unlike the Keynesian revolution, does not have a single Great Book as its source, and thus is much less of a unified whole than is Keynesian theory. In studying the quan-

[1] A major new theory opens up many exciting research opportunities because it raises questions that were previously ignored. After some time the more promising of these research opportunities have been exploited, and the profession is again in a receptive mood for a new theory.

tity theory and monetarism in this and the following chapter we will therefore have to take up several distinct approaches.

THE CHICAGO APPROACH

The best-known version of the monetarist approach is the work of Milton Friedman, a Nobel laureate, and of his former students at the University of Chicago. (Friedman is known to a much wider audience as a leading free-market advocate. While his views on monetary theory are consistent with a general free-market position, they do not require it. One can accept his views on monetary theory and policy without having to accept his general political views, and vice versa.) A major part of the work of Friedman and his students has centered on explaining the demand for money Recall the Cambridge equation, $M=kYp$. If, as Cambridge economists believed, k is stable, then we can predict how nominal income has to change when the money supply changes. But is k some stable number like, say, ⅕? Surely not. In Chapter 12, we saw that the real quantity of money demanded is a function of the interest rate. One can think of real money as being like any other commodity, with the quantity that people want to hold depending on the cost of holding it, on the cost of holding related commodities, on income or wealth, and on tastes.

Hence, Friedman's version of the quantity theory treats the quantity of money demanded (and thus k) not as a stable *number,* but as a stable *function* of other variables.[2] If the demand for money is, in fact, a stable function of a few measurable variables, then, if the values of these variables are known, one can predict how much money will be demanded. Suppose that, as we assumed in drawing the *LM* curve, the demand for nominal money is a function of nominal income (Yp) and the nominal interest rate (R), that is:

(1) $M^d=f(\overset{+}{Y}p, \overset{-}{R})$.

Since the empirical evidence suggests that supply and demand for money are fairly soon equilibrated by the money market, we can write:

(2) $M^s=M^d=f(\overset{+}{Y}p, \overset{-}{R})$

or, more specifically

(3) $M^s=M^d=a+b\overset{+}{Y}p+c\overset{-}{R}$

where a, b, and c are coefficients that can be estimated statistically. Now suppose that we also know R. In this case, *once we are told what will happen to the nominal money stock M^s we know how nominal income must change to make equation* (3) *hold.* This is the approach of Friedman's refurbished quantity theory.

[2] Another way in which Friedman has modified the traditional quantity theory is that he uses it primarily to determine nominal income rather than prices. The traditional quantity theory was a theory of the long run in which prices adapted to changes in the quantity of money while output was unaffected.

Keynesian theory teaches us that the factors that bring about changes in income are changes in the propensity to consume, the marginal efficiency of investment, liquidity preference, and the stock of money. What happens to these factors in this theory? One of them, the stock of money, is obviously included, and, in fact, plays the starring role. Another one, an autonomous change in the liquidity preference curve, is deemphasized because of the quantity theorist's belief that the money-demand function is stable.

The other two factors, changes in the propensity to consume and in the marginal efficiency of investment, enter only indirectly. Suppose that households decide to raise their consumption, or firms their investment. In either case nominal income starts to rise. But equation (3) tells us that if the money supply is constant and nominal income rises, then the interest rate must rise too. Put another way, if the public wants to spend more, it tries to get hold of more money to finance these increased expenditures. This increase in the demand for money raises the interest rate. This, in turn, reduces the Cambridge k, that is, it raises velocity. Thus, since changes in the propensity to consume and in the marginal efficiency of investment enter Friedman's theory indirectly, there is no substantive difference between the two theories on this formal abstract level. The real disagreements relate to two empirical issues. First, quantity theorists believe that the demand for money function is stable, while Keynesians believe that it varies more. In terms of equation (3) Keynesians believe that the coefficients, a, b, and c are not stable.

The second difference relates to the role of the rate of interest. Suppose that the quantity theorists are correct in saying that the money-demand function is stable, but contrary to their views suppose that the interest elasticity of demand for money is very high. (Alternatively, one could assume that the interest elasticity of investment and consumption is very low.) *Assume also that prices are constant.* If so then, as the quantity theory claims, when the stock of money rises, the stable money-demand function allows us to predict by how much income rises. *But,* contrary to the quantity theory, this rise in income is quite small instead of being strictly proportional to the rise in the money stock. Most of the increase in the money stock finds willing holders, not because nominal income has increased, but because the interest rate is lower.

This has an important implication. If a given change in the money stock generates only a relatively small change in income, this makes it at least somewhat more probable that the variations in the money stock that have actually occurred are not the main cause of the observed fluctuations in income.

Consequently, to maintain the quantity theory, one must take one or more of the following three positions. One is that the interest elasticity of the demand for money is very low. The second is that an increase in the supply of money does not lower the interest rate by much. (Insofar as the interest rate does not change much, the interest elasticity of demand for money has little room for play.) The third is that historically fluctuations in the money stock have been much greater than fluctuations in the chief Keynesian variable, investment. If the money stock has actually varied much more, then the fact that a significant part of the resulting variation in kYp has been absorbed by changes in k would still allow changes in the money stock to be responsible for most of the observed variation in nominal income.

Friedman has taken all three of these approaches by examining empirically the relation between fluctuations in money and in income. First, his statistical analysis of the demand for money since 1869 has convinced him that most of the observed changes in the demand for money are the result of changes in permanent income, and that the interest rate plays only a small role in explaining the demand for money. But this empirical analysis has been disputed by other economists who argue, from the same or similar data, that a decline in the interest rate *does* play a significant role in making the public willing to hold additional money. And the evidence they have presented is persuasive. The second approach, which focuses on the way interest rates respond to changes in the money stock, needs discussion.

The Behavior of Interest Rates

Suppose that the money stock increases and that this causes the interest rate to fall. If so, k increases, and hence nominal income cannot rise in proportion to the rise in the money stock. The quantity theory seems refuted! But does an increase in the money stock actually lower the expected real interest rate? In the short run it does. It takes some time for nominal income to rise and, in the meantime, the interest rate must have fallen by enough to make the public willing to hold the additional money.

Friedman agrees that the initial effect of an increase in the money stock is to reduce the expected real interest rate, but he argues that this initial effect will not last long. In Figure 15.1 (which takes real income as given) let R_0 be the real interest rate that corresponds to an unemployment rate equal to the natural rate, that is, to the interest rate at which prices are stable. Now the quantity of money rises from M_0 / p_0 to M_1 / p_0, with prices not yet having had a chance to adjust. With the real interest rate now being lower aggregate demand rises, so that prices increase. As prices rise the real quantity of money falls, first to M_1 / p_1 and then to M_1 / p_2. But M_1 / p_2 cannot be an equilibrium because the interest rate, R_3, is still below the interest rate, R_0, that corresponds to the natural unemployment rate at which prices are stable. Prices must therefore continue to rise until the interest rate is back at R_0, so that the real money stock is back at $M_0 / p_0 = M_1 / p_3$. But once the interest rate is back at R_0, k is back at its initial value too, and therefore nominal income must have risen in proportion to the increase in M. And with the interest rate being back at its initial value real income must be back at its initial value too, so that all the increase in nominal income is an increase in prices. With both k and Y being constant, M and p must have risen proportionally. Thus the quantity theory is vindicated despite the fact that the interest elasticity of demand for money is not zero.

The crucial question is how long this process takes. Keynesians would agree that an increase in the quantity of money *ultimately* results in a proportional change in prices and in an unchanged interest rate. But they believe

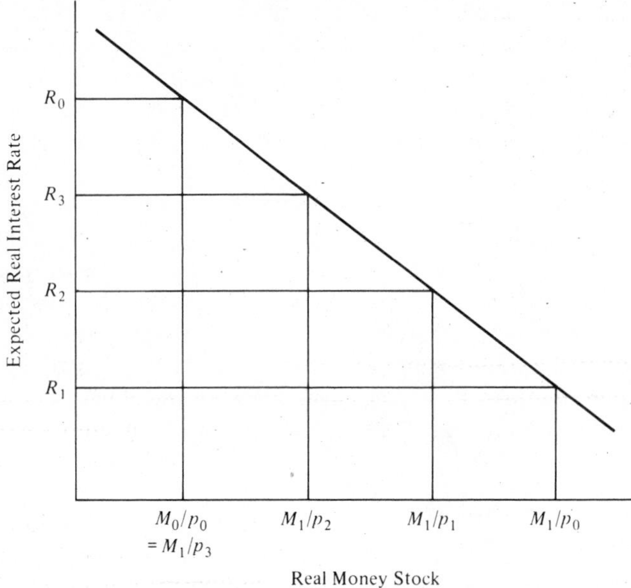

Figure 15.1 Behavior of Interest Rates

that, due to prices being slow to adjust, it takes many years until they have risen in proportion to the increase in the quantity of money. In the meantime the real interest rate is below its initial level. As a result both k and Y are higher than before. And with k being higher nominal income cannot have risen in proportion to the increase in the money stock. By contrast, Friedman believes that it takes only about a year and a half to two years until prices have adjusted.

An important point of disagreement between Friedman and the Keynesians is therefore the speed with which prices adjust. Who is right is an empirical question, but unfortunately the empirical evidence can be interpreted in two ways. While some statistical studies support Friedman's contention, others support the Keynesian case.

Friedman has elaborated his analysis further. For a time period long enough to be relevant for most of the important problems, he takes the *real* rate of interest as constant, and hence unaffected by changes in the quantity of money. If the supply of money is increased, nominal income rises, and the resulting expectations of a rise in prices cause the *nominal* interest rate to rise since borrowers and lenders add an inflation premium to the interest rate, thus keeping the expected real rate constant. This increase in the nominal interest rate in turn raises velocity. This may seem like a contradiction of the quantity theory since nominal income now rises *more* than strictly proportionately to the rise in the stock of money. But the sequence of events is that the previous increases in the money stock caused prices to rise, which raised the nominal interest rate, which, in turn, raised velocity. Hence, that part of the rise in nominal income that is not due directly to the increase in the money supply is due indirectly (via the increase in velocity) to a previous rise in the money stock. Thus the quantity-theory conclusion, that it is changes in the money stock that ultimately drive income, is vindicated.

The Transmission Process

What is the mechanism by which money affects income? Friedman's explanation of *how* money affects nominal income differs from the Keynesian explanations discussed in previous chapters in several ways. First, he does not refer to the interest rate, but instead says that when people hold excess money balances they raise their expenditures in an attempt to bring their money holdings into equilibrium. This difference between the Friedmanian and Keynesian approaches is not basic. In a formal sense, one can relate any point on a demand curve to either the price or the quantity axis, and no fundamental issue of theory is involved in whether one says that the quantity of money has increased or that the interest rate has fallen. The reason Friedman looks at the quantity of money rather than at the interest rate is that he believes that the relevant interest rate is not measured properly by the available data. Hence, an analysis that focuses on interest rates is likely to give misleading advice when applied to practical problems.

A second difference between *some* Keynesian versions of the transmission process and Friedman's version is that in the latter changes in the money supply affect not only investment but also consumption. Friedman does not try to determine which is the bigger effect. Since consumption is a much larger total than investment, a change in the money stock *could* have the major part of its impact on income via consumption even if the interest elasticity of investment is greater than the interest elasticity of consumption. But while Keynes himself assumed that changes in the money stock would directly affect only investment and not consumption, many modern Keynesians believe that consumption is affected too.

A third and related difference is that Friedman believes that changes in the money stock affect expenditures in so many and such complicated ways that it is useless to try to discover them all. Any attempt to do so would surely fail to find some of them, and would therefore underestimate the total effect that money has on income. Hence, instead of setting up an ambitious econometric model, Friedman (who, in any case, has little faith in large econometric models) prefers to follow a different approach. This is to compare changes in the money supply and in nominal income over time without trying to trace through the particular channels by which money affects income. This has caused many economists to criticize him for relying on a sort of "black box" where changes in the money stock are seen going in at one end and changes in income emerge at the other end, without anyone knowing how the process works. This point is often put by saying that Friedman is relying on a mere correlation of changes in money and in income, and that there are numerous examples in economics of correlations that do not prove that one variable is causing the other. For example, there is a correlation between the number of school teachers in a city and per capita alcohol consumption. On the other hand, Friedman believes that the empirical evidence shows that the correlation between money and prices is causal rather than spurious. Moreover, economic theory explains in detail why, if the supply of a good increases, its price falls. This can be applied directly to explain why the purchasing power of money falls, that is, prices rise, when the supply of money increases. Do we really need much more than that?

Fiscal Policy

Another difference between Friedman's theory and Keynesian theory concerns the role of fiscal policy. In a Keynesian model an increase in government expenditures (or any other outward shift of the *IS* curve) has several effects on income. It raises aggregate demand both directly and indirectly via the multiplier and the accelerator, but it also tends to lower aggregate demand by raising the interest rate (as we move along the *LM* curve). Except in the extreme case of a completely vertical *LM* curve, the net effect of an increase in government expenditures or of a tax cut is to increase aggregate demand. In Friedman's analysis, however, while a rise in government expenditures could, in principle, raise aggregate demand (since k is falling as government borrowing pushes up interest rates), as an empirical matter government expenditures have virtually no effect on aggregate demand; they simply "crowd out" an equivalent amount of investment and consumption.[3] This does not mean that Friedman looks upon increases in government expenditures with equanimity. Far from it. First, on broad philosophical grounds, he opposes the growth of the public sector and, second, as an increase in government expenditures raises the interest rate there is often pressure on the Fed to increase the money supply at a faster rate in an (ultimately vain) attempt to lower the interest rate again. And these increases in the money supply can, of course, be inflationary.

The Behavior of Money and Income: Empirical Evidence

Figure 15.2, taken from a recent book by Friedman and Schwartz, shows the relation of money, income, and velocity in the United States and Britain for over a century. Since Friedman and Schwartz were concerned with longer run movements they charted these variables, not on a year-to-year basis, but as averages for each expansion and for each recession. As Figure 15.2 illustrates for such periods the relation between changes in money and income is remarkably close. Most of the variations in the rate of change of income are explained by variations in the rate of change of money rather than by the rate of change of velocity.

[3] This crowding out does not occur right away, and hence an increase in government expenditure does raise nominal income for some time. In Friedman's analysis complete crowding out does not require a vertical *LM* curve because the rise in interest rates is supplemented by certain effects on wealth that also reduce consumption and investment.

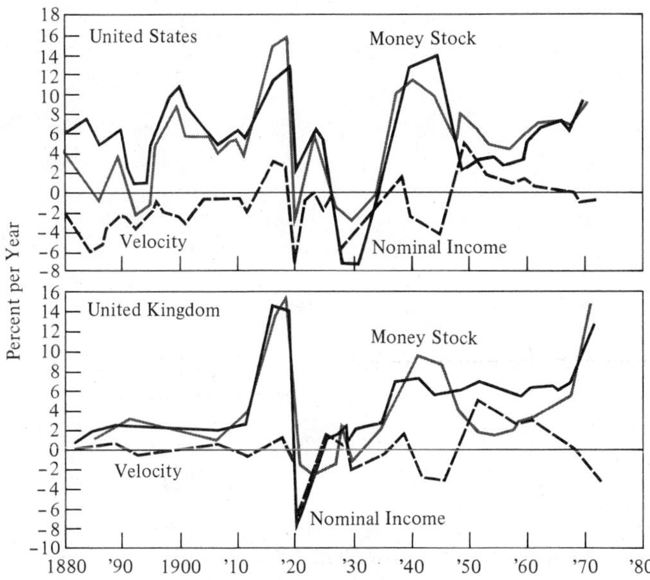

Figure 15.2 Rates of Change of United States and United Kingdom Nominal Income, Nominal Money Stock, and Velocity

Source: Milton Friedman and Anna Schwartz, *Monetary Trends in the United States and the United Kingdom,* p. 168.

The importance of changes in the growth rate of money in the shorter run has been shown by Byron Higgins. He calculated the ratio of the actual level of the money stock to what it would have been if it had grown over the last twelve months at the same rate as it was growing during the previous two years. This ratio, which he called the A / E (actual / extrapolated) ratio, is, of course, below unity if the money stock has grown at a lower rate during the past twelve months than during the previous two years. As Figure 15.3 illustrates, in the period covered, this ratio always has fallen prior to a recession.

Does this high correlation between money and income mean that changes in the money growth rate cause changes in nominal income, or should the correlation be interpreted the other way round, as changes in income causing changes in the money growth rate? In the latter case the correlation would certainly not be evidence supporting the quantity theory. Friedman and Schwartz support the hypothesis that causation runs from money to income in several ways. One is that they, as well as Phillip Cagan of Columbia University, have undertaken extensive historical studies of what factors caused the money stock to change. They concluded that in severe recessions like 1920–21 or 1929–33 the money stock fell for some specific reason other

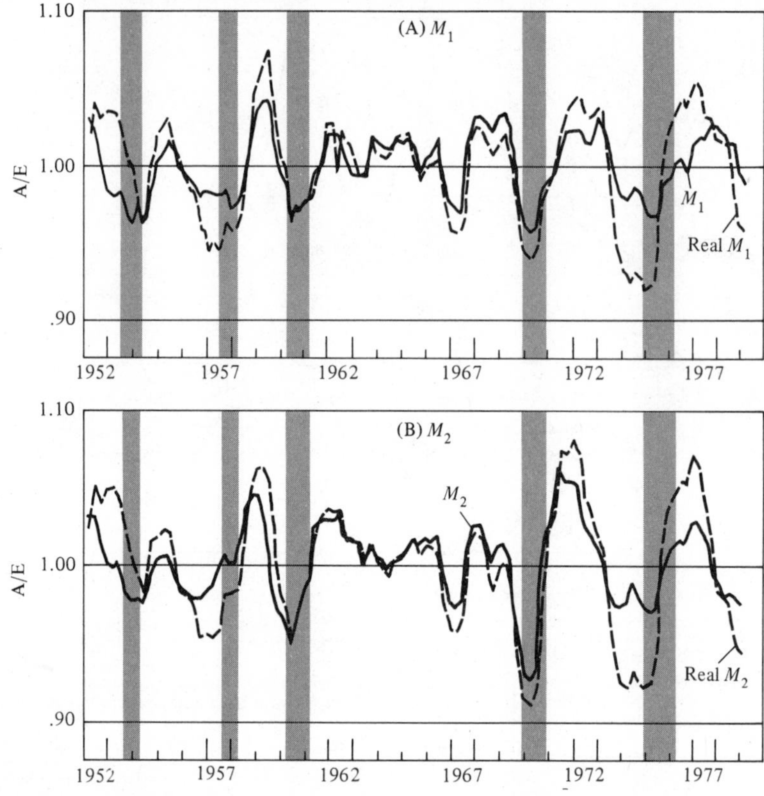

Figure 15.3 A/E Ratios of Real and Nominal Money
1952–78

Note: Shaded areas indicate recessions.

Source: Byron Higgins, "Monetary Growth and Business Cycles," *Economic Review* (Federal Reserve Bank of Kansas City) 64 (April 1979): 18–19.

than a fall in income, such as widespread bank failures or a restrictive Fed policy. Hence, they argued, in these cases causation *must* have run from money to income since we know that what caused the decline in the money stock was something other than the drop in income. Similarly, large increases in the money stock can be explained by factors such as the development of new techniques for refining gold. For the minor business recessions—which are by far the more common ones—Friedman and Schwartz concede that the historical evidence is not nearly so clear-cut. (This allows one to develop a compromise between the Keynesian and Friedmanian theories, by saying that Keynesian theory can explain the usual minor recessions, but that major recessions are caused by a decline in the money growth rate.)[4]

[4]Friedman and Schwartz have also pointed to the fact that the peak in the growth rate of the money stock usually occurs prior to the peak in business cycles, but they consider this to be much less important evidence for their hypothesis that causation runs from money to income than the just discussed historical evidence. In any case, as James Tobin ("Money and Income: Post Hoc, Ergo Propter Hoc," *Quarterly Journal of Economics* 84 [May 1970]: 301–17) has shown, this evidence is of doubtful value because one can develop a model in which income change is the cause and the change in the money growth rate the effect, and yet the money growth rate shows an earlier peak than does income.

Critics of the quantity theory, on the other hand, have argued that a rise in income can bring about a rise in the money stock. As shown in Chapter 10 the money multiplier increases to some extent when interest rates and income do. Moreover, the Fed has tended to increase the growth rate of the base when the growth rate of income increases.

SOME MONETARIST PROPOSITIONS

There is more to monetarism than just the quantity theory. The authors believe that it is possible to isolate twelve major issues in the Keynesian-monetarist dispute.[5] Underlying the debate on these issues is a basic difference relating to the length of the horizon of one's analysis, and the speed with which the economy adapts. Keynesians accept many monetarist views as correct in the long run, but not in the shorter run that is relevant for economic policy.[6] Six of these differences relate to economic theory and will be discussed now; the remaining six relate to policy, and will be deferred until Chapter 25.

The first and most basic is the monetarist's belief in the quantity theory. The second is an hypothesis about the way in which changes in the money stock affect income, that is, the transmission process. We have already discussed Friedman's version of the transmission process, and in the next chapter we will look at the transmission process of two other prominent monetarists, Brunner and Meltzer.

Third, monetarists believe that the private sector of the economy is inherently stable. If the government would not destabilize the economy by ill-considered policies, there would still be *some* fluctuations in income but we would have tolerable levels of unemployment and little inflation. Keynesians, on the other hand, by and large, believe that the private economy is inherently unstable, and that fiscal and monetary policies are therefore needed to stabilize it.

The next monetarist proposition is a subtle one relating to research strategy. It asserts that to determine nominal income one need look only at the factors changing aggregate demand as a whole, such as changes in the quantity of money, and can ignore the allocation of this demand among different sectors of the economy. By contrast, Keynesians determine aggregate demand by combining the demands in various sectors of the economy since they think of aggregate demand as being determined by the incentives to spend in these sectors. For example, suppose the money stock increases. Monetarists focus on the fact that money holdings are now out of equilibrium and say that expenditures on goods and services will increase without specifying what goods and services. By contrast, Keynesians think in terms of the increase in the money stock lowering the interest rate, and then investigate the effect that lower interest rates have on various sectors of the economy, such as residential construction, industrial plant and equipment, etc.

[5] For a further discussion of these issues see Thomas Mayer et al., *The Structure of Monetarism* (New York: W. W. Norton, 1978).

[6] Keynes made his famous statement, "in the long run we are all dead," as a response to the quantity theory. (*A Tract on Monetary Reform* [London: Macmillan, 1924], p. 80.)

As a result, there is a fifth difference: while Keynesians generally use large-scale econometric models that describe various sectors of the economy in detail, monetarists prefer to use smaller, highly aggregated models, such as the St. Louis model described in the next chapter.

Finally, monetarists and Keynesians view the price level in a different way, with monetarists believing that prices are much more flexible—downward as well as upward—than Keynesians do. For example, suppose that the price of oil rises, say, by 20 percent. Keynesians tend to say that if oil accounts directly and indirectly as a raw material for, say, 10 percent of GNP, then this 20 percent rise in oil prices will raise the overall price level by 2 percent. Monetarists, on the other hand, say that, with the nominal money stock held constant, much of the rise in the price of oil and oil products will be offset by declines in other prices relative to what they would otherwise be. This is so because if, as oil prices rise, the price level were to rise by 2 percent, then the demand for nominal money would increase and exceed the supply, with the result that aggregate demand would fall, and hence prices would decline again.

These propositions are connected in many ways. Thus, one can readily see the quantity theory at work in the example of the rise in oil prices, and also in the monetarist proposition that one does not have to look at demands in various sectors of the economy to determine aggregate demand.[7] Similarly, the hypothesis that the demand for money is stable fits in well with the view that the private sector is stable. And if the private economy is stable, then there is less reason to bother about demand in particular sectors. Moreover, if one thinks of the price level as a single unit, so that wage and price increases in one sector are offset by wage and price decreases (or a slowdown in the rate of increase) in other sectors as in the above example of oil prices, then the economy is much less subject to cost-push inflation, and hence is stable in this sense. Furthermore, if one does not have to bother with allocative detail in various sectors, then why use a large econometric model? Thus these six monetarist propositions form an interconnected whole, though they are *not* so closely connected that to accept any one of them means that one *has* to accept the others as well.

THE STABILITY ISSUE

An important issue on which Keynesians and monetarists disagree is the stability of a private enterprise economy, that is, its ability to avoid—without the help of government stabilization policies—substantial periods of extensive unemployment and severe inflations.[8] The Keynesian approach developed as a response to the unstable behavior of the economy. For nearly two hundred years before World War II, the progress of capitalist countries was periodically interrupted by panics, recessions, and depressions. The Great Depression of the 1930s was the last straw. Although monetarists attribute

[7] But one has to look at much more than aggregate demand to determine what will be the change in prices as opposed to changes in output.

[8] For an example of the Keynesian view, see Hyman Minsky, *John Maynard Keynes* (New York: Columbia University Press, 1975).

this and other severe depressions to sharp declines in the growth rate of the money stock, the Great Depression was widely interpreted as a result not of poor monetary arrangements but as an inherent fault in the capitalist system. Governments in all developed market economies became committed to interventionist policies aimed at preventing or limiting the erratic movements of production and employment that had caused so much waste and suffering in the past. Keynesian income-expenditure analysis provided a rationale for interventionist stabilization policy and a paradigm for the analysis of alternative stabilization policies.

Keynes's theory emphasized the instability of private investment and at the same time deprecated the notion that the private economy contained adjustment mechanisms that could offset the variations in income generated by variations in investment. Keynesians attributed the instability of investment to variations in the investment opportunities generated by new techniques and new products. They also supposed that those variations in investment were accentuated by speculation in security markets. Moreover, Keynes and his followers emphasized the tendency for swings in investment to feed on themselves. Increasing investment would increase consumption spending through the multiplier, and the resulting improvement in capacity utilization would cause further increases in investment in sectors not originally involved in the investment boom. When the original impetus weakens, the whole process could go into reverse.

In analyzing the sources of instability in an economic system, we have to make a distinction between primary causes of instability and the secondary responses of the system to those primary impulses. The oil shock of 1973–74 stands as a classic example of a primary shock or cause of instability. Multiplier response to a change in investment is a simple example of a secondary response.

Inventory cycles provide a more complex case. A rise in the rate of growth of income will tend to increase the rate of inventory investment, and that, in turn, will contribute to a further increase in the rate of growth of income. Exhaustion of the original impulse that sets off the boom not only slows down the growth of income directly but will cause inventory investment to decline and might even cause an absolute drop in output. In that case, producers will have excessive inventories, and will for a time attempt to reduce them so that inventory investment becomes negative. That, of course, will make the situation even worse, causing a further decline in income and accentuating inventory problems. Because inventory investment is only a small part of the total GNP, it will usually be possible to work off excess inventories. Nonetheless, the inventory mechanism can cause a fluctuation in output out of proportion to the original impulse that changed investment and the rate of growth of output.

Monetarists agree with Keynesians that all of these factors can, *in principle,* create economic fluctuations. However, monetarists argue that *as an empirical proposition* much the greater part of the income fluctuations we have actually experienced have been due to variations in the growth rate of the money stock. Second, monetarists put less emphasis than Keynesians on the *macroeconomic* effects of a given exogenous shock because they focus on the supply and demand for money, which works as an automatic stabilizer. Suppose, for example, that an innovation greatly raises investment in the airline industry. This tends to raise nominal income. But with the money stock constant and nominal income rising, k must be falling. Ignoring changing interest rates for the moment, why should the public be willing to reduce its k? Since people are initially holding their desired ratio of money to nominal income, as nominal income rises, everyone will try to increase his or her money holdings. And they do this by cutting expenditures (or selling assets), so that the increases in output and prices in the industries producing the new capital goods for the airlines are offset by falling output or prices in other industries.

To be sure, the assumption that the public wants its k to remain constant despite the rise in the interest rate is extreme and implausible. But monetarists believe that the interest elasticity of the demand for money is not very great, so that an investment boom lowers k only moderately. With the money stock constant and k falling only moderately, income rises only moderately. In monetarist analyses shocks, such as innovations, have much more effect on *relative* outputs and *relative* prices than they do on total output and the overall price level.

Moreover, while monetarists agree that the economy is subject to *some* shocks, they do not believe that these shocks (apart from those resulting from government policy) are as frequent and as big as many Keynesians claim. And the previously discussed secondary responses of consumption and investment need not be large either. One issue involved here is whether consumption depends mainly on income in the current year, or on income over a much longer period of time. If consumption is heavily dependent on income of previous years, then the marginal propensity to consume out of *current* income is relatively low, so that the short run multiplier is low too. Hence, changes in investment have relatively little effect on income. Similarly, if investment depends on the change in sales over several years, rather than in just one year, investment is more stable, because erratic swings in sales in any one year tend to offset each other.

The question whether a capitalist economy is stable or needs government intervention to avoid an unacceptable level of unemployment or inflation is obviously an extremely important one. Unfortunately, it is a question easier to pose than to answer. In the authors' view there is no convincing empirical evidence that would allow one to decide who is right. The following illustrates some of the problems encountered in trying to answer this question. One possible approach is to take an econometric model and put into it a stable monetary and fiscal policy in place of the policy actually followed, to see if the model then shows less fluctuation in income than was actually experienced. But monetarists doubt that these models are reliable enough to evaluate the effects of various policies, which is a more difficult task than forecasting income. Another possible approach is to ask whether the economy has been more stable in the postwar years in which stabilization policy was used than before 1932 when it was not used. It turns out that it is more stable now, but monetarists can reply that this is due to the more erratic fluctuations in the money stock before 1932. A third approach is to ask whether in those countries in which the government does relatively little to stabilize income, income is actually more stable than it is in those countries that follow stronger stabilization policies. But the problem here is to determine the direction of causation. Certain countries may follow stronger stabilization policies precisely because they experience more income fluctuations.

SUMMARY

1. The quantity theory focuses on equilibrium and disequilibrium in the money market. Changes in aggregate demand are interpreted as attempts to bring *real* money holdings into equilibrium.
2. The Chicago approach treats the demand for money as a stable function of a limited set of other variables rather than as a stable number. Permanent income is taken as the most important of these variables.
3. Dependence of the demand for money on the interest rate is consistent with the quantity theory if a change in the quantity of money changes the interest rate only for a short time. Once the expected real interest rate has returned to its previous level nominal income and money have changed proportionately.
4. The transmission mechanism of the Chicago approach is formulated in terms of changes in the quantity of money rather than in terms of interest rates, and is agnostic about whether the effect of changes in money operate via investment or consumption. Moreover, it does not try to analyze the particular channels by which money affects income in detail, in part because there are too many of them.
5. There is much empirical evidence showing a close correlation between nominal money and nominal income or prices. A debated issue is direction of causation. Friedman and Schwartz argue that historically major changes in the money stock have not been the result of previous changes in income. Many Keynesians disagree.
6. Monetarism can be described as a conjunction of several related propositions. Leaving aside the ones relating to policy, they are the validity of the quantity theory, a particular transmission process, the stability of the private sector, a focus on aggregate demand as a whole rather than on demand in particular sectors, a focus on the price level as a unit, and a skeptical attitude towards large econometric models.
7. In the Keynesian view the economy is unstable, due both to external shocks and to internal factors, such as inventory cycles. Monetarists question the empirical significance of such destabilizing factors.

Questions and Exercises

1. Describe, in your own words, the *basic* idea behind the quantity theory.
2. If both the interest rate and real income are constant, and there is no money illusion, then a 10 percent rise in the money stock results in a 10 percent rise in nominal income. Discuss.
3. Show why a rise in the money stock would lead to a proportional increase in prices if (a) the demand for money is completely interest inelastic, or, alternatively, (b) if prices are flexible and the economy is at full employment.
4. "The disagreements between the Friedmanian theory and the Keynesian theory are not matters of economic theory, but are empirical issues." Discuss.
5. What are the main reasons why Friedman and the Keynesians come up with different answers?

6. Look up recent data on the money stock and on income. (They can be found in the appendix of the *Economic Report of the President*, for example.) See if these data support Friedman's theory. Also calculate the Cambridge *k*. How stable has it been?
7. Germany experienced a hyperinflation after World War I. In November 1923 wholesale prices were one *billion* times what they had been sixteen months earlier. But in this period, the stock of money (as measured by the currency circulation of the central bank) was only (!) about twenty-one million times what it was sixteen months before. How can this be explained? Does it contradict the quantity theory?
8. Suppose income increases because of an increase in the marginal efficiency of investment. Describe the process in quantity theory terms.

Further Reading

DAVIS, RICHARD. "The Role of the Money Supply in Business Cycles." *Monthly Review* (Federal Reserve Bank of New York) 50 (April 1968): 63–73. A powerful critique of the Friedman-Schwartz evidence for the quantity theory.

FRIEDMAN, MILTON. "Money." In *International Encyclopedia of the Social Sciences*. An excellent survey of monetary theory from a quantity theory standpoint.

———. "The Role of Monetary Policy." *American Economic Review* 58 (March 1968): 1–17. A powerful argument that changes in the money stock depress interest rates only temporarily, and that the Phillips curve is in real terms.

———. *Studies in the Quantity Theory of Money*. Chicago: University of Chicago Press, 1956. A classic statement of Friedman's view together with essays by his students providing empirical evidence. Chapter one is particularly useful.

FRIEDMAN, MILTON, and SCHWARTZ, ANNA. *Monetary Trends in the United States and the United Kingdom*. Chicago: University of Chicago Press, 1982. An outstanding piece of scholarship. (For review articles that survey its highlights see the December 1982 issue of the *Journal of Economic Literature*.)

———. "Money and Business Cycles." *Review of Economics and Statistics* 45 (February 1963) supplement: 32–64. An important survey of the empirical evidence for the quantity theory.

GORDON, ROBERT J., ed. *Friedman's Monetary Theory*. Chicago: Aldine Publishing Co., 1974. This is the definitive statement of Friedman's monetary theory together with criticisms by eminent economists and Friedman's reply.

LAIDLER, DAVID. "Money and Money Income: An Essay on the Transmission Mechanism." *Journal of Monetary Economics* 4 (April 1978): 151–92. An excellent survey of one of the major disputes about the quantity theory.

MAYER, THOMAS, et al. *The Structure of Monetarism*. New York: W. W. Norton, 1978. A survey of, and debate about, the broader aspects of monetarism by both monetarist and nonmonetarist economists.

POOLE, WILLIAM. "The Relationship of Monetary Decelerations to Business Cycle Peaks: Another Look at the Evidence." *Journal of Finance* 30 (June 1975): 697–712. An update of the Friedman-Schwartz evidence.

SELDEN, RICHARD. "Monetarism." In *Modern Economic Thought*, edited by Sidney Weintraub, pp. 253–74. Philadelphia: University of Pennsylvania Press, 1976. A very useful survey.

Monetarism: Additional Models 16

In the previous chapter we discussed some issues that are basic to the quantity theory and to monetarism, and took up one major variant of this approach, the work of the Chicago School. In this chapter we consider the three other leading variants, the St. Louis model, the work of Karl Brunner and Allan Meltzer, and Don Patinkin's real balance effect.

THE ST. LOUIS APPROACH

It may seem that the way to settle the Keynesian-monetarist debate is to undertake the following test. Let both Keynesians and monetarists select the variables that according to their theories explain income, and put them into so-called regression equations. (Regression analysis is a statistical technique that tries to show how one or more independent variables affect a dependent variable. For example, if consumption (C) is regressed on the money stock (M) the computer is told to find values for a and b in the equation $C = a + bM$, so that the square of the differences between the predicted and actual values for C are minimized.) We can then see which regression better explains past movements in income. Specifically, to have a test that is directly relevant to the question of what policy tools the government should use, let us see if income can be predicted better by looking at fiscal policy or at monetary policy. Since Keynesian theory asserts that changes both in the deficit and in the money stock bring about changes in nominal income, a finding that fiscal policy, as well as monetary policy, does so supports Keynesian theory. But if the data show there is little, if any, correlation between the deficit and changes in nominal income, while changes in the money stock have a powerful effect on income, then the quantity theory is vindicated and Keynesian theory is rejected.

This test was undertaken by two economists, then at the Federal Reserve

Bank of St. Louis, Leonall Andersen and Jerry Jordan, who built on an earlier test by Milton Friedman and David Meiselman. The variables they used to explain income were the narrow money stock (M_1), and the monetary base as well as high employment federal government receipts, expenditures, and deficits.[1]

The results Andersen and Jordan obtained were dramatic. Changes in the nominal money stock, or in the monetary base, had powerful effects on nominal income, but the fiscal policy variables had no lasting effect. They raised income in the calendar quarter in which they increased, and in some equations, in the next calendar quarter too, but in the subsequent quarters they lowered income, so that over a year, their *net* effect was close to zero. And a reworking of their analysis using more recent data showed fiscal policy having no effect in any calandar quarter. These results suggest that fiscal policy is not a useful stabilization tool. Monetary policy—that is, changing the quantity of money—on the other hand, is a much more powerful tool. In addition, monetary policy affects income quicker and to a more predictable extent than fiscal policy does, and for these reasons too monetary policy appears to be the better policy tool. A subsequent study by Michael Keran (then also at the St. Louis Fed) found similar results for several other countries. These results surprised most economists. They led to an extensive debate of which we will discuss only a few highlights.

One set of criticisms relates to the monetary variables used by Andersen and Jordan, that is, the money stock (M_1) in some regressions and the monetary base in others. For their analysis to be valid, causation should run from these monetary variables to income, but not from income back to these monetary variables. Otherwise the observed correlation between changes in nominal income and in nominal money could hardly be used as an argument that changes in the money stock *cause* changes in income. But does the correlation run almost only from money to income, and not from income to money? The critics of Andersen and Jordan point out that as income rises so do interest rates, and when interest rates rise the Fed tends to increase the monetary base. Moreover a rise in the interest rate tends to raise the money multiplier. Hence these critics believe that the high correlation Andersen and Jordan found between changes in money and in nominal income

[1] These high employment fiscal variables need explaining. Suppose one compares actual federal government deficits with nominal income, and observes that there is no correlation between them. This would not necessarily mean that increases in the deficit have no effect on income. What *may* be going on is the following: when an increase in government expenditure and hence in the deficit occurs, it raises nominal income, as Keynesian theory predicts. However, it is also true that, if for some reason, say, a decline in the marginal efficiency of investment, income falls, this fall in income reduces tax receipts and thus results in an increase in the deficit. In the first case—an increase in government expenditures—there is a positive correlation between the deficit and nominal income, and in the second case—a drop in income—there is a negative correlation since the deficit increases whenever income drops. The net result may well be that data that combine instances of both of these cases show very little, if any, correlation between the deficit and nominal income, even though, in the situation we have posited, an increase in the deficit *does* raise nominal income. To minimize this problem Andersen and Jordan used, not the *actual* figures on the government's expenditures and deficits, but estimates of what government receipts and deficits would have been at a *given* level of income that corresponds to high employment.

does not confirm the quantity theory. Andersen and Jordan, however, believe that causation does run *primarily* from money to income.

It may seem that this criticism focuses on the wrong thing because what is surprising about the Andersen-Jordan study is not that the monetary variables are powerful, but that the fiscal variables are so weak. However, since the monetary and fiscal variables are correlated in their data, these two results are connected. In their regressions, reducing the role that monetary variables play raises the importance of the fiscal variables.

Another criticism focuses on Andersen and Jordan trying to explain nominal income by using a single equation rather than a large-scale econometric model. To investigate whether the single equation approach that Andersen and Jordan prefer is adequate, Franco Modigliani of MIT and Albert Ando of the University of Pennsylvania undertook a test to see whether this approach can yield a misleading answer.[2] They approached the problem indirectly. Suppose it can be shown that in a special situation, where we *know* that fiscal policy has a strong effect, the Andersen-Jordan technique shows fiscal policy as having no effect. If this is the case then one can argue that since the Andersen-Jordan technique gives a wrong result in one situation it should not be trusted in other situations. Accordingly, Modigliani and Ando used the Federal Reserve's large-scale econometric model to predict the change in income resulting from changes in monetary and fiscal policies. They then used the income data it predicted as though they were *actual* observations on income that should be explained by monetary and fiscal policy using Andersen and Jordan's technique. When they did this the answer they got was that fiscal policy has no lasting effect on income. But we *know* that this is wrong because the model that generated the income data is one in which fiscal policy does have a strong effect on income. Thus, the Andersen-Jordan technique can yield a misleading result, and hence their findings should be rejected. (But this test is not quite conclusive since Modigliani and Ando did not use exactly the same technique as Andersen and Jordan.) The Andersen-Jordan analysis has been used as a foundation of a formal model of the economy which is discussed in the Appendix to this chapter.

THE BRUNNER-MELTZER ANALYSIS

When discussing Friedman's monetary theory we mentioned that (rightly or wrongly) he is often criticized for not sufficiently explaining *how* money affects income, and for relying on "mere correlations." And the same criticism has been made of the work of Andersen and Jordan. But this criticism is certainly not applicable to the work of two other leading monetarists, Karl Brunner and Allan Meltzer. They have developed an extensive and very complex analysis of the transmission process. Brunner and Meltzer reject the standard Keynesian *IS-LM* transmission mechanism as oversimplified. In its simplest version, it takes the price level as fixed and ignores wealth.

[2] Franco Modigliani and Albert Ando, "Impacts of Fiscal Actions on Aggregate Income and the Monetarist Controversy: Theory and Evidence," in Jerome Stein (ed.) *Monetarism* (Amsterdam: North Holland Press, 1976), pp. 17–42.

Even in our modified version in Chapter 13 that allows for variations in prices, the public is viewed as having to choose between only two assets, money and bonds. But how about capital, which the public can hold either directly, for example, as houses or equity in unincorporated business, or indirectly as corporate stock? In the *IS-LM* analysis such capital is combined into a single asset with bonds, so that people choose between holding money or holding bonds-capital. Their choice depends (given income and wealth) on a single yield called the rate of interest on bonds. This is a valid simplification if the yield on capital bears a fixed relation to the yield on bonds. But if it does not, then in explaining the quantity of money that people choose to hold one has to introduce the yield on capital as well as the rate of interest. Beyond this, the *IS-LM* approach usually ignores changes in the stock of assets.

Hence, Brunner and Meltzer developed a different transmission mechanism, one that stresses changes in the stock of assets and in the relative price of assets. In their model (built on some earlier work of Carl Christ of Johns Hopkins University) suppose that government expenditures increase. There is, as in the standard Keynesian model, a direct expansionary effect and also a multiplier effect. But, in addition, there is a stock effect. The government has to finance the deficit; it must pay for the increased expenditures by issuing either bonds or money.[3]

Consider first the case in which it issues money. Microeconomics tells us that if the supply of any one item increases its *relative* price must fall to clear the market. But an increase in the supply of money cannot lower the price of money in dollar terms; a dollar always sells for a dollar. However, it can lower the *relative* price of money by raising the prices of all other items, that is, of consumer goods, capital goods, and bonds. As the prices of both consumer goods and of capital goods rise, it becomes profitable to produce more of them, so that output now increases. And, similarly, the rise in bond prices makes it profitable for firms to issue more bonds and to buy capital goods with the proceeds of these bond sales. (Or, to express this in Keynesian terminology, the fall in the interest rate stimulates spending.) At first, all of this results in both output and prices rising. But output rises only as long as it is profitable to produce more because the price of output is high relative to the price of labor and other inputs needed to produce it. Once wages and other costs rise in proportion to the increase in output prices the additional production is no longer profitable, so that output now falls back to its previous equilibrium level. Thus, an increase in the money stock raises real income only temporarily, but prices, and hence nominal income, rise permanently.

Consider now the opposite case in which the government finances its rising expenditures by selling bonds to the public, instead of increasing the money stock. The increased supply of bonds lowers bond prices relative to the prices of other assets. The critical question is now what this fall in bond

[3] Actually the Treasury does not, except to a trivial extent, pay for its expenditures by issuing money. What happens in this case is that the Treasury issues bonds, and that, at the same time, to keep the interest rate stable, the Fed buys government securities in the open market. But as a result of its security purchases bank reserves, and hence the money stock, increase.

prices does to the demand for capital, and hence to investment. If one assumes as the *IS-LM* model does that bonds and capital are similar, and therefore good substitutes for each other, then as the public holds more bonds its demand for capital is reduced. Hence, stock prices and prices of capital goods such as houses fall, and firms cut their investment. But Brunner and Meltzer (as well as some Keynesians, such as James Tobin) make the opposite assumption. In their view government bonds and capital are complements rather than substitutes. Hence, an increase in the supply of government bonds *raises* the demand for capital as the public tries to sell its excess government bonds to buy corporate stock and physical capital instead. As a result, stock prices rise, so that corporations now have an incentive to issue more stock and build more plant and equipment. Investment and income therefore increase. Thus in the Brunner-Meltzer model, not only monetary policy, but also the size of the government deficit—fiscal policy—and the way it is financed can, at least in principle, have a powerful effect on income. This effect of fiscal policy is partly a direct effect through government purchases, partly a multiplier effect, and partly an effect via an increased stock of government bonds.

Another important role that fiscal policy plays in the Brunner-Meltzer model arises from the fact that this model takes account of disequilibrium in the government sector. Most macroeconomic models look at the commodity and labor markets and at money or bond markets, and say that the economy is in equilibrium if all these markets are. But suppose the government is running a deficit. Can one still say that the economy is in equilibrium? Brunner and Meltzer say no because the government has to finance the deficit by issuing bonds or money, and hence—as long as there is a deficit—the public's stock of bonds or money must be growing. And with its wealth growing in this way the public's expenditures will be growing too. Hence as long as the government runs a deficit the *IS* and *LM* curves are continually shifting so that the economy is not in equilibrium. And the same is true (though now with wealth and expenditures falling) if there is a surplus. Equilibrium requires a balanced budget.

How is it then that so many other economic models ignore the need for a balanced budget in equilibrium?[4] The answer is that they define equilibrium less comprehensively. Thus, they treat the rise in the public's stock of bonds and money due to the deficit in one period as an exogenous factor that disrupts equilibrium in the next period, and therefore they analyze the effects of the increase in these stocks separately. By contrast, Brunner and Meltzer look at the whole process as a single unit.

What makes equilibrium analysis so attractive to economists is that there usually exist forces that move the economy towards equilibrium. In the absence of new shocks, one can predict where the economy will end up. Does this work for the Brunner-Meltzer model? What mechanisms, if any, bring the economy to such a broader equilibrium in which the government's budget is just balanced?

[4]Not all other models ignore the effects of the deficit. Some Keynesian economists have built models incorporating these effects much along the lines of Brunner and Meltzer.

Assume the government raises its expenditures, thus running a deficit. This has several effects. It increases aggregate demand both directly and also through multiplier effects as consumption increases. With income thus rising, tax receipts rise too. But they do not rise by enough to balance the budget. There are, however, additional effects. One is that the deficit, by raising the public's holdings of bonds and money and hence its wealth, raises the proportion of income consumed. Investment too increases as the rise in the stock of money and bonds lowers interest rates. And both the rise in consumption and investment raise nominal income, and hence tax receipts. Moreover, rising prices lower the real value of the interest payments the government makes on its debts. For all of these reasons the increase in aggregate demand reduces the deficit. And since aggregate demand continues to increase as long as there is a deficit, eventually the deficit is eliminated entirely. At this point the economy is in equilibrium. A similar analysis applies if the government cuts its expenditures or raises taxes so that it runs a surplus; this too will be eliminated.

In this model where equilibrium requires that the government's budget be balanced fiscal factors, such as the progressivity of the tax system, play an important role. The more progressive the tax system the smaller is the rise in income required to generate the revenue needed to eliminate a given deficit. Such a large role for fiscal policy has caused some economists to question whether the Brunner-Meltzer model is really monetarist and not Keynesian. *In principle,* their model could even produce the old-fashioned and rigid Keynesian conclusion that fiscal policy has a powerful effect on income, while monetary policy is almost powerless. But Brunner and Meltzer believe that this is as it should be: a theory sets out various possibilities, and empirical tests then determine which of these possibilities corresponds to the real world. And Brunner and Meltzer have undertaken extensive empirical tests from which they conclude that the dominant impulse that drives nominal income is not fiscal policy, but changes in the nominal money stock. Since they have also shown that the Fed, if it wants to, can control the nominal money stock they hold the Fed largely responsible for inflation and for fluctuations in real income.

THE REAL BALANCE APPROACH

Another approach to the quantity theory, called the real balance approach, has been developed by Don Patinkin. This is concerned primarily with establishing two propositions. The first is that under certain specified conditions a change in the stock of money brings about a strictly proportional change in the price level, and the second is that Keynes was wrong when he claimed that there could be an equilibrium at less than full employment in an economy in which wages and prices are *completely* flexible. Patinkin does not deny that reestablishing full employment when, say, the marginal efficiency of investment falls, may *perhaps* mean a much greater drop in wages than would be feasible; he is just concerned with showing that, in principle, falling wages and prices would bring about full employment.

Patinkin organized his analysis around the real balance effect. As a convenient, though hardly realistic, expository device, suppose that a helicopter flies over a city and drops currency. The lucky inhabitants now find that they hold more money than they desire to hold, given their incomes, wealth, and the interest rate. Hence, they use this excess money to buy securities and physical assets. This basic idea of the real balance effect is obvious, and we have already discussed it at various points. But to understand it fully, one must put it into a model that starts out with certain quite specific assumptions.

The Assumptions

The most dramatic assumption is that wages and prices are completely flexible so that as long as the supply of labor exceeds the demand for labor, wages continue to fall. Patinkin is not saying that this is the way wages actually behave—he is merely trying to show what would happen if this assumption were to hold.

The second assumption is that people do not suffer from a "money illusion." This needs explaining. Suppose that prices double and the real interest rate is constant, but that your income and wealth double also, so that you are as well off as before. Will you also double the *nominal* value of your expenditures, thus keeping your real expenditures constant? If you are fully aware of what has happened, and behave rationally, you will do so. Your propensity to consume depends on your real income, real wealth, and the real interest rate, and these variables are all unchanged. But it is certainly possible that you may not be fully aware that your real income and wealth are unchanged; for example, you may underestimate the rise in prices, and hence believe that your real income and wealth have risen. If so, you are said to suffer from a money illusion.

As prices rise or fall some redistribution of income takes place and if gainers and losers have different marginal propensities to consume or to invest, aggregate demand is affected. But to simplify the analysis Patinkin assumes such redistribution effects do not occur. In addition, he assumes that as prices change people do not hold back or accelerate purchases in the expectation of further price changes. Purely for expository convenience, he also assumes that the government's budget is balanced. In addition to these assumptions, we will assume *temporarily* that there are no government bonds outstanding, and that all the money in existence is outside money, specifically, for example, currency. Finally, we assume that taxpayers are indifferent to the real value of the government's debt, and do not feel poorer, and hence cut their consumption, when the real value of the government's debt rises.

The Model

Aggregate all the numerous markets in the economy into three. One is the commodity market in which a person's real expenditure on consumer goods and a firm's expenditure on capital goods are functions of real income, the interest rate, and real wealth.

The second market is the labor market in which both the supply and demand for labor depend upon the real wage; the higher the real wage the greater is the supply of labor willing to work, but the smaller is the demand for labor. Third, there is the money market in which the interest rate depends on nominal income and upon the nominal money stock. The higher nominal income, the greater is the demand for money, and hence, the higher is the interest rate. And the greater the supply of money, the lower is the interest rate.

Another aspect of the model is that real expenditures (that is, consumption plus investment) are functions of real income and real wealth. This is not so much an assumption as something that follows directly from microeconomic theory.

Real wealth consists of three types of assets, physical capital or claims thereon, claims that the public has on the government (currency, government securities, and reserves that depository institutions hold with the Fed), and claims that one member of the public has on another, for example, corporate bonds or mortgages. For the public as a whole, these latter claims wash out, since each person's claim is balanced by some other person's debt. We first consider a model in which there are no government bonds and no reserves with the Fed, so that net wealth for the public as a whole consists only of capital and currency, and money is the same as currency.

Workings of the Model

We now put this model through its paces by considering five cases: an expansion of the labor force, a rise in the money stock, an increase in the demand for money, a rise in the average propensity to consume, and an exogeneous rise in prices. To simplify we describe some processes that actually operate simultaneously as though they would operate sequentially.

An Expanded Labor Force. As more people seek work wages fall. And given our assumption of complete wage and price flexibility wages must fall until all those who want jobs have them. But with wages and, hence, prices falling won't aggregate demand fall too, so that real wages are constant and firms have no incentive to employ the additional workers? To see why this will *not* happen assume at first that it *does* happen and then see why this cannot be an equilibrium. Suppose that both wages and prices fall equally by, say, 10 percent. Real income is then constant. But real wealth has increased. With the money stock being constant in nominal terms, the real money stock has risen by 10 percent, so that both the economy's wealth and liquidity have risen. This increased liquidity lowers the interest rate which induces a rise in expenditures. The increase in wealth also raises consumption. These increases in expenditures in turn raise prices. Hence, in equilibrium prices have fallen less than wages. The decline in real wages permits the additional workers to find jobs.

A Rise in the Nominal Money Stock. Suppose that due to a benevolent helicopter, the money stock increases by 10 percent. People now try to get rid of their excess money holdings by raising expenditures. As long as their real money balances are higher than before, their expenditures will also be greater than before. Only after prices have risen by 10 percent, too, will real money balances be back in equilibrium.

What happens to the rate of interest? The factors that determine it are saving, the yield on capital (and hence the demand for capital), and any gap that exists between the real quantity of money demanded and supplied. In the Patinkin model a rise in the supply of money does not change the flow of saving or the yield on capital. And, as just discussed, the price level adjusts to eliminate the gap between the real quantities of money demanded and supplied. Hence, with none of the determinants of the interest rate being different, the rate of interest must be the same as it was before the money stock increased.

An Increased Demand for Money. Suppose people want to hold 10 percent more real money. To do so they must reduce their demand for something else since their total assets are fixed. We assume that they reduce their demand for commodities and bonds proportionately. As they reduce their expenditures on commodities unemployment develops so that wages and prices fall. Once prices have fallen by 10 percent, the real quantity of money available has risen by 10 percent, thus matching the 10 percent increase in the demand for real money. The economy is back in full employment equilibrium and wages and prices no longer fall. And as in the previous case of an increase in the supply of money the interest rate must be back at its previous level too.

An Increase in the Average Propensity to Consume. Initially the rise in consumption raises prices. However, this reduces the real money stock, and with falling wealth and rising interest rates there is downward pressure on prices. But prices do not fall all the way back to their initial level. With the propensity to consume having risen, there is, of course, less saving. Hence, the interest rate rises, and at the higher interest rate the public wants to hold less money. To make people willing to hold all the existing money, prices must be higher than they otherwise would be. Thus, prices cannot fall all the way back to where they were before the propensity to consume increased. Instead, they settle at some point in between their initial level and the level they rose to right after the propensity to consume had increased and before the wealth effect had come into play.

An Exogenous Increase in Prices. Suppose that for some reason producers mistakenly believe that the equilibrium price level has risen and accordingly raise prices. This reduces real wealth, and also the real money stock so that the interest rate rises. Both the rise in the interest rate and the decline in wealth reduce expenditures. And as expenditures fall prices are forced down again. Equilibrium is restored only at the previous price level and interest rate.

Concluding Note. In two of these five cases (an increase in the money stock, and an increase in the demand for money) there were no effects on the real economy. In this model purely monetary changes, such as these, have no *real* effects; money is just a veil. But in two cases, an increase in the labor force and a rise in the propensity to consume, the interest rate changed too. These were cases of changes in the real factors (the supply of labor and the supply of saving) so that one would expect a change in the relative price of labor and capital, and not just in the price level. In the final case, an autonomous price increase, neither the interest rate nor the equilibrium price level changed because all that had happened was that prices had been raised by mistake.

Inside Money, Outside Money, and Government Bonds

The time has come to remove two assumptions—the absence of government bonds and currency being the only type of money. If there are government bonds denominated, as they usually are, in nominal terms, then a 10 percent increase in the money stock must raise prices by *less* than 10 percent. Suppose prices would rise by 10 percent. The real value of government bonds would then fall by 10 percent, so that the public would be poorer. It would therefore cut consumption. This, in turn, would force down prices. Hence, a new equilibrium can be reached only when prices have risen less than proportionately to the rise in the money stock.

Now assume that there exists inside money, that is, money which is a claim on someone within the private sector such as deposits which are claims on banks. Assume that such inside money increases by 10 percent. If prices were to rise by 10 percent too, then people would be poorer because the real value of their currency plus government bonds would then have fallen by 10 percent so that they would cut their consumption. Hence, when inside money increases by 10 percent prices must rise by less than 10 percent. (Prices will rise to some extent because the money stock having increased, the interest rate falls.)

The upshot of all this is that if there are government bonds or inside money, money and prices will generally not change proportionately as they do in the Chicago version of the quantity theory. But we must qualify this last statement by saying that some economists believe that inside money is also net wealth, and others believe that the taxpayers do treat an increase in the real value of the government debt as a corresponding reduction in their wealth. If they are right the above discussion has to be modified.

SUMMARY

1. The St. Louis approach attempts to see whether changes in the money growth rate or in fiscal policy explain changes in income better. It found that changes in the money growth rate have a powerful effect, while the fiscal variables have no or little effect. However, critics have argued that causation runs also from income to money, and that the statistical technique in the St. Louis approach is too simple to be reliable; that in at least one case it can be shown to give the wrong result.

2. Brunner and Meltzer have criticized the *IS-LM* model for treating capital and bonds as homogeneous and for ignoring changes in stocks of assets. Their own version of the transmission process emphasizes relative prices and stocks of assets. It also emphasizes the government budget constraint which requires that the budget be balanced in equilibrium.
3. The real balance approach is a formalized model of the quantity theory that brings out its assumptions. It shows that if prices and wages are completely flexible, then the economy tends to full employment, and that (if there are no government bonds or inside money) a change in the money stock brings about strictly proportional changes in prices. The driving mechanism is that changes in prices change the real value of outside money. Once inside money and government bonds are allowed into the analysis the strict proportionality between changes in money and prices need not hold.

Questions and Exercises

1. Describe in your own words what Andersen and Jordan did and what they found. How convinced are you by this?
2. Describe the ways in which the Brunner-Meltzer model differs from Friedman's approach.
3. Discuss Brunner and Meltzer's criticism of the *IS-LM* model.
4. Show how the real balance effect operates to stop a wage-price spiral.
5. Describe the distinction between inside and outside money. Why is this distinction relevant?
6. Suppose that inside money (but not outside money) increases. What does this do to the equilibrium level of the interest rate?
7. (On Appendix) In what way does the St. Louis model exhibit the various characteristics of monetarism?

Further Reading

ANDERSEN, LEONALL, and CARSON, KEITH. "A Monetarist Model for Economic Stabilization." *Review* (Federal Reserve Bank of St. Louis) 52 (April 1970): 7–25. A detailed exposition of the St. Louis model.

ANDERSEN, LEONALL, and JORDAN, JERRY. "Monetary and Fiscal Actions: A Test of Their Relative Importance in Economic Stabilization." *Review* (Federal Reserve Bank of St. Louis) 50 (November 1968): 11–23. A classic.

DORNBUSCH, RUDIGER. "Comments on Brunner and Meltzer." In *Monetarism,* edited by Jerome Stein, pp. 104–25. Amsterdam: North Holland Publishing Co., 1976. Contains a remarkably clear exposition of the Brunner-Meltzer model.

PATINKIN, DON. *Money, Interest, and Prices*. 2d ed. New York: Harper and Row, 1965. This is an advanced treatise, but well worth reading.

PESEK, BORIS, and SAVING, THOMAS. *Money, Wealth and Economic Theory*. New York: Macmillan, 1967. An interesting argument that inside money is wealth too; therefore, the distinction between inside and outside money is irrelevant.

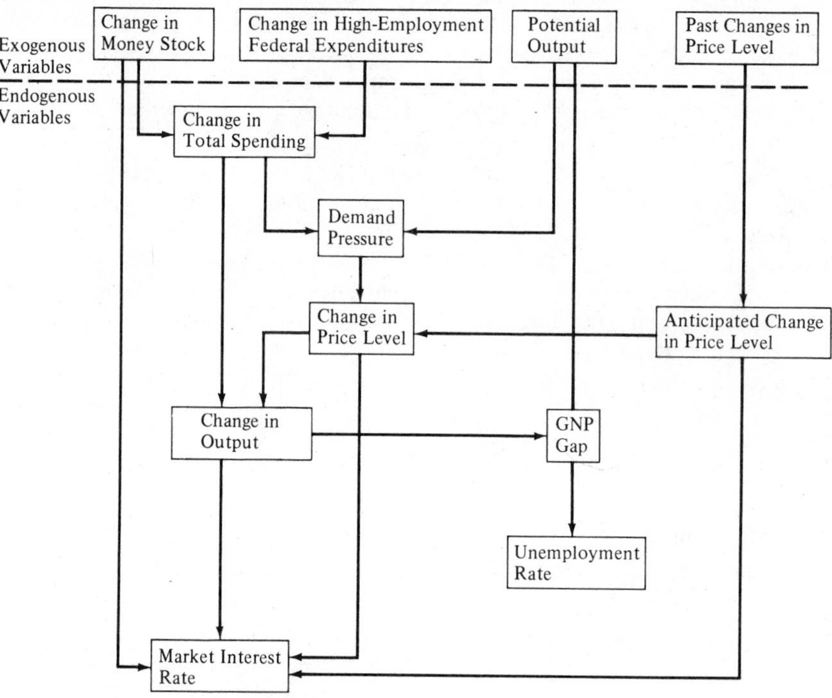

Figure 16.1 Flow Chart of the St. Louis Model

Source: Leonall Anderson and Keith Carson, "A Monetarist Model for Economic Stabilization," *Review* (Federal Reserve Bank of St. Louis) 52 (April 1970): 10.

APPENDIX: THE ST. LOUIS MODEL

Figure 16.1 shows the flow chart of this model. The top line consists of the four exogenous variables—the variables whose values are determined outside the model and taken as given. The first two of these, the money stock and high-employment government expenditures, were already discussed. The two new ones are potential output and previous changes in the price level.

The role of the previous price-change variable is to determine anticipated price changes, since in this model people form their expectations of future inflation by looking at past inflation rates. The *anticipated* price level is therefore an endogenous variable, and it, in turn, affects two other endogenous variables, the actual price level and the rate of interest.

The other new exogenous variable, potential output, has two functions. First, it affects demand pressures on prices since it measures the potential supply that is available to meet aggregate demand. Second, along with the level of aggregate demand, it determines the GNP gap, that is, the gap between high-employment output and actual output.

In this model, changes in the money stock and changes in high-employment federal expenditures determine changes in total spending. And changes in total spending, along with potential, output affect demand pressures on commodity markets, and these demand pressures, along with anticipated inflation, determine prices. The model assumes that firms set prices on the basis of two considerations; the expected rate of inflation and the extent to which demand for their own products is excessive or insufficient. Output responds to changes in total spending. The change in output, in turn, affects the GNP gap and thus the unemployment rate. But since firms are willing to produce more if prices rise, the change in output depends not only on the change in total spending, but also on the change in the price level.

Finally, the market rate of interest is determined by four factors. Apart from the anticipated rate of price change, these are the actual change in prices and the change in output, as well as changes in the stock of money. The changes in output and in actual prices affect the rate of interest by determining the demand for money. Juxtaposed to this change in the demand for money is the change in the supply of money.

This model differs in several ways from Keynesian models, ways closely related to the characteristics of monetarism discussed in the last chapter. One of these is that in this model there is no way one can introduce changes in private demand, due to changes in, say, the marginal efficiency of investment or the propensity to consume. It therefore implies that private demand does not generate major fluctuations in the economy. By contrast, in the Keynesian model such changes in private demand can show up in any of the numerous equations that describe private expenditures. Second, in this model aggregate demand is treated as a single unit. Similarly, the results of this model consist only of aggregates, that is, real income, the price level, unemployment, and the interest rate, while Keynesian models generally provide much more detail about individual sectors of the economy.

Third, the price level is determined directly by the interaction of aggregate demand and potential output. By contrast, in Keynesian models aggregate demand often does not enter *directly* into price-determination equations. Instead, prices are taken as just a markup on standard labor costs and other costs. Fourth, in the St. Louis model the interest rate does not help to determine any other variables, while in Keynesian models changes in the interest rate are a stepping stone in the transmission process by which monetary policy and other variables affect income.

The Monetarist-Keynesian Debate in Perspective

17

It is sometimes difficult to get a clear view of the differences between monetarists and those who use the income-expenditure approach, because they appear to be using different languages to express their views. To compare their views, it is necessary to translate from one language to another, and there is always the danger that something will be lost in the translation.

In the income-expenditure approach, each component of the expenditure side of the national income accounts is "explained" in terms of other variables. Thus consumer expenditures are explained in terms of disposable income, wealth, and perhaps some other factors. Investment is supposed to vary with capacity utilization and interest rates. Price changes reflect changes in wages and in capacity utilization, but are also influenced by "exogenous" changes in food prices, taxes, and other factors. All of these linkages interact with one another in the complex system sketched out in Chapters 13–15. In that kind of system, prices, output, and unemployment are strongly influenced by both monetary and fiscal policy, but they can be influenced by many other variables as well. Moreover, the structure of the system itself is subject to change without notice. The relations between unemployment and wage change can be influenced by changes in the strength of trade unions, by import competition, and by changes in regulation as well as by expectations of future government policy. Investment expenditures can be influenced by "speculation" about the rapid growth of new industries, by threats of war, and by confidence or lack of confidence in government policy.

The income-expenditure approach is built up from a great many pieces. Economists who use this approach have disagreements about the relative importance of the many variables entering the system. For example, some think that changes in wealth have a powerful influence on consumer expenditures. Others are skeptical about the effect of wealth. Statistical studies do not yield sufficiently precise results to resolve the controversy. The result is that there can be considerable differences in judgments about the effects of any proposed policy. What links Keynesians is not their conclusions but their basic way of approaching the analysis of the economy.

Much the same thing can be said of monetarists. They too have their differences, but they share a belief in the critical importance of variations in the rate of growth of money in the explanation of changes in prices and outputs. They tend to emphasize the existence of direct links between money on the one hand, and expenditures, prices, and output on the other, thus bypassing the complex causal chains appearing in Keynesian models. Some of the direct linkages relate prices and outputs to actual and expected changes in asset markets, particularly money markets. They give great weight to the role of stocks of assets in determining flows of expenditures so that, for example, they emphasize the link between stocks of wealth and flows of consumer expenditures. Moreover, monetarists tend to emphasize, more than Keynesians do, the importance of expectations, especially those connected with the rate of growth of the money stock. In addition, as already discussed in Chapter 15, they consider that prices and wages are relatively flexible, that is, more flexible than Keynesians usually assume. And they also think of the private economy as relatively stable.

Finally, as mentioned in Chapter 15, monetarists tend to have a longer time horizon than Keynesians. They are often concerned, for example, with the consequences of an increased rate of growth of money supply persisting over a period of years. Keynesians are more often concerned with short-run changes. Some misunderstandings arise from this source, because the short-run effect of a policy change may be quite different from its long-run effect.

At a very general theoretical level, Keynesians and monetarists often agree about the nature of the factors influencing prices, expenditures, and output. In summary paragraphs they often sound very similar. Unfortunately, the apparent agreement often amounts only to Robert Solow's summary of a student's progress in economics: In the elementary course he learns that everything depends on everything else. When he becomes a graduate student, he learns that everything depends on everything else in two ways.

For practical purposes, it is necessary to simplify things to some extent. Interactions considered to have minor effects must be neglected. The result is that Keynesians often neglect matters that monetarists consider important, and vice versa. In using different simplifications, they often appear to be talking different languages.

In many ways, however, the monetarist description of the qualitative linkages between money and expenditures, prices and output does not sound so very different from the Keynesian approach. Milton Friedman's analysis of the demand for money is not fundamentally different from the Keynesian analysis. Patinkin's model of real balance effects can certainly be given a Keynesian interpretation. The Brunner-Meltzer model overlaps the Keynesian one in many ways—though containing its own special features. Up to a point one can think of Keynesians and monetarists as using a common model and differing about numerical magnitudes such as the interest elasticity of demand for money or the flexibility of prices. At one time, until the mid-1960s, the debate centered on the relative slopes of *IS* and *LM* curves, to which we now turn.

INTEREST ELASTICITIES IN THE *IS-LM* MODEL

In any debate, it is helpful to define the question in your own way. In the early stages of the Keynesian-monetarist debate, Keynesians treated monetarism as a special case of the Keynesian model. They argued that the quantity theory of nominal income would be correct if the demand for money were inelastic to interest rates, or if investment demand were highly elastic to interest rates. They then proceeded to make empirical arguments to show that neither was true. Monetarists were never very enthusiastic about that formulation of the issue, but they did debate some of the questions involved. The result of a long statistical wrangle and the accumulation of experience was to bring both positions together. The result of convergence, however, was not to produce agreement, but to shift the argument to new grounds.

Demand for Money

Many early Keynesians believed that (especially at the low rates prevailing after World War II) the interest elasticity of demand for money was almost infinite. Consequently, velocity would adjust to any change in GNP with very little change in interest rates. That view, of course, reflected the experience of the late thirties, World War II, and the early postwar years.

However, statistical studies covering longer periods as well as the experience of monetary restraint indicated that the interest elasticity of demand for money was not as high as some Keynesians had thought. On the other hand, those estimates were not so low as to justify a simple fixed-velocity quantity theory in which "only money matters." A moderate interest elasticity of demand for money leaves room for fiscal and other influences on the *IS* curve as well as for monetary influence through the *LM* curve shifts. Milton Friedman's permanent-income approach offered an alternative explanation. He showed that a model in which demand for money is made to depend on the trend of income could explain much of the cyclical variation in velocity. Later studies showed that even after taking the permanent-income effect into account, demand for money is generally still sensitive to interest rates. Nonetheless, Friedman's point was well taken, and most current formulations do use some average of past and current incomes as part of the explanation of demand for money.

Monetarists, including Friedman, as well as Keynesians, agree that demand for money is responsive to interest rates. On the other hand, they also agree that the short-run interest elasticity of demand for money is fairly low so that changes in the growth rate of money can have substantial effects on aggregate demand. There is still disagreement in this area, but it is no longer the basis for fundamental differences between monetarists and Keynesians.

Interest Elasticity of Expenditure

A somewhat similar convergence of views about the interest elasticity of expenditures has taken place. Early Keynesian expositions linked money to expenditure through the effect of money on interest rates and the effect of interest rates on investment. While that linkage played an important role in Keynes's exposition, his followers tended to argue that investment demand is very inelastic to interest rates. That argument provided another justification for a "money-doesn't-matter" position.

Again, a long series of statistical studies and accumulating experience showed that interest-rate variations can have significant effects on business investment. However, the difficulty of measuring the expected *real* interest rates makes precise measurement difficult.

The effect of interest-rate variations on residential constructions is well established, and in that case, nominal as well as real interest rates appear significant. In addition, the effects of interest rates extend to consumer expenditures through the influence of interest rates on wealth. Indeed, in a leading Keynesian econometric model, about half the total impact of monetary change results from the wealth effect.

As in the demand for money case, Keynesians have moved away from the "money-doesn't-matter" position. At the same time, interest elasticities are not so high as to provide any basis for an "only-money-matters" position. Again, there is room for disagreement about numbers, but the interest elasticity of expenditures is no longer a critical element in the division between Keynesians and monetarists.

RECENT MODELS

As discussed in the preceding two chapters, the Keynesian-monetarist debate drifted away from the issue of the slopes of the *IS* and *LM* curves in the 1960s. Milton Friedman argued that the slopes matter only for a relatively short time, because if the money stock is increased, the interest rate soon rises back to its previous level. On this issue of the behavior of the interest rate, there has so far been little convergence. Monetarists and Keynesians both can point to empirical studies that support their positions; regressions of the interest rate on changes in the money stock generally support the monetarist position, while econometric models tend to support the Keynesian position. And there is an extensive debate on the relative validity of simple regressions of one variable on another versus econometric models. This debate deals more with issues in econometrics than with issues of monetary theory.

Another important development in the debate has been the construction by Brunner and Meltzer of their model with its focus on changes in the relative prices of money, securities, and commodities (including capital), which was discussed in the previous chapter. While many Keynesians would dispute the practical relevance of this model, arguing that these relative price and wealth effects are unimportant in the short run, which is what they think matters for policy making, there has been some convergence, since some Keynesian economists have built models that are more or less similar to the Brunner-Meltzer model. All in all, among economists this debate is by no means as dogmatic as some newspaper reports suggest. Many economists take an intermediate position, and agree with monetarists on some issues and with Keynesians on others.

One important aspect of the debate, which we want to single out for further discussion, is whether in a three-asset model, bonds are closer substitutes for money than for real capital or vice versa. If bonds are more like real capital than like money, an increased supply of bonds will depress the price of real assets. On the other hand, if bonds are more like money than like real capital, an increased stock of bonds will raise the price of real assets.

Why is that so important? Because government deficits financed without money creation have to generate bonds. If bond issues depress real capital prices, the expansive effect of deficit financing is blunted. If government bond issues raise the price of capital, the effect of deficit finance is enhanced.

Monetarists have emphasized this consideration much more than Keynesians. Many monetarists and some Keynesians consider government debt to be a relatively close substitute for real capital, which weakens the force of fiscal policy. Finally, some economists think that long-term debt is close to real capital, while short-term debt is close to money.

In spite of their disagreements, monetarists are linked together by their emphasis on the relevance of asset-market issues. At the one extreme an antifiscalist monetarist considers that (1) government debt is not wealth (in terms of its influence on consumption), and (2) government debt is a close substitute for real capital in asset portfolios. Those assumptions minimize the effect of fiscal policy. Other monetarists see more power in fiscal policy.

What makes them both monetarists is their emphasis on the asset-stock implications rather than the expenditure-flow aspects of fiscal policy. Their treatment of fiscal policy is parallel to their treatment of monetary policy. In both cases the influence of policy is from change in asset stocks (money, government bonds) to wealth and the relative prices existing and currently produced assets to spending on consumption and investment. In the same way, a change in tax rates is thought to influence spending not only through its effect on the deficit, but also through its effect on the value of assets and on the perceived present value of future aftertax earnings.

POLICY DIFFERENCES

The monetarist-Keynesian debate has gone on for a long time, and it has not become any simpler. Indeed, as interest in monetarism has increased, the number of monetarists has grown and they now disagree among themselves as much or more than the Keynesians do. However, monetarists tend to unite with one another in their disagreements with Keynesians about economic policy. In this section we will outline some basic differences between the Keynesian and monetarist approaches to the art of policy making, leaving a more detailed discussion until Part Five.

We can start with something everybody agrees about. At any one time there is a fairly well marked, practical limit to real GNP and a corresponding lower limit to unemployment. The corresponding unemployment rate is the natural rate or NAIRU (nonaccelerating inflation rate of unemployment). It is agreed that no policy can sustain an unemployment rate below the natural rate or NAIRU for long.

Does the opposite proposition hold? Can unemployment remain above NAIRU for a long time? Keynesians generally think so. Monetarists certainly recognize that disturbances from various sources (especially from rapid changes in the money growth rate) can cause unemployment to rise above the natural rate. However, they tend to believe that in the absence of new disturbances, price and wage adjustments will soon bring the system back to equilibrium.

It follows immediately that fiscal and monetary policy have only short-run effects on real output. Moreover, an activist policy is likely to do more harm than good. Managing monetary and fiscal policy to counter short-run shocks could help in principle, they say, but in practice, forecasting errors and politically motivated decisions will worsen rather than improve the economy's performance.

Keynesians, of course, are not nearly so sanguine about the self-adjusting capacity of the system. In their view, the balance between full-employment saving and investment is often disturbed. It needs to be corrected by shifts in monetary and fiscal policy. Moreover, they believe that the batting average of forecasters is good enough to permit policy actions to make the economy more rather than less stable and that policymakers can use these forecasts efficiently. Hence the dispute about policy involves much more than differing views about economic theory. It also involves differing views about the efficiency of the political process. A typical example of this difference is that Keynesians often point to sophisticated mathematical procedures by which the Fed could stabilize the economy, while monetarists point to blunders that the Fed has made in the past.

These days the big dispute is about inflation control. How can we keep the inflation rate from accelerating? Can we make it decelerate? Monetarists argue that we can prevent acceleration by keeping the growth of the money supply at a level equal to the existing rate of inflation, plus the growth of potential output, less the trend of velocity. If oil prices rise or if food prices are driven up by poor crops, there will be a temporary acceleration of inflation, a temporary rise of unemployment, but we will soon get back on the track. Those who think that fiscal policy has some power would also want to avoid any strong fiscal stimulus. A widespread monetarist prescription for deceleration of inflation is a gradual deceleration in money growth. Again some extra unemployment would occur, but it would be temporary.

Keynesians on the other hand find themselves in a dilemma. They think it will take a lot of unemployment for a long time to bring the inflation rate down. Moreover, price pressures from oil, food, and increased tax rates would have to be offset by even more unemployment. Many Keynesians think that we must live with a continuing inflation, or use guidelines or other interference in the wage and price-making process. These problems are discussed in Chapter 18.

Aggregate Supply, Aggregate Demand, and the Wage-Price Spiral

18

Inflation has been a chronic problem in almost all market economies in the years since World War II. The problem is hardly a new one. Readers of Gibbon's *Decline and Fall of the Roman Empire* can find a lively account of the inflation problems of the Roman Empire and the Emperor Diocletian's unsuccessful effort to enforce price control. Chinese history records inflation more than one thousand years ago. More recent examples include a period of inflation during the American Revolutionary War, when prices rose so much that the currency issued by the Continental Congress became virtually worthless. Both the Union and the Confederacy suffered from runaway inflation. During the U.S. Civil War, for example, a bag of groceries cost a basketful of Confederate currency, even before Appomattox. The German inflation that began with World War I is charged with destroying the savings of the German middle classes and helping to bring Hitler to power.

Viewed in purely economic terms, inflation tends to reduce economic efficiency. Everyone finds it harder to make price comparisons when prices are changing rapidly. It is more difficult to negotiate contracts for future deliveries and payments and to calculate the true return on investments in periods of rapid price change. Those costs would be much smaller if the rate of inflation could be fully anticipated but that is seldom possible. Unexpected changes in the rate of inflation cause arbitrary redistributions of income and wealth between debtors and creditors. Old people who depend on pensions in dollar amounts and on savings invested in bonds or mortgages are likely to be the big losers.

Inflation is a political as well as an economic problem. Widespread uncertainty about the future value of assets produces political as well as economic instability. Recent public opinion polls show fear of inflation to be of greater concern to the American public than unemployment, crime, pollution, or nuclear war.

This chapter provides a review of the major theoretical and empirical issues in the analysis of inflation, starting with a discussion of the theory of inflation. The occurence of inflation is first interpreted in terms of aggregate supply and demand and changes in expectations. A different approach, somewhat more suitable for empirical analysis, is then used to explain what is popularly called the wage-price spiral.

Since we have already discussed aggregate demand, most of our attention is given to the supply side. Much of the chapter is devoted to discussion of theories of the response of wages and prices to changes in demand, and to changes in expectations of future price changes. The student has to remember, however, that changes in demand induced by changes in monetary and fiscal policy play a fundamental role in the causation of inflation. To bring that point home, we outline some scenarios showing how prices will respond to several different sequences of changes in monetary and fiscal policy. We then show how some changes in the structure of labor markets help to explain the simultaneous occurence of increasing unemployment and more rapid inflation during the 1970s. The roles of such "cost-push" factors as increases in the prices of raw materials, food, and fuel are then reviewed. Finally, we note some of the issues raised by recent "experiments" in monetary policy.

CAUSES OF INFLATION

Most of the inflations previous to World War II were associated with wars that had been financed with huge issues of paper money or, in earlier times, by recoining silver coins into silverplated copper ones, which made one silver coin into several "debased" ones. In those circumstances the occurrence of inflation was never very hard to explain. The government's expenditures and the induced expenditures of consumers whose incomes were increased, created a demand for more goods than could be produced at the initial prices. Merchants, selling out their inventories, marked up prices; manufacturers, working at capacity, raised their prices and hired as much labor as they could get. Employers were ready to pay higher wages because increased output was profitable even at higher cost, and with help-wanted signs everywhere, they had to pay more. Everyone then had a higher income; and the government, having to pay more for military supplies, spent faster and printed money faster. "Too much money chasing too few goods" was a simple but adequate slogan for the typical wartime inflation.

Postwar Inflation

Since World War II inflation has been a chronic problem in market economies throughout the world. Inflation has occurred in peacetime as well as during wars, and in countries with budgetary surpluses as well as in those with chronic deficits. Worst of all inflation has continued during slumps as well as in booms. Inflation in depressed economies has been prevalent enough to get a name—"stagflation"—a stagnant economy suffering from inflation. Chronic and worldwide inflation is a new phenomenon harder to explain than the earlier inflations associated with wars, revolutions, or profligate monarchs. A new and complex phenomenon inevitably breeds controversy and there has been no lack of that. Books and articles purporting to explain inflation or to provide a remedy number in the thousands.

In spite of all the controversy, economists have reached a very substantial measure of agreement on the broad outlines of the theory of inflation though they continue to disagree about the importance of many substantive points. The starting point is agreement on the proposition that the rate of inflation involves an *interaction* between aggregate demand and the structure of markets in which prices and wages are determined. With a given level of real GNP (relative to potential output) we can have more inflation with one kind of market structure than another—for example, tariffs and quotas may increase the inflationary response to a rise in real GNP. On the other hand the amount of inflation produced by any given market structure will depend on what happens to aggregate demand (in relation to potential output).

In previous chapters we showed that the equilibrium price level is determined by the intersection of the aggregate-demand curve and the potential output line. When the aggregate-demand curve shifts to the right faster than potential output, the equilibrium price level rises. During transition the system is out of equilibrium. Prices are below equilibrium.

The position and slope of the aggregate demand curve depends on all the factors underlying the *IS–LM* analysis. These include "real factors" such as capital stock and technology and the long-term expectations of investors and consumers with respect to the growth of output. They also include "nominal" factors. Of these, the most important are the nominal money stock, the nominal level of government expenditures, the nominally fixed elements in the tax system, for instance, the "brackets" in the income-tax schedule, and the outstanding debt. The aggregate-demand curve slopes downward to the right—lower price level, higher output—because the real value of the nominal magnitudes in the system increases with lower price levels. Both monetarists and Keynesians use the aggregate-demand apparatus. Monetarists emphasize the money supply as a major determinant of the position of the curve, while Keynesians give weight to other factors, but the demand-curve concept can be used by both.

In the long run, with all prices in equilibrium relative to one another, one absolute price level generates the same output as another. Doubling all prices and wages leaves output unchanged so that the long-run aggregate supply curve is vertical. It is possible, however, to think of a short-run disequilibrium supply curve. It is only a short-run curve based on a given price history and, as we will see, it will shift with the passage of time, but it is helpful in understanding the inflationary process.

In Chapter 13 we showed how cyclical movements in aggregate demand could cause cyclical swings in both prices and output. When demand shifts upward prices rise but not enough to offset fully the effect of the demand expansion. A fall in demand has the opposite effect. The immediate adjustment of prices to shifts in demand is usually incomplete for several reasons. Wage and price movements are often limited by contracts. In oligopolistic

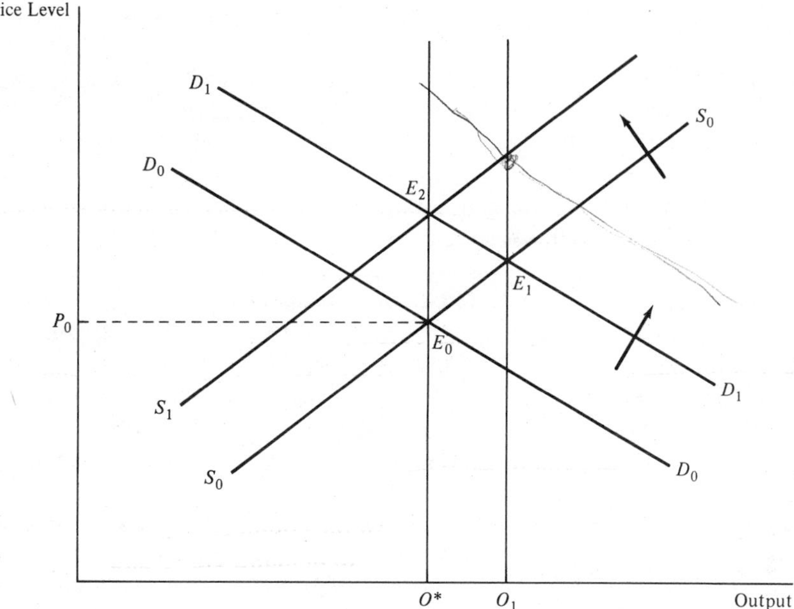

Figure 18.1 Interaction of Shifting Aggregate-Demand and Aggregate-Supply Curves

industries firms will not change list prices until they are convinced that rivals will follow (though they may offer discounts). Wage movements will be slowed by administrative and labor relations considerations.

During a temporary cyclical upswing output as well as price will rise. In those sectors with little or no initial slack producers will have to use overtime work or let postponable work slide until the period of peak demand is over. In sectors with some initial slack, unemployment will decline.

When demand shifts downward both price and output will decline. They will follow a short-run supply curve like S_0S_0 in Figure 18.1 (S_0S_0, D_0D_0, and D_1D_1 are taken from Figure 13.17). The "Lucas supply function" used by rational expectations theorists emphasizes the significance of differences between actual and perceived changes in relative wages and prices. Lucas argues that the inability to distinguish between general and relative price changes is important in the explanation of variations in output.

Persisting Shifts in Demand

Now suppose that the boom has come to stay. Demand shifts upward to D_1D_1 and remains at the higher level. Will prices and output stay fixed at E_1? They will not because S_0S_0 is supposed to represent the response of prices to shifts in demands perceived as temporary. Once it appears that demand is not going to shift down, a new set of price adjustments will occur.

There are two reasons for further adjustment in prices. First, price and wage policies suitable for a temporary situation will not work well in the longer run. Administrative costs are large relative to the gain from a temporary price change but they are not important if the price can be raised and kept up. In concentrated industries, firms will be able to recognize their mutual interests in a price rise when they are all convinced that the rise in demand will continue. Trade-union contracts expire, and in addition nonunion employers will prefer to adjust their wage schedule rather than continue to operate with overtime, use temporaries, or get the work out while they are short-handed. Thus we can expect that as time passes there will be a further round of price and wage increases.

Second, the price response shown on the aggregate-supply curve is the response of each producer to the change in demand given the prices of all the others. But some of the price increases in the first round depicted in the S_0S_0 curve will increase costs to other producers. That will lead to a second round of price increases. In labor markets firms that made some wage adjustment will find that they did not improve their relative position as much as expected because other wages also rose. Those who made no adjustment find their competitive position has worsened. Workers who got a higher starting rate or a merit increase now find that the cost of living has risen and opportunities elsewhere have improved. Thus, to the extent that everyone finds actual prices higher than expected, a further round of price adjustment is required.

Thus if everyone regards the new price level as a permanent baseline, the whole short-run supply schedule S_0S_0 shifts upward to a new equilibrium with a higher price level and somewhat lower outputs.

In time there should be a further reaction as all market participants respond to the second round of price increases and to the fact that they are still out of equilibrium. As long as output is above O^*, the level of vacancies, overtime work, and capacity utilization is still too high. Price and wage adjustments, which would have eliminated those problems for individual firms, fail to do so because their effect is canceled out by other price and wage increases. Prices will stop rising only when the short-run supply schedule shifts up enough so that it cuts the demand curve at E_2 where output is back to O^*.

The end result is the same as in the price flexibility case, but since the price adjustment process takes time, prices rise at a certain rate per year instead of in one jump. While they are adjusting, output is above normal.

We have argued that a one-shot persistent increase in demand would lead to a rise in output accompanied by a rise in prices, and then a further rise in prices over a period of time accompanied by a decline in output. Now suppose that the initial increase in demand occurred because the government wanted to achieve a higher level of output and a lower level of unemployment. Suppose it wants to keep output at O_1. It can do so, for a time at least, by making a further increase in aggregate demand. As the short-run supply curve shifts up from S_0S_0 to S_1S_1 an increase in money supply and government expenditure will shift demand up again so that output remains at O_1. This will, of course, make the supply curve shift up again since the movement of prices toward equilibrium has been offset by an upward movement in the equilibrium price level. However, that new upward shift in supply schedule can be offset by a further increase in demand. If the lags in the price-adjustment process remain the same as before and in particular if each price is adjusted on the expectation that prices will stay the same, it will be possible to maintain output at O_1 with some annual rate of inflation.

We should expect that the rate of inflation associated with any given output level will be higher as the difference between the actual output level, for example, O_1, and potential output, O^*, increases. In that case we can draw a curve showing the level of output in excess of O^* on the horizontal axis and the rate of inflation on the vertical axis. That curve shows the trade-off between output and employment on the one hand and rate of inflation on the other.

Before going on to consider the problems that arise when people come to expect continuing inflation, it is important to remember what is involved in maintaining a continuing inflation. If output is to be maintained at a fixed level above O^*, the aggregate-demand curve must be continually shifted upward. This can be done if nominal government expenditures, nominal money supply, and nominal outside money all grow at the rate of inflation. One might envisage other possibilities—perhaps a "stronger" fiscal expansion and a "weaker" monetary expansion—that could do the trick. However, we need not pursue the matter because the outcome will in fact be dominated by the expectational considerations discussed next.

Price Expectations

As usual, however, there are other complications. The notion that a particular rate of inflation will be associated with a given level of output depends upon the proposition that the price-wage responses of the system remain independent of the experienced rate of inflation. In fact, of course, that is not likely to be the case. The shifting supply-curve model used in the last section depended on (1) assuming that there are good reasons for avoiding price and wage adjustments that will have to be reversed and (2) that the price and wage adjustments that do occur will be based on the assumption that other prices remain fixed. An absolute price increase is expected to be a relative price increase because other prices are expected to be the same. But as soon as everyone expects that prices generally are going to keep rising at, say, 2 percent per year the whole game is changed. Firms have much less incentive to avoid price and wage increases because they do not expect them to be reversed. And anyone who feels that a relative price increase is profitable has to make a larger absolute increase to reach the same relative price target.

The result of that process will be to step up the rate of inflation from 2 percent per year to a higher figure. If, nonetheless, the government continues to engage in enough fiscal and monetary expansion to maintain the level of output at O_1 everyone will come to expect continuance of the new higher rate of inflation and that will set the stage for a new acceleration.

Thus to maintain a level of output in excess of O^* the aggregate-demand curve must be shifted upward at a progressively more rapid rate. We will discuss the implications of that conclusion at the end of the chapter. First, however, we will look at the inflation process in a way that can be linked more directly to empirical work on inflation.

The use of aggregate-supply curves combines the wage-setting process in labor markets with the price-setting process in product markets. It is not very convenient for dealing with the special problems posed by fluctuations in raw material and farm prices. In empirical work on inflation, it is often convenient to analyze the forces leading to changes in wages, and then show how wages and other factors influence prices. In the following sections, we will outline the conclusions of that approach.

REAL OUTPUT, EMPLOYMENT, PRICES, AND WAGES

The determination of prices and wages in modern industrial economies is obviously a very complicated affair. Some industries more or less approximate the competitive model. Some look more like pure monopolies. Many have characteristics of both models. Prices in some industries are regulated, for example, by public utility commissions; government enterprises produce quite a lot of output and have their own pricing procedures. Prices of agricultural products are influenced by fluctuations in weather as well as by government price-support programs. Sales and excise taxes, real-estate and corporate income taxes can influence prices. Finally, even in a relatively closed economy like the U.S. prices are influenced by foreign prices. Foreign prices are obviously important for imports like coffee, and prices charged by U.S. firms making steel, autos, and many other things are influenced by the prices offered by foreign competitors.

Labor markets are equally complicated. There are unions of varying strengths. Markets for unskilled labor appear to differ from those for lawyers, scientists, or business executives. Labor markets can be influenced by minimum wage legislation, unemployment compensation, and welfare payments.

In the face of all this complexity it is obviously difficult to find an overview. We can be pretty sure that most labor and products markets do not work like simple auction markets. But it is hard to know where to go from there.

In fact it turns out that a few relatively simple empirical generalizations will take us a long way although we have to beware of the oversimplification involved. Simplicity is what we want now, because we have to connect up some generalizations about wages and prices with other generalizations about demand, money, and prices in order to understand the whole picture. Once this picture is sketched, we can examine some more details, qualifications, and complications without getting hopelessly lost.

Wages, Prices, and Unemployment

One of the most familiar and distressing phenomena of our era is the wage-price spiral. Everyone knows that big wage increases produce price increases and everyone knows that an increasing cost of living drives up wages. So business managements say we have a wage-price spiral—wage increases lead to price increases, which lead to wage increases, and so on. Labor leaders say it is the other way around, price increases lead to wage increases, wage increases lead to price increases, and so on. A great deal of rhetoric is wasted on the question of who started it. In fact, though wage-price or, if you prefer, price-wage spirals are a reality, they are much more complex than the "who-dun-it" rhetoric suggests.

In the next two sections we will look briefly at the effect of wages on prices and then at the effect of prices on wages. Then we can look at the interaction process to try to understand wage-price spiral dynamics.

Prices and Labor Costs

In spite of all the complexities arising from variations in competitive structure and regulation, in practice prices of private nonfarm output produced in the U.S. are dominated by movements of labor costs. In a way this is not so surprising. Compensation of employees accounts for two-thirds of total costs. Moreover, in the long run, product prices must cover depreciation on the cost of capital goods. Capital-goods prices in turn are strongly influenced by labor costs. Even indirect business taxes are influenced by the wages of government employees, which move with the rest. There is obviously room for variation in the relation of prices to labor costs especially in the short run. There is even more room for short-run variation in that relationship in individual industries. But when we take them all together a lot of nonwage factors affecting individual industries come out in the wash. In the aggregate the trends of average prices for privately produced nonfarm products and the corresponding unit of labor costs are surprisingly close as shown in Figure 18.2.

Unit labor costs are defined as compensation of employees (wages plus fringe benefits) divided by output per hour. The corresponding measure of prices is the GNP deflator for the nonfarm private sector. It is not affected by prices of farm products or imported materials. From year to year or quarter to quarter, changes in the private nonfarm deflator and the corresponding unit labor cost are less closely correlated than in the long run.

Part of the deviation is explained by erratic and cyclical movements in productivity. Cyclically, when output rises fast and capacity utilization improves, productivity rises sharply. It increases slowly in slumps. Firms do not raise prices in slumps or lower them in booms. Their prices behave as though they were based on the trend of unit labor costs. There are some variations in profit margins in the short run, but statistical studies show that a good approximation of the nonfarm deflator is reached if it is supposed to move with the trend value of unit labor costs. The trend value has to be calculated so as to eliminate the ups and downs of productivity caused by fluctuations in output. In the U.S. the trend growth of productivity was about 2¾ percent per year from 1955 to 1966. During the 1970s it slowed to less than 1 percent.

A rough generalization about prices is to assert that the price level is proportional to unit labor costs so that $P=\frac{W}{OH}L$ where P is the private nonfarm deflator, W is compensation per hour, OH is the physical volume

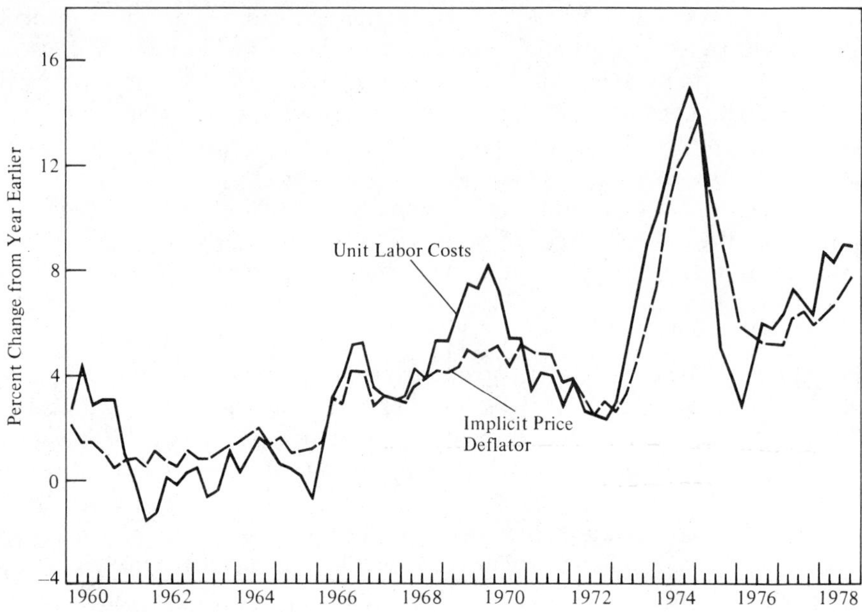

Figure 18.2 Unit Labor Costs and Deflator, Nonfarm Business

of output per hour, and L is a "markup" factor. Since percentage changes can be added if they are small, the average percentage change in price level equals the percentage change in wage, plus the percentage change in markup, less the percentage change in productivity. If we neglect the small changes in markup we can drop the last item so that changes in prices are related to changes in wages and the slowly changing productivity growth rate. In the short run the rate of change of wages will be the active cause of price change.

The consumer price index is more relevant than the nonfarm GNP deflator for some purposes. It is affected by farm prices and import prices.

Wage Determination

As in other markets, the price of labor services is essentially a matter of supply and demand. We expect to find money wages rising relatively rapidly when demand for labor is high in relation to supply—that is, when unemployment is low and vacancies high. And we expect to find money wages rising slowly or even falling a little when demand for labor is low in relation to supply with unemployment high and vacancies low. Of course, that is only a crude generalization. With any given level of overall unemployment, demand for some particular types of labor will be strong relative to supply while other markets are in the reverse condition. Moreover, experience shows that some trade unions can get wage increases even in the face of heavy unemployment in their own occupation. Nonetheless, the record does show that, other things equal, wages increase faster when unemployment is low than when it is high. As we shall see, however, the other-things-equal clause covers a multitude of complexities.

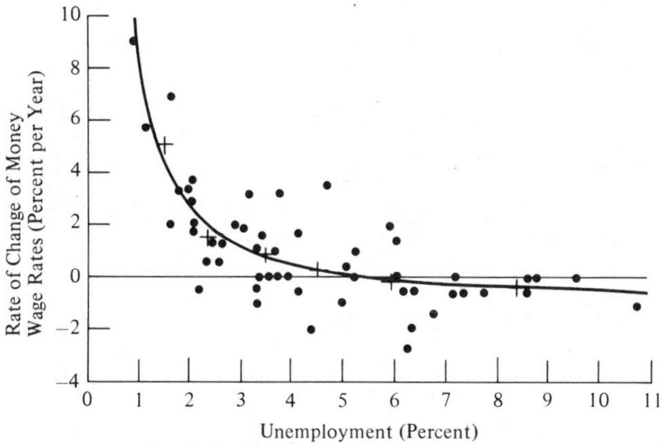

Figure 18.3 The Original "Phillips Curve"
1861–1913

Source: A. W. Phillips, "The Relationship between Unemployment and the Rate of Change of Money Wages in the United Kingdom, 1861–1957," *Economica* 25 (November 1958): 285.

The Phillips Curve

The empirical relationship between wage changes and the level of unemployment was reviewed by A. W. Phillips in 1958 using wage and unemployment data for the United Kingdom over a long period. He summarized his conclusion that wage changes are influenced by the level (not the change in level) of unemployment in Figure 18.3. A relationship of that type with percentage wage changes on the vertical axis and the unemployment level on the horizontal has since been called a Phillips curve.

Figure 18.4 shows the relation between wage changes and unemployment in the U.S. for the period 1913–59. Though the relationship is far less clear than in the British case, American economists began to use the Phillips curve as a basic tool in the analysis of inflation.

From Wage Phillips Curve to Price Phillips Curve

We can turn the relationship of Figure 18.4 into one linking unemployment with price changes by using the wage-price-productivity relationship. Earlier we argued that roughly speaking the percentage change in prices equaled the difference between the percentage change in wage rates and the percentage change in productivity. The annual percentage change in prices is the percent change in money wages minus the annual percentage increase in output per hour. We can derive a price Phillips curve from the wage Phillips curve by just shifting the origin up by the annual growth in output per hour.

In Figure 18.5 the left-hand panel is a wage Phillips curve and the right-hand panel is a price Phillips curve drawn on the assumption that the annual increase in productivity is 3 percent. The price Phillips curve is exactly the same as the wage curve except that the vertical axis represents annual per-

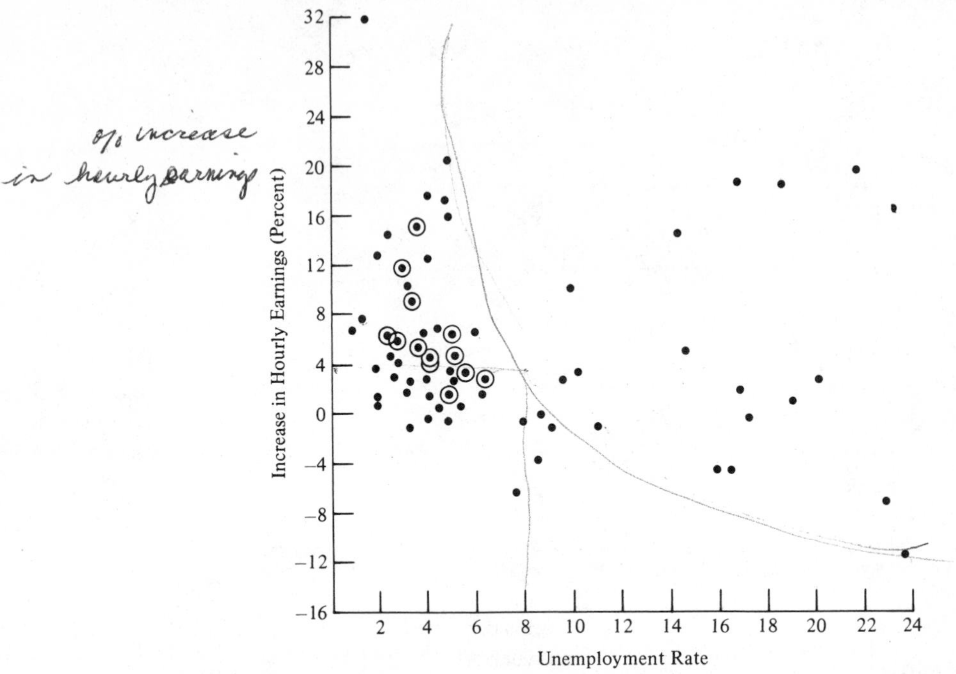

Figure 18.4 Phillips Scatter Diagram for U.S. *1913–59*

(The circled points are for recent years.)

Source: Paul A. Samuelson and Robert Solow, "Analytic Aspects of Anti-Inflation Policy," *American Economic Review* 50 (May 1960): 188.

centage increases in prices and the origin is moved up 3 percent. A horizontal line across the wage Phillips curve was drawn at a height of 3 percent.

At point *A* where the wage Phillips curve crosses the 3 percent line, wages are rising 3 percent per year, but since productivity is also rising 3

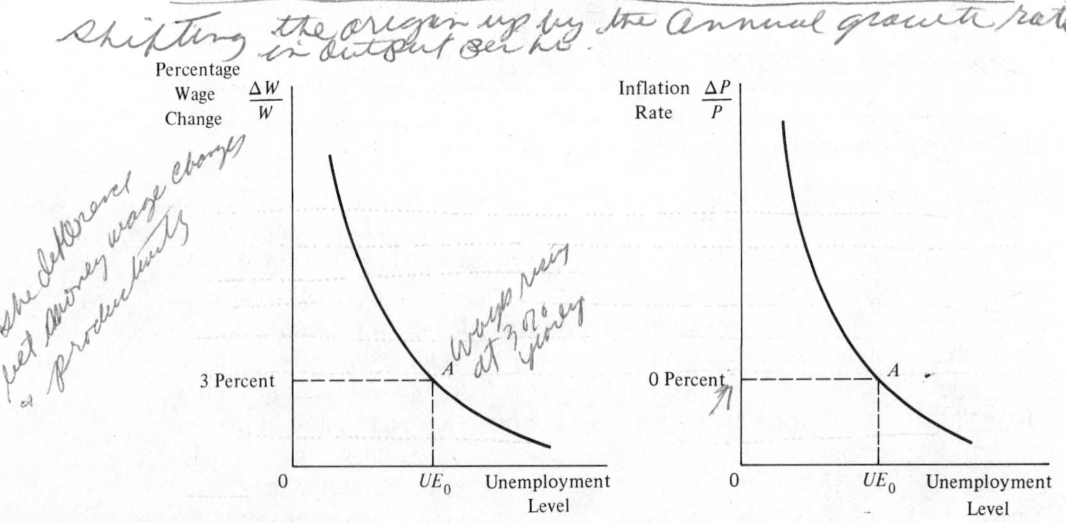

Figure 18.5 Wage and Price Phillips Curve

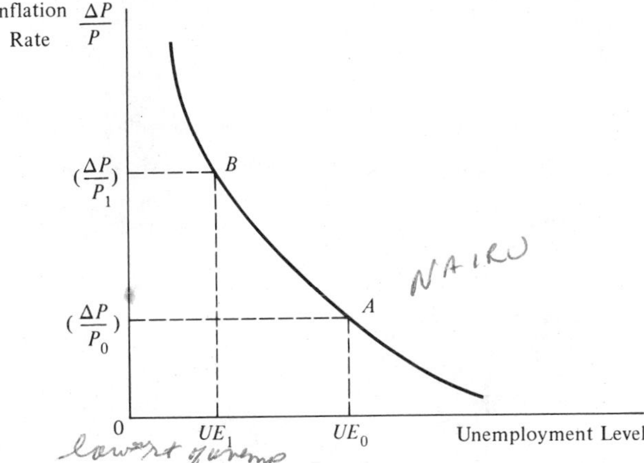

Figure 18.6 Shifts in the Phillips Curve

percent per year, prices are stable; so *A* is on the origin (zero price increase level) of the price Phillips curve. To the right of *A*, wages are still rising but prices are falling. To the left of *A* prices are rising 3 percent less than the rate of wage increase.

Acceptance of the Phillips curve approach led to the notion that public policymakers (and the public they serve) had a choice or "trade off" between a high rate of unemployment with a low rate of inflation—for example, point *A* on Figure 18.6—or a low rate of unemployment and a high rate of inflation—for example, point *B* on Figure 18.6. This gave opportunity for lots of philosophical discussion of the relative social cost of inflation and unemployment. Those issues are still alive but in a much more complicated form than in the Phillips curve discussion of twenty years ago.

Real Wages versus Money Wages

Experience in the late sixties showed that there was something fundamentally wrong with the simple Phillips curve approach. After 1966 the inflation rate increased, even when the level of unemployment showed little change or actually rose. Figure 18.7 shows the apparent shift in the Phillips curve of the U.S. since 1965.

The problem seemed to lie in the implicit assumption that the Phillips curve is invariant to the history of prices. Empirical studies of the process of wage change showed that the rate of increase in money wages in any one period is influenced by the past history of wage and price changes. They showed that after several years of inflation, the Phillips curve defined in nominal terms had shifted up. The rate of wage increase associated with a given level of unemployment was higher than before. Moreover, it appeared that a further rise in the rate of inflation resulted in another upward shift in the Phillips curve.

Employers are willing to raise money wages to improve or maintain their wage scale relative to the scale of wages offered by their competitors.

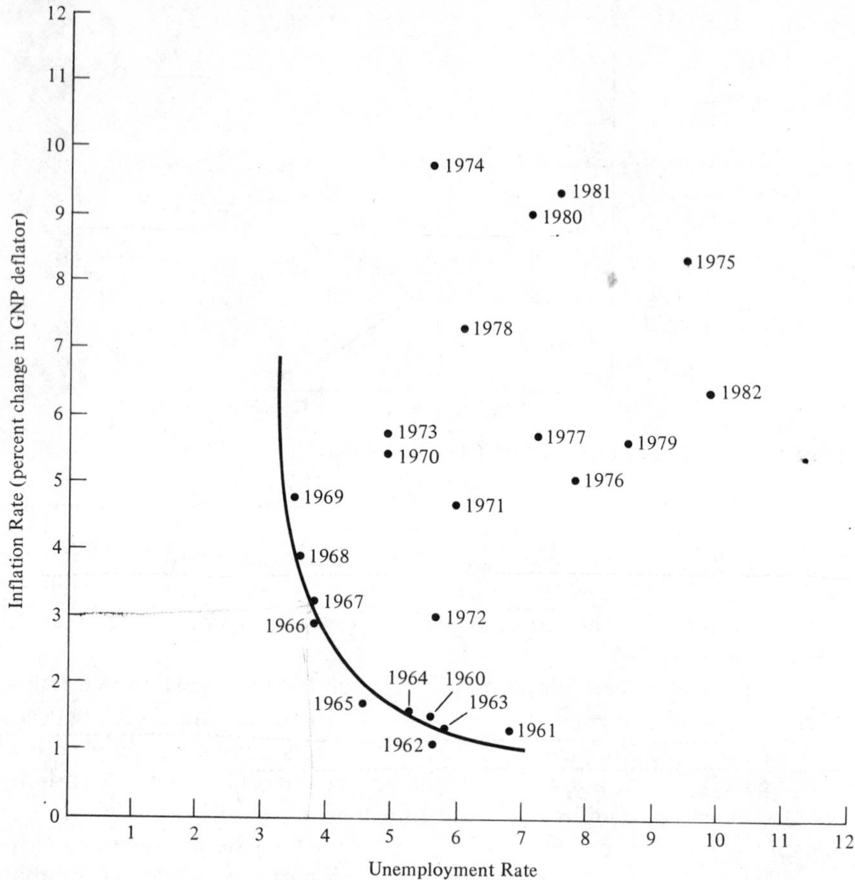

Figure 18.7 The U.S. Phillips Curve *1960–82*

They want to be able to recruit and retain workers with a certain level of skill and experience. Obviously, an employer's willingness to raise wages depends on the tightness of the labor market, but it also depends on what has happened and what is expected to happen to other wages and prices. An employer will be more willing to push up wages if his competitor's prices have risen recently, or if he expects that they will rise. He will also have more recruiting problems if other firms have recently raised wages, or if he expects them to do so.

Trade unions, of course, want protection against expected price increases. They try to bargain for a wage increase large enough to cover expected price increases or for an "escalator" clause providing for automatic wage increases when prices rise. Trade-union leaders are often under pressure to keep up with gains of other unions in the same area or industry. Thus we expect that at any given level of unemployment, wages will tend to rise more rapidly if (1) wages have risen rapidly in the past, (2) wages are expected to rise rapidly in the future, (3) prices have risen rapidly in the past, or (4) they are expected to rise rapidly in the future. Notice that in both the wage-wage interaction and the price-wage interaction, firms and workers may be backward looking—making catch-up adjustments to past changes; or forward looking—getting the jump on what they expect to happen to wages and prices. Some economists think that attempts to catch up with past wage and price movements are the most important part of the shifting Phillips curve. However, the most widely accepted view puts the emphasis on expectations of future inflation. Today's average wage change consists of two parts: the money-wage change that would result if no one expected the price level to rise, and the additional amount that would compensate for expected inflation.

Formation of Expectations

The rate of price increase that employers and workers expect can be influenced by many factors. The dominant factor, however, seems to be the actual price increases that they have experienced in the past. People do not just expect this month's inflation rate to persist but they do seem to act as though they expect the next year's inflation rate to be about the same as the average rate over the past couple of years.

Price Expectations and Shifting Phillips Curve

One way to adjust for inflation expectations is to shift the Phillips curve with changes in inflation expectations. In Figure 18.8 the solid curve I shows a wage Phillips curve for a period when prices have been stable and no inflation is expected. At unemployment rate *A* both money and real wages are rising at 3 percent per year, just enough to balance 3 percent productivity when prices are stable. The dotted curve II is a Phillips curve drawn on the assumption that prices have been rising at 2 percent per year and are expected

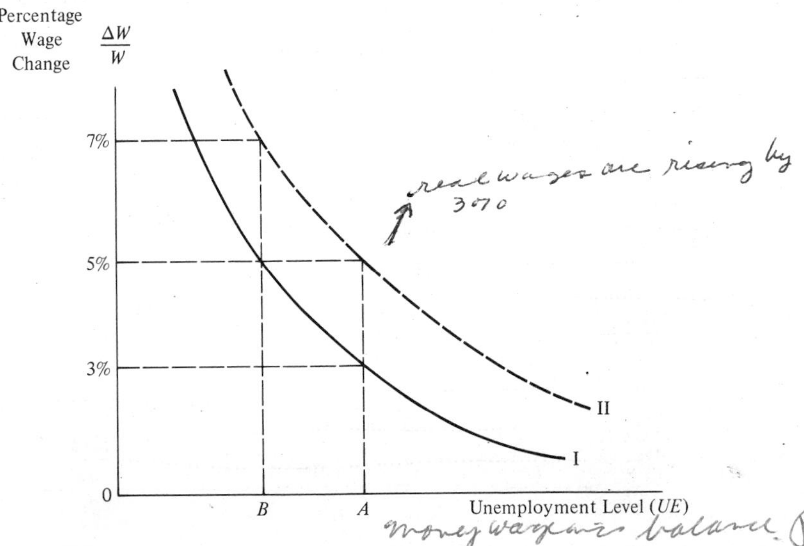

Figure 18.8 Changes in Inflation Expectations Shift the Phillips Curve

to continue doing so. The dotted curve is higher than the solid one by 2 percent at every level of unemployment. At unemployment rate *A* money wages are rising at 5 percent per year but *real* wages are rising at 3 percent just as on the solid curve.

The notion of a shifting Phillips curve together with the established link between wage and price changes leads to the conclusion that any attempt to maintain a level of unemployment sufficiently low to start an inflation will lead to an indefinite increase in the rate of inflation. Suppose, for example, that starting from a period of price stability, with an initial Phillips curve like I, it is decided to expand demand and push the unemployment rate down to *B*. That produces a 5 percent rate of wage increase and a 2 percent inflation rate. But as everyone gets used to the 2 percent inflation rate the Phillips curve shifts up to II, wages rise at 7 percent, and inflation accelerates to 4 percent. After a while the higher rate of inflation will push the Phillips curve up and the rate of inflation will rise again. The sequence will repeat until unemployment rises again.

Moreover, raising the unemployment rate back to *A* will not stop the inflation. It will only stop it from rising. The inflation will continue indefinitely at whatever rate was built into people's expectations before the shift back to *A*.

Consider the effect of a rise in unemployment to *A* after the hypothetical events just outlined. Suppose that the last rise in the inflation rate from 2 percent to 4 percent is still regarded as temporary. Curve II based on expectations of 2 percent inflation is still relevant. When unemployment returns to *A*, the rate of wage increase will decline to 5 percent, and prices will rise at 2 percent per year. Expectations of 2 percent inflation will be confirmed by events. The inflation rate will continue at 2 percent as long as unemployment remains at *A*.

Notice that the unemployment rate *A* is the only one at which that can be true. At any unemployment rate below *A*, it will turn out that the actual rate of inflation exceeds the expected rate. Expectations will be adjusted upward, causing a further rise in the inflation rate. The reverse will be true for unemployment rates above *A*.

The unemployment rate *A* is a neutral one—where money-wage increases just balance productivity increases—but at that point the real wage increases permitted by productivity increases can be realized with any rate of inflation and money-wage increases that exceed the inflation rate by just the amount of productivity increase.

To reduce the inflation rate in the example it would be necessary to maintain a rate of unemployment higher than *A*. That would shift the Phillips curve down and slow the inflation. Ultimately unemployment could go back to the stable level *A*.

Milton Friedman called the unemployment rate corresponding to *A* "the natural rate of unemployment." Others who feel that high rates of unemployment are neither natural nor desirable have used the more neutral but more cumbersome term *nonaccelerating inflation rate of unemployment* or NAIRU.

The conclusion—contrary to the earlier Phillips curve trade-off view—

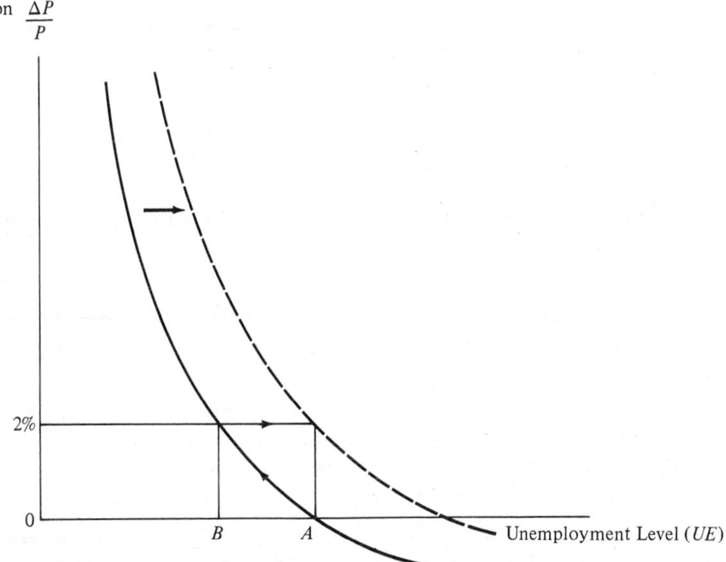

Figure 18.9 Changes in Unemployment and a Shifting Phillips Curve

is that no steady rate of inflation is possible if unemployment is below NAIRU. If prices have been stable in the past and the unemployment rate is held at A on Figure 18.9 where the rate of price change is zero, then price stability will continue. If the unemployment rate is now pushed down to B, prices will start to rise—an initial trade-off of some price rise for a reduction in unemployment. However, if unemployment remains at B, the rate of inflation will rise again the next year, and again the year after. The trade-off for the reduction of unemployment from A to B is not a once-and-for-all rise in inflation rate from zero to 1 percent, but an indefinite succession of increases in the inflation rate until the level of unemployment is increased once more.

The dynamic Phillips curves shown in Figure 18.9 are oversimplified in two respects. First, they neglect lags. In fact, considerable time is likely to elapse after a change in the rate of inflation before the adjustment of expectations about future inflation is completed. Moreover, the initial expectational response may vary with people's views about the causes of inflation and their perception of the probable response of monetary and fiscal policy. Their response to a one-time rise in energy or food prices may differ from their response to an inflation generated by a change in monetary and fiscal policy that is expected to persist.

Second, the models underlying the diagrams assume a literal one-for-one-response of the Phillips curve to increases in the rate of inflation. A 2 percent increase in the rate of inflation shifts the whole Phillips curve by *exactly* 2 percent. The reality is almost surely more complicated. The shift in the Phillips curve in response to inflation *may* be greater in the low unemployment range than in the high unemployment range. Moreover, the response *may* be different when the initial inflation is generated by tight labor markets than when it is generated by oil and food prices or changes in productivity.

That *may* be so because wage changes reflect the product market as well as labor-market conditions.

SHIFTS IN AGGREGATE DEMAND

So far in this chapter, we have emphasized supply problems and the reaction of prices to changes in demand and to the past history of price changes. In our discussion of the dynamics of aggregate supply and the Phillips curves, we simply assumed that demand is being manipulated to maintain some level of real GNP and unemployment. Now we have to return to the demand side of the picture to reexamine how the levels of real GNP and unemployment are affected by changes in prices.

We have already given the central message. In equilibrium terms a rightward shift in the aggregate-demand curve (starting from full equilibrium) first causes output to rise above potential. Prices then begin to rise and must continue to do so until movement along the aggregate-demand curve reduces output to its old level. With any fixed aggregate-demand curve, a rise in prices reduces the amount of goods and services demanded by reducing the real value of the nominal magnitudes underlying the aggregate-demand curve. A one-time shift in the aggregate-demand curve leads to a one-time rise in the price level. It will not produce a continuing inflation without a continuing rightward shift in the aggregate-demand curve. However, the adjustment process may not be a smooth one. In the next section we will examine the adjustment to a one-time rightward shift in aggregate demand in a little more detail.

A "One-Shot" Increase in Demand

A boom period with the aggregate-demand curve shifting rapidly to the right and outrunning the trend increase in potential output is a fairly common occurrence. Booms in private investment or in consumer durables often occur. Changes in fiscal policy, involving a rapid increase in government expenditures or a sharp reduction in tax rates, can readily occur. Shifts in the rate of growth of money supply can start or support a rapid increase in aggregate demand. Periods of rapid expansion, lasting for a couple of years, are not uncommon, and if at the start the economy is near its potential output, prices will rise for a time, but such events need not lead to continuing inflation. In fact they are unlikely to do so if there is no further increase in nominal government expenditures and nominal money supply after the initial demand shift.

If the economy is initially in equilibrium at UE^*, increased demand will first lead to increased output and reduced unemployment, but prices will also start to rise. In equilibrium, the level of output must be one at which prices do not tend to rise. That by hypothesis is the output corresponding to UE^*. The equilibrium price level must rise enough to crowd out enough expenditures to bring output back to potential. The crowding-out process has three elements: (1) higher prices mean lower real money supply and higher interest rates, thereby reducing investment and consumption (because higher interest rates reduce wealth); (2) higher prices reduce real money balances and thereby reduce consumption; (3) higher prices also reduce the real value of other nominal magnitudes—government debt, tax exemptions, and government expenditure.

Dynamic adjustment. We can assert that the economy will not be in equilibrium until the price level has risen to its new equilibrium position and output is back to normal, but it does not follow that the adjustment will be a smooth one. If the rise in expenditure takes place very gradually, the adjustment might be smooth, but if there is a rapid increase in expenditure, the adjustment process may be rather bumpy. Three types of dynamic considerations have to be taken into account: those arising from expectations of rising prices; those arising from changes in the rate of growth of income; and credit-crunch problems.

Expectations. If prices rise for a while before monetary restraint takes hold, people may begin to project continued price increase. That will, of course, speed up the price rise. It will also imply that the expected real rate of interest rises less than the nominal rate. Indeed, the expected real rate may fall before it begins to rise again. This will stimulate demand and add to inflationary pressure.

Rate of change responses. The adjustment process implies some significant changes in the rate of growth of output. The initial impact of the increase in expenditures will accelerate the growth of output. Inflationary expectations may cause a further acceleration. If a higher rate of growth continues, it will tend to produce an acceleration-principle response in plant and equipment and inventory investment and in consumer durables purchases, pushing total demand up even further. Ultimately, however, rising prices working against a fixed money supply and other fixed nominal magnitudes will check the expansion. The rate of growth of output must fall in order to restore equilibrium. As it begins to do so, acceleration-principle effects may go in the reverse so that the boom ends in a recession instead of a smooth transition to the new equilibrium.

Credit crunch. The likelihood that the boom will end with a bang instead of a whimper is increased by the likelihood of a credit crunch. Monetary restraint in collision with expansionary fiscal policy (or any other nonmonetary source of expansion) is likely to produce sharply rising short-term interest rates. The result may be mortgage-market problems of the type described in Chapter 6. There may also be bankruptcies or fears of bankruptcy for firms that have weak credit standing and heavy dependence on short-term financing.

The upshot is, first, that a rise in expenditures working against a fixed money supply will produce a rise in the equilibrium price level with the amount depending on the slopes of the *IS* and *LM* curves, and the importance of real money balance effects and the system's response to deflation of the real value of other fixed, nominal magnitudes. Second, it is quite likely that adjustment to the new equilibrium will cause some fluctuations in output.

Accommodating Inflation

In the case just outlined, the rise in prices was brought to a halt because rising prices deflated the value of real money supply, government expenditures, and other nominal magnitudes in the system. We assumed that nominal money supply did not grow (or did not grow any faster than potential output) while the government held fixed the dollar magnitudes in its budget in the face of rising prices.

Suppose, instead, that the government raises expenditures in pace with the rise in prices, so as to keep real expenditures intact. At the same time, suppose that the central bank allows the money supply to expand as fast as prices. (You may suppose that they do not want to be blamed for a credit crunch.) Then the automatic braking effect of the rise in prices is eliminated. The aggregate-demand curve keeps shifting upward; output is maintained at a level above potential output, and prices continue to rise.

In fact they not only continue to rise, they tend to rise faster and faster. The initial shift in aggregate demand produces a reduction in unemployment and leftward movement along the Phillips curve continues until prices rise at, say, 2 percent per year. But after a time, everyone gets used to inflationary conditions and the Phillips curve shifts upward by 2 percent. That causes a further increase in the rate of inflation.

If budget expenditures and money supply are adjusted upward to keep pace with the higher rate of inflation, unemployment will remain low, the Phillips curve will continue to shift upward, and the rate of inflation will continue to increase.

Sooner or later, of course, someone will call a halt. When the rate of inflation gets high enough, the public will support measures aimed at reducing the rate of inflation, or at least preventing any further increase in the rate of price increase.

Checking the upward spiral. Even the less ambitious objective of leveling off the inflation will not be easy. To prevent further acceleration in the rate of price increase, it will be necessary to do what should have been done in the first place. The rate of unemployment has to be raised to the NAIRU. The real money supply and the real value of government expenditure must be reduced enough to bring real GNP back to the potential output level. That will not be any easier than in the one-shot inflation case. The same credit-crunch problems and the same uneven adjustment to a change in the rate of growth of demand are likely to occur. The result is likely to be a recession with output falling below potential output.

An Equilibrium Inflation

In principle, at least, one can visualize an economy operating with an equilibrium rate of inflation. The level of real GNP would grow with potential output, the unemployment rate would be constant at NAIRU, and wages and prices would rise at a constant rate. To maintain the equilibrium, underlying factors, such as capital stock in relation to expected real output, would have to be constant. At the same time all of the nominal magnitudes in the system would grow steadily at a rate of growth equal to the rate of growth of potential output plus the rate of increase of prices. Maintenance of such a complete equilibrium over any long period is implausible. After all, there are hundreds of nominal magnitudes in the system: Government debt is not likely to maintain a fixed relationship to income, since the outstanding amount at any time is an inheritance from the past, unrelated to current demand conditions. Nonetheless, it is possible for an economy to maintain a fairly steady rate of inflation with expectations and the approximate growth rate of money supply and government expenditures adjusted to a continuing steady rate of inflation.

Notice that under these conditions, the inflation continues with no appearance of demand pressure. Real GNP equals potential output, unemployment is at the NAIRU. In contrast with the conditions ruling when the inflation rate is accelerating, the rise in prices cannot be attributed to high capacity utilization or labor shortages. The economy is just as much in balance as it would be with stable prices. Moreover, because prices and wages do not quickly respond to short-run fluctuations in demand, the inflation appears to be unconnected with demand movements, and it seems to continue inexorably.

Getting rid of inherited inflation. Once a situation approximating an equilibrium inflation has been established, it may be difficult to reach a new equilibrium with a substantially lower inflation rate. Experience strongly suggests that a brief, mild recession will not do the trick. In fact, experience and the logic of the Phillips curve argument indicate that to get a well-established rate of inflation down significantly, it will be necessary for unemployment to remain well above the NAIRU for several years.

To start the deceleration process, it would be necessary to break the equilibrium by holding down the growth of government expenditure and money supply in nominal terms and to let their real growth rates decline. The result would be to reduce real GNP and raise the unemployment rate. As usual the adjustment would not be a smooth one. It could not be accomplished without a sharp decline in output, a rise in unemployment followed by a partial recovery. That recession episode would reduce the rate of inflation but would not eliminate it. To make further progress, it would be necessary to manage monetary and fiscal policy to avoid a full recovery and keep unemployment above NAIRU. One would then hope to see a reversal of the accelerating price increase sequence, described earlier. The initial recession should first produce a reduction in the rate of inflation. That reduction should, after some lag, cause a downward shift in the Phillips curve, a further reduction in the inflation rate, and so on.

It appears, however, that the road back to price stability can be a long and bumpy one. Our experience shows that several years of high unemployment could be required for a return to full price stability, unless expectations can be changed drastically. We will discuss our experience with high unemployment and disinflation at the end of the chapter. First, however, we must take account of some other factors affecting wage and price determination.

STRUCTURAL CHANGES IN THE WAGE PHILLIPS CURVE

The Phillips curve summarizes the response of the average wage rate to changes in the balance of supply and demand for labor in the many overlapping submarkets in which wages are established. A great variety of factors can influence the position and shape of the curve. Many of those changes cancel each other out but significant and persistent changes do occur from time to time. Two such changes are noted in the following sections.

Trade Unions

Legislative changes adopted in the 1930s greatly increased the strength of trade unions in the years just before the Second World War. Many economists believe that the increased strength of trade unions is one cause of the persistence of inflation since the Second World War. Others have argued that trade unions may be able to raise their relative wages once but cannot account for continuing inflation.

Empirical studies indicate that trade union wages tend to be less sensitive to changes in unemployment, rising more in slack periods and less in booms than those of unorganized workers.

Trade union wages seem to be more sensitive to price changes than others. On balance trade union wages and fringe benefits have risen substantially faster than others over the whole postwar period. Those gains may be eroded in the future. Nonetheless, it seems likely that trade union action has raised the money wages of union members (and probably of others as well) at any given level of employment.

The Effects of Stabilization Policy

At the end of the war, memories of the Great Depression of the 1930s were still vivid. The aggressive use of fiscal policy to maintain high employment, and especially to avoid a recurrence of major depressions, became the accepted basis of economic policy in all the industrial countries. By comparison with earlier times, that policy has been relatively successful. There have been no deep depressions, and recessions have been relatively brief and mild. Unfortunately, there are grounds for believing that the partial success of full-employment policy has made inflation control more difficult.

Policies aimed at maintaining full employment have direct and indirect effects on price stability. A commitment to full employment leads to accommodation of any established rate of inflation.

In addition, however, a commitment to quick recovery from any recession weakens the effect of antiinflation measures when they are undertaken. In most markets, prices and wages are influenced by the expectations of buyers and sellers about future demand conditions as well as by the current state of demand. Firms faced with declining demand during a recession are under pressure to reduce prices and wages or at least to limit increases. The pressure is much less when they expect a quick recovery than it is when they fear worsening recession. The result is that successful pursuit of full employment may change the structure of the system so that a bigger dose of unemployment is required to achieve a given reduction in the rate of inflation.

SUPPLY SHIFTS I: UNEMPLOYMENT VACANCIES AND WAGE INCREASES

One of the puzzling aspects of the inflation problem is the upward trend in unemployment which accompanied the persistent inflation of the 1970s. That paradoxical pattern reflected changes in the composition of the labor force and in work incentives. Table 18.1 shows how those changes have shifted the relationship between unemployment and other measures of labor market tightness. Those other measures such as the new hire rate or the quit rate indicate how hard it is for employers to find and retain satisfactory workers. Recent research has shown that the help wanted index and quit rate give a better explanation of wage increases than the Phillips curve. Thus a part of the explanation for the rise in both unemployment and inflation lies in the change in labor market structure implied by the rise in unemployment relative to other measures of labor market tightness.

Table 18.1 Selected Measures of Labor Market Tightness, 1950–80

Year of period and descriptive statistic	Unemployment rate (percent)	Perry unemployment rate (percent)[a]	Help-wanted index[b]	Layoff rate[c]	Quit rate[c]	New hire rate[c]
Year or period						
1950–54	4.0	3.3	112.8	1.3	2.4	3.5
1955–59	5.0	4.2	72.1	2.0	1.6	2.4
1960–64	5.7	4.6	69.1	2.0	1.4	2.4
1965–69	3.8	2.6	112.8	1.3	2.4	3.5
1970	5.0	3.6	94.6	1.8	2.1	2.8
1971	5.9	4.4	82.7	1.6	1.8	2.6
1972	5.6	4.0	100.0	1.1	2.3	3.4
1973	4.9	3.3	119.6	0.9	2.8	3.9
1974	5.6	3.9	101.9	1.5	2.4	3.1
1975	8.5	6.5	73.0	2.1	1.4	2.0
1976	7.7	5.8	84.7	1.3	1.7	2.6
1977	7.0	5.2	102.2	1.2	1.9	2.9
1978	6.0	4.3	125.3	0.9	2.1	3.1
1979	5.8	4.2	128.9	1.1	2.0	3.0
1980	7.1	5.7	103.6	1.8	1.5	2.2

a. George Perry's weighted unemployment rate as described in "Changing Labor Markets and Inflation," *Brookings Papers on Economic Activity,* 3:1970, pp. 411–41.

b. Help-wanted advertising in newspapers divided by the civilian labor force, indexed to 1972 equals 100.

c. All manufacturing, per 100 employees per month.

d. Numbers in parentheses are *t*-statistics.

Sources: U.S. Department of Labor, Bureau of Labor Statistics, establishment and household data in *Employment Situation* and *Employment and Earnings;* BLS Bulletin 1312; and U.S. Department of Commerce, Bureaus of the Census and of Economic Analysis, *Business Conditions Digest,* series 3 and 46.

There remains the question of the underlying cause of the change just noted.

Part of the change can be explained by the increase in the proportion of young workers in the labor force. The proportion of workers under 25 in the labor force increased markedly from the early 60s until the late 70s. Because young workers enter and leave the labor force more often than older ones the increase in their numbers has increased the amount of "frictional" or "job search" unemployment relative to the number of vacancies. Moreover many of these workers with few specific skills, little work experience, and a high turnover rate, have not been attractive to employers seeking adult workers. Thus in periods of expansion employers have pushed up wages in competition for experienced workers even though there were plenty of unemployed younger workers.

Some economists argue that the minimum wage law has prevented the fall in relative wages which would in theory make it possible to employ a greater proportion of young and inexperienced workers. But we do not know how much wages would have to drop to cause the required adjustment. Nor do we know how many young workers would lose interest in jobs if wages fell.

In any case, youth unemployment is only part of the problem. The unemployment rate for men between 25 and 54—prime age males—has risen relative to the help wanted index and quit rate.

Here too, free market fans argue that expanded coverage and favorable tax treatment of unemployment compensation have made being unemployed more attractive compared to working. Others argue that the explanation is more complex. Highly paid workers in such industries as steel and automobiles are unemployed while employers in such "high tech" industries as computers lament the shortage of trained workers.

Some economists argue that those problems reflect the need to adapt to new technology and new patterns of international trade. They emphasize the need for extensive retraining of the work force; others argue that the rapid rise in relative wages in highly unionized industries is responsible. In any case, the problems of unemployment and inflation are labor market problems as well as demand management problems.

SUPPLY SHIFTS: II

In the last few sections we have been concerned with shifts in the wage Phillips curve. Those shifts are of course reflected in the price Phillips curve. However, the price curve may be influenced directly by factors affecting the relation between wages and prices. The most important of those factors is the trend of productivity growth.

The productivity slowdown. Since 1973 the rate of growth of productivity has shown a marked decline. Output per hour has risen less than 1 percent per year. (See Table 18.2.) Some of the decline can be explained by such factors as the expenditure of resources on pollution abatement and safety. A decline in the rate of capital formation has also played a role. Economists studying productivity have noted a number of other factors accounting for

Table 18.2 Labor Productivity Growth
1948–82 (Percent change per year)

Sector	1948 to 1955	1955 to 1965	1965 to 1973	1973 to 1978	1978 to 1982[a]
Private business sector	2.5	2.4	1.6	0.8	+0.1
Nonfarm	2.4	2.5	1.6	.9	−0.1
Manufacturing	3.2	2.8	2.4	1.5	(b)
Nonmanufacturing	2.1	2.2	1.2	.5	(b)

a. Preliminary.
b. Not available.
Note: Data relate to output per hour for all employees.
Source: *Annual Report of the Council of Economic Advisers,* February 1980, p. 85, and February 1983, p. 208.

minor parts of the decline. However, much of the decline remains unexplained. Whatever the explanation, the productivity slowdown makes the containment of inflation more difficult. For a given wage Phillips curve the price Phillips curve will be 2 percent higher at every level of unemployment with productivity growth at 1 percent per year instead of 3 percent per year.

Of course, the wage Phillips curve is not entirely independent of the growth of productivity, since employers are concerned about the effect of using unit labor costs on profits and market position. Nonetheless, the productivity slowdown is a significant factor in the explanation of recent inflation.

SUPPLY SHIFTS: III

"Cost-Push" Factors in Inflation

In addition, several different types of supply or cost factors have influenced the course of inflation. First, rapid changes in raw materials, food, and fuel prices, partly generated by changes in demand, but partly due to events on the supply side, had a significant influence on price movements. Second, a variety of actions by government tended to increase the rate of inflation.

RAW MATERIALS, FOOD, AND FUEL

The prices of food and raw materials are usually more volatile than those of manufactured goods or of services. Demand for them is inelastic and so is supply. Consequently cyclical variations in demand are likely to cause disproportionate changes in price. Shifts in supply curves due to weather conditions, strikes, revolutions, and long cycles in development of mineral resources may offset or reinforce the cyclical movements of demand. In the long run we may expect most of those factors as well as the influence of demand cycles to cancel out. However, a decade is not the long run and price movements in the 70s were significantly influenced by large increases in oil prices in 1973 and 1979, and by large price increases for food in 1973. Reductions in food and fuel prices helped to slow inflation in the early 80s.

Cost Push from Government

The list of cost-push factors must include a number of items attributable to government actions. These include the cost of pollution abatement and safety requirements, and increases in employer contributions for social security (which are often passed forward into prices). The rapid rise in medical costs is due in considerable measure to the reimbursement practices of the Medicare and Medicaid systems.

SUPPLY AND DEMAND INTERACTIONS

The combined effect of the factors discussed in the last few sections may seem more than sufficient to explain the simultaneous rise in unemployment and prices. All the developments outlined in the last few sections can be described in terms of their influence on wage and price Phillips curves.

Changes in the demographic composition of the work force or changes in incentives to work have shifted the wage Phillips curve to the right.

The price curve was shifted up directly by a decline in the rate of productivity growth. Increases in oil prices caused "one shot" but large changes in prices.

An upward shift in the Phillips curve working against a fixed aggregate demand curve will cause prices to rise but will also cause employment and output to fall. If, however, aggregate demand is increased to prevent a fall in employment, prices and wages will rise again. The pattern outlined under "accommodating inflation" will apply and a wage-price spiral will continue until the policy of accommodation is abandoned.

Thus expansion of aggregate demand plays a dual role in starting or continuing inflations. In some cases a rapid expansion of demand may start an inflation. In other cases prices may be driven up from the supply side while fiscal and monetary policy are adjusted to accommodate the rise in prices and avoid a rise in unemployment.

INFLATION: 1970s

The legacy of the 1960s was an inflation rate of 4½ percent and an unemployment rate of 3½ percent in 1969. The brief recession of 1970 checked a further buildup of inflationary expectations but did not reduce the rate of inflation. A decade later, at the beginning of 1980, the inflation rate (again measured by the GNP deflator) was 11 percent while the unemployment rate was 6 percent. Three years later the figures were nearly reversed. Unemployment hovered around 10 percent while the inflation rate was about 5 percent.

The inflation of the late 1960s can be explained by the demand expansion which was generated by the 1964 tax cut, expenditures on Great Society programs, and on the Vietnam War.

The inflation of the 1970s involved a far more complex interaction of supply and demand. On the supply side the decade was marked by the slowdown of productivity growth especially after 1973, adverse changes in labor markets, and oil and food shocks.

Stabilization of inflation at the 1970 level by demand control alone would have required:

1. a gradual rise in unemployment to offset changes in labor market conditions;
2. a further rise to offset the effect of the productivity slowdown;
3. enough recession to offset the oil and food shocks of 1973 and a further one to offset the 1979 shock.

Still more restraint would have been required to eliminate the inflation inherited from the 1960s.

Actual policy reflected the compromise between desire to restrain inflation and to maintain "full employment" which has governed policy ever since World War II.

Unemployment averaged 54 percent in the first half of the 1970s and 7 percent in the second half. That was enough to offset some, but evidently not all, of the supply side pressures noted above. The inflation rate stood at 8 percent in early 1979 before the oil price increase.

Thus fiscal and monetary policy were restrictive enough to permit a very significant rise in unemployment but not firm enough to prevent a rise in the inflation rate let alone pushing the 1970 rate back down to zero. The 1979 oil price increase caused a new surge of price increases which brought inflation back into the double digit range. As the inflation speeded up controversy intensified. While some people argued for new forms of price control, monetarists pressed the case for steady growth of monetary aggregates. They emphasized the link between expected money supply growth and price expectations and maintained that the cost of inflation could be greatly reduced if the Fed would adopt a consistent predictable money supply policy. They argue first that the equilibrium rate of inflation is determined by the rate of growth of the money supply. Moreover, they believe everyone knows that. Accordingly, if people are rational, they will form their expectations about future inflation by observing what is happening to the rate of growth of the money supply.

They argue that if the Federal Reserve were to make a firm commitment to the maintenance of a limited rate of growth of the money supply at, say, a rate of 4 percent, or to a gradual decrease in the rate of growth of the money supply, the public's expectational response would make it possible to bring down the rate of inflation without a long period of high unemployment. They argue that everyone would know that the Fed's commitment to limited monetary growth would ultimately bring the inflation to an end. The only uncertainty would be about the rate at which inflation would decelerate. Moreover, everyone would believe that if the rate of inflation did not decelerate rapidly, there would be a recession. Workers would tend to moderate their wage demands and employers would tend to resist demands for wage increases more strongly. There would, therefore, be some immediate deceleration in the rate of inflation. A little success on the inflation front would confirm the expectations of those involved in determining wages and prices and lead to further deceleration in the rate of inflation. Ultimately, the policy would work, and it would work much faster and with much less cost in terms of unemployment than one would expect from the use of the extended Phillips curve model.

Keynesians are generally skeptical of this scenario, though at least some of them recognize that expectations about monetary growth could make a significant contribution to the control of inflation. However, because they tend to give less weight to the objective, nonexpectational force of monetary factors, many Keynesians doubt the strength of the public's response. Moreover, they feel that as a practical matter the monetarists' proposal amounts to asking the Federal Reserve to play a game of chicken. The Federal Reserve is supposed to announce a policy that will only work if the public believes that the Fed is prepared to maintain its schedule of monetary growth, even in the face of a severe recession. Some Keynesians argue that the monetarists' expectational proposal might work, if the Fed could really establish the credibility of its intentions, but they do not believe that that is possible in the present American political situation. In general, however, Keynesians regard proposals of the type under discussion as very risky and potentially costly, while monetarists are more sanguine about the probable outcome or more fearful of the ultimate consequences of continuing inflation.

THE GREAT MONEY SUPPLY EXPERIMENT

The severity of the problem induced the Fed to take drastic action. In November 1979 the Fed announced that it would adhere much more closely to its monetary aggregate targets and announced target rates of growth of money supply which implied a relatively slow growth of nominal GNP. Adherence to the targets implied either rising unemployment, lower inflation, or both.

During the next three years interest rates reached record highs, output stagnated, and unemployment rose to over 10 percent.

It took a while before the inflation rate responded but by 1983 severe unemployment aided by falling oil and food prices brought inflation down to less than 5 percent (as measured by the GNP deflator).

Everyone agreed that the experiment was a great demonstration of the power of monetary policy but they didn't agree about much else. Keynesians claimed that things had worked just as they had predicted. It took a lot of unemployment to bring the inflation rate down and the job still was unfinished after four years. Monetarists said that the Fed had not really followed a monetarist prescription. Money growth rates moved erratically from 1979 to 1982 so that the Fed had never really established the credibility of its anti-inflation posture. It could no longer be said that the Fed was accommodating inflation, but in view of the erratic movement of money supply they were not following the monetarists' steady growth formula. Monetarists still argue that their formula for disinflation with few tears has not been given a proper trial. The issues raised by this experience are discussed in more detail in the following chapters.

SUMMARY

1. As a first approximation, prices rise when the aggregate-demand curve shifts to the right under the impact of a private sector boom, increasing government expenditure, increasing money supply, or any combination of those factors.
2. Initially, prices and output rise together following the short-run supply curve.
3. However, if the high level of demand persists, the supply curve will shift upward so that prices rise further and output falls back toward its equilibrium.
4. A continuing inflation will occur if money supply, government expenditure, and other nominal magnitudes are increased in pace with prices.
5. After a time, expectations of continuing inflation will cause further shifts in the supply curve.
6. Output cannot be maintained above the equilibrium level without a rising rate of inflation supported by progressively larger increases in money supply and government expenditures.
7. The wage Phillips curve summarizes the relation between the level of unemployment and the rate of change of wage.
8. The price Phillips curve translates wage increases into price increases on the assumption that prices rise in proportion to unit labor costs (increases in wages, adjusted for the trend growth of productivity).
9. Given the wage Phillips curve and the trend growth of productivity, there is some level of unemployment at which prices will remain stable.
10. Starting with an initial equilibrium, an increase in aggregate demand will first reduce unemployment, and cause wages to rise more than productivity so that prices rise.
11. If demand grows fast enough in nominal terms to maintain the new lower level of unemployment, prices will continue to rise.
12. Expectations of continuing inflation will shift the Phillips curve up and if aggregate demand is pushed up to maintain the low level of unemployment, price increases will accelerate.
13. It is possible to have a continuing equilibrium inflation. Note the difficulties of getting rid of an inherited inflation. Finally, we considered the possibility of a direct link between money growth and inflation expectations and reviewed the effects of inflation on interest rates.
14. It may take a long time to get rid of an inflation which has persisted for a long time.
15. The cost of eliminating inherited inflation may depend on expectations about the continuity of antiinflation policies.
16. Inflation has been a continuing problem since World War II. Periods of accelerating price increases have alternated with intervals of slower price rises, but there has been an upward trend in the rate of inflation.
17. The history of inflation reflects an interaction between demand factors and a variety of other factors that directly influence costs and prices or indirectly affect the response of wages and prices to changes in demand. The latter factors include changes in raw material, food supply, and energy prices as well as some cost-raising actions of the government.
18. The response of wages to changes in the level of demand and unemployment reflect some long-standing imperfections in the labor market. In addition, changes

in the composition of the labor force have increased the rate of unemployment consistent with price stability.

19. There is controversy over the role of trade unions, minimum wage policy, and unemployment compensation.

Questions and Exercises

1. Using aggregate-demand and supply curves, show how a rightward shift in aggregate demand will increase both prices and output.
2. If there is no further change in aggregate demand, will output remain at the new higher level?
3. List some of the events that can cause a shift in aggregate demand.
4. What actions by government would be required to maintain the level of output reached after the initial increase in demand?
5. Assume a given wage Phillips curve. How would the price Phillips curve be affected by a reduction in the rate of productivity growth?
6. "We can reduce unemployment if we are willing to tolerate a little more inflation." What evidence can be cited to support the quoted statement? Is the statement true? Why or why not?
7. A one-time increase in money supply or government expenditure can cause prices to rise for a time, but the rise in prices will in itself cause changes in output and employment that reduce the tendency for prices to rise. Explain.
8. "Inflation may continue in the face of high unemployment simply because everyone expects it to continue." Illustrate, using the shifting Phillips curve analysis.

Further Reading

FEDERAL RESERVE BANK OF BOSTON. *After the Phillips Curve*. Federal Reserve Bank of Boston Monetary Conference, 9 November 1978, Boston, Massachusetts. This volume contains a number of essays by leading economists on the most recent developments in inflation theory. The papers and discussions include a number of spirited debates between monetarists and Keynesians.

FRIEDMAN, MILTON. "The Role of Monetary Policy." *American Economic Review* 58 (March 1968). In this Presidential Address to the American Economic Association, Milton Friedman outlines his views on the theory of inflation and the effect of monetary policy on prices and economic activity.

———. "Nobel Lecture: Inflation and Unemployment." *Journal of Political Economy* 85 (May–June 1977): 451–72. In this paper Friedman restates his views in light of the experience of the decade since his Presidential Address.

GORDON, ROBERT J. "Recent Developments in the Theory of Inflation and Unemployment." *Journal of Monetary Economics* 2 (April 1976): 185–219. A well-organized summary and critique of competing theories of the inflationary process.

HUMPHREY, T. "Changing Views of the Phillips Curve." *Monthly Review* (Federal Reserve Bank of Richmond), July 1973. A very useful exposition of the development of the Phillips curve approach to wage determination. The student will find the graphical exposition particularly useful.

PHELPS, EDMUND S., et al., eds. *The Microeconomic Foundations of Employment and Inflation Theory*. New York: W. W. Norton, 1970. An interesting and influential study of the influence of inflationary expectations on the determination of wages and employment.

PHILLIPS, A. W. "The Relation between Unemployment and the Rate of Change of Money Wage Rates in the United Kingdom, 1861–1957." *Economica* 25 (November 1958): 283–99. The original "Phillips curve" study.

TOBIN, JAMES. "Inflation and Unemployment." *American Economic Review* 62 (March 1972). In this Presidential Address to the American Economic Association, Professor Tobin emphasizes the role of imperfect markets in explaining the simultaneous occurrence of inflation and unemployment.

Monetary Policy

PART FOUR

Having taken up monetary theory, we can now discuss monetary policy. With a small loss in accuracy we identify monetary policy with Federal Reserve policy, brushing aside the fact that the Treasury also has some very limited monetary policy powers. In the first chapter of this Part we therefore take up the Fed's goals, and in the following chapter we will look at the tools it has available to reach these goals. The subsequent chapter deals with how these tools operate in the money market, and the very controversial question of exactly how the Fed should use them. Chapter 22 then investigates how monetary policy affects aggregate demand. Chapter 23 then asks whether monetary policy can be used successfully to stabilize the economy, or whether it generates further instability. In Chapter 24 we illustrate by specific historical examples some of the previously discussed points. The concluding chapter of this part then brings much of the material together by asking whether, given all the problems it has, countercyclical monetary policy is really desirable.

One warning. Part Four relates entirely to the United States. In other countries monetary policy is very different both in its goals and techniques. In the less-developed countries the big issue in monetary policy is the extent to which the central banks should finance development projects by creating money, and what should be done about the resulting inflation. But even in other developed countries the relative emphasis on various goals of monetary policy differs.

Moreover, institutional differences provide countries with very different milieus for monetary policies. For example, in most countries, the government securities market is not large enough to allow the use of government securities in large open-market operations. Thus, in Switzerland, the central bank has to conduct its open-market operations by buying or selling foreign currencies. And, much more significantly, most countries are more open to foreign trade than the United States and have to take foreign exchange rates and the balance of payments much more into account than the United States does. In addition, differences in the structure of the government influence the way monetary policy is used. Thus, in the United States monetary policy is frequently treated as a more flexible tool than fiscal policy because often—though by no means always—it takes a long time for Congress to change fiscal policy. In countries with a parliamentary system this can be done much more rapidly.

The Goals of Monetary Policy

19

Monetary policy shares the goals of general macroeconomic policy: high employment, price stability, exchange-rate stability, and a high rate of economic growth. But although monetary policy therefore has the same overall goals as fiscal policy it also has some specialized goals. These are interest-rate stability, an acceptable distribution of the burdens of restrictive monetary policy, and the prevention of large-scale bank failures and financial panics.

THE GOALS

We will first discuss these goals individually, and then take up the question of whether they are consistent in the sense that it is possible to meet all of them at the same time, or whether we have to sacrifice one to obtain another.

High Employment. High employment is an obvious goal. Regardless of whether one focuses on the loss of output or on the human misery involved, practically everyone prefers high employment to large-scale unemployment. But an employment goal does raise serious issues. One is its definition. Obviously, it does not mean zero percent unemployment. There is always some *frictional unemployment* that results from workers leaving one job to look for a better one, from new entrants to the labor force starting out as unemployed, and from a geographical or occupational mismatch of workers and jobs. A certain level of unemployment is optimal for economic efficiency. By analogy consider the rental market in a city. If the vacancy rate for apartments were zero, then newcomers and those who want to change their housing would be in great difficulty. Despite the *apparent* "waste" of having some empty apartments, this is not really a waste. Similarly, firms keep inventories to meet their customers' needs. These "idle" inventories may seem a great waste, but an economy without such inventories could not function efficiently. Unemployed workers function, to some extent, like idle inventories. Unfortunately, it is far from clear, even conceptually, how great the optimal level of frictional unemployment is.

And further, we do not have a good statistical measure of actual unemployment. The unemployment data, which are gathered by monthly household surveys, are polluted in several ways. On the one hand, they understate the true extent of unemployment because they count only those looking for work, thus leaving out those who have ceased to hunt for a job because they believe that there is little chance of finding one. Second, part-time workers, who would prefer to work full time, are not counted as partially unemployed. On the other hand, if a male worker loses his job, his wife as well as he might then look for work so that the data count two people as unemployed, although the family is really looking for only one job. In addition, in some states people on welfare have to look for jobs, though presumably a number of them are not employable. Moreover, some people who work surreptitiously because they evade taxes, or are engaged in illegal activities, might classify themselves as unemployed. Beyond these statistical problems, the number of people actually unemployed also depends on the level and duration of unemployment-compensation payments. If these payments are high and obtainable for a long time, then workers have an incentive to look for good jobs rather than taking the first one that comes along. This is not necessarily bad. For example, if a skilled tool and die maker takes a job as a janitor when, with a few days' more search he could have located a job in his trade, there is a clear loss in national income.

Thus, not only do we not know what the proper level of unemployment is, we also cannot accurately measure current unemployment. This means that it is sometimes difficult to decide whether unemployment is too high or too low. Obviously, this is not always the case. In the 1930s when at times over a quarter of the nonfarm labor force was unemployed, there was little doubt the unemployment rate exceeded its desirable level, but this is much less clear if the unemployment rate is, say, 5 or 6 percent. However, even a 5 percent level of unemployment may well be undesirable in the sense that with some better manpower programs, such as job training, and broader and better information on job vacancies, the appropriate level of frictional unemployment could be reduced.

So far we have talked about the optimal unemployment rate in terms of that level of unemployment that balances at the margin the social loss from having idle labor, with the loss from not being able to find the workers needed to increase production. But probably a more relevant consideration is that a reduction in unemployment can generate inflation. If unemployment is kept below a certain level inflation accelerates. Many economists define the proper level of unemployment, and hence by implication full employment, as the minimum level that is consistent with the inflation rate not accelerating. Unfortunately, nobody knows for certain whether this level is 6 percent, 6½ percent, 7 percent, or some other number still?

Price Stability. The next goal, price stability, may seem an obvious one, but actually it is far from obvious. Consider an economy in which prices have been rising at a rate of, say, 100 percent per year for the last fifty years, and everyone knows with certainty that the inflation rate will continue to be 100 percent. What damage does this inflation do? It does not redistribute income because all wages and all contracts, as well as tax laws and accounting procedures, are adjusted for it. For example, if productivity is growing at a 2 percent rate, wages rise at a 102 percent rate each year, and the interest rate is, say, 103 percent instead of 3 percent. Such a fully anticipated inflation imposes only three types of losses. First, there is the bother and inconvenience of having to change price tags and catalogue prices frequently, and furthermore, the buyer's knowledge about what is an appropriate price of a certain good is quickly outdated. Second, since prices cannot be changed continually, they will be out of equilibrium for the presumably short periods between price changes. Third, inflation creates an incentive to hold too little currency because currency holdings lose their real value without having the compensation of the higher nominal interest rate that other assets have. Hence, people are put to the inconvenience of continual trips to the banks to get currency. Yet, this seems a rather minor problem.

But the inflations we actually experience are not fully anticipated, and our economy is not fully indexed. Thus inflation raises tax payments. This can be criticized on equity grounds since some taxpayers are hit harder than others, as well as on the grounds that it reduces capital formation by taxing corporate profits and interest receipts particularly hard. This is so because the depreciation that corporations deduct against taxable income is figured on an original cost basis, and because nominal rather than real interest income is taxed. For example, if the interest rate is 12 percent and the inflation rate is 10 percent, a taxpayer in the one-third marginal tax bracket receives an after-tax real rate of return of −2 percent ($12 \times 2/3 - 10$).

Since inflation affects the tax burdens faced by corporations to varying degrees it also leads to a socially inefficient allocation of investment funds, because after-tax profits become a less reliable guide to the true productivity of capital in various industries. Moreover, as discussed in Chapter 8, the high nominal interest rates that result from inflation create serious problems in the residential construction market. In addition, inflation, for reasons that are still much disputed, lowers stock prices.

Another effect of unanticipated inflation is its impact on the distribution of income and wealth. Obviously, it hurts creditors, and hence the retired, and benefits debtors. In addition, it may help or hurt wage earners depending upon whether or not wages lag behind prices. All in all, the evidence suggests that in recent years inflation has helped the poor, thus making the distribution of income less unequal. But, this may not hold true for all inflations.

But regardless of what inflation does to the distribution of income among different income classes, it generates a substantial income redistribution *within* each income class, since some households are net borrowers and others net lenders. And this type of redistribution is surely deplorable. It is no more equitable than would be a tax on everyone who was born on an even-numbered day. To anyone genuinely concerned with equity, this redistribution must be a major loss from inflation.

Another loss from inflation is that it creates uncertainty and insecurity. Households can no longer plan confidently for the distant future since they do not know what their fixed dollar assets will then be worth in real terms. More generally, people have been taught the virtue of saving for a rainy day. But such prudent behavior is punished rather than rewarded by unanticipated inflation. This is likely to cause people to lose faith in the government and in the equity and reasonableness of social conditions in general. While this effect of inflation cannot be quantified, it may well be a major, perhaps even *the* major, disadvantage of inflation. Thus in the 1979 *Economic Report of the President,* President Carter wrote:

> The corrosive effects of inflation eat away at the ties that bind us together as a people. One of the major tasks of a democratic government is to maintain conditions in which its citizens have a sense of command over their own destiny. During an inflation individuals watch in frustration as the value of last week's pay increase or last month's larger social security check is steadily eroded over the remainder of the year by a process that is beyond their individual control. All of us have to plan for the future. . . . The future is uncertain enough in any event, and the outcome of our plans is never fully within our own control. When the value of the measuring rod with which we do our planning—the purchasing power of the dollar—is subject to large and unpredictable shrinkage, one more element of command over our own future slips away. It is small wonder that trust in government and in social institutions is simultaneously eroded.[1]

Economic Growth. We defer the foreign exchange rate goal until Part Five and turn now to the growth rate of potential output. There is some dispute about the desirability of a high rate of economic growth. However, the majority of Americans do believe that a high rate of economic growth is desirable. In fact, there is now much concern that our current rate of growth is low relative to its trend in the postwar period, and relative to that in other countries. This lower growth rate is due to many factors, most of which are beyond the Federal Reserve's control, but the Fed can influence one important determinant of the economic growth rate: investment. A higher rate of investment not only means more capital per worker, but is also an important way in which technological progress comes about, since innovations are often embodied in new equipment. For example, the invention of a new machine does not increase productivity until firms invest by installing it.

One way of raising investment is to keep the real interest rate fairly low. But this is inherently expansionary, and to prevent inflation such a policy would have to be accompanied by a restrictive fiscal policy, that is, by a large government surplus. This depends, of course, on Congress and the administration, and is beyond the Fed's control. And, to raise total invest-

[1]Executive Office of the President, *Economic Report of the President* (Washington, D.C.: 1979), p. 7.

ment, the surplus would have to be achieved either by raising taxes that impinge primarily on consumption, or by cutting government expenditures on items other than those that are government investment, such as expenditures for research and development. But now when the federal government is running large deficits any talk about a budget surplus seems utopian.

Another way the Fed can raise the rate of investment is by controlling the rate of inflation since the uncertainty created by an unpredictable rate of inflation lowers investment.

Prevention of widespread bank failures and financial panics. The prevention of bank failures and panics is in a way not a separate goal, since the main loss resulting from large-scale bank failures is likely to be a depression with very high unemployment. We list it here among the goals just as a reminder of the importance of the Fed's lender of last resort function. American economic history prior to 1934 shows a number of examples of massive bank failures that resulted in financial panics and depressions. This certainly does not mean that the Fed has to be concerned about every single bank failure, or even about the failure of several banks at the same time. These cases can safely be left to the FDIC. But if somehow banks holding, say, 5 or 10 percent of total bank deposits were in danger of not being able to meet depositors' withdrawals, then it would be the Federal Reserve's job to step in and, through massive open-market operations, provide the banking system with enough reserves (and hence access to currency) to meet depositors' demands. Less dramatically, in the summer of 1982 when there was much concern about large potential bankruptcies and the fragility of the banking system, it was widely believed on Wall Street that the Fed eased policy for that reason. This, of course, cannot be verified.

Interest Rate Stability

Although the Fed has allowed increasing fluctuation of interest rates since October 1979, interest rate stability has traditionally been one of its goals. A reason for this is that fluctuating interest rates hurt those who, when interest rates rise, have to sell securities at a loss. Such losses are perceived as inequitable. Moreover, with sharply fluctuating interest rates firms that plan to borrow have to spend time and effort trying to predict the best time to do so, and financial institutions that borrow short and lend long are in trouble. In addition, as will be explained in Chapter 27, interest rate fluctuations generate fluctuations in exchange rates and thus are disruptive to foreign trade and investment. In general, the Fed is subjected to bitter criticism when interest rates rise sharply.

Sharing the Burden of a Restrictive Policy

This is certainly not a major goal of the Fed, but it does have to be concerned if the main impact of a restrictive policy is felt primarily by one industry, particularly if this industry has a lot of friends in Congress.

CONFLICT AMONG GOALS

Thus the Fed has many different goals, and its task is greatly complicated by the fact that there are numerous conflicts among them. Hence, it has to estimate the trade-offs and to decide the extent to which it will sacrifice one goal to attain the other.

Economic Growth

The conflict between price stability and high employment in the short run has already been discussed in the previous chapter; the conflict between exchange rate stability and the other goals will be discussed in Part Five. Hence, we turn now to the relation of economic growth to price-stability and high-employment goals. Since inflation that is not fully anticipated reduces economic growth there is no conflict between high economic growth and the price-stability goal in the long run. But in the short run there may be a conflict. To eliminate or reduce an existing inflation generally requires that unemployment and excess capacity increase. And the more excess capacity firms have, the less is the incentive to invest.

Bank failures and financial panics. The prevention of widespread bank failures does not clash with the employment goal, but it can, at times, conflict with the price-stability goal, and hence in this way also with the economic growth goal. For example, in 1966 the Federal Reserve called a halt to the severely restrictive policy it had adopted to fight inflation because it was afraid that a financial panic might occur. Admittedly this situation arises only rarely. Beyond this, bank regulation, by inhibiting banks in financial innovations, also has some, though presumably small, deleterious effects on economic growth.

Interest-rate stability. The relation between price stability and interest-rate stability is very different in the long run and the short run. In the long run there is no conflict between the two: the lower the rate of inflation, the lower is the nominal interest rate, and similarly, the more erratic the inflation rate the more erratic is the nominal interest rate. But the short run presents a very different picture. Suppose that aggregate demand increases because investment has become more profitable. As firms try to invest more the rate of interest starts to rise. The only way the Fed can postpone this rise (it cannot prevent it permanently) is to allow the quantity of money to increase at a faster rate. But this is obviously inflationary. A similar short-run conflict arises if an inflation is already underway. To stop the inflation the Fed would have to cut the money growth rate, which would result in temporarily higher interest rates.

Interest-rate stability has some, but probably only a small, effect on the rate of economic growth. But insofar as it changes the inflation rate and the capacity utilization rate it does affect economic growth indirectly in the ways we just discussed. Interest-rate stability is helpful in preventing bank failures since a bank can be seriously hurt by the fall in the market value of its security holdings when interest rates rise.

Sharing the Burden

The final goal is minimizing the special burden that monetary policy imposes on particular sectors of the economy. Here too, one must distinguish between the long run and the short run. In the long run it is an expansionary policy that, by generating inflation, creates special problems for particular sectors of the economy because many of our institutions are predicated more or less on price stability. For example, the problem that thrift institutions face is mainly due to the inflation-induced rise in nominal interest rates. Thus, in the long run, the moderately restrictive monetary policy that is needed to curb inflation is consistent with minimizing distortions. But in the short run such a restrictive policy raises interest rates, and thus hurts sectors like residential construction.

WHAT SHOULD THE FED DO?

This whole problem of conflicts among goals would not arise if the Fed had as many independent tools as it has targets and constraints. But this is not the case. All its major tools operate by changing bank reserves and interest rates, so that in this sense it has but a single tool. Hence it frequently faces a dilemma; some of its goals suggest that it should increase bank reserves, and others that it should reduce them.

One possible solution would be to give the Fed only a single goal, or at least a predominant goal. *If* this is to be done, this should *perhaps* be price stability rather than full employment since a consistent attempt to reduce unemployment would probably result in only a very small reduction in unemployment and a high inflation rate. In the long run the Phillips curve is vertical or almost vertical.

But during a substantial inflation, a policy to stabilize prices would probably result in much unemployment for some time. Besides, an overriding price-stability goal would prevent the Fed from taking expansionary action at those times when unemployment is very high, but a supply shock, such as a rising cost of oil imports, is raising prices. Most economists therefore believe that the Fed should deal with the conflict among its goals in an ad hoc manner, flexibly balancing the gain with respect to one goal against the loss with respect to another goal.

This raises the obvious question, what does the Fed actually do? How much importance does it attach to each of the above goals? Unfortunately, this is difficult to determine. The Fed does not issue statements revealing its trade-offs between various goals, nor does it tell us which one it considers the most important.[2] Instead, it tends to deemphasize the conflict between its goals, and sometimes suggests that the achievement of any goal is necessary to attain another. Such an unwillingness to reveal its hard choices is not surprising. If the Fed were to say that it is relinquishing one goal for the

[2] Some economists have tried to explain the Fed's behavior by a regression equation in which the dependent variable is some measure of the Fed's actions, such as the growth rate of the base, and the independent variables are factors like the unemployment rate, the inflation rate, and the balance of payments. They have often found that unemployment and the balance of payments variables explain Fed behavior.

sake of the others, the proponents of this goal would react angrily and might join a coalition that would trim its independence. But the reluctance to face conflict among goals is probably more than just a matter of political expedience. A governor who votes to adopt a restrictive policy knowing that it will create substantial unemployment, and hence much misery, would probably feel very uncomfortable about this, particularly since it is not certain that this restrictive policy is really needed to curb inflation. It is much easier for the governor to say to himself or herself that the restrictive policy is needed, both to curb inflation and to prevent greater unemployment subsequently.

The Fed's reluctance to spell out its goals has another great advantage for it. It makes it hard to evaluate its actions since, when accused of failing with respect to one goal, the Fed can frequently point to another goal that, perhaps for reasons having little to do with monetary policy, has been attained. The exasperating task involved in evaluating monetary policy is well exemplified by the following comment of Senator Proxmire to former Federal Reserve Chairman Martin:

> I have the greatest respect for your ability, and I think that you are an outstanding and competent person, and everybody agrees with that, but the fact is, that when you try to come down and discuss this in meaningful specific terms, it is like nailing a custard pie to the wall. . . . And frankly, Mr. Martin, without specific goals, criteria, guidelines, it is impossible to exercise any Congressional oversight over you, and I think you know it.[3]

The problem of determining the Fed's trade-offs between its goals is complicated not only by its reluctance to reveal its trade-offs, but also by the fact that its trade-offs probably vary from time to time. Given the great power and influence of the chairman of the Board of Governors, goals may change when a new chairman takes over. In addition, as pointed out in Chapter 7 the Fed tends to accept the president's goals, and in general it is influenced by changing political attitudes. In the late 1970s, for instance, the occurrence of double-digit inflation generated a strong constituency for curbing inflation. This caused—or permitted—the Fed to take a more restrictive stance. On the whole it *seems* that in the 1950s the Fed was relatively more concerned with price stability, and that in the early and mid-1970s it placed more emphasis on employment. In the late 1970s and early 1980s it then focused again more on curbing inflation. This emphasis then seemed to change in 1982 due to the severity of the recession.

Monetary Policy and Fiscal Policy

The goals of monetary and fiscal policy overlap since both are macroeconomic stabilization tools. This raises the question whether one can use fiscal policy to ameliorate the problem that the Fed has too many and conflicting goals. Or, on the contrary, does fiscal policy interfere with monetary policy?

[3]Cited in John Culbertson, *Full Employment or Stagnation?* (New York: McGraw-Hill, 1964), pp. 154–55.

Coordination of Fiscal and Monetary Policy

An obvious way in which fiscal policy can support monetary policy is by taking over part of the general stabilization task, so that monetary policy can be used in a more moderate manner. If taxes are raised or expenditures cut when aggregate demand is excessive, then this reduces the severity of the restrictive monetary policy that is required to prevent unacceptable inflation. But fiscal policy cannot help monetary policy in one important way. It cannot remove the conflict that exists in the short run between price stability and high employment. Both fiscal and monetary policies operate by changing aggregate demand, while the price stability–unemployment conflict is inherent in the way product markets and labor markets react.

Can monetary and fiscal policy be made to share the burden in a way that uses the comparative advantages of each? One possibility might be to make use of a possible difference in their timing. Unless there is widespread agreement in Congress, changing taxes and government expenditures takes a long time. On the other hand, the Fed can change monetary policy fairly rapidly. However, what matters is not just how long it takes to change policy, but also the lag until the change in policy has its impact on income. When one takes account of this lag it is not obvious that monetary policy is necessarily faster-acting than fiscal policy.

Another possibility is to use fiscal policy to moderate the loss that a restrictive monetary policy imposes on some particular sectors. Thus, during periods of sharply rising interest rates, one tool of fiscal policy—lending by government credit agencies—has been used to provide additional funds to thrift institutions. But, on the whole, the idea of employing fiscal and monetary policies as a team founders on the fact that government tax and expenditure policies usually are not employed as countercyclical tools. Rather, government expenditure goes up when there is a perceived need for additional government services. Tax rates are raised primarily because government expenditures are going up, or are cut because the public is fed up with high taxes. Countercyclical considerations play some, but only a quite limited, role in actual fiscal policy.

The Government Budget Constraint

Fiscal and monetary policies are inevitably related in one way. This is that the government, like everyone else, has a budget constraint. The Treasury must finance its expenditures either from its revenues or by borrowing from someone. But the government, unlike other sectors of the economy, has an apparent "out." It can borrow from itself, that is, from the Fed. As the Treasury sells securities to the public, the Fed can at the same time buy securities from the public, so that the public's holdings of government securities do not increase. In effect, the Fed "lends" to the Treasury. But this "out" has a nasty side to it. As the Fed buys government securities it provides banks with additional reserves, so that the money stock increases. This process is called *monetizing* the debt, and is, of course, inflationary.

Does the Fed monetize increases in the Federal debt? One way it did so in the past—and *perhaps* still does so now—is by trying to stabilize interest rates. As the Treasury sells more securities interest rates tend to rise, and if the Fed tries to stabilize interest rates it undertakes open market purchases of government securities to increase the money stock. Some economists believe that apart from this indirect way via interest rate stabilization, the Fed, at least in the past, has also monetized part of the Treasury's security sales by increasing its open market purchases when the Treasury ran a larger deficit.

But regardless of whether the Fed does monetize deficits it is obvious that at least at those times when inflation is a serious problem, large deficits complicate the Fed's task. It is therefore not surprising that Federal Reserve chairmen like to lecture both Congress and the administration on the need for fiscal prudence. These lectures also have the advantage of giving the impression that the Fed is a staunch foe of inflation, even though it may at the same time be allowing the money stock to grow at much too fast a clip.

SUMMARY

1. The Federal Reserve has several goals—high employment, price stability, economic growth, exchange rate stability, prevention of bank failures, interest rate stability, and an acceptable distribution of the burden of restrictive policy.
2. Unemployment creates an obvious loss, but it is hard to determine what level of unemployment is appropriate. Inflation creates relatively few problems *if* it is fully anticipated. But if not fully anticipated then it reduces and distorts investment, has arbitrary effects on the distribution of income, and creates uncertainty and a feeling of loss of control.
3. There is a potential conflict among goals, but the Fed tends to downplay this conflict and does not spell out its priorities.
4. Fiscal policy and monetary policy share the same goals, but there are serious problems in coordinating them. Government deficits can be monetized. The avoidance of large deficits would make the Fed's task easier.

Questions and Exercises

1. What are the goals of Federal Reserve policy? Either argue that one of them should not be treated as a serious goal, or argue that there is an additional goal that should be included.
2. Why does the Fed have an interest-rate stabilization goal? Do you think it is important?
3. Describe the problems an inadequate fiscal policy can create for the Fed. Do you think fiscal policy is currently helping or hindering monetary policy?
4. Read through the current *Economic Report of the President* and prepare a statement of the trade-offs between various goals that are either explicit or implicit in it. Do you agree with these trade-offs?

Further Reading

ABRAMS, RICHARD, FROYEN, RICHARD, and WAUD, ROGER. "Monetary Policy Reaction Functions, Consistent Expectations and the Burns' Era." *Journal of Money, Credit and Banking* 12 (February 1980): 30–42. This is one of a series of articles that tries to estimate by regression analysis how the Fed reacts to unemployment, inflation, and foreign-exchange market pressures.

BACH, G. L. *Making Monetary and Fiscal Policy*. Washington, D.C.: Brookings Institution, 1971, pp. 3–25. A good discussion of the Fed's goals with emphasis on their evolution.

BLINDER, ALAN. "Issues in the Coordination of Monetary and Fiscal Policies." Federal Reserve Bank of Kansas City, *Monetary Policy Issues in the 1980s*. Kansas City, Mo: 1983, pp. 3–34. An excellent response to much idle rhetoric.

BURNS, ARTHUR. *The Anguish of Central Banking*. Washington, D.C.: American Enterprise Institute, 1980. An excellent short discussion by a former Fed chairman.

FISCHER, STANLEY, and MODIGLIANI, FRANCO. "Towards an Understanding of the Real Effects and Costs of Inflation." *Weltwirtschaftliches Archiv* 114, 4 (1978): 810–33. A useful summary of the losses from inflation.

JOHNSON, HARRY. *Essays in Monetary Economics*. London: George Allen, 1967, ch. 6. Although dealing directly with Canadian conditions, it contains many insightful points relevant to the United States.

LEVY, MICKEY. "Factors Affecting Monetary Policy in an Era of Inflation." *Journal of Monetary Economics* 8 (1981): 351–73. A statistical analysis of the Fed's goals that brings out the Fed's monetization of government debt.

MAISEL, SHERMAN. *Managing the Dollar*. New York: W. W. Norton, 1973. Provides an excellent "feel" for the pressures under which the Fed operates.

Tools of Monetary Policy 20

In this chapter we take up specific tools of the Fed's. These tools can be divided into two groups: **general controls** that *affect the whole economy,* and **selective controls** that are *designed to reinforce, or ameliorate, the impact of general monetary policy in specific areas of the economy,* such as the stock market. This distinction between general and selective controls is, however, not watertight; selective controls also have some effects on the rest of the economy.

OPEN-MARKET OPERATIONS

Open-market operations are now by far the most important tool of monetary policy, a fact that would have greatly surprised the framers of the Federal Reserve Act. The original idea of the Fed was that, like the Bank of England, it would use discounting, that is, lending to member banks, as its main tool. But, more or less by accident, a much more efficient tool was discovered: open-market operations. In the early years of the Fed, the Federal Reserve Banks bought government securities to provide themselves with earnings, with no realization of the effects of this on reserves. They soon discovered that their purchases or sales of securities had a powerful effect on reserves and on the money market. In 1923 they therefore agreed to carry them out with "primary regard to the accommodation of commerce and business."[1]

The present organization for open-market operations has already been discussed in Chapter 7. The FOMC sends a directive to the account manager (or "Desk") at the New York Federal Reserve Bank who undertakes the

[1] Statement by Federal Reserve Board, quoted in W. Randolph Burgess, *The Reserve Banks and the Money Market* (New York: Harper and Row, 1946), p. 241. This book provides a very good survey of pre-World War II Federal Reserve functioning.

actual purchases and sales of securities. He deals, not with the general public, but with a small number of security dealers, some of them banks and others specialized wholesalers of government securities. The Desk is in continual contact with them, asking them for bids or offers on securities. It therefore knows the price and the interest rate on these securities at all times, and has precise knowledge of money-market conditions, of what the Fed calls "the feel of the market." The Fed does not force anyone to buy or sell securities; it buys or sells at the prices the dealers quote to it.

Paul Meek gives the following description of the operations of the Trade Desk.[2]

> The time is just before noon on the Tuesday before Thanksgiving Day. The place is the eighth floor trading room of the Federal Reserve Bank of New York. The manager of the Federal Reserve System's Open Market Account has made his decision. He tells his second in command to buy about $500 million in United States Treasury bills for immediate delivery.
>
> The decision made, the officer-in-charge turns to the ten officers and securities traders who sit before telephone consoles linking them to more than 30 primary dealers in U.S. Government securities. "We're going in to ask for offerings of all bills for cash," he says. Each person is quickly assigned two to four dealers to call.
>
> Joan, a New York Federal Reserve trader, presses a button on her telephone console, sounding a buzzer at the corresponding console of a Government securities dealer.
>
> "Jack," Joan says, "we are looking for offerings of all bills for cash delivery."
>
> Jack replies, "I'll be back in a minute." The salesmen of his firm quickly contact customers to see if they wish to make offerings. Jack consults the partner in charge about how aggressive he should be in offering the firm's own holdings.
>
> Ten minutes later Jack calls back. "Joan, I can offer you for cash $5 million of January 5 bills to yield 5.85 percent—$10 million of January 26 bills at 5.90—$20 million of March 23 bills at 6.05—and $30 million of May 30 bills at 6.14."
>
> Joan says, "Can I have those offerings firm for a few minutes?"
>
> "Sure."
>
> Within minutes the "go-around" is completed. The traders have recorded the offerings obtained from their calls on special preprinted strips. The officer-in-charge arrays the individual dealer offerings on an inclined board atop a stand-up counter. A tally shows that dealers have offered $1.8 billion of bills for cash sale—that is, with delivery and payment that very day.
>
> The officer then begins circling with a red pencil the offerings that provide the best—that is, the highest—rate of return for each issue. The large quotation board facing the open end of the U-shaped trading desk tells him the yields on Treasury bills as they were in the market just before the "go-around" began. An associate keeps a running total of the amounts being bought. When the desired amount has been circled, the individual strips are returned to the traders, who quickly telephone the dealer firms.
>
> "Jack, we'll take the $5 million of January 5 bills at 5.85 and the $30 million of May 30 bills at 6.14 both for cash; no, thanks, on the others," Joan says.
>
> Forty-five minutes after the initial decision, the calls have been completed, and $523 million in Treasury bills purchased. Only the paper work remains. The

[2]Paul Meek, *Open Market Operations* (New York: Federal Reserve Bank of New York, 1978), pp. 1–2.

traders write up tickets, which provide the basic authority for the Bank's government bond department to receive and pay for the specific Treasury bills bought. The banks that handle the dealers' deliveries—the clearing banks—will authorize deductions of the securities from the book entry list of their holdings at the Federal Reserve. In return, they will receive credit to the reserve accounts the banks maintain at the New York Reserve Bank.

The Federal Reserve credits to the dealers' banks immediately adds over $500 million to the reserves of the U.S. banking system.

The Fed is authorized to deal in its open-market operations in U.S. Treasury securities, securities of government agencies such as GNMA (Ginnie May), certain state and local government securities, bankers' acceptances, and so on. But in practice the great bulk of open-market operations is in Treasury securities. And further, most of the transactions are in Treasury bills. This is so because the Fed wants to minimize the extent to which it changes security prices in its open-market operations. Since the market for Treasury bills is extremely large, it can buy or sell a substantial volume without changing their price much. By contrast, if the Fed were to sell an equal volume of, say, twenty-year government securities, their price could drop more. This would create unwarranted capital losses for many holders. Specifically, government-security dealers, who hold a large volume of securities relative to their capital, could be seriously hurt. And the Fed is afraid that as a result they might cease to "make a market" in such securities, that is, that they would cease to hold an inventory of them, but would act merely as brokers who bring buyers and sellers together. This would reduce the efficiency of the capital market. Hence, while the Fed *does* deal from time to time in longer-term securities, it conducts most of its operations in Treasury bills.

Actually, most open-market operations are not really sales or purchases in the usual sense of the words. The great bulk of "purchases" are done under repurchase agreements, often called **repos,** that is, under an agreement with the "seller" that he will buy the securities back again at a fixed price at a certain date. Similarly, most of the Fed's security sales are done under so-called **reverse repos,** more formally known as matched sale-purchase transactions, with the Fed pledging itself to buy these securities back at a fixed price at a particular time. The reason why the Fed uses such repos and reverse repos is that most open-market purchases or sales are intended to affect reserves for only a very short time. By using repos and reverse repos the Fed lets the market know that these transactions will soon be reversed.

Such reversal results from the fact that most open-market operations are "defensive" rather than "dynamic." Dynamic operations are those in which the Fed wants to change the volume of reserves. By contrast, the Fed undertakes defensive operations when it wants to keep reserves constant. To do this it has to undertake open-market operations to offset the impact on reserves of "market factors," such as changes in float or currency holdings.

Fluctuations in market factors generate very large—but temporary—

changes in reserves. To stabilize the money market and the supply of money, the Fed tries to offset these changes, except insofar as they happen to go in the direction the Fed wants. To do this the Fed expends considerable effort in predicting the probable behavior of various market factors. In addition, the Fed tries to gauge the *overall* impact of market factors by obtaining the "feel" of the money market in its contacts with government security dealers. Hence, something that frequently triggers open-market operations is changes in the federal funds rate as market factors supply or withdraw reserves. Defensive operations account for the great bulk of open-market operations.

The effect of open-market operations on bank reserves has already been demonstrated in Chapter 11 by means of T accounts.

Advantages of Open-Market Operations

Open-market operations are the prime tool of monetary policy for several reasons. First, the Fed can buy or sell enough government securities to set the size of reserves as it pleases. This tool is always strong enough to do the job. Second, open-market operations occur at the initiative of the Fed, unlike bank borrowing where the Fed can only encourage or discourage borrowing but has no precise control over the volume involved. Third, open-market operations can be carried out in small steps, very small ones if need be. This allows the Fed to make exact adjustments in reserves. Fourth, open-market operations enable the Fed to adjust reserves on a continuous basis as the federal funds rate changes, and as it receives new information about the impact of market factors on reserves. Fifth, and finally, open-market operations are easily reversed.

THE DISCOUNT MECHANISM

The discount mechanism is a device by which institutions that are required to keep reserves with the Fed can borrow from it.[3] It serves several functions. One is to fulfill the Federal Reserve's lender-of-last-resort function, particularly in those cases where only a few institutions experience a liquidity crisis. If many depository institutions are short of liquidity, then the discount mechanism has to be supplemented by extensive open-market purchases, but even then it is important in channeling funds to those institutions that are particularly vulnerable. Second, the discount mechanism provides a way in which the Fed can provide temporary liquidity to a partic-

[3]Discounting is a process of deducting the interest due from the face value of the borrower's promissory note. For example, someone who borrows by discounting, receives in exchange for a promise to pay, say, $10,000 next week, not the full $10,000, but only $9,990, the $10 interest being subtracted in advance. Banks normally borrow from the Fed by discounting their own promissory notes (using government securities as collateral), but they can, under certain conditions, instead discount a second time certain promissory notes they have discounted for their customers. Hence the term *rediscounting* is sometimes used.

ular institution that is in difficulty, such as the Franklin National Bank discussed in Chapter 3. This prevents runs on other banks by large depositors and other providers of managed liabilities. Third, by changing the discount rate the Fed can encourage or discourage borrowing, and this is one way it has of changing the volume of reserves.

Borrowing can take the form of "adjustment credit" or else "extended credit." The former, which accounts for the bulk of the borrowing, can be done fairly automatically, often over the telephone. It is intended to tide depository institutions over until they can get other funds when they face a sudden liquidity drain, due for example, to a large deposit loss, or a rapid upsurge in loan demand. It is short-term credit only, in fact the largest banks are supposed to repay the next business day. However, banks that have a substantial seasonal pattern in their deposits or lending activities, such as banks in ski areas, can borrow for these seasonal needs.

Extended credit is available under several circumstances. One is if a depository institution faces special difficulties, for example, extended deposit drains. A second situation is when a broad group of depository institutions experience liquidity strains. Institutions obtaining extended credit have to explain the need in some detail and submit an acceptable plan for restoring their liquidity.

Since depository institutions can at times borrow from the Fed at less than prevailing market rates it is necessary to limit such borrowing. They are not supposed to borrow for the sake of reinvesting the funds at a profit, but only in case of need. The Fed tries to enforce this provision by scrutinizing the activities of borrowing institutions. But the prohibition against borrowing for profit is vague, and hence hard to enforce. For example, suppose, to increase its interest earnings, a bank buys securities even though it knows that it may soon experience a deposit outflow. Then, when this deposit outflow does occur, and the bank is short of reserves, it borrows from the Fed. Is it borrowing for "need" or for "profit"? What the Fed *can* enforce is checks over how frequently and for how long a bank borrows. Hence the Fed has set out specific limitations on the quantity and frequency of borrowing by individual banks. All the same, it is hardly surprising that, as Figure 20.1 shows, borrowing increases when the discount rate is low relative to the federal funds rate.

This does not mean, however, that all banks try to take advantage of any federal funds rate-discount rate gap. Some may hold off borrowing because they know that if they borrow now the Fed may make it more difficult for them to borrow at a later time, a time when their need to borrow may be greater or the federal funds rate much higher than it is now. Others, as a way of demonstrating their conservative management, are reluctant to borrow from the Fed.

When banks do borrow they are under pressure to repay. The Fed believes that when a borrowing bank obtains additional funds its first priority should be to repay these loans, and not to buy securities or make loans. Whether banks actually behave this way is a disputed issue. It may depend on how much—and for how long—they have borrowed.

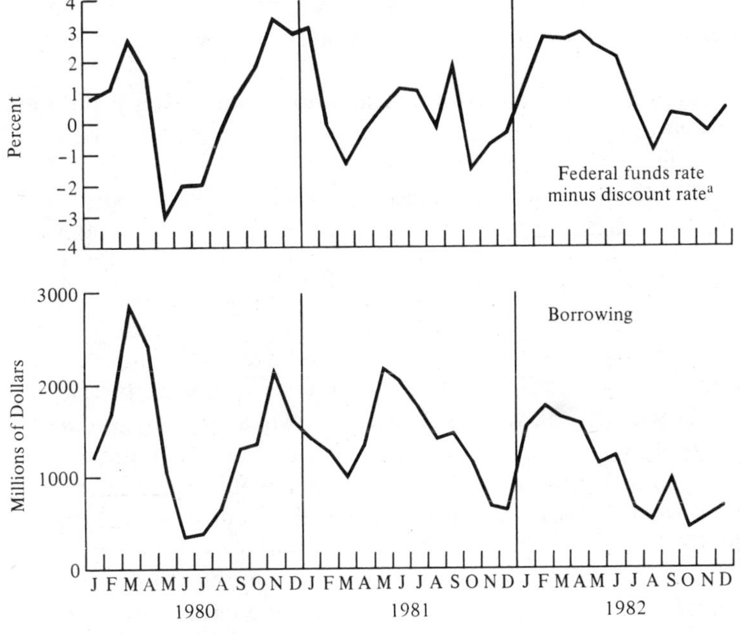

[a]Discount rate including surcharge

Figure 20.1 Relation of Discount Rate to Federal Funds Rate and Member Bank Borrowing

Source: *Federal Reserve Bulletin,* May, 1983, and *Economic Reports of the President* 1981–1983, Table B65.

Moreover, one should distinguish between the behavior of individual banks and of the whole banking system. Banks that have made extensive use of the discount privilege in the past may be under strong pressure to repay. But as they do so, and borrow on the federal funds market instead, the funds rate increases, which then sends other banks that have not borrowed much in the past to the Fed's discount window. Hence, even if the Fed effectively controls borrowing by individual banks, it may exercise less effective control over the total volume of borrowing.

Whether a bank treats repayment of Fed loans as its first priority when it obtains additional funds has a bearing on the proper measure of bank reserves. If banks do feel under strong pressure to repay Fed loans, then unborrowed reserves and the unborrowed base are better predictors of how bank deposits will change than are total reserves or the total base.

THE DISCOUNT RATE

The Fed can vary the interest rate it charges borrowing institutions. Thus it can induce banks and thrift institutions to increase or to reduce their borrowing, and can in this way change reserves.[4] But the volume of reserves involved is usually small compared to the change that results from open-market operations.

The inducement to borrow can, and does, vary even if the Fed keeps the discount rate unchanged. If the federal funds rate rises, say, from 8 percent to 8.5 percent, and the discount rate stays put at 8 percent, then banks and thrift institutions have a greater incentive to borrow; so that discount rate policy has become more expansionary without the discount rate itself changing. To keep its discount policy constant the Fed would therefore have to change the discount rate frequently. But this creates a problem. Many people interpret a rise in the discount rate as a restrictive policy, even if it is merely a response to rising interest rates on the open market. They argue that by increasing the discount rate the Fed has validated the rise in interest rates by showing that it thinks interest rates will stay high. And a restrictive monetary policy has many critics. Hence, the Fed is sometimes under considerable political pressure not to raise the discount rate. There have been occasions when a President has criticized the Fed for raising the discount rate and Congress has held hearings on the matter.

Reductions in the discount rate have less political fallout, though foreign central bankers and others might interpret a cut in the discount rate as a policy that will cause the dollar to decline on the foreign-exchange market. Beyond this, the Fed is reluctant to lower the discount rate because it knows the criticism that will follow if it has to raise it again later on. Thus, the Fed has in actuality only limited freedom to change the discount rate.

If the discount rate is too low relative to the federal funds rate so that borrowing increases, the Fed can offset the resulting increase in reserves by undertaking additional open-market sales. Hence, the main effect of having a discount rate that is too low relative to open-market interest rates is that banks make a profit at the Fed's expense by borrowing from it and lending at a higher rate.

The Announcement Effect

In addition to its effect on borrowing, and hence on reserves, the money stock, and on interest rates, a change in the discount rate also affects people's expectations to some, albeit to a limited, extent. Not only the financial community, but also the general public read about it in the newspapers. Thus, in November 1978, when President Carter wanted to stop the fall of the dollar on the foreign-exchange market by indicating to the world that the United States was ready to adopt a firm antiinflation policy, he announced that he had asked the Federal Reserve to raise the discount rate.

When the Fed raises the discount rate the public *may* interpret this as a sign that the Fed is acting to curb excessive expansion and feel that there is

[4] Although we always speak of the "discount rate," there are actually several rates depending upon the collateral offered by the borrower. In addition, as a result of the Franklin National Bank experience, the Fed added a proviso that allows it to charge an unusually high discount rate should such a case occur again.

now less reason to fear inflation. It may therefore reduce such inflationary activities as buying ahead to beat price increases or demanding higher wages to offset expected inflation. By contrast, when the Fed cuts the discount rate this may be interpreted as a sign that the Fed is now taking action to moderate an economic downturn. However, the public *may* also react in just the opposite way, and treat a rise in the discount rate as a sign that the Fed shares its prediction that inflation is becoming a more serious problem.

Unfortunately, the public may also take the change in the discount rate as an indication of the Fed's predictions even in those cases where the Fed changes the discount rate only because market rates have changed. All in all, it is far from clear that on the whole the announcement effect of a change in the discount rate is helpful. For reasons we will take up in the next chapter some economists believe that the Fed should tie the discount rate to some open market rate, making it, say, ¼ of 1 percent more than last week's federal funds rate. This would eliminate the announcement effect of discount rate changes entirely.

The change in the discount rate is not the only tool of monetary policy that has an announcement effect. Changes in reserve requirements are also reported in the newspapers. Moreover, the financial and business specialists whose decisions have the important effects are sophisticated enough to know how to interpret open-market operations and changes in the federal funds rate. Large financial institutions employ economists—many of them former Fed employees—to predict what the Fed will do before the Fed either does it or announces it. "Fed watching" has become an important industry.

RESERVE-REQUIREMENT CHANGES

Congress has given the Fed the power to vary reserve requirements within broad limits. Raising the reserve requirement affects the money stock in two ways. First, previously excess reserves of banks are now transformed into required reserves. Second, the reserve ratio is one of the components of the denominator in the money multiplier. Hence, a rise in the reserve ratio lowers the money multiplier, and thus lowers the deposit expansion that banks can undertake on the basis of their remaining excess reserves. Given the wide range within which the Fed can change reserve requirements it has a *potentially* powerful tool here. But despite its strength, the Fed uses the reserve-requirement tool relatively infrequently. For example, the reserve requirements against demand deposits that were in effect September 1983 were set in December 1976.

Although the Fed changes the reserve requirements ratio only infrequently, the *average* reserve requirement per dollar of deposits changes all the time. Since large depository institutions have a higher reserve requirement than small ones, a shift of deposits from small institutions to large ones raises the average reserve requirement ratio, and thus lowers the money multiplier. Although the Fed can predict, and hence offset, the impact of such deposit shifts, it cannot do so without some error. Hence, having reserve requirements that depend on the size of the depository institution substantially weakens the Fed's control over the money stock in the short run. Fortunately this problem will be greatly reduced as the new reserve requirement system is phased in.

There are several other proposals for reforming the reserve requirements system. They are discussed in the Appendix to this chapter.

ARE ALL THREE TOOLS NEEDED?

Why have all three tools—open-market operations, discount-rate changes, and changes in reserve requirements? Clearly, they are not all equally important. Open-market operations is by far the dominant one since it has many advantages. One might therefore suggest that the Fed rely entirely on open-market operations and relinquish the two other tools by hooking the discount rate to the federal funds rate, and by announcing that it will keep reserve requirements fixed. While some economists support this, the Fed believes that it helps to have all three tools.

Although this is irrelevant from the strict viewpoint of monetary policy these three tools have different distributional effects. If the Fed lowers reserve requirements depository institutions can make more loans or purchase more securities. Hence, unless demand for their credit is inelastic their profits rise. (This is hardly surprising since as discussed in Chapter 4, the reserve requirement operates as a tax.) By contrast, if the Fed increases reserves by open-market purchases, then the depository institutions that sell securities to the Fed have to give up some of their securities in exchange for the additional reserves. However, for each dollar of securities they sell to the Fed, depository institutions as a whole can have more than one dollar of deposits—and hence of loans and securities, outstanding—so that presumably their total earnings increase. If the Fed lowers the discount rate the cost of funds to depository institutions is reduced, so that their profits are likely to increase.

Selective Controls

The tools discussed so far operate on aggregate demand by changing reserves and interest rates, and thus affect the whole economy. By contrast, "selective controls" have their initial impact on specific markets that some economists think are relatively insulated from the effects of overall monetary policy. These controls are also designed to focus on trouble spots where demand may be excessive.

Stock-Market Credit

The Fed controls the use of credit to purchase stocks listed on stock markets plus certain unlisted stocks. It has set the down payments, or *margin,* for stock purchases, limiting the percent of the purchase price that may be borrowed. The Fed's regulations T, U, and G control credit for stock purchases extended respectively by brokers (and dealers), banks, and other lenders, while Regulation X closes certain loopholes, such as borrowing abroad, by controlling the borrower directly. The Fed varies the margin requirement from time to time, and can raise it up to 100 percent to control a speculative stock-market boom.

The reason the Fed was given this power in 1934 can be seen by looking back at the situation in the years 1927 through 1929. Then prices were stable or gently falling, but there was a speculative boom in the stock market. The Fed was in a quandary. It had no power to affect the stock market directly. By raising the discount rate or by open-market operations it could have made credit generally less available and, hence, could to some extent have limited the purchase of stocks on credit. But with stock prices rising rapidly, it would probably have taken a *very* substantial boost in interest rates to have a significant effect on stock-market borrowing. And such a substantial rise in interest rates would have been too restrictive for the rest of the economy. If the Fed had had margin regulations available at that time it could have limited stock-market credit without such a restrictive effect on the rest of the economy.

As so often happens, the barn door was locked after the horse was stolen. Since 1934 there has been no disastrous boom in the stock market, so that while the Fed has used its margin controls—occasionally even raising them to 100 percent—there has been no great need for them.

Consumer Credit

Potentially more important are selective controls over consumer credit. During World War II, as well as during the Korean War and briefly in 1948–49, the Fed set minimum down payments and maximum maturities on loans for consumer durable purchases. During World War II the Fed also controlled mortgage credit in a similar way.

Then, in 1981, in part as a way to create confidence in the government's determination to fight inflation, President Carter had the Fed impose a 15 percent reserve requirement on unsecured consumer credit. Whether in response to this, or to the accompanying moral suasion to cut spending, consumer credit fell; probably by much more than the administration intended. Since this came shortly before the onset of a recession it was hardly very helpful. The law permitting the Fed to impose direct controls over consumer credit has since expired.

Regulation Q

This regulation is concerned with protecting a sector of the economy from rising interest rates, rather than with curbing demand in sectors that are supposedly hard to reach with conventional monetary policy. It has already been discussed in detail.

MORAL SUASION

Another tool is **moral suasion.** This simply means that the *Fed uses its powers of persuasion to get banks, or the financial community in general, to* *behave differently*. Since the interests of the Fed frequently coincide with the long-run self-interest of financial institutions, this form of control may *in certain cases* be more effective than appears at first. For example, during an inflationary expansion, the Fed may urge lenders to be more cautious in their loan policies, and lenders *may* treat this as sound business advice from someone who can forecast business conditions better than they can. To be sure, sometimes banks and other institutions may feel that the stress is more on the "suasion" than on the "moral." For example, in 1965 when the Fed laid down guidelines to limit foreign lending, some banks, at least according to some reports, were afraid that if they ignored the guidelines, they might find it more difficult to borrow from the Fed. Admittedly, these fears may have been groundless; for an outsider it is hard to say. But in 1966 the Fed openly informed banks that discounting would be easier for banks that curbed their business loans and made more mortgage loans. The Fed's control over bank holding company activities, and its power to prohibit proposed mergers, has given it another potential threat over recalcitrant banks.[5] Some people think that this gives the Fed a powerful weapon, despite its questionable legal status.

PUBLICITY AND ADVICE

The Fed has many ways of making its opinions known to the general public. The chairman of the Board of Governors frequently testifies before congressional committees, and journalists pay attention to press releases by the Fed, and the chairman's speeches. In addition, the Board of Governors publishes each month the *Federal Reserve Bulletin,* and the individual Federal Reserve banks publish *Reviews*. Given the high regard in which the business community and its journalists hold the Fed, it has no difficulty in getting its views across to the general public. In these ways it can affect business expectations, and hence actions. In addition, as discussed in Chapter 7, the Fed also acts as an informal economic adviser to the administration.

SUMMARY

1. Open-market operations are the dominant tool of monetary policy. This is a strong tool that can, however, be used in very small steps, and can be used frequently and with predictable effects on reserves. The great bulk of open-market operations are defensive rather than dynamic.
2. Depository institutions that are required to keep reserves with the Fed can borrow from it. Borrowing is supposed to be for need rather than for profit. But this rule is difficult to administer. Banks are supposed to repay their borrowings as soon as possible.
3. The Fed can vary the discount rate to influence the volume of borrowing. Borrowing responds to the gap between the federal funds rate and the discount rate, which means that, to keep borrowing stable, the Fed would have to change the discount rate frequently. But this creates political problems. Discount rate

[5] See Edward Kane, "The Central Bank As Big Brother," *Journal of Money, Credit and Banking* 5 (November 1973): 979–81.

changes, as well as the use of other tools of monetary policy, have an announcement effect.

4. The ability to change reserve requirements gives the Fed a potentially powerful tool. However, the Fed does not use this tool frequently.
5. In principle, the Fed could get along with just one tool, open-market operations. But it prefers to have all three.
6. The Fed also has tools of selective control over stock market credit and at one time had controls over consumer credit.
7. Moral suasion and publicity and advice round out the tools the Fed has available.
8. One final word of warning: this discussion of tools applies only to the United States. Thus, open-market operations require a broad well-developed capital market, something that exists in only a few countries. In countries with only a few banks, moral suasion is a much more effective and frequently used tool than in the U.S.

Questions and Exercises

1. Write an essay describing the use the Federal Reserve has made of its various tools in the last three years. (Information on this is available in the Federal Reserve's Annual Reports.)
2. Using T accounts show why an open-market sale reduces reserves.
3. Discuss the distributional effects of various Fed tools.
4. Borrowing from the Fed is supposed to be for need rather than for profit. How is it then that the volume of borrowing is correlated with the gap between the federal funds rate and the discount rate?
5. Describe the Fed's selective controls.

Further Reading

FEDERAL RESERVE BANK OF NEW YORK (Paul Meek). *Open Market Operations*. New York: Federal Reserve Bank of New York, 1969. A lively and authoritative description.

FRIEDMAN, MILTON. *A Program for Monetary Stability*. New York: Fordham University Press, 1960. Chapter 2 is a stimulating discussion of reforms.

MEEK, PAUL. *U.S. Monetary Policy and Financial Markets*. New York: Federal Reserve Bank of New York, 1982. A highly informative and authorative statement by a senior Fed official.

ROOSA, ROBERT. *Federal Reserve Operations in the Money and Government Security Markets*. New York: Federal Reserve Bank of New York, 1956. A fascinating description of the "nuts and bolts" of open-market operations by a former manager of the Desk.

U.S., BOARD OF GOVERNORS, FEDERAL RESERVE SYSTEM. *Consumer Installment Credit*. Washington, D.C.: Board of Governors, Federal Reserve System, 1957. Volumes 1 and 2 are an exhaustive treatment.

U.S., BOARD OF GOVERNORS, FEDERAL RESERVE SYSTEM. *Reappraisal of the Federal Reserve Discount Mechanism*. Washington, D.C.: 1971. Volume 1, chapter 1, and volume 2, chapter 3, reprint two of the papers from the Federal Reserve study that led to reform of the discount mechanism. The former is the report of the Federal Reserve committee; the latter summarizes academic views on discounting.

APPENDIX: RESERVE REQUIREMENTS: SOME CONTROVERSIES AND REFORM PROPOSALS

The prevailing reserve-requirement system has been subjected to numerous criticisms and proposals for reform. Here are the major ones.

Elimination of Reserve Requirements

The most radical suggestion has been to do away with the reserve requirement altogether. Reserve requirements no longer serve the function of protecting depositors to any significant extent. An obvious counterargument is that reserve requirements are absolutely necessary for monetary policy, that if there were no reserve requirements banks could create as many deposits as they wanted. Thus, using the simple deposit multiplier, where deposits are equal to one divided by the reserve ratio, it might seem that with a zero-reserve requirement there would be no determinate volume of deposits. But this is obviously wrong. After developing the simple deposit multiplier we developed more complex multipliers in which the legal reserve requirement is only one of several terms in the denominator. In particular these multipliers include a term for the banks' excess reserves. Surely, even if there were no legal reserve requirements banks would still want to hold some reserves to meet a deposit outflow. And the public would hold currency in a certain ratio to its deposits. Hence a legally imposed reserve requirement is not really necessary. The reserve ratio that banks hold for their own purposes and the public's currency ratio could serve as the fulcrum of monetary policy instead.

Granted that a system without legal reserve requirements *could* work, would it work better than a system with legal reserve requirements? This depends in large part on how predictable a voluntary reserve ratio would be. If banks, on their own, want to keep a stable ratio of reserves to deposits, then the abolition of the *legal* reserve requirement would not hinder monetary policy. And the same would hold if the voluntary reserve ratio, while varying from time to time, would do so in a predictable way. The Fed could then simply offset any changes in the reserve ratio of banks by open-market operations.

The real argument for a legal reserve ratio is therefore, not that it is necessary, but rather, that by setting a floor below which reserves cannot fall, it makes the actual reserve ratio more predictable, and hence facilitates monetary policy. Unfortunately, there are no data on how predictable the reserve ratio would be in the absence of a legal reserve requirement.

One Hundred Percent Reserves

At the opposite extreme from eliminating the legal reserve requirement entirely is a proposal to raise the reserve requirement to 100 percent, thus abolishing deposit creation by the banking system. This 100 percent reserve plan would eliminate commercial banks as we know them, and replace them by two types of institutions: one would be a type of bank that accepts deposits and transfers them by check, but cannot make any loans—its income would come entirely from service charges. The second type of bank would be an institution that accepts longer-term savings and makes loans. It would pay interest to its depositors, but their deposits would not be available on demand. To prevent a radical reduction in the money stock at the time when the scheme is inaugurated, additional reserves would have to be provided, perhaps by having the Fed buy securities and loans held by banks.

A major advantage of the 100 percent reserve proposal is that it would abolish multiple-deposit creation and, hence, give the Fed more precise control over the money stock. Each dollar of reserves would now result in one dollar, and in no more than one dollar, of money. There would not be the slippage existing under the present system where, at times, banks can add to the money stock by running down excess reserves and, at other times, can reduce the money stock by holding more excess reserves. Moreover, changes in currency holdings of the public would no longer change the potential money stock. At present, if the public decides to hold more currency there occurs a *multiple* decline in bank deposits, so that the total money stock (deposits plus currency) falls. The second advantage of 100 percent reserves is that it would eliminate bank failures except for some possible cases of fraud. Fewer government regulations over banks would then be needed.[6]

The most obvious disadvantage of the 100 percent reserve plan is the trouble and dislocation involved in setting it up. The banking system would have to be split into two parts, bank personnel and bank customers would have to be reeducated, and much uncertainty and confusion would result. Those who believe that even moderate fluctuations in the money supply have a powerful effect on income *may* consider these once-and-for-all costs as unimportant when compared to the gains resulting from 100 percent reserve banking, but others are unlikely to consider the changeover worthwhile. But whatever its merits and demerits, it is hard to imagine Congress adopting the 100 percent reserve proposal.

Reserves against Time Deposits

Leaving aside this radical proposal, another proposal would exempt all time deposits and not just personal time deposits, from any legal reserve requirement, while still another one goes in the opposite direction, and would apply the same reserve requirement to all time deposits as to demand deposits.

[6] However, the currency flow problem could also be handled by a much simpler reform. See William Poole, "A Proposal for Reforming Bank Reserve Requirements in the United States," *Journal of Money, Credit and Banking,* 7 (May 1976): 137–48.

The reason we control the money stock is that it affects aggregate demand. The required reserve ratio on various liquid assets should therefore reflect the impact of these items on aggregate demand. For example, if an additional dollar of time deposits raises aggregate demand only by as much as 50 cents of demand deposits do, then the reserve requirement against time deposits should be half the reserve requirement against demand deposits.

But, as discussed in Chapter 9, there is no generally accepted definition of money that would allow one to say that a dollar of time deposits has, say, 50 percent of the moneyness—and impact on aggregate demand—that a dollar of demand deposits has. Hence, reform proposals that treat time deposits as though they have the same moneyness as demand deposits, or alternatively, as though they have no moneyness at all, are hard to evaluate.

The Fed's Targets and Instruments 21

In the two previous chapters we have discussed the Federal Reserve's ultimate goals and its tools. But these tools do not operate directly on the goal variables. Primarily, they change bank reserves and the short-term interest rate, and it is a long way from there to high employment and price stability. This problem is exacerbated by the fact that it takes time until changes in bank reserves and short-term interest rates affect nominal income, and hence employment and prices. Thus, if the Fed changes bank reserves in the wrong direction, or by the wrong amount, by the time it notices that income is moving inappropriately and hence reverses its policy, it is too late; the damage has been done.

Hence, the Fed interposes between its tools and its ultimate goals two sets of intermediate variables. The first set, called **targets,** *consists of variables,* such as the money stock or long-term interest rates, *that have a direct effect on nominal income.* But the Fed cannot reach even these targets directly with its tools. It determines directly and immediately, not the money stock, but only bank reserves and short-term interest rates. It therefore has another set of lower-level targets called **instruments** or **proximate targets** that *stand between its tools and its targets.* These are variables like the federal funds rate and bank reserves that it can affect directly. Figure 21.1 shows the relation between the Fed's goals, targets, short-run targets, and tools.

To illustrate, suppose that the Fed wants nominal income to grow by, say, 7 percent. What open-market operations should it undertake? Suppose it believes that a 7 percent increase in nominal income requires a 6 percent increase in the money stock, which in turn requires a 6¼ percent increase in unborrowed reserves. The Fed now undertakes open-market operations that raise unborrowed reserves by 6¼ percent. But it turns out that the money stock is growing not at the predicted 6 percent rate, but at an 8 percent rate.

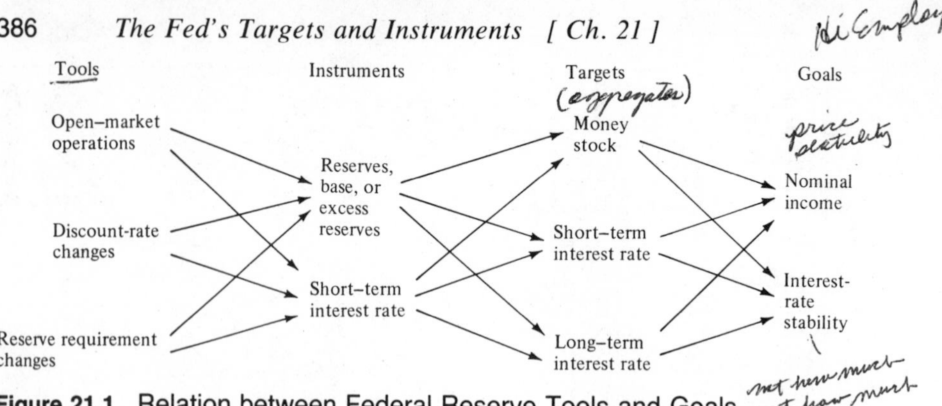

Figure 21.1 Relation between Federal Reserve Tools and Goals

Note: The short-term interest rate appears as a long-run target as well as an instrument because it affects certain types of investment. It is also a goal variable if the Fed is concerned about interest-rate stability.

Something has gone wrong, income will probably rise too much, and the Fed should now reverse its open-market operations until money growth is back at the 6 percent rate that the model says is consistent with the desired 7 percent growth rate of nominal income. After all, it is not open-market operations per se, but the resulting changes in the money stock and the interest rate that affect income. In doing so the Fed is using the money stock as its *target* and is setting its tools with a view to this target rather than focusing directly on its ultimate goal.

But while the money stock is something the Fed can influence more directly than nominal income, it is still some distance removed from its tools. Hence, in aiming at its money stock target the Fed uses *instruments*, such as bank reserves or the federal funds rate as the immediate target of its open market operations.

By using such targets and instruments it can make midcourse corrections if the incoming data tell it that the economy is departing from the path charted out for it. By contrast, if the Fed were to aim directly at its nominal income target it would not be able to make such midcourse corrections because data on the way its policy is affecting income are available only with a much longer lag than are the money-stock data—it takes a long time until the effects on income occur. This does not *necessarily* mean that the use of targets and instruments is beyond criticism. Later on in this chapter we will discuss some alternatives.

TARGET VARIABLES

The choice of a target, or intermediate target as it is sometimes called, is a crucial step in formulating monetary policy, since different target variables frequently tell the Fed to do very different things. For example, the interest-rate target may tell it to adopt an expansionary policy, while the money-stock target tells it to follow a restrictive policy. The selection of the proper targets is a major issue in monetary policy.

Criteria for Target Variables

To be a good target for monetary policy a variable, such as the interest rate, or the money stock, must meet three criteria: measurability, controllability, and relatedness to the goal variables.

The measurability criterion implies two things. First, accurate data must be available quickly. Unless the Fed can tell where it is relative to the target, it does not know what it should do to attain this target.

The second criterion for a target variable is controllability. Unless the Fed has a reasonable chance of achieving, or at least approximating, its target, having the target does not do much good. For example, suppose that the Fed would use as its target changing business expectations. This target is certainly related to its nominal income goal, but there is not enough that the Fed can do (apart from actually changing its policy) to affect expectations. Hence, changing expectations is not a useful target. Unrealistic targets are not just unhelpful, but also make for sloppy policy; if a target is not achievable there seems to be little purpose in even trying very hard to reach it. (The use of unattainable targets does, however, provide a bureaucracy—or for that matter, all of us—with a wonderful excuse for failure and hence is a popular device.)

The third criterion, relatedness, is what using a target variable is all about. The only reason why the Fed uses a target is precisely because it believes that achieving the proper value for this target variable will result in it attaining, or at least coming close to, its ultimate goals. For example, suppose that the money stock had no effect on nominal income, why then should the Fed care whether it is growing at a 2 percent or a 20 percent rate?

Potential Targets

There are three leading contenders for the role of target. They are the money stock, interest rates, and a credit or debt variable. The Fed has to make a choice. If it wants to aim precisely at one of these targets it must usually relinquish control over the other two. Suppose, for example, that the Fed brings about a particular money supply. To make the public willing to hold exactly this amount of money requires a particular interest rate. And if the Fed prefers a different interest rate this is unfortunate; there is nothing it can do about it. If it wants a different interest rate it can reach that interest-rate target only by relinquishing its money-stock target, and giving the public the money stock it wants to hold at *that* interest rate. In the short run (until income, and hence the demand for money curve, have changed) the public's existing demand curve for money tells us the interest rate that corresponds to each particular quantity of money, and the Fed must settle for a combination of money stocks and interest rates that lies on this demand curve. A similar thing applies to bank credit. If the Fed selects a particular interest rate the quantity of bank credit outstanding at that interest rate depends upon the public's demand for bank credit, and not on the Federal Reserve's wishes. And a credit target also implies a specific money stock and vice-versa.

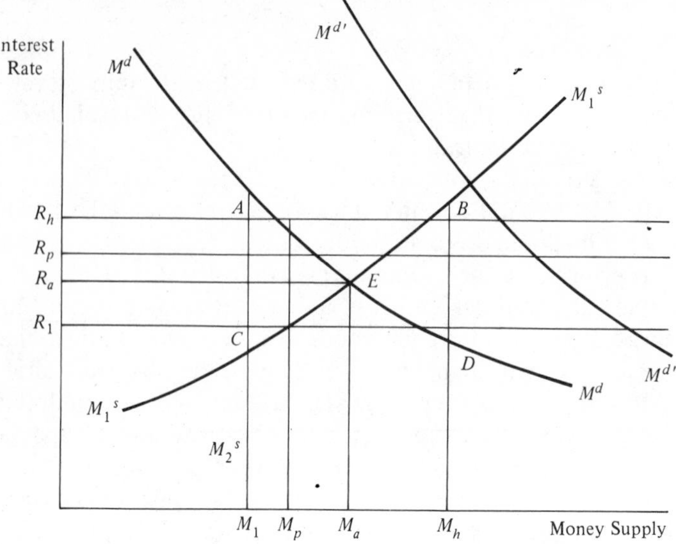

Legend: M^d = money demand curve
M^s = money supply curve
R_h = highest interest rate acceptable to the Federal Reserve
R_p = Federal Reserve's preferred interest rate
R_a = actual interest rate
R_1 = lowest interest rate acceptable to the Federal Reserve
M_1 = lowest money stock acceptable to the Federal Reserve
M_p = Federal Reserve's preferred money stock
M_a = actual money stock
M_h = highest money stock acceptable to the Federal Reserve
$ABCD$ = area within which both the interest rate and the money stock are acceptable to the Federal Reserve

Figure 21.2 The Conflict of Money-Stock and Interest-Rate Targets

Hence, the Fed must either choose to concentrate on only a single target variable, or else it must straddle by using a broad enough range for its targets, so that within this range two or more targets are consistent. This is illustrated in Figure 21.2, where the ranges set for the interest-rate target and the money-stock target (shown by the rectangle *ABCD)* are broad enough so that they are consistent, even though the Fed's preferred target points, R_p and M_p, are inconsistent. And at times, as illustrated by the money demand curve $M^{d'}$, even a broad range around the target points may not suffice to make two target ranges consistent. In such cases the Fed has to make a choice, or else broaden the range.

With this background let us now see how well the potential target variables meet the criteria. We will first discuss the choice between the money stock and the interest rate.

Measurability. In Chapter 9 we discussed the inaccuracies in the early estimates of the money stock, and it is these early estimates that the Fed has to work with. In addition, there is the conceptual problem of whether to focus on *M-1, M-2,* or *M-3*. This depends on which of these measures is more closely related to income, and which one the Fed can control better. Unfortunately, the empirical evidence does not give us unequivocal answers to these questions. And as Figure 9.1 demonstrated, the growth rates of *M-1* and *M-2,* while showing substantial correlation, also show some differences. The fact the *M-2* is growing at a faster rate than *M-1* is not bothersome. What matters is differences in *changes* in their growth rates. Suppose that the growth rates of both drop, say, by half. This would indicate a tightening of monetary policy despite the fact that *M-2* is still growing faster than *M-1*. But if the growth rate of *M-2* rises while the growth rate of *M-1* falls, then it is hard to decide whether the "money stock" is rising or falling. But however severe the measurement and conceptual problems are for the money stock, many—though certainly not all—economists believe that they are just as bad, if not worse, for the interest rate. The term "the interest rate" as used in economic theory is a theoretical term referring to the weighted average of all the interest rates at which borrowing takes place. But the interest rates recorded by our data do not cover all of these rates. They include mainly the interest rates charged on public markets. For example, they do not cover the imputed interest rates that firms charge themselves on internally generated funds.

Second, some of the recorded rates are of doubtful accuracy. For example, while the rate on government securities is measured precisely, this is not true of interest rates charged on bank loans. The data on bank interest rates fail to take into account certain costs of borrowing, such as the need to keep compensating balances, or the various restrictions that a bank imposes on the borrowing firm. More generally, the cost of borrowing—which is what affects investment decisions—contains much more than just the interest rate. The more a firm borrows now the smaller the additional amount it can borrow in the future if it suddenly needs funds. Moreover, the more it borrows the greater is the proportion of its earnings that it is required to pay to its lenders. A relatively small drop in its revenues may therefore cause a firm that has borrowed a great deal to go bankrupt.

Third, as discussed in Chapter 4, banks and other lenders ration credit, so that for many borrowers the prevailing interest rate is of only limited relevance. Suppose, for example, that the interest rate is constant, but that credit becomes tighter, so that a firm that was previously a marginal borrower is now rationed out of the market. In one sense the interest rate for this firm has now become infinite, but this has no effect on the published interest rate data.

Fourth, even if we had accurate data on interest rates charged on all borrowing, and if there were no capital rationing, we would still face the problem of how to combine the observed plethora of interest rates into a single weighted average that represents *the* interest rate. What weights are to be given, for example, to the Treasury bill rate, to the rate on twenty-year bonds, and to the five-year rate? The actually observed volume of borrowing at each rate does not provide us with a meaningful set of weights, because in deciding how much importance to attach to the rise in any particular interest rate, one should look at the amount of borrowing that is choked off by this increase in the interest rate, and not at the amount of borrowing that occurs.

Fifth, what motivates investment decisions are *after-tax* yields and costs. For a firm that is in a 33 percent tax bracket, a 15 percent interest rate represents an after-tax cost of only 10 percent. Unfortunately, it is not easy to determine what the applicable tax rate is for the marginal borrower whose investment depends on the after-tax interest rate. For firms with no income against which to write off costs, the relevant tax rate is zero, and a 15 percent before-tax rate is also a 15 percent after-tax rate.

But the most serious difficulty results from the distinction between the nominal and the real interest rate. Obviously, our data record only the nominal rate. But what is relevant for most expenditure decisions is the expected real rate of interest. Hence, unless we know the price expectations of borrowers we do not know how to interpret a given nominal rate. For example, if the nominal rate is 9 percent, this is a high expected real rate (4 percent) if people think prices will rise at a 5 percent rate, but is a low expected real rate (2 percent) if they think prices will rise at a 7 percent rate. Thus an entirely reasonable error in estimating the public's price expectations leads in this example to an error in estimating the expected real interest rate that is equal to 100 percent of the lower of the two rates. And very little is known about the public's price expectations, so that such an error is far from implausible.

The significance of having to estimate the expected real interest rate from data on the nominal interest rate varies from time to time. In a period when prices are stable, and have been stable for a long time, it is not significant because then one can assume that the public expects prices to be stable, so that the nominal rate and the expected real rate coincide. But in a period of high and variable inflation rates this is not so.

Controllability. The second criterion for a monetary target is controllability. There is no question that in the long run, say, over a period of a year or two, the Fed can reach or come close to its money-stock target. But the critical question is whether the Fed can do so in the short run. In a business-cycle context a year is a long time. The median contraction in postwar cycles has lasted only eleven months.

If changes in reserves had a rapid effect on the rate at which the money stock is growing, then the Fed's task would be much simpler. If money is growing too slowly it could simply inject more reserves, and adjust the amount of reserves to get precisely the money growth rate it wants. But unfortunately, there is a significant lag between changes in reserves and money growth. This creates two problems for the Fed. One is the difficulty of interpreting any deviations of money growth from its target: Suppose that it wants the money stock to grow by $4 billion. Suppose also that only 10 percent of the effect of additional reserves shows up in the first month. At the end of that month the Fed notices that money has grown, not by the anticipated $400 million, but only by $200 million. Does this mean that it should inject more reserves, or will subsequent revisions of the data show that money was growing that month by $400 million after all? Or perhaps the $200 million shortfall is due to some factor that is only temporary. If, despite these doubts, the Fed responds to the shortfall by injecting reserves, it may have to withdraw them again later on. In the process it will destabilize interest rates, first lowering them, and later, when it withdraws reserves, raising them.

Moreover, the existence of a substantial lag in the money creation process means that if the Fed wants to attain its money target right away it will have to allow reserves to overshoot at first. For example, suppose that the Fed wants to raise the money stock by $1 billion within the first month, but that in this time only 10 percent of the effect of an open-market operation on the money stock takes place. If so, the Fed will have to buy a volume of securities that would raise the money stock ultimately by $10 billion. Subsequently it will have to reverse itself sharply and adopt the opposite policy to offset the major part of the first policy when this first policy begins to have its main effects. Since major changes in bank reserves tend to bring about large changes in the federal funds rate, the Fed does not like such erratic policies.

This brings us to a major issue in money-stock control. Many critics of the Fed, particularly monetarists, argue that the Fed could control the money stock much better *if* it were willing to let interest rates fluctuate more.

Turning from the general to the specific, it is obvious that the Fed cannot control the money growth rate with any degree of accuracy on a week-to-week basis. Quite apart from the lag in response of money to changes in the base, the measurement problems discussed in Chapter 9 imply that the Fed's error in estimating the money stock is large, probably much larger than the change the Fed is trying to bring about in that week. Suppose, for example, that the Fed thinks that the money stock is $200 million too low. Even if it succeeds in raising it by exactly $200 million, due to measurement errors the money stock may be $300 million above (or below) what the Fed wants. Fortunately, neither week-to-week nor month-to-month changes in the money supply have much impact on income.

Year-to-year changes in the money stock—which certainly do matter for the behavior of income—can be controlled much better. Within a year most of the response of the money stock to changes in the base has taken place, erratic fluctuations have had a chance to wash out, and also measurement errors are fairly small when compared to the, say, $25 billion by which the Fed wants to change the money stock over the year rather than to the corresponding $500 million change it is trying to bring about during a week. Hence, as Table 9.4 showed on a year-to-year basis, the standard error of the money growth rate is fairly small (0.8 percent for *M-1*). Some monetarist critics of the Fed believe that it could, if it really wanted, hit its money targets more accurately than Table 9.4 suggested.[1]

[1]Thus James Johannes and Robert Rasche believe that the Fed could hit its *M-1* target with a monthly error of 1.5 percent and a year-to-year error of 0.5 percent: "Can the Reserves Approach to Monetary Control Really Work?" *Journal of Money, Credit and Banking,* 13 (August 1981): 298–313.

Can the Fed attain any specific interest-rate target? At one time this was questioned on the argument that at a low enough interest rate the liquidity-preference curve is infinitely elastic. Few economists worry about this any more. But, there is another limitation on the Fed's ability to lower interest rates. A fall in the rate of interest generates a rise in income and prices that raises the interest rate again. Is this a serious limitation on the Federal Reserve's power? To the extent that it is an increase in real income that raises the interest rate back towards its previous level the Fed has nothing to worry about, because presumably it initially lowered the interest rate precisely to obtain this increase in real income. However, if the Phillips curve is vertical, and all the increase in nominal income stimulated by the lower interest rate is a rise in prices, then the Fed is obviously not achieving its purpose. But the problem then is not that the Fed has no power over the interest rate, but rather that the Fed's target, a rise in output, is unattainable, at least by conventional macro policies.

Even if the Phillips curve is not vertical, there is another limitation on the Fed's ability to lower interest rates. This is that besides its income-stabilization goal it also has another goal, exchange-rate stability. As we will explain in Part Five if interest rates fall this tends to reduce the value of the dollar on the foreign-exchange market.

So far, we have talked about the interest rate without specifying what interest rate it is. Since the Fed conducts its open-market operations primarily in short-term securities, its initial impact is on the short-term interest rate. The effects on the long-term or intermediate-term interest rates may be much attenuated and late to arrive. Many, though by no means all, economists believe that it is the long-term rather than the short-term interest rate that has the most effect on investment.[2] They therefore view the fact that monetary policy affects the long-term rate primarily via the short-term rate as a serious limitation on monetary policy.

Relatedness. The third criterion for a target is its relatedness to the Fed's higher-level goals. What is important here is *not* by how *much* a given change in the target variable changes nominal income; if it has only a small effect on income, the Fed can simply change the target variable by a large amount. What is important is how *accurately* the Fed can predict by how much income changes when it changes its target setting.

Does the money stock or the interest rate have a more predictable relation to income? This is a tough question. To see why, consider a situation where the interest rate is initially at the Fed's desired level but then suddenly rises. The Fed does not know why. But it must make a decision. Should it take the interest rate as its target, and keep it stable temporarily by increasing the money stock at a faster rate, or should it treat the money stock as its

[2] However, Robert Hall of Stanford University has argued that it is the short-term interest rate that is relevant for investment decisions. In any one year a firm has to decide whether to invest this year or postpone the project until next year. Hence it compares the yield from investing this year with the cost of investing this year instead of next year, which is the one-year interest rate. See Robert Hall, "Investment, Interest Rates and Stabilization Policy," *Brookings Papers on Economic Activity*, 1 (1977): 61–103.

target, and keep *it* growing at the previously decided-upon rate, even though this means a higher interest rate?

The answer depends on why the interest rate is rising. With the supply of money growing at a constant rate, the unexpected rise in the interest rate must be due to a rise in the demand for money. And in terms of the Cambridge equation, $M = kYp$, this rise in the demand for money must in turn be due either to a rise in k (the proportion of its income the public wants to hold in the form of money), or else to a rise in Yp nominal income.

Suppose first that a rise in k is responsible. In this case the Fed should use the interest rate as its target, and since the desired level of income has not changed, it should keep the interest rate constant. With the demand for money per dollar of income having increased, to prevent a decline in income, the Fed must meet the increased demand for money by increasing the supply of money by the same amount. Otherwise the interest rate rises and causes income to fall. *Thus in this case where the increase in the interest rate is due to a rise in the Cambridge* k *the Fed should use the interest rate as its target.*

But in the alternative case where the unexpected rise in the interest rate is due to a rise in Yp rather than in k, the Fed should use a money-stock target. Since it does not want the rise in nominal income (for if it did, it would already have adopted a policy to change nominal income), it should keep the growth rate of money constant, and allow the interest rate to rise. This rise in the interest rate is desirable because it inhibits expenditures. In other words, when expenditure incentives, such as the profitability of investment, rise and income increases, the resulting rise in the interest rate acts as an automatic stabilizer that moderates the increase in income. *If the Fed uses an interest-rate target in this case, where the rise in the interest rate is due to an increase in income, the Fed acts in a destabilizing manner.* By preventing the rise in the interest rate it removes an important automatic stabilizer. In other words, with an interest-rate target the Fed generates the money to finance an increase in nominal income that it does not want.

This principle can be illustrated with *IS-LM* diagrams.[3] In (A) of Figure 21.3, the *IS* curve shifts around anywhere between IS_1 and IS_2. If the Fed uses a money-stock target, it generates a fixed supply of money and lets the interest rate increase as a rise in income raises the demand for money. Hence, the *LM* curve slopes upward in the usual way. As a rise, say, in the profitability of investment, or in government expenditures, shifts the *IS* curve from IS_1 to IS_2, income increases from Y_0 to Y_1. By contrast, assume that the Fed uses an interest-rate target. It then keeps the interest rate fixed at the desired

[3]Our previous discussion in terms of income and the Cambridge k can be translated into *IS-LM* as follows. An increase in expenditure incentives shifts the *IS* curve. (This curve tells what income will be, given the interest rate, while an increase in expenditure incentives means that at each interest rate firms or consumers want to spend more.) The *LM* curve is drawn to equilibrate the money market by selecting those combinations of interest rates and incomes that equate the supply and demand for money. If people now want to hold more money, the curve shifts outward since it now takes a higher interest rate, or lower income, to make them demand no more money than is available. A problem with using a simple *IS-LM* diagram is that this assumes that prices are stable, which is not necessarily the case here. Fortunately, the results illustrated here with the *IS-LM* diagram can be reached also in algebraic ways that do not require price stability.

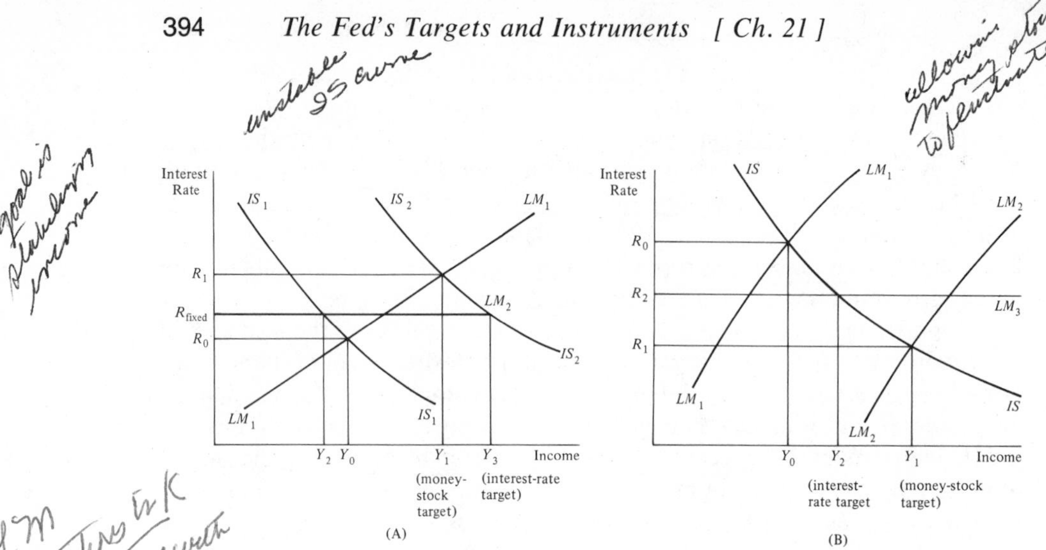

Figure 21.3 Comparison of Money-Stock and Interest-Rate Targets

level by meeting changes in the demand for money with corresponding changes in the supply, so that the LM curve becomes a horizontal line, LM_2. As the IS curve shifts from IS_1 to IS_2 income now rises from Y_2 to Y_3, that is, by more than before.

In 21.3 (B) the IS curve is stable, but the demand for money fluctuates instead, so that the LM curve varies between LM_1 and LM_2. Suppose the Fed has a money stock target that keeps the money stock constant (since it does not want income to change) and lets the interest rate fluctuate. Income then varies between Y_0 and Y_1. Now suppose instead that the Fed uses an interest-rate target, that is, it varies the supply of money enough to keep the interest rate fixed all the time at R_2. This changes the LM curve to LM_3, so that income stays at Y_2.

Thus we have the following rule: *If the change in the interest rate is due to a change in the Cambridge* k *the Fed should follow an interest-rate target, but if the change in the interest rate is the result of a change in income as expenditure incentives change, in other words, a shift of the* IS *curve, then the Fed should use a money-stock target instead.* And now here is the problem. *When the interest rate changes, the Fed does not know whether this is due to changes in the Cambridge* k *or in expenditure incentives*. All it observes is that the interest rate is, say, rising and it has to decide whether or not to prevent this rise by increasing the money stock.[4] Whatever decision it makes, under *one* set of circumstances it will be the wrong decision, and will destabilize the economy.

[4]There is an additional complication. The above conclusions depend critically on the *IS* curve sloping downward. If, instead, it should have a positive slope the conclusions just obtained would be reversed. And one cannot be certain that the *IS* curve does not have a positive slope. See David Geitman, "Optimal Choice of Monetary Policy," *Quarterly Journal of Economics* 85 (November 1971): 712–15.

This is a horrible situation. It would not be so bad if the Fed would know whether unexpected changes in the interest rate are *usually* due to a change in the Cambridge *k* or to a change in expenditure incentives. It could then do that which would *usually* yield the right result. But the Fed does not really know which is the usual case and which is the unusual one. Monetarists believe that the Cambridge *k* is stabler and more predictable then expenditure incentives, and hence support a money-stock target, but Keynesian theory can be interpreted to favor either a money-stock or interest-rate target. But it can be shown that if unexpected shifts in the *IS* and the *LM* curves are equally likely, then the money stock is a better target than is the interest rate.[5] Hence, unless there is some halfway reliable evidence that the unexpected changes in the interest rate are more likely to be due to a shift in the *LM* curve, the Fed should adopt a money-stock target.[6]

In Conclusion

To summarize, on the first criterion, measurability, both the money stock and the interest rate perform very badly. Similarly, both target variables have some, though lesser, problem on the second criterion, controllability. And their relative performance on the third criterion, relationship to the income goal, is much disputed.

Before leaving the targets issues there is one more important, practical consideration. We have talked about the Fed choosing an interest-rate target consistent with its desired income level. But the Fed is also concerned with keeping interest rates stable. With an interest-rate target the Fed is therefore continually tempted to keep the level of its target unchanged, even though income is changing in an undesired way. On the other hand, with a money-stock target the Fed would quite clearly be required to let interest rates change. Hence, a money-stock target is less subject to abuse; it does not lend itself to the temptation of overemphasizing a day-to-day concern (interest-rate stability) at the expense of the longer range, but much more important, task.

All in all, the selection of a target variable for monetary policy involves

[5]The argument is complex, but comes down to the following. First, assume that the Fed wants to minimize the square of the deviations of actual income from the desired income level. Second, assume that when the interest rate changes the Fed does not know at all whether the *IS* or *IM* curve has shifted. In this situation, the Fed should adopt a policy that is intermediate between what it would do if it knew with certainty which curve had shifted. But, it turns out that the money-stock target is just such an intermediate policy. To see this, assume that the Fed was certain that the *IS* curve has shifted outward. Should it then adopt a policy of keeping the money stock constant? No, it shouldn't. While this policy would be better than keeping the interest rate constant, the Fed could do better still. It could *reduce* the money stock, thus offsetting the rise in income produced by the shift in the *IS* curve. Keeping the money stock constant is therefore already an in-between policy, and hence is the appropriate policy if shifts in the two curves are equally likely. See Steven LeRoy and David Lindsey, "Determining the Monetary Instrument: A Diagrammatic Exposition," *American Economic Review* 68 (December 1978): 929–34.

[6]Although we have discussed only the problem of choosing between a money-stock target and an interest-rate target, a similar analysis can be developed for the bank-credit-interest-rate targets choice.

controversies on three levels. First, there are narrow technical disagreements about the measurability of the variables, and the extent to which they can be controlled. Second, there are disputes about basic macroeconomic theory. Are fluctuations in income due more to fluctuations in the expenditure incentives, so that by using a stable money growth rate as its target the Fed could stabilize income, or are income fluctuations due more to variations in the Cambridge *k* that the Fed should offset? More specifically, does economic analysis tell us that there is a particular monetary variable, such as *M-1* or *M-2,* that has a stable relation to income? Third, there is a dispute about what might almost be called the sociology of central banking. If the Fed uses an interest rate target will it be able to resist the temptation to keep the interest rate stable rather than move it to the proper level?

CREDIT OR DEBT VARIABLES

In recent years another potential target, outstanding credit or debt, has appeared, or rather reappeared, on the scene, primarily due to the work of Benjamin Friedman of Harvard University. He has argued that the total outstanding debt of all nonfinancial borrowers (that is, all borrowers other than financial institutions) is as good or better a target variable than is money.

While the deregulation of the financial system and the resulting growth of new types of accounts has made the meaning of *M-1* and *M-2* uncertain, the outstanding debt of nonfinancial borrowers has retained its meaning. Moreover, it bears as stable a relationship to nominal income as does money. And the Fed can control it because its open-market operations provide banks with the wherewithal to extend credit.

Benjamin Friedman does not suggest that the Fed cease looking at money. Instead the Fed should set target ranges for the growth rates of both money and the total debt of nonfinancial borrowers. What if these two targets conflict, what if, say, bringing the money growth rate up within its target range would mean allowing debt to grow at a rate above its growth rate range? This, says Friedman, should serve as a signal to the Fed to reconsider its ranges for both variables, and to decide which to readjust. Being guided by the behavior of two variables is better than looking at just one variable since it avoids putting all ones eggs into one basket. This idea is still quite new and so far (late 1983) has not yet received much professional discussion. However, some economists have questioned whether the Fed can control the debt variable as accurately as it can control money.

INSTRUMENTS

The problems that the Fed faces in controlling nominal income apply also to its control over its target variables. It therefore uses instrument variables. The criteria for these are similar to those for the targets: measurability, controllability, and relatedness (now to the targets themselves rather than to the income goal).

The Instrument Variables

The Fed can use as its instrument variable any of the several measures of bank reserves and the base discussed in Chapter 11. These measures, together with measures of money, are often referred to as *"the aggregates"* to distinguish them from a very different instrument, the federal funds rate. (The funds rate can also be a target variable because it affects certain types of investment directly. And insofar as the Fed tries to stabilize the funds rate it is also a goal variable.) The Fed has used the federal funds rate as its instrumental variable by operating on the demand for money. Thus, if it wanted the money stock to grow it would lower the federal funds rate so that the public would want to hold more money, and presumably the banks would create this additional money by running down their excess reserves or by borrowing from the Fed.

Another instrument is called **money-market conditions.** It is a rather nebulous amalgam of a number of variables that gauge supply and demand in the money market, such as the federal funds rate, and bank borrowings (which indicates the pressure on banks to repay their borrowings from the Fed) and free reserves, as well as the Fed's general subjective evaluation of the money market, sometimes called "color, tone, and feel." This proximate target played an important role in the Federal Reserve's thinking in the 1950s and early 1960s and then faded away.

Evaluation of Instruments

Now let us see how good each of these instruments is at controlling one of the target variables, the money stock. Total reserves and unborrowed reserves pass the measurability test with flying colors. The Fed can at any time read off its own books the reserves that depository institutions keep with it and the amount of their borrowings. And it can easily estimate the other part of reserves, vault cash, from the reports filed with it. Similarly, the Fed can readily estimate the reserve base and the extended base by estimating the currency holdings of the public. All of these variables also meet the attainability criterion very well since the Fed can use open-market operations to change reserves by any desired amount.

The money-market-conditions instrument has a measurement problem since it is subjective. The Federal Reserve can control it well. But, in any case, this instrument has a fatal disease; money-market conditions do not have a consistent—and hence usable—relation to any of the target variables.

ALTERNATIVE APPROACHES

The Base

The targets and instrument approach just discussed is used both by the Fed and by many academic economists. But some have rejected it. They argue that the Fed can achieve more accurate control over income by using a single variable, the base, than by using separate target and instrument variables. The usual procedure of going from the base to the money stock, and then from the money stock to income, introduces two errors: an error in the equation estimating the money stock from the base, and a second error in the equation linking the money stock to income. Some economists believe that the error in the single equation linking the base directly to income is as small or smaller than the error in the equation linking the money stock to income. Hence, the total error in estimating income is greater if the money stock is interposed as a target since we then have the additional error involved in going from the base to the money stock. However, other economists believe that using separate equations to go from the base to money, and then from money to income gives smaller errors. Unfortunately the data do not give an unequivocal answer as to which is the better procedure. One reason some economists object to relating the base directly to income is that approximately 70 percent of the base is currency. And although we can predict the demand for currency quite well, we do not really *understand* why people are holding so much currency. Reliance on badly understood statistical regularities can be dangerous.

Control Theory

A more basic criticism of the instruments and targets approach has been presented by Benjamin Friedman. We began this chapter by discussing the case where the Fed observes that the money stock differs from what it had predicted, and therefore adjusts the money stock to keep it on target. But, Friedman asks, why does the money stock differ from the predicted one? Obviously something has gone wrong in one of the equations of the Fed's model. This is useful information since it is likely to affect also the model's prediction of the relation between the money stock and income. This information should not be discarded as it is by saying, oh, well, we will just bring the money stock to the level we originally planned for it. Moreover, the money stock and the interest rate are not the only variables that affect income. Hence he suggests that the Fed should not use the money stock or the interest rate as its only target, but should instead use all the available information to predict how income is changing, and use this information in deciding on open-market operations.

Along similar lines, a number of economists (including Benjamin Friedman) have tried to extend the traditional analysis by focusing on the fact that when the Fed observes an unexpected rise in the interest rate or in the money stock it is being told by the data that one of its equations (or informal forecasts) is wrong. And this error may well be due to shifts in *both* the *IS* and *LM* curves rather than in just one of them, so that the simple rule we developed in Figure 21.3 is not applicable. Hence, there is no easy way the Fed can respond. But the Fed is not the only one who faces this problem of being off-target. Electrical engineers experience it too and have designed optimal mechanisms for bringing a variable back to its target. (The familiar furnace thermostat is an example of such a mechanism.) They have developed a branch of mathematics called "control theory" that can be used to decide how a mechanism should respond to information that it is off-target. This control theory has been applied to the problem of selecting a monetary policy target. Unfortunately, it requires some quite complex mathematics, and therefore having looked the problem firmly in the eye we will pass on.

Nominal Income Target

Another alternative is to have the Fed focus directly on nominal income rather than on some intermediate target such as the money stock. The meaning of this proposal is not obvious. It is not a simple choice between using only income or only money as the target. Using a money stock target already implies a nominal income target because the money stock target is not picked out of thin air. A particular money stock is selected precisely because it is thought to bring about a particular level of nominal income. Similarly, if the Fed were to announce that it has selected a nominal income target, it would still have to translate this target into specific targets for open-market operations at various times. And in the process of determining what open-market operations are compatible with the nominal income target the Fed would have to think in terms of money, or interest rates, or some other financial target.

But this does not mean that announcing a nominal income target is almost the same thing as announcing a money stock target or an interest rate target. If the target is set and announced in terms of a particular money growth rate the Fed will tend to stay with that money target for some time. Thus, if it achieves its money target, but income is not growing at the desired rate, it will not change the money growth rate right away. By contrast, if it focuses on an income target it will make the change sooner. Unfortunately, it is far from clear how fast the Fed *should* adjust. There is also a political problem. By stating its target in terms of a money growth rate the Fed can hide the fact that it is aiming at an income level that seems too low to many people. Is this good or bad?

THE FEDERAL RESERVE'S POLICY PROCEDURES

How does the Fed actually conduct its policy? What targets, instruments, and indicators does it use? To get some perspective on this question it is useful to back up, and look first at the Fed's previous procedures.

The 1950s and 1960s

In the 1950s and early 1960s the Fed relied more on intuitive judgment than on economic analysis. William McChesney Martin, who was then chairman, believed that the informed judgment of market participants, even though not always well articulated, is superior to abstract economic analysis, that central banking is an "art" and not a "science." The Fed did not think that the quantity of money was central and instead emphasized short-term nominal interest rates, credit conditions, and bank credit. It did not see itself as determining the long-term interest rate, but rather as generating sufficient credit to finance "sound" expansions, while curbing inflationary and unsustainable expansions. Its policy was expressed in phrases like "leaning against the wind." This preference for vague, intuitive notions over quantifiable magnitudes was quite explicit, with several Governors arguing that not enough is known to quantify the targets of monetary policy. Hence, the FOMC would change its policy, for example, from one of "ease" to one of "active ease."

In formulating its Directive the FOMC used, without distinguishing between their employment as targets and instruments, free reserves, the short-term interest rate, and money-market conditions. The emphasis on free reserves, that is, excess reserves minus borrowed reserves, money-market conditions, and the short-term interest rate had some definite advantages for the Fed. A major aim of the Fed at the time was to keep interest rates from fluctuating too much. Essentially what the Fed did was to accommodate the demand for reserves. As the demand increased, and interest rates rose, it would provide additional reserves, primarily through open-market purchases. This tended to make its policy procyclical rather than countercyclical because the demand for credit, and hence the banks' demand for reserves, rises in the expansion and falls in the recession, so that the Fed tended to supply more reserves in the expansion and fewer in the recession.[7]

This questionable policy was due, in part, to the Fed's use of a nefarious target, free reserves. It believed that banks first want to repay all their borrowing from the Fed, and then use most of the excess reserves they have left over to extend loans and purchase securities. Hence, the Fed thought that it could control deposit creation, and thus bank credit and the money stock by controlling the volume of free reserves. But the assumption that banks want to keep only a fixed amount of free reserves is invalid. Free reserves are an inventory that banks keep, and their desired inventory of free reserves depends on the opportunity cost of holding these reserves (for example, the federal funds rate) and the benefit of holding excess reserves, such as avoiding having to borrow at the Fed if there is a deposit outflow.

To see the damage a free-reserves target can do, assume that the Fed wants to prevent excessive ease by reducing the free reserves that banks have, say, from \$100 million to \$50 million. It therefore undertakes open-market sales of \$50 million. But, given prevailing interest rates, banks *want*

[7]The money growth rate being procyclical is not *necessarily* bad. It is *not* true that to stabilize the economy one should raise income in the recession and lower it in the expansion. During the first part of the recession income is still above its normal level, and during the first part of the expansion it is still below its normal level. Hence, to stabilize income around its trend, monetary policy *should* lower income during the early stages of the recession. Thus, instead of seeing whether the money growth rate behaves pro- or anti-cyclically, one should compare it to some indicator, such as the unemployment rate, that tells us whether aggregate demand is insufficient or excessive. And if one compares changes in the growth rate of either *M-1* or *M-2* to cyclical changes in unemployment, then the money growth rate is seen to respond fairly well to unemployment. Does this mean that the Federal Reserve is actually stabilizing the economy? Not necessarily, because changes in the money growth rate affect aggregate demand with a lag, so that monetary policy could very easily be destabilizing after all. But whether or not it is destabilizing cannot be determined unless one knows the lag in the effect of monetary policy. In addition, there is a problem with how one reads the data. While monetary growth rates were procyclical in the 1950s, for the 1960s it depends on whether one starts with recessions or expansions.

to keep $100 million of free reserves. They therefore reduce their loans and security holdings, and thus deposits and the money supply fall. The Fed now sees that free reserves are still $100 million, so it undertakes another open-market sale of $50 million, to which the banks respond again by cutting their deposits and hence the money stock, to hold on to their $100 million of excess reserves. This process goes on until either the Fed finally gives in, or else interest rates change enough to make banks want to hold only $50 million rather than $100 million of excess reserves. But either of these could take a long time, and in the meantime the money supply keeps on shrinking. By using a totally inappropriate target the Fed lost control of the money supply.

What made this policy particularly bad is that during a recession as interest rates fell banks wanted to hold more free reserves. The Fed, using free reserves as an indicator as well as a target, then interpreted the rise in excess reserves as showing that its policy was easy, when in fact the growth rate of the money stock was falling.

Its use of the short-term interest rate enhanced this confusion. During a recession interest rates fall as the demand for credit decreases. But the Fed interpreted this decline as showing that it was following an expansionary policy. With interest rates falling, sometimes substantially, the Fed concluded that its policy was too easy and reduced the growth rate of bank reserves.

As a result of a great deal of criticism from academic economists, particularly Brunner and Meltzer, by 1966 the Fed started to change its policy procedures. Not surprisingly, this has taken the form of an evolutionary series of steps rather than a once-and-for-all radical change.

The 1970s

During the 1970s the Fed's emphasis on the growth rate of money slowly increased, so that by the late 1970s it used the growth rate of money as its target. The federal funds rate was *seemingly* used as an instrumental variable; if the Fed wanted the money growth rate to rise it would lower the funds rate to increase the public's demand for money. But, in addition—and this is a most important addition—the FOMC also set a tolerance range for the funds rate. Usually this federal funds rate range was set as a quite narrow band, for example, 8¼–9½ percent, while the range for the money growth rate might be, say 4–8 percent for M_1 and 6–10 percent for M_2.

As discussed earlier in this chapter (see Figure 21.2) the ranges for the funds rate and the money growth rate may turn out to be inconsistent. What happened then? In the great majority of cases the Fed decided to keep the funds rate within its range, and allow the money growth rate to fall outside its range. Hence, the Fed was *not* actually following a procedure of using the money growth rate as a target and the funds rate as an instrument. Instead, the process was dominated by the Fed's reluctance to allow large changes in the funds rate. The longer run target of a specific money growth rate—as is so often the fate of long-run targets and other good intentions—was sacrificed to the short-run target, which was interest rate stability.

Starting in 1975, Congress entered the picture. The Fed chairman now appears before congressional committees to reveal and justify annual growth targets for money, and to explain any misses from the previous targets. There is, however, less to this than meets the eye, in part because the target growth rate is stated as a broad range, say 2½–5½ percent, even though a 5½ percent growth rate may be consistent with a 3 percent higher inflation rate than is a 2½ percent money growth rate. Moreover, the Fed can shift its focus of attention among *M-1, M-2,* and *M-3* to that measure whose growth rate is easiest to justify, and in general Fed chairmen are highly skilled in conducting defensive operations against congressional probes.[8]

The Fed's slowly growing emphasis on the money growth rate did not satisfy its critics, particularly the monetarists. They accused the Fed of only paying lip service to the money growth rate while really being much more concerned with stabilizing interest rates. The Fed replied that interest rate stability is important for an efficiently functioning money market, and argued that if the money stock is moderately off its target for up to six months this has little effect on GNP. (But remember that 0.01 percent of GNP is still a lot of money.) Besides, the Fed said, the money data are so bad, and subject to such large revisions, that one should not worry so much if the currently available figures show the money growth rate being off target. The next revision of the data might well change this. Moreover, the Fed argued that the Cambridge *k* changes from time to time and that the money growth rate should be varied to accommodate these shifts.

In any case, there was an institutional factor that limited effective control over the money stock. This was a system of *lagged reserve accounting* whereby banks had to keep reserves against their deposits two weeks earlier, rather than against their deposits during the current week. This meant that in any week in which banks did not have sufficient reserves to meet their reserve requirements they could do nothing about it. Any single bank could increase its reserves by buying federal funds, etc., but this did not help the banking system as a whole. Accordingly, to allow banks to meet their reserve requirements the Fed had to provide them with the needed reserves.

Many economists criticized this system, arguing that instead of controlling the money stock the Fed was simply letting the banks determine the money stock and then supplying them with the needed reserves. The Fed replied that since it provided these reserves by forcing banks to borrow from it, rather than through open-market operations, banks had an incentive to cut back their deposits, and hence their need for borrowed reserves during the next week. Many other economists, however, doubted that banks are that much concerned about their level of borrowing. In any case, the Fed substantially modified this system in 1983 making the lag only two days. Whether this will solve the problem is too early to tell.

[8] In addition, if the Fed say, overshot its target in one quarter it would apply the previously decided-upon rate of growth for the next quarter, not to what the level of money should have been, but to what it actually was, that is, to a higher base. Thus errors were compounded. Under subsequent legislation this "base drift" can now occur only once a year.

While this debate was waxing fast and furious events took a hand. As will be described in Chapter 24, in October 1979 there was a crisis of confidence in U.S. monetary policy because it seemed to many foreign central banks, as well as to many Americans, that the Fed was unable to control the money growth rate and hence the inflation rate. As a result the Fed announced a new procedure to which we now turn.

The Early 1980s

The new procedure is that the Fed adopts longer-run (twelve months) monetary targets. Since these targets are announced six months earlier it amounts in effect to an eighteen-month plan, though the Fed reserves the right to change it if circumstances change. At its meetings the FOMC also sets out shorter-run targets, say for the next two or three months. It also establishes a range for the federal funds rate. But since this range is much broader than before, say 5 percent, a conflict between the funds rate target and the money growth rate target is now much less likely than it was before. And, if such a conflict does arise, the funds rate target is not binding. The account manager then asks the FOMC for new instructions, and usually the funds rate target is adjusted. Apart from the money target, the Fed also uses a credit target.

The instrumental variable used is unborrowed reserves. The Fed first estimates the volume of total reserves required to reach its money stock target, and then subtracts its estimate of what borrowings will be.[9] This gives it an estimate of the unborrowed reserves it has to supply through open market operations. But, suppose the Fed's estimate is off, and borrowings are greater than it expected. If this continues for some time the Fed will eventually offset the higher level of borrowings by lowering unborrowed reserves. Until then, however, the Fed allows total reserves to be above target because it thinks that such increased borrowing acts as a safety valve if the demand for reserves per dollar of deposits is increasing due to some factor, such as a shift of deposits to banks that have a higher reserve requirement. In addition, it believes that a rise in borrowed reserves is not likely to lead to much of an increase in the money stock because banks are reluctant to expand deposits on the basis of borrowed reserves.

How has this new procedure worked? The federal funds rate has fluctuated *much* more. This is hardly surprising. What *is* surprising is that the money growth rate has also been more variable. One would expect that once the Fed was no longer so constrained by the wish to stabilize interest rates it would hit its monetary targets more accurately than before. The Fed's explanation is that the observed variability reflects the instability in the demand for money. In its view academic economists were simply wrong when they had previously argued that the money growth rate would be stabler if only the Fed would relinquish its urge to stabilize the funds rate. Moreover, as previously discussed, due to data errors and to random fluctuations around the trend, a stable *underlying* money growth rate is consistent with the data

[9] Borrowings depend, in turn, on the discount rate and the federal funds rate. The Fed sets the latter at a level that it believes will induce the public to hold the target level of money.

showing large month-to-month variations in the estimated money growth rate.

The Fed's critics who had lambasted the Fed's previous narrow constraints on the funds rate for causing it to miss its money targets are now on the defensive. One of their answers is that the Fed has not really changed its policy significantly, that it is still trying to stabilize interest rates. For example, suppose that the funds rate that is consistent with the desired money growth rate is 18 percent. If so, it matters little whether the permitted range on the funds rate is 16–17 percent or 12–17 percent. Second, by using unborrowed reserves, rather than total reserves or the base as its target the Fed is still allowing the demand for money to bring about corresponding changes in the supply of money. For example, suppose that firms want to borrow more. This drives up interest rates and, with a fixed discount rate, gives banks an incentive to borrow from the Fed.[10] As long as the Fed focuses on unborrowed reserves it will allow such increased borrowing to result in a higher level of total reserves, and hence in a higher money stock. The debate here centers on what is the main cause of changes in borrowings. If it is changes in the demand for money, then accommodating the change in the demand for reserves will cause the money stock to depart from the Fed's target, and accommodation is therefore bad. But if the increased demand for reserves is due to a greater demand for reserves per dollar of money, then the Fed should accommodate it.

SUMMARY

1. It takes a long time until the effect of the Fed's actions shows up, and even then these effects are hard to isolate. Hence, the Fed measures the impact of its actions on a set of intermediate target variables.
2. The selection of a target variable is a crucial step; the relevant criteria are measurability, controllability, and relatedness to the higher level goals. The two main rival targets are the money growth rate and interest rates, but total debt of nonfinancial borrowers has also been suggested as a target. The Fed must choose between them, or else use a compromise, since they are generally not simultaneously achievable. Both variables have serious measurement problems. Controllability is also a serious problem. On the relatedness issue the rule is that if the *IS* curve is unstable while the *LM* curve is stable the Fed should use a money stock target, while in the opposite case it should use an interest rate target.
3. Since the Fed does not *directly* control any of the target variables, it uses instrumental variables to attain its targets. The two main candidates here are reserves (or the base) and the short-term interest rate.
4. This targets-instruments approach is not accepted by all economists. Some prefer to use the base as both an instrument *and* a target, while others believe that the Fed should abandon both targets and instruments, and look at nominal income rather than focusing just on financial variables.
5. The Fed's use of targets has changed over time. From an emphasis on money market conditions in the 1950s it has shifted to a focus on the money stock. In

[10] However, the higher interest rates also reduce the demand for money, and hence the money stock.

the 1970s, however, the Fed's reluctance to change the federal funds rate meant that it frequently missed its money targets.

6. At present the Fed has both long-run and short-run money growth targets, and uses unborrowed reserves as its instrument. Surprisingly, the money growth rate fluctuated more in the early 1980s than in the 1970s. The Fed attributes the sharp fluctuations in the money growth rate to the inherent difficulties of controlling money, while monetarists believe that it has not tried sufficiently hard to control the money growth rate.

Questions and Exercises

1. To what extent is the money stock a good target? To what extent is the interest rate?
2. Using the data provided in the *Economic Report of the President* make a judgment about whether the Federal Reserve actually does offset borrowing and currency flows.
3. What are the criteria for targets and instruments? Explain in your own words.
4. Discuss: "Given the uncertainties about targets and instruments the Federal Reserve is just as likely to act in a destabilizing as in a stabilizing way."
5. Compare the Directives in recent issues of the *Federal Reserve Bulletin* with the data (also in the *Federal Reserve Bulletin*) on the *actual* changes that occurred in the money stock and the federal funds rate. Is it still true that the Fed is putting little emphasis on its interest-rate target?
6. Explain in your own words why the Fed should use an interest-rate target if the observed change in the interest rate is due to a change in the amount of money demanded per dollar of income, and a money-stock target if it is due to a rise in income.

Further Reading

BERKMAN, NEIL. "Open Market Operations and the New Monetary Policy." Federal Reserve Bank of Boston, *New England Economic Review* (March/April 1981): 5–20. A useful discussion of the Fed's post-October 1979 procedures.

BOARD OF GOVERNORS, FEDERAL RESERVE SYSTEM. *New Monetary Control Procedures*. Washington, D.C.: 1981. The first essay by Stephen Axilrod provides a useful summary of this massive and highly technical Fed study of targets and instruments.

FEDERAL RESERVE BANK OF ST. LOUIS. *Review*. Early each year this *Review* has an article on the previous year's FOMC decisions and discusses changes in Fed procedures.

FRIEDMAN, BENJAMIN. "The Inefficiency of Short Run Monetary Targets for Monetary Policy." *Brookings Papers on Economic Activity*, 1977:2, 292–346. A stimulating critique of the targets and instruments approach.

GAMS, CARL. "Federal Reserve Intermediate Targets: Money or the Monetary Base." Federal Reserve Bank of Kansas City, *Review* 65 (January 1980): 3–15. A provocative discussion of the issue of the base vs. money as a target.

LINDSEY, DAVID. "Nonborrowed Reserve Targeting and Monetary Control," in Laurence Meyer (ed.) *Improving Money Stock Control*. Boston: Kluwer-Nijhoff, 1983, 3–41. An important discussion of current operating procedures.

MELTZER, ALLAN, RASCHE, ROBERT, AXILROD, STEPHEN, STERNLIGHT, PETER. "Is the Federal Reserve's Monetary Control Policy Misdirected?" *Journal of Money, Credit and Banking,* 14 (February 1982): 119–47. The record of a very interesting debate on the Fed's new procedures.

MORRIS, FRANK. "Do the Monetary Aggregates have a Future as Targets of Federal Reserve Policy?" Federal Reserve Bank of Boston, *New England Economic Review* (March/April 1982): 5–14. A powerful critique of the use of monetary targets.

WALLICH, HENRY, and KEIR, PETER. "The Role of Operating Guides in U.S. Monetary Policy." *Federal Reserve Bulletin* 65 (September 1979): 679–91. An excellent survey of the Fed's changing targets and indicators.

The Impact of Monetary Policy

22

Having seen how the Fed changes the money stock and interest rates we now look at how changes in money and interest rates affect nominal GNP and various sectors of the economy. But before doing so, a few words about the strength of monetary policy.

STRENGTH OF MONETARY POLICY

From the 1930s until the late 1950s or early 1960s the predominant view among economists was that monetary policy has little effect on GNP; changes in the money stock would be largely offset by changes of velocity in the opposite direction. But nowadays, few if any doubt that a sharply restrictive monetary policy can bring about a recession or prevent a recovery. Any remaining doubts about this were stilled by the experience of the early 1980s. The evidence is less clear on whether an expansionary monetary policy could terminate a really severe recession within a reasonable time. Some—though by no means all—Keynesians argue that massive open-market purchases during a severe recession would be ineffective, because lower interest rates would do little to stimulate investment in a slump; "you can't push on a piece of string." But this is a minority view.

THE TRANSMISSION PROCESS

As pointed out in Chapter 15 a major difference between the monetarist and Keynesian analyses of *how* money affects the economy is that monetarists do not spell out this transmission process in detail, while Keynesians do. Hence, before turning to the detailed Keynesian story we present just a brief discussion of a portfolio process that summarizes the monetarist version of the transmission process, but is also entirely acceptable to Keynesians.

Portfolio Equilibrium

Everyone has a portfolio of assets and liabilities and tries to keep the (monetary plus imputed) yields of all its assets equal at the margin. Now suppose that the quantity of money increases, so that at least some portfolios now include more money. Given, for the usual reasons, declining marginal utility, the yield on money is now less than before, and therefore also less than the yield on other assets. Hence, portfolio holders now exchange money for other assets. What assets they buy depends upon the cross-elasticities of demand, which, in turn, depends on the similarity between assets. For example, money and Treasury bills, being similar, are close substitutes (have a high cross-elasticity of demand). Not only are they both very safe assets, but the type of risks to which they are subject are alike. They are both subject to inflation risk, but not to default risk. Similarly, there is no significant fall in their values if interest rates rise. Hence, those who initially hold excess money balances use them to buy mainly securities, like Treasury bills. But the sellers of Treasury bills now receive these excess money balances and they buy mainly assets that are not too dissimilar to Treasury bills, for example, commercial paper and three-year government securities. The sellers of these items, in turn, then buy other assets, and eventually the increased demand for assets spreads (in principle) to all assets in the economy, until in the new equilibrium the (monetary plus imputed) yields on all assets are again equal. Among the assets whose prices are raised in this way are common stocks, and thus the value of corporations. And if the value of existing corporations exceeds the cost of creating new ones, investment takes place. For example, suppose that it costs $100 million to construct a new plant and that the public is willing to pay $110 million for the stock of a corporation that owns just this plant. It is now profitable to start a new corporation that owns such a plant, or to add such a plant to an existing corporation. Moreover, as the yield on various assets such as money, stocks, and bonds declines, the imputed yield on consumer durables starts to exceed these other yields, so that households buy more durables. And similarly, nondurable consumption may rise.

The Keynesian Approach

The Keynesian version of the transmission process accepts the foregoing, but spells it out in greater detail and formulates it in terms of interest rates rather than in terms of the stock of money relative to other assets. In this analysis two relations are central in determining by how much a given increase in the money growth rate raises income. One is the slope of the liquidity preference (demand for money) curve. This slope determines how much the interest rate will decline as the money stock increases. The second is the slope of the marginal efficiency of investment curve which determines how much investment increases in response to the fall in the interest rate. The third is the multiplier relating investment to income.

Impact of Money Market Imperfections

In Chapter 14 we showed why a decline in interest rates induces firms to invest more. This discussion assumed a perfect capital market in which firms can borrow as much as they want to invest. We will now extend this analysis by dropping this assumption and consider how a change in the interest rate affects investment by changing the availability of funds.

In Chapter 4 we discussed capital rationing and how some firms are unable to obtain bank loans. If banks now obtain additional reserves they are more willing to make loans to some of these potential customers. These previously unsatisfied borrowers have a number of investment projects that they thought worth undertaking even at the previous higher interest rate, and they are even more eager to undertake these projects now that the interest rate has fallen.

Moreover, when interest rates fall another imperfection in the capital market is reduced. Some financial institutions are sometimes "locked in." They bought securities previously at a high price, and since then security prices have fallen. The managers do not want to admit that they made a mistake in buying these securities by selling them at a loss; instead they hold onto them.[1] But once interest rates fall and security prices rise again, financial institutions can sell these securities without taking a loss. Hence they sell them and make loans with the proceeds from these sales. This means that business borrowers get loans, and when they spend them, aggregate demand increases. But how about the buyers of the securities? As they buy them they have to reduce other expenditures. But they are not likely to reduce other expenditures dollar for dollar. Securities, particularly short-term government securities, are very liquid. Hence, a firm that buys government securities can satisfy part of its demand for liquidity in this way and can now run down its money holdings to some extent. Thus, the decline in expenditures by the purchasers of securities is less than the increase in expenditures by those who now get loans from banks and other financial institutions, so that there is a net increase in aggregate demand.

In the past market imperfections also played a role in the impact of monetary policy on residential construction. As interest rates rose disintermediation reduced the volume of mortgage loans that thrift institutions could make. But now with the demise of Regulation Q, this is much less of a problem.

Finally, some economists have pointed to an institutional factor that they believe substantially reduces the impact of monetary policy. This is the existence of trade credit. (Trade credit is the credit that a firm, say a wholesaler, extends to another firm, say a retailer, by shipping goods with payments to be made only in the future, perhaps in thirty or ninety days.) They

[1] Such a locking-in effect may seem irrational. Why *not* sell securities at a loss and get the benefits of a tax write-off? The answer is that some portfolio managers are maximizing, not the income of their institutions, but their own welfare. Moreover, writing losses off makes the company's balance sheet look worse, something some companies cannot afford.

have argued that if firms extend more credit to their customer firms this can, at least partially, offset the effect of a restrictive monetary policy. However, the empirical evidence suggests that, at least as far as manufacturing firms are concerned, trade credit does *not* expand when the Fed reduces the growth rate of the money stock. This suggests that trade credit does not inhibit the impact of monetary policy.[2]

Monetary Policy and Stock Prices

To see how changes in monetary policy affect stock prices we will deal first with a situation in which there is not much fear of inflation. Assume that the Fed adopts an expansionary policy and the growth rate of money rises. The way stock prices are affected can be formulated in three ways. The first is to say that the public now holds more money in its portfolio, and since its money holdings were previously in equilibrium it now holds excessive money, and tries to exchange some of it for other assets including corporate stock. Another way of putting this is to look at relative yields and notice that as people get more money the yield on money falls at the margin, so that it is now less than the expected yield (adjusted for risk) on stock. As they buy stock they bid stock prices up until at the new price the expected (risk-adjusted) yield on a dollar invested in stock is no greater than the marginal yield on a dollar held as money. A third way of putting it is to say that the present value of a stock, and hence its price, is equal to expected streams of future yields discounted at the interest rate. An increase in the quantity of money temporarily lowers the interest rate, and hence increases the present value of the expected future earnings on the stock, and thus its price.

Knowing this can you go out and make money on the stock market? Unfortunately not. The trouble is that other people have this information too. So when you rush down to your broker you find that there are already other people there who want to buy stock too, and potential sellers who know what is happening are demanding a higher price. Information that everyone else has too is of no use to you in the stock market.[3] Only if you know something (something right, that is) that others don't, can you cash in on it. Suppose, for example, you discover that in every month in which there is a full moon on a Thursday, the Fed raises the money growth rate. Then, until others discover this too, you can predict stock prices in time to buy stocks before they go up. But it is extremely difficult to predict what the Fed will do, though many smart people will try.

Just to complicate things, there is the problem that in an inflationary period it is possible for the stock market to act "perversely." Many people

[2] M. I. Nadiri, "The Determinants of Trade Credit in the U.S. Total Manufacturing Sector," *Econometrica* 37 (July 1969): 408–23; Paul Junk, "Monetary Policy and the Extension of Trade Credit," *Southern Economic Journal* 30 (January 1964): 274–77.

[3] This is an implication of the "random walk" theory of stock prices. For very clear discussions of this theory, see Burton Malkiel, *A Random Walk Down Wall Street*, New York: W. W. Norton, 1975; and Neil Berkman, "A Primer on Random Walks in the Stock Market," *New England Economic Review* (Federal Reserve Bank of Boston) September/October 1978, pp. 32–50. The latter contains a formal model of how money affects stock prices.

know by now that an increase in the money growth rate is inflationary. And for reasons that are still somewhat obscure, inflation drives stock prices down. Hence, at a time when people are highly sensitized to inflation, perhaps you should sell rather than buy stock, when your study of geese entrails tells you that the money growth rate is rising.

If stock prices fall this stimulates investment since firms can finance a given investment project more cheaply. To raise a given amount of money for new investment they have to hand over to new stockholders a smaller share of the company than was true before.

Consumption

Monetary policy affects consumption as well as investment. This is important because, while gross private domestic investment accounts for only about 15 percent of GNP, consumer purchases account for about 64 percent of GNP. Hence, even if the interest elasticity of investment is much higher than the interest elasticity of consumption, much of the impact of monetary policy *could* still come from consumption.

A fall in real interest rates affects consumption in several ways. First, it changes the allocation of income between current consumption and saving. Unfortunately, the direction of this effect is hard to determine. A fall in the real interest rate lowers the reward for saving which, taken by itself, should cause people to lower their savings ratio. At the same time, there is an income effect pulling against this substitution effect; if interest rates fall then interest recipients are poorer, and hence, to restore some of their income losses, they increase their productive efforts, both by working more and by saving a larger proportion of their incomes. To take an extreme example, suppose someone insists on accumulating an estate of, say one million dollars in twenty years. Such a person must save substantially more if the interest rate falls from 10 percent to 5 percent.

A second way in which a change in interest rates affects consumption operates through the way in which households want to hold their wealth. Households divide their wealth so that at the margin the yield they obtain from holding consumer durables is just equal to the yield they obtain by holding financial assets, such as securities or bank deposits. When the interest rate on securities and bank deposits falls, households then have an incentive to hold fewer of these assets and to buy more consumer durables. Hence consumer expenditures increase. Third, as interest rates fall credit rationing is relaxed. For example, sales finance companies find it easier and cheaper to borrow, and hence they are willing to grant loans to applicants whom they otherwise would have turned down.

Fourth, with interest rates falling the value of securities rises, so that households feel richer. And the higher their perceived wealth, the greater is their consumption. Fifth, a rise in the value of any of its assets raises a household's liquidity in the sense of raising its ratio of net worth to liabilities. And if households become more liquid they are more ready to trade some of their liquid assets for such illiquid assets as consumer durables.

The MPS Model

The time has come to put these various effects together. One way to do so is in an econometric model. In Chapter 16 we discussed the monetarist St. Louis model, and now we will see how monetary policy functions in one large Keynesian model.

Although there are many such models that could be used, we will employ the Federal Reserve's MPS model. (The acronym MPS stands for M.I.T., the University of Pennsylvania, and the Social Science Research Council, which contributed to its financing.) This large model, while essentially Keynesian, has a much more detailed monetary sector than most other models since it was built for the Fed. It is used in two ways. One is to forecast income, prices, unemployment, and so on. In forecasting, the Fed combines the predictions obtained from this model with judgmental forecasts, that is, forecasts made in an informal manner by experts familiar with developments in various sectors of the economy. The Fed also uses the MPS model to simulate how its policies affect the economy. For example, it may use the model to predict how income would change if unborrowed reserves would rise by $1 billion.

Do not treat this model as though it were *the* model of the economy. Some other models, that predict approximately as well, have different monetary sectors, and hence describe the impact of monetary policies differently. Moreover, the MPS model is constantly being revised. The latest versions are not publicly available and the version described here is somewhat outdated. Hence, treat it more as an illustration than as the last word.

In this model, monetary policy affects income in three ways. One channel is the wealth effect; as interest rates rise, bond and stock prices fall, households feel poorer and respond by cutting consumption. This wealth effect is very important in the model, and at some times accounts for roughly half the *direct* impact (that is, the impact excluding the indirect multiplier and accelerator effects) of monetary policy as measured by the model. The second channel is the effect of changes in interest rates on the demand for capital, that is, a cost of capital channel. This applies not only to industrial plant and equipment, but also to consumer durables, to residential construction, and to nonresidential construction both by the private sector and by state and local governments. The third effect, called the *credit availability channel,* operates through credit rationing; as policy becomes more restrictive, more potential borrowers are unable to obtain mortgage loans.

Figure 22.1 shows the flow chart of the MPS model for the first-round effects of monetary policy. Since it deals only with the first round it excludes the various feedbacks, such as the effects of rising income on interest rates, consumption, and investment. To include these would make the figure much too complex. We start out by assuming a rise in the Aaa bond rate; that is, the interest rate paid on the highest-quality corporate bonds. Part A shows the wealth-consumption channel. This has already been discussed, and the only thing that may need mentioning is that the model does not stop with the change in consumption, but breaks it down into its major components. It also shows the effect of the rise in the interest rate on the distribution of

Figure 22.1 First-Round Effects of Monetary Policy in the MPS Model

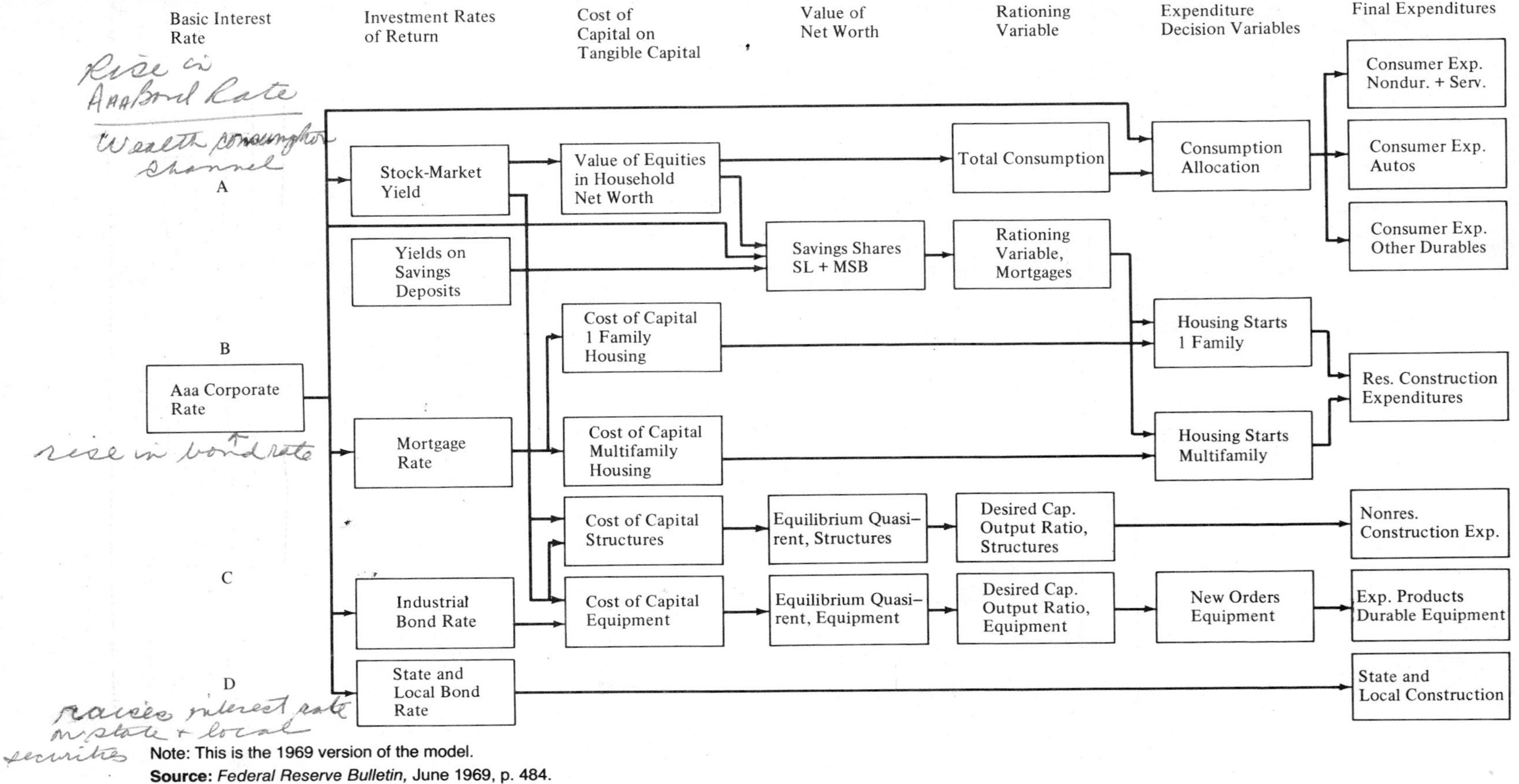

Note: This is the 1969 version of the model.

Source: *Federal Reserve Bulletin*, June 1969, p. 484.

consumption between durables and nondurables. This is a cost of capital effect.

Part B deals with the impact of monetary policy on mortgage lending by thrift institutions, an impact that will be greatly reduced as Regulation Q is phased out. The rise in the corporate bond rate causes deposits to flow out of thrift institutions. Hence thrift institutions now have to reduce their mortgage lending, and do so, in part, by rationing credit. This is the credit availability channel. As a result, in part C, housing starts and residential construction decline.

Part B also shows the direct cost effect of the rise in the Aaa bond rate. Since bonds and mortgages are substitutes in the portfolios of lenders, a rise in the bond rate raises the mortgage rate. This increase in the cost of borrowing lowers the profitability of investment in houses, so that housing starts and residential construction again fall.

Part C shows the effects on industrial plant and equipment and on private nonresidential construction. A rise in the yields on stocks, bonds, and mortgages raises the yield that firms must expect to obtain on investment in industrial plants to make them willing to undertake such investment. As this rate—called the equilibrium quasi-rent—rises the desired stock of capital per dollar of output is reduced. Hence new orders for equipment fall, and investment declines. Finally, as part D shows, the rise in the corporate bond rate raises the interest rate on state and local securities, and this discourages state and local construction expenditures. The version of the model shown in Figure 22.1 does not include an effect on inventory investment. A later version of the model has such an effect as well as a liquidity effect on consumption, and a Phillips curve that becomes vertical in the long run. Hence, the MPS model shows monetary policy as affecting many components of aggregate demand.

Figure 22.2 shows the impact of a rise in the federal funds rate on various components of GNP and on the GNP deflator as estimated by the Chase econometric model. Figure 22.3 compares the impact of a change in unborrowed reserves on GNP shown by various models. The difference is quite substantial. (But *some* of the difference reflects the fact that in some models the unborrowed reserves injections are larger than in other models, that they occur at different stages of the business cycle, and that the models make different assumptions about the behavior of some exogeneous variables.)

INTERNATIONAL TRADE EFFECTS

So far we have dealt only with a closed economy. But if exchange rates are flexible, monetary policy affects income also through its impact on foreign-exchange rates. Suppose that the United States adopts a restrictive monetary policy so that interest rates in the U.S. rise temporarily. Since, in the first instance, interest rates in the rest of the world are constant, foreigners now have an incentive to buy U.S. securities. But to do so they must demand dollars on the foreign-exchange market. At the same time with higher interest rates in the U.S., Americans have less of an incentive to buy foreign securities, so that their demand for foreign currency (which is needed to buy

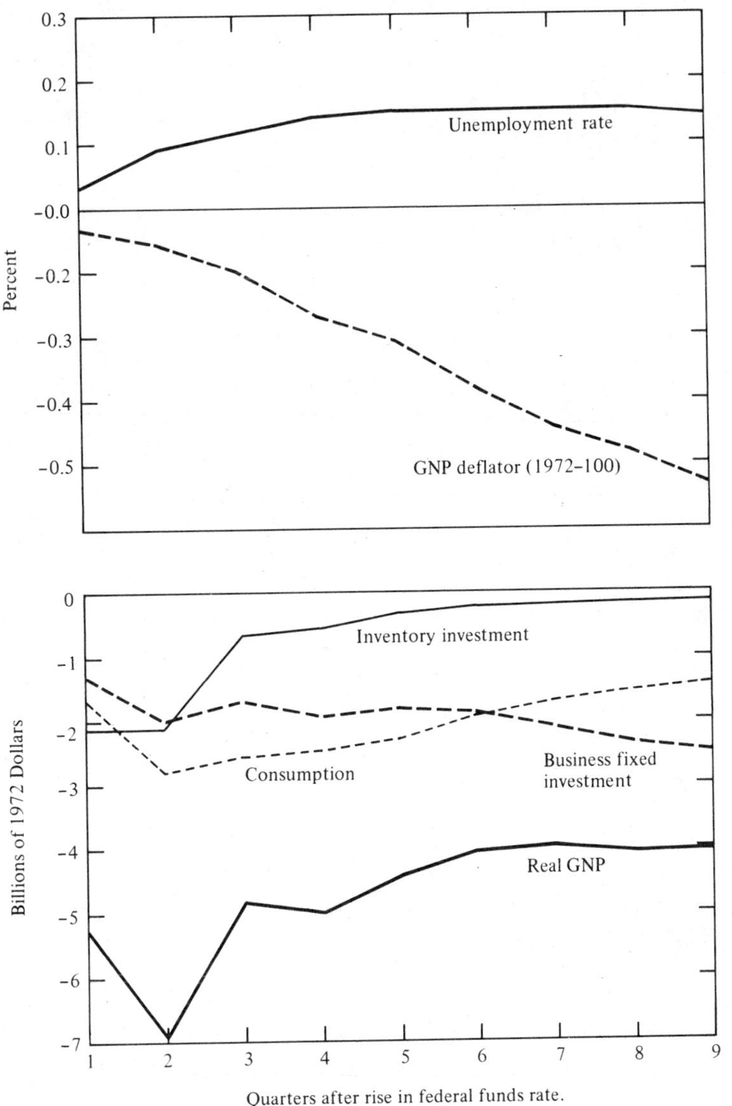

Figure 22.2 Effect of a 1 Percent Increase in the Federal Funds Rate—Chase Econometric Model

Source: David Cross, *Model Notes—Part I.* Chase Econometrics.

foreign securities) is reduced. Hence, on the foreign-exchange market, with more dollars and less foreign currency being demanded, the value of the dollar rises. Foreigners therefore find that U.S. goods cost more in terms of their own currency, and so they buy fewer. Similarly, with foreign goods being cheaper in terms of dollars (since the dollar buys more British pounds, German marks, and so on) U.S. imports increase. For both of these reasons the demand for goods produced in the U.S. falls. This reinforces domestic effects that a tight money policy has in constraining demand.

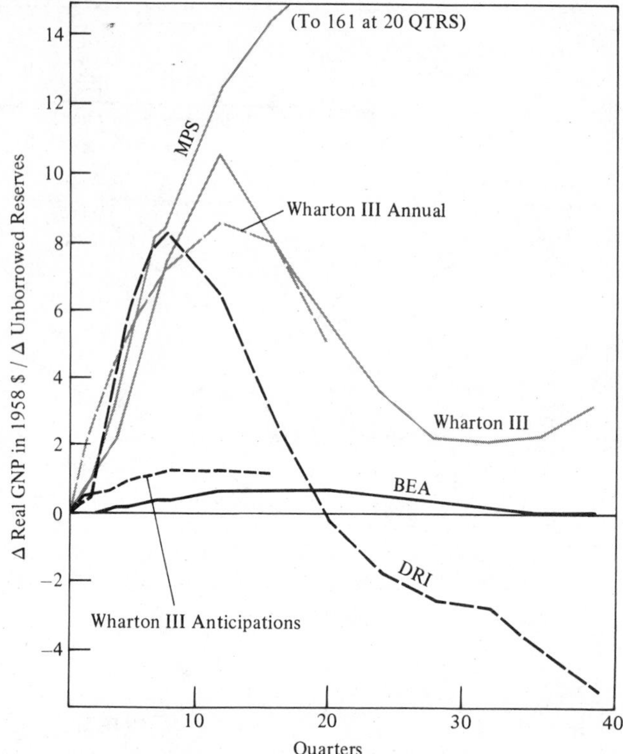

Figure 22.3 Impact of a Maintained $1-Billion Increase in Unborrowed Reserves upon Real GNP

Note: In later versions of the MPS model real GNP turns down again.
Source: Carl Christ, "Judging the Performance of Econometric Models of the U.S. Economy," *International Economic Review* 16 (February 1975): 71.

What has been presented so far is the traditional explanation. But in recent years another approach, which emphasizes the supply and demand for money, has been developed. Suppose that the Fed adopts a restrictive policy. The decline in the growth rate of money results in the supply of money being less than the demand for money. Hence, Americans *try* to increase their money holdings by selling more goods and securities to foreigners, and by buying less from them.[4] But this succeeds in raising the dollar holdings of Americans only to the extent that foreigners relinquish dollars they hold, and this is rather minor. However, there is a more important—albeit indirect—effect. As Americans sell more goods and securities to foreigners, and buy less from them, the supply of foreign currency on the foreign-exchange market increases, and the demand for it falls. Hence, the

[4]Of course, Americans do not consciously decide to sell more to foreigners. Instead, Americans simply try to sell more regardless of whether it is to domestic residents or to foreigners. But since other Americans also try to sell rather than to buy, they end up, on the whole, selling more only to foreigners.

price of foreign currency in terms of dollars falls; that is the dollar rises. And as the dollar rises relative to other currencies, the price of internationally traded goods *in terms of* dollars falls. This reduces prices in the United States both directly and indirectly as producers who compete with imported goods have to reduce their prices. This in turn puts pressure on other producers who compete with those who have reduced their prices to compete with imports. And in an ultimate sense, all goods compete with each other. Moreover, with the inflation rate thus falling workers are willing to settle for smaller nominal wage increases. Thus, the rise of the dollar on the foreign exchange market helps the Fed to curb inflation.

There is, however, another international-finance effect of monetary policy that tends to weaken it. This is that as the interest rate rises in the United States the increased purchases of U.S. securities by foreigners (and by those Americans who would otherwise have bought foreign securities) works to moderate the rise in the interest rate. This, in turn, reduces the impact of the Fed's restrictive policy on investment and consumption. However, in a system of flexible exchange rates this offset is limited. Since exchange rates fluctuate, foreigners take a risk in buying securities denominated in dollars rather than in their own currencies, and this limits capital inflows. This will be discussed further in Part Five.

RATIONAL EXPECTATIONS

So far, this discussion of the way monetary policy affects the economy has been rather mechanistic. It is high time to allow for the fact that people do not just react to events that have already occurred, but also respond to what they expect to happen. If one leaves room for expectations, there is yet another way in which monetary policy can affect prices, and hence nominal income.

Assume that at a time of full employment the Fed substantially increases the reserve base. Not only will this initially reduce interest rates, and hence stimulate expenditures, but people, particularly well-informed decision makers, will realize what is going on. They will expect aggregate demand to increase. More specifically, with the economy already operating at capacity they will expect wages and prices to rise. But if prices are expected to rise isn't it rational for people to try to protect themselves against this by buying ahead now, by withholding goods from the market to sell them in the future, and by raising wages and prices right away? Hence, an increase in the growth rate of the base can lead to an immediate increase in prices. This is, of course, much more likely to happen at a time when high and variable inflation rates have conditioned people to watch the growth rate of the base, than at a time when people have had little or no experience with inflation.

At the cost of some unrealism one can carry this example to an interesting conclusion. Assume that everyone knows that an increase in the base is inflationary, and, also, that all contracts have escalator clauses, and that laws and regulations do not inhibit a rapid adaption to inflation (for example, tax laws are fully indexed, and all outside money somehow is indexed too). If so, an increase in the growth rate of the base will result immediately in a rise in nominal interest rates as the higher rate of inflation is embodied in the inflation premium that is included in the nominal interest rate. Hence neither investment nor output rise, but the inflation rate responds instantly and fully to the higher growth rate of the base.

Admittedly the assumptions that people can predict accurately the impact of the higher growth rate of the base on prices, and that long-term contracts, tax laws, and so on, are fully indexed are extreme. But this example does warn us to watch for the way in which monetary policy affects expectations. Suppose, for example, that Congress would suddenly direct the Fed to aim at keeping unemployment to 3 percent, or to bring the Treasury bill rate down to 3 percent. This would probably bring about an immediate and very substantial increase in the inflation rate. Conversely, if Congress were to order the Fed to make price stability its only goal, the inflation rate would start to decline even before the Fed takes any action.

AN EMERGING PROBLEM: A FLEXIBLE INTEREST RATE ON MONEY

Financial innovation is permitting an increasing number of depositors to receive on their transactions accounts an explicit interest rate that varies along with open-market rates. This *may* have an important effect on the impact on the economy of monetary policy and of changes in expenditure incentives. Since this emerging problem is just beginning to be discussed by economists we can only offer a sketch of what might happen.

Suppose the Fed reduces the growth rate of money. As before, interest rates rise temporarily, but now the interest rate paid on money rises too. Hence there is now less of an incentive to switch out of money into securities. The liquidity preference curve (the demand curve for money) therefore becomes steeper, as does the *LM* curve. In the extreme case suppose that the interest rate paid on money moves precisely with the open-market interest rate, and that banks hold no reserves. If so, an increase in the interest rate provides no reason at all to hold any less money than before, and the *LM* curve is completely vertical. However, as long as banks have to hold some reserves, the *LM* curve will not become completely vertical since banks have to pass along to their depositors the cost of holding these reserves, which is the foregone interest. And the higher is the interest rate, the greater is this foregone cost, and hence the greater is the margin by which the open-market rate exceeds the interest rate paid on deposits.

With a steeper *LM* curve, a shift in the *IS* curve brings about a smaller change in income. Suppose that government expenditures increase. As the government borrows more the interest rate rises, and as a result private expenditures are cut back. The steeper the *LM* curve is, the greater is the rise in the interest rate that is required to equilibriate the money market, and hence the greater is the cut-back in private expenditures. In the extreme case with a completely vertical *LM* curve, an increase in government expenditures lowers private expenditures dollar for dollar and nominal income is unchanged. Hence, the payment of a flexible interest rate on money makes income more stable with respect to a shift in the *IS* curve. But it becomes less stable with respect to a shift in the *LM* curve. Suppose that the supply of money decreases, or that the demand for money per dollar of income increases. The resulting rise in the interest rate then provides an incentive to hold less money, partially offsetting the initial decrease in the supply of money or the increase in the demand for money. But to the extent that the interest rate on money rises too, this offsetting effect is weakened.

The payment of a flexible interest rate on money also creates a transitional problem that *may* be serious. There is now an incentive to hold as checkable deposits some funds that would otherwise have been invested in other assets. The interest elasticity and the income elasticity of these checkable deposits may well differ from the elasticities of previous deposits. Hence the average interest elasticity and income elasticity of money has changed. It may take the Fed some time to discover what these new elasticities are, and in the meantime, its forecasts will be less accurate.

ALLOCATION EFFECTS

All in all, there is little doubt that monetary policy—or at least a restrictive policy—can be strong enough to do the job if it is carried far enough. But this alone does not suffice to recommend its use as the main stabilization tool. One should look also at its efficiency and its side effects. If monetary policy turns out to be extremely inequitable or to discourage certain types of socially desirable investment too much, then one *may* want to adopt a policy mix that gives a smaller role to monetary policy and a greater one to fiscal policy or credit allocation (a system described below). We therefore conclude this discussion of the impact of monetary policy by seeing if the *relative* impact of a restrictive monetary policy on various sectors of the economy is appropriate. The following chapter then deals with other aspects of the efficiency of monetary policy.

The Criteria

Obviously, the first step in deciding whether the impact of monetary policy is appropriately distributed is to select a criterion for an appropriate distribution. We will discuss two rival criteria.

One possible criterion is a competitive free market allocation. According to this the price of credit, i.e., the interest rate, should be set to clear the market. There should be no credit rationing or use of market power. Everyone uses credit until the point at which its marginal cost (the interest rate) equals the perceived marginal benefit. Hence, when the Fed reduces money growth, and the interest rate rises, borrowers cut back until the marginal utility of borrowed funds for each of them rises enough to equal the higher interest rate. There is no reason why all borrowing activities should be cut back equally. By analogy, when a family decides to cut back on its expenditures it does not cut its outlays for vacation trips and for bread equally! *If* one takes the distribution of income (after interest rates have risen) as beyond question, and assumes that there is adequate competition, and that there are no uncompensated externalities, then this free market criterion is applicable and there is no reason to be concerned about the allocation effects of monetary policy.

A popular alternative criterion is proportionality: a restrictive monetary policy should cut back borrowing and expenditures in each sector more or less in the same proportion. This criterion has no economic justification; it seems to represent an underlying ethical judgment that sacrifices should be shared equally. This ethical judgment, however, is not clearly formulated. It is usually employed only in an implicit way in arguments that a restrictive monetary policy is imposing too high a cost on some worthy sector or group.

Impacted Sectors

In the 1960s and 1970s there were massive complaints about the unduly harsh impact of restrictive monetary policy on several sectors. One of these sectors is investment in general. Some economists argued that a restrictive monetary policy cuts back investment substantially, but has little, if any, effect on consumption. Hence, by using a restrictive monetary policy and an easy fiscal policy, growth of the capital stock and hence the growth of productivity are reduced. It would be better to have a restrictive fiscal policy that curbs consumption and an expansionary monetary policy that stimulates investment.

Residential Construction. But most criticism of the allocation effects of monetary policy concentrates on its impact on residential construction, a sector generally agreed to be highly sensitive to rising interest rates.

A sharp impact of a restrictive monetary policy on residential construction is not hard to explain. First, residential construction represents unusually long-term investment, and hence is more sensitive than most other types of investment to the cost of borrowing. Second, for many years, residential construction financed under the government's (FHA and VA) mortgage insurance and guarantee programs had a maximum interest rate ceiling that was changed only with a significant lag. In the meantime, as interest rates rose such loans became harder and harder to obtain. Third, a number of states had restrictive usury law ceilings that inhibited mortgage lending when interest rates rose. Last, but not least, there was the disintermediation that resulted from Regulation Q ceilings.[5]

To the extent that the cut-back in residential construction was due to it being long-lived investment, it was justified under the free market criterion, but to the extent that the other factors just discussed played a significant role, the plight of the construction industry could be justified on neither that criterion, nor the proportionality criterion.

The problem was exacerbated by the fact that many people implicitly reject the free market criterion, and look upon residential construction as a particularly meritorious type of investment. They believe that housing

[5] An additional reason for the sharp impact of tight money on residential construction was the prohibition of interest payments on demand deposits which gave banks an incentive to reward business depositors by giving their loan requests priority over those of mortgage borrowers.

investment should be carried beyond the point that the free market would select on its own.[6] Hence, having it cut back by a restrictive monetary policy is reprehensible.

Moreover, it is not only builders or purchasers of new houses that are hurt when interest rates rise; those who want to buy or sell old houses are hurt too. This is so because in many cases the seller of a house cannot pass on to the buyer the implicit capital gain obtained from having an old low-cost mortgage. The potential buyer would have to take out a new mortgage at the new, higher interest rate. Hence, the sale of old houses is reduced. This is an interference with efficient resource allocation that does little to help curb inflation.

It is not surprising that the government has tried to ameliorate the impact of rising interest rates on residential construction by providing massive infusions of mortgage funds from federal and federally sponsored agencies such as the Federal National Mortgage Association ("Fanny Mae"). Thus, in the first quarter of 1970 when private mortgage funds were scarce, federally sponsored credit agencies accounted for about a half of the net increase in outstanding mortgage debt. Whether this really helped the mortgage market is another question. The government-sponsored agencies borrow on the open market to obtain the funds they provide to the mortgage market. But as they borrow on the open market they drive up interest rates which draws deposits out of savings and loans who then reduce their mortgage loans. Some studies have therefore argued that these government rescue operations are useless.

Small Business. Another sector said to be hurt too severely by a restrictive monetary policy is small business and particularly new firms. At first glance, this may seem implausible since profit-maximizing banks have an incentive to lend to those firms, regardless of size, that promise to pay the highest rate of return. But until the 1970s interest rates on bank loans changed only sluggishly toward market equilibrium, so that they would lag behind when a restrictive monetary policy raised interest rates. With the demand for credit then exceeding the supply at the below-equilibrium interest rate, banks had an incentive to ration credit more tightly. In doing so they eliminated the riskier applicants—often small firms. Moreover, large firms that are turned down by one bank can go to another bank or sell securities on the open market. Small firms often do not have these alternatives. The *extent* to which there is discrimination against small firms, is, of course, a matter of empirical judgment and one that has generated much dispute.

Income Distribution. Finally, there is the distribution of income. It may seem obvious that a restrictive monetary policy, by temporarily raising the real rate of interest, helps the rich and hurts the poor. This is not necessarily so. With aggregate demand being excessive one has to be specific about what is the alternative to a restrictive monetary policy. Is it to raise taxes on the top

[6]One reason for this solicitude about housing is a wish to improve living conditions in slums, though it is not obvious that support for housing across the board is the best way to achieve this. Also, it seems to be widely believed that homeownership makes people into better citizens, or that there are important aesthetic benefits received by the public from good housing beyond those received by its owners.

quarter of the income distribution, or to cut government welfare programs? Or is it to let inflation accelerate by doing nothing? Moreover, the poor tend to hold a larger proportion of their assets (though not necessarily of their incomes) in fixed-rate assets, such as bank deposits, than do the rich.

Another distributional effect of a rising interest rate is the impact on buyers and sellers of assets. Someone who sells a long-term bond when interest rates have risen suffers a capital loss. This *seems* inequitable since he or she may not have had any choice about when to sell the asset. One might reply that, in terms of opportunity costs, those who hold on to their assets rather than selling them suffer an equal loss. Nonetheless, people seem to feel worse about taking actual losses than book losses, and in this respect, those who have to sell assets when interest rates rise do suffer.

Increased Financial Flexibility. The criticisms of restrictive monetary policies just discussed became less prominent in the early 1980s. By then the financial system was becoming much freer, reducing the imperfections of financial markets. Regulation Q was going out—if not with a bang then at least with a whimper. Thrift institutions—if willing to pay the price—can now obtain additional funds. Hence, they no longer have to turn down applications for mortgage loans from those willing to pay the higher equilibrium rate. And state usury law ceilings were repealed or eased in many states. FHA and VA interest rate ceilings too are now much more flexible. And the lender can reduce his risk by making variable rather than fixed-rate mortgages. At the right price mortgage loans are available to those who can meet the higher income qualifications that are imposed due to higher monthly payments.

Similarly, with banks being able to purchase funds through liability management, and with so many bank loans being made on a floating rate basis, banks have less need to ration credit, so that discrimination against small firms is reduced.

Moreover, in 1981–82 the suffering from high interest rates could be seen to be widely diffused. With auto sales way down nobody could argue that the costs of a restrictive monetary policy are confined to the construction industry, or that consumer expenditures are unaffected by rising interest rates.

But while the freeing of the financial system reduced the burden of a restrictive policy in one way, it also created its own problems. Previously, as rising interest rates caused disintermediation, the funds leaving the housing sector would be lent in other sectors, thus holding down interest rates there. Put differently, as long as Regulation Q ensured that as interest rates rose the residential construction sector would be forced to relinquish demand over resources, interest rates did not have to rise as much to choke off a boom as they do now. Hence, while there are now fewer complaints about the discriminatory impact of a restrictive policy, there are more complaints about high interest rates. Thus while housing was hurt less in 1981–82 by market imperfections it was hurt more by high interest rates. There was massive unemployment in the building industry, and monetary policy was blamed for the high interest rates that caused it.

What can be done to meet these complaints? One possibility, a much tighter fiscal policy, is not politically feasible. A more expansionary monetary policy would result in only a very short-run decline in nominal interest rates since it would raise the inflation premium embedded in the nominal interest rate. Even so, it might reduce the real after-tax rate, since this rate does not seem to adjust fully for inflation. But most of the complaints are directed at nominal rates. And indeed, complaints that relate to the discriminatory effects that result from market imperfections *should* be directed at nominal rates, since it is sticky nominal rates rather than real rates that cause the discrimination. An expansionary monetary policy is therefore not an adequate answer; in fact it is just such a policy rather than a restrictive policy that is the cause of the problem because by generating inflation it raises nominal rates.

This leaves the possibility of returning to the previous system of rationing some borrowers out of the market to increase the supply of credit available to other borrowers, thus reducing the interest rate they have to pay. Given the pace of financial innovation this can no longer be done by a device like Regulation Q. But there is another way of rationing out some borrowers—credit allocation. This is discussed in the Appendix.

SUMMARY

1. In the 1930s, 1940s, and 1950s a substantial majority of economists believed that monetary policy has little effect on GNP. This view is now generally rejected.
2. The monetarist transmission channel of monetary policy focuses on the excess supply or demand for money, and does not provide much detail.
3. One can describe the transmission process in terms of portfolio balance. As firms and households receive more money they bring their portfolios back into equilibrium by acquiring other goods and assets instead.
4. In the Keynesian transmission story an increase in the money stock lowers interest rates which raises investment via a lower cost of borrowing. Certain market imperfections, such as Regulation Q ceilings and the locking-in effect, increase the impact of interest rates on investment. In addition, interest rates also affect consumption.
5. The Fed has sponsored an elaborate econometric model, whose flow chart is shown in Fig. 22.1.
6. Changes in interest rates affect the exchange rate of the dollar, so that, as interest rates fall, exports increase and imports decline, thus reinforcing the expansionary domestic effects.
7. Monetary policy also works through expectations; wages and prices could rise before the increase in the money stock actually takes place.
8. In deciding whether to use monetary policy as a stabilization tool its allocational effects should be considered. One criterion for evaluating these effects, the free market criterion, takes as optimal the allocation that would occur in a competitive economy. The proportionality criterion, on the other hand, takes as optimal that each sector suffers a roughly proportional cut-back from a restrictive policy.
9. In the 1960s and '70s there was much complaint about restrictive monetary policy imposing excessive burdens on investment in general, on residential con-

struction, small business, and the poor. The sharp impact on residential construction could be explained by its being long-term investment and by market imperfections: Regulation Q, usury laws, FHA and VA interest ceilings. This caused much concern, given the belief that housing is a particularly meritorious good, and special government credit programs were invoked.

10. By the early 1980s these allocation problems due to market imperfections became less important, but had been replaced by the problem of high interest rates.
11. Many of those who complain about either high interest rates or the discriminatory effects of tight money want a more expansionary policy. But, by raising the inflation premium embedded in nominal interest rates, such a policy would, after some time, just make the nominal rate rise even more.

Questions and Exercises

1. Do you think monetary policy has had much influence on the behavior of income over the last ten years? To answer this question look at data presented in the *Economic Report of the President*. Document your conclusion by references to these, or other, data.
2. Compare and contrast the monetarist and the Keynesian approaches to the impact of monetary policy on income. Explain why this impact seems stronger in the monetarist than in the Keynesian approach.
3. Describe the ways in which an expansionary monetary policy increases consumption.
4. Discuss the portfolio effect and the locking-in effect of rising interest rates.
5. Describe the impact of monetary policy in the MPS model.
6. "With exchange rates being flexible, the Fed's power to combat a recession is increased." Discuss.
7. Suppose you are an executive of a trade association in the construction industry. Write a "letter to the editor" of a newspaper objecting to a restrictive monetary policy because of its impact on your industry.
8. Write another "letter to the editor" answering the letter from the previous question.

Further Reading

DE LEEUW, F., and GRAMLICH, E. "The Channels of Monetary Policy." *Journal of Finance* 24 (May 1969): 265–90. This is an exposition of how monetary policy works in the MPS model.

JUDD, J., and SCADDING, J. "Financial Change and Monetary Targeting in the United States," Federal Reserve Bank of San Francisco, *Interest Rate Deregulation and Monetary Policy*. San Francisco, Federal Reserve Bank of San Francisco, 1983. An interesting discussion of the impact of deregulation on monetary policy.

LAIDLER, DAVID. "Money and Money Income: An Essay on the Transmission Mechanism." *Journal of Monetary Economics* 4 (April 1978): 151–93. An excellent survey, particularly strong on the expectational aspects.

MISHKIN, FREDERIC. "Monetary Policy and Liquidity: Simulation Results." *Economic Inquiry* 16 (January 1978): 16–36. An interesting analysis of the importance of changes in household liquidity.

WOJNILOWER, ALBERT. "The Central Role of Credit Crunches in Recent Financial History." *Brookings Papers on Economic Activity,* 2 (1980): 277–326. A fascinating piece of "analytic description" arguing that monetary policy can curb a boom only by plunging the economy into a recession. It is brilliantly written—a pleasure to read.

APPENDIX: CREDIT ALLOCATION

In a system of credit allocation the government limits the amount of credit made available to certain sectors of the economy. This increases the availability of credit to all other sectors and lowers interest rates. Such a system has been used occasionally in the United States (World War II, 1948–49, 1950–52, and 1980) as well as in several European countries, particularly in France.[7] Credit allocation might be used only on special occasions, for example, at a time when a restrictive monetary policy has temporarily raised interest rates, or it might be used permanently.

The mechanics of credit allocation can take several forms. One is to prohibit certain types of loans. For example, the Fed's Regulation W in the 1940s set minimum downpayments and maximum maturities for installment sales of consumer durables, thus prohibiting low downpayment, long maturity loans. A less rigid approach imposes a ceiling on certain types of loans. This could take the form of a maximum growth rate of all loans of certain lenders or ceilings on specific types of loans. For example, banks might be told that they could not increase their business loans by more than 5 percent per year. Instead of such ceilings, floors could be used, for example, banks being required to increase their mortgage loans by at least 10 percent per year. Alternatively, instead of setting rigid floors or ceilings, banks and other lenders could be given an incentive to make—or to cut back upon—certain types of loans. For instance, banks could be given a credit against their reserve requirements for a certain proportion of their additional mortgage loans, or special reserve requirements could be imposed on other loans. Thus, in March 1980 the Fed temporarily imposed a 15 percent reserve requirement against increases in the outstanding volume of certain consumer loans of all significant types of consumer lenders. Since then, the law has changed, so that the Fed no longer has the authority to allocate credit in these ways.

The case for credit allocation takes two forms. One is to argue that certain types of investment have large external benefits and hence deserve a government subsidy. By requiring banks and other lenders to make more loans to these sectors, the cost of credit to them is reduced, and their investment is stimulated without any expenditure of government funds. The second form the argument can take is to say that the discriminatory effects of tight money are so severe that they have to be offset by another policy, credit allocation. Admittedly, while credit allocation would, in part, abro-

[7] To a small extent credit allocation has been used in the United States at other times too. For example, in making certain types of loans, but not others, eligible for discounting, the Fed tried to influence the characteristics of loans made by banks. At other times it has indicated that member banks that extended certain types of loans could borrow more readily from it.

gate the market mechanism, credit rationing by banks and other lenders already does so too. And if we are to have credit allocation it should be done by the government, which takes social usefulness into account, rather than by bankers just concerned with profits.

But there exists a cogent case against credit allocation. It is not at all clear that governmental decisions about where credit should flow would be superior to the decisions of the private market. In principle, they should be since the government can take into account any externalities that the private market ignores (though it is far from clear that the externalities that could be taken into account by credit allocation are all that large). But in practice, various pressure groups may succeed in obtaining undeserved preference for their credit demands. In effect, with credit allocation, the distribution of political power may well determine access to credit.

Furthermore, while a system of credit allocation could work in the short run, eventually it would become ineffective. If banks or other financial intermediaries were forced to make less profitable loans, they would reduce the interest rate they pay on deposits. Depositors would then switch to other intermediaries. If necessary, new types of uncontrolled intermediaries would spring up. Moreover, borrowers can also confound a system of credit allocation. For example, a family buying a house can take out a larger mortgage, and use its own funds thus freed to buy securities. *In the long run* one cannot control the allocation of credit by controlling the portfolio choices of financial intermediaries. Britain, which made heavy use of controls over bank lending as a tool of monetary policy in the 1950s and 1960s, found that this device became less and less effective with the passage of time and with the growth of nonbank financial intermediaries.

Moreover, credit allocation reduces the efficiency of the financial system. New institutions may spring up that are viable merely because they can avoid this regulation, though they are otherwise less efficient than existing institutions. Efficiency is also reduced by a decline in intermediation below its optimal level. If financial intermediaries cannot invest the saver's funds in the most profitable way, savers and ultimate borrowers both have an incentive not to use financial intermediaries and to undertake direct finance. All in all, our experience with Regulation Q does not make tampering with the financial system look particularly appetizing.

If credit allocation *is* instituted, what industries would be the intended beneficiaries? In the 1970s when there were several attempts in Congress to impose credit allocation it seemed to be just one more scheme for subsidizing residential construction. Currently (1983) when there is much concern about the competitive position of certain manufacturing industries, credit allocation might be slanted towards industries such as steel or automobiles.

Can Countercyclical Monetary Policy Succeed?

23

The old-fashioned, traditional functions of monetary policy were to maintain the gold, or silver, standard and to prevent financial panics. In the early 1920s when Keynes advocated using monetary policy to stabilize the domestic economy on a continuous basis, this was considered a radical proposal. Since then this idea has become generally accepted. But this conventional wisdom has now been challenged by a number of economists who have argued that it is a vain hope; that in attempting to stabilize the economy, monetary policy is more likely to generate further instability and inflation. In this chapter we take up the reasons why they think so, and in Chapter 25 we examine their preferred alternative of keeping the growth rate of the money stock constant regardless of the stage of the business cycle.

The belief that a monetary policy that tries to be countercyclical will actually worsen economic fluctuations and inflation is based on any or all of five grounds. First, there is the problem of choosing the correct target, which we discussed in Chapter 21. As explained there, if the Fed uses an interest-rate target when it is the *IS* curve that is shifting, then the Fed will cause income to fluctuate more.[1] The second reason why countercyclical, or discretionary, monetary policy could enhance fluctuations is that it takes time for monetary policy to affect income. Thus, the Fed may adopt an expansionary policy in a recession, and this policy may raise income only after a long time when the recession is over, and aggregate demand is excessive. Third, the public's reactions to the Fed's policy may cause it to be destabilizing. Fourth, due to political pressures, the Fed may follow a policy that is highly inflationary and destabilizing. Finally, the Fed may lack the administrative competence required for stabilization policy. We will now take up

[1]However, if it uses a money-stock target when that target is inappropriate then it will not seriously worsen the fluctuations of income; it will simply not reduce them.

each of these potential problems in turn except for the already discussed targets problem. Although the discussion will deal only with monetary policy, similar problems also confound fiscal policy.

THE PROBLEM OF LAGS

This problem arises only with respect to a policy that tries to reduce the fluctuations of income around its trend rather than with a policy that tries to raise, or lower, the trend of income. But before we discuss the problem that lags create it is necessary to clarify what this term means. Do not think of the lag as the time that elapses from the date at which policy changes to a specific date at which income changes. Not all the change in income occurs at one particular time. Some of the change in income occurs quickly, but it takes a much longer time until the full effect is reached. We are dealing here, not with a point-input-point-output situation, but with a "distributed lag," so that, instead of saying that it takes monetary policy, say, fifteen months to change income, we should say for example that 30 percent of the effect is reached after four months, 60 percent after twelve months, and 100 percent after twenty-four months. This is the type of situation that was shown in Figure 22.3, which compared the impact of monetary policy shown by several econometric models.

If monetary policy had all of its effect on income immediately, the Fed's task would be greatly simplified. Once it becomes aware that the economy is in a recession it could simply adopt an expansionary policy, and, conversely, if demand is too high it would adopt a restrictive policy. By looking at the current level of income it could make sure that its policy is just strong enough to keep nominal income close to the right level. Admittedly, the fact that accurate data on current income are not available right away would create a problem, but this would be relatively minor.

Unfortunately, this is not the way it works; once the Fed changes policy it takes quite a long time for its main effects on income to show up. And when they do, economic conditions *may* have changed so that an expansionary policy initiated in the recession raises income when income is already too high, or a restrictive policy adopted during the previous boom lowers income during the subsequent recession. When the Fed then reverses itself and adopts a new policy, the effects of this new policy may again come at the wrong time. We may therefore get the stabilizer's nightmare shown in Figure 23.1 in which monetary policy increases the amplitude of the business cycle. This possibility has to be taken seriously because in the postwar period business cycles have been short. In the years 1945–83, the median length of a recession was only eleven months, and the median length of an expansion was forty-five months.

A Formal Model

Milton Friedman has developed a model that highlights the importance of the proper timing of countercyclical monetary and fiscal policy. Assume that the trend of aggregate demand is just right, and that we want to minimize

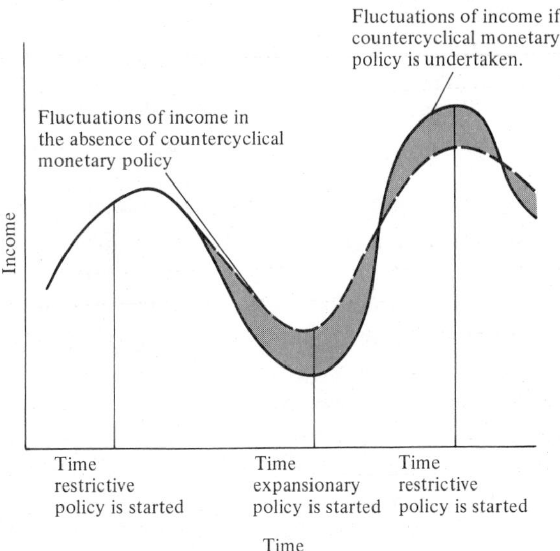

Figure 23.1 Effects of Badly Timed Stabilization Policy

fluctuations around this trend. A convenient way of measuring fluctuations is a statistical measure called the **variance.** (To obtain the variance take the difference between each observation and the mean and square it. Then take the average of these squared differences.) Since the variance involves the *squared* deviations from the mean, treating the minimization of the variance as the goal of stabilization policy implies trying to minimize, not the differences of aggregate demand from the desired level, but instead trying to minimize the *squares* of these differences. In turn, this implies that we are more than proportionally concerned about a few large differences than about more frequent small ones.[2] Another implicit value judgment is involved in the treatment of a dollar of excessive income as being exactly as undesirable as a dollar of shortfall in income.

All the same, let us assume that we *do* want to minimize the variance of nominal income. Changes in the marginal efficiency of investment, government expenditures, etc., cause income to vary. We designate the variance of income that is due to these "private sector" fluctuations and is independent of policy by σ_x^2. Stabilization policy then consists of generating changes in income that offset these independent fluctuations. Since the average level of aggregate demand is just right, these policy-induced changes are sometimes positive and sometimes negative and have a mean of zero. Their variance

[2] For example, compare two policies. Policy A generates the following series of deviations from the mean: 0, 4, 0; while policy B results in deviations: 2, 2, 1. If the criterion is to minimize the absolute deviations, policy A is superior. But if we are trying to minimize the square of the deviations, policy B (with a sum of 9) is better. Specifically, we are using what is called a quadratic utility function, such as $U=f(P^2, U^2)$ where P is the excess of the actual inflation rate over the desired inflation rate, and U the excess of the actual unemployment rate over the full-employment rate. (Since both inflation and unemployment lower utility, f denotes a negative function.) This use of a quadratic utility function involves a value judgment, which not everyone may wish to accept.

around this mean of zero we will call σ_y^2. The total variance of income, designated by σ_z^2, will be the result both of the original fluctuations in income and of the policy-induced fluctuations. A theorem in statistics tells us that this is:

$$\sigma_z^2 = \sigma_x^2 + \sigma_y^2 + 2R\sigma_x\sigma_y,$$

where R is the coefficient of correlation between the original variance of income, σ_x^2, and the variance induced by the stabilization policy, σ_y^2.[3]

Applying this formula for the sum of two variances to the problem at hand one can see the great importance of the correlation between the original variations in income and the variations induced by policy—that is, the timing of policy. If a policy is badly timed—R being positive—so that it raises nominal income when nominal income is already above its mean, and lowers it when it is below its mean, then we have the case of the stabilizer's nightmare.

If this obvious point were all that the above equation shows we would not have bothered to introduce it. But it also shows two other, not so obvious things. One is that it does not suffice for the policy to be "neutral" in its timing, that is, to be right half the time. If it is, $R = 0$, the last term in the previous equation drops out, and the variance of income is equal to $\sigma_x^2 + \sigma_y^2$, which is, of course, greater than σ_x^2. Hence, if the Fed's timing is half-right it is *de*stabilizing income. This suggests that there is a genuine danger that stabilization policy may actually be destabilizing. Second, by algebraic manipulation one can obtain the maximum effective size of the stabilization policy's impact on income for each R. This is $\sigma_y^2 = (R\sigma_x)^2$. Any policy that *tries* to do more than this will actually do less. For example, assume that the Fed adopts a policy powerful enough to offset all the fluctuation in income; that is, that it sets $\sigma_y = \sigma_x$. If the correlation coefficient is -0.5 such a policy will not succeed in reducing the net fluctuation of income at all.[4] And if the correlation coefficient were, say, -0.4, it would actually *in*crease income fluctuation.[5] Too much can be even worse than nothing at all.

This way of looking at policy therefore has much to teach. It shows the great importance of the timing of the impact of the policy since this deter-

[3] The correlation coefficient can best be explained by considering the regression equation $y = a + bx + u$ in which a is a constant, b measures the effect of x on y, and u is a randomly distributed variable. The computer is then kindly requested to select those values of a and b that allow x to explain most of the squared variation in y, that is to minimize the square of u. If u is zero, then x and y are perfectly correlated; that is, since we know the constants, $a + b$, once given x we know what y has to be. In this case the correlation coefficient is unity (or minus unity if b is negative). Now suppose that there is no relation at all between x and y: assume, for example, that x is your age and y the last digit of your driver's license. In this case knowledge of x would not allow you to predict y at all. In this case the correlation coefficient is zero. The square of the correlation coefficient tells you that proportion of y "explained" by x.

[4] If $\sigma_x^2 = \sigma_y^2$ and $R = ½$, then the expression $\sigma_x^2 + \sigma_y^2 + 2R\sigma_x\sigma_y$ reduces to σ_x^2, which is the original fluctuation of income in the absence of stabilization policy. If the correlation coefficient is -0.5, the maximum by which policy could reduce the variation of income is 25 percent; any policy more powerful than that would be less effective.

[5] In this case the variance of income would be $2\sigma_x^2 - .8\sigma_x^2 = 1.2\sigma_x^2$ compared to σ_x^2 in the absence of policy.

mines R. It warns us that it does not take great errors in timing to be destabilizing, and it shows that one must beware of adopting a policy that is too strong. But remember that it has two limitations. First, it applies only to what is strictly a *stabilization* policy, that is, to a policy that tries to even out fluctuations in nominal income. Policy may be more concerned with changing the average level of income. For example, a policy that causes the unemployment rate to fluctuate between, say, 5 and 7 percent is surely better than one that causes the unemployment rate to be absolutely stable at 12 percent. Second, it requires that we are concerned with the *squares* of the deviations of income from its mean, and that we attribute equal importance to positive and negative deviations. But despite these qualifications, R, the coefficient of correlation between the original fluctuations in income and the fluctuations induced by policy, is obviously critical for stabilization policy. To avoid destabilizing the Fed must ensure that R is negative and large enough for the size of the policy being used. This requires that it forecast sufficiently well (1) future income in the absence of policy, and (2) the effect of its policy on income.

Problems Created by the Lag

If monetary policy would have most of its effect on income almost immediately, the prediction of "future" income would not create a problem for the Fed. Since income changes very little over a short span of time, such as a calendar quarter, the Fed could use as its estimate of income, when the policy becomes effective, the income level prevailing currently at the time with perhaps a small adjustment for the growth trend. But, obviously, this does not work if monetary policy takes a long time to affect income. Assume that most of the effect occurs only after two years. In two years the economy may well be in a different business-cycle stage. Hence, if the Fed selects its policy on the basis of what income is currently, the correlation between the original income fluctuations (σ_x^2) and the income fluctuations caused by policy (σ_y^2) is likely to be close to zero, and monetary policy will destabilize the economy. If monetary policy has a long lag—as much of the empirical evidence suggests—then the Fed has to use a forecast of income. Since obviously the Fed's forecasts are not without errors, this provides a limitation on the effectiveness with which the Fed can stabilize income.

A second way in which the length of the lag is important is the leeway the Fed has to offset errors it has made. Suppose that it expected income to decline and adopted an expansionary policy; nominal income now turns out to be much higher than expected. If the lag is short, the Fed can quickly reverse itself, and offset the effect of its previous action, but it cannot if the lag is long.[6]

[6] In principle, the Fed could avoid this problem by adopting a corrective policy that is much stronger than the initial policy it is trying to offset. For example, assume that only 20 percent of the impact on income occurs in the first quarter, and that after one year monetary policy has 80 percent of its full effect. The Fed could then fully offset within a quarter a policy action that it took a year ago, *if* it were willing to adopt an offsetting

And there is still a third problem. To use stabilization policy effectively, the Fed must know, *R*, the correlation between fluctuations in income and its policy. But to know this it must also know the impact of its policy in each period, say each quarter, that is, the distributed lag of the impact of its policy. This would be a difficult econometric problem even if the lag were fairly constant. But the problem is much worse if the lag is highly variable. Thus suppose that the Fed's staff were to tell the FOMC that the lag is, *on the average*, one year, but that in one-third of the cases, it is only three months, and in another third it is two years. In deciding whether to adopt an expansionary, or a restrictive, policy the FOMC would then not know whether to orient its policy towards the income level it expects to prevail in three months, in a year, or in two years. What the FOMC must consider is not the average lag, but the lag for the particular action it is contemplating. Hence, knowledge of the average lag is sufficient only if the lags cluster closely around the average. If the Fed uses the average lag from its econometric model this *could* make its policy destabilizing in the majority of cases, even if the model estimates the average lag correctly. However, this is not so if the Fed avoids all explicit forecasting and simply bases its actions on the current level of income.[7]

Thus the existence of a significant lag in the effect of monetary policy creates three problems for the Fed. It must forecast income, even if only by saying that income will not change, it cannot offset past errors easily and quickly, and it must estimate the effect of its policies in each period.

Hence, to evaluate whether the Fed has reliable enough information to be an effective stabilizer we would have to know how accurate its forecast of income is and how well it predicts the effect of its policy in each period. Neither can be known precisely since the Fed does not make available its forecast for the most recent years. However, data for an earlier period suggest that the Fed forecasts about as well as good private forecasters do.[8] Hence, the forecast record of a sample of private forecasters, shown in Table 23.1, provides some indication of how well the Fed can predict economic conditions. But unfortunately, no data are available on how well the Fed can predict the second item, the effect of its policies on GNP.

---

policy that is four times as strong as the original policy. But such large policy changes have costs; in particular, they lead to violent swings in interest rates. There is also the *possibility* that a continual policy of quick offsets via stronger and stronger offsetting policies would cause an explosive increase in the size of policies. However, this does not appear likely.

[7] If the Fed bases its policy entirely on current income, then, surprisingly, the variability of the lag does no harm. In fact, the more variable it is, the greater is the probability that policy is stabilizing. We know of no intuitive explanation of this strange result that emerges from a mathematical analysis. See Haskell Benishay, "A Framework for the Evaluation of Short-Term Fiscal and Monetary Policy," *Journal of Money, Credit and Banking* 4 (November 1972): 779–810.

[8] See Raymond Lombra and Michael Moran, "Policy Advice and Policymaking at the Federal Reserve," *Carnegie-Rochester Conference Series on Public Policy,* 13 (Autumn 1980): 9–68.

Table 23.1 Mean Absolute Errors of 4 Quarter Ahead Forecasts 1976 I–1980 III[a]

	Mean error	Mean error as percent of average annual change 1976–80
Nominal GNP (current dollars)	40.2	17.6
Real GNP (1972 dollars)	13.6	8.0
Consumers Price Index	4.8	25.1

a. Error of sample of forecasters forecasting early in quarter.

Sources: Based on Stephen McNees, "The Recent Record of Thirteen Forecasters," Federal Reserve Bank of Boston, *New England Economic Review*, September/October 1981, Table 2 and *1983 Economic Report of the President*, Tables B–1, B–2, B–54.

Empirical Estimates of the Lag

It is convenient to divide the lag into two parts. There is first the *inside lag*, that is, *the lag from the time the need for action arises until the Fed takes action*. This lag can be divided into two further components: (1) the lag from the time the need arises until the Fed recognizes that a new policy is needed, and (2) the lag between the time the Fed recognizes this and the time it takes action. This is a distributed lag since the Fed is unlikely to undertake all its action at one time. Usually it will undertake its new open-market policy in a series of steps spread out over several months because it is uncertain whether the new policy is really the appropriate one, and hence wants to move slowly.

Then there is the *outside lag*. This is *the distributed lag from the time of the Fed's action until income changes*. Obviously, an increase in the money stock and a decrease in interest rates do not raise income immediately. For investment firms have to make a decision to invest, they have to draw up plans, place orders, and so on. For consumption, it takes some time until interest rates on consumer credit decline and until households respond to the rise in their money holdings or the increase in security prices that results from lower interest rates.

The inside lag can, but need not, be very short; it depends upon the extent to which the Fed is willing to take action on a forecast as opposed to waiting until conditions have actually changed. It also depends upon whether the Fed is willing to take much of the required action in one fell swoop, or spreads its action out over many months, either because it wants to avoid a rapid change in interest rates, or because it is not sure of itself. Thus if it is willing to undertake much of its open-market purchases before a business downturn actually occurs, the inside lag will be negative. The inside lag therefore depends upon the Fed itself, and hence depends on who the chairman of the Board of Governors is.

The outside lag is more objective and less subject to Fed control. Many economists have tried to estimate it. Some have used econometric models, and we showed some of their results in Figure 22.3, while others have regressed income on money, or have measured the lag between turning points in the money growth rate and business-cycle turning points. Several economists have measured how long it takes firms to invest, while still others have (following the analysis described in Chapter 15) looked at the length of time it takes interest rates to return to their previous levels after changes in the money growth rate. Unfortunately, little agreement has been reached, though most, but not all, of these studies show that it takes *at least* two quarters for monetary policy to reach half of its ultimate effect.[9] Beyond this, the range of estimates is large with the big econometric models usually showing long lags. A major reason for the long lags shown by econometric models is that most of them use a term-structure equation that shows a very slow adaption of long-term interest rates to the changes that the Fed brings about in short-term rates. However, these term-structure equations with their long lags are questioned by some economists. But the other methods of measuring the lag in monetary policy are also open to serious criticism. The wide range of estimates is disturbing and suggests that some skepticism is in order about the accuracy of all of them. Moreover, although little empirical work has been done on the extent to which the lag of monetary policy varies from case to case, the limited amount of information that is available suggests that the lag is highly variable. If correct, this is most disturbing.

Policy Tools: A Further Consideration

We are now in a position to return to the discussion of the tools of monetary policy, and take up briefly a sophisticated problem that we could not discuss before. Suppose several tools are available, such as open-market operations, discount-rate changes, and reserve-requirement changes or, alternatively, fiscal policy and monetary policy, all of which are strong enough to change income by the required amount. Which one should be used? One possible answer is the strongest. But a moment's reflection will show that unless there is a cost from using a tool too much or too often, there is no reason for choosing the strongest. Instead of looking at the strength one should use that tool that has the most predictable impact. Moreover, it is generally better to use several tools at the same time. This is so because if their variances are not perfectly correlated, then an averaging-out process ensures that the variance of the impact is less for several tools jointly than it is for any single tool. The exact mixture in which the tools should be used depends upon their relative variances and upon the correlation of their variances.

RATIONAL EXPECTATIONS

The lag in the effect of monetary policy is not the only factor that may cause countercyclical policy to be ineffective. Rational expectations may do this too. Firms do not act to maximize *actual* profits, they act to maximize *expected* profits. Hence, to predict how firms will act one has to find some way of determining what profits they *expect* to earn from various alternatives. There

[9] A complication here is that it is quite possible that the effect of monetary policy does not build up smoothly to a peak, but rises to a certain level, and then declines again to a lower level or cycles around some level.

are several ways of doing this. One is to assume that they form their expectations by looking only at the current and past behavior of the variable they want to predict. For example, if prices have been rising, they will expect them to rise in the future too. A useful specification of this approach is the error-learning model, in which a firm makes a forecast for one period ahead, and then, at the end of the period, looks at the errors in its forecast and adjusts its prediction for the second period accordingly. For example, if you predict that prices will rise at an 8 percent annual rate this month, but they actually rise at a 6 percent rate, it is reasonable for you to adjust your prediction for the next month down to, say, 7 percent.[10]

But such a backward-looking method of prediction is not always the best possible one. Suppose, for example, that at the end of the month you hear that Congress has ordered the Fed to bring the Treasury bill rate down from, say, 10 percent to 5 percent and to keep it there. Surely, you should use this piece of information in predicting what will happen to prices in the future. Since there has been an important change in the economy it would not be rational to predict prices merely by projecting the past behavior of prices into the future. When discussing the term structure of interest rates in Chapter 6, we mentioned rational expectations, and also made use of this approach in Chapter 22, to explain why you cannot make a killing in the stock market merely because you know that stock prices rise when the money growth rate does. But rational expectations are much more important than these examples suggest; they *may* make countercyclical stabilization policy both unnecessary and impossible.

What are Rational Expectations?

According to the rational-expectations approach, people forecast in a fully rational way, given all the information available to them. This is quite different from just projecting the past behavior of a series, such as interest rates, as is done in the error-learning model. In the error-learning model, when interest rates decline more than expected, people do not bother to ask why their previous forecast was wrong. Moreover, since they usually adjust their forecasts only part of the way each period, they tend to make systematic errors, for example, they overestimate for several periods. By contrast, in the rational-expectations approach people use all the information they can get at reasonable cost to make their forecasts. To do this they must have in their minds some model of the economy that allows them to interpret the incoming information. For example, using what they have learned from economics courses, they predict that inflation will speed up substantially if Congress orders the Fed to lower interest rates. But, how about those who have never taken an economics course? They too will have some information that will allow them to make a judgment about how the inflation rate will be affected. Everyone has an explicit or implicit theory that is used to interpret incoming information.

[10] Why not adjust your expectations down all the way to 6 percent? Well, you used quite a lot of information in deciding that prices will rise at an 8 percent rate. Do you really want to discard all of this information merely because you were wrong in one month?

Economics would be much further advanced if we knew these (largely inchoate) theories that people use. But we do not, so we have to make some assumptions. One possible assumption is that people's theories correspond fairly well to the economists' theories. This does not mean that everyone reasons the way economists do, but merely that their conclusions average out to what is shown by the economists' models. This is not as unrealistic as it sounds at first, because the most important decisions are made mainly by experienced managers who have reached their positions because they usually predict correctly. These managers can reach the same conclusions as economists without having the economists' theories in their toolbox. For example, someone may not know the theories that explain the term structure of interest rates, but may simply observe that long-term interest rates behave in a certain way when short-term rates change; birds can fly without having studied aerodynamics.

Moreover, assuming that expectations are rational is not the same thing as assuming that people have perfect foresight; economic models certainly do not. What it does mean is that, unlike in the error-learning model, people will not make *systematic* errors for any length of time. They will still make errors, but these errors will be random, and have a mean of zero. To illustrate, here is an example from everyday life. Suppose that without this being announced, trains are now running slower, so that the average trip takes ten minutes longer. On the first day almost everyone will arive at work late. Someone using an error-learning model will leave the next day, say, six minutes earlier and be four minutes late. But someone operating according to rational expectations may remember that in previous years when the weather was like this, trains were usually ten minutes late, or else may call the railroad to get a new timetable. Such a person will still not always be exactly on time; some days the train is slower, and some days it is faster. But this person will be late (or early) no more frequently than before.

This example assumes that people act on the available information, and leave ten minutes earlier, and this assumption that people do *act* on their available information is an important part of rational-expectations theory. Specifically, the theory assumes that if workers realize that the demand curve for their services has shifted downward they will be ready to accept wage cuts. Many Keynesians, on the other hand, assume that workers do not behave this way.

Rational Expectations and Unemployment

Assume that people act rationally in the sense just described, and consider a labor market in which workers and employers set wages for the following week at the level that they think will clear the market. Since they lack perfect knowledge this wage will sometimes be too high, so that unemployment occurs, and sometimes too low, so that there is an unsatisfied demand for labor. Now assume that aggregate demand falls suddenly so that extensive unemployment develops. At first workers and employers may think that this unemployment is merely a random event just as likely to be followed next week by an unsatisfied demand for labor as by a recurrence of unemployment. But after some time they will realize by looking at all the available information that the unemployment they are observing is not just the previously experienced random unemployment, but is more persistent and widespread. Hence they will negotiate lower wages. As wages fall, so do prices, and the resulting real balance effect restores employment to its equilibrium level.

This picture of a self-equilibrating economy was rejected by Keynes. He maintained that workers are reluctant to accept money wage cuts. Hence, Keynesians argue, if aggregate demand falls, why go through a lengthy and painful process of reducing wages and other costs, why not instead raise aggregate demand back to its previous level by expansionary fiscal and monetary policy?[11] And it is this reasoning that underlies the widespread support for countercyclical policies.

But in recent years a number of economists have challenged this. They interpret unemployment very differently and argue that it is due, not to any stickiness of money wages, but to the fact that it takes time for workers and employers to realize that aggregate demand has fallen permanently and that money wages should fall too. As soon as one makes unemployment the result of ignorance rather than of an unwillingness to accept lower money wages, the traditional justification for countercyclical stabilization policy becomes suspect. Ignorance is not confined to the labor market; the government has its share too. Assume that the government is exactly as well informed as those who set wages. In this case by the time the government realizes what has happened and raises aggregate demand, wages are being cut and the real balance effect brings about full employment in any case. Hence expansionary policy is not needed. If one assumes that money-wage stickiness is due entirely to lack of information, rather than to a reluctance to take a wage cut, then, only if the government is better informed than the private market will stabilization policy be useful. And there is no reason to assume that this is the case.

It is therefore an important issue whether money wages are flexible and fall when it is realized that aggregate demand has fallen, or whether they are sticky. Many economists rationalize wage stickiness in several ways. One way is to say that a person's wage affects his or her self-respect, so that workers are willing to risk unemployment rather than take a wage cut, or, more questionably, to try to argue that unions keep wages up.[12] Another way is to point out that workers do not set wages on their own; in nonunionized firms—which employ about three-quarters of the labor force—wages are set by the employer subject to a minimum wage floor, and in unionized industries they are set by employers and workers jointly. And, it may well

[11] Keynes was not the only one who advocated raising aggregate demand in the 1930s. Economists who then constituted the "Chicago School" advocated that the government should increase the quantity of money, and put it into circulation by using it to pay for public works.

[12] Despite the substantial increase in unionization since the Great Depression days, the cyclical sensitivity of wages to unemployment did not decline much; it was never large. (See Charles Schultze, "Some Macro Foundations for Micro Theory," *Brookings Papers on Economic Activity*, 1981:2, 521–75.)

be employers rather than workers who are unwilling to cut wages during a recession. There is a theory, known as the implicit-contract theory, that argues that the employer makes an implicit contract with the employee along the following lines: "I cannot supervise you all the time, and I expect you to work efficiently even when I am not watching you. In return for this, I will not try to take advantage of every slight decline in your equilibrium wage: for example, even if I could hire an unemployed worker in your stead at, say, 10 percent less than I am paying you, I will neither fire you nor ask you to take a 10 percent wage cut." If such mutual loyalty arrangements are common, then many wages will not fall even after it becomes apparent that aggregate demand has fallen.

Wage rigidity may therefore furnish a justification for stabilization policy. But in the previous section of this chapter we raised the question whether, given its lags, stabilization policy can be effective. Can these two arguments be combined? Yes, to some extent they can since they both concern lags. (Wage stickiness is a matter of lags; if large-scale unemployment persists long enough, eventually wages will fall.) Suppose that aggregate demand drops. If money-wage cuts and the resulting real balance effect occur quicker than the effect of expansionary monetary policy does, then monetary policy should not be used. But if money wages are very slow to respond, then unemployment *may* continue for a long enough time for monetary policy to do some good.

The Impact of Stabilization Policy

If the rational-expectation theorists are correct, countercyclical policy not only does no good, it does positive harm because it is inflationary. To see why, consider first an economy with rational expectations and high employment. The government now undertakes a long-run expansionary policy. The traditional story is that firms react to the increase in aggregate demand for their products initially by raising their output and raise their prices only with a lag. This is so primarily because firms do not know whether this increase in demand is permanent or just temporary, and they want to avoid frequent price changes. But, say the rational-expectations theorists, this story is wrong. Entrepreneurs read newspapers, and, hence, *in this case,* when demand increases, they realize that it is because of an expansionary policy, and that the higher demand will persist. Hence, they raise prices right away instead of raising output.

This example has the government raising aggregate demand during a period of high employment, which is hardly an example of a good stabilization policy; so now assume instead that it raises aggregate demand only during a recession, but does so consistently. If so, whenever a recession occurs firms know that the government will raise aggregate demand, and hence they raise their prices. Or more realistically, they refrain from doing what they otherwise would have done during the recession, cutting prices.

Suppose, for example, that the government were to announce that every time unemployment exceeds, say, 6 percent, it will raise the money growth rate by 3 percentage points. Both firms and unions would then take an unemployment rate of over 6 percent as an indication that they should raise their wages and prices. Carrying this approach a bit further, rational expectations theorists have argued that an *expected* increase in the money growth rate only raises prices and does not raise output even temporarily. Output rises temporarily only in response to an *unexpected* increase in the money growth rate. Hence, the only way the Fed could raise output and employment would be if it could adopt expansionary policies that are unexpected. But sooner or later the public will figure out any consistent Federal Reserve policy; and even if the Fed could somehow fool the public in the long run, it is far from clear that it should do so since this would cause people to make wrong decisions.

This theory is highly controversial. While the empirical evidence was initially favorable to it, on recent empirical tests its performance has, on the whole, not been good.

Although rational expectations theories, if correct, eliminate the argument for stabilization policy, they enhance the efficacy of one type of stabilization policy. This is a policy to end inflation by cutting aggregate demand. The usual story is that if a restrictive monetary or fiscal policy cuts aggregate demand the initial result is a much greater fall in output than in the inflation rate. Firms and unions do not realize that the government is serious about ending inflation. They continue to expect inflation, and therefore raise their wages and prices. Only after a long time of great unemployment will the inflation rate decline substantially. Rational-expectations theory suggests such a period of high unemployment is not necessary; the government should let the public know that it really will cut aggregate demand sufficiently to bring the inflation rate down. If this is done, then prices and wages will adjust relatively quickly.

But what is needed is not just a statement by the government that it is "against inflation"—such talk is cheap. The government would have to show that it means what it says, perhaps by a dramatic gesture, such as directing the Fed to concentrate on price stability, or even by a constitutional amendment requiring price-stabilizing policies.

But such measures would be strongly opposed by organized labor and others who cherish high employment. They would not be convinced that such a policy would succeed. They could reply that while the rational-expectations theory sounds plausible, it may not work, and people's jobs are too important to experiment with. Moreover, by making such a commitment, the government would have to give up its flexibility. It would then be costly for it to change the anti-inflation policy even if it does not work. The cost is that if the government changes its mind, and, for example, changes the directive given to the Fed, then later on if it wants to change expectations again by a similar method it will not be believed.

But even if for these reasons the government does not want to abandon the employment goal completely, rational-expectations theory still has an important lesson: this is that if the Fed adopts a restrictive policy and intends to stick with it, the public should be told. In general, one does not have to accept rational-expectations theory completely to conclude that expectations do matter, and that monetary policies will have different effects depending on what expectations they generate. For example, some of the variation in the lag with which changes in the money stock affect income *may* be due to differences in the extent to which the public realizes what is happening.

Predicting the Effects of Policies

The rational-expectations approach has another important implication for policy. This is that policy may quite unintentionally change the way the public reacts to events. For example, take a policy that cuts personal income taxes during a recession and raises them again during the following expansion. To find out how big a tax cut is needed economists may calculate the marginal propensity to consume from past data on consumption and disposable income, or they may look at how consumption changed every time taxes were cut previously. But they may be in for a disappointment. When income taxes are now cut as a countercyclical policy, the public *may* raise its consumption very little. It knows that, unlike in the past, from now on income taxes will be raised again when the economy expands. And since it sets its consumption on the basis of its long-run disposable income, it now reacts very differently to a tax cut than it did before.

Thus, the adoption of a new policy has outdated and made inapplicable the information obtained from past experience. This implies that it is dangerous to use the information generated by econometric models, regression equations, or economic history in general, to predict the effects of any policy that may change people's expectations. Hence, rational-expectations theorists argue, we know very little about the effects that economic policies have, and this too makes it questionable that stabilization policy can succeed.

POLITICAL PROBLEMS

The technical problems created by long and variable lags and by rational expectations are not the only difficulties that confront discretionary policy. Political difficulties too may prevent effective policy. The political assumption underlying economic policy is that the electorate knows what is best for it and that the technicians who operate the government carry out policies that will achieve these ends. Now obviously this is an idealization, and the question is not whether it mirrors reality exactly, but whether it is close enough to reality, so that stabilization policy does more good than harm. Although economists generally assume that this is the case, some economists, particularly monetarists, are challenging it. Unfortunately, this discussion is still in its very early stages, so that we can only give a rather impressionistic sketch of the problem.[13]

Several things can go wrong in a process that has the public decide on its desired goal, which the technicians in government then carry out. One is

[13] Although the political problems of monetary policy have received little discussion, those of fiscal policy have been discussed more. See, for instance, James Buchanan and Richard Wagner, *Democracy in Deficit* (New York: Academic Press, 1977), and the symposium on this book in the *Journal of Monetary Economics* 4 (August 1978): 567–636.

that the public may not know what is best for it. A second is that special-interest groups may be able to substitute their wishes for those of the majority, and a third problem is that the majority may override the legitimate interests of a minority. And finally, the bureaucracy may be unresponsive.

The public may at times mistake its own interests in the goals it indirectly sets for monetary policy through its elected representatives. This does not imply that the public is unintelligent, but merely that any one person has so little influence on monetary policy that it is not worth his or her while to devote even a trivial amount of time to it. Consequently, the public may sometimes support policies that are clearly wrong. More specifically, the public *may* have a short memory about recent economic policy. This creates a danger of the political business cycle discussed in Chapter 7. Whether this has actually occurred in the United States is a debated issue.

A second possibility is that monetary policy may be used to hide the true costs of government programs. The government may undertake popular expenditures and run a deficit. If this occurs at a time of high employment, the resources used by the government must be withdrawn from the private sector. If the money growth rate is kept constant, then the government obtains these resources by selling securities to the public, and this raises interest rates. This rise in interest rates makes the private sector willing to give up some current resources since it raises the cost of using resources currently rather than in the future. But rising interest rates are unpopular, and hence there is pressure on the Fed to generate a sufficiently large increase in the money stock to hold interest rates down temporarily. The public is thereby fooled into believing that it has obtained a desirable government program at no cost since it attributes the then resulting inflation to big business or big labor.

Another variant of this approach has the Fed act as a scapegoat for politicians. The public demands high employment, price stability, and low and stable nominal interest rates. But these goals are incompatible, and hence the politicians need an "out." As Edward Kane of Ohio State University has put it:

> The Fed is a political institution designed by politicians to serve politicians. . . . Fed officials are expected to let Congressmen and Senators blame them for whatever financial or economic developments their constituents back home dislike. In exchange for playing economic-policy scapegoat, Fed officials are offered unusually long terms in office and substantial budgetary autonomy. . . . The Fed has allowed elected politicians to make it responsible for a series of impossible economic-policy tasks, with the implicit understanding that, when the Fed fails, how loud these politicians and their successors will bark (and whether or not they will also bite) depends on the quality of Fed efforts to get along.[14]

Further, by not being vigilant about monetary policy the public may allow special-interest groups to exert excessive influence on monetary policy. One special-interest group consists of banks and other financial institutions. Some economists attribute the Fed's previous emphasis on interest-rate stabiliza-

[14] Edward J. Kane, "Politics and Fed Policymaking: The More Things Change the More They Remain the Same," *Journal of Monetary Economics* 6 (April 1980): 209.

tion, and its permissive attitudes toward fudging of the line between money and near-moneys, both to the Fed's self-interest, and to the pressures on it from banks and other financial institutions.

Moreover, as discussed in the previous chapter, rising interest rates have particularly strong effects on certain industries, such as the politically powerful residential construction industry.[15] These industries can be expected to pressure the Fed, both directly and through Congress, or by arousing public opinion, into adopting an expansionary policy to postpone the rise in nominal interest rates. The costs of adopting a too expansionary policy are diffused over the general economy, while the short-run benefits from such a policy are much more concentrated. Hence, those who gain from such a policy organize to pressure the Fed, while those who lose from it do not.

The last potential problem with government policy is that the majority might override the legitimate interests of the minority. This may not be a problem with monetary policy except insofar as the Fed *might* show too little concern about unemployment because it is a problem that directly affects only a minority of the electorate.

ADMINISTRATIVE PROBLEMS

There are highly competent economists on the Board of Governors, on its staff, and in the Reserve Banks. One might therefore expect that in the absence of insuperable political pressures the Fed should be able to handle its stabilization task as successfully as technical factors, such as lags and inevitable forecasting errors, permit. But this need not be the case. Internal problems of the Fed *might* create serious difficulties for stabilization policy. This is an area in which little research has been done so far. All we can do here is to sketch some potential problems rather than present documented conclusions.

One set of factors that might interfere with efficient stabilization policy is that the Fed has its own bureaucratic interests. For example, suppose—for the sake of argument—that to break inflationary expectations the correct policy would be for the Fed to commit itself absolutely to a particular money growth target for the next three years. Regardless of the true merits of such a policy, the Fed might well be reluctant to do this because it would mean relinquishing flexibility and hence autonomy.

Moreover, the Fed, like everyone else, might indulge in the natural tendency to put the urgent ahead of the important; to solve today's problems today even if it creates greater problems in the future. In addition, if the Fed responds too slowly it will be destabilizing. But given the great uncertainty it faces, the FOMC may well be willing to act only on the basis of currently prevailing conditions, and not a forecast. The likelihood of this is increased by the fact that the FOMC usually changes its policy only as a result of a widespread consensus rather than on a mere majority. Since the liberals on

[15] The residential construction industry is so powerful in part because there are contractors and construction workers in every congressional district, and because of the industry's alliance with the influential thrift industry. Part of its power probably comes from the public's susceptibility to the emotional arguments for fostering housing.

the FOMC are generally unwilling to concede that a more restrictive policy is required until the need for it has become clear, while the conservatives are reluctant to accept a more expansionary policy until the need for that policy is obvious, one would expect the FOMC to be tardy in changing policy.[16] Thus, the very way the FOMC is organized may cause monetary policy to be destabilizing. (Perhaps this problem could be reduced substantially by not publishing the FOMC's votes.)

Or consider the following hypothesis: The members of the FOMC, being decent people, would like to reduce unemployment to any feasible extent. But unfortunately, it is not clear what the natural rate of unemployment is. Suppose that it seems to be 6 percent. Given the great misery unemployment causes, it is only natural for the FOMC to try to see if it would not be feasible to operate with somewhat lower unemployment. Hence, it may adopt a more expansionary policy. Initially, little, if any, inflation results. Later on, when some inflation does occur, the FOMC may be reluctant to return to a more restrictive policy because the observed increase in the inflation rate may turn out to be only a temporary blip, or it could be due to some other factors. Eventually, of course, the inflation rate rises enough so that the FOMC is forced to adopt a more restrictive policy—and can do so with a good conscience because inflation, not unemployment, is now *the* problem. Thus, one can tell a story in which good intentions cause a business cycle. Whether this actually occurs is hard to say; no evidence for it has yet been presented. But there is much evidence that Fed decisions were made, not on the basis of rigorous technical analysis, but on a rather casual basis, where considerations such as just now sketched *could* play a role.[17]

SUMMARY

1. Monetary policy affects income with a distributed lag. Hence, it might be badly timed and therefore destabilizing. This depends upon the correlation between the policy and the original fluctuation in income, and on the strength of the policy.
2. The existence of the lag creates several problems. The Fed must forecast income, it must predict the strength of its policy, and its distributed lag. All of these predictions are subject to substantial errors. Moreover, the lag prevents the Fed from quickly offsetting any errors it made. The lag can be divided into an inside lag and an outside lag. Estimates of the latter vary widely.
3. The Fed should use not necessarily the strongest tools, but those with the most predictable effects. Usually it is best to employ several.
4. Rational expectations (which means that people predict on the basis of all available information and do not make consistent errors) creates another potential

[16] See Robert Shapiro, "Politics and the Federal Reserve," *The Public Interest,* 66 (Winter 1982): 119–39.

[17] For descriptions of the thinking that went to make relatively recent Fed policy, see Lombra and Moran, *loc. cit.;* Thomas Mayer, "A Case Study of Federal Reserve Policymaking: Regulation Q in 1966," *Journal of Monetary Economics,* 10 (September 1982), and "Federal Reserve Policy in the 1973–75 Recession: A Case Study of Fed Policy in a Quandary," in Paul Wachtel (ed.), *Crises in the Economic and Financial Structure,* Lexington, Mass.: Lexington Books, 1982.

problem for the Fed. Under rational expectations stabilization policy can be effective only if the government has better information than the public, or if its policy affects the economy before the public can act. This raises the question of whether wages are sticky or merely respond slowly due to limited information.

5. Rational expectations theory also argues that if the Fed reacts to a recession by a predictable expansionary policy, this policy will have its effects only on prices and not on output. However, this is much disputed. Rational expectations theory also implies that if the government changes its policy, then the economy will change too, so that the policy—which is based on past data—may no longer be valid.
6. The Fed does not make policy in a vacuum; political pressures impinge on it and may deflect it from the correct policy. One example of this is a political business cycle. Politicians may use the Fed as a scapegoat.
7. Administrative problems, such as concern with its own interests, an overemphasis on current problems and an attempt to do too much, *may* also inhibit effective policy. Very little is known about this.

Questions and Exercises

1. "The problem with monetary policy is not, as was once thought, that it is too weak, but that it is too strong." Explain.
2. Explain why monetary policy is destabilizing if the correlation coefficient between σ_x^2 and σ_y^2 is zero or positive.
3. Discuss the problem that the lag in the effect of monetary policy creates for the Federal Reserve.
4. Why does a variable lag create a more serious problem than a stable one? What factors could account for it being variable?
5. Read one of the empirical studies trying to measure the lag. (The items by Hamburger and Uselton in Further Reading have references to these studies.) Write a critique of it.
6. Explain in your own words the rational-expectations criticism of stabilization policy.
7. "If expectations are rational, an expansionary monetary policy will raise only prices and not output." Discuss.
8. Is it sometimes more reasonable to use an error-learning model than rational expectations? If so, under what conditions? How do you form your own expectations?
9. What are the political problems that may hinder effective stabilization policy? Do they apply to fiscal policy as well as to monetary policy?

Further Reading

BRAINARD, WILLIAM. "Uncertainty and the Effectiveness of Monetary Policy." *American Economic Review* 57 (May 1967): 411–25. An excellent discussion of how to use various policy tools that have different degrees of predictability.

FRIEDMAN, MILTON. "The Effects of a Full Employment Policy on Economic Stability: A Formal Analysis." In his *Essays in Positive Economics*. Chicago: University of Chicago Press, 1953. This is a classic.

HAMBURGER, MICHAEL. "The Lag in the Effect of Monetary Policy: A Survey of Recent Literature." *Monthly Review* (Federal Reserve Bank of New York) 53 (December 1971): 289–98. An excellent survey of several empirical studies.

HAVRILESKY, THOMAS. "A Theory of Monetary Instability." In *The Political Economy of Policymaking: Essays in Honor of Will E. Mason,* edited by M. Dooley, H. Kaufman, and R. Lombra. Beverly Hills: Sage Publications, 1978, pp. 59–88. An interesting attempt to explain Fed actions.

KANE, EDWARD. "Politics and Fed Policy-Making: The More Things Change the More They Remain the Same." *Journal of Monetary Economics* 6 (April 1980): 199–211.

SHEFFRIN, STEVEN. *Rational Expectations*. New York: Cambridge University Press, 1983. An excellent survey.

TOBIN, JAMES. "How Dead Is Keynes?" *Economic Inquiry* 15 (October 1977): 459–68. A very good defense of Keynesian economics against the rational expectations criticism.

USELTON, GENE. *Lags in the Effects of Monetary Policy*. New York: Marcel Dekker, 1974. Chapter two is a useful survey. Both this, and the article by Hamburger above, contain references to the numerous empirical studies the reader may wish to consult.

The Record of Monetary Policy 24

Having looked in the abstract at the problems that face monetary policy we now see how monetary policy has actually functioned in the past. In doing so we try to evaluate the Fed and see what mistakes it has made because such mistakes may again occur in the future.

We therefore try to evaluate the Fed's performance rather than to study monetary history for its own sake. While history is certainly worth studying for its own sake, the history of monetary policy, taken out of the context of the society in which it functions, is hardly the most life-enhancing type of history. Since we are concerned with evaluating Federal Reserve performance we will stress critical episodes rather than try to cover all of the more than sixty years of Fed history in a balanced manner.

THE EARLY YEARS

When the Federal Reserve System was inaugurated in 1913 one of its major goals, perhaps *the* major goal, was the maintenance of the gold standard, which at the time was generally considered the foundation of sound money. We will discuss the gold standard in Part Five. Here it suffices to note that under the gold-standard "rules of the game" the Fed should let the quantity of money be determined by the country's gold stock. A gold inflow is supposed to increase the quantity of money, and a gold outflow to decrease it.

Although it also had some belief in the quantity theory, a second guiding idea of the Fed was the real-bills doctrine. According to this, now discarded, theory what matters is the *quality* rather than the *quantity* of money; as long as deposits are created as a result of short-term self-liquidating loans that finance real (as opposed to financial) activities, deposit creation cannot be inflationary.[1] Member banks could borrow from the Fed only by rediscounting **eligible paper,** that is, those *promissory notes they had discounted for their customers that met the requirements of the real-bills doctrine,* or by discounting their own promissory notes backed by government securities. The theory was that this would provide an "elastic" currency that would allow the money supply to expand when the demand for money for real transactions increased. At that time banks would discount more eligible promissory notes for their customers, and could then rediscount this eligible paper with the Fed.

Another guiding idea was the need to avoid financial panics. It was widely believed that recessions were often the result of financial panics that were, in turn, caused by excessive speculation. Hence, one of the tasks of the Fed was to limit speculation. In addition, the provision of an elastic currency would also help to prevent financial panics, as would the Fed's supervision of member banks, and the centralization of member bank reserves in the Federal Reserve Banks. The law of large numbers makes centralized reserves a more effective barrier against failure than are reserves kept individually by each bank.

Another goal of the Fed was to stabilize interest rates. It was to eliminate, or at least reduce, the pronounced seasonal swings in interest rates that occurred before 1914, and to avoid the sharp interest-rate increases that would accompany periods of financial stringency and panics.

All in all, the initial goals of the Fed were those that seemed reasonable to a small-town merchant in 1913, rather than those that an economist would now set for a central bank. Full employment had not yet been "invented"—there were not even unemployment statistics. Although in the 1920s there were attempts in Congress to add a price-stabilization goal to the Federal Reserve Act, these attempts failed. But, while we now set other goals for the Fed, these 1913 goals have not completely disappeared. We no longer have the gold standard, but the Fed has as one of its minor goals an appropriate exchange rate of the dollar. The Fed is still opposed to excessive speculation—a dislike of speculation being one of the few Puritan ideas not challenged in the turmoil of the 1960s. The Fed is still concerned about interest rate fluctuations, and even the real-bills doctrine lives on in occasional admonitions to banks to avoid "unproductive" loans.

But in its early years the Fed had little chance to aim at these goals. Shortly after it got underway, World War I broke out. Belligerents increased their purchases in the U.S., resulting in a large gold inflow. The Fed could not offset the impact of this on bank reserves since it did not yet have enough securities to sell.

In April 1917 the United States entered the war. It has been said that in every war, truth is the first casualty. It might be added that sound ideas on finance are the second. During the war the Fed became subservient to the

[1] The argument was that a loan to finance short-term productive activity would increase output by as much as it increased demand. And with supply and demand increasing equally, prices would be constant. This argument is invalid because part of the increase in the *value* of output may be due to higher prices. Under the real-bills doctrine the Fed could be financing ever-increasing inflation.

Treasury Department. Its policy was therefore dominated by the Treasury's goal of raising funds. Two-thirds of the government's wartime expenditures were financed by borrowing. The Treasury wanted to borrow at below-market interest rates and to rely on patriotic appeals to sell its securities. But to provide a material incentive too, individuals could borrow from banks to buy government securities at an interest rate equal to the rate they received on these securities, that is, at no net interest cost. Banks could borrow from the Fed on their promissory notes secured by Treasury certificates at an interest rate below what the banks earned on these Treasury certificates. Hence, they had an incentive to borrow. This was highly inflationary. And with this policy continuing after the war, so did the inflation. In the postwar expansion, March 1919 through January 1920, the wholesale price index rose by about 50 percent, and the GNP deflator by about 10 percent.

Although the Fed was concerned about the inflation, it was more or less willing to go along with the Treasury's inflationary policy until late 1919. Then in January 1920 it raised the discount rate applicable to commercial-paper borrowing from 4½ percent to 6 percent, the sharpest jump in the discount rate that has ever occurred. In June 1920 this discount rate was raised to 7 percent where it stayed despite the recession until May 1921.

The month, January 1920, in which the Fed shifted to such a highly restrictive policy was also the month of the upper turning point of the business cycle. The ensuing recession started mildly, but then turned into one of the deepest recessions in American history, though fortunately it was short-lived. Real GNP declined by 12 percent and, due to a sharp price decline, nominal GNP fell by 31 percent. Clearly the Fed is not to blame for *initiating* this recession since the upper turning point occurred before the restrictive policy could have become effective. However, Milton Friedman and Anna Schwartz have blamed the Fed for the subsequent severity of the recession. It is obvious that, at the very least, the adoption of a severely restrictive policy just when the economy turned down was not what was needed. And the continuation of this policy despite a major recession was hardly a proud moment for monetary policy.

What were the reasons for this blunder? One was the Fed's concern about inflation. Another was the decline in the Fed's ratio of gold holdings to the currency and deposits it had issued. (At the time the law specified minimum ratios.) But this was probably more a public justification for the policy than its main reason since the Fed had the legal power to suspend this reserve requirement. Instead, the main reason was probably the inadequacy of the Fed's underlying monetary theory. Thus, it did not understand that once high interest rates have succeeded in breaking the boom they should be lowered again to ameliorate the ensuing recession, and not be kept at a high level that would continue to exert deflationary pressures. This is so, particularly when sharply falling prices raise very substantially the expected real interest rate corresponding to a given nominal rate.

Moreover, the Fed held to the pernicious real-bills doctrine. It believed that it should provide additional reserves only temporarily for seasonal needs or to prevent panics, and did not realize that it should provide additional reserves to take care of secular growth. It therefore wished, in accordance with the real-bills theory, to eliminate the money creation that had resulted during the war from the discounting of notes secured by government securities. It also wanted to reduce the seeming excessive liquidity of bank portfolios that resulted from banks holding large amounts of government securities. In addition, the Fed believed that a deflation was desirable to offset the previous inflation, and it feared that an easy money policy would lead to excessive speculation. In general, the Fed did not think that it should manage the money stock with a view to cyclical factors and to secular growth in the demand for money. Rather it saw its function as increasing reserves only temporarily to stabilize interest rates on a seasonal basis and during potential panics.

OTHER EVENTS IN THE 1920s

In the 1920s Fed policy was influenced by several considerations. One was the gold standard, though there is still considerable dispute about how important this really was in determining Fed policy. European countries, particularly Britain, were trying to return to the gold standard. To ensure that Britain had enough gold for this, the Fed wanted low interest rates in New York so that gold would not flow from London to New York. Later on, the Fed was concerned with preventing a gold outflow that could drive the United States off the gold standard. However, at the same time, the Fed was also paying attention to domestic conditions, and in particular, there was now some emphasis on the quantity of credit rather than just on the quality of credit. There was some attempt at countercyclical monetary policy, and the Fed began to pay attention to the level of output as well as to prices.

The great stock-market boom of 1928–29 placed the Fed (which, at that time, did not have the power to set margin requirements) in a difficult position. It wanted to raise the discount rate to stop the boom, but this would have raised interest rates to business when business conditions did not call for this. Moreover, it would have stimulated a gold flow from London to New York, thus hurting British stabilization policy. Hence, the Fed decided to try indirect pressures, that is, moral suasion and the denial of discounts to banks making excessive loans for security purchases. Finally, in August 1929 the discount rate *was* raised. But by then the stock-market boom was so strong that the relatively small increase in the price of credit did little to curb it, while it did hurt ordinary business borrowing. Had the Fed raised the discount rate earlier, it might have succeeded in stopping the stock-market boom before it gathered steam.

THE GREAT DEPRESSION

Understanding the Great Depression is important, not only for evaluating the Fed's record, but also for an understanding of how the economy reacts to monetary policy. At the time, and since then, many economists have argued that the 1930s demonstrated that, at least during a major depression, monetary policy is ineffective. It was the experience of the Great Depression, as well as the publication of Keynes's masterpiece in 1936, that swung economists away from the quantity theory toward the income-expenditure approach. On the other hand, monetarists point to the Great Depression as showing exactly the opposite: the immense damage a perverse monetary policy can do, and hence, the great importance of money. It is therefore not surprising that of all the historical episodes discussed here only the Great Depression is still debated extensively.

Before turning to the rival explanations, here are some facts about the depression. The upper turning point was reached in August 1929, that is, a few months prior to the stock-market crash. The recession continued until March 1933 when an upswing started. This upswing reached a submerged peak, a peak that still had very substantial unemployment, in May 1937. The following recession reached its trough in June 1938. The ensuing expansion carried into and through World War II. In the period 1929–33, net national product fell by more than one-half when measured in current prices; real net national product fell by more than one-third, as did the wholesale price index. Table 24.1 shows the appalling unemployment rates as well as the GNP deflator. Note, incidentally, that despite very high unemployment, prices rose after 1933. Contrary to the impression given by many commentators, "stagflation" is not a new development. To some extent, price increases in the 1930s can perhaps be attributed to a government program that tried to raise wages and prices.

Turning to the monetary data, from August 1929 to March 1933 nominal M_1 fell by one-quarter, and nominal M_2 fell by more than one-third. This decline in the stock of money was the accompaniment of wide-spread bank

Table 24.1 Unemployment, Prices, and Money
1929–41

Year	Unemployment as percent of nonfarm employees	GNP deflator (1958 = 100)	Per capita nominal money stock as percent of 1929[a] M_1	M_2
1929	5.3%	50.6	100.0%	100.0%
1930	14.2	49.3	95.6	97.6
1931	25.2	44.8	89.5	91.1
1932	36.3	40.2	76.2	73.2
1933	37.6	39.3	71.2	63.5
1934	32.6	42.2	77.5	69.4
1935	30.2	42.6	92.1	79.3
1936	25.4	42.7	107.5	89.8
1937	21.3	44.5	110.4	93.0
1938	27.9	43.9	104.5	90.1
1939	25.2	43.2	115.8	96.6
1940	21.3	43.9	136.4	109.0
1941	14.4	47.2	158.1	121.8

a. Money-stock data are for June of each year.

Source: Stanley Lebergott, *Manpower in Economic Growth* (New York: McGraw-Hill, 1964), p. 512 (used with permission of McGraw-Hill Book Co.); U.S. Bureau of the Census, *Historical Statistics of the United States* (1976 ed.), p. 224; Milton Friedman and Anna Schwartz, *A Monetary History of the United States* (Princeton: Princeton University Press, 1963), pp. 712–16.

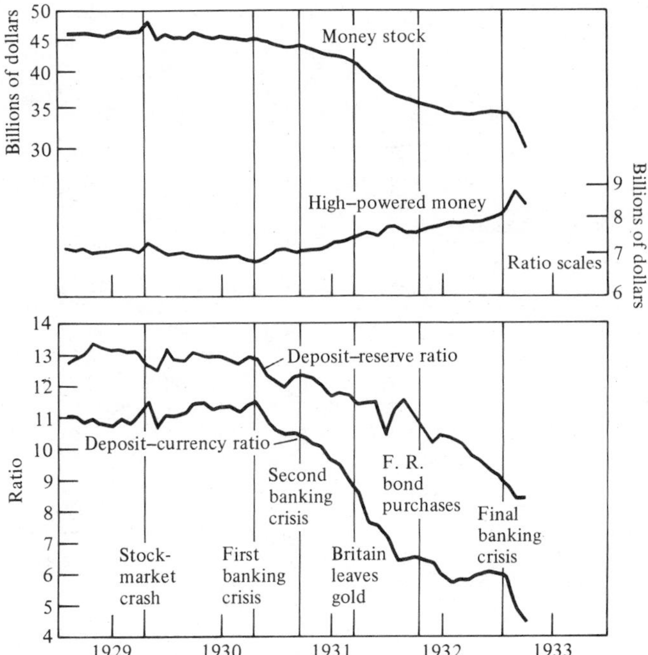

Figure 24.1 The Stock of Money and Its Proximate Determinants, Monthly *1929–March 1933*

Source: Milton Friedman and Anna Schwartz, *A Monetary History of the United States* (Princeton: Princeton University Press, 1963), p. 333.

failures, failures which occurred in three waves, in October 1930, in October 1931, and the final one, which led to the bank holiday when all banks were closed for a time, in March 1933.

Figure 24.1 shows that the decline in the money stock was not due to a decline in the reserve base (high-powered money) but resulted from a fall in the deposit-reserve ratio and in the deposit-currency ratio. Not surprisingly, as many banks failed, the surviving banks tried to ensure their own safety by holding more reserves, while the public tried to avoid losses by withdrawing deposits.

The discount rate fell radically in this period. It was reduced from a level of 5 to 6 percent in various Federal Reserve Banks in the fall of 1929 to a level of 1½ to 3 percent in September 1931. A Figure 24.2 shows other short-term rates declined sharply, too. However, in this period the rate on long-term government securities did not decline as much, and the rate on Baa corporate bonds, that is, bonds of "lower medium grade" quality, actually rose substantially in the early part of the period, then fell, and in 1939 was not far from its 1928 level. Moreover the price declines that occurred in the early 1930s meant that for these years the real rate of interest was substantially greater than the nominal rate shown in Figure 24.2. For subsequent years the real rate of interest was less than the nominal rate. But since the

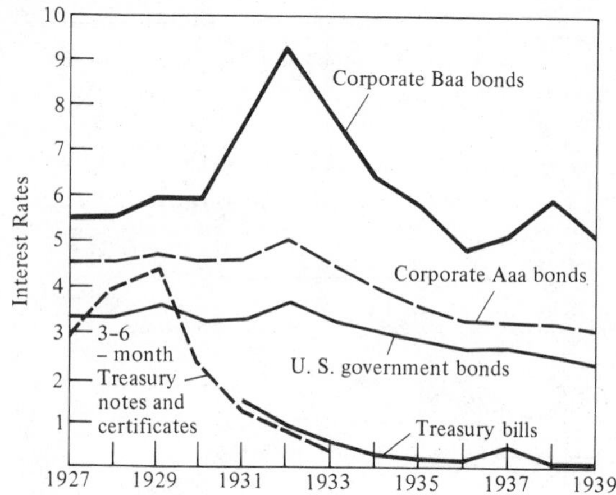

Figure 24.2 Selected Interest Rates
1927–39

Source: Thomas Mayer, *Monetary Policy in the United States* (New York: Random House, 1968), p. 219.

price level was lower in 1939 than in 1929, for the decade as a whole, the real rate exceeded the nominal rate of interest.

FEDERAL RESERVE POLICY

Where was the Fed while all of this was going on? For many years it was widely believed that, on the whole, it behaved well. Right after the stock-market crash it cut the discount rate, and kept it low except in late 1931 when there was a gold outflow as fears developed that the United States would follow Britain off the gold standard. The Fed did make a serious mistake in raising reserve requirements in 1936 and 1937, but it certainly cannot be blamed for the depression. This resulted from a massive collapse in the marginal efficiency of investment, and monetary policy is almost powerless in such a situation. The Fed kept the discount rate, and other short-term rates low, but business had little incentive to borrow. The Fed made reserves available, but banks simply held them as excess reserves. And even if they had not, the liquidity-preference curve was so flat at the extraordinarily low Treasury bill rates of much less than one percent, that it would not have been feasible to reduce rates any further. You cannot push on a piece of string.

Although some economists had challenged this view of monetary policy earlier, it was the prevailing orthodoxy until the 1960s, when it was powerfully challenged by Friedman and Schwartz and by Elmus Wicker. Although Friedman and Schwartz present a strongly monetarist interpretation, many Keynesians have to a considerable extent accepted their interpretation of Federal Reserve policy.

Given their monetarist outlook, Friedman and Schwartz placed much more emphasis on what was happening to the reserve base and the quantity of money than on interest rates. But even as far as interest rates are concerned, they pointed out that while the discount rate and the commercial-paper rate were low during most of the depression, this was not true for the interest rates that are more important for business borrowers, for instance, the Baa bond rate. The public, fearing further financial crises, bid up the prices of highly liquid securities such as commercial paper, thus creating an unusually large gap between interest rates on highly liquid securities and on less liquid and safe ones. Moreover, in the first part of the depression, with prices falling, the expected real rate of interest was presumably much higher than the nominal rate. Also, the discount rate, while low by historical standards, was not low relative to open-market rates, thus providing little incentive to discount. In addition, the low discount rate may not have had much significance because, as Warburton had pointed out earlier, it was accompanied by a very restrictive policy of discount administration—"the Federal Reserve authorities had discouraged rediscounting almost to the point of prohibition. . . ."[2]

But the main focus of the reinterpretation of Federal Reserve policy is not on interest rates, but on the Fed's open-market operations, or lack thereof. The Fed did not undertake large-scale open-market purchases until 1932. In fact, until then it was offsetting the expansionary impact on the base that would have occurred naturally from large gold inflows. Friedman and Schwartz described the policy as:

> . . . one of monetary "tightness" not "ease." During a period of severe economic contraction extending over more than a year, the System was content to let its discounts decline by nearly twice its net purchases of government securities, and to let its total credit outstanding decline by almost three times the increase in the gold stock. . . . The System's holdings of government securities plus bills bought were nearly $200 million lower at the end of July 1930 than they were at the end of December 1929.[3]

In 1932 the Fed finally undertook large-scale open-market purchases. Friedman and Schwartz suggested that the reason was political. Congress was considering expansionary legislation, such as a bill to pay a bonus to World War I veterans, and the Fed thought that an activist policy could reduce support for such proposals. After Congress adjourned in July these open-market purchases ceased. (Friedman and Schwartz suggest that in general Congress' judgment on monetary policy has often been better than the Fed's.)

Why did the Fed not adopt a more expansionary policy? One reason Friedman and Schwartz suggested was the Fed's choice of the wrong indicators, that is, its almost exclusive focus on certain interest rates (such as the discount rate), on excess reserves, and on the availability of credit, and its disregard of the decline in the quantity of money. A second reason was the Fed's failure to understand the nature of excess reserves. Although some of its officials realized that banks wanted to hold more excess reserves because

[2]Clark Warburton, *Depression, Inflation and Monetary Policy, Selected Papers, 1945–53* (Baltimore: Johns Hopkins University Press, 1966), p. 340.

[3]Friedman and Schwartz, *Monetary History of the United States,* p. 375.

the successive waves of bank failures had made banks afraid of further runs on them, the Fed persisted in thinking of excess reserves as *unwanted* reserves, that is, as reserves that banks held only because they had too few customers for loans, and had little incentive to buy securities at the prevailing low interest rates. It is therefore not surprising that it treated the fact that banks held more reserves than they were legally required to, as evidence that nothing would be gained by giving banks even more reserves by open-market purchases. Moreover, the Fed did not consider itself under any great obligation to prevent bank failures. It believed that these failures resulted in large part from too much risk taking, and hence were the fault of the banks. Besides, failures were concentrated among nonmember banks, who the Fed believed were not its responsibility. In addition, the failing banks tended to be small banks, and the Fed may perhaps have been influenced by the belief that there were too many small banks in any case. All in all, Wicker concludes that by 1932 "it was becoming increasingly clear that System officials did not recognize any strong obligation to maintain the solvency of the banking system."[4]

Perhaps two things should be said in defense of this dismal record. First, the advice the Fed obtained from the writings of academic economists was not good either, and, second, by no means did all Fed officials agree with the prevailing policy. The New York Federal Reserve Bank generally advocated much more expansionary policies, but it did not prevail.

Effects of Federal Reserve Policy

How much difference would it have made had the Fed aggressively undertaken substantial open-market operations and been able to prevent bank failures in this way? There already was an unusually severe depression in 1930 before there were any large-scale bank failures. This part of the depression is not really explained by the Friedman-Schwartz analysis. But the economy had suffered such depressions in 1908, 1914–15, and 1921, and each time had recovered within a reasonable time. What was unique about the Great Depression was not only its depth, but also the tardiness of the recovery. Can these characteristics be attributed to the waves of bank failures, and could the Federal Reserve have prevented these failures?

The answer to the first of these questions depends in large part upon how important the quantity of money is. It also depends upon whether there were other factors at work that caused this depression to be so severe and prolonged. And the answer to the second question, whether the Fed could have prevented the bank failures, depends upon whether banks were basically sound or whether they held too many bad assets.

On the first question, the importance of money, we have little to add to our previous discussion. But one does not have to be an out-and-out monetarist to accept a monetary interpretation of the 1930s given the great drop in the money stock. Modern Keynesians too consider such a decline to be a

[4] Wicker, *Federal Reserve Monetary Policy, 1917–33* (New York, Random House, 1966), p. 173.

disaster. To be sure, the fall in the money supply was not the only thing that happened, velocity also fell, but Friedman and Schwartz argued that this decline was not an independent factor causing the depression, but was induced by the fall in income. Hence, they say that the fall in velocity was ultimately the result of permitting banks to fail. Keynesians, on the other hand, usually do not accept Friedman's theory of velocity that underlies the calculation that velocity dropped just because of the decline in income; they stress instead the effect of low interest rates on velocity. But even if it turns out that there were many other factors at work that could have caused a depression, it seems plausible to attribute much of its persistence and severity to the great fall in the money stock.

Critics of the monetary explanation frequently argue that the drop in the money stock was only an intermediate cause and not the real (or interesting) cause. In their view, bank failures resulted from banks having acquired unsound assets, and hence could not have been prevented by expansionary Fed policy. Friedman and Schwartz, on the other hand, argue that the massive bank failures would not have occurred if the Fed had undertaken large-scale open-market purchases. In their view, any deterioration in the quality of bank assets that occurred in the 1920s was minor. They not only blame the Federal Reserve for dereliction of duty, but also suggest that most of the bank failures would not have occurred had the Fed not existed. Prior to 1913, when massive bank failures threatened, banks would all agree to suspend currency payments for a time, while still clearing checks among themselves. The public could then still use its deposits to make payments from one account to another. Banks that were temporarily short of currency and other liquid assets did not fail. But the existence of the Fed with its discount mechanism reduced the interest of strong banks in initiating—as they had usually done in the past—such a suspension of currency payments.

But how can Friedman and Schwartz blame the Fed in view of the fact that starting in 1934 member banks had large excess reserves? Member bank excess reserves, which had averaged 0.2 percent of deposits in 1929–31 amounted to 6.8 percent of deposits in 1935. After falling sharply in 1936–37 as a rise in reserve requirements converted excess into required reserves, excess reserves then rose to 12 percent of deposits in 1940. Their answer is that these reserves were not "excess" reserves in an economic sense, as distinct from a legal sense. They believe that bank failures had frightened the surviving banks enough for them to want to keep a large volume of "excess" reserves. In terms of a liquidity-preference analysis, which relates bank holdings of excess reserves to the interest rate, the Friedman-Schwartz interpretation of the rise in excess reserves is that the curve had shifted outward as banks realized that they could not rely on the Fed to act as a lender of last resort. By contrast, in the Fed's view at the time, and in the view of many economists since then, the banks' liquidity-preference curve had not shifted outward; instead as interest rates fell banks had simply moved down *along* the curve. With a Treasury bill rate of less than 0.2 percent in 1936, banks had little incentive to buy securities, and there were few sound customers for loans. Which of these two interpretations is the correct one is still a disputed topic.

An Alternative View

In 1976, the Friedman-Schwartz interpretation of the Great Depression was challenged by Peter Temin of M.I.T., who raised many important issues. One of these is whether the observed decline in the money stock was the result of a shift in the supply curve of money, as Friedman and Schwartz claim, or the result of a shift in the demand curve for money. Suppose that the depression was actually caused by a collapse of the marginal efficiency of investment or an exogenous drop in consumption. As income declined the demand for money declined too, and so did interest rates. And a fall in interest rates can reduce the money supply by inducing banks to hold more excess reserves, and to borrow less from the Fed, and perhaps also by raising the currency-deposit ratio. Someone might then observe the reduction in the money supply along with the fall in income, and conclude that the decline in the money supply caused income to fall, whereas actually the story is just the other way around. And Temin argued that Friedman and Schwartz failed to show that the decline in the money stock was the cause rather than the effect.

In Temin's view there is no evidence that money was tight, at least in the earlier part of the depression. The per capita *real* money stock was slightly higher in 1931 than in 1929, though it did fall after that. Hence he argues that since into 1931 prices fell enough to offset the decline in the nominal money stock, it was the decline in velocity, rather than a decline in the nominal money stock, that was responsible for falling output. What is going on here is the following: money, velocity, prices, and output all fell. Temin rather arbitrarily allocates the fall in prices to the fall in the money stock, and thus attributes the drop in output to the decline in velocity. Friedman and Schwartz might well reply that this is, totally arbitrary; that in response to joint changes in money and velocity, that is, in aggregate demand, prices and output change jointly, with the aggregate supply curve determining by how much each of them changes.

In addition, Temin argues, interest rates on liquid securities were low, which again suggests that there was no shortage of money. However, Friedman and Schwartz explain the decline in these interest rates by a rise in the demand for highly liquid securities (which raised their prices and lowered their yields) because the public was afraid to hold less-liquid assets. In particular, banks bid up the price of commercial paper because it could be discounted with the Fed. And, as Figure 24.2 shows, the yield on less-liquid and safe securities was *not* low.

Moreover, Temin criticizes Friedman and Schwartz for not explaining the causes of bank failures sufficiently. Temin argues that part of the decline in the stock of money should be attributed to falling prices of farm products and to the agricultural distress that caused rural banks to fail. Many bank failures, Temin argues, were ultimately due to a real factor, the relative decline of agricultural prices, rather than to a monetary factor, such as Federal Reserve policy.

In addition to the rural banks, a large New York bank, the Bank of the United States, failed. Temin argues that, contrary to the Friedman-Schwartz view, this failure was due to fraud and illegal activities by the bank's management, so that the Fed could not have prevented this failure. And all of these bank failures then frightened depositors into runs on other banks. When these banks tried to meet deposit withdrawals by selling bonds, bond prices fell. This then forced other banks to write down the prices at which they carried these bonds on their books, which, in turn, impaired the capital position of many of these banks, and forced them to close.

Beyond the question of what caused bank failures, Temin accuses Friedman and Schwartz of overemphasizing the role of the Fed and underemphasizing what the private sector did. Thus, Friedman and Schwartz wrote that the discount rate, while falling, was still too high because market rates were falling even faster, and they blame the resulting decline in discounting on the Fed. Temin, on the other hand, puts the blame for the decline in discounting on falling market rates. In his view the changes in the money stock that occurred were not *caused* by the Fed merely because the Fed could have prevented them.

An important issue arises here. Friedman and Schwartz blame the Fed for the depression because it was passive, and did not move aggressively through open-market operations to provide banks with the reserves they needed. They take some bank failures as a given and focus on the behavior of the Fed that allowed these failures to spread to other banks. By contrast, Temin takes the inaction of the Fed as his given and treats as the cause of the decline in the money stock those factors that initially caused some banks to fail. Hence, to a considerable extent, the protagonists are talking past each other since they are discussing different questions. Temin's work does not really vindicate the Federal Reserve.

Temin believes that changes in the supply of money played only a subsidiary role. Thus he points to Friedman and Schwartz's concession that the first banking crisis (1930) left no pronounced imprint on the major economic indicators. In his view, the initial downturn resulted from an unexplainable drop in consumption, and he believes that the unique severity of the depression resulted from a whole series of other factors. The most dramatic, though by no means the largest, was the stock-market crash, which, by reducing wealth, reduced consumption and caused people to reduce their financial leverage. There was also a big drop in consumption due to some unknown factor.[5] Agricultural developments (a bad harvest in the United States and a good harvest in Europe) also played a role. And in the fall of 1930 when no recovery appeared, businessmen lost confidence. Then in 1931, there was an international financial crisis triggered by the failure of an Austrian bank. This endangered German banks that had lent to it and caused Germany to impose exchange controls, which limited foreign payments by Germans. The British pound then came under pressure because British banks had made large loans to German banks. This brings Temin up to 1931. "After that time the story becomes so complex and the interactions so numerous that it is no

[5] But Temin's evidence for an unexplained drop in consumption is very much open to question. See Thomas Mayer, "Consumption in the Great Depression," *Journal of Political Economy* 86 (February 1978): 139–47.

longer possible to envisage separate movements in different parts of the world."[6]

All in all, Temin has presented the monetary explanation of the Great Depression with a sharp challenge. But this is not the place to argue its pros and cons; we must hurry on to the next episode.

WAR FINANCE AND INTEREST-RATE PEGGING

During World War II, as in World War I, the Fed's overriding goal was to ensure that the goverment could borrow all it wanted at a low interest rate. The traditional concerns of stabilization policy were shelved. But in contrast to its restrictive policy after World War I, after World War II the Fed continued its expansionary policy.

Pegged Rates

The policy adopted during World War II was to "peg" interest rates by having the Fed stand ready to buy all government securities offered to it at least at par, that is, at 100 percent of face value. The level at which interest rates were pegged was the then prevailing low level of the Great Depression, ranging from 3/8 of one percent on Treasury bills to 2½ percent on long-term securities, though after the war the bill rate was allowed to rise to over one percent. The decision to maintain the currently prevailing level of interest rates was an obvious one at the time. It would allow the deficit to be financed cheaply. Moreover, it would, most economists believed, be appropriate for the postwar period when, according to the generally prevailing view, the economy would again be depressed. It should have been obvious, but it was not, that a policy of pegging short-term interest rates much lower than long-term rates would generate trouble. If the Fed stands ready to buy long-term bonds at par, long-term bonds are in effect as liquid as short-term securities, so that everyone has an incentive to sell 3/8 of one percent Treasury bills to the Fed and hold 2½ percent bonds instead. And, eventually, the Fed did end up holding nearly all the Treasury bills in existence.

During the war there was little dispute about monetary policy, and even in the early postwar years the Fed accepted interest-rate pegging with few complaints. This was so despite the fact that this policy had an obvious inflationary potential, since it eliminated the Federal Reserve's control over the stock of money. The Fed had to provide reserves to any bank that offered it government securities in exchange. Monetary policy was therefore completely passive in the sense of being unable to curb an expansion of the money stock.

Why was such a policy more or less acceptable to the Fed? One reason was the tardiness with which the persistence of the postwar inflation was recognized. Almost everyone expected a depression after the war, and it took some time for people to realize that the problem was excessive, rather

[6] Peter Temin, *Did Monetary Forces Cause the Great Depression?* (New York: W. W. Norton, 1976), p. 173.

than insufficient, aggregate demand. Another reason was the low repute of monetary policy, that is, the widespread belief that the Great Depression had demonstrated the unimportance of the quantity of money, and that one should therefore rely on fiscal policy rather than on monetary policy. This belief was, of course, connected with the victory of Keynesian theory and the eclipse of the quantity theory. Still another important reason for the widespread acceptance of pegging was that this policy seemed harmless. Pegging interest rates provided the potential for an explosive rise in the money stock, but the explosion did not occur. Just the opposite; in 1949 the money stock was slightly lower than in 1947. For much of the period the equilibrium interest rate was below the pegged 2½ percent bond rate, so that the Fed was not called upon to protect the peg by increasing bank reserves and the money stock. With velocity rising rapidly, the demand for money did not grow.

The Debate

All the same, as time went by, the Fed became more and more uneasy about its lack of control. With the outbreak of the Korean War in 1950, the Federal Reserve's restiveness turned into open opposition. As long as pegging was taking place it was the Treasury, and not the Fed, that was, in effect, conducting monetary policy since the Fed was bound to support the Treasury's decisions about interest rates paid on government securities. Now with renewed war, accompanied by inflation (the consumer price index rose by 11 percent between June 1950 and December 1951), the Fed wanted to reclaim monetary policy. A great debate occurred. The Treasury argued that a small rise in interest rates would be insufficient to restrain aggregate demand significantly, while a large increase could throw the economy into a recession. The Fed replied that somewhere between too little and too large there must be "just right," which was open to the rejoinder that nobody knows where this "just right" level of interest rates is.

The Treasury pointed out that a rise in interest rates would, given the large size of the public debt, raise government expenditures significantly, but the Fed's supporters replied that the Treasury got back in higher taxes approximately half of its interest payments. Apart from these technical issues there were also some broader ones. President Truman had populist suspicions of high finance, and wanted interest rates to remain low in the belief that this would help the average citizen. Moreover, the Treasury held the bizarre notion that if government bond prices fell below par this would reduce confidence in the United States government and have terrible effects. Besides, there was the danger that the Korean War would turn into World War III, with massive financing needs that the Treasury did not want to meet at high interest rates. This does not mean that the Treasury and administration were oblivious to inflation; rather, instead of monetary policy, they wanted to rely on fiscal policy and price controls which were then in effect. The Fed has less faith in price controls.

In its dispute with the Treasury the Fed had substantial support among academic economists, and, what is much more important, also in Congress.

It therefore felt powerful enough to challenge the Treasury. In August 1950 it allowed some short-term securities to fall slightly below par. A major row occurred, but was resolved in March 1951 by an agreement known as the "Accord" under which short-term interest rates were allowed to rise moderately and long-term rates to rise very slightly. The Fed was relieved of the burden of complete pegging, but, de facto, agreed to prevent government securities from falling much below par. This Accord lasted only until after the 1952 election, when the incoming Eisenhower administration restored the Fed's full freedom.

THE MID- AND LATE-1950s

After receiving its freedom the Fed maintained a low money growth rate. From 1952–53 to 1959–60, M_1 grew only at a 1.9 percent rate per annum and M_2 at a 3.2 percent rate. But since velocity was rising, GNP grew at a faster rate, and the price level rose at an average rate of 1.4 percent. About half of the total price rise in the period occurred in the short span, 1957–59. From June 1957 to June 1958 the consumer price index rose 2.9 percent, which at the time was considered an unacceptable inflation. Since unemployment was not abnormally low in 1957 by the standards of those days, this led to a rather inconclusive debate about cost-push inflation. This debate was intensified in 1958 when, despite a 6.8 percent unemployment rate, a very high rate for those days, prices continued to rise.

The Fed was much criticized at the time for following a too restrictive policy, and many economists thought that the administration's fiscal policy was also too restrictive. By hindsight one possible interpretation is that the Fed was "drying out" the economy and eliminating the inflationary expectations that had developed during the post-World War II and Korean War inflations. If so, this is a fascinating experiment deserving of much discussion. However, it will not get this discussion because we know much too little about how expectations changed, or even whether the Fed was actually trying to change them. But certainly one *possible* explanation for why during the subsequent long expansion of the 1960s there was so little inflation until 1965, is that the Fed set the stage in the 1950s by creating the expectation that prices would be stable.

Another characteristic of Fed policy in this period was a change, albeit small, in its targets. It started to place *some,* though still quite limited, emphasis on the growth rate of the money stock, rather than looking *just* at credit conditions and interest rates. Countercyclical monetary policy, "leaning against the wind" as a favorite Fed phrase puts it, received more emphasis too. But this policy was mistakenly undertaken by using money-market conditions and free reserves as its targets. This prevented the Fed from having the desired effects on the money stock and on income.

A major dispute arose in the 1950s about the types of securities the Fed should use in its open-market operations. Under a policy called "bills-only" the Fed decided to confine its open-market trading normally to Treasury bills. In this way it could affect bank reserves without greatly affecting relative interest rates, and with most open-market operations being defensive operations there is no reason for changing relative interest rates. The Account Manager would no longer decide whether to sell, say, five-year bonds and lower their price relative to other securities. Much of the impetus for this policy came from government security dealers who were afraid that large sales by the Fed could lower the prices of securities they held in their portfolios, thus imposing great losses on them. The Fed was afraid that such losses could drive many of them out of business, which would make the securities market function less efficiently.

Critics of the bills-only policy objected to such concern about the welfare of government security dealers. They argued that by operating only in bills the Fed's open-market operations would have only little—and long-delayed—effects on the long-term interest rate, and hence on investment. From a monetarist standpoint, on the other hand, the bills-only policy was unimportant since what matters is the volume of bank reserves, and not whether open-market operations make credit more available in the long-term, or short-term, security markets. The bills-only policy was abandoned in 1961. However, most, though not all, open-market operations are still conducted in short-term securities.

THE 1960s AND 1970s

The following decade, which witnessed the longest expansion in United States history (February 1961–December 1969), saw a number of important developments for monetary policy. (Some relevant data are shown in the endpaper inside the front cover.)

One important development was an increasingly severe balance-of-payments problem. The dollar was overvalued and large balance-of-payments deficits were the norm. It should have been clear, but for a long time was not, that unless the United States was willing to curb the growth rate of the money stock—and accept the accompanying unemployment—the dollar would *have* to be devalued. But instead of taking such a drastic step, various palliatives were tried.

Exchange control was tried in a modest way; a special tax was levied on interest earnings on foreign securities to eliminate the gains from buying foreign securities with a higher yield than domestic ones. And there were restraints on large-scale capital exports by banks and other firms. Moreover, it is likely that, had it not been for the balance-of-payments problem, the Fed would have followed at least a somewhat more expansionary policy. But it is hard to know whether balance-of-payments considerations really were important in making monetary policy.

In the 1960s there also occurred a major internal change in the Fed; increased professionalization. For the first time since 1936 there was a professional economist on the Board of Governors, and eventually economists became a majority on the Board, and also among Reserve Bank presidents. Moreover, there occurred a great improvement in the professional quality of the staff of the Fed's research departments, and research started to deal less with the details of banking and to focus more on macroeconomic analysis. Thus, in the MPS model, which we discussed in Chapter 22, the

Board of Governors now has one of the country's major macroeconomic models, while the St. Louis Federal Reserve Bank is a leading center of monetarist thought. And formal forecasts are now presented at FOMC meetings, which was not the case in the 1950s.

A second—again informal—change was the rise of monetarist influence in the Fed. There was a shift in its targets from money-market conditions to at least somewhat greater emphasis on monetary targets. A third change was that, as discussed in Chapter 5, in 1966 the Fed made Regulation Q constrictive.

Another very important development was that, as the endpaper figure shows, the growth rate of the money stock increased substantially in the second half of the decade, particularly in 1967 and 1968. A reason for this was the large deficits that resulted from the Vietnam War and the "Great Society" programs. In principle, this deficit could have been allowed to raise interest rates and crowd out private expenditures. But it was decided to hold interest rates down and monetize the deficit. This rapid growth of the U.S. money stock in the late 1960s proved to be inflationary. The basis for long-run inflation was laid.

This period also saw two examples of sharply restrictive policies. The first of these, sometimes called "the crunch," occurred in 1966. As former Fed Governor Maisel explained it:

> The 1966 experience was a rude awakening. The degree of inflationary demand from the expanding Vietnam War was greater than United States monetary policy had attempted to cope with since 1920. The decision to fight inflation vigorously caused high costs elsewhere. A choice became necessary. It appeared that there was a limit to what traditional monetary policy could do. . . . In 1966 it became apparent that the Federal Reserve could not neglect the side-effects of decreased money and credit, and higher interest rates. Three of these side-effects reached critical dimensions with relation to (a) the composition of demand and output, (b) the maintenance of viable financial markets, (c) the protection against large-scale failures of financial institutions.[7]

The Fed's response to the gathering inflationary pressure was strong, even brutal. The growth rate of M_1 had been 4.6 percent in both 1964 and 1965; in the second half of 1966 it was cut to zero. As the endpaper shows, interest rates rose sharply. In addition banks gave preference to their steady business cusomers and cut back on their mortgage loans. Moreover, the net flow of funds into savings and loans fell to one-quarter of the previous year's level. A sharp drop in residential construction occurred that was widely blamed on tight money. Signs of financial strain appeared. There was a danger of widespread failures of savings and loans. Moreover, the restrictive Regulation Q ceiling prevented banks from "buying" deposits as they had been able to do previously. The Council of Economic Advisers concluded that in August 1966 "monetary policy was probably as tight as it could get without risking financial disorder."[8]

[7] Sherman Maisel, *Managing the Dollar* (New York: W. W. Norton, 1973), pp. 63–64.
[8] *Economic Report of the President, 1967* (Washington, D.C.: 1967), p. 60.

By October 1966 it was apparent that an economic slowdown was more likely than a continuation of the excessive expansion, and monetary policy was eased. Though a slowdown did occur in 1967 it was not severe enough to be a full-blown recession. The Fed, after stepping heavily on the brake, had released it in time. The Fed then became more expansionary again, and subsequently the inflation rate rose.

1969 to 1980

In 1969 the Fed then tried to break this inflation, even at the cost of risking a recession. In December 1969 there was a downturn with a trough in November 1970. This cycle too was accompanied by severe financial strains, and if the Fed had not acted promptly as a lender of last resort there could well have been a financial panic. The money market was extraordinarily tight, which is hardly surprising given the Fed's restrictive policy, and the fact that the United States incursion into Cambodia had created great political tensions. By June 1970 stock prices had declined by more than 20 percent below their 1969 average.

In that month the Penn Central Transportation Company, one of the country's major corporations, filed for bankruptcy. Shock waves spread throughout the financial market. Penn Central's credit rating had been high enough for it to have issued commercial paper. Lenders were now asking themselves who would be next. There were rumors that Chrysler Corporation would not be able to sell new issues of commercial paper to replace the maturing ones, that is, to "roll over" its commercial paper. And this would have made lenders afraid to buy the commercial paper of some other firms. Firms issuing commercial paper frequently arrange bank lines of credit as a back-up measure. There was now a danger that if firms were unable to roll over their commercial paper, banks would suddenly have to find the wherewithal to increase their business loans substantially, and they might not be able to honor all their lines of credit.

Fortunately, the Fed stepped in promptly, and did what a central bank is supposed to do. It calmed the money market by announcing that the discount window was wide open for banks that had to make loans to firms unable to roll over their commercial paper. In addition, it suspended the Regulation Q ceiling for certain large CDs, so that banks would be able to buy funds readily. In August 1970 it also lowered reserve requirements. All in all, the Fed emerged as the hero of this episode; however, one might suggest that had it not been for its sharply restrictive policy in 1969 (which itself was the consequence of its previously too-expansionary policy), the market could have handled the Penn Central failure, so that there would then have been no emergency that required heroic action.

In the early 1970s another event occurred that was just as dramatic as the incipient panic of 1970, and was to have a much longer-lasting effect. This was the collapse of the fixed exchange-rate system discussed in Chapter 28. In 1971 President Nixon imposed wage and price controls. These controls reduced inflation temporarily. After the removal of controls in April

1974, prices rose rapidly; the consumer price index rose by over 12 percent that year. The removal of price controls was not the only cause: oil prices had been raised by OPEC, and other raw material prices had risen due to poor harvests in much of the world and due to the coincidence of booms in many major industrial countries.

All the same, one can make a reasonable case that price controls actually *increased* the inflation rate. Some studies show that once controls were taken off prices rose by enough to reach, or surpass, the level they would have reached had there been no price controls. And they had an additional inflationary effect that these studies do not take into account. This is that in response to price controls the Fed adopted a more expansionary policy than it otherwise would have. It did this to hold down interest rates for the following reason: Many people complained that it was unfair to impose controls on wages and not on interest rates. Hence the Fed was afraid that controls would be imposed on interest rates. This would have meant either a total disruption of the money and capital markets, or else forced the Fed to increase the money growth rate enough to bring the equilibrium interest rate down (in the short run) to the controlled rate. The Fed thought that the best way to avoid this danger was to meet the demand for lower interest rates part way. But this required an inflationary increase in the money growth rate.

In 1973–1975 the economy suffered what until 1981–82 was the most severe postwar recession. The inflation rate rose as the economy was hit by the effects of the oil shock and other supply shocks, as well as by effects of the previous acceleration of the money growth rate. The term stagflation entered the public's vocabulary.

Due to the high inflation rate the Fed adopted a restrictive policy in the second half of 1974. This policy was much criticized. The inflation rate had risen in 1973–74 in part because of supply shocks and the Fed seemed intent to offset these shocks partially by putting downward pressure on other prices. Keynesians objected that while monetary policy should perhaps be used to fight demand-pull inflation, it should not be used to fight that part of the inflation that resulted from such obvious cost-push factors as bad harvests and the rise in oil prices. Specifically, they opposed adopting a sharply restrictive policy in the midst of a recession. Monetarists also objected to changing the money growth rate so rapidly. The Fed caught it from both sides.

Defending the Dollar

Not only was the inflation rate high in the recovery from the 1973–75 recession, but it was accelerating as the Fed allowed the money stock to grow at a high rate. Largely as a result of this, in late 1978 the dollar fell rapidly on the foreign-exchange market, and there was a danger that some foreign central banks, as well as private holders, would now dump their dollar holdings, thus accelerating the dollar's fall. In response, on 1 November 1978, President Carter followed up his earlier call for ''voluntary'' wage and price ceilings with a series of measures. He announced that the United States would borrow 30 billion dollars of foreign currencies it could use to support the dollar in the foreign-exchange market. More fundamentally, he asked the Fed to adopt a restrictive policy. For a President, particularly a Democratic President, publicly to ask the Fed to raise interest rates was an extraordinary step with great symbolic significance.

But what matters are not dramatic gestures, but the consistency with which they are followed up. The initial follow-up was strong; the money growth rate fell sharply—but not for long. In the second quarter of 1979 it rose again and stayed high for the rest of the year. It seemed as though the Fed had lost control over it. This by itself might not have caused a radical change in policy, but two other obviously connected events occurred: the inflation rate accelerated sharply and the dollar fell heavily on the foreign exchange market as foreigners lost confidence in the dollar. The seemingly strong policy changes of the previous November had bought less than a year's respite.

One can make a reasonable case that the Fed faced disaster. It seemed unable to control the money stock. A rapid rise in the price of gold (by $100 an ounce between late August and early October) and of certain raw materials suggested that the high inflation rate was generating a belief that the only safe thing to do was to dump dollars and buy commodities. Obviously, if such a belief spreads it results in much more inflation. In addition, there was a danger that the dollar would plummet on the foreign-exchange market as foreigners saw that the Fed's action of November 1978 had failed. Foreign central banks held a large volume of dollars they could dump on the market to cut their losses.

In October 1979 the Fed therefore took another dramatic step. Despite the fact that it was widely (though wrongly) believed that the economy had already entered a recession the Fed adopted a highly restrictive policy. It raised the discount rate by another percentage point to 12 percent, and it imposed an 8 percent reserve requirement on increases in certain managed liabilities of banks. And in a more important step it announced that it would try to get a better grip on the money stock by allowing the federal funds rate to fluctuate much more.

The October 1979 policy initiative succeeded in stopping the threatened collapse of the dollar on the foreign-exchange market. In addition, the Fed succeeded in bringing the money growth rate down, though subsequently it was still high relative to the midpoint of the Fed's target ranges. Nominal interest rates rose sharply.

Although successful in the foreign-exchange market, domestically the October 1979 program failed. Financial markets did not believe that the Fed would control inflation. Had they anticipated that the Fed would succeed, long-term bond prices would have risen, and long-term interest rates would have fallen along with the anticipated inflation premium that is contained in interest rates. But instead, bond prices fell!

And the market was right. In three months, December 1979–February 1980, the consumer price index spurted at an annual rate of 17 percent. Credit markets became demoralized by the fear that the inflation rate, and hence interest rates, would zoom. How could market participants determine what interest rates to set on new bonds? They couldn't. As a result the long-term bond market as well as the mortgage market in large part suspended operation for a time, and even short-term markets, such as the commercial-paper market, ceased to function properly. Some major banks were reported to have difficulties in selling large CDs.

By March 1980 the October 1979 policy was in shambles. Strange as it may seem many people were actually hoping for a recession that would reduce both the inflation rate and interest rates. It is reported that when Federal Reserve Chairman Volcker was asked whether monetary and fiscal tightening would result in a recession, he replied, "yes, and the sooner the better."[9]

It was clear that something had to be done, and in March 1980 President Carter announced a multifaceted program to break inflationary expectations. As part of this he revised the budget he had just sent to Congress to eliminate the projected deficit (though, as it turned out, not the actual deficit). The Fed's role was twofold. One part was to tighten conventional monetary policy by raising reserve requirements on certain managed liabilities, and to impose a special three percentage points surcharge on the discount rate charged large banks that borrow frequently. The second part was to impose credit allocation.

Banks were told to let their loans expand by no more than 9 percent, with banks that were growing slowly in any case, or had low capital and liquidity ratios, staying well below this ceiling. This part of the program was voluntary, but there is an old saying, "you don't have to, but you'll be sorry if you don't." Since large and medium banks frequently come to the Fed for permission to undertake mergers or to start holding-company affiliates, the Fed is not exactly powerless.

To cut consumer spending, which was growing rapidly, the Fed also imposed a 15 percent reserve requirement on unsecured consumer loans, such as credit-card and charge-account borrowing. This reserve requirement applied not only to banks, but also to other financial institutions, as well as to retailers. Finally, a 15 percent reserve requirement was also imposed on increases in the assets of money-market funds.

This credit control program was effective—much more effective than had been intended. The public seemed to respond to the President's wish that consumer credit be cut from a mixture of patriotism and fear of worsening economic conditions. Outstanding consumer credit stopped growing and fell. This response would have been most gratifying had it not been for one little fact—just two months earlier the economy had entered a recession!

The 1981–82 Recession

The 1980 recession was shortlived, but so was the ensuing expansion. In mid-1981 before the recovery was completed another recession occurred. This was the most severe recession since the 1930s with unemployment rising to 10.8 percent. Helped along by favorable supply-side developments the inflation rate responded to the recession; the GNP deflator rose by only 4.6

[9] Clyde Farnsworth, "Washington Watch," *New York Times*, 17 March 1980, p. D2.

percent compared to 10.2 percent the previous year. Over the first three months of 1983 the consumer price index was virtually stable.

There was concern about the possibility of a financial collapse. The failure of some government security dealers, as well as of a medium-sized bank, Penn Square, combined with the threatened failures of some large firms, and the inability of some countries, e.g., Mexico, to repay their loans, all generated such fears. Many thrift institutions failed, or had to be merged into other ones. Interest rates declined, but not by as much as the inflation rate did, so that, at least on short-term loans, real rates were unusually high. While some blamed this on the large current and prospective federal deficits, other blamed the Fed for not raising the money growth rate sufficiently.

The Fed was in a quandary. On the one hand it wanted to continue with its disinflationary policy, but on the other hand, it wanted to ameliorate the recession. Four factors complicated its task. First, raising the money growth rate could generate fears that the inflation rate would rise again. This would result not only in more inflationary wage and price decisions by the private sector, but would also raise the inflation premium that is included in the nominal interest rate. Second, there was much pressure on the Fed to lower interest rates, and bills to curb the Fed's independence gathered extraordinarily strong support in Congress.

Third, with deregulation fostering new types of accounts the problem of measuring money became much more severe. For instance, NOW accounts were growing rapidly. Should the Fed interpret this just like an ordinary increase in *M-1* and take offsetting action, or did it merely represent a shift of long-term savings out of other accounts and securities into these NOW accounts, and hence not call for reducing the *M-1* growth rate?

Finally, there was a puzzling fall in the velocity of *M-1*. After rising at a trend rate of about 3 percent per year, it suddenly fell by 4 percent between 1981 and 1982, the first significant drop in about thirty years. *M-2* velocity also fell. The Fed had not anticipated these declines in velocity.

The Fed responded by easing policy. The *M-1* growth rate accelerated rapidly in the second half of 1982. While some criticized the Fed for thus laying the groundwork for an acceleration of inflation, others complained that it still left interest rates too high. The Fed defended the rapid rise in *M-1* by arguing that financial innovations had greatly reduced, at least temporarily, the significance of *M-1*. It therefore shifted its focus towards *M-2*. Thus in October 1982 the FOMC set targets for *M-2* and *M-3*, but not for *M-1*. And in early 1983, while it did set a target for *M-1*, it also set a target for the total debt of nonfinancial borrowers. Moreover, it seemed to pay more attention to interest rates. Does all of this mean that the monetarist revolution of October 1979 has been abandoned, or will the Fed again place more emphasis on money once the data are less distorted by new financial innovations? Right now (late 1983) it is too early to tell.

HOW MUCH HAS THE FED LEARNED?

This excursion into history shows that the Fed has learned some things from past experience. It has definitely learned to be a lender of last resort, and to take aggressive action to avoid financial panics. Were it faced today with a sharp decline in the money stock, such as occurred in the 1930s, it would surely undertake massive open-market operations.

Similarly, if it were to adopt a sharply restrictive policy in the same month as a really major cyclical downturn, as happened in 1920, it would probably reverse its policy more rapidly unless the ongoing inflation rate was very high. How much it has learned from the bond-pegging episode is harder to say because the exigencies of wartime finance leave few options. But should a similar situation arise again it is unlikely that it would try to peg as lopsided a term structure as it did during World War II.

Has the Fed also learned to avoid substantial inflation? On a technical level it surely has learned that to avoid inflation it has to control the money growth rate. It has also learned that to do this it must concentrate its efforts on that job and let interest rates rise. But whether it will make use of these lessons is a harder question to answer. This will depend to a large degree on the political pressures to which it is subjected.

SUMMARY

1. The Fed's original ideas were the great importance of maintaining the gold standard, the need to avoid financial panics, a wish to stabilize interest rates and adherence to the real-bills doctrine. But during World War I the Fed focused on facilitating the government's financing task.
2. In 1920 the Fed adopted a highly restrictive policy just when the economy went into a very severe recession. Later during the 1920s the Fed tried to facilitate the restoration of the gold standard in Europe, and in the late 1920s it faced the dilemma of a runaway stock market boom while business activity was not excessive.
3. In the Great Depression the money stock fell substantially. Friedman and Schwartz blame the Fed for not undertaking massive open-market purchases as the public drained bank reserves by withdrawing currency. But Temin argues that the fall in the money stock was due to a decline in the demand for money. Excess reserves of banks rose substantially, a fact which some economists interpret as a shift of the banks' liquidity-preference curve, and others as a movement along this curve.
4. During World War II the Fed pegged interest rates at the depression level. After the war the continuation of this policy led to a great debate. It was modified by the "Accord" and finally dropped in 1953. Many economists criticized the Fed during the 1950s for a too-restrictive policy, and also for adopting the bills-only policy.
5. The balance of payments deficit became an important consideration in the 1960s. The Fed became more professionalized and somewhat more monetarist, but the money growth rate rose substantially. The Fed then became sharply restrictive in 1966 and 1969, to the point that there was a danger of financial panic. In the early 1970s the fixed exchange rate system collapsed and price controls were

imposed. Following the oil shock the Fed subsequently adopted a highly restrictive policy for which it was much criticized.

6. In late 1978 the dollar fell sharply on the foreign exchange market and a flight from the dollar was a real danger. The Fed responded with a temporarily restrictive policy which was insufficient, and in October 1979 the Fed had to adopt a stronger policy and to change its operating procedures by letting interest rates fluctuate much more. By early 1980 it was clear that even this policy was insufficient. In March policy was tightened again and credit controls were imposed. 1981–82 saw the most severe postwar recession with fears about financial collapse. The Fed's task was complicated by factors, such as the danger of fostering inflationary expectations, and the problem of measuring money in a time of financial innovations.
7. The Fed has learned to be a lender of last resort and also is not likely to repeat its 1920–21 mistake again. It has also learned that it must control the money growth rate. But whether it—and the public—have learned enough to curb inflation is another question.

Questions and Exercises

1. Use the description of monetary policy in recent issues of the *Economic Report of the President* and the Federal Reserve *Annual Report* to bring the discussion of this chapter up to date.
2. "In the Great Depression the Federal Reserve did all it could reasonably have been expected to do." Discuss.
3. "Prior to World War II the Federal Reserve usually did the wrong thing." Discuss.
4. "There has been little real improvement in the conduct of monetary policy. What looks like improvement is merely that the Fed, instead of being too soft on unemployment, as it used to be, is now too soft on inflation." Discuss.
5. What do you think has been the Fed's biggest mistake in the postwar period?
6. For what action does the Fed deserve the most credit in the postwar period?
7. What were the ideas with which the Fed started out? To what extent, if any, were they responsible for the Fed's actions in 1920?
8. Take one issue in the dispute between the rival interpretations of the Great Depression given by Friedman and Schwartz and by Temin and write an essay on it.
9. What do you think is the most effective argument used by (1) Friedman and Schwartz and (2) Temin in their discussions of the Great Depression?

Further Reading

BERNANKE, BEN. "Nonmonetary Effects of Financial Crisis in the Propagation of the Great Depression." *American Economic Review* 73 (June 1983): 257–76. An interesting hypothesis that bank failures had their main impact by disrupting financial channels.

BRUNNER, KARL, ed. *Contemporary Views of the Great Depression*. Amsterdam: Martinus Nejhoff, 1981. A series of important articles on the Great Depression.

FRIEDMAN, MILTON, and SCHWARTZ, ANNA. *A Monetary History of the United States.* Princeton: Princeton University Press, 1963. A classic. The chapter on the Great Depression has been published separately as *The Great Contraction.*

MAISEL, SHERMAN. *Managing the Dollar.* New York: W. W. Norton 1973. An important source for the history of the Fed in the 1960s.

PIERCE, JAMES. "The Political Economy of Arthur Burns." *Journal of Finance* 24 (May 1979): 485–96. A very good survey of monetary policy in the 1970s.

POOLE, WILLIAM. "Burnsian Monetary Policy: Eight Years of Progress?" *Journal of Finance* 24 (May 1979): 473–84. Another very good survey of monetary policy in the 1970s.

TEMIN, PETER. *Did Monetary Forces Cause the Great Depression?* New York: W. W. Norton, 1976. A major response to Friedman and Schwartz by a leading economic historian.

TOBIN, JAMES. "The Monetary Interpretation of History." *American Economic Review* 55 (June 1965). A response to Friedman and Schwartz by a leading monetary theorist.

U.S., EXECUTIVE OFFICE OF THE PRESIDENT. *Economic Report of the President.* Washington, D.C. Each issue carries a history of monetary policy in the previous year.

WICKER, ELMUS. *Federal Reserve Monetary Policy 1917–1933.* New York: Random House, 1966. A very thorough piece of historical research.

Alternative Monetary Policies

25

Chapter 23 dealt with some very serious criticisms of countercyclical monetary policy while Chapter 24 suggested that it is far from obvious that the Fed has been a stabilizing influence in the past. This leads naturally to the question of what is the alternative to countercyclical monetary policy, sometimes called discretionary monetary policy. This chapter discusses the main alternative, a fixed money growth rate, as well as some other monetary policy stances.

RULES VERSUS DISCRETION

A number of economists, of whom Milton Friedman is the most prominent, have advocated that instead of trying to counteract the business cycle, the Fed should ensure that money grows at a constant rate. To the supporters of this stable growth-rate rule, keeping money growing at *some* stable rate is much more important than the particular rate that is chosen.[1] They believe that a stable growth-rate rule would result in a relatively stable rate of change of the price level. Whether this rate is positive, zero, or negative is not as important as that it be stable—and hence predictable. The unfavorable results of inflation are largely due to its being unanticipated.

[1] Some versions of the rule choose a zero growth rate, that is, a constant *stock* of money, and others would allow the money stock to rise at the same rate as the population, but not rise with increased productivity. Increased productivity would then show up as falling prices. This continually increasing purchasing power would mean that the public is earning an imputed yield from holding currency, and hence would have no incentive to spend valuable resources to economize on its currency holding. But the most popular variant has money growing at a rate equal to the growth of productivity minus the growth rate of velocity, both of these being estimated for the long run.

Before looking at the specific arguments for, and against, the rule, there are several characteristics of the rule that should be kept firmly in mind. First, it is a second-best policy. Supporters of the rule do not claim that it would give us perfection. They believe that even with a monetary growth-rate rule there would still be some fluctuations in output. But, they argue, these fluctuations would be less severe than the ones now experienced, since currently the net destabilizing effects of monetary policy are added to the fluctuations that are inherent in the economy. They therefore advocate the use of a monetary growth-rate rule as the best that can be done under present conditions.

Second, since the main argument for a stable growth rate is that at the present stage of our knowledge about monetary policy we can do no better, it follows that one might advocate the rule as a temporary device until more is learned about monetary policy. And indeed, Friedman has suggested that eventually we may want to return to discretionary monetary policy.

Third, the adoption of the rule is not necessarily a matter of all or nothing. One might adopt the rule in a partial form by, for example, telling the Fed to keep the money growth rate within certain bounds. Thus in 1967 the Congressional Joint Economic Committee recommended that the Fed normally keep the growth rate of M_1 in a 3–5 percent range, except insofar as very special conditions require otherwise.

The Case for a Monetary Rule

The leading proponent of a rule, Milton Friedman, has argued that the lags in the effect of monetary policy are highly variable, so that even if the Fed knew the average lag, it would not be able to conduct a stabilizing monetary policy. To be sure, this argument is vulnerable to the rejoinder that even if the Fed knows very little about the lag, so that the correlation coefficient (R) between the initial fluctuations in income and the policy-induced changes in income is very close to zero, as long as it is negative, there exists some small policy that will stabilize income to some limited extent. Only if our ignorance is so great that R is zero or positive will a *very small* policy do more harm than good.

Adherents of the rule can reply that although the Fed could in principle stabilize the economy to a very small extent *if* it would conduct its policy solely to this end, in actuality it is constantly being distracted from its stabilization task by other claims on it, as well as by political pressures, so that its policy is often wrong. One example is the bond-pegging episode after World War II; another is the reluctance to let interest rates fluctuate enough to control the money growth rate. Friedman therefore believes that the Fed has often followed a policy that is perverse from a stabilization viewpoint. A leading Keynesian, Abba Lerner, once likened stabilization policy to a steering wheel that is needed to keep the economic car on the road. Reviewing the history of monetary policy Friedman replied:

> In light of experience, the most urgent need is not to have some everpresent back-seat driver who is going to be continually correcting the driver's steering, but to get off the road the man who has been giving the car a shove from one

> side to the other all the time and making it difficult for the actual driver to keep it on the straight and narrow path. . . . I am tempted to paraphrase what Colin Clark once wrote about the case for free trade. Like other academicians, I am accustomed to being met with the refrain, "It's all right in theory but it won't work in practice." Aside from the questionable logic of the remark in general, in this instance almost the reverse of what is intended is true. There is little to be said in theory for the rule that the money supply should grow at a constant rate. The case for it is entirely that it would work in practice. . . .[2]

More generally, in a debate with Franco Modigliani, a supporter of discretionary policy, Friedman stated:

> My major difference of opinion with Franco is in two respects: First, with his assumption that he knows how to accommodate [changes in the demand for money] (or that I do, for that matter, or that anybody does); and second with the assumption that if in fact you adopt a policy of accommodation, Franco Modigliani will be twisting the dials. . . . Once you adopt a policy of accommodating to changes, there will be all sorts of changes that he and I know should not be accommodated, with respect to which there will be enormous pressure to accommodate. And he and I will not be able to control that. . . . The real argument for a steady rate of monetary growth is at least as much political as it is economic; that it is a way of having a constitutional provision to set monetary policy which is not open to this kind of political objection.[3]

Beyond the problem of lags and political pressures there is also, as discussed in Chapter 23 the more basic rational-expectations case against discretionary policy. In a more positive vein, another argument for the monetary rule is that it would generate confidence. If businessmen know that the money stock will increase at a given rate, they know what to expect and can confidently plan ahead, instead of having to watch continuously for changes in monetary policy. Finally, the rule has also been advocated on the broader philosophical ground that it is desirable to reduce government interference by replacing the "rule of men" by the "rule of law."

The Case against the Rule

But these arguments favoring a monetary rule have been accepted only by a minority of economists. First, many economists doubt that the lag of monetary policy is really so long and variable that countercyclical policy is likely to be destabilizing. It is generally agreed that the lag makes countercyclical policy less effective, but does it reduce its effectiveness to zero? This is a tough, technical question. Second, many economists, while disappointed with the Fed's past policies, are not disillusioned, and believe that in the future it will conduct a more successful stabilization policy. Third, the rational-expectations case against countercyclical policy is accepted by only a dis-

[2] U.S., Congress, Joint Economic Committee, *Employment, Growth and Price Levels, Hearings* (Washington, D.C.: 1959), p. 615; Milton Friedman, *A Program for Monetary Stability* (New York: Fordham University Press, 1960), p. 98.

[3] Milton Friedman and Franco Modigliani, "The Monetarist Controversy: A Seminar Discussion," *Economic Review* (Federal Reserve Bank of San Francisco) supplement, Spring 1977, pp. 17–18.

tinct minority of economists because of its assumption of a high degree of wage and price flexibility.

The monetary growth-rate rule is also criticized for ignoring the occurrence of major supply shocks. For example, in 1973 when OPEC and poor harvests raised oil and food prices, the Fed had the *choice* of validating these price increases by raising the money growth rate, or keeping it constant, so that the increased prices of food and oil would exert downward pressure on prices in other sectors. Under a rule the Fed would not have had this choice.[4]

Moreover, are the proponents of the rule right in asserting that a stable money growth rate would generate a stable trend of prices? Are the growth rates of velocity and output really that stable? If not, there would be some fluctuations in prices. A related argument is that if the rule is set to aim at price stability, and if velocity then grows at a rate lower than expected or potential output at a faster rate, high employment would require falling prices. Would firms be willing to cut prices rather than output? To be sure, eventually they would become accustomed to cutting their prices every year, but it *may* take many years of unemployment and excess capacity to overcome downward price inflexibility, and to make workers accept money-wage cuts. Similarly, if the rule results in inflation because velocity is growing faster or output less, eventually the inflation will be fully anticipated, and hence do little damage. But this takes time.

This raises a nasty problem. Suppose one decides to adopt a monetary rule. How does one get there? Does one incorporate the existing inflation rate into the rule by setting the monetary growth rate accordingly, or does one bring the inflation rate down first at the cost of unemployment?

Another problem with the rule is the danger of evasion. After the Civil War when a tax was imposed on state bank notes, banks turned to checks. If the growth rate of money is limited, near-monies may take over more and more of the work of money, so that the monetary growth-rate rule would become irrelevant. But with respect to the deposit component of the money stock this would not be much of a problem if Regulation Q and the prohibition of interest payments on demand deposits are eliminated, and if the Fed pays the market rate of interest on required reserves. Deposits would then pay a market determined rate of interest, so that there would be no temptation to develop substitutes for them.

There would still be a temptation to find substitutes for currency since it does not pay interest, but if the inflation rate is low, so that the interest rate is also low, this would not be an insuperable problem. A more serious problem might be that the Fed could evade a monetary growth-rate rule if it

[4]Supporters of the growth rate rule could reply that the Fed responded to the rise in food and oil prices by adopting a restrictive policy in the second half of 1974. This suggests that it did not use its freedom from a confining monetary growth rate rule very effectively. However, one study found that the results of this policy were better than those that would have followed from adherence to a monetary rule. But it could not take into account that the adoption of a rule would have changed the public's expectations, and hence its behavior. See Roger Crane, Arthur Havenner, and James Barry, "Fixed Rules vs. Activism in the Conduct of Monetary Policy," *American Economic Review* 68 (December 1978): 769–83.

wants to. Whichever way "money" is defined for the rule, there are some excluded items that are not much less liquid than some items that are included. By adopting regulations that increase the liquidity of some of these excluded items, the Fed could make them into de facto money. Similarly, through its regulatory powers the Fed could increase the quantity of near-monies in general.

A related problem is that the "money" which should be growing at a fixed rate is not, in the view of some economists, any particular country's money. Given the ease with which foreign currencies can be traded, if, say, British interest rates are higher, Americans will hold some of their money in the form of British pounds rather than as dollars, while if U.S. interest rates are higher more dollars will be held by Britons. Hence, to be effective, a monetary growth-rate rule should be applied not just to any one country, but to, say, four major currencies jointly. But it would be hard to get these countries to collaborate on a monetary rule. Insofar as they do not, the Fed might have to reduce its money growth rate because, say, the German central bank is expanding its money at too fast a rate. The American public might not sit still for this. But other economists think that the international money market is not all that integrated; that people are reluctant to hold foreign currencies, so that you can still control domestic prices by controlling domestic money.

More generally, at a time of rapid financial innovation one might well doubt one's ability to select a particular measure of money, and to define the correct monetary policy as having this measure grow at the appropriate rate for the next, say, thirty years. It might be necessary to redefine money from time to time and that would create an opening for discretion.

In addition, there is the fact that a monetary rule would require the Fed to ignore all targets other than the money stock. For example, it could not act to moderate swings in the exchange rate and in interest rates. While many economists would welcome this, others believe that the goals the Fed would have to relinquish are desirable goals.

And the argument that the rule would reduce government interference has drawn the response that this interference is not so terrible. Then, there is the question of the political feasibility of adherence to a rule. If the rule is adopted, wouldn't it be abandoned as soon as interest rates fluctuate sharply, or unemployment rises substantially? The late Jacob Viner has argued that:

> In the economic field important rules affecting important social issues have in fact been extremely scarce, and to the extent that they have had a substantial degree of durability this has been largely explicable either by the fact that they evolved into taboos, or ends in themselves, and were thus removed from the area of open discussion and rational appraisal, or by the tolerance of widespread evasion. The most conspicuous instances of economic rules with a substantial degree of durability were the prohibition of lending at interest and the maintenance of fixed monetary standards in terms of precious metals. The most enthusiastic advocate of rules can derive little comfort from the availability of these historical precedents.[5]

[5]Jacob Viner, "The Necessity and Desirable Range of Discretion to Be Allowed to a Monetary Authority," in *In Search of a Monetary Constitution,* ed. Leland Yeager (Cambridge: Harvard University Press, 1962), p. 248.

Some Possible Compromises

Given these arguments for, and against, the monetary growth-rate rule, it is not surprising that some economists have looked for a compromise position. One compromise already mentioned would give the Fed, not a single-valued target, but a range, say, 4–6 percent for *M-1*, and perhaps allow it to move outside this range under special circumstances.

Another possible compromise is to adjust the monetary growth rate each quarter to offset the changes in velocity in the most recent quarter, or quarters. This would prevent the drift in the price level that would result if the long-term trend in velocity differs from what was assumed in setting up the rule.

Still another compromise is known by the inelegant name of "semirules." These are rules, not for a constant monetary growth rate, but for a constant reaction to changes in income. For example, the Fed could announce as its policy an equation that relates the growth rate of the money stock to the rate of change in income in the recent past. Some studies using both an earlier version of the MPS model and the St. Louis model have shown that, *if* either of these models is a correct description of the economy, there exists such a semirule that would have performed better than a constant monetary growth rate.[6] But these studies have two great weaknesses. First, by assuming that the lag of monetary policy in each individual case is equal to the average lag, they assume away a good part of the case for the monetary rule, and, second, as discussed in Chapter 22, the adoption of a rule would change the public's expectations, and thus the way it acts. Hence, even if the MPS model or the St. Louis model were absolutely true descriptions of how the economy functioned before the rule was adopted, this need no longer be so once a monetary rule is adopted.

All in all, the issue of whether the Fed should continue using discretionary monetary policy, a growth-rate rule, or a semirule is far from settled.

THE MONETARIST POSITION

Support of a monetary growth-rate rule is a major characteristic of monetarism. Thus Franco Modigliani has stated that this is *the* basic issue dividing monetarists and Keynesians, since nowadays Keynesians agree that money is a highly important variable.[7] However, this may go a bit too far; Keynesians generally still attribute *less* importance to changes in the money stock than do monetarists.

Moreover, there is much more to monetarism than just a preference for a stable money growth rate. In Chapter 15 we discussed briefly six attributes that characterize monetarist theory: the money supply as the dominant factor driving money income, a particular view of the transmission process, the

[6] See J. Phillip Cooper, *Development of the Monetary Sector, Prediction and Policy Analysis in the FRB-MIT-Penn Model* (Lexington, Ky.: Lexington Books, 1974), ch. 4.

[7] Franco Modigliani, "The Monetarist Controversy; or, Should We Forsake Stabilization Policy?" *American Economic Review* 67 (March 1977): 1–19.

stability of the private sector, the irrelevance for the determination of nominal income of the allocation of demand among various sectors, focus on the price level as a whole rather than on individual prices, and a preference for small models.

In discussing monetary policy we have, so far, looked at three other monetarist propositions: use of the money stock rather than the interest rate as the target (together with the belief that the Fed can control the money stock), the use of total reserves or the base as the instrument, and support of a monetary growth-rate rule. Three remaining policy propositions serve to round out a set of twelve propositions that constitute a description of monetarism. One is that there is no useful trade-off between unemployment and inflation since the Phillips curve is in real terms. Most Keynesians probably agree that *ultimately* there exists little or no trade-off between unemployment and inflation, but believe that there is such a trade-off for a long enough time to be usable for stabilization policy. Second, monetarists are more strongly opposed to unanticipated inflation than are Keynesians, and are *relatively* less concerned with unemployment. Finally, monetarists usually favor free-market processes, and oppose government intervention, more than Keynesians do.

These characteristics of monetarism can generally be related to the monetarist's tendency to take a long-run point of view, and are connected. For example, if most of the historically observed fluctuations in nominal income are due to changes in the money growth rate rather than to variations in velocity, then a stable money growth rate seems desirable. (One proviso, however: Suppose that velocity has been fairly stable in the past only because the Fed met changes in the demand for money by changing the money supply correspondingly, so that interest rates, and hence velocity, did not change. If so, adoption of a stable money growth-rate rule need not reduce income fluctuations, because it will make velocity more variable.)

Moreover, if, in the absence of fluctuations in the money growth rate, the private sector is stable, then countercyclical monetary policy is not needed. Similarly, someone who wants a stable monetary growth rate obviously wants the Fed to use a money-stock target rather than an interest rate target. In addition, if one looks at the price level as a whole, then, cost-push inflation seems less of a danger, and hence there is less need for the Fed to adopt the policy of increasing the money stock to maintain high employment despite rising prices. Besides, if there is no usable trade-off between unemployment and inflation, then there is one less thing that stabilization policy could potentially do. A monetary growth-rate rule also eliminates the danger that the Fed will shift to an inflationary policy, and it gets rid of one type of government interference.

But this does not mean that one can accept the monetary growth-rate rule only if one accepts all the other monetarist propositions too. Suppose, for example, that there are long and unpredictable lags in the effects of monetary policy, or that there is irresistible political pressure on the Fed, or else, that the rational-expectations criticism of discretionary policy is correct. If any of these conditions prevail, then the monetary growth-rate rule would be preferable to discretionary policy.

THE LONG-RUN STABILIZATION APPROACH

The two main disadvantages of the monetary growth-rate rule are first, that it requires abandoning attempts to stabilize the economy and second, that the development of money substitutes and new ways of managing payments *may* make the fixed money growth rate that is chosen inappropriate at a later time. Yet it has the great advantages that it prevents the Fed from actually destabilizing the economy, and that it pays attention to the long run, thus avoiding the inflationary bias of a countercyclical policy. Because it focuses on the short run, countercyclical policy tends to be biased in favor of too expansionary policies since the favorable effects of such policies show up in the short run, while their unfavorable effects occur only later on. Someone making policy that concentrates on the short run is under great temptation to be a "nice guy" and do something to reduce unemployment.[8]

A new compromise position appears now to be emerging that is still evolving and not yet fully formulated. But it does seem to have some influence on the Fed. It represents a retreat from the Keynesian position accepted during most of the post-World War II period, that the Fed should try to smooth out business cycles. But while agreeing with the monetarists in rejecting countercyclical stabilization, the new approach does not accept their solution of a fixed long-run money growth rate because it is hard to predict how velocity will change over the long run. Hence, it sets money growth-rate targets as a fairly broad range for a year or two ahead. This range is chosen more with an eye to bringing down the inflation rate at a tolerable pace than with concern about the current stage of the business cycle.

THE EASY-MONEY POSITION

This is a populist position that has considerable support among the general public and in Congress. It is also supported by some economists, particularly those who reject "orthodox theory," such as John Kenneth Galbraith of Harvard University. It comes in various degrees of strength. For the sake of contrast with the foregoing we will summarize a strong version.

Proponents of the easy-money position argue that contemporary inflations are often not caused by excess demand, but result from cost-push factors, such as increasing industrial concentration, supply shocks, or the unwillingness of low-income groups to put up with the existing distribution of income. Consequently, a restrictive monetary policy is a most inappropriate way to fight inflation. It would create a totally unacceptable amount of unemployment without bringing the inflation under control. In fact, it would

[8] In fact one might speculate that a major proximate cause of the postwar inflation is a rise in social concern and in pragmatism. At one time central bankers saw their task as the preservation of a justified faith in the financial system and in the value of money. They were not afraid to be rigid in serving that task and had the required political support. But in recent years the ethic of helping people has tended to replace the ethic of preserving the social structure.

make the inflation worse because firms pass on in higher prices any increases in their costs, and higher interest rates certainly raise costs.

Consequently, the government should make sure that aggregate demand is always sufficient for full employment. In other words, the Fed should decide what interest rate is low enough to generate full employment, and then provide sufficient reserves to keep it at that level. Inflation should then be curbed, not by the immoral policy of creating massive unemployment, but by incomes policy—wage and price guidelines, or outright controls—perhaps in combination with a policy to redistribute income so that low-income groups no longer feel it necessary to demand inflationary wage increases.

If aggregate demand is to be reduced this should be done through fiscal policy rather than monetary policy, since a restrictive monetary policy distorts resource allocation. Specifically, it discourages such socially useful investment as low- and middle-income housing, while allowing large corporations to carry out some investment projects that do little to enhance public welfare. Moreover, rising interest rates hurt the poor and help the rich.

Adherents to the easy-money position frequently want to reduce or eliminate the Federal Reserve's independence. They look on the Fed as having a deflationary bias since it is controlled by financial interests, such as banks, that profit from high interest rates.

THE GOLD STANDARD

A rule that has achieved considerable public attention, though most economists oppose it, is a return to the gold standard. With money being redeemable in gold, the Fed would, in effect, have to stabilize the price of dollars in terms of gold. If—and this is a big if—the relative price of gold in terms of a representative market basket of other goods is stable, then the Fed would, in this way, be stabilizing the overall price level. There are, however, a number of serious problems with a gold standard. Thus, if the price of gold is set too high then there would be a massive gold inflow from other countries which the Fed would have to monetize with obvious inflationary consequences. Similarly, a gold outflow would require a contraction of the money stock which would probably cause a major recession. It is therefore not surprising that the majority of a commission on the gold standard appointed by President Reagan rejected a return to the gold standard.

THE MONETARY STANDARD

The debates reviewed in this chapter deal with the monetary standard—that is, with the rules and conventions that underlie day-to-day monetary policy and provide the long-run framework. For almost fifty years our monetary standard has been that the Fed would try to counteract unemployment and inflation, focusing on the current situation rather than on the longer-run effects of its policies.

As a result of the great inflation that has occurred since the mid-1960s there is now much dissatisfaction with this standard. Inflation is not a normal and inevitable fact of life. Over the long historical run there have been *very* roughly as many years of inflation as years of falling prices. (However, with the percentage change in prices being greater during years of inflation than during years of falling prices, the price level has risen substantially.) At one time people could be reasonably confident that the value of money would be preserved over the long run because adherence to the gold standard prevented the central bank from giving in to political pressures for inflation. After the collapse of the gold standard during the Great Depression, the wish to maintain exchange-rate stability provided at least a partial substitute until 1971. But what is to protect us against inflation now? Can we rely on ad hoc policies or do we have to constrain the central bank by some sort of rule?

SUMMARY

1. A number of economists have advocated a stable money growth-rate rule as the best that can be done given our limited knowledge. They point to long and variable lags, as well as to political pressures that are likely to interfere with discretionary monetary policy.
2. Supporters of discretionary policy doubt that the lag is really all that variable, and point to the occurrence of supply shocks, to the variability of velocity and productivity growth, as well as to the development of near-monies as vitiating the case for a fixed money growth-rate rule.
3. Some economists advocate a compromise position, such as setting a band for money growth or the use of semi-rules.
4. One can identify a monetarist position on policy that consists of the use of the money stock as the target, a fixed money growth-rate rule, use of total reserves or the base as the instrument, rejection of a Phillips curve trade-off, relatively greater concern about inflation than about unemployment, and a relatively greater preference for free-market processes. While these monetarist positions are mutually connected, and are connected with those discussed in Chapter 15, one does not have to accept—or reject—them as a bundle.
5. There is now developing a position that, while it does not advocate a long-term fixed money growth-rate rule, also rejects the countercyclical use of monetary policy. Instead, monetary policy should focus on the long run, and on bringing down the inflation rate.
6. There has also been some support for a return to the gold standard as a way of ensuring price stability, but there is the danger that massive gold flows would then require major inflations or deflations.
7. Adherents to the easy-money position want monetary policy to focus on achieving full employment and to keep interest rates low. Inflation should be fought by incomes policy and fiscal policy.
8. A monetary standard is the set of rules that underlies day-to-day monetary policy. Our monetary standard since the Great Depression has been one of ad hoc intervention. The desirability of this standard has now been challenged.

Questions and Exercises

1. Write an essay defending the easy-money position.
2. Write an essay criticizing the easy-money position.
3. Consider the monetary policies that have been followed over the last ten years. Do you think they are superior to what would have resulted from a rule?
4. List the major arguments for a monetary rule. Which do you find most persuasive?
5. List the arguments against a monetary rule. Which do you find most persuasive?
6. Formulate your own position on the issue of policy.

Further Reading

BRONFENBRENNER, MARTIN. "Monetary Rules: A New Look." *Journal of Law & Economics* 8 (October 1965): 173–94. An excellent discussion of the rules debate.

BRUNNER, KARL. "The Case Against Monetary Activism." *Lloyds Bank Review* 139 (January 1981): 20–30. A sweeping attack on discretionary policy.

FRIEDMAN, MILTON. *A Program for Monetary Stability*. New York: Fordham University Press, 1959. A classic statement of the rules position.

———. "Monetary Policy: Theory and Practice." *Journal of Monetary Economics* 14 (February 1982): 98–118. A powerful indictment of the Fed's procedures.

LAIDLER, DAVID. "Monetarism: An Interpretation and an Assessment." *Economic Journal* 91 (March 1981): 1–28. An excellent survey.

LERNER, ABBA. "Review of Milton Friedman's *A Program for Monetary Stability*." *Journal of the American Statistical Association* 57 (March 1962): 211–20. An outstanding criticism of the monetary growth-rate rule.

MILLER, ERVIN. *Microeconomic Effects of Monetary Policy*. London: Martin Robertson, 1978. A fervent statement of the easy-money position (but watch for the distinction between nominal and real rates).

MODIGLIANI, FRANCO. "The Monetarist Controversy; or, Should We Forsake Stabilization Policy?" *American Economic Review* 67 (March 1977): 1–19. An excellent criticism of monetarist policy prescriptions.

MODIGLIANI, FRANCO, and FRIEDMAN, MILTON. "The Monetarist Controversy." *Economic Review* (Federal Reserve Bank of San Francisco) supplement, Spring 1977. An extremely stimulating debate.

TOBIN, JAMES. "The Monetarist Counter-Revolution Today—An Appraisal." *Economic Journal* 91 (March 1981): 29–42. A powerful criticism of monetarism.

International Money and Finance

PART FIVE

When monetary policy is analyzed in a world of more than one hundred national currencies—an open economy—the primary question is whether the major conclusions about its effectiveness in a one-currency nation—a closed economy—are seriously changed, and, if so, how. A related question is how changes in U.S. monetary policy affect the exchange rate and the U.S. balance-of-payments surplus or deficit.

Changes in U.S. monetary policy may have two effects on the foreign-exchange value of the U.S. dollar and the U.S. payments balance. One is immediate and direct and operates through the relationship between investor demand for financial assets denominated in the U.S. dollar and for comparable assets denominated in the mark, the yen, the Swiss franc, and various other foreign currencies. The second effect is delayed and indirect, and operates through the impacts of changes in consumption and investment spending in the United States on the demand of U.S. residents for foreign goods and securities.

One issue in the analysis of the effectiveness of monetary policy in an international context involves the substitutability between domestic securities and foreign securities: the more perfect the substitutability, the smaller the impact of a given change in monetary policy on consumption and investment spending, and the larger the immediate impact of a given change in monetary policy on imports of foreign securities. The less perfect the substitutability between domestic bonds and foreign bonds, the greater the impact of a given change in U.S. monetary policy on interest rates on dollar securities and consumption and investment spending. As U.S. income increases, U.S. commodity imports increase; at the same time, some domestic goods will be diverted to the U.S. markets from export markets. The increase in U.S. income leads to increased demand for securities, and more foreign bonds may be imported and fewer domestic bonds exported.

To the extent investor views about the substitutability between domestic and foreign securities vary with whether foreign currencies are pegged to the U.S. dollar or instead float, the impact of a given change in U.S. monetary policy on domestic income varies with the exchange-rate system. If the monetary authorities abroad peg their currencies to the dollar, then the increased investor confidence that the exchange rates will not change greatly is likely to strengthen investor views about the close substitutability between dollar securities and comparable securities denominated in other currencies. In contrast, the less investors believe in their ability to predict future exchange rates, perhaps because the price of the dollar in terms of foreign currencies moves freely in response to changes in supply and demand, the smaller is the substitutability of domestic and foreign securities. Consequently, a given change in U.S. monetary policy is likely to have a larger impact on domestic interest rates and domestic incomes under a floating-exchange-rate regime than under a pegged-exchange-rate regime.

Floating or Pegged

Changes in the exchange-rate regimes as the international payments arrangements have evolved in the last century are discussed in Chapter 26. During the gold standard of the nineteenth century and under the Bretton Woods system of the 1945–70 period, exchange rates were pegged. During the 1970s and 1980s, the currencies of major countries have not been pegged; they have floated freely. The pattern of evolution in the arrangements of international payments is discussed in this chapter.

The organization of the foreign-exchange market and the relation between spot-exchange rates and forward-exchange rates are considered in Chapter 27 along with the determinants of the level of the exchange rate, and the various explanations for the large movements in exchange rates. This chapter concludes with a brief discussion of the central concepts of balance-of-payments accounting.

The structure of the banking system in an international context, with special attention to the growth of the Eurodollar market and its impact on the effectiveness of national monetary policies, is analyzed in Chapter 28. The rapid growth of international banking and the expansion of banks headquartered in the major countries in foreign markets are examined.

Chapter 29 evaluates several of the major continuing policy issues in international money and banking, including the choice of exchange-rate regimes and the changes in the organization of the foreign-exchange market, and the monetary roles of gold and the dollar as the system continues to evolve.

The Evolution of the International Monetary System

26

The international monetary system provides a framework enabling residents of one country to make payments to residents of other countries. Such payments are necessary because importers in one country must pay exporters in other countries; either the importers must first acquire the currencies of the countries in which the exporters live, or the exporters must, after being paid in the importer's currency, exchange it for their own.

The business and financial needs of industry and trade are served by the minimization of the additional costs and inconvenience and risks of international transactions relative to domestic transactions. These costs, while generally small, have varied with changes in the international payments arrangement. Over the last century, the international monetary system has evolved from primary reliance on gold to primary reliance on national monies to meet the demand for international reserve assets, monies which provide the basis for international payments. The changes in these arrangements for international payments have not been accidental, but instead are responses to economic disturbances, both monetary and structural, and to changes in political relationships among the major countries.

An international monetary system can be identified by three key features—the organization of the foreign-exchange market, the types of assets used for financing or settling payments imbalances, and the mechanisms of adjustment to payments imbalances.

As the institutional basis for organizing the foreign-exchange market and for producing international reserve assets has changed, so has the name given to the international monetary system. Before World War I, the term *the gold standard* was applied to international financial arrangements; after World War I the *gold-exchange standard* described the mechanism.

The term *standard,* when used in reference to the gold standard or a bimetallic standard, suggests a measure or unit of account, like a yard or a liter. National monies at that time had values that were stated in terms of gold; thus the U.S. dollar was equal to 1.672 grams of gold of .900 fineness.

A treaty-based system known as the Bretton Woods system developed after World War II and functioned until the early 1970s. With the breakdown of the Bretton Woods arrangement in the 1971–73 period, arrangements for payments among countries have become more varied and eclectic, and no comprehensive term now describes the payments arrangements. The term *system* has been applied since World War II to the arrangements for organizing the foreign-exchange market and for producing international reserves.

This chapter first describes the three international monetary systems that prevailed for nearly a hundred years. Then attention is given to the economic and political factors that may explain the evolution of the institutional features of the system, especially the rise of the United States as a dominant economic power.

THE GOLD STANDARD

The nineteenth century is frequently described as the gold-standard era, although more detailed analysis suggests that for most countries the term is more appropriately applied to the years 1880–1913 (some countries had been on the gold standard earlier). A country "joined" the gold standard when its national legislation required that its major banks and financial institutions redeem or repurchase their monetary liabilities at a fixed price, the mint parity, that indicated the value of the national currency unit in terms of a specified amount of gold. Thus at the beginning of January 1879, the United States went back on the gold standard, having abandoned it in 1863, and U.S. commercial banks were once again obliged to convert their monetary liabilities into gold. The mint parities of major countries are shown in Table 26.1, together with the price of major foreign currencies in terms of the U.S. dollar. Thus, the Act of Parliament of 1816 obliged the Bank of England to buy gold at three pounds, seventeen shillings, nine pence per ounce and to sell gold at the price of three pounds, seventeen shillings, ten and one-half pence per ounce: the gold was .916⅔ fine or pure. Some countries pegged

Table 26.1 Parities of Major Currencies under the Gold Standard

Country	Unit	Weight[a]	Fineness[b]	Value of one ounce	U.S. dollar parity
United States (1879)	1 dollar	1.672	.900	US 20.67	—
Great Britain (1816)	1 pound	7.988	.917	BP 3/17/10½	$4.86
France (1878)	1 franc	.3226	.900	FF 107.1	$ .193
Germany (1871)	1 mark	.398	.900	DM 86.8	$ .238
Italy (1878)	1 lira	.3226	.900	IL 107.1	$ .193
Netherlands (1875)	1 florin	.672	.900	DF 51.4	$ .402

a. Weight of standard coin in grams.

b. Fineness of standard coin = proportion pure gold.

Source: M. L. Muhleman, *Monetary Systems of the World* (New York: Charles H. Nicoll, 1894).

their currencies to silver as well as to gold, and so they were on a bimetallic standard; monetary institutions in these countries were obliged to buy and sell gold and silver on demand at the respective parities. Managing a bimetallic system proved difficult because of the need to maintain the fixed-price relationship between the mint parity for gold and the mint parity for silver. From time to time, when large new discoveries of silver or gold were made, changes in one mint parity were necessary.

Adherence to the gold standard did not involve participation in an international treaty or agreement at an international conference. Rather the choice was decentralized, and individual countries pegged their currencies to gold at somewhat different times.

A major by-product of commitments of individual countries to peg was a system of pegged exchange rates. Thus, given the willingness of the Bank of England to buy and sell one ounce of gold at 77 shillings and 10½ pence and the willingness of the U.S. Treasury to buy and sell one ounce of gold at the parity of $20.67, the dollar price of one pound sterling could be calculated as $4.865 (once an adjustment was made for the somewhat greater purity of the British gold coin).[1]

Some central banks bought and sold gold at their mint parities. Most central banks, however, bought gold at prices fractionally below their mint parities and sold gold at prices fractionally above their mint parities. These small differences between the mint parities and the gold buying and selling prices were called handling charges, and were intended to compensate the national central banks for their costs in buying and selling gold. In addition, some central banks varied their gold selling prices modestly, increasing these prices when the demands for gold was strong so the amount demanded would be smaller; these countries were said to be on the "limping gold standard."

Gold and International Reserves

A key aspect of the gold standard was that central banks held a large part of their international reserves in the form of gold. The Bank of England held virtually all its assets in the form of gold; other central banks held a large proportion of their assets in gold and the rest in assets such as government securities denominated in the pound sterling, French francs, and their own currencies. Differences among central banks in the proportion of gold in their international reserves reflected differences in their business needs. One reason that these banks outside Great Britain held such a large proportion of their assets in sterling was that they sold sterling-denominated debt in London; London was then the world's principal financial center. Similarly, they received French francs after selling franc-denominated debt in Paris. Moreover, these countries were obliged to acquire these currencies to repay debts denominated in these currencies.

[1]Thus if an ounce of gold equals both 77 shillings 10½ pence times $\frac{.917}{.900}$ (the adjustment for differences in the proportion of pure gold in the several coins) and $20.67, then 20 shillings, or one pound, equals $4.865.

Gold and Payments Imbalances

A second feature of the gold standard was that gold might flow from the countries with payments deficits—broadly, those whose imports of goods, services, and securities exceeded their exports of goods, services, and securities—to countries with payments surpluses. Gold flows were supposed to settle payments imbalances. One of the paradoxes of the gold standard was that relatively little gold was actually transferred among countries. Shipments of gold between New York and London incurred costs of freight and insurance as well as the forgone interest on the wealth invested in gold between the date the payer acquired the gold in one country and the date the payee received gold in the second country. Consequently, traders and investors sought less costly methods to make international payments.

As an alternative to the gold transactions, a market developed in bills of exchange, which were a type of check. These bills were issued by importers or buyers, and were IOUs indicating that payment for the purchase would be made in thirty, sixty, or ninety days. Thus, a U.S. importer with a payment to make in London would buy a sterling-denominated bill of exchange in New York from a U.S. exporter who previously had received this sterling bill from a London importer of U.S. wheat. The U.S. wheat exporter wanted dollars, not sterling; he could sell the sterling bill in London, and buy gold to ship to the United States, or he could sell the bill of exchange in New York to a U.S. importer and avoid the costs and inconvenience of the gold shipment. The U.S. importer would pay for the sterling bill in dollars, and the U.S. wheat exporter would receive dollars and avoid the costs of shipping gold from London to New York.

Because the costs of shipping the bill of exchange to London were much lower than the costs of shipping the gold to London, the U.S. importer would pay a higher dollar price for the bill of exchange than for the amount of gold that would generate the same volume of sterling payments. The ability to make the London payment by shipping gold set an upper limit to the dollar price of the sterling bills. Similarly, the ability to make a payment from London to New York by shipping gold set a lower limit to the dollar price that the U.S. exporter would accept for his sterling bills; if the dollar price were lower, the exporter would instead ship gold.

"Rules of the Game"

The third feature of the gold standard was the concept of "rules of the game"—the idea that countries with balance-of-payments surpluses would follow expansive monetary policies because the gold inflows would lead to an increase in the monetary liabilities of the central bank. Conversely, the countries with balance-of-payments deficits and gold outflows would follow contractive monetary policies: their money supplies would decline. Commodity price levels would rise in the countries with the payments surpluses and fall in the countries with the payments deficits. As the international competitiveness of the two groups of countries changed, the imports of the first group would rise, and their exports would fall; in contrast, the imports of the second group would fall and their exports would rise. The change in national price levels would continue until balance-of-payments equilibrium was achieved. Hence international payments imbalances would be automatically self-correcting without the need for discretionary monetary policies.

This adjustment process appeared to be automatic, guided by an invisible hand. The evidence that countries followed the rules of the game is mixed. Yet countries, once they accepted gold parities, were able to maintain their parities, and so some mechanism in the system facilitated restoring payments equilibrium once disturbances occurred that led to imbalances.

One important aspect of the operation of the "rules of the game" should be noted—in order to maintain the fixity of one price, their gold parities, countries accepted variations in their national price levels. Increases in these price levels occurred when countries had payments surpluses, and decreases in these prices occurred when countries had payments deficits. Without such variations in national price levels, maintaining the gold parities would have been impossible.

Gold and Commodity Prices

The fourth feature of the gold standard was the promise of commodity price-level stability in the long run. If on a worldwide basis monetary gold stocks were increasing rapidly, either because of new gold discoveries or because of new and lower cost techniques for gold ore refining, then central banks in many countries might experience gold inflows simultaneously, and their money supplies would rise in many countries at the same time. At the new and higher commodity price levels, gold mining would be more costly, the level of gold production would decline, and a damper or brake would be placed on further increases in the commodity price levels. Conversely, if the demand for gold increased relative to the supply, the commodity price levels would fall because less gold would be available for monetary purposes. At the lower price levels, more gold would be mined, and eventually the decline in the commodity price levels would be checked. So just as national price levels changed to restore balance-of-payments equilibrium, so changes in the world price level would prove self-limiting. Thus, price-level stability would be achieved over a period of several decades if not on a year-to-year basis.

The U.S. and British commodity price levels for 1800–1950 are shown in Figure 26.1. The commodity price levels at the outbreak of World War I are not very different from the price levels a century earlier. The average annual change in the price levels was small, certainly less than one percent. And there are very few years, except those at the times of major wars, in which the annual change in the price level exceeded three percent.

The attractions of the gold standard were inherent in its anonymous, automatic, self-correcting properties. Balance-of-payments adjustments could be made easily and without fuss. Moreover, this system promised price-level stability in the long run, even though price levels might vary modestly from one year to the next. Finally, the tremendous economic growth in the inter-

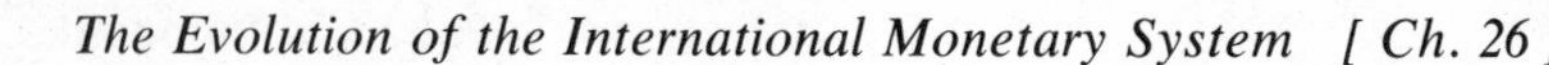

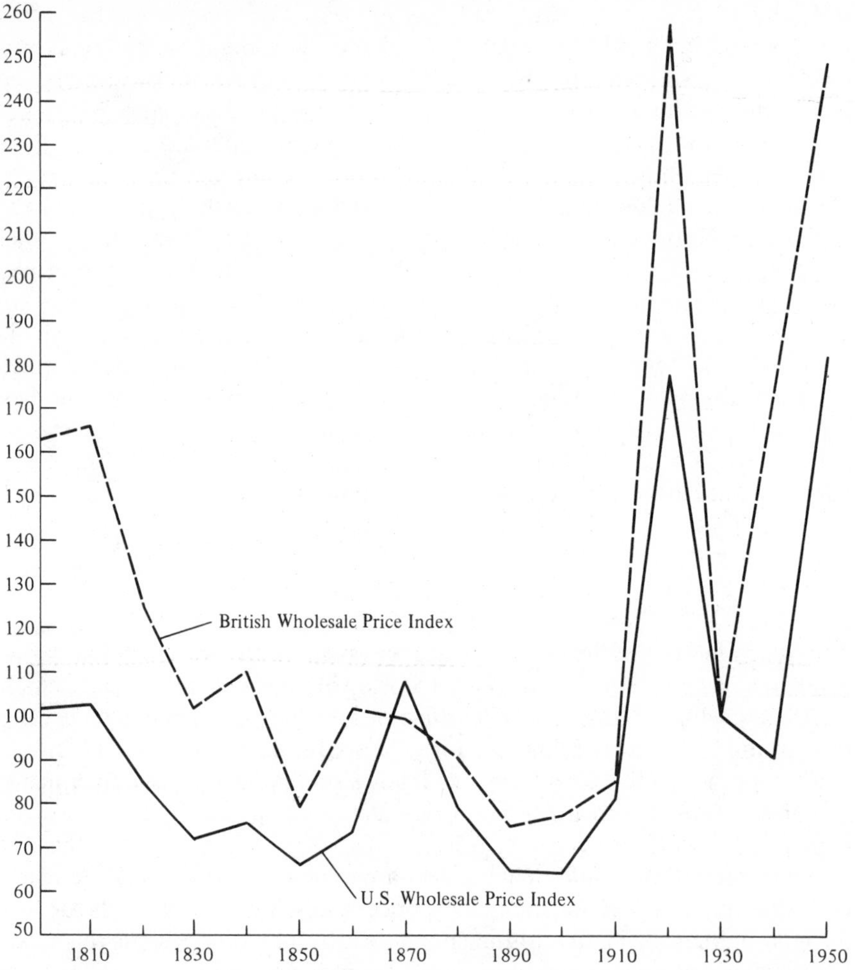

British Wholesale Price Index

U.S. Wholesale Price Index

Figure 26.1 The U.S. and British Wholesale Price Indexes, *1800–1950*

national economy during the half-century before World War I, which may have been helped by national commitments to the gold standard, contributed to the view that this monetary arrangement was ideal.

During World War I most countries ceased pegging their currencies to gold. Moreover, their price levels increased sharply. After the war some countries, the neutrals as well as Great Britain, managed to return to their prewar parities but at considerable cost. High levels of unemployment resulted, since the needed changes in commodity price levels required deflationary monetary policies. Others eventually gave up, and increased the price of gold in terms of their currencies. In retrospect, it appears that it would have been easier and less costly to reestablish the gold standard if countries had been willing to increase the price of gold in terms of their currencies to match the increase in the price levels.

THE GOLD-EXCHANGE STANDARD

The gold-exchange standard developed in the early 1920s in response to an anticipated gold shortage due to reduction in the supply of gold and an increase in the demand. The anticipated reduction in the supply would result from the combination of the increase in national price levels and the concomitant increase in costs of gold production together with the fixed selling price for gold. The increase in demand would result both from an increase in the number of central banks due to the breakup of the Austro-Hungarian Empire and an increase in the demand for gold for monetary uses because of the increase in the national price levels during and after World War I.

The possible shortage of gold was extensively discussed at two conferences sponsored by the League of Nations, one in Brussels in 1920 and one in Genoa in 1922. Because central banks were reluctant to raise the price of gold in terms of their currencies, the participants sought to economize on the use of gold. The use of gold coins for private payments was discouraged; monetary gold holdings would be concentrated in central banks. Moreover, a practice that had been evident before World War I received formal recognition and approval: some central banks would hold their reserves in the form of foreign exchange, such as bank deposits, Treasury bills, and bankers' acceptances, denominated in sterling, or the dollar, or some other currency.

The intent of the gold-exchange standard was supposed to modify only the composition of international reserves. Central banks were still supposed to follow the "rules of the game" for balance-of-payments adjustment. Countries would still maintain parities for their currencies in terms of gold. Yet there was a change: If the United States or Great Britain incurred payments deficits and the countries with the payments surpluses acquired assets denominated in dollars or in sterling, the United States and Great Britain would not follow the rules of the game; only the countries with the payments surpluses would do so. The automatic adjustment tendencies of the gold standard were maintained, but in a somewhat more asymmetric way than before World War I.

The rationale for the development of the gold-exchange standard was that it would provide a stable framework in which national currencies would again exchange at their mint parities. Yet exchange rates were not pegged during most of the period between the two world wars. In May 1925 Great Britain pegged sterling to gold at its 1913 parity. In September 1931 Great Britain decided that maintaining the gold parity was too costly in terms of domestic employment, so sterling was allowed to float until World War II with the difference that the British authorities intervened much more extensively in the foreign-exchange market. The 1930s was a decade of sharp changes in parities, which followed a domino-like pattern: the U.S. dollar was devalued in 1933-34, and the French franc and the Dutch guilder in 1936. The alignment of the exchange rates at the end of the 1930s was not very different from that at the end of the 1920s. After the sequence of devaluations, the monetary price of gold was 75 percent higher.

The growth of international reserves denominated in sterling, the dollar, and other major currencies during the 1930s was reasonably small. At the end of the 1920s, holdings of foreign exchange accounted for 20 percent of international reserves. At the end of the 1930s this ratio was lower because of the effective worldwide increase in the price of gold and the sharp increase in the value of monetary gold holdings. In the 1940s, in contrast, the foreign-exchange component amounted to 30 percent of international reserves; most of the reserves involved claims on the United States and Great Britain.

The monetary instability in the interwar period was reflected in the combination of sharp movements in exchange rates, high unemployment, and the growth of ad hoc restrictions on international payments. This instability is sometimes associated with the tension between Great Britain, whose economic power was declining, and the United States, whose economic position was getting stronger. One aspect of this tension was that interest rates the United States felt appropriate for its domestic economy attracted funds from London, and so the British had to counter by raising sterling interest rates. In the early 1930s, there was a conflict about the appropriate value for the dollar-sterling exchange rate. The value preferred by the U.S. authorities would have increased the competitiveness of U.S. goods more than the British found acceptable.

This shift in economic power from Great Britain to the United States was almost inevitable given the differences in economic size and long-term growth rates. Whether this shift could have been accommodated without the instability that actually occurred is conjectural. Major policy errors led to some instability. One error was the unwillingness to adjust exchange parities to reflect the changes in the post-World War I price levels. A second error was the unwillingness of many countries to raise the monetary gold price to correspond with the increase in the national price levels.

THE BRETTON WOODS SYSTEM

Early in World War II, the United States and Great Britain took the initiative in development of economic institutions to deal with anticipated problems of the postwar period—and to avoid a repetition of monetary and trade disturbances of the previous twenty years. Thus, the International Bank for Reconstruction and Development (the IBRD or World Bank) was established to facilitate the postwar recovery in Western Europe; once this task was completed at the end of the 1940s, the bank focused on extending financial assistance to the developing countries. Plans for the International Trade Organization (ITO) were developed to provide a framework for reducing tariffs, for establishing commodity arrangements to limit variations in prices of basic raw materials, and to coordinate antitrust policies. Although the ITO never came into existence, the first article in its charter led to the General Agreement on Trade and Tariffs (GATT), which has been the dominant agency promoting a reduction of tariffs and other trade barriers. The third institution, the International Monetary Fund (IMF), was established to enhance stability in international payments in several ways: by providing rules for changes in exchange parities, and for exchange controls on international payments, and by acquiring a pool of national currencies that individual countries might borrow from to help finance their payments deficits.

The International Monetary Fund

The IMF, which is the institutional embodiment of the Bretton Woods system, is based on an international treaty; the system took its name from the resort in New Hampshire where the treaty was signed. Hence, this system differs sharply from both the gold standard and the gold-exchange standard in its legal aspects, as the earlier systems had no international legal basis. Moreover, the Bretton Woods system was to be managed by international civil servants, responsible to the Board of Governors selected by its members (usually their secretaries of the treasury or ministers of finance) and a full-time board of Executive Directors, essentially ambassadors from its members.

Each member country of the IMF was required to state a parity for its currency in terms of gold or in terms of the U.S. dollar. Most subsequent changes of the exchange parities required consultation with or approval by the Fund.

When the Fund was established, its capital was projected to be the equivalent of $10 billion. Countries joining the IMF were obliged to subscribe to its capital; the amount of each country's capital subscription or quota was based on a formula that included its share of world imports and its gold holdings. One-quarter of each country's capital subscription was made payable in gold and the remaining three-quarters in its own currency in the form of a non-interest-bearing demand note.

Whenever a member country had a payments deficit, it could borrow one of these currencies from the pool held by the Fund, with the amount it might borrow geared to its quota. About one-quarter of its quota was automatically available, and the rest was available on a discretionary basis. To finance these loans, the Fund would cash part of the non-interest-bearing demand notes. For example, in 1956, at the time of the Suez crisis in the Middle East, Great Britain borrowed nearly $2 billion from the Fund. In the Fund's terminology, Great Britain "drew" or bought dollars from the Fund with sterling, with the consequence that the Fund's holdings of dollars declined while its holdings of sterling increased. The Fund obtained the dollars by cashing part of its non-interest-bearing demand note at the U.S. Treasury. Great Britain paid interest to the Fund, with the interest rate based on the size of the borrowing in relation to its quota, and the length of the loan. When Great Britain repaid the loan, it purchased sterling with dollars or some other currency acceptable to the Fund.

Several other features of the Bretton Woods system merit attention. One was its position on exchange controls, various types of licenses, special tariffs, and other devices to limit foreign payments; the Fund rules sought to eliminate the use of exchange controls on payments for goods and services like shipping and tourism, although members were to be allowed to retain such restrictions during the postwar reconstruction period. Members could maintain restrictions on transactions in securities, such as stocks and bonds, for an indefinite period.

The Fund rules also provide that the IMF might declare a currency "scarce" in the Fund if some members wished to borrow more of a given currency than the Fund holds. IMF members would then be entitled to apply discretionary exchange controls on their payments to that country, which might force an appreciation of that country's currency. The scarce-currency clause was never invoked.

Special Drawing Rights

The Fund's Articles of Agreement provided that the ability of a member to borrow would not be conditional on its approval of the member's economic and social policies. Over the years, however, the Fund management has taken the view that credit should be extended if there is a reasonable prospect that the member country could resolve its balance-of-payments problems. By 1980 the capital of the Fund was the equivalent of $50 billion, with the increase a result of increases in quotas. Two important institutional innovations, one in the early 1960s and the second in the late 1960s, complemented periodic increases in IMF quotas as a way to increase the funds available to the IMF and the supply of international reserves. To alleviate a possible shortage of currencies in the Fund, the General Arrangements To

Borrow was attached to the Fund structure in 1963; this agreement formalized the terms on which the Fund could borrow the currencies of member countries.

A major modification involved the establishment of Special Drawing Rights (SDRs), a new international reserve asset. The value of the SDR is based on five major currencies (the U.S. dollar, the Japanese yen, the British pound, the German mark, and the French franc); the IMF determines the value of the SDR each day on the basis of the weight of each country's currency in the basket, and the value for each country's currency in terms of the U.S. dollar. Ten billion dollars of SDRs were produced in three years, through a form of international open-market operation; each member country received newly produced SDRs in proportion to its share of total IMF quotas. Each member country could then use SDRs to buy foreign currencies from other members or from the Fund. For example, if Great Britain had a payments deficit, it might sell some of its holdings of SDRs to the U.S. Treasury to get the dollars to use to support sterling in the foreign-exchange market, or instead it might sell SDRs to the Fund to get dollars or marks or some other national currency. In addition, SDRs began to develop some characteristics of a unit-of account, and some countries began to state the parities for their currencies in terms of SDRs, just as, at earlier dates, they had stated their parities in terms of gold and then the U.S. dollar.

During the 1950s and 1960s, international trade and payments grew rapidly, and exchange controls or international payments that had been adopted by countries in Western Europe in the 1940s were reduced. For the major industrial countries, the increase in national incomes was very large, so that the contrast between the post-World War I and post-World War II eras was sharp.

One interpretation was that this boom in national incomes and international trade was attributable to the Fund and especially to the orderly arrangements both for changes in exchange rates and the reduction in exchange controls. Indeed, one of the surprising features of the 1950–70 period was the infrequency of changes in exchange parities of major currencies. Thus British sterling was devalued once, the French franc was devalued twice, while the German mark was revalued twice and the Dutch guilder once. Parities for the Japanese yen, the Swiss franc, the Italian lira, and the Belgian franc were not changed. An alternative explanation was that the United States provided a stable framework for the growth of national incomes abroad by maintaining a relatively stable price level. According to this view, the growth of the international economy reflected the underlying economic stability of the major countries.

The irony of the IMF system was that although the IMF rules were established to avoid frequent changes in parities, changes in parities proved to be quite infrequent. Payments imbalances were extended because there were no longer any "rules of the game" for the balance-of-payments adjustment. Countries were committed to their domestic full-employment policies, and were reluctant to adopt measures to reduce payments deficits when one of the consequences might be an increase in unemployment. There was no agreement or understanding about whether the countries with the payments deficits or those with the payments surpluses should take the initiative to reduce extended payments imbalances. The reluctance to change parities reflected that the countries with deficits believed that devaluations would be viewed as evidence of the failure of economic policies, while the surplus countries believed that the persistent imbalances reflected the inflationary policies of the deficit countries.

The Fund's successes and failures are closely linked to the successes and failures of U.S. economic policy. When the U.S. inflation rate was low, the Bretton Woods system worked. As U.S. economic policies became less successful—as the U.S. inflation rate increased in the late 1960s—the U.S. payments deficit became larger than could be readily explained by the demand of other countries for payments surpluses and international reserves. The Fund was virtually powerless to effect a change in the alignment of exchange rates of the major countries. As long as international payments imbalances were those of smaller industrial countries, the Fund had been useful in inducing the return to payments equilibrium. But when the imbalances involved the largest industrial countries, the Fund mechanisms proved ineffective.

With the increase in the inflation rates in the 1970s, a move to floating exchange rates became inevitable because countries could no longer successfully maintain their parities. The Fund rules on exchange parities became obsolete. And with the explosion in the growth of international reserves in the 1970s, the Fund mechanisms seemed irrelevant in meeting the need for international reserves.

THE MOVE TO FLOATING EXCHANGE RATES

When the Bretton Woods system was established, the U.S. international economic position seemed supreme. There was considerable concern about a perpetual dollar shortage—that Europe's desire to spend dollars would exceed its ability to earn dollars at *any* exchange rate, so that Western Europe would have a persistent payments deficit. Even though the 1949 devaluations immediately led to a deficit in the U.S. payments balances the concern with a dollar shortage remained for a decade.

The story of the U.S. payments balance after 1950 can be segmented into three stages. In the first, which runs from 1950 to the mid-1960s, the annual U.S. payments deficits were small, and largely reflected the desire of other countries to add to their holdings of gold and dollars. Their demand for these assets was the cause of the U.S. deficit. During this period, U.S. price-level performance was more impressive than that of any other industrial country. In the mid-1960s the U.S. inflation rate began to increase, and to exceed that in some other industrial countries; in the late 1960s, the U.S. payments deficits began to increase above the levels that could be readily explained by the foreign demand for gold and dollar assets. In a three-year period, 1969–71, the cumulative U.S. payments deficit reached $40 billion, partly as a consequence of a decline in U.S. competitiveness in an array of manufactured products and increasingly in response to speculation about a devaluation of the dollar. In the fall of 1969, the German mark was revalued; in the spring of 1970, the Canadian authorities ceased pegging their currency, and the Canadian dollar immediately appreciated by nearly ten percent. For the next fifteen months, the pressures for changes in parities became increasingly intense.

The Smithsonian Agreement

In August 1971 the U.S. Treasury formally suspended gold sales to foreign official institutions, and the U.S. government adopted a tariff surcharge of ten percent to induce other industrial countries to revalue their currencies; the premise was that the surcharge would be dropped after they devalued. Negotiations with the Europeans and the Japanese formalized this bargain; at the end of 1971, in the context of the Smithsonian Agreement of 1972, the dollar price of gold was increased to $38, the dollar was effectively devalued by about 12 percent, and the tariff surcharge was withdrawn. The new system of pegged exchange rates lasted little more than a year, and there was renewed speculation against the dollar. Because of the inability of national monetary authorities to adopt policies that would have made the new system of pegged exchange rates viable, floating rates again became inevitable, as in the immediate post–World War I period.

The move to floating rates occurred because there was no viable alternative mechanism to accommodate the changes in the international economy. One change was the more rapid inflation in the United States than in some of its major trading partners. Whereas greater success in achieving price stability had increased the foreign demand for dollar assets in the 1950s and early 1960s, the failure to maintain a low inflation rate in the United States in the 1970s led to a reduction in this demand. Moreover, the foreign demand for dollar assets might have fallen because the United States seemed to have lost its dominant lead in world manufactures. Finally, the sharp increase in the world price of petroleum and the large payments surpluses of OPEC nations led to sharp changes in money flows; movements in exchange rates were necessary to accommodate the sharp changes in payment surpluses and deficits.

In the context of the floating-rate system, the dollar was weaker than would have been predicted from the change in relationship between the increase in the U.S. price level and the increase in the foreign price level. Moreover, the cyclical movements in exchange rates were much larger than would have been predicted on the basis of changes in national price levels.

Until the 1980s, investors—both central banks and private institutions—had tried to develop alternatives to the dollar as international reserve asset. The problem was partly circular. Investors moved out of dollar assets because the dollar was weak in the foreign-exchange market; however, the weakness of the dollar in the exchange market reflected that the foreign demand for dollar assets had declined as foreign official institutions were diversifying the currency denomination of their assets.

Analogies with the decline of U.S. economic power in the 1970s, the breakup of Bretton Woods, and the weakness of the dollar were made to the decline of British economic power in the 1920s, the breakdown of the gold standard, and the weakness of sterling. One factor common to both experiences was the reluctance to increase the monetary price of gold to compensate for the worldwide inflation during and after both world wars. One shortcoming to this analogy is that the dominant U.S. economic position in the 1940s and 1950s was bound to be temporary, and last only as long as Germany and Japan were still recovering from the economic decline associated with the war. Hence, part of the decline in the U.S. international economic position was almost certainly inevitable. In this sense, the ability of the United States to provide a framework for global monetary stability also declined.

In the early 1970s, the Fund charter was modified to accommodate the adoption of floating exchange rates by the major industrial countries—these practices were, in fact, in violation of treaty commitments. The purpose of the modification was to attempt to develop a set of rules to reduce the likelihood of competitive exchange market intervention practices that would be costly to the interests of their trading partners.

The historical evidence suggests that there will again be a move back to pegged exchange rates, for such a system has been maintained for nearly ninety years of the last century. Yet such a move seems unlikely until inflation rates among the major countries are similar and at a very low level.

SUMMARY

1. An International Monetary System is identified by three key features—the organization of the foreign-exchange market, the assets used to finance payments imbalances, and the mechanism for adjustment to payments imbalances.

2. The gold standard involved a set of mint parities for each national currency in terms of gold, transactions in gold to finance payments imbalances, and changes in national money supplies as a means to facilitate balance-of-payments adjustment induced by gold inflows and outflows.
3. Stability in U.S. and British price levels was greater during 1800–1920 then in the subsequent decades.
4. The gold-exchange standard was developed in the 1920s to provide a new source of international reserve assets in the form of assets denominated in the British pound, the U.S. dollar, and other national currencies.
5. The International Monetary Fund was established in the 1940s to ensure that changes in exchange rates would be orderly. The Fund was endowed with a pool of national currencies which might be lent to countries with balance of payments deficits.
6. Special Drawing Rights (SDRs) were a new reserve asset established in the late 1960s within the framework of the IMF.
7. One notable feature of the 1970s was that currency parities of the industrial countries were changed infrequently.
8. The move from pegged exchange rates to floating exchange rates in the early 1970s occurred at a time of significant differences among the major industrial countries in their rates of inflation.

Questions and Exercises

1. Describe the major differences between the key features of the gold standard and of the Bretton Woods system of adjustable parities.
2. List the major alternative ways a country might achieve equilibrium in its payments balance when a disturbance has led to a payments deficit or a payments surplus.
3. Why did the gold standard break down at the beginning of World War I? Why did the Bretton Woods system of adjustable parities break down in the early 1970s?

Further Reading

ALIBER, ROBERT Z. *The International Money Game*. 4th ed. New York: Basic Books, 1983. A romp through the major issues in international finance.

COOMBS, CHARLES. *The Arena of International Finance*. New York: John Wiley and Sons, 1976. A central banker's brief for pegged exchange rates.

MAYER, MARTIN. *The Fate of the Dollar*. New York: Times Books, 1980. A journalist's view of international monetary developments.

SOLOMON, ROBERT. *The International Monetary System, 1945–1976*. New York: Harper & Row, 1977. A comprehensive blow-by-blow account of negotiations.

TEW, BRIAN. *The Evolution of the International Monetary System, 1947–77*. London: Hutchison, 1977. A succinct analysis of the Bretton Woods system and its breakdown.

TRIFFIN, ROBERT. *Gold and the Dollar Crisis*. New Haven: Yale University Press, 1961. A classic on the U.S. international financial dilemma.

YEAGER, LELAND B. *International Monetary Relations*. New York: Harper & Row, 1966. An excellent text with comprehensive historical treatment.

The Organization of the Foreign-Exchange Market

27

Trade and payments across national borders require that one of the parties to the transaction contract to pay or receive funds in a foreign currency. If an American wishes to buy a Japanese car, then at some stage in the chain of payments between the purchaser and the producer U.S. dollars must be used to buy Japanese yen. Moreover, knowledgeable investors based in each country are aware of the opportunities to buy assets when the anticipated returns are higher abroad and to sell debts denominated in foreign currencies when the interest costs are lower; these investors also must use the foreign-exchange market whenever they invest or borrow abroad.

One unique feature of any international financial system is the exchange rate; and a second the payments balance. The *exchange rate* which is the *price of foreign monies in terms of domestic money,* is determined in the foreign-exchange market. The *payments balance,* which is frequently viewed as a measure of "how well" a country is doing, is one entry in the *balance of payments,* which is the *accounting record of all international transactions.* The payments balance is the value of the transactions of the central bank or monetary authority in liquid assets, such as gold, U.S. Treasury bills, bank deposits, and claims on the International Monetary Fund.

At any moment, the exchange rate provides a basis for comparing prices of domestic goods, services, and securities with comparable goods, services, and securities available in other countries. Few individuals or investors use the foreign-exchange market because they want to hold foreign monies; rather they buy foreign exchange as a necessary intermediate transaction before they can buy a foreign good or security or sell a debt denominated in a foreign currency. Merchants in each country seek to take advantage of any significant difference between the prices of domestic goods and comparable foreign goods; the exchange rates permit them to compare the price of Chevrolets with the prices of Toyotas and of Fiats. Similarly, producers in each country use the exchange rate to determine whether they have a competitive advantage in foreign markets and to judge whether their production costs are below those of firms producing similar goods abroad.

If imports of goods, services, and securities exceed exports of goods, services, and securities during any time period, the country has a deficit in its payments balance that must be financed by selling assets or borrowing abroad. Under a floating exchange-rate regime, the exchange rate would change to restore equilibrium; under a fixed- (or pegged-) rate regime, the equilibrium is restored by changes in national price or income levels.

The terms on which national currencies trade with each other determine the significance of the segmentation of the world into separate currency areas. If the exchange rates were fixed and known with certainty, then the differences among national monies would be a trivial matter (except for differences in political risk, which involves the application of exchange controls to international payments), of little more significance than the difference between \$50 bills and \$100 bills, or between the notes issued by the Federal Reserve Bank of San Francisco and the Federal Reserve Bank of New York. Individuals and investors would be indifferent about the currency mix of their assets and liabilities. Changes in the consumer price level in one country would fully correspond to the changes in similar price levels in other countries. National money supplies would be readily summed into a world money supply.

If exchange rates moved freely, and at the same time, the exchange rates for all future dates were known with certainty, individuals and investors would still be indifferent about the currency mix of their assets and liabilities. In this world, the differences in interest rates on similar assets denominated in different currencies would fully reflect anticipated changes in exchange rates. These differences in interest rates would compensate investors for forthcoming changes in exchange rates.

The assumption of the perfect substitutability between assets denominated in different currencies is too extreme. Substantial uncertainty about future exchange rates characterizes the foreign-exchange market. Even if countries pledge to maintain fixed or pegged exchange rates (for instance, when £1 was equal to \$2.80 in the 1950s and 1960s), the parities could still be altered. Because of the uncertainty about future exchange rates, traders and investors are concerned with the currencies in which they denominate their assets and liabilities. The ease with which traders and investors can alter their holdings of assets and liabilities denominated in different currencies complicates the management of national monetary policies, and has an impact on both the supply of domestic money and the demand for domestic money. Hence the critical question is the significance of the factors that segment the dollar currency area from the currency areas for the mark, the yen, and other national currencies.

THE MARKET FOR FOREIGN EXCHANGE

Although each of the financial centers in the major countries is sometimes said to have its own foreign-exchange market, the markets for foreign exchange in London, New York, Frankfurt, and Tokyo are geographic components of one, worldwide market. The banks in each financial center are linked by telephone and telex to each other and to the major banks in other centers. The units traded are demand deposits; the basic unit in dollar-sterling trading is a sterling deposit of £100,000 while the basic unit in dollar-mark trading is DM200,000. At any moment, the prices or exchange rates for one currency in terms of another are virtually the same in every center, with the differences in prices quoted for comparable large transactions significantly smaller than one-tenth of one percent, and frequently no more than several one-hundredths of one percent.

The foreign-exchange market is the largest market in the world in terms of the volume of transactions; on some days, the volume of trading may reach $150 billion. The volume of foreign-exchange trading is many times larger than the volume of international trade and investment; individuals and firms involved in international trade and investment participate in less than 10 percent of the foreign-exchange transactions. Most transactions involve banks.

The foreign-exchange market is extremely competitive; there are many participants, none of whom is large relative to the market. Prices—exchange rates—change continuously, and the change can be as small as one one-hundredth of one percent. The major international commercial banks act as both dealers and brokers. In their dealer role, banks maintain a net long or short position in a currency, and seek to profit from changes in the exchange rate. (A long position means their holdings of assets denominated in one currency exceeds their liabilities denominated in this same currency.) In their broker function, banks obtain buy and sell orders from commercial customers, such as the multinational oil companies, both to profit from the spread between the rates at which they buy foreign exchange from some customers and the rates at which they sell foreign exchange to other customers, and to sell other types of banking services to these customers. If a U.S. firm wishes to buy $150 million of marks to make a payment in Frankfurt, the bank that offers marks at the lowest price is most likely to get the business; almost immediately, the bank will seek to buy an equivalent amount of marks to minimize its risk of loss from any subsequent appreciation of the mark.

In their transactions with their customers, banks quote both the price at which they will buy and the price at which they will sell, usually in the form of 1.8380–90 marks per dollar, for a standard volume; the small price difference reimburses the banks for their costs incurred in their foreign-exchange transactions. If an investor or trader wants to buy dollars, the bank will buy marks at the rate of 1.8390. If the investor or traders wants to buy marks, the bank will buy dollars at the rate of 1.8380. The bid-ask spread of one hundred marks, or about $60 on a purchase of DM200,000, is six one-hundredths of one percent of the dollar value of the transactions. The size of the bid-ask spread differs by currency and by the bank providing the quotation. The major international banks quote smaller bid-ask spreads than those in provincial centers, where the competition may be less extensive. The rates quoted also indicate whether the bank wants to increase or reduce its position in a currency; if a bank owns more marks than it thinks optimal, it will set its quotes low enough to discourage sellers of marks and encourage buyers of marks.

Foreign-exchange brokers are used in some centers to bring buyers and sellers together in an anonymous fashion; the brokers relay the exchange rates quoted by particular banks to various customers. Most commercial customers do not use brokers; instead they may "shop" the banks for the most attractive rate quotations. Commercial banks frequently deal with each other through brokers, and central banks deal with commercial banks through brokers.

Organization of the Foreign-Exchange Market

The pattern of the organization of the foreign-exchange market follows the pattern of trade financing. More international trade transactions are denominated or invoiced in the U.S. dollar than in any other currency. Thus, in U.S.–Canadian trade, Canadian exporters to the United States quote a price in U.S. dollars and receive payment in U.S. dollars. Similarly, Canadian importers agree to pay U.S. dollars for their purchases of U.S. goods. The Canadian importers and exporters prefer to undertake their foreign-exchange transactions close to home—in Canada rather than the United States—so relatively more U.S.–Canadian dollar transactions occur in Toronto than in New York. Both for convenience and to reduce indirect transaction costs, importers and exporters with the need to undertake foreign-exchange transactions prefer to deal with banks closer to their home offices rather than with banks in distant foreign centers. Because the volume of foreign-exchange transactions in each currency pair is so much larger in the centers outside the United States, the markets may be modestly more competitive and the rates quoted by banks to commercial customers somewhat more favorable than the rates quoted in the United States. Hence, the paradox is that because such a large volume of international trade and financial transactions is denominated in the U.S. dollar, most foreign-exchange transactions involving the U.S. dollar occur outside the United States.[1]

The principal center for mark-dollar transactions is Frankfurt; New York is the secondary center. Similarly, Tokyo is the principal center for yen-dollar transactions and London for sterling-dollar transactions. Banks in each center specialize in trading the domestic currency against the U.S. dollar. New York is a secondary center in all foreign currencies. Table 27.1 shows the distribution of banks and foreign-exchange traders among centers. Paris is a tertiary center for trading in the dollar relative to all currencies other than the French franc, while Zurich is a tertiary center for trading in the dollar relative to the mark, sterling, and the French franc.

Within most of the major financial centers—London, Frankfurt, New York—a large number of banks participate actively in the foreign-exchange market. A few banks are dealers in the currencies in which they specialize; these banks hold large inventories of foreign exchange. When banks are not

[1]Paradoxically, prior to World War I much more of U.S. trade was denominated in foreign currencies, so relatively more of the foreign-exchange transactions associated with U.S. trade occurred in New York.

Table 27.1 Distribution of Banks and Traders in Foreign Exchange

North America	Number of banks with foreign-exchange department	Number of traders
New York	96	667
Toronto	12	88
Chicago	14	84
San Francisco	8	52
Los Angeles	8	38
Western Europe		
London	227	1645
Luxembourg	68	356
Paris	64	378
Zurich	30	199
Frankfurt	47	300
Milan	35	212
Brussels	29	186
Asia and Middle East		
Tokyo	27	150
Singapore	49	234
Hong Kong	54	246
Bahrain	26	106

Source: *Foreign Exchange and Bullion Dealers Directory,* 1983, Hambros Bank, London.

dealers, they participate as brokers, buying and selling foreign currencies on the basis of exchange-rate quotations from dealers.

Once the rates for two currencies such as the mark and the yen are known in terms of the dollar, the price of the mark in terms of the yen, or the cross-rate, can be inferred. For example, on 31 December 1982 the yen-dollar rate was 234.70 per dollar, and the mark-dollar rate was 2.3755 marks per dollar, so the cross-rate was 101.21 yen per mark.

One consequence of the organization of the market along the lines of a series of currency pairs, each involving the U.S. dollar, is that the financial counterpart of many international trade transactions involves two foreign-exchange transactions. Assume, for example, that a German distributor of automobile parts buys Japanese-produced components. The banks in Frankfurt quote a yen-mark rate based on their rates for the dollar in terms of both the mark and the yen. The banks in Frankfurt are not likely to hold a significant amount of yen, so the bank supplying the yen to the Frankfurt importer undertakes two transactions: marks are used to buy dollars and dollars are then used to buy yen. Since the yen-dollar market is primarily in Tokyo, the bank may act as a dealer in the first transaction and as a broker in the second.

Trading in foreign exchange occurs on almost a continuous time basis, since the markets in various cities are located in different time zones. The Tokyo market closes for the day before the market in London opens.

THE RELATION BETWEEN THE SPOT-EXCHANGE AND THE FORWARD-EXCHANGE RATES

Traders and investors who desire to alter the currency mix of their assets or liabilities can readily do so by *leading and lagging;* they increase their loans denominated in the dollar and reduce their loans denominated in another currency, say, the mark. Alternatively, they can increase their holdings of assets denominated in the mark and reduce their holdings of assets denominated in the dollar.

Foreign-exchange transactions are either **spot transactions,** which *involve an exchange of deposits two days after the date of the contract,* or **forward transactions,** which *involve an exchange of deposits at specified future dates.* Most foreign-exchange transactions are either forward transactions, or swaps—an exchange of deposits over two days against deposits at a specified future date. Traders and investors frequently prefer forward exchange contracts because they do not "tie up" scarce working capital.

Forward contracts are generally available on maturities up to a year or longer in the major currencies. Some maturities are standardized—three months, six months, and one year—reflecting the standardization of terms of payment on commercial-trade transactions. Banks also offer maturities to match traders' needs; the banks can readily supply a thirty-nine-day forward contract or a seventy-eight-day forward contract. (Forward contracts in foreign exchange which are bought and sold by the major banks should be distinguished from currency futures contracts, which are traded on financial exchanges in Chicago and in London; these futures contracts have standardized maturities and amounts.) Transactions costs associated with forward-exchange contracts are modestly higher than those on spot-exchange contracts. Moreover, these costs are higher on distant forward maturities than on near forward maturities and higher on the more volatile currencies than on the less volatile currencies. The spot-exchange rates and forward-exchange rates for major currencies relative to the dollar are shown in Table 27.2.

If a currency is less expensive in the forward market than in the spot market, the currency is at a forward discount. And if the currency is more expensive in the forward market, then the currency is at a forward premium.

The banks act as intermediaries between buyers and sellers in the forward-exchange market, just as they do in the spot-exchange market. A bank may combine a long spot position with a short forward position in a particular currency to limit its exposure in the currency; if the currency appreciates, the value of the spot position increases and so, however, does the value of the short forward position. Or it may have a long position in some forward maturities and a short position in others.

One of the basic propositions in international finance is that the difference between forward- and spot-exchange rates, when expressed in percentage terms, equals the difference between domestic and foreign interest rates for assets with the same maturity as that on the forward contract. This relationship, known as the Interest Rate Parity Theorem, results from the profit-maximizing behavior of individual investors. Those same investors who seek to profit from anticipated changes in exchange rates continually com-

Table 27.2 Foreign-Exchange Rates

Closing market rates on 31 December 1982
(Foreign currency units per U.S. dollar)

	Spot rate	Forward rates			
		1 Month	3 Months	6 Months	12 Months
Canadian dollar	1.2316	1.2323	1.2336	1.2361	1.2386
British pound[a]	1.6145	1.6132	1.6107	1.6086	1.6065
Belgian franc	46.85	47.10	47.35	47.75	48.15
French franc	6.7300	6.8100	6.9800	7.1600	7.3300
German mark	2.3755	2.3681	2.3550	2.3550	2.2940
Italian lira	1368.00	1390.00	1424.00	1472.00	1543.00
Dutch guilder	2.6250	2.6150	2.5952	2.5710	2.5175
Swiss franc	2.0020	1.9905	1.9722	1.9445	1.8820
Japanese yen	234.70	234.05	233.25	231.65	228.70

a. U.S. dollars per British pound.

Source: Harris Trust and Savings Bank, *Weekly Review: International Money Markets and Foreign Exchange Rates* (Chicago: Harris Bank, 31 December 1982).

pare whether it will be more profitable to alter their position in foreign exchange by spot transactions or by forward transactions. They prefer the forward market if the currency is cheaper there than in the spot-exchange market. Other investors take advantage of profit opportunities by buying a currency in the financial center in which it is cheap and selling the same currency in the center in which it is expensive, after adjustment for any difference between the spot- and forward-exchange rates and the interest-rate differential. The first group are called *speculators;* by definition *they seek to profit from anticipated changes in exchange rates*. The second group are known as *arbitragers; they seek to profit from deviations between the interest-rate differential and the interest equivalent of the spread between the forward- and spot-exchange rates*. Arbitragers avoid exchange risk.

Assume a U.S. firm has agreed to pay 10 million marks to buy some machinery in Germany. The actual payment will be made in three months. The U.S. firm might buy marks in the spot market and invest the mark funds in Frankfurt either in the money market or in a bank deposit, at the prevailing interest rate. At the maturity of the investment the importer will pay the German seller of the machinery. If the importer can invest funds in Frankfurt at 8 percent, the importer would buy 9,804,000 marks to be invested at 8 percent for ninety days to yield 10 million marks. If the spot exchange rate is 2 marks per dollar the investor would need $4,902,000 to acquire the 9,804,000 marks. The cost of this transaction is the interest rate of 10 percent that the importer might earn on a comparable dollar investment for ninety days.

Alternatively, the importer might buy the mark forward, and pay for the forward marks with the proceeds of the ninety-day dollar investment. If the mark is at a forward premium of 2 percent, the importer would pay $5,025,000 for ten million marks. An investment of $4,902,000 for ninety days at a 10 percent annual rate would yield $5,025,000. So the cost to the importer of buying the mark in the spot market and buying the mark in the forward market are the same, if the forward premium on the mark is equal to the difference between the interest rate on dollar assets and the interest rate on mark assets.

In the real world, one form of payment may be slightly less expensive than the other, and the importer will normally prefer this form of payment. Some U.S. importers may decide to acquire marks immediately prior to the date when payment is due; in the interval between the dates when they enter into commitments to pay foreign exchange and the dates when they buy the foreign exchange they have a foreign exchange exposure.

For both groups of importers, the financing pattern depends on the relationship between the spot- and forward-exchange rates, the interest rate on mark assets, and the interest rate on comparable dollar assets. The equivalent relationship between the money-market interest-rate differential and the difference between the spot- and forward-exchange rates is known as the Interest-Rate-Parity Theorem. The formal expression is

$$a\frac{(F-S)}{S}=\frac{1+r_d}{1+r_f}$$

where a is the factor to convert the percentage difference in the two exchange rates to an annualized rate of return (a is 4 if the forward-rate quotation is on a three-month contract), F the forward-exchange rate, S the spot-exchange rate, r_d the domestic interest rate, and r_f the foreign interest rate.

Empirical studies indicate that the differences between the forward-exchange rates inferred from the interest-rate differential and the observed forward rates are most always less than one percent, and frequently only several tenths of one percent. That there is any measurable deviation from interest-rate parity reflects either that investors encounter costs and incur risks in undertaking transactions to take advantage of the "apparent" riskless arbitrage profit opportunity, or that the securities available in the several centers are not perfect substitutes for each other.

Traders and investors prefer forward transactions to leading and lagging as a way to alter their exposure because of the greater convenience. But traders and investors lead and lag if the costs of acquiring foreign exchange in the forward market exceed the costs in the spot market—the forward discount is significantly larger than the discount "predicted" by the interest-rate differential.

FORWARD-EXCHANGE RATES AS FORECASTS OF FUTURE SPOT-EXCHANGE RATES

One empirical question involves the relationship between the values of the forward-exchange rates and the values for the spot-exchange rates on the dates when these forward contracts mature. The key question is whether investors who buy and sell forward-exchange contracts demand a risk premium; if this premium seems appropriately related to the risk, there would be a systematic difference between the forward rates and the spot-exchange rates on the maturity of forward contracts. Each forward contract is not likely to "predict" accurately the spot-exchange rate on the dates when the forward contracts mature, because of the large number of unforeseen disturbances or shocks between the dates when traders and investors buy forward contracts and the dates when these same contracts mature. Those who argue that the forward-exchange rates are likely to be biased predictors of future spot-exchange rates—that is, that investors demand a risk premium for buying foreign exchange in the forward market—rely on the analogy of payment for risk-bearing in other markets. They assert that if investors are risk averse, then the *average* of the exchange rates on a set of forward mark contracts would be below the *average* of the spot-exchange rates on the dates when these forward contracts mature, so that the sellers of forward marks would incur—on average—a loss. If these investors sought to avoid this loss by leading and lagging they might fail, for the difference between the interest rates on mark assets and the interest rates on dollar assets of comparable maturities would be large—on average—relative to changes in the exchange rate during the period when the assets denominated in the several currencies mature.

The response to this argument is that while some traders and investors are sellers of forward marks, others are buyers of forward marks. If the first group pays a risk premium, then the second group, who are also hedging their foreign-exchange positions, would receive a profit, which is the mirror of the cost incurred by the sellers. Few empirical studies support the idea that there is a significant risk premium; either the marginal investors are not risk averse or the willingness of each group of importers to pay a risk premium has proven to be more or less offsetting.

Uncertainty about future exchange rates can deter international trade and investment, even though traders and investors can hedge any commitments through forward contracts or through leading and lagging, and at no apparent cost. The explanation for this paradox is that the cost (or profit) from hedging the foreign-exchange exposures will be known only at the conclusion of their investments—when the forward contracts mature, and the rates on these contracts can then be compared with the spot rates. The impact of uncertainty in deterring trade and investment is an empirical issue on which there is modest evidence.

THE LEVEL OF THE EXCHANGE RATE

The foreign-exchange market is one component of the international money market, which also includes the various national markets in bank deposits and money-market assets, such as Treasury bills, bankers' acceptances, and commercial paper. The unique aspect of the foreign-exchange market is that neither of the assets traded in a particular transaction, domestic demand deposits and foreign demand deposits, is unique to that market in the sense that gold is unique to the gold market and wheat to the wheat market. Instead, the demand deposits denominated in different currencies are acquired and held to facilitate payments. Thus, U.S. traders and investors buy marks so they can then acquire commodities or securities available in Germany.

Since all foreign-exchange transactions are intermediate to some other economic transaction, the basic question is how the exchange rate is deter-

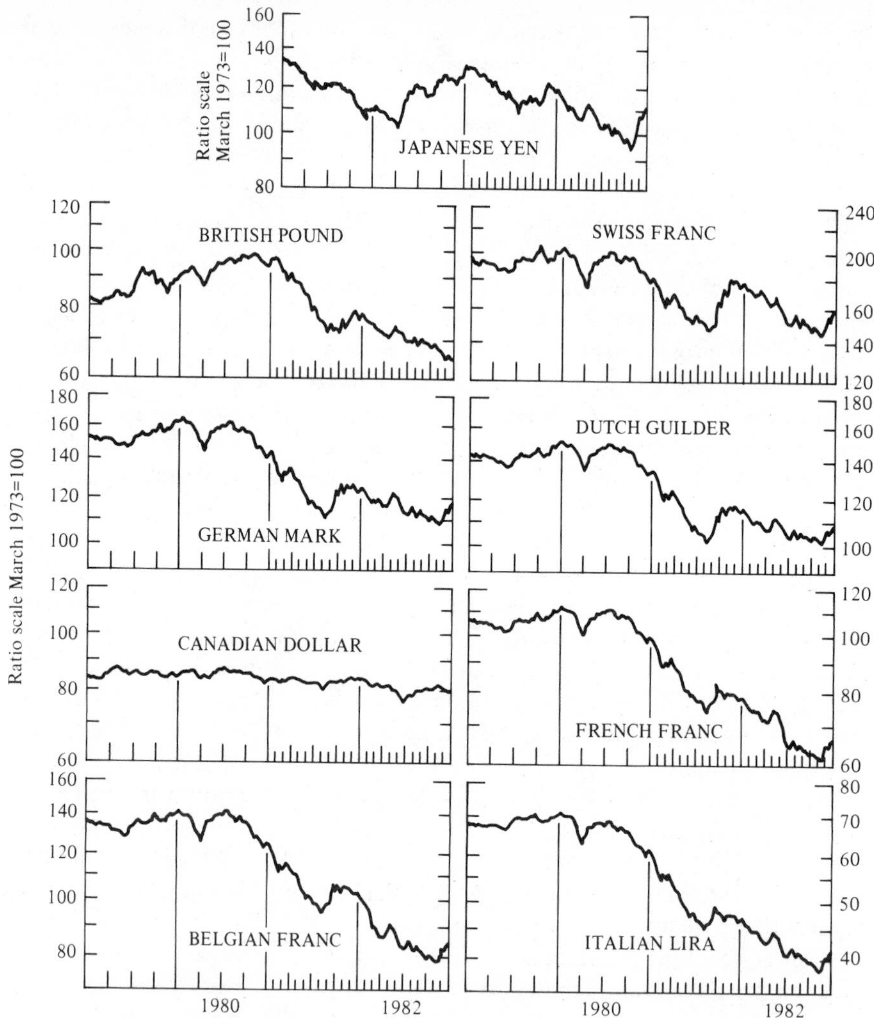

Figure 27.1 Spot-Exchange Rates
Dollar Prices of Foreign Currencies—Averages for Week Ending Wednesday

Source: Board of Governors of the Federal Reserve System, *Selected Interest & Exchange Rates: Weekly Series of Charts* (Washington, January 1983).

mined and why exchange rates vary so extensively within a year or a few months, as evident in Figure 27.1. One response is that the exchange rate is the price of national monies that causes the prices of similar goods available in the several national markets to be more or less equal. The story is that if the prices of similar goods available in the several countries differ significantly at the prevailing exchange rate, traders would buy the goods in the country in which they are cheap and ship them to the country in which they are dear, and profit from the price differential. The prices of these goods would rise in the first country and fall in the second; at the same time, the foreign-exchange value of the first country's currency would increase. Arbitrage in commodities would continue until the difference in the prices of similar goods at the new exchange rate would be no greater than transaction and transportation costs. In this case, then, the exchange rates move to reduce differences in the prices of comparable goods available in different countries.

This relationship between the prices of tradable goods and the exchange rate is the *purchasing-power-parity* (PPP) *theory*. At times the prices of similar goods available in the several countries are compared at the exchange rate in an absolute version of this relationship; usually, however, *changes* in the commodity price levels in the several countries are compared with changes in the exchange rate in the relative version of PPP. The expression is $F\dot{C}/\$ = (\dot{P}_F/P) - (\dot{P}_{US}/P_{US})$ where $F\dot{C}/\$$ is the rate of change of the dollar in terms of foreign currency, $\dot{P}_F/P$ is the rate of change in the foreign price level, and $\dot{P}_{US}/P_{US}$ *is the rate of change in the U.S. price level.*

During the 1970s, as in the 1920s, changes in the exchange rates in a month or a quarter or a year were 15 to 25 percent greater than the contemporary change in relative national price levels. Thus, during the summer of 1976, sterling became greatly undervalued when it appeared that the British government would not be able to limit increases in wage rates and price levels. In six months, the sterling price of the dollar increased by nearly 25 percent (or at an annual rate of 50 percent). Sterling goods became greatly undervalued; Parisians flew to London for Saturday shopping. Then sterling subsequently appreciated, so that by the end of 1977, exchange rates were back to the early 1976 levels. Similarly in 1977 and the first ten months of 1978, the dollar became substantially undervalued; after a dramatic change in the Fed's monetary policy in October 1978, as was discussed in Chapter 24, the dollar appreciated. Yet for an extended period, U.S. goods remained undervalued. Then with the sharp increase in U.S. interest rates following the change in the operating procedures of the Federal Reserve in late 1979, interest rates on dollar assets rose to peak values, and the dollar appreciated sharply in the foreign exchange market. The statement, then, that the exchange rate moves to reflect changes in national price levels is not consistent with much recent data.

Transactions in commodities provide one of the reasons firms and investors participate in the foreign-exchange market. The demand and supply of foreign exchange also are affected by investment or security transactions, as funds are moved between currencies to profit from the differences in interest rates on comparable assets denominated in different currencies, or from anticipated changes in exchange rates. From the investors' point of view, the spot-exchange rate is "just right" when, given the interest rates on domestic securities and the anticipated rate of change of the exchange rate, the interest rates on foreign securities are at levels such that no significant profit can be made from buying or selling them.

Thus $r_d = r_w + (\dot{E}/E)^*$, where r_d is the interest rate on domestic financial assets, r_w the interest rate on comparable foreign financial assets of the same maturity, $(\dot{E}/E)^*$ the anticipated rate of change of the exchange rate during the interval until the maturity of the two securities. This statement is the *Fisher Proposition*.[2] As new information about possible changes in government policy becomes available and investors alter their demand for assets denominated in the several currencies, the spot-exchange rate changes. If the new information about the trade accounts, inflation rates, national monetary policies, or election campaigns leads investors to conclude that the mark-denominated assets will prove a less attractive investment than dollar-denominated investments, they will sell mark assets and buy dollar assets, and the mark will depreciate. The mark will continue to depreciate until the return on the mark assets adjusted for the anticipated change in the exchange rate equals the return on dollar assets.

The anticipated rate of change of the exchange rate, $(\dot{E}/E)^*$, depends both on investors' estimates of where the spot-exchange rate will be at various future dates, and the current spot-exchange rate. In equilibrium, the anticipated rate of change of the exchange rate must equal the money-market interest differential. If investors believe there is a disequilibrium—that $r_d \neq r_w + (\dot{E}/E)^*$—then in the move to equilibrium, the adjustment may occur in the current spot-exchange rate, the anticipated spot-exchange rate, or either of the two money-market interest rates. But the adjustment is not likely to occur in the anticipated spot-exchange rate, since this rate is set to be consistent with the domestic and foreign price levels expected to prevail. Some adjustments may occur in the two interest rates as investors shift funds from one money market to another; however, the volume of funds shifted may be small relative to the size of the two money markets. Consequently, much of the adjustment must occur in the current spot-exchange rate, with the consequence that the changes in the current spot-exchange rate may be much greater than the changes that would be inferred from the contemporary changes in the several national price levels.

Analyzing Exchange-Rate Disturbances

Two different types of disturbances that affect the foreign-exchange market—nonmonetary and monetary—should be distinguished. Assume investors believe that the mark will depreciate in value at a time when interest rates on mark assets and dollar assets remain the same because the German and U.S. monetary policies are unchanged; increased "bearishness" does not lead to any increase in interest rates on mark assets. In this case, the value for the mark in the spot-exchange market will move to the level of the anticipated spot-exchange rate, perhaps abruptly.

Alternatively, assume that the Bundesbank follows a more contractive monetary policy, and interest rates on mark assets increase. At the same time, the anticipated spot-exchange rate is unchanged, perhaps because

[2]The relationship between the money-market-interest differential and the anticipated spot-exchange rates is identified as the Fisher Proposition, or Fisher Open, after Irving Fisher. Analysts frequently confuse the Interest-Rate-Parity Theorem with Fisher Open: the former involves the efficiency of arbitrage in circumstances in which all values are known, while the latter involves investment decisions in an uncertain environment.

investors believe that the move to a more contractive monetary policy will be reversed. Then investors would acquire mark-denominated assets because of the higher interest rate, and the mark would appreciate. As long as interest rates on mark assets are higher than those on dollar assets, the only factor that can equalize the return to investors from holding dollar assets and mark assets is the subsequent depreciation of the mark. The paradox is that in response to the increase in interest rates on mark assets, there is a sudden unanticipated appreciation of the mark, so the mark may then subsequently depreciate, with the anticipated rate of depreciation equal to the excess of interest rates on mark assets over those on dollar assets.

Price movements in other financial markets, in the stock and the bonds market and in the wheat, soybeans, and gold markets, also are large, and comparable to those in the foreign-exchange market. At any moment, the spot prices in these markets in equilibrium are the discounted values of anticipated future prices. In the foreign-exchange market, the discount factor is the difference between the money-market interest rates on similar securities denominated in different currencies. For example, if interest rates on dollar Treasury bills are 10 percent and interest rates on mark Treasury bills are 8 percent, the discount rate is 2 percent a year. If the anticipated values are unchanged, then during each week and each month the mark price of the dollar should increase at the rate of 2 percent a year, or 0.166 percent a month, 0.038 percent a week, or 0.0055 percent a day. Even a weak currency—one that might depreciate at a rate of 20 percent a year—would depreciate at an average daily rate of 0.0624 percent or by much less than the observed daily changes in foreign currency rates. But this cannot be the whole story. That the changes in exchange rates on a daily and weekly basis are many times larger than these values, means that they reflect sharp movements in anticipated exchange rates.

Many factors affect anticipations of future exchange rates, including investor estimates of inflation rates or money-supply growth rates. Thus traders and investors may extrapolate recent changes in domestic and foreign price levels to obtain estimates of future national price levels, which serve as a basis for their anticipations of exchange rates. Moreover, changes in money-supply growth rates may be used to generate estimates of the national price levels, which in turn lead to estimates of the future exchange rates.

Some analysts believe that the mark appreciates when U.S. monetary policy becomes more expansive or German monetary policy becomes more contractive. When the interest-rate differential changes, the exchange rate may change sharply. If investors focus on spot-exchange rates anticipated in several years, then the change in exchange rates may be substantially larger, in percentage terms, than the change in the interest-rate differential. For example, assume U.S. monetary policy becomes more expansive and interest rates on dollar assets fall by one percentage point. If investors expect U.S. interest rates to remain at this level for two years, then the dollar might depreciate by two percent in the spot-exchange market to equalize the anticipated returns on short-term mark and dollar investments.

CENTRAL BANK INTERVENTION IN THE FOREIGN-EXCHANGE MARKET

For most of the last one hundred years the currencies of the major countries have been pegged to each other, initially because each currency had a mint parity that was the price of a standard unit of gold. After World War II, many foreign countries expressed the parities for their currencies in terms of the U.S. dollar. Under a pegged-rate arrangement, each central bank commits itself to limit the range of movement in the price of its currency around its parity. These limits were narrow under the gold standard, usually set by the costs of gold shipments. In the post-World War II period, these limits were set by central banks, usually about 1 percent either side of parity or less. Within these limits, currencies were free to float, although many monetary authorities intervened within these limits to smooth the hour-to-hour, day-to-day exchange-rate movement.

Intervention involved purchases or sales of demand deposits denominated in the national money against a foreign money, most frequently the U.S. dollar. A central bank was obliged to prevent its currency from depreciating below its lower support limit, or appreciating above its upper support limit. The central bank would buy its own currency from commercial banks operating in the exchange market and sell them dollars. These transactions were effectively an open-market sale using dollar demand deposits rather than domestic bonds. Such transactions reduced the central bank's domestic liabilities in the hands of the public.

The ability of a foreign central bank to prevent its currency from depreciating depended upon its holdings of dollars, together with dollars that might be obtained by borrowing. Even if a national monetary authority had the foreign exchange necessary for intervention, its need to support its currency in the exchange market might be inconsistent with its efforts to undertake a more expansive monetary policy to achieve its domestic economic objectives.

Similarly, if a country's currency was strong, its central bank was obliged to sell more of its currency to limit its appreciation in the exchange market. In effect, this central bank undertook an open-market purchase of dollars, with the purchase of dollars financed by the expansion of its own monetary liabilities. Such open-market purchases might confound its desire to limit the expansion of its monetary liabilities, perhaps because of its concern about the domestic inflationary implications. Thus Germany, with a strong currency in the 1960s and early 1970s, faced the choice between maintaining the established exchange parity for the mark with the consequence of a more rapid than desired increase in the German money supply or limiting the growth in the reserves of the banking system in Germany at the cost of either revaluing the mark periodically or permitting the mark to float. While the German central bank might have undertaken open-market sales of mark-denominated securities to counter or neutralize its open-market purchases of dollar securities, such transactions were not costless, for they raised interest rates on German securities more than was deemed desirable for domestic objectives. Moreover as German interest rates went up, investors would

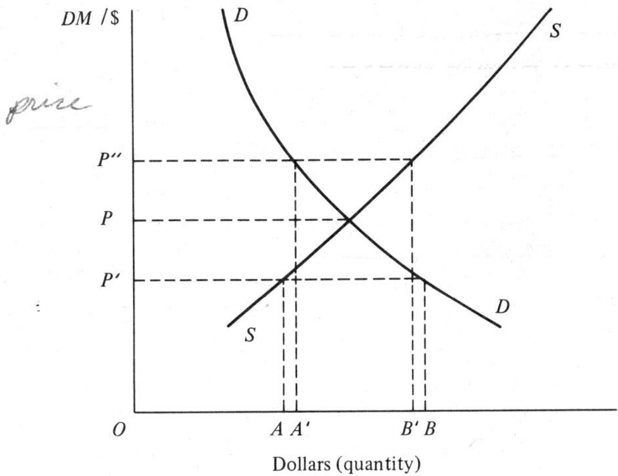

Figure 27.2 The Market For Foreign Exchange

have shifted out of dollar-denominated securities into mark-denominated securities, intensifying the problem for the Bundesbank.

Thus the Bundesbank's transactions in the foreign-exchange market are shown in Figure 27.2. The price of the dollar in terms of marks is measured on the vertical axis, the volume of dollars demanded and supplied is measured on the horizontal axis. The demand of traders and investors for dollars is shown as *DD;* as the mark price of the dollar increases, the amount of dollars demanded declines. The supply of dollars by graders and investors is shown as *SS;* as the mark price of the dollar increases, the amount of dollars supplied increases. At *OP* the demand and supply of dollars are equal; *OP* is the rate that clears the exchange market without official intervention. If the Bundesbank had pegged the mark at *OP*′, the demand for dollars would have exceeded the supply. Each period the Bundesbank would have sold dollars equal to *AB* and Germany would have had a payments deficit. If instead, the Bundesbank had pegged the mark at *OP*″, the Bundesbank would have bought dollars equal to *A*′*B*′, and Germany would have had a payments surplus.

The maintenance of the exchange parity appeared to conflict with the achievement of domestic economic objectives. No such conflict was supposed to occur with floating exchange-rate systems, since the exchange rates would change to neutralize any tendency to a payments surplus or deficit. Hence monetary policy could be directed solely to attainment of domestic objectives; changes in the exchange rate would continuously insure that payments and receipts would be equal. Hence central banks would not have to undertake open-market operations in foreign exchange that might offset either partially or fully their open-market operations in domestic securities. However, in practice under the floating exchange-rate system market forces sometimes caused the exchange rate to deviate from the level deemed appropriate for domestic objectives and so central banks again felt the need to intervene in the exchange market even at the cost of complicating attainment of their domestic objectives.

The paradox is that central bank intervention in the foreign-exchange market has been much more extensive in the floating exchange rate period, at least as judged by changes in their holdings of international reserve assets. Some central banks have intervened to limit or smooth the day-to-day, week-to-week, and month-to-month variability in their exchange rate. Some have intervened because they wanted to add to their holding of international reserve assets; in a few countries the growth in the holdings of international reserve assets provides the basis for the growth in their domestic money supplies. Some have intervened because changes in the exchange rates complicated the attainment of their domestic economic objectives.

THE SEGMENTATION OF NATIONAL MONEY MARKETS

One of the key policy issues in international finance, known as the optimum currency-area issue, involves whether there are any economic gains from maintaining independent national central banks, each with its own currency. Does the Bank of Canada have the capacity to cause interest rates in Canada to change and deviate significantly from U.S. interest rates? If the Bank of Canada attempts to follow a more expansive monetary policy, and buys bonds denominated in the Canadian dollar, is it possible that the sellers of Canadian bonds will buy U.S. bonds, so that the interest rates on Canadian bonds would remain virtually unchanged? If Canada is following a pegged exchange rate, is it possible for interest rates in Canada to differ significantly from U.S. interest rates? And if Canada is on a floating rate system, can changes in Canadian monetary policy affect any real variables, such as the level of employment, or will the impacts of these changes be limited to altering nominal values such as the Canadian price level and the exchange rate?

The scope for national monetary independence depends on how fully investors believe that assets that are alike in all attributes except for currency of denomination are close, near, or good substitutes for each other. Transactions costs might deter investors from shifting funds among assets denominated in different currencies; similarly, exchange controls might deter these shifts. Such shifts might also be deterred by exchange risk in the form of uncertainty about future exchange rates, or political risk in the form of uncertainty about future changes in exchange controls. Investors are likely to shift funds to profit from differences in interest rates only if they are compensated for these costs and for the associated risks. At most, the differential in interest rates on similar assets denominated in different currencies adjusted for any anticipated changes in exchange rates cannot exceed the sum of these costs and the payments demanded by investors for incurring the risks associated with the movements of funds across the borders between currency areas.

Transactions costs are small or even trivial, especially for the large international firms; transactions costs are smaller still for the major international banks. Transactions costs have two components—one involves those external to the firm, the actual costs incurred in buying and selling foreign exchange, and the second involves those internal to the firm and incurred in managing their foreign exchange or international monetary investments.

Transactions costs to the commercial customers are measured by the bid-ask spread—the difference between the prices at which traders and investors could buy and sell a relatively large amount—$3 to $5 million—of a particular currency at any moment. The costs encountered by commercial customers in using the foreign-exchange market are substantially smaller than those they would incur with transactions of equivalent value in most other markets—the government securities market or the stock market. Depending on the currency, the time, and the maturity of the forward contracts, the cost of a foreign-exchange transaction of $1 million would be $100 to $500, or from one one-hundredth of one percent to one-twentieth of one percent. Transactions costs are smaller, the less volatile the currency; thus, bid-ask spreads in the Canadian dollar have generally been lower than the bid-ask spread in sterling, the German mark and other European currencies, and the Japanese yen. Transactions costs on forward contracts with relatively distant forward maturities—those longer than six months—are larger than those on shorter maturities; transactions costs on the spot transactions are below those on forward transactions. That transactions costs are so small reflects the technical efficiency of payments, the virtually riskless character of the transactions, and the large size of the transactions.

Transactions costs on interbank transactions in the foreign-exchange market are smaller than those on the transactions between banks and customers—less risk is associated with interbank transactions. The lower level of transactions costs encountered by banks than by their commercial customers means that the banks have an advantage in responding to any potential profit opportunities.

Measuring the payments demanded by investors for carrying exchange risk and political risk is more difficult. One issue is whether firms are risk-averse, and require payments for bearing these risks. It is sometimes argued that firms are (or should be) risk-neutral and seek to maximize profits; if so, they would require no special payments for carrying these risks. Even if firms are risk-averse, the cost they would incur in hedging their exposure to this risk is trivial in the long run (because forward rates are on average unbiased "predictors" of future spot rates) if not in the short run. Yet firms may nevertheless be deterred from movement of funds internationally by the uncertainty about this cost.

National financial markets appear segmented to a greater extent than can be readily explained by transactions costs, exchange risk, or political risk. Segmentation provides some opportunity for national monetary independence under pegged exchange rates. If over time, traders and investors become more knowledgeable about the returns and the risks and costs from altering the curency mix of their assets and liabilities, so that the segmentation of national money markets declines, changes in monetary policies will be less effective in altering real variables.

THE BALANCE-OF-PAYMENTS ACCOUNTS

The data on international transactions of a country are presented in its balance-of-payments accounts, a record of payments and receipts, organized by major type of transactions, between residents and nonresidents during a particular period such as a quarter or a year. Table 27.3 summarizes U.S. international transactions for 1979, 1980, and 1981.

The approach used in developing such accounts is based on the system of double-entry bookkeeping. All transactions represent exchanges of equal value, and so for every import of a good, service, or security there must be a corresponding export of a good, service, or security—so the balance-of-payments accounts must necessarily balance. When U.S. residents import Scotch whiskey, they export dollars, usually in the form of demand deposits, in payment. The U.S. accounts then show an increase in U.S. exports of demand deposits and in U.S. imports of whiskey. The British payments accounts, in contrast, show an increase in the export of the Scotch whiskey and an increase in the import of U.S. security (demand deposits).

The data for the entries in the balance-of-payments accounts are obtained in various ways. Data on commodity imports and exports are obtained from U.S. tariff collection authorities. Data on tourist expenditures are estimated by sampling travelers. Data on exports of securities are obtained from reports filed by banks and brokerage firms. Because the sum of all recorded receipts and the sum of all recorded payments in a time period are unlikely to be equal, a statistical discrepancy results, which is line 34. The value for this entry is the residual between recorded payments and recorded receipts (the

difference between receipts and payments is added to the smaller figure so that the two are set equal to each other).

The millions of international transactions are summed into three major categories or groups. The trade balance (line 2) is the difference between the values of commodity exports and commodity imports, usually with imports valued at their landed price, so the value of imports exceeds that reported by the exporting countries by the amount of cargo insurance and freight (CIF) costs. A country has a trade surplus if the value of its commodity exports exceeds the value of its commodity imports. The current-account balance (line 1) includes all transactions in commodities, together with all transactions in services such as transportation, tourism, royalties and license fees, film rentals, investment income, and private remittances such as Social Security payments, and various gifts, such as religious charity, UNICEF, and foreign aid. The characteristic of all international transactions not included in the current-account balance is that they involve transactions in assets or securities with non-residents ranging from equities and direct investment to non-interest-bearing demand deposits; transactions in monetary gold, government securities, and bonds are included in the capital-account balance. Lines 10 through 33 summarize various capital-account transactions.

The most important conceptual relationship in the balance-of-payments accounts is the relationship between the current-account balance and the capital-account balance; all international transactions are included in the calculation of one of these balances and no transaction is included in both. (Although purchases of foreign investments are in the capital-account balance and the dividends and interest on these investments are in the current account, these are separate transactions, even in time.) Because of the double-entry character, a surplus on the current account means a deficit on the

Table 27.3 U.S. International Transactions Summary (millions of dollars[a])

Item credits or debits	1979	1980	1981
1 Balance on current account	−466	1,520	4,471
2 Merchandise trade balance	−27,346	−25,338	−27,889
3 Merchandise exports	184,473	224,237	236,254
4 Merchandise imports	−211,819	−249,575	−264,143
5 Military transactions, net	−2,035	−2,472	−1,541
6 Investment income, net	31,215	29,910	33,037
7 Other service transactions, net	3,262	6,203	7,472
8 Remittances, pensions, and other transfers	−2,011	−2,101	−2,104
9 U.S. government grants (excluding military)	−3,549	−4,681	−4,504
10 Change in U.S. government assets, other than official reserve assets, net (increase, −)	−3,743	−5,126	−5,137
11 Change in U.S. official reserve assets (increase, −)	−1,133	−8,155	−5,175
12 Gold	−65	0	0
13 Special drawing rights (SDRs)	−1,136	−16	−1,823
14 Reserve position in International Monetary Fund	−189	−1,667	−2,491
15 Foreign currencies	257	−6,472	−861
16 Change in U.S. private assets abroad (increase, −)[a]	−59,469	−72,746	−98,982
17 Bank-reported claims	−26,213	−46,838	−84,531
18 Nonbank-reported claims	−3,307	−3,146	−331
19 U.S. purchase of foreign securities, net	−4,726	−3,524	−5,429
20 U.S. direct investment abroad, net	−25,222	−19,238	−8,691
21 Change in foreign official assets in the United States (increase, +)	−13,697	15,442	4,785
22 U.S. Treasury securities	−22,435	9,708	4,983
23 Other U.S. government obligations	463	2,187	1,289
24 Other U.S. government liabilities[b]	−73	561	−69
25 Other U.S. liabilities reported by U.S. banks	7,213	−159	−4,083
26 Other foreign official assets[c]	1,135	3,145	2,665
27 Change in foreign private assets in the United States (increase, +)	52,157	39,042	73,136
28 U.S. bank-reported liabilities	32,607	10,743	41,262
29 U.S. nonbank-reported liabilities	1,362	6,530	532
30 Foreign private purchases of U.S. Treasury securities, net	4,960	2,645	2,932
31 Foreign purchases of other U.S. securities, net	1,351	5,457	7,109
32 Foreign direct investments in the United States, net[a]	11,877	13,666	21,301
33 Allocation of SDRs	1,139	1,152	1,093
34 Statistical discrepancy	25,212	28,870	25,809

a. Includes reinvested earnings of incorporated affiliates.

b. Primarily associated with military sales contracts and other transactions arranged with or through foreign official agencies.

c. Consists of investments in U.S. corporate stocks and in debt securities of private corporations and state and local governments.

Source: Bureau of Economic Analysis, *Survey of Current Business* (U.S. Department of Commerce).

capital account of the same arithmetic value. Thus if a country has a current-account surplus (its exports of goods and services exceed its imports of goods and services) it must necessarily—by definition—have a capital-account deficit, and so its imports of securities must exceed its exports of securities. The country's net international creditor position is increasing.

The last major group is the payments balance, at one time thought a measure of how well a country "was doing"; this balance is the sum of lines 35 and 36. Payments surpluses were considered indicative of a successful economic performance, and payments deficits of a less successful performance, perhaps because of the association of payments deficits and domestic inflation. Initially payments surpluses were associated with gold inflows, deficits with outflows. Subsequently transactions in other types of assets, including liquid assets denominated in the major currencies and claims on the International Monetary Fund, were included in the calculation of the payments balance.

At times, the entry "payments balance" was thought of as the sum of "financing transactions"; all international transactions were segmented either into an autonomous category or an induced category, and those items in the induced category were considered to be the payments balance. Because of the reliance on the concept of double-entry bookkeeping, the value for the entry on the autonomous payments necessarily equals the value for the entry for the induced payments, but with an opposite sign. So if a country's exports of goods, services, and long-term securities exceed its imports of goods, services, and long-term securities, so that there is a surplus on the autonomous account, there must be a deficit on the induced account—the country's imports of monetary gold and foreign-exchange reserves exceed its exports of monetary gold and foreign exchange reserves.

An alternative approach considers the payments balance as the sum of transactions in money—liquid assets including gold—by the monetary authorities. A country with a payments surplus imports monetary assets. In effect the country has a deficit in the money account—its imports of monetary assets exceed its exports of monetary assets. The shorthand approach is that a country's payments surplus or deficit should be measured by the change in its central bank's holdings of international money.

Over the last twenty years various agencies in the U.S. government have debated which transactions are to be included in the measurement of the payments balance. Prior to 1964, changes in the foreign holdings of liquid dollar assets of foreign commercial banks and foreign private parties as well as of foreign central banks were included in the measurement of the U.S. payments balance. In the 1960s, the U.S. authorities took the view that only transactions of foreign monetary authorities should be included. The decision to exclude changes in liquid dollar holdings of foreign commercial banks and foreign private parties at a time when they were adding to their holdings of liquid dollar assets led to a reduction in the measured U.S. payments deficit. The United States was exporting money because these foreign groups had a secular demand for dollar assets. With the move to the floating exchange-rate system, the U.S. authorities downplayed the significance of the payments balance.

SUMMARY

1. A foreign-exchange market is necessary in a multiple currency world. The assets traded in this market are demand deposits denominated in different currencies. The price is the exchange rate.
2. London is the principal center in the world for trading in foreign exchange; New York is the next busiest center.
3. Most foreign-exchange transactions are either forward contracts, which provide that deposits will be exchanged at specified future days, or swaps, which involve an exchange of a forward contract against a spot exchange contract.
4. Forward exchange contracts are available from banks and should be distinguished from currency futures contracts which are traded on financial exchanges in Chicago, New York, and London.
5. The Interest Rate Parity theorem stipulates that the percentage difference between the spot and forward exchange rates will be equal to the difference between interest rates on domestic and foreign securities with maturities equal to that of the forward contract.
6. Some evidence suggests that forward rates may be thought of as the market's "best-view" of the spot exchange rates on the dates when the forward contracts mature.
7. The Purchasing Power Parity theory states that changes in the exchange rates should reflect the difference between changes in the price of comparable market baskets of goods available in different countries.
8. The Fisher Proposition is that domestic interest rates should equal world interest rates plus the anticipated rate of change of the exchange rate.
9. Central bank intervention in the foreign-exchange market has been much larger in the period when currencies have been floating than in prior decades with pegged exchange rates.
10. The balance of payments accounts is the accounting record of transactions in goods, services, and securities between domestic residents and foreign residents.
11. The payments balance measures the purchases and sales of reserve assets by the national monetary authorities.

Questions and Exercises

1. Discuss why the costs and risks associated with the transactions in the foreign-exchange market are important for the effective operation of monetary policy in an open economy.
2. Why is the volume of dollar-sterling foreign-exchange transactions in London larger than the volume in New York?
3. Describe how the values for exchange rates for forward-exchange contracts for various maturities are related to the spot-exchange rate. What are the consequences of an increase in the interest-rate differential on the relationship between the spot-exchange rate and the forward-exchange rates?
4. Describe the determinants of the level of the spot-exchange rate. If interest rates on sterling-denominated assets fall, why might the price of the dollar in terms of sterling increase? Why might the sterling price of the dollar increase even if the interest-rate differential remains unchanged?

Further Reading

ALIBER, ROBERT Z. *Exchange Risk and Corporate International Finance.* New York: Halsted Press, 1979. A systematic guide for analysis of exchange-rate movements.

FEDERAL RESERVE BANK OF BOSTON. *Managed Exchange Rate Flexibility: The Recent Experience.* Boston: Federal Reserve Bank, 1978. A conference volume with numerous essays analyzing the movement of exchange rates in the 1970s.

FRIEDMAN, MILTON. "The Case for Fluctuating Exchange Rates." In his *Essays in Positive Economics.* Chicago: University of Chicago Press, 1953. A classic statement of the case for floating exchange rates.

INTERNATIONAL MONETARY FUND. *Annual Report.* Washington, D.C.: yearly. This report discusses annual developments in the foreign-exchange markets.

KUBARYCH, ROGER. *The New York Foreign Exchange Market.* New York: Federal Reserve Bank, 1979. A comprehensive description of the institutional aspects of the foreign-exchange markets in the United States.

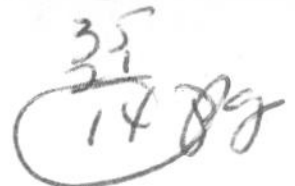

International Banking and National Monetary Policies

28

Traditionally, studies in international finance have implicitly assumed that the banking structure in each country was self-contained. In the last several decades, commercial banking has become internationalized in two important, distinct, but related ways: branch systems of U.S. banks have been extended into the domestic markets abroad, and branches of U.S. banks in other countries have been established to compete with domestic banks for dollar deposits. The key concern is how these changes in the structure of banking affect the management of monetary policy in the major countries.

THE INTERNATIONALIZATION OF COMMERCIAL BANKING

The commercial banking systems of the major industrial countries have become internationalized in the last decade and banks headquartered in New York, Chicago, Tokyo, Frankfurt, Zurich, and Toronto have begun to compete aggressively in each other's domestic market. United States banks have nearly one thousand branches and subsidiaries in Western Europe, Asia, and Latin America. Banks headquartered in Western Europe and Japan have set up over three hundred banking offices in New York, Chicago, San Francisco, and Los Angeles, and account for 15 percent of U.S. banking assets.

One consequence of the internationalization of commercial banking is that there is now more extensive competition in the major international centers due to the presence of foreign banks that seek to increase their shares of markets for loans and deposits. Banking in Great Britain is dominated by four major banks (National Westminster, Barclays, Midland, and Lloyds); twenty major non-British banks compete for the sterling deposits and loans of major and modest customers. Similarly, the three big German banks (Deutsche, Dresdner, and Commerz) have encountered increased competition for loan and deposit business from forty or fifty branches of foreign banks in Frankfurt, Düsseldorf, and Hamburg.

The Eurodollar Market

The surge in international banking competition has been facilitated by the growth of the external currency market, sometimes called the Eurodollar or offshore banking market. A Eurodollar is a *dollar-denominated deposit issued by a banking office located outside the United States*. Similarly a Euromark deposit is a mark-denominated deposit issued by a banking office located in Luxembourg, London, or any other center outside Germany. These offshore offices engage in an intermediation function virtually identical with that of the domestic banks; the major difference is that they sell deposits and buy loans denominated in a currency other than that of the country in which they are located. Thus the London offices of U.S. and German banks sell deposits and buy loans denominated in dollars, marks, Swiss francs, and perhaps ten currencies other than sterling. Foreign banks with U.S. branches obtain a substantial part of their funds by selling dollar deposits in London and other offshore centers.

At the end of 1981, offshore deposits issued by banks in Western Europe totaled $891 billion. About 70 percent of these deposits were denominated in the U.S. dollar, 14 percent in the German mark, and 7 percent in the Swiss franc. About 25 percent of these deposits were owned by firms and individuals; the rest were owned by banks. The offshore dollar deposits owned by non-banks were about 27 percent of domestic money.

Offshore banking occurs in "monetary havens" such as London, Luxembourg, Singapore, Panama, and the Cayman Islands. Tax havens are an analogy—firms and investors shift funds to tax havens to take advantage of the lower tax rate. Similarly investors acquire offshore deposits because the interest rates exceed those on domestic deposits by more than enough to compensate for the additional costs, inconveniences, and risks. And offshore banks can pay higher interest rates than domestic banks because they are not subject to interest rate ceilings and because they are not obliged to hold reserves.

International Banking and Domestic Monetary Policy

The internationalization of banking and the growth of the offshore dollar market raise important questions for the management of U.S. monetary policy. Should offshore dollar deposits be included in the calculation of the U.S. money supply? If so, should the dollar deposits of the offshore offices of U.S. banks be distinguished from dollar deposits of offshore offices of non-U.S. banks? Should the dollar deposits of U.S. offices of foreign banks be included in the calculation of the U.S. money supply, just as if they were U.S. banks? Should the deposits of the offshore offices of U.S. banks denominated in the German mark, the Swiss franc, and the Japanese yen be included in the measurement of the U.S. money supply? Should the Federal Reserve regulate only the domestic branches of U.S. banks, or should regulation of the offshore branches of U.S. banks be identical with the regulation of domestic branches?

The critical question for monetary analysis is whether the money supply should be measured to include the volume of bank deposits produced within a country (say, the United States or Germany) regardless of currency, or the volume of bank deposits denominated in a particular currency (say, the U.S. dollar or the German mark) regardless of the country in which the deposits are produced, or the volume of deposits produced by banks headquartered in particular countries (say, U.S. banks or German banks) regardless of currency and location of the country in which the deposits are produced. The most appropriate answer depends on how well each of these alternative approaches to the measurement of the money supply can explain changes in the level of prices within a country. The narrowest definition of the money supply involves dollar liabilities of U.S.-owned banks produced only by their U.S. offices. This measurement might be expanded in the ownership dimension to include the dollar liabilities produced by the U.S. offices of non-U.S. owned banks, or in the geographic dimension to include the dollar liabilities produced by the foreign offices of U.S. banks, or in the currency dimension to include the nondollar liabilities of U.S. banks.

One view is that the most relevant measure of the U.S. money supply includes the total of dollar-denominated bank liabilities regardless of whether dollar deposits are produced by U.S. banks or by foreign banks and regardless of whether the deposits are produced in the United States or abroad. The rationale is that the borders among currency areas—between the dollar area and the mark area, for example—are significantly higher than the borders between the domestic and external segments of a particular currency area, which in turn are probably higher than the distinctions between domestic and foreign-owned banks producing similar types of bank deposits. There is general agreement that the liabilities of foreign-owned banks operating in the United States should be included in the measurement of the U.S. money supply. Households and firms generally view their deposits in foreign-owned banks in the United States as close substitutes for their deposits in U.S. banks; otherwise the branches and subsidiaries of foreign banks would be at a significant competitive disadvantage in selling deposits. However, there is less agreement that offshore deposits denominated in U.S. dollars should be considered part of the U.S. money supply, even though offshore dollars can ultimately only be spent in the United States.

The first issue discussed in this chapter involves the structural differences among countries in the character of banking regulations and the significance of these differences for the management of monetary policy. The second issue involves the relation of the offshore dollar deposits to domestic dollar deposits, and the monetary implications of the development of offshore markets. Special attention is given to the implications of the growth of offshore dollar deposits for the management of U.S. monetary policy.

THE STRUCTURE OF INTERNATIONAL BANKING

The traditional approach to the analysis of the structure of international banks examines the market shares within each country for loans and deposits of foreign-owned banks. If data were available, it would be useful to examine the extent to which residents in each country acquire deposits from foreign banks and sell loans to them. Thus, as the costs incurred by residents of any country in acquiring deposits abroad or obtaining loans abroad decline, the size of the market in which banks located in a particular center expands.

The growth of international banking is important because foreign-owned banks may have easier access to external funds than domestic banks, and so may be able to sidestep changes in domestic monetary policy, more than domestic banks can. For example, if the Bank of England pursues a more contractive monetary policy, so that British banks find it difficult to extend sterling loans, U.S. and other foreign banks with ready access to dollar and mark funds may sell these funds for sterling and buy more sterling loans. Alternatively, borrowers in London may go to banks in New York and Frankfurt to offset their reduced ability to borrow in London.

One of the striking differences in the comparisons of the domestic banking systems in the major countries is in the size distribution of banks. Another is in the form and extent of bank regulation. Although the largest banks in terms of assets are in the United States, the number of banks in the United States is much larger than the number in any other country. In most other countries, three, four, or five banks, each with hundreds of branches, account for 60 or 70 percent of bank deposits and loans.

That U.S. banks are both very large and yet much more numerous than in other countries reflects two factors—one is that the total bank deposits are much larger in the United States than elsewhere because the U.S. economy is much larger. The second is the concern in the United States with maintaining competition in banking, which has led to regulations against expansion of bank branches across state lines (the McFadden Act of 1927), and, in many cases, across political jurisdictions within states, or even across the boundaries between zip code areas.

Paradoxically, in a few cases, the large size of major U.S. banks contributed to the mergers among foreign banks so they would not be at a size disadvantage relative to the U.S. banks in meeting the financial needs of large multinational firms. Thus, in Great Britain in the early 1970s, the National Provincial Bank merged with Westminster Bank while Lloyds merged with British and Overseas Bank. In The Netherlands, Amsterdam Bank and Rotterdam Bank merged.

Most of the foreign offices of U.S. banks are branches; they are not incorporated in the country in which they are located. In a few cases, however, the parents have set up subsidiaries, which have a separate legal status abroad. Frequently, host countries require that foreign-owned banks have minority domestic ownership so that the subsidiary form is essential. The distinction between branch and subsidiary is important for determining U.S. corporate income tax liability, for the income of offshore branches is included in U.S. income in the year in which the income is earned, while income of the foreign subsidiaries is subject to U.S. taxation only when the subsidiaries pay dividends to their U.S. parents. Conceivably the subsidiary could close with a loss to its shareholders while the parent remained in business; in contrast a branch could not fail while the parent remained open for business.[1]

COMPETITION AND REGULATION

The rapid growth of foreign banks in the United States in the last decade focused attention on bank regulation, and especially on whether foreign banks had regulatory advantages in the United States relative to U.S. banks. Moreover, this rapid growth led to concern regarding the possibility that the regulations applied by foreign authorities to the activities of U.S. banks within their jurisdictions are more restrictive than the regulations applied to the activities of foreign banks within the United States—that is whether there was reciprocity in banking. A key feature of banking regulation within the United States is the multiplicity of regulatory authorities, which was extensively discussed in Chapter 3. The regulatory dilemma is that if U.S. regulation of foreign banks seeks to follow the principle of reciprocity, then the severity of regulations applied to U.S. offices of banks headquartered abroad may vary, depending on the country in which the bank is headquartered.

The growth of offshore banking has facilitated the growth of international banking in several important ways. Branches of U.S. banks established in London to sell dollar deposits could easily compete for sterling deposits and loans at the same time. Similarly, branches established to do offshore banking business in Brussels could sell deposits and buy loans denominated in the Belgian franc. These Brussels branches could obtain funds to make loans by issuing Belgian franc deposits to Belgian residents or by borrowing Belgian francs from the major Belgian banks in the interbank market. Or these branches might have issued Belgian franc deposits in the offshore market, or issued deposits denominated in various foreign currencies in the offshore market and converted the funds to Belgian francs. Because transactions costs encountered by banks are very low, the costs of the currency swap would be insignificant. Similarly, foreign banks that wanted to develop a loan business could obtain the funds to buy dollar loans by obtaining dollar deposits in the offshore dollar market and by borrowing in the U.S. interbank market.

The major expansion of U.S. banks abroad occurred in the 1960s (although a few U.S. banks had established foreign branches in the 1920s and several in the latter part of the nineteenth century) for several reasons. One was to follow the foreign expansion of U.S. firms. A second was to avoid domestic limits on growth; this was especially true for U.S. banks headquartered in New York City. Finally, a large number of U.S. banks went abroad to participate in the offshore money market, and especially to avoid the loss of deposits to U.S. and foreign banks offering higher interest rates on dollar

[1] A subsidiary is a legally incorporated firm that is owned by the parent bank. A branch is an unincorporated extension of the parent bank.

deposits than those available on domestic dollar deposits. The distribution of foreign offices of U.S. banks matches the pattern of U.S. foreign investment with two major exceptions: U.S. banks are underrepresented in those countries in which entry was restricted or prohibited, including Canada and Mexico, and overrepresented in London, Luxembourg, the Bahamas, and other monetary havens.

Foreign-owned banks also set up offices in London, Luxembourg, Singapore, and other monetary havens to participate in the offshore market for deposits denominated in the dollar, the mark, and the Swiss franc. Setting up branches abroad to engage in the offshore market was generally less costly or more profitable than setting up additional offices to compete for domestic business. The major expansion of foreign banks in the United States took place in the 1970s for several reasons. One was to circumvent the domestic constraints on growth and to participate directly in the dominant international center of finance. Another was to participate in the financing of international trade between their own countries and the United States; because much of the trade was denominated in dollars, foreign banks may have been at a disadvantage in trade financing. A third was to serve the particular ethnic markets in the United States, both the expatriate business community and immigrants. Moreover, foreign investment was also increasing in the United States, and the German, Japanese, and British banks did not want to lose their customers to the U.S. banks.

Foreign banks contemplating entry in the U.S. faced a number of key decisions—one was whether to set up offices in New York or in other cities; a second was whether to enter by starting a new office or through purchase of a U.S. bank; a third was whether to set up a branch, a subsidiary, or an agency. Foreign banks initially had certain advantages in the United States. One was that although they were not allowed to branch across state lines, they might place branches in one state and a subsidiary in another (or subsidiaries in several other states). A second was that their U.S. branches were not required to join the Federal Reserve, nor were they required to hold reserves. Capital ratios were below those of the U.S. banks; indeed the U.S. branches of foreign banks had no separate capital of their own.

The International Banking Act of 1978 (IBA) significantly reduced the competitive advantages previously available to foreign banks in the United States by treating them as if they were U.S. banks; the principle of "national treatment" was established. All foreign banks operating in the United States are to be treated as if they were U.S. banks, regardless of the treatment afforded U.S. banks in their home countries (the national treatment principle has priority over the reciprocity principle). While foreign banks might not join the Federal Reserve, they were required to hold reserves, providing they had deposits in excess of $1 billion, comparable to those held by the U.S. banks. The U.S. branches of foreign banks were provided with the option of federal licenses; previously they had only state licenses. Those branches of foreign banks that were involved in retail banking were required to participate in Federal Deposit Insurance. Foreign banks could set up Edge Act corporations, and the powers of the Edge Act corporations of U.S. banks were expanded.[2] The U.S. branches of large foreign banks now are subject to the same supervisory and supervision requirements as comparable U.S. banks.

The impact of the IBA will slow the growth of foreign banks in the United States. Yet these banks are sufficiently numerous and large to increase significantly competition in banking, especially in the wholesale market, but also in the retail markets in New York and California. By subjecting foreign-owned banks to reserve requirements, the effectiveness of U.S. monetary control will be increased.

THE GROWTH OF OFFSHORE BANKING

The growth of offshore deposits has generated considerable controversy about their impact on the rate of world inflation, about the stability of the international financial system, and about the effectiveness of national monetary control. One assertion is that the growth of the offshore dollar deposits led to a surge in the rate of world inflation in the 1970s, largely because offshore banks were not subject to reserve requirements and hence were in a position to create a massive amount of credit on the basis of a modest increase in their reserves. A second concern is that the offshore banking system might collapse along the lines of the failure of banks in the Great Depression. One scenario has the closing of one or two poorly managed offshore banks due to losses on their loans to high-risk borrowers triggering the collapse of better managed banks from whom they had borrowed; the metaphor sometimes used is that of a collapsing "house of cards." The third concern is that the growth of the offshore market has reduced the segmentation among national financial markets, so there is less scope for independent national monetary policies. A variant of this argument is that the weakness of the dollar in the foreign-exchange market has resulted from the monies "sloshing about" in the offshore market. Finally, there is concern that the effectiveness of monetary control has declined because U.S. banks can circumvent domestic monetary tightness through their offshore activities.

The rapid growth of offshore deposits denominated in the U.S. dollar reflects investor response to the excess of interest rates on offshore deposits over the interest rates on comparable domestic deposits. Two factors explain this interest-rate differential. One is that offshore banks incur lower costs than domestic banks, largely because they are located in financial centers where they are not obliged to hold reserves against dollar-denominated deposits. Similar statements can be made about offshore deposits denominated in marks. Reserve requirements are an implicit tax on deposits. The second factor is that offshore banks are not constrained by ceilings from paying interest rates higher than those they can pay on domestic deposits;

[2] Edge Act corporations are permitted by an amendment to the Federal Reserve Act that relaxes restrictions on U.S. banks engaged in financing international trade and investment. Thus U.S. banks headquartered in Chicago and San Francisco are permitted to establish subsidiaries in New York to engage in international financial activities. Similarly, New York banks are able to establish subsidiaries in other U.S. cities.

thus they can pay interest on demand deposits. Both factors reflect that banking is less extensively regulated in offshore financial centers than in domestic financial centers.

Offshore banks are virtually unregulated by the authorities of the countries in which they are located; thus, the British authorities recognize that dollar transactions in London are a matter of geographic convenience and believe these dollar, mark, and other foreign currency transactions have no more significance for the management of the British economy than if they had occurred in Luxembourg or New York. Great Britain benefits from exporting more banking services. Indeed, to the extent *dollar* banking services occur in London, the British have "poached" the banking activities that almost certainly would have occurred in New York or other U.S. cities. Employment in banking and related industries is higher in London and lower in the United States.

Competition for deposits among offshore banks means they pass on to investors or depositors most, if not all, of the cost savings realized by producing deposits in the offshore market. Fifty international banks—the dominant banks in each country—are important competitors in the London offshore market, while another two hundred banks from various countries also participate. Competition among different political jurisdictions such as Great Britain, Luxembourg, the Bahamas, and Singapore for offshore banking business causes each to be reluctant to apply any regulations on offshore banks, because these banks might then move to less extensively regulated offshore centers.

INTEREST RATES IN DOMESTIC AND OFFSHORE BANKS

Once major international banks have established offices to produce and sell offshore deposits, large investors have a new set of investment alternatives. They can buy domestic deposits, or alternatively, they can buy offshore deposits denominated in the same currencies, even from the branches of the same banks from which they can buy domestic deposits. Interest rates on the offshore deposits are higher than those on comparable domestic deposits. If owners of domestic dollar deposits know about the higher interest rates available on offshore deposits, their continued demand for domestic deposits even at the cost of forgone interest income must be explained. They perceive additional risks associated with offshore deposits, especially in the form of exchange controls which might be applied to the repatriation of funds from the offshore market to the domestic market either by the country in which the deposit is located or by the United States. While the probability of these controls may seem slight, the additional interest income is also modest.

To the extent interest rates on offshore dollar deposits exceed those on comparable domestic deposits by the amount that reflects differences in costs (primarily those of reserve requirements) of the two kinds of deposits, each U.S. bank is indifferent between selling an additional offshore deposit and selling an additional domestic deposit. In the absence of exchange controls, banks can use offshore deposits as well as domestic deposits to finance domestic loans. There is no necessary link between where a bank sells a deposit and where this bank buys a loan. Interest rates charged to a borrower on an offshore loan are comparable to the interest rates the same borrower would be charged on a domestic loan, for banks have no financial incentive to charge customers lower interest rates on offshore loans.

Once a bank has decided on the maximum interest rate it can pay on an offshore deposit denominated in U.S. dollars, the bank can readily determine the maximum interest rate it can pay on offshore deposits denominated in the German mark, the Swiss franc, and other currencies, and still be no worse off than if it had sold an offshore dollar-denominated deposit. Thus the London branch of a U.S. bank may issue deposits denominated in the mark and then use the funds to purchase a dollar loan, after first buying dollars in the foreign-exchange market. To reduce or eliminate the exchange risk, the bank would buy the German mark in the forward market at the same time the bank sells the German mark in the spot market. If banks sought to fully cover any possible exchange exposure (or to be compensated for carrying the exposure), differences in interest rates on offshore deposits denominated in various currencies would reflect the cost of covering the exchange risk, or the percentage difference between the forward-exchange rate and the spot-exchange rate.

Some U.S. banks have branches in London, Zurich, Luxembourg, and Paris. At any moment, the branches of a U.S. bank in these centers would offer virtually the same interest rate on a dollar-denominated deposit of a particular maturity. In general, there is no economic incentive for the London branch to offer a higher interest rate on a dollar deposit than the Zurich branch does, especially if the funds realized from issuing the deposits are to be used to finance the purchase of a loan in New York. If interest rates on offshore deposits sold by the branches of a given bank in different centers are the same, then the volume of deposits produced in each center will depend on investor appraisal of the differences in the risks associated with deposits in the various centers; relatively more deposits will be produced in centers in which the risk of exchange controls is lower. If investors believe the risk attached to London dollar deposits is increasing relative to the risk attached to Luxembourg dollar deposits, they would shift funds from London to Luxembourg. Nevertheless, the interest rates on London dollar deposits would not change significantly relative to interest rates on Luxembourg dollar deposits.

Occasionally, branches of a bank in a particular center seek to sell offshore deposits there because they wish to buy loans in that country. If investors associate higher risk with offshore deposits available in a particular country because of greater likelihood of exchange controls, then the offshore offices located there must offer higher interest rates on deposits than the offices located in the principal offshore centers. For example, offshore offices in Milan, Italy have had to pay modestly higher interest rates on dollar deposits than have the branches of the same banks in London; investors perceive larger risk is attached to offshore deposits in Italy. The banks that sell dollar deposits in Milan use the funds to buy dollar loans from Italian banks. If these banks offered the same interest rate on Milan dollar deposits as on London dollar deposits, they would sell a smaller volume of deposits, or perhaps not sell any at all.

Just as some offshore centers are judged riskier than others, so some offshore banks are judged riskier than others. The riskier banks must pay higher interest rates to sell offshore deposits. The differences in the perception of risk reflect several factors, including the size of each bank, measures of its solvency such as its capital-deposit ratios, the country of domicile of its parent, and the total of offshore deposits sold by the bank relative to its total domestic deposits. Investors rank offshore banks into three or four major groups, so there is a "tiering" of offshore interest rates (an analogy is the rating of bonds issued by various firms and governments). The spread between the lowest interest rates paid by banks at any time and the highest interest rates paid by other banks has ranged from less than one-half percent to nearly two percent.

At each moment, investors have a large range of deposits available to them. They can choose between domestic deposits and offshore deposits denominated in the U.S. dollar, the German mark, the Swiss franc, and other currencies. Moreover, they can choose among offshore deposits denominated in a particular currency in various offshore centers and among offshore deposits and domestic deposits offered by several hundred banks that differ in size and country of domicile.

The much more rapid growth of offshore deposits than of domestic deposits reflects two factors. One is that the interest incentive to shift to offshore deposits has increased as interest rates have increased, since the tax implicit in non-interest-bearing reserves has increased. The second is that the assessment of the risk associated with offshore deposits has decreased.[3]

THE MONETARY IMPLICATIONS OF OFFSHORE DEPOSITS

The rapid growth of offshore deposits in the 1970s, at a time when the world inflation rate increased, led to the assertion that the growth of offshore deposits caused or intensified increases in the world price level. The analysis of this proposition depends on whether the growth of offshore deposits has been in addition to the growth of domestic deposits or instead a substitute for the growth of domestic deposits. A related issue is whether the supply of reserves to the commercial banking system has been independent of the growth of offshore deposits.

Two extreme views about the process of credit creation in the offshore deposits have led to different conclusions about the inflationary implications of the growth of offshore deposits. One is that the offshore banking system

[3]The U.S. payments deficit may have contributed modestly to the growth of offshore deposits, to the extent that foreign central banks hold part of their dollar reserves in offshore banks. But such holdings are small. And offshore deposits denominated in the Swiss franc and the German mark have increased, even though Germany and Switzerland have had payments surpluses.

is comparable to the domestic banking system, with the exception that the offshore system lacks a central bank. This view implies that a modest increase in the reserves of the offshore banks leads to a substantial expansion of deposits and credit in the offshore banking system, because offshore banks are not required to hold reserves. Thus, the story is that once an individual shifts funds from a domestic bank to an offshore bank, the latter in turn lends to some other individual who buys goods or securities from someone who in turn deposits the receipts in another offshore bank, which in turn lends funds to someone who buys goods, and so on. Thus the size of fractional-reserve multiplier is higher. Those who argue that the growth of offshore deposits has had a significant impact on the rate of world inflation generally share this view about a segmented and independent offshore banking system.

The competing view is that the offshore market is exclusively an interbank market, the international counterpart of the U.S. federal funds market. According to this view, no credit is created in the offshore system; rather, the market facilitates more efficient allocation of credit. Thus, banks in countries with balance-of-payments surpluses extend credit to banks in countries with balance-of-payments deficits. Extensive interbank transactions in the offshore market support this view.[4] But this view is inconsistent with the data that show that a substantial proportion of liabilities of offshore banks are to private firms and investors, including central banks.

Offshore banks are not part of a segmented financial system but rather are the branches and, to a much lesser extent, the subsidiaries, of major international banks located in centers where they are not obliged to hold reserves. There are virtually no important offshore banks that are not branches or subsidiaries of major international banks; the offshore offices of major international banks compete with the domestic offices of these same banks to sell deposits. If the domestic office of a U.S. bank sells an additional domestic deposit, its required reserve holdings increase; if the offshore office of the same bank sells an additional deposit, its required reserves are unchanged. The U.S. banks mingle the reserves held against offshore deposits with those held in domestic deposits. By selling an additional offshore deposit, a bank is able to reduce the effective or economic level of reserves below the legal level required against domestic deposits. Hence the ratio of non-interest-earning assets to interest-earning assets declines as offshore deposits increase relative to domestic deposits.

The more rapid growth of offshore deposits than of domestic deposits means that the effective reserve requirements applied to each bank has declined. So there almost certainly has been a larger than anticipated increase in the supply of dollar credit for a given increase in the supply of dollar reserves because of the increase in the money multiplier. To the extent that

[4]One reason for the large volume of interbank transactions is that banks that are deemed less risky lend to riskier banks. A second is that banks seek to match maturities of their assets and liabilities to economize on the need for liquidity. A third is that some countries have an advantage in taking deposits while others have an advantage in making loans. A fourth is that offshore banks engage extensively in credit rationing; they have limits on their willingness to acquire loans of individual borrowers, or loans of borrowers in a particular country or loans of borrowers in a particular industry. Once a bank's loans in each category are at its ceilings, it extends credit to banks less able to sell deposits to investors.

growth of offshore deposits has been unanticipated by the central bank, there has been a more rapid than anticipated increase in the volume of credit. Estimating the impact of this unanticipated increase in the supply of credit on the U.S. inflation rate and on the world inflation rate is difficult, in part because this source of growth of credit may have been a substitute for some other source of credit that otherwise would have grown more rapidly.

Hence the growth of the offshore deposits has reduced the effectiveness of monetary control because the authorities can never be confident of the changes in the money supply associated with a given change in reserves of the banking system. The source of their uncertainty lies in the changes in the money multiplier as the volume of offshore deposits increases relative to the volume of domestic deposits. On a year-to-year basis, the trend has been variable and appears unpredictable.

The growth of offshore deposits has probably decreased the significance of the barriers among currency areas, and complicated the management of monetary policy. Both investors and banks are more conscious of the returns associated with crossing the borders between currency areas. The growth of offshore deposits has increased the willingness of firms to estimate the costs and risks associated with altering their currency exposures, although it has not reduced these costs or risks in any significant way. Thus, the segmentation of currency areas has declined, and so the scope for independent national monetary policies has declined.

Since the major offshore banks are branches of the major international banks, the concern that their failure might trigger the collapse of the banking system is greatly exaggerated. Most offshore banks are unlikely to make riskier loans than their head offices; indeed the offshore branches and subsidiaries of U.S. banks are examined by the same U.S. authorities that examine the domestic offices. Legally, holders of deposits in offshore offices are not likely to incur losses even if these offices make numerous loans that prove faulty. The solvency of these offshore offices is not independent of the solvency of their head offices. Finally, the various central banks that participate in the activities of the Bank for International Settlements have agreed that each central bank is responsible for the liquidity needs of the offshore offices of its domestic banks.

Reducing the Advantages of Offshore Banks

One proposal to reduce the incentive to export the U.S. banking system is that reserve requirements be applied to offshore deposits. Reserve requirements might be applied to all offshore deposits produced in a particular center. The response was that investors would shift funds to other offshore centers, which, in order to increase their share of offshore deposits, choose not to apply reserve requirements. Hence, if reserve requirements were applied to offshore deposits in London, owners of offshore deposits would shift their funds to Luxembourg, Paris, and Panama. Alternatively, reserve requirements might be applied by the monetary authorities in each country to the offshore offices of banks headquartered in their jurisdictions; thus, the U.S.

authorities could extend domestic reserve requirements to the offshore offices of U.S. banks. The German authorities might extend their own domestic reserve requirements to the offshore offices of German banks. The response to this proposal was that the owners of offshore deposits would shift their funds to offshore deposits produced by British, French, and Swiss banks. A third proposal is to pay market interest rates on reserves held by the central bank. But this proposal, if implemented, would reduce the government's income.

In 1980 the Federal Reserve permitted banks operating in the United States to establish International Banking Facilities (IBFs)—offices that can issue deposits not subject to reserves. Only nonresidents are permitted to acquire these deposits. They now receive higher interest rates on dollar deposits in the United States than U.S. residents. Perhaps the approach toward segmenting the markets will work.

The regulatory problem is that the U.S. authorities must choose between reducing the incentive for investors to acquire offshore deposits or adjusting to the more rapid growth of offshore deposits than of domestic deposits. In a period of high interest rates and low-cost communications, banks and their customers have found it easy and profitable to circumvent the tax on domestic deposits inherent in reserve requirements. The U.S. authorities must recognize that the structure of U.S. financial regulation cannot be independent of that elsewhere; they cannot maintain a level of reserve requirements significantly higher than those abroad, or more of the banking business will go abroad.

If U.S. residents were permitted to hold deposits in IBFs, many would shift funds from offshore banks in London and Zurich to IBFs in New York, Chicago, and San Francisco. Yet many holders of domestic deposits in Minneapolis and Salt Lake City and other U.S. cities, who were deterred by the possibility of exchange controls from acquiring dollar deposits in London or Zurich, would find it attractive to shift funds to the IBFs in New York, Chicago, and San Francisco. So the potential rush to acquire deposits in the IBFs would mean that banks in each major metropolitan area in the United States would seek to establish an IBF, and reserve requirements would be circumvented since a smaller and smaller share of deposits would be subject to these requirements. The implication is that efforts of the Federal Reserve to maintain high reserve requirements on one class of deposits while virtually identical deposits are not subject to reserve requirements would be readily circumvented. While regulations might be adopted to limit shifts of funds to the banks in the free-banking zone, these regulations would be avoided. Thus, the implications of establishing free-banking zones in the United States only highlights the problems for monetary management in a world in which similar deposits are subject to different reserve requirements. As long as banks operating in the United States are subject to higher reserve requirements than are banks operating in London and other offshore centers, the reserve requirement creates an incentive to export the U.S. banking system.

Bank Regulation and Monetary Policy

The varied approach to the regulation of banks may reduce the effectiveness of monetary policy. Several anomalies are evident. The domestic transactions of U.S. banks are regulated on one basis; their offshore transactions on another. The offshore transactions of U.S. banks are regulated on a different basis than those of non-U.S. banks. And the domestic transactions of U.S. banks and the transactions of foreign banks in the countries in which they are headquartered are regulated in different ways.

The question of whether U.S.-owned or foreign-owned banks provide banking services to U.S. residents should be distinguished from broader questions about the effectiveness of U.S. monetary policy when national regulations differ. Differential regulation has an impact on the competitive position of different groups of banks, and on their growth rates. The question of the ownership of the institutions that provide banking services is independent of the monetary implications, with one exception: namely, to the extent foreign-owned banks may have easier access to funds at their home offices, they may be able to circumvent changes in monetary policy. The significance of this source of funds is an empirical matter. On an a priori basis, the argument would appear to be much more significant for smaller countries than for the United States.

Currently, U.S. monetary control is weakened because of the differential in reserve requirements and the lack of a stable relationship between the growth of offshore dollar deposits and the growth of domestic deposits. In periods of monetary contraction, as interest rates rise and the effective interest cost of reserve requirements applied to U.S. banks increases the share of U.S. banks in the dollar deposit markets declines. To reduce the disadvantage of U.S. banks, either domestic reserve requirements might be lowered to reduce or eliminate the financial incentives in favor of offshore deposits, or interest might be paid on required reserves. The argument for such adjustments demonstrates that the U.S. regulatory authorities cannot operate independently of foreign regulations; more severe regulation tends to lead to the export of U.S. financial transactions.

SUMMARY

1. In the last several decades, commercial banking has become much more international as banks headquartered in the United States, Western Europe, and Japan have established systems of branches in other countries.
2. The growth in international banking has been facilitated by the expansion of offshore banking—banking offices operating in particular centers sell deposits denominated in a currency other than that of the country in which they are located. Thus banks in London, including the London branches of U.S. banks, sell deposits denominated in the U.S. dollar or the German mark or the Swiss franc.
3. Offshore deposits denominated in the U.S. dollar have grown significantly more rapidly than domestic deposits denominated in the dollar (even after adjustment for the growth of interbank deposits) with the result that the growth in the dollar money supply has been understated.

4. The rapid growth of offshore deposits in the 1970s, like the rapid growth of money market funds, is a result of the cost of reserve requirements in a period when interest rates increased sharply.
5. The growth of offshore deposits denominated in the U.S. dollar and other currencies has facilitated the integration of national money markets, since banks can sell deposits denominated in one currency, convert the funds into some other currency in which they wish to make the loan, and cover the exchange risk with a forward exchange contract.
6. The growth of offshore deposits denominated in the dollar has meant that the effective reserve requirement applied to dollar deposits is lower; the effective requirement is the weighted average of the reserve requirement applied to domestic deposits and the zero requirement applicable to offshore deposits.
7. The regulatory change which permitted U.S. banks to establish IBFs will reduce a major incentive for non-residents to acquire offshore deposits. U.S. residents will continue to acquire offshore dollar deposits as long as they offer higher yields than domestic deposits.

Questions and Exercises

1. Discuss the conditions necessary for the growth of an external currency market. Why do interest rates on offshore deposits exceed those on comparable domestic deposits? What is the upper limit to this difference? If interest rates on external deposits are higher than those on domestic deposits denominated in the same currency, why does anyone continue to hold domestic deposits?
2. Why might the growth of an offshore market in dollar deposits weaken the effectiveness of monetary control of the Federal Reserve?
3. Is it possible or likely that a financial collapse or disaster might develop in the offshore banking system, and be independent of the domestic banking system?
4. Discuss the ways in which the growth of offshore dollar deposits has contributed to the growth of branches of foreign banks in the United States.

Further Reading

FIELEKE, NORMAN. *Key Issues in International Banking*. Boston: Federal Reserve Bank of Boston, 1977. A conference volume with good descriptive material.

LITTLE, JANE SNEDDON. *Eurodollars*. New York: Harper & Row, 1975. A descriptive survey of actors in the offshore money market.

U.S., CONGRESS, HOUSE, COMMITTEE ON BANKING, CURRENCY, AND HOUSING. *International Banking*. Washington: Government Printing Office, 1976. A comprehensive survey of international banking; background materials for the International Banking Act of 1979.

The Issues in International Finance

29

Over the next several decades, the monetary authorities in the major countries will remain concerned with developments in international financial arrangements. Many will seek methods to reduce the range of movement in exchange rates, and the frequency and severity of the disturbances that countries import from their trading partners. Some will seek to develop arrangements that will enhance the effectiveness of monetary policy without infringing on freer international trade and payments. And the prospects that the debt burdens of developing countries will prove too burdensome to be manageable worry many.

TOWARD A NEW INTERNATIONAL MONETARY SYSTEM

Since the breakdown of the Bretton Woods system of pegged exchange rates, the arrangements for organizing the foreign-exchange market and producing international money are seen as too haphazard to qualify as an international monetary system. To pass this hurdle, the arrangements must have more "order," be more systematic, or be based on an international treaty. Some proposals to modify existing arrangements to achieve greater order seek to improve the operation of the floating exchange rates, while others favor a return to pegged exchange rates, either on a global or a regional basis. Other proposals seek to alter the roles of assets used as international reserves; one issue is whether gold should continue to be phased out of the international monetary system, or whether gold should again be used as an international reserve asset. The future international monetary roles of dollar assets and assets denominated in other currencies would be modified under some proposals.

A key issue is how the changes in these institutional frameworks would affect the management of monetary policy—both the need or demand for monetary independence in the major countries and the ability of the U.S. monetary authorities and those in other countries to follow policies appropriate for domestic objectives with minimal external constraints. The need or demand for monetary independence arises because the phases of the business cycle are not perfectly correlated across countries; even if they were, however, countries differ in the importance they attach to full employment and to price stability. Even if individual countries decide they wish to pursue greater monetary independence, there may be significant external constraints and the changes in monetary policy may have significant impacts on the flows of capital or on the level of the exchange rates. In modifying the international monetary arrangements, the goal is to develop arrangements so that countries can pursue their domestic objectives without forgoing the advantages of openness and specialization possible in the international economy.

Some proposals are ambitious in the extent to which they would modify current arrangements for the organization of the foreign-exchange market and the supply of international reserves. A new system implies a set of rules—perhaps based on an international treaty like the Bretton Woods agreement—that would affect the intervention practices of central banks in the foreign-exchange market. The participating countries would commit themselves to follow particular practices about exchange-market intervention and international reserve holdings and refrain from adopting other actions. Adhering to many of these commitments is likely to have *no* significant cost; even without the treaty, the countries would have behaved much as if they were following the commitments. To the extent adherence to the commitments has a cost in that several of the participating countries are obliged to pursue measures they would not have in the absence of the treaty, the key question is how long they will abide by the commitment, and forgo pursuing their own interests to satisfy an international obligation. One issue is how far "in front" of the consensus the treaty can get; treaties that are expensive to domestic interests may, like the Smithsonian Agreement, soon fall by the wayside.

So a major question involves the impact of changes in international arrangements on national economic policies. The relevant question is how long efforts of central banks to peg or manage exchange rates can cause these rates to assume significantly different values than they otherwise would have. Intervention can have a greater impact on the exchange rate in the short run—a period of a few months or even a year—than over a more extended period. In the long run, exchange rates are determined by relative prices and incomes and expectations about charges in relative price levels.

The success in devising an international financial arrangement that will remain viable for some time depends on the relationship between the implied commitments and the prevailing set of monetary and even political relationships. An attempt to adopt a system of pegged exchange rates is not likely to be viable in an inflationary period; one characteristic of inflation is that rates of price level increase differ sharply across countries and vary significantly from one year to the next and so countries are likely to find the costs of pegging their currencies for an extended period too high.

If the proposed international financial arrangements are to be viable, they must be consistent with the distribution of political and economic power. Thus, the gold standard succeeded during a period of British economic dominance, and broke down as U.S. economic power was increasing. The Bretton Woods system flourished during a period when U.S. economic and political power was dominant. As the relative U.S. economic position declined with the resurgence of the German and Japanese economies, the fragility of the Bretton Woods system became more apparent. The new set of arrangements must be consistent with a dispersion of economic power among at least three major economic centers—the United States, Germany and the European Community, and Japan.

Proposals that require extensive centralization of authority are not likely to be viable if nationalist pressures become stronger. Changes in institutional arrangements involve complicated interplay of interests of various countries. Few central bankers and treasury officials attempt to optimize or maximize a cosmopolitan or universal interest. Rather, in developing positions on these issues, each deals with a national variant on a familiar theme, "What's in it for me?" Implicitly, the policymakers in each country develop a cost-benefit analysis of the impacts that the adoption of each proposal would have on the well-being of their constituents and on the ability of their own governments to realize their objectives. Relatively few national monetary authorities would agree to proposals that might advance the cosmopolitan interest if the cost to their own constituents is high.

International monetary problems develop because national interests diverge. Differences across nations are more extensive, usually, than the differences within nations. Moreover, within countries, there are usually established legal procedures, frequently based on a written constitution, for determining the public interest, whereas across nations procedures for determining the cosmopolitan interest tend to be vague. Developing solutions to the questions might be easier if national interests were more malleable or alterable. A frequent proposal is that the national authorities coordinate their policies. But such proposals often ignore the divergence of interest. Because such interests change only slowly, the problem is how to devise a set of international arrangements that will best accommodate many different countries.

This chapter first traces developments in international monetary arrangements in the last decade. Then attention is given to the modification of exchange market arrangements, the development of reserve arrangements, and the unified currency area. Three issues are considered—the scope for mergers of national currencies and the optimum currency area issue, the choice between pegged rates and floating rates, and the future roles of competing international monies, especially the role of gold, the dollar, and IMF monies.

INTERNATIONAL MONETARY DEVELOPMENTS IN THE LAST DECADE

Change in international monetary arrangements in the last decade was much more extensive than in any previous period. The market price of gold, which had been $35 at the end of the 1960s, exceeded $600 a decade later; in January 1980 the gold price reached $970. The gold price had fallen to $300 in the summer of 1982; by the end of the year, the price had reached $500.

At the end of the 1960s, the IMF system of adjustable parities came under pressure because of the delay in the necessary changes in exchange parities to the increasing overvaluation of the dollar. The system broke down once in August 1971, was patched and stumbled through 1972, only to break down again in early 1973, because the monetary authorities could no longer convince traders and investors that monetary policies consistent with a system of pegged exchange rates would be pursued. Yet the floating-rate system did not conform to the textbook model; the range of movement in exchange rates was much greater than the difference in the increases in national price levels. The authorities intervened extensively to dampen movement in the exchange rates; indeed, by the measure of purchases and sales of international reserves, intervention was more extensive than in the previous decade with pegged exchange rates.

The changes in the foreign exchange value of the dollar were large and frequently abrupt. And when the dollar was weak the monetary authorities in many countries sought to diversify their reserves to include relatively more assets denominated in currencies other than the dollar, especially the mark, the Swiss franc, and the yen. In the 1960s, one of the major concerns was the shortage of international reserves, which culminated in the establishment of the SDR arrangement and the production of $10 billion in SDRs. In the decade of the 1970s, total reserves minus gold had increased sevenfold, from $40 billion at the end of 1969 to $270 billion at the end of 1979. Total reserves including gold increased from $80 billion to $600 billion if monetary gold is valued at $300 an ounce and to $700 billion if monetary gold is valued at $400 an ounce.

The Impact of Inflation

The factor that relates all these changes in international financial relationships is the surge in the world inflation rate, from an annual average rate of 4.3 percent in the 1960s to one of 11.1 percent in the 1970s; the U.S. inflation rate increased from an average of 2.3 percent in the 1960s to 7.1 percent in the 1970s. Inflation rates were at their highest-ever levels at the end of the decade. While this inflation rate was intensified by the succession of increases in the price of crude petroleum promoted by OPEC in 1973–74 and again in 1978–79, the world inflation rate was already at the double-digit level before the fourfold increase in 1973–74. Nevertheless in 1974 and again in 1979, the sharp increases in the price of oil probably caused the world inflation rate to be higher by two to three percentage points. In some countries, the impact was greater, because the oil price increase triggered increases in other prices, and expectations of future price increases.

In periods of inflation, the private demand for gold increases because investors believe gold is a hedge against inflation. Those investors with the highest inflationary expectations set the price in this market. While gold was clearly undervalued at the end of the 1960s, since its price had remained constant since 1934 while the world price level had increased by a factor of four, the increase in the gold price in the 1970s suggests expectations of continued and accelerating inflation. From time to time, the rules concerning official transactions in gold have been changed. For a while the national monetary authorities agreed not to deal in gold at a price other than the official price, then the official price was abandoned. A few monetary authorities have raised the valuation attached to their holdings of gold; many monetary authorities consider gold an important component of their international reserves, and are not likely to demonetize gold.

The experience with floating rates in the 1970s demonstrated that countries can have somewhat greater control over their price level than they could in a world with pegged rates. But no country was able to maintain an inflation rate as low as the average in the 1960s.

OPTIMAL CURRENCY AREAS AND MONETARY UNIONS

One of the central issues in international finance involves the span of the use of particular currencies. Should each country have its own currency, as virtually all do, or should countries merge their currencies, which is frequently contemplated as the monetary counterpart of integration in the European Community? Or would it be worthwhile for certain large countries, say China or Brazil, to develop two or more currencies for distinct regional areas? In the nineteenth century, currency unification was extensive within Germany, Japan, and Italy—in each case as part of the program of political unification, and in each case, among people who shared the same language and culture.

The dominant tendency in the last several decades has been an increase in the number of currencies. Thus the Irish pound, which had been firmly pegged to the British pound since Irish independence in 1922, now floats relative to the British pound. With the breakup of British, Dutch, French, and Portuguese empires and the establishment of new, independent countries, there was a sharp increase in the number of national currencies. Initially, these currencies were pegged to those of their former metropoles. Over time, as the monetary policies in the new countries became more independent and more expansive, parities have altered. Moreover, some countries have changed the currencies to which their own currencies are pegged; thus the Australian dollar, formerly pegged to sterling, is now pegged to the U.S. dollar.

On a more abstract level, the issues about unification of national currencies involve the attributes of countries whose currencies might be merged so as to maximize the economic welfare of the participating countries. The gains from currency unification involve the more efficient allocation of resources and capital and the reduction in the costs associated with the use of the foreign-exchange market. If there were only one currency in the world, these costs would disappear. The United States might be viewed as a unified currency area, comprising twelve Federal Reserve districts and fifty states. Financial capital flows smoothly and efficiently from high saving–low growth areas to low saving–high growth areas; one indication of the almost frictionless movement is that interest rates on comparable securities are virtually the same. Payments can be made on a virtually costless basis from Maine to

California by check. Internationally, the segmentation of Western Europe into currency areas incurs costs that would be avoided if the national currency areas were merged into one European currency.

The costs of currency unification are those associated with the loss of a central bank in one of the areas or countries, and thus with the decline in the ability to manage monetary policy to enhance employment and price-level objectives in the area, country, or region. If the Federal Reserve Bank of Chicago was independent of the other units in the Federal Reserve System, it might pursue a more expansive monetary policy than the other parts of the Federal Reserve in order to counter the surge in the unemployment rate in the Midwest. The value of having a separate currency area centers on the advantages attached to being able to alter the rate of growth of the money supply. The significance of these costs of unification varies with the choice of countries involved, and with the similarity of their economic structures.

One logical proposition relevant to optimizing the number of currency areas is that there should be no more central banks than there are labor markets. If there were, some of the central banks would be redundant (as eleven of the regional Federal Reserve banks are), in that the unemployment rates in these labor markets would always be identical with those other labor markets. A labor market is defined as an area in which excess demand for labor and excess supply of labor of the same type cannot exist at the same time. If labor is perfectly mobile between or among several labor markets, then they effectively are components of one larger labor market, in that the levels of money wages and the changes in these levels cannot differ significantly in geographic subsectors of this larger labor market. The explanation is straightforward; if the unemployed workers would move to the firms with excess demand for labor and competition among workers maintains reasonable uniformity of wages, no firm would pay a higher wage to attract labor than the prevailing market wage.

Hence the necessary condition for having separate national central banks is that there are segmented labor markets and that labor is not perfectly mobile among them. Economic welfare might be enhanced if the central banks in the areas with high unemployment followed an expansive monetary policy while the central banks in the areas with inflation followed a more contractive policy. However, a second condition is that if financial capital is perfectly mobile between these currency areas, then an independent central bank would be redundant, for the central bank could not, by changes in its monetary policy, induce a change in domestic interest rates relative to world interest rates. In the case where capital mobility negates the efforts at monetary independence, central banks should merge their currencies to eliminate the costs of servicing the exchange market. Hence the *sufficient* condition for separate currency areas is that national capital markets are partially segmented.

Even if both labor markets and capital markets are partially segmented, so that independent monetary policies are needed and feasible, the costs of maintaining separate national currencies may exceed the benefits. The tradeoff associated with the merger of currencies involves whether the welfare gains from the enhanced flow of goods and securities and the elimination of the costs of servicing the foreign-exchange market are larger than the welfare costs of higher unemployment because of a reduction in the number of central banks.

These general economic propositions about when currencies should be merged must be made operational. One proposal is that currencies be merged if the countries' economies are complementary, a second if their trade patterns are similar, and a third, if their business cycles are similar in timing and amplitude. The rationale is that the central banks in these countries would be following similar monetary policies. Small countries would have much to gain from mergers of their currencies with each other, or with the currency of a large country as a result of the increased flow of goods and financial capital. Large countries like the United States have already realized the gains from flows of goods and capital between quite different areas. Canada and Mexico might gain from merging their currencies with the U.S. dollar because each would have much better (and cheaper) access to the U.S. financial market. In addition, currency unification has been suggested for countries that are physically adjacent or share the same language. Proximity appears to be a dominant factor in the choice to merge currencies.

The European Community and Currency Unification

The historical evidence suggests that currencies are merged to secure political objectives rather than economic objectives. Currency unification is seen as an important step toward political unification.

The most ambitious effort to merge national monies in recent years has been that of the European Community. This effort followed the Treaty of Rome (1957), which led to the elimination of tariffs on internal trade among members of the community, to the development of a common external tariff and a common agricultural policy, and to the harmonization of social security, welfare policy, and business taxes in the member countries. So it might seem natural for the member countries to harmonize or coordinate monetary policies, and to move toward a common community-wide money, a change that would eventually require mergers of their central banks.

One motive for currency unification in Western Europe is that political unification is viewed as a desirable objective. A merger of currencies would be a meaningful step toward this objective. Some note the growth of intra-European trade; an increasing share of the trade of various European countries is with other members of the community. Payments from one country in Europe to another would be facilitated if there were only one currency, and if there were only one currency in the community, then trade within Western Europe would be promoted. Hence the move to a European currency would provide a modest amount of trade protection to European firms in competition with non-European firms. A third motive for currency unification is that the development of a European currency area might provide a larger center of monetary stability and better enable the European countries to insulate their economies from monetary shocks generated by the United States.

Once a decision has been reached to merge currencies, the authorities must decide on how to realize this objective. One approach is to harmonize monetary policies and then, if inflation rates are similar, to peg each currency to a common unit of account. An alternative approach involves pegging these currencies in the exchange market, and then harmonizing monetary policies so as to reduce the likelihood of extended payments imbalances at the established parities.

The likelihood that countries outside Western Europe will merge their currencies in the near future is very modest. Moreover, there may be substantial setbacks in efforts to move to currency unification in Western Europe. Nevertheless, the insights generated by the analysis of the costs and benefits of currency unification are applicable to two other questions. The first is whether a country's interests are better served by pegging its currency or permitting its currency to float. The second is that if a country decides to peg its currency it must then decide whether its interests are advanced by pegging to the U.S. dollar, the German mark, the Japanese yen, or some other currency.

THE CHOICE BETWEEN FLOATING AND PEGGED EXCHANGE RATES

For most of the last century, the U.S. dollar has been a pegged currency. Prior to World War I, a system of pegged rates resulted because the dollar and other major currencies were pegged to gold. The usual story is that central banks were able to maintain their parities because they followed the "rules of the game" for adjustment to payments imbalances, deflating when in deficit and inflating when in surplus.

The 1920s (really, 1919–26) was the first extensive period with floating currencies. At the outbreak of World War I, the European central banks stopped pegging their currencies at their mint parities; they embargoed gold exports and supported their currencies at levels five to fifteen percent below their prewar parities. Inflation was extensive and at different rates in various countries. Returning to the 1913 parities, while the dominant objective in most countries, was not immediately feasible at the end of the war because of the wartime inflation. Countries permitted their currencies to float, and some countries attempted to deflate so it would again be possible to peg to gold at their 1913 parities.

A few countries—Great Britain and the various neutrals, including Switzerland, The Netherlands, and the Scandinavian countries—succeeded in again pegging their currencies at their 1913 parities. The other Allies—France, Belgium, Italy, and Japan—eventually pegged their currencies in the late 1920s, after continued inflation and extended depreciation of their currencies, at levels one-third to one-fourth of their previous parities. In effect, gold was three to four times as expensive in terms of their currencies than before the war. The defeated belligerents—Germany, Austria, Hungary, and Russia—also pegged their currencies to gold after hyperinflations forced the adoption of new currencies.

The exchange-rate experience in the 1930s was substantially different from that of the 1920s. Great Britain permitted sterling to float in September

1931; a few countries—Ireland, Denmark, Sweden, and some Commonwealth countries—decided to peg to sterling and their currencies floated in terms of the dollar and other currencies pegged to gold. Then when President Roosevelt took office in early March 1933, he closed all U.S. banks, nationalized private U.S. gold holdings, and eliminated the gold parity for the dollar. For the next ten months, the dollar price of gold varied, for the most part increasing; the dollar was depreciating in terms of gold and most foreign currencies. At the end of January 1934, the dollar price of gold was again fixed, this time at $35 an ounce, so the effective increase in the dollar price of gold was 75 percent. Then speculative pressures developed against currencies that still pegged their currencies to gold, and, in mid-1936, the French franc, the Belgian franc, and the Dutch guilder were all devalued.

The interwar experience led to a number of assertions about the operation of floating exchange rates. One was that floating rates would disrupt international trade and investment; a second, that speculation would be destabilizing, both that the amplitude of exchange-rate movements would be wider and that speculators would cause the trend value of the exchange rate to follow a path different from what it would have followed in their absence. Thus if speculators sold a weak currency, the price of foreign exchange would increase, and so would the price of imports. The domestic price level would increase more rapidly; in contrast, the domestic price level would increase less rapidly in those countries whose currencies were acquired by speculators. So speculation would be self-justifying. At a later stage, this behavior led to what has been called "vicious and virtuous cycles."

The proponents of floating exchange rates criticized these conclusions, but only after asserting that the primary advantage of a floating exchange rate system was that countries would be able to pursue or realize greater monetary independence. They claimed that countries would be able to follow monetary policies independent of an external constraint because any tendency towards a payments deficit would automatically lead to a depreciation of their currencies. For example, if a country followed a more expansive monetary policy, one that would be associated with a larger payments deficit than it could readily finance with a pegged-exchange-rate system, its currency would depreciate. Similarly, no country would be obliged to purchase large amounts of foreign exchange and hence increase its own money supply to maintain its exchange parity; instead, its currency would appreciate and the monetary base would not be affected by its currency flows. The pro-floaters argued that trade and investment would not be disturbed by uncertainty about exchange-rate movements because traders and investors would hedge their foreign-exchange commitments through forward-exchange contracts. Hence countries would have greater freedom to follow policies so their price levels would differ from those in other countries; similarly, they would have greater freedom to pursue different employment objectives. They also argued that speculation would not be destabilizing, or that destabilizing speculators would soon go bankrupt because they would be betting against long-run trends.

A litany developed between the critics and the proponents of floating exchange rates. The critics argued that there were inadequate forward-exchange-market facilities in most currencies, and that, besides, hedging was not a costless activity. They also asserted that monetary independence was a chimera, and that countries would have much less control over their own price and income targets than the proponents promised. Moreover, the critics noted that the removal of the exchange parities would eliminate one of the last barriers to domestic inflation, so that the average level of inflation would be higher with a floating exchange-rate system.

Uncertainty and Independence under a Floating-Rate System

The resolution of the issue between the proponents and the critics of floating rates partly involves the nature and consequences of uncertainty under the floating-rate system. The greater monetary independence under a system of floating exchange rates than under a system of pegged exchange rates is possible only because the increased uncertainty about future exchange rates increases the segmentation of national money markets. Without segmentation, there is no scope for greater monetary independence. Yet the uncertainty that enhances monetary independence also deters trade and investment. True, trader and investor uncertainty about future exchange rates can be hedged through the purchase of forward contracts, and hedging may be costless to the extent that forward rates are unbiased predictors—on average—of future spot-exchange rates. Yet hedging is not riskless because forward rates individually are not very good predictors of the spot-exchange rates on the dates when the forward contracts mature. The "forecast" errors are substantial; the reason that the forward rate is an unbiased predictor of future spot rates is that two types of forecast errors are more or less offsetting—the forecast errors that underpredict the appreciation of the foreign currency offset those that underpredict its depreciation.

The benefits of monetary independence with floating exchange rates cannot be attained without increased uncertainty, and the cost of this increased uncertainty is a reduced level of trade and investment—or, in a growing world economy, a reduction in the rate of growth of trade and investment. The economic significance of this cost and its value relative to the value of greater monetary independence remain important and unresolved empirical issues.

The critics of floating rates base their assertion that speculation would be destabilizing on the observation that changes in exchange rates have been much sharper than might be inferred from contemporaneous changes in the differences in national price levels. The proponents of floating rates respond that the period-to-period movement in the exchange rates follows a random walk, that there is no systematic or predictable movement, and hence the exchange market is efficient.[1] There are no "runs" in the time-series—periods when the direction of changes in exchange rates can be accurately predicted from past changes. But if the exchange-rate movement follows a trend, then

[1] A financial market is said to be efficient when market prices of assets adjust immediately and fully to any new information. If "good news" and "bad news" occur randomly, then the changes in the price of the asset should follow a random walk.

the forces "driving" the exchange rate also may follow a trend. Alternatively the monetary authorities may have been "leaning against the wind"—and while intervening in the foreign-exchange market—retreating. In the last several years, some analysts have concluded that the foreign exchange market is not efficient—that day-to-day changes in exchange rates have been serially correlated when there have been large changes in the rates.

The efforts of national monetary authorities to follow independent monetary policies must inevitably lead to large movements in the spot-exchange rate since the current spot rate primarily reflects the anticipated future rates. Changes in monetary policy affect the anticipations of future exchange rates because of the impacts on the price-level developments and the interest rates at which these future exchange rates are discounted to the present. So a move toward a more expansive monetary policy would be associated with an anticipation of a more rapid increase in the domestic price level and a decline in the domestic interest rate; both factors would cause the currency to depreciate. The large swings in the exchange rates that are evident from hindsight reflect that the changes in monetary policy have been offsetting, either a domestic contractive policy is followed by a domestic expansive policy or by contractive policies abroad.

If these swings in exchange rates induced by changes in monetary policy are substantial, then the authorities may be obliged to intervene in the exchange market to limit the swings in the exchange rate; a "would-be" clean float becomes a managed float. Assume the U.S. authorities follow a more expansive monetary policy. If the dollar tends to depreciate, then foreign monetary authorities may buy dollars to limit the appreciation of their own currencies. The purchase of dollars leads to an increase in their money supplies. Unless these sales are offset when the currency movement is reversed, there is upward bias in the growth of the money supplies and the price-level movement. The authorities may have less control over their money supplies in the floating-rate period than in the pegged-rate period, because the private capital flows are so much larger.

Problems of Managing a Pegged-Rate System

The proponents of floating exchange rates frequently point to the difficulties of managing a pegged-rate system. Changes in parities almost always occur after too great a delay because the authorities hope that divine providence will intervene so that almost certain change in a parity will not be necessary. The move to floating exchange rates in the early 1970s did not occur because the proponents of floating exchange rates won the arguments; rather, in a period of growing inflation and increased divergence among countries in their inflation rates, the authorities were unwilling to pay the domestic political costs of maintaining the pegged-rate system. The pegged-exchange-rate system might have been maintained if the foreign monetary authorities, especially those in Germany, had been willing to accept the U.S. inflation rate.

The evidence of the last one hundred years suggests that the monetary system has a tendency to gravitate to pegged rates—as long as such a system is feasible. If inflation rates among major countries are similar and low (and they cannot be high and similar), a return to pegged rates seems likely. Countries will peg their currencies to that of a nearby and larger metropole, which is the pattern of the European monetary system. Hence the number of major countries with floating rates will decline, currency blocs will develop, and eventually pegging will reduce the exchange-rate movements among the major currency blocs.

A crawling-peg system has been proposed as an arrangement that combines the advantages of both a pegged- and a floating-rate system. On frequent occasions, perhaps as often as once or twice a month, the authorities change their parities, usually by no more than two or three percent. Because the changes in parities are frequent, no political trauma is associated with these changes. Because the amount of the change is so small, few traders and investors deem it worth their while to attempt to predict these changes, and profit from them. Between the time of changes in parities, the monetary authorities would peg the rate; however, because of the frequency of changes in the parity, the domestic monetary implications of pegging the rate would be slight.

THE SYSTEM OF RESERVE ASSETS

In the 1960s, monetary authorities in many countries were concerned that international reserves were increasing at too slow a rate, and then primarily because the United States incurred payments deficits. In the 1970s, there was an unplanned and unanticipated surge in reserves. The surge in reserves contributed to the surge in the inflation rate; and so one of the major concerns is how the growth of reserves might be managed to limit inflationary impacts. A related question involves the components of reserves, and whether gold and liquid financial assets denominated in the dollar, the mark, and other currencies will continue to serve as reserves, along with SDRs.

The surprise in the 1970s was the growth in the volume of reserve assets even during a period of floating exchange rates. Foreign central banks acquired dollar assets to limit the appreciation of their currencies when private parties, both American and non-American, "unloaded" their dollar holdings.

At the end of 1965, international reserves totaled \$67 billion; when floating began in 1973, reserves totaled \$150 billion. Determining the value at the end of 1981 is complicated by the need to place a value on monetary gold holdings. If monetary gold is valued at \$500 per ounce, reserves exceed \$800 billion, and if, instead, gold is valued at \$400 per ounce, reserves total above \$700 billion. Even if gold is valued at \$250 per ounce, international reserves amount to \$600 billion or about five times the 1970 level. Even after an adjustment for the increase in commodity price levels, the increase in reserves has been substantial in real terms. If gold remains in monetary limbo, countries in deficit will be able to sell gold at or near its market price (or else borrow against their gold holdings) to obtain currencies to finance their payments deficits.

A second concern of the 1960s was that the "system" then could not produce international reserves without forcing the United States to incur "payments deficits"; the United States was the major supplier of reserves, both in the form of gold and liquid dollar assets. During the fifteen-year period 1950–65, U.S. gold sales to foreign official institutions were almost as large as new gold production. As foreign holdings of dollars increased and U.S. gold holdings declined, the ability of the United States to maintain the $35 parity of gold for an indefinite future appeared increasingly questionable. The conundrum was that to the extent the United States was successful in reducing its payments deficit, most other countries would no longer be able to increase their holdings of gold and other reserve assets at the desired rates. But unless the United States could reduce its payments deficit, the $35 parity could not be maintained. As U.S. gold holdings declined, numerous other countries became more reluctant holders of dollar assets; they could not readily sell dollar assets to buy gold without jeopardizing the U.S. ability to maintain the gold parity.

A third problem was the asymmetry between the apparent ease with which the United States financed its payments deficits and the difficulties other countries encountered in financing their payments deficits. Other countries "spent" owned reserves and reserves borrowed from international institutions; either they had first to acquire reserve assets before they could use these assets to finance payments deficits, or, if they borrowed from foreign official institutions to finance deficits, they had then to repay these loans. In contrast, the United States financed much of its deficits by "passive borrowing" to the extent other countries were willing to acquire dollar-denominated assets. Thus that part of the U.S. deficit not financed by gold sales could be financed "automatically." Such automatic financing led to the concern that there could be an "uncontrolled" growth of international reserves.

GOLD AS INTERNATIONAL MONEY

Whether gold will again have a role as an international reserve asset depends on the outcome of two forces. One is a continuation of the pressures for economic efficiency that led to the progressive decline in gold's monetary role in the last century. At this point in time, gold no longer is used as a domestic money, nor do any countries peg their currencies to gold. Gold seems a "barbaric relic." The U.S. authorities have sought to reduce the international monetary role of gold, "to remove it from the center of the monetary system." They have succeeded, for in the last decade since the price of gold has been variable, gold has rarely been traded among central banks. Yet central banks have hoarded their gold, because its market price has been so much higher than the official price.

Gold has been an important monetary asset for centuries; investors and monetary institutions acquired gold because gold held its value better than other assets. Moreover, partly because of its underlying commodity value, gold maintained its value over a wider geographic span than any other monetary asset; gold had a credibility as a monetary asset that other assets lacked. More importantly, there was relative price level stability in the century of the gold standard, if not on a year-to-year basis, then over several decades. Whether price-level stability was a cause or a consequence is arguable. But the period since gold has been shifted from the center of the system is one of much more rapid inflation than experienced during the previous century.

The case for reducing the monetary role of gold further is that gold is not readily manageable as a reserve asset. Once a generation, the monetary price of gold would have to be increased, otherwise there would be a cumulative reserve shortage. And investors would continually speculate about the timing and amount of these increases. Such increases, however, are likely to be necessary only if inflation continues; with a stable price level, there is no evidence that the monetary price of gold must be raised.

The case for maintaining gold as a reserve asset has several elements—gold already is an important monetary asset, gold has a large constituency, and considering gold as an acceptable reserve asset would restore a balance to central bank portfolios, now overloaded with dollars. The importance attached to gold suggests that once again a monetary role will develop for gold, for the value of gold in reserves is so large that no substitute can readily be found. Several scenarios for enhancing the monetary role of gold are feasible. One is that central banks will develop arrangements so that countries in deficit will have greater confidence that they will be able to sell gold to other central banks to obtain the foreign exchange necessary to support their currencies in the exchange market. Alternatively, the United States and other countries might agree to a new monetary price for gold in terms of their currencies as part of a complex negotiation involving the roles of gold and other reserve assets.

THE DOLLAR AND OTHER FIAT ASSETS

A major concern in the evolution of the international financial system is the role of the dollar as a reserve asset. While holdings of dollar assets are increasing, holdings of assets denominated in the German mark, the Swiss franc, and the Japanese yen are likely to increase. International institutions are also likely to continue producing reserve assets. Nevertheless, it seems highly unlikely that the dollar will be phased out as an international reserve, or that its role will even decline significantly. The growth of reserves denominated in various national currencies is a result of the decisions of foreign central banks; almost always each acquires the currencies of the countries with whom it has major trade and financial relations, provided those countries have a reasonable record for commodity price-level stability. Inevitably, only the currencies of a very few countries are acquired as reserve assets.

Over the long run, the growth of reserve assets denominated in different currencies is usually demand determined; the countries acquiring these assets first decide on the volume of reserves they wish to acquire and then decide on the currency denomination of these assets. On several occasions, however, changes in the volume of reserve assets represent excess production, as with sterling during World War II, or with the dollar during the 1969–71 period. Excess production of reserve assets occurs because countries with the payments surpluses are reluctant to revalue their currencies.

A key policy issue is whether U.S. interests are served by having the dollar used as an international reserve asset. The dollar became a reserve asset because foreign monetary authorities found it to their advantage to acquire dollar assets; the development of the dollar as a reserve asset was not the result of a plan of the U.S. authorities. The United States gains several advantages from being an international banker. One, the seigniorage gain involves the profits from the production of money—the difference between the cost of producing money and its purchasing power in terms of other assets. In a competitive banking system, such gains would be competed away in the form of higher interest rates on dollar deposits. But U.S. interest rates may be lower, not higher, because of the foreign demand for dollar assets.

A second advantage of being banker is the flexibility advantage that became apparent in the late 1960s. The U.S. payments deficit was financed by the willingness of foreign central banks to add to their holdings of dollar assets. The U.S. payments deficit could be financed more easily than the payments deficits of other countries to the extent that there was an "automatic" demand for dollar assets at the prevailing exchange rates.

In the 1960s, some analysts concluded that the use of the dollar as a reserve-asset currency was *not* in the U.S. interest. One criticism was that the United States had less control over its monetary policy because there was a greater constraint on changes in U.S. interest rates due to the concern of the Federal Reserve that shifts of funds to foreign financial centers by private parties would be larger because of the volume of central bank-owned dollars. To the extent that foreign official institutions were buyers of dollar assets rather than of gold, these shifts of private funds presented no problem; the constraint became apparent only if foreign official institutions might sell dollars and buy gold as U.S. interest rates fell. A second criticism was that the United States had less control over its exchange rate than did other countries; a U.S. devaluation would be more likely to be followed by comparable devaluations of other countries. The evidence of the early 1970s suggests that offsetting devaluations probably reflect the unwillingness of other countries to incur the adverse change in their international competitive position due to a U.S. devaluation, rather than the possible losses on their holdings of dollar assets. Finally, increases in U.S. exports of securities led to smaller U.S. exports of commodities, which was a cost to the producers of commodities if not to the U.S. economy.

Now that foreign holdings of dollar assets exceed $300 billion, the question is whether changes in the demand for these assets can have a significant impact on the U.S. economy. If foreign holders of dollar assets decide to shift to reserve assets denominated in a foreign currency, the U.S. dollar would depreciate in the foreign-exchange market.

When the dollar has been weak in the exchange market, there have been proposals for new arrangements to manage foreign dollar holdings. One proposal is that the United States extend exchange guarantees on foreign dollar holdings; if the dollar depreciated by more than a specified amount, the U.S. authorities would make a direct payment to some or all foreign official holders of dollars to compensate them for their exchange losses. Alternatively, some or all of foreign central bank holdings of dollar assets would be transferred to the International Monetary Fund; the Fund in turn would acquire these claims on the United States. The U.S. authorities would extend a maintenance-of-value guarantee on these dollar holdings of the Fund, and the Fund in turn would be able to extend a similar guarantee on its liabilities to foreign official institutions. A third proposal is that the U.S. authorities begin to support the dollar in the foreign-exchange market to limit the variations in the foreign-exchange value of the dollar; in this case, the U.S. authorities might draw on U.S. reserves and borrow foreign currencies from the International Monetary Fund and from foreign central banks.

The common feature of all these proposals is that the U.S. authorities incur the exchange risk on some or all U.S. liabilities held by foreign official institutions. The presumption is that the U.S. willingness to acquire the exchange exposure would limit variations in the foreign-exchange value of the dollar. Foreign central banks would be less reluctant to intervene in response to sharp movements in exchange rates that seem out of line with general underlying economic movements.

THE ROLE OF MULTINATIONAL MONETARY INSTITUTIONS

One proposal to resolve the problems resulting from the use of assets denominated in major national currencies as reserve assets is to establish an international institution to produce reserve assets. Member countries would hold reserves in the form of deposits in this institution; when in payments deficits, they would transfer part of their deposits to the countries with the payment surpluses. This type of arrangement has a number of advantages; one is that reserves could be produced without the need for any particular currency to become overvalued. The seigniorage attached to the production of international money could be distributed to all countries. The rate of growth of international reserves could be managed on a planned basis; the overproduction of reserves could be limited.

The movement toward an international reserve-providing institution has been slow for several reasons. Since few countries can manage their growth of money to achieve price stability, it seems unlikely to conclude that the growth of international reserves can be managed to avoid a bias toward inflation. In the international context, the decisions about the rate of growth of reserves appear likely to be dominated by the inflation-prone countries. Hence the countries with the strongest commitments to price stability would realize larger-than-desired payments surpluses from holding the liabilities of the international institution, and face the choice of either accepting a higher-than-desired inflation rate or else be continually revaluing their currencies. If, as seems not unlikely, reserves were produced at too rapid a rate, the surplus countries would be reluctant to acquire deposits in the new institution.

From the point of view of individual countries, the relevant question is whether the attainment of national objectives will be eased by the activities of an international reserve-providing institution. Thus the U.S. authorities would necessarily be concerned with the implications for the management of domestic monetary policy of U.S. participation in such an institution. If the United States tended to be in payments deficit, financing the deficit might be more difficult than under the current arrangement because foreign official institutions would no longer acquire dollar assets, and so monetary policy might have to be directed to reduce the deficit. If the United States is in payments surplus, it would be obliged to extend credit to countries with payments deficits; as a consequence, the U.S. authorities might face the choice between monetary expansion to reduce the U.S. payments surplus or monetary contraction to dampen or counter the expansive impacts of the large surplus.

National attitudes toward the idea of a central reserve-producing institution generally reflect whether a country is more likely to incur payments deficits or payments surpluses. The countries with a tendency toward higher inflation and payments deficits generally favor the development of such an institution, since they believe financing their deficits in the future would be easier. Countries with a tendency toward payments surpluses are more skeptical since they would be obliged to extend credit to countries with the payments deficits.

Developing a new reserve-producing institution does not resolve the problems of accommodating the differences among countries in their inflation rates and their growth rates. Some countries would have payments surpluses, others would have payments deficits, and the problem under the new arrangement, as under previous arrangements, is which group of countries would take the initiative in adopting measures to reduce the payments imbalance.

SUMMARY

1. The source of international monetary problems is that national interests diverge.
2. The Bretton Woods system of pegged exchange rates broke down because of the surge in the world inflation rate, and the efforts of several countries to realize inflation rates lower than those in the United States.
3. If countries were to join a currency or monetary union, they would benefit from the elimination of the various costs of using the foreign exchange market on their transactions with each other; however, their economic welfare might be adversely affected unless their business cycles and trade patterns are similar.
4. For most of the last century, the major industrial countries have pegged their currencies with the exception of two periods—the first half of the 1920s and from 1973 on.
5. The movements in foreign exchange rates in the 1970s have not conformed with the claims previously advanced by their proponents. Thus the range of movements in exchange rates has been large, and countries have had much smaller monetary independence than they would have preferred.
6. In the 1960s, there was an almost uniform belief that there would be a shortage of international reserve assets; in contrast, in the 1970s, international reserve assets have increased at a very rapid rate.
7. The increase in the market price of gold has had a major impact on the value of central bank holdings of monetary gold. The self-interest of many banks will be advanced if arrangements develop so they can once again use gold to finance payments deficits.

8. Holdings of dollar-denominated assets are the next largest component of international reserve assets after monetary gold holdings. The United States has almost certainly benefited from the foreign demand for dollar assets.
9. SDR and reserve positions in the International Monetary Fund account for only a small part of international reserves. Because nations must agree before these components can be increased significantly, the likelihood of significant growth in this component of reserve assets is low.

Questions and Exercises

1. Discuss the costs and the benefits of the maintenance of the separate national currencies. Why might the major countries in Western Europe now think the time appropriate to merge their currencies?
2. Discuss the basic argument for floating exchange rates and the arguments for a system of adjustable parities. What conditions must be satisfied if the major countries are again to peg their currencies?
3. During the 1960s financial officials in the major countries were concerned with the shortage of international reserves. Discuss the conditions that might lead to the conclusion that the volume of international reserves is too small or too large.
4. Why has the relationship between the demand for reserves and the supply of reserves changed in the last decade?

Further Reading

MURPHY, J. CARTER. *The International Monetary System: Beyond the First Stages of Reform*. Washington: American Enterprise Institute for Public Policy Research, 1976. A liberal's approach to international monetary developments.

SCHMIDT, WILSON E. *The U.S. Balance of Payments and the Sinking Dollar*. New York: New York University Press, 1979. The title tells the story.

Index

Interest rates go up, bonds go down

Rule of 72 divide Interest into 72 gives you how long it will take for your money to double

14 yrs
.05⟌72
5
22

Cyclical + Counter cyclical

To offset a recession govt should lower taxes and increase spending thereby purposely incurring a deficit.

Inflationary upswing – taxes raised and govt. spending slashed
resulting surplus could be used to retire Fed debt incurred in financing the recession

Rational expectations – people forcast in a rational way, given all the information.

Crowding Out – increase the interest rate + reduce private spending